THE LIFE AND CORRESPONDENCE OF
RUFUS KING

Volume IV
1801-1806

THE LIFE AND CORRESPONDENCE OF
RUFUS KING

*Comprising His Letters, Private and
Official, His Public Documents, and His Speeches*

Edited by Charles R. King

Volume IV
1801-1806

DA CAPO PRESS • NEW YORK • 1971

A Da Capo Press Reprint Edition

This Da Capo Press edition of *The Life and Correspondence of Rufus King* is an unabridged republication of the first edition published in New York in six volumes between 1894 and 1900. It is reprinted by permission from copies of the original volumes in the collections of the Newark Public Library and of the Library of Temple University.

Library of Congress Catalog Card Number 69-16653

ISBN 0-306-71125-7

Published by Da Capo Press, Inc.
A Subsidiary of Plenum Publishing Corporation
227 West 17th Street, New York, New York 10011
All Rights Reserved

Manufactured in the United States of America

THE LIFE AND CORRESPONDENCE

OF

RUFUS KING

VOLUME IV.

1801-1806

Rufus King

From a painting by Gilbert Stuart, 1820

THE LIFE AND CORRESPONDENCE

OF

RUFUS KING

COMPRISING HIS LETTERS, PRIVATE AND OFFICIAL
HIS PUBLIC DOCUMENTS AND
HIS SPEECHES

EDITED BY HIS GRANDSON

CHARLES R. KING, M.D., LL.D. (Trin.)

FELLOW OF THE COLLEGE OF PHYSICIANS, PHILADELPHIA, AND
MEMBER OF THE NEW YORK AND PENNSYLVANIA
HISTORICAL SOCIETIES

VOLUME IV.

1801-1806

NEW YORK
G. P. PUTNAM'S SONS
The Knickerbocker Press
1897

The Knickerbocker Press, New York

PREFACE TO THE FOURTH VOLUME.

This fourth volume presents the correspondence to the time of the close of Mr. King's mission to Great Britain, and gives an account of several interesting events which occupied attention, and in which he was an interested actor. He returned to the United States finding the friends with whom he had been closely associated before his departure for Great Britain out of power, the political principles upon which they had founded the government discredited and supplanted by others of which they saw the dangerous tendency; a condition of things which made many loyal men suggest disloyal expedients. Mr. King was not of these but was, indeed, an earnest opposer of their plans; and when he came home untrammelled by personal connection with the political animosities which prevailed, he was put forward by the leaders as the representative of the old Federal Party, but only to be defeated. The circumstances connected with these efforts to recover power will be found explained in the correspondence. The relations with his friend Alexander Hamilton; his connection with the duel which deprived the country of its leading statesman; his interest in seeing provision made to relieve the family, whose head had been taken away; are all clearly stated, showing the warmth of his friendship, and the earnestness with which he sought to avert the consequence of this sad event.

The threatened attempt of some of the New England men to seek relief from the political troubles of the time by severing the Union, received, as will be seen, his positive rebuke, as it had received that of Hamilton and of other sound men of the Federal party. It was not in that way that relief was to be found, but by a steadfast adherence to their principles and earnest appeals to the patriotism of the people.   Without going into detail to show the events of the period covered by the correspondence, it may be proper to say that the Louisiana purchase occupies a considerable space, in which Mr. King in his letters to Mr. Livingston lays down clearly, in reference to the pending negotiation with France, the principle, since named the Monroe doctrine —that the United States would look with disfavour upon the attempt of any European nation, but Spain, to colonize on its borders.   There is another subject which enlisted the warm sympathy of Mr. King during his residence in England, the liberation of the Spanish American colonies from the parent state.   Full correspondence relative to this will be found in this volume, extending over several years, and in which its projector Genl. Miranda earnestly sought his help, especially, when, despairing of the often promised help from the British Government he came to the United States to enlist, if possible, the assistance of the Government and of individuals to enable him to carry out his plans. Mr. King, much as he desired to help him, could not do so, because the expedition could only be carried out by an infringement of the laws of the United States.   The result proved his wisdom ; the parties who were instrumental in sending it out were indicted, though not convicted, and the venture disastrously failed.

In all the matters adverted to in the following paper, are evinced the intelligent understanding, sound judgment, wise foresight and prudent counsels which mark the life of Mr. King and the love of his country which was never shaken however much its welfare was threatened.

CONTENTS OF VOL. IV.

CHAPTER V.

CHAPTER VI.

CHAPTER VII.

CHAPTER VIII.

CHAPTER IX.

CHAPTER X.

CHAPTER XI.

CHAPTER XII.

CHAPTER XIII.

CHAPTER XVIII.

CHAPTER XIX.

CHAPTER XXXI.

CHAPTER XXXII.

CHAPTER XXXIII.

THE LIFE AND CORRESPONDENCE OF RUFUS KING.

CHAPTER I.

At the beginning of this fourth volume it is well to look
over the state of affairs in the United States, tho' perhaps
this has only an indirect interest in shaping the actions
of Mr. King abroad, for his now long residence in England
prevented him from taking any personal share in the current events at home. His correspondence with old personal
and political friends, however, kept him well informed on

what was passing among them, and he was thus enabled to understand the changes in political matters that were daily taking place, and especially with regret to learn that the principles of the government, which he had so faithfully sought to establish, were gradually changing under the new administration in a way that boded no good to the country. Among these most valued and intelligent correspondents was Fisher Ames, who gives, in the first letter presented below, a clear statement of the affairs in the country and a well-considered view of the opinions of their old federal friends under the changes which were taking place, which they deprecated but could not check.

<hr>

F. AMES TO R. KING.

BOSTON, October 27th, 1801.

DEAR SIR :

While Mr. Gore * is on the Continent, I may be allowed to address a letter to you, and if I could give either clear or comforting information about our affairs I might hope that my letters wd. be acceptable to you without that excuse. But Democracy rides the high horse. Bradley is chosen a Vermont Senator, yet they say the assembly of that State is federal. Others say that all goes there by barter and that offices are trucked off to Feds & Jacobins without much discrimination, provided the high-contracting parties find their individual amount in it. Royal Tyler is a Judge of their Supreme Court, Israel Smith Ch. Justice. A motley bench which ought to try *per mediatatem.*

N. Jersey is said to be democratic. Delaware has a demo. Governor chosen by the people. Connecticut still shews a bold face, and vaunts of its Federalism which I fear is losing ground— yet so slowly that the pendulum may swing back again before the Demos get the majority. N. Hampshire still chuses Gilman, yet their " intriguans " intend to run Langdon as soon as the full-

* During the suspension of the sitting of the Commission under the Seventh Article of the Treaty with Great Britain, Mr. Gore, a member of the Committee, made a visit to the Continent of Europe.

ness of time has come—which is expected to be next spring.
Here, Govr. Strong will be rechosen, but the most zealously federal parts of the state are leavening and souring with the same
fermentation that in other parts has passed beyond the vinous
almost to the putrid.   Where Jacobinism triumphs, it is probable,
it's numbers do not increase—but it's insolence does,—and the
Feds in those places yield the ground to them with less contest
than formerly.   So that on a fair calculation of force, we are weak
indeed.   New England ought to be roused and all our efforts
ought to be directed to saving the remnants of federalism ; our
life and being would be lost, if the skill of our masters had been
equal to the felicity of the conjuncture when they conquered us.
They had only to promise well—indeed they did—and to keep on
promising smoothly, which they have not done, easy as the task
was.   Instead of it, they write foolish letters of excuse for themselves and inculpating the Feds as a Sect.   There is hardly anything that a skilful statesman may not *do*, but there is very little,
he can *say*.   This prating vain letter * has certainly alarmed the
Feds, who consider it as a manifesto announcing a violent
Jacobin administration.   And the knowing ones among the
Jaco'. think it stiff.   Already they whisper that little B. alone
has the needed energy of character, and party for him will
be form'd whenever it can be employed with effect.   In the
mean time he will push his Captain forward to do obnoxious
things, and when resentments are concentered on him, then perhaps he will think the Feds despairing of victory will only seek
revenge.   To secure which, *he* will be wanted.   It is indeed evident that a govt. too democratic in it's structure, or a people too
democratic in their notions to support any energetic form, will
breed endless factions.   We have hoped that our system was, as
Mr. Jefferson says very sagely, the *strongest* in the world and that
we are the people the fittest in it for such a system.   I presume
not to decide so grave a question.   I think however our experience soon will.   In New York the rights & the property of the
city and state are subject to the vice and folly and poverty of the
society.   The like will be brought about in every other state as
in Pennsylvania unless the quill shall be found a weapon of power

* Probably Jefferson's New Haven letter.

enough to counteract the progress we have commenced. Even
that weapon will be wielded by champions who do not think all
is at hazard. The popular consolation still is as much as ever
that all goes well—Prosperity smiles on everybody—Wealth increases, and the New men promise to make great savings. The
displacing a few exasperates a few hundreds, who soon forget
their anger and the circumstances and occasion of it. Those
who affect great concern for the people will be the men to have
popular power committed to them and newspaper writers will fail
as formerly in the attempt to make the understanding of those
who will not reason an overmatch for the blind impulses of those
who can only feel. Accordingly as I see the propensities of
things, as I estimate the feebleness of the means to hinder their
further and fatal decline, judge whether I am sanguine as to the
effect of Federal Gazettes. Yet I think despair ought not to be
confessed—still less circulated. Soon if the evil apprehended
should be deemed inevitable, which is rather more than my belief
—yet a certain manner of meeting it is necessary—otherwise it
will come with aggravation. We must openly and zealously and
with all our skill labor to prevent it. We must honestly and
faithfully cling to the Govt and Constitution and to the rules of
virtue and real patriotism to the last ; so that our fall, if fate decrees it, shall be incontestibly due to our political adversaries,
not to ourselves. As what is best and what is practicable are
points depending on events, and not to be foreseen or decided
before they happen, we shall thus stand ready to act as may be
proper—we shall keep ourselves united with the public sentiment
and when danger is obvious, the good and able will feel an impulse as strong as we vainly wish to inspire beforehand. Therefore the Gazettes are now of importance and the Feds are
preparing this kind of ammunition in Pennsylvania, N York &
Boston. Such gazettes will keep alive all the yet surviving respect
for principles, and if the Jacos. in Congress are not callous may
check their most outrageous designs. It is however obvious to
me that charges of violating the constitution affect the Jacos. very
little, while you know that the Feds when in power were exceeding affected by them—even when palpably false and frivolous—
as if the Feds were rather cowards who feared to be indicted for
breaking the Constitution, not really lovers of it who will not

suffer any others to do it. The bold liberties taken with the power of displacing and appointing are *abuses* if not infractions—yet as the Jacos. care little for principles and as the Feds are averse to making a great clamor for what to most persons will appear a little thing, I do not expect much check from that source. On the contrary, I expect a repeal of the late Judicial Law and an ousting of the new Circuit Judges will be received with patience by all, and with approbation with some federalists. If repealing a law will deprive a Judge of his office and salary, there will be no independence of the Judiciary on the Legislature.

As to the views and plan of politics of the ruling party in respect to foreign nations and to their own ultimate objects all is but conjecture. Probably one great man is a Democrat and thinks the extremes of Democratic principles are wise principles.

Madison certainly knows better and yet there ever was a strange vein of absurdity in his head. But the *second* has no such nonsense, Jacobinism now uses and urges Democracy, as it did in France—We are now in the Roland & Condorcet act of our Comedy—Whether we go on to the Danton and Robespierre acts depends on time and accident and not on the discernment energy or force of the Feds. This I sometimes hope ; Jacobins will not hold power contentedly only for fair honest purposes and they cannot proceed to use it to any very profitable extent for any other, without rousing a late opposition that would delay if not prevent the crisis—They cannot oppress and rob without our knowing ; and the oppressed will not be coaxed. Excuse my running on thus into infinite space. I stand again on old firm ground when I assure you of my cordial regard with best respects to Mrs King—

Yours &c.

R. KING TO C. GORE, PARIS.

LONDON, Oct. 30, 1801.

. . . The K.'s speech & the addresses you will see in all the papers. Sheridan has in a sentence expressed a very just notion of the public opinion ; " the peace everybody is glad of, but nobody proud of." There will be an animated Debate in both houses on Tuesday next. . . . In respect to our affairs here, they remain as they were when I last wrote to you. At present we cannot gain a hearing—every one is armed with weapons of attack or defence for the Battle of next week. This over, perhaps we may again find a moment for our affairs. . . .

R. K.

R. KING TO MR. MADISON.
Private.

LONDON, Oct. 31, 1801.

DEAR SIR :

It is confidently believed that a considerable Expedition composed of land and sea forces is preparing in France and will soon proceed to St. Domingo and perhaps to the Mississippi. Should Toussaint resist, our commerce may experience fresh embarrassments in the West India Seas. On this account among others the presence of our Minister at Paris, becomes more and more desirable.

To my surprise the Ship Frederick of New York, the first of our vessels detained upon the charge of having broken the Blockade of Havre de Grace, was two days ago tried and condemned in the High Court of Admiralty. I had been assured that the trial of these vessels should stand over, until the Cabinet should find time to consider the subject, and I had, moreover, reason to expect that an intimation would be given to the Judge, that under all circumstances these vessels, at least such of them as had not been warned, ought to be discharged. As soon as I heard of this sentence, I called on Sir Wm. Scott (to whom I had already sent a copy of my correspondence with Lord Hawkesbury concerning the Blockade of Havre) who told me that not having received the communication he had expected from the Government when the case of the Frederick came on, he intimated the expediency of suffering it with such other cases as were in similar circumstances, to stand over ; that the King's advocate who on a former day had stated an expectation that he might receive particular instructions respecting these cases, signified his readiness to acquiesce, but that the claimant's counsel pressed for a trial, and he could do no otherwise than condemn the vessel and cargo. The other vessels will not be tried before the Cabinet has decided whether it will interfere ; and that this decision may no longer be delayed I have required Lord Hawkesbury explicitly to inform me whether it is intended to make the cases of these vessels a subject of ministerial consideration.   Should the Cabinet interfere, the vessels will be discharged with their cargoes ; if it decline, or delay to do so, I shall put my correspondence with Lord Hawkesbury into Mr. Erving's hands with directions to deliver it to the advocate of the claimant to be used on the Trials.

With great respect &c.

RUFUS KING.

R. KING TO JAMES MADISON, ESQ.
(*Private.*)

LONDON, Nov. 2d, 1801.

DEAR SIR :

The Newspapers, among which is the Porcupine, the paper of the new opposition, which Mr. Dawson's repeated disappointments enable me to add to those I had before delivered to him, afford a pretty just view of the public sentiment concerning the Peace.   Mr. Sheridan in a single sentence has happily expressed this sentiment—" It is a Peace everybody is glad of, and nobody proud of."   Of the old Ministry Mr. Windham (the friend of Burke, and the Legatee of his opinions respecting the French Revolution) in one house, and Lord Grenville in the other, will censure the Preliminaries ; but a very large majority of both houses will approve them : there are notwithstanding some able, reflecting and influential men, both in and out of Parliament, who behold with deep concern the decided superiority that France has obtained over all her adversaries, and which in their opinion endangers the repose and independence of every State in Europe. The Peace according to these gentlemen is only the end of the first Punic war ; and tho' they may not live to see the last, they make no secret of their apprehension that it will prove fatal to the independence of their country.   I have this morning seen Mr. Addington, and had an opportunity of explaining to him the extraordinary situation of the negotiation respecting the 6th Article.   The light in which he sees the subject, encourages me to expect that the business will yet take a satisfactory turn ; in the meantime I am pressing Lord Hawkesbury for a definitive answer.

I am no stranger to the feelings which would be gratified by a more peremptory mode of discussion ; but having from a pretty thorough acquaintance with the subject, become strongly impressed with the policy of our getting rid of a controversy which nobody seems willing to examine and in which we have to encounter much interested misrepresentation ; I am led to doubt the suggestion of every measure that would afford a Pretext to decide the Question, upon which we are at issue upon any other than its true principles ; and it is to considerations of this sort, that I must refer myself, for the justification of the yet unexpected stock of Patience, with which I have pursued the settlement of this unpleasant discussion.

With sentiments of sincere Respect &c.

RUFUS KING.

On the 2d of November a conversation * upon the state of the American negotiations was held with Mr. Addington, which was followed the next day by a private note to him from Mr. King presenting the steps by which it had reached its present condition. This note is dated on the 3d, and follows. Mr. King states that the conversation then turned to politics.

Mr. A. was evidently contented with the state of parties. The King was at first staggered but finally acquiesced by saying as he had no allies upon the Continent the best must be done that could be. The Prince of Wales had written to him that he should have his full support, and Lord Camden, who some days ago appeared decided to oppose, had just written to him, to say he shd. go out of town on Tuesday when the Preliminaries are to be discussed and that he shd. give Mr. Addington his support.

Speaking of Windham, he did credit to his integrity, sincerity and disinterestedness, and added that he shook hands with him at court with the observation of Sir Wm. Temple "friends here but enemies at Breda," alluding to the debate upon the Preliminaries, to which Windham replied *enemies nowhere.*

* Memorandum Book.

Of Ld. Grenville Mr. A. spoke with displeasure, and was willing to impart his and the Marquis of B.'s opposition to factions and interested views. Lord Grenville was already tired of retirement &c.; but he miscalculated & his views are understood. It was utterly inconsistent that he who negotiated at Lille should censure the minister who had concluded the Peace. Lord Radnor was a particular man, he shd. a priori have inferred his opposition. Lord Carnaervon was a wild and irregular character. The whole Bench of Bps. with the exception of Rochester would support him. He felt that he deserved support. If the war had gone on, could he have abridged the power of France, could he have delivered any of the Dominions which had fallen under its government? If not, why prolong the war, especially when he found he could not make another campaign without bringing upon his country an additl. permanent burthen of two millions annually. Add to that, the probability that France wd. have completely overrun Spain and Portugal and made irruptions into other States. For it wd. have been necessary even for Bonaparte to have employed his army abroad in order to get rid of the expence of maintaining it at home.

That on the whole, he was in hopes the Peace wd. be permanent, and he did not perceive anything in the relative condition of the countries wh. made it more likely than on former occasions to be of short duration. If it shd. not continue wd. not G. Br. be better able to measure herself apart with France, than she wd. have been had the war continued another year or two, which wd. have enormously increased the public burthen and weakened and exhausted those resources upon wh. the public safety must depend in the event of a future war.

Speaking of the Negotiator, he thanked me for the character I had early given him of Mr. Otto, and said he had found it to be perfectly merited. That the King had lately expressed himself favourably respecting him and intimated a wish that he might be the Ambassador here. Mr. A. then said two circumstances respecting him were highly creditable to his integrity and discretion —one that he certainly did not gamble in the stocks and the other that he had not any intercourse with the discontented people of G. Britain. Jos. Bonaparte he expected wd. be the Ambassador.

R. King to Mr. Addington.

Private.

Nov. 3, 1801.

Mr. King sends him a statement of the " Origin, Changes and present state of the Negotiation concerning the 6th Article of the American Treaty of 1794."

1799, December.   As soon as the Commission in America under the Sixth Article of the Treaty of 1794, discontinued its meetings, the American Government proposed to that of Great Britain an explanatory Article for the regulation of its future Proceedings.

1800, April.   The British Government declined agreeing to the proposed explanatory Article, but offered to accept a Sum of between one and two millions in satisfaction of the Debts contracted before the Peace of 1783 ; to abolish the American Commission, and take upon itself the distribution of the Money among the British Creditors.   This offer was not accompanied by a proposal in like manner to convert the American Claims under the Seventh Article of the Treaty of 1794 into a definite sum ; on the contrary, it was explicitly declared that the Commission in London, charged with the examination of these Claims, should be suspended only until a settlement could be made respecting the Commission in America.

1800, August.   The Government of the United States declined the proposal of giving a sum in satisfaction of the Debts, and offered a Sum in satisfaction of the Claims of the Creditors upon the American Government, leaving the Creditors to pursue the recovery of their debts in the ordinary Course of the Judiciary.

At this Stage the British Government inquired if the American Minister were authorized to convert the American Claims upon the British Government into a definite Sum, and abolish the Commission in London in like manner as it was proposed to abolish that in America ; and on receiving an explicit answer in the negative, a discussion was *immediately* commenced for the purpose of ascertaining the Sum to be given in satisfaction of the Claims upon the American Government, and most certainly with the mutual expectation that, this Sum being agreed upon, the Commission in London would be free to proceed in ascertaining the amount of the American Claims upon the British Government.

1801, August. After a tedious discussion, this sum has been mutually ascertained and settled, as well as the Terms of its Payment ; It follows, therefore as a matter of course, and good faith requires, that the Commission in London should be at Liberty to proceed in the execution of its duties.

R. King to James Madison, Esq.

Private.

LONDON, Nov. 5, 1801.

Dear Sir :

The War having ended has given occasion to a review of the diplomatic Corps of this Country, but few of which have lately been in service ; and I hear that Mr. Liston will be sent to Holland, instead of returning to America. Mr. Jackson, who was Secretary of Legation at the Hague and at Madrid before the war, and who was named Ambassador to the Porte soon after its commencement, but did not proceed to Constantinople, has been appointed Min. plenipo. to France and will reside at Paris during the Congress at Amiens.

As soon as the definitive Treaty shall be concluded, Lord Whitworth (formerly in Russia) will go as Ambassador to Paris, and Mr. Jackson as Mr. Liston's successor to America.

With great Truth &c.

RUFUS KING.

G. Cabot to R. King.

Nov. 6, 1801.

My Dear Sir :

Perhaps there never were six months of more perfect tranquillity than we have last enjoyed ; yet like the Seaman who calls a *Summer* day in the winter Season a *weather breeder* I look for Storms. I am however less solicitous than formerly about all these things. While I hoped, & believed it possible, to save our country from the terrible evils of Democracy I was full of anxiety, but perfectly convinced as I am now, that no human means cou'd have prevented them I reconcile myself, as Nature kindly disposes us, to all unavoidable events.—We are going the course decreed by the Author of man for every popular State. . . .

Our friend A. lately put into my hands a letter for you which I thought so good as to deserve transcribing that it might have two chances of arriving—my son therefore made a copy which I now enclose.—You will see by it that he adheres to the good old maxim of *never despairing of the Commonwealth* yet if you observe his details I think you will determine that his faith is not only without evidence but in fact against it. Indeed I sometimes believe that a few hundred of such men as he is, properly distributed thro' our Country, might save it, but we have only one in this quarter & not many elsewhere. After all I have said to chill, your hopes I ought to say that the more enlightened part of our society think more justly & more alike than at any former period & from thence some good expectations are formed.

Yours truly,

G. C.

R. King to Lord Hawkesbury.

Great Cumberland Place, Nov. 11, 1801.

My Lord :

I had the honour on the 28th ulto. to recall to your Lordship's recollection the several representations which I had before made to you in behalf of the American Ships and Cargoes, detained in their passage to the Port of Havre de Grace ; the greater part of these vessels has been nearly three months in the Ports of England, during which time the Crews, tho' engaged on war wages, have been kept together in daily expectation of an answer from your Lordship to my repeated applications in their favour.

As I cannot consistently with a due regard to the Interest and Rights of the Owners of these Ships and Cargoes, recommend to their Masters to remain here with their respective Crews, at the enormous expence which attends their detention, without a certainty that their cases will be examined without farther delay, I take the liberty again to request your Lordship's answer to the representations I have made on their behalf.

With great consideration &c.

Rufus King.

G. Morris to R. King.

MORRISANIA 13 Novr., 1801.

DEAR SIR:

I am much oblig'd by yours of the twentieth of last December which I ought sooner to have acknowledged but my Hermitage offers nothing to communicate to a Man in the Great World.

I never believed that the Northern League would last long. Indeed I ventured to predict the speedy Dissolution of it and to ground some Reasonings as to our affairs on that Position. I do not now believe that Peace will soon be made. Necessity, or the Feebleness of Soul which calls Difficulty by that Name, may procure the assent of the British Ministers to an armed Truce under the Semblance of Peace; but if they leave France in Possession of her present Dominion and Authority they reduce their Country to the Rank of a secondary, perhaps a dependent Power. This seems so evident that it is wonderful Buonaparte did not propose an uti possidetis as the Ground Work of a Treaty. If it be said that War is necessary to him, one would think he might turn his Arms North Eastward: for if Austria, Russia and Prussia have not the Good Sense to aid England in restoring the Ballance of Power, the two first might be induced to agree with the first Consul on eating up the last. No more convenient Morsel could be found nor any which would better cut up into Indemnities. But whether the War shall now continue or the Parties agree to take a short breathing Time; one of two things seems inevitable; either that a Grand Alliance be formed against France, as at the Beginning of the last Century, or that all other Powers submit to her Domination. The part we may act must depend much on Circumstances, but I question whether our present Administration (tho' quite as able as the last) be equal to the Business, which they will probably have to manage. I hope they may, and rely much on the scriptural Assurance that Heaven tempers the Wind to the shorn Lamb. . . .

Believe me ever and truly yours

GOUVR. MORRIS.

R. KING TO LORD GRENVILLE, &c. &c.

GR. CUMBERLAND PLACE, Nov. 14, 1801.

MY LORD :

In the Morning Chronicle of to-day your Lordship is stated to have said in the debate of last evening in the House of Lords, that while you were in his Majesty's service " a foreign Minister had by misrepresentation, and the most flagrant perjury, been instructed to complain of the conduct of a British official of high reputation, and on enquiry it was found to be most grossly false, and the charge scandalous." It having been my duty during my residence in this country, as the Minister of the United States, to prefer various complaints founded upon proofs of delinquency against certain of the King's naval officers, I take the liberty of requesting your Lordship to inform me, whether the complaint alluded to by your Lordship, in the House of Lords, was made by the Minister of the U. S. and if so, that you would have the goodness to mention the date of the complaint, and the Tribunal before which the falsehood and perjury ascribed to it were established.

With high consideration and respect, &c.

RUFUS KING.

————

LD. GRENVILLE TO R. KING.

CAMELFORD HOUSE, Nov. 14, 1801.

DEAR SIR :

If an accurate report were made of what I said last night in the House of Lords, you would, I am sure, see, what I trust you would readily believe even without this assertion of it, that no part of my speech did, or could, in the smallest degree reflect on your character, or conduct, to both which I have always borne, both in public and in private, the testimony of that sincere esteem and respect which I feel towards you.

Having said this, which was no less due to my own feelings than to your's, you must allow me to add that I cannot think it consistent with my duty as a Peer of Parliament to enter into any particular explanations with a foreign Minister, respecting an unauthorized publication in a newspaper, of opinions supposed to have been delivered by me in my place in the House of Lords.

I have the honor to be with sincere respect & regard

Dear Sir your most faithful & most obedient humble Servant.

GRENVILLE.

RUFUS KING ESQ. &C., &C., &C.

This letter is thus endorsed in R. King's handwriting.

LORD GRENVILLE, Nov. 14, 1801—In consequence of this answer I deemed it expedient to consult with my corps, and after stating the subject to Count Woronzow, who was of opinion that this Reply was satisfactory and that I could not require of Ld. Gr. to enter into fuller explanations, I concluded to suffer the Business to stop here—purposing however to express any opinion to Ld. Gr. of the unfitness of his Language when I next meet him.

Having myself heard his Speech, I know it to have been as exceptional as stated in the Morng. Chronicle.

R. KING TO SECRETARY OF STATE.   No. 42.

LONDON, Nov. 20, 1801.

SIR :

If the annexed copy of the Treaty * between France & Spain, respecting the establishment of the Prince of Parma in Tuscany, be genuine, of which I have no reason to doubt, you will perceive the value which these Powers seemed to have placed upon Louisiana ; the cession whereof to France is confirmed by the 5th article of this Treaty.

I am in hopes that I shall be able to obtain and send you a copy of the Treaty ceding Louisiana to France ; this would enable us to determine whether it includes New Orleans and the Floridas.

There is doubtless an understanding between England and France in respect to the expedition now nearly ready to proceed to Saint Domingo ; and I think I am not mistaken in the belief, whatever may be the intentions of France in respect to the occupation of Louisiana, that no part of the Forces now collect-

* See p. 19 of this volume for Article 5.

ing, and which are going to St. Domingo, will be employed for this purpose.

It is not a little extraordinary that during the whole negotiation between France and England, not a word was mentioned on either side, respecting Louisiana, though this Government was not ignorant of the views of France in this quarter.

With perfect respect & Esteem &c.

RUFUS KING.

R. KING TO LORD ELDON, &c.

GREAT CUMBERLAND PLACE, Nov. 22, 1801.

MY LORD :

With view of explaining the origin and progress of the discussion in which I have now for upwards of two years been engaged, on the subject of the Sixth Article of our Treaty of 1794, I have drawn up the enclosed Paper,* which I ask the favour of your Lordship to peruse.

I wished to have made it shorter, but could not without omitting what appeared to be material to the elucidation aimed at. If I be not altogether mistaken the Point upon which the Business continues to be delayed, will appear to your Lordship, from the perusal of this Paper, in a light somewhat different from that in which you have before seen it, and I am willing to hope that it may have some influence in bringing the affair to a satisfactory conclusion.   With perfect consideration & respect &c.

RUFUS KING.

P.S.   I shall be obliged to your Lordship to put the Paper into Lord Hawkesbury's hands after you shall have read it.

LEWIS LITTLEPAGE TO R. KING.
Private.

PHILADELPHIA, 28th of Novbr., 1801.

DEAR SIR :

I have never forgotten the important conversation which passed between us the last time we met in St. James's Park. In a conversation which I had with the President about a week past, I

---

* The paper alluded to above, covers nearly six pages of folio.

mentioned the affair in question to him. He told me he had been informed of it for *four months*, that it would be *unfortunate*, but what were the means of *prevention?* That question you may suppose, I was ill prepared to answer, totally ignorant as I am, of the politics and resources of my own County. I have here met with our Vice President Col. Burr, with whom I spoke a little on the same subject. He assured me that he had long studied it, had conversed upon it with Toman and Talleyrand, in this Country, had his opinion *irrevocably fixed* upon it, but could not declare to me what that opinion was, except in *presence of the President.* So far for *external* politics. With respect to our internal affairs the President thinks himself sure of a Majority in both houses. With respect to changes he is less precipitate than many expected. I believe he does not mean to descend to the lower offices. I was happy to hear him speak in high terms of you, and can assure you his opinion of you is general in this Country. I am surprised at the conditions of Peace between England and France. For Heaven's sake let me know how it came to pass.

 I have the honor to be with high respect &c
    Sir, &c
      Lewis Littlepage.

Endorsed by R. King
 " Ans'd Mar. 22nd *private ;* (probably 1802)
 Subject generally state of Exped'n to Louisiana—in wh. Eng. will not interfere and concern'g wh. the public welfare must be promoted or risqued by our own Exertions or omission."

———

Mr. King having asked for a conference with Lord Hawkesbury it took place on Nov. 25, 1801.*

I began by saying I had desired to see him chiefly with regard to the negotiation about the 6 & 7 articles ; stated my solicitude for its conclusion, and that I must present a note upon the subject in case it was not likely soon to be again taken into consid'n.

He said the Chancellor was much engaged in his Court, but that he hoped soon to have an opportunity of conversing with

    * Memorandum Book.

him, &c ; and then repeated what Hammond had before mentioned to me, that Lord Grenville said he had agreed to nothing
wh. committed the Government, and moreover that the Commission under the 7 art. going on was a circumstance wh. wd. naturally have an influence (which it had not had as Lord H.
observed) in deciding upon the sum for wh. the 6 article shd. be
commuted.

I told his Lordship that I had drawn up a paper upon this subject wh. was in the Chancellor's hands with a request that it shd.
be sent to him, & that I felt persuaded that it w'd shew the
business in its true light and prove that the discussion upon the
6 art. proceeded upon the basis of that article's being commuted
and the 7 article's being executed.

I then enquired concerning the Expedition to San Domingo,
preparing in the French Ports. Asked if it wd. proceed before
the definitive Treaty ; if its object were approved by Eng. and
whether Louisiana formed a part of it.

He replied that an understanding existed with respect to the
Expedition to St. Domingo ; intimated that the Expedition cd.
not wait for the defin. Treaty. On the subject of Louisiana not
a word had passed during or since the negotiation with France
abo. Louisiana—he would not speak positively and what he did
say was confidential, but he shd. rather conclude that no part of
the Expedition now preparing was destined for Louisiana. Spain
had certainly ceded Louisiana. But he did not exactly comprehend the Territory included under that Term.

I said by *Louisiana* without other words one wd. understand
only lands west of the Mississippi ; but we apprehended the
Floridas and New Orleans likewise to be ceded. We then turned
to a map and I pointed out to L. H. the boundaries of Louisiana
as I understood them making the Mississippi on the East and the
River Norde on the West the limits. He asked where *New
Orleans* was and I pointed it out to him, and also explained the
ancient claim of the Limits of Louisiana and such as was advanced before the 7 years' war—adding that the Treaty of Paris
in 1762 gave the countries east of the Mississippi to England,
leaving Louisiana solely on the west of that River. I then
enlarged upon the value and importance of Louisiana to Fr.,
provided New Orleans & the Floridas were added. His Lord-

ship seemed to have never considered the subject, and remarked that it must be a very long time before a country quite a wilderness could become of any considerable value.

I observed that we saw the subject in a different light and were desirous that this region shd. remain in the quiet hands of Spain, and then asked if Spain shd. continue to desire it, as well as we, and we shd. employ such influence as we might have to engage France to relinquish the cession, whether England wd. coöperate at Amiens by using her influence in favour of the restoration of this country to Spain. Lord H. said he wd. give me no answer on that point, adding what he had before asserted that they had taken no notice of the cession & he would not think that it wd. soon become of importance.

Speaking of the act of cession, he said that they had seen a copy of it & on my asking for a copy he said he wd. give it to me. (He sent me the copy of a Treaty between Fr. & Sp. of March 1801, securing Tuscany to the Prince of Parma, and wh., referring to the cession of Louisiana, confirms it.*

* Traité signê à Madrid le 21 Mars 1801 par le Prince de la Paix et Lucien Bonaparte.

The fifth Article of this Treaty reads thus : "Ce Traité étant en conséquence de celui deja conclu entre Le Premier Consul et S. M. E. par le quel le Roi cède à la France la Possession de la Louisiane les Parties Contractantes conviennent d'effectuer le dit Traité et de s'arranger à l'égard de leurs Droits respectifs."

CHAPTER II.

Nov. 27. 1801.

Nov. 27. 1801.* Dined at Mr. Addington's with eight or ten individuals, his personal friends he called them ; Otto & myself the only strangers. In my morning ride I fell in with Mr. Addison ; we rode together and conversed on different subjects. . . . He said, speaking of Mr. Otto, what he had before told me that his conduct had been most excellent and correct ; for him and his colleagues to have acted with fairness in respect to the funds was precisely their duty : but Otto had not been precisely in the same situation, yet he was persuaded that he had abstained with as much discretion and as entirely as they themselves had. I

* Memorandum Book.

20

observed that it was certainly very creditable to Otto, but that it had surprised me that Talleyrand had not made use of his knowledge to job in the Eng. funds. Without replying, Mr. Addington in a sort of ejaculation, said he was glad Lord Cornwallis had left Paris for Amiens ; as he believed things wd. do better at a distance from that Man ! (Talleyrand)

One of two inferences may be made from these words—either that Talleyrand was not trusted by Bonaparte in the negotiation carried on by Otto in London and might not be in that to be entered upon at Amiens ; or that the ex-Bishop had already gained an influence over Lord Cornwallis. Sitting by Wilberforce at Dinner I glanced at the latter interpretation which I thought he assented to—and in a loose conversation with Hammond I perceived the same idea was admitted by him. But Otto some time since told me that certain of his dispatches were sent with unbroken seals to Bonaparte.

Wilberforce told me that he had not much hopes, that the Article abolishing the Slave Trade would be inserted in the definitive Treaty. Lord Cornwallis knew & cared little about it, but wd. act fairly, whereas Malmesbury, knowing the King's opinion, like a mere courtier as he was, wd. be sure to defeat any hopes wh. might exist in its favour. Addington was well enough disposed, as well as others of his colleages, but Hawkesbury partook of his Father's sentiments on this topic and he had fairly told him that so long as he entertained these principles *he W.* would never look upon him with the friendship he desired to do. Wilberforce seemed to think (in wh. I believe he is quite mistaken) that Bonaparte was disinclined or lukewarm, on account of his wife, who is a creole !

MR. PITT.

Wilberforce spoke in high terms of Mr. Pitt and especially with regard to his disinterestedness and support of the new Ministry— adding that before he went out of office, he sent for him W. and explained his intentions, as well in regard to his own resignation as the forming of one new Ministry, asking him what he thought of his project. W. replied that he approved of it and encouraged him to persevere. Pitt replied that he was glad to receive his approbation especially as others had told him the new min. wd.

not do, and desired him to counteract that opinion. Mr. P., said, Wilberforce, is the only one of the old ministry who wd. have made the Peace the new Ministry has done and he has acted nobly in supporting them.

Speaking of the Expedition to Egypt he lamented that they had been so misled by Canning's foolish Book (referring to the Preface and Notes to Bonaparte's intercepted Letters). Had Menou been an able instead of a weak General, they shd. have been defeated & disgraced at Aboukir : and after all Providence had saved them, for poor Abercrombie (who was certainly brave and whose gallant death shd. cover all his errors) was most completely surprised by the French in the morning in which he was mortally wounded !

Anecdote.

Lord Molesworth, the Eng. Envoy in Denmark, wrote an acct. of that Country which unveiled *the tyranny* of its Government. Scheel, the Dan. Envoy in Eng., complained to King William of this Publication and demanded reparation &c. The King who was attached to Lord Molesworth evaded the complaint of Scheel who renewed his representation and added that for such like offense committed by the Dan. Envoy in England, his Dan. Majesty wd. cut off the offender's head and send it to the offender's ally.

King William good humouredly expressed his acknowledgments and said that such were not the laws of England and that he wd. command Lord Molesworth to put in his book what were the laws of Denmark upon this subject.

KING TO LORD PELHAM.

GREAT CUMBERLAND PLACE, Nov. 28, 1801.

MY LORD :

It seems not the least extraordinary of the wonderful things of the age in which we live, when reforms of almost every sort, and in every direction, have been aimed at, and powerful Leagues to effect them have been formed and dissolved on all sides, that no one has thought of a confederacy to repress the piratical practices of the States of Barbary, which, at the very doors of the great Nations of Europe, have for so many Centuries laid them with the rest of the commercial world, under Contribution.

It is true Great Britain, on account of her naval superiority, feels this Evil but lightly ; but were it permitted to others to express an opinion on this head, it might be said, that the reason why she does not feel it more heavily is precisely that which should free her, as well as the rest of the World, from feeling it at all.

For these Reflections, I ought, however, to crave your Lordship's indulgence, though in Truth they are not altogether foreign to the particular object of this Letter, which serves to communicate to your Lordship the enclosed complaint against the British Agent residing at Tripoli. The Bey of Tripoli has lately declared War against the United States, which, in consequence thereof, have been compelled to send a squadron of Frigates into the Mediterranean to protect their Commerce and curb the cruisers of this Regency.

Bryan McDonough, the British Agent at Tripoli, has, as we are informed, materially contributed by his misrepresentations and influence over the Bey, to engage him to make war upon the United States. In addition to the information derived from the American Consuls at Tripoli and Tunis, Commodore Dale, Commander of the American Ships in the Mediterranean, after particular inquiry confirms, in the fullest manner, the complaint against McDonough.

It will naturally occur to your Lordship, that this complaint, from its nature, does not admit of exact Proof, since it is from various and connected circumstances only that we are enabled to satisfy ourselves, in cases of this sort, that our suspicions are well founded : in the present instance, however, although we cannot accompany the complaint against his Majesty's Agent at Tripoli, with such Proofs as would judicially establish his Guilt, it is my duty to state to your Lordship that the evidence of delinquency is such as to convince us that the war in which we are engaged with Tripoli has been excited by the false and unfriendly representations of this agent, if not chiefly produced by his mischievous influence over the mind of the Bey. How far his malignant views may have been promoted by his abuse of his public character is matter of conjecture ; but there can be no doubt that his influence, whatever it may have been, must have arisen principally from his official situation.

Relying, as we do, upon his Majesty's friendship and Justice, I flatter myself that this complaint will meet with a ready and impartial consideration ; and that his Majesty will not only manifest his displeasure at this highly criminal and injurious Proceeding, but that he will moreover give explicit instructions to his Consuls and agents throughout the States of Barbary, to pursue for the future a conduct in respect to the United States and their affairs, conformable to the harmony and good understanding that so happily subsists between our respective Countries.*

With the most perfect consideration &c &c

RUFUS KING.

LORD PELHAM TO R. KING.

WHITEHALL Dec., 5, 1801.

SIR :

I have received the honor of your Letter, dated 28th. ulto., inclosing a Copy of one from Mr. William Eaton, Consul for the American States at Turin, to Mr. Magra, his Britannic Majesty's Consul General at the same place, in which the conduct of Mr. Bryan McDonough at Tripoli is stated as highly reprehensible.

It is, I should hope, unnecessary to assure you that any conduct observed by Mr. McDonough hostile to the interests of the American Government in the Barbary States is totally unauthorized, and that every possible disposition is felt by the British Government to preserve in every quarter that harmony and good understanding, which so happily subsists between it and the United States of America.

Were Mr. McDonough likely to continue in his present station, the circumstances of the charges against him (although the authenticity of them rests merely on the assertion of Mr. Eaton) should certainly undergo a full investigation, but as he is almost immediately to be superseded, such investigation is unnecessary. Lest, however, from any accidental cause, his supercession should not take place as soon as it is intended, a Letter shall be immediately written to him, cautioning him against persisting in the

* To this is appended a report from Com. R. Dale, stating the charges against B. McDonough.

conduct he is charged with, and his successor shall be fully apprized of the friendly sentiments, entertained by the British Government towards the American States.

I have the honor to be &c

PELHAM.

R. KING TO LORD HAWKESBURY.

Private.

GREAT CUMBERLAND PLACE, Nov. 30, 1801.

MY LORD :

If your Lordship will advert to the really unpleasant situation in which I am placed by the great and continued delay of the settlement concerning the 6th article of our Treaty, I am persuaded you will be disposed to do justice to my encreased solicitude upon the subject. Preserving always a due confidence in the assurances which have given me reason to expect a satisfactory conclusion of this affair, I have from month to month and from year to year (for it is near three years that the business has been depending) endeavored to satisfy my Government in respect to this unusual and inconvenient Delay.

Having nothing to add, or to alter upon a subject we have so fully considered, and as I thought settled, I may without further apology, appeal to your Lordship's impartiality for my justification in claiming, as it is my duty to do, a final decision of this affair. The season of the year offers but few opportunities to America ; the regular mail for New York will be made up in the course of this week, and I am anxious to give to my Government positive and explicit information upon this subject. I will only add, that I shall be happy to be enabled to say, that the business is finally and satisfactorily closed.

With perfect respect &c., &c,

RUFUS KING.

R. King to Secretary of State.

No. 43.

Sir :

London Nov. 30 1801.

It is understood that Lord Cornwallis will leave Paris for Amiens in the course of a day or two, and as soon as the Ministers of France, Spain, Portugal and Holland shall arrive there, that the negotiation of the definitive Treaty will be commenced. As the principal Points were settled in the Preliminaries, and those of inferior note have been since discussed at Paris, the prevailing opinion seems to be that not much time will be required to bring the negotiation to a conclusion.

The expedition to St. Domingo has not yet sailed ; but as England has really a squadron of ten or twelve ships of the Line, which is to be sent immediately to the Jamaica station, it is supposed that the French Expedition will proceed as soon as it shall be ready and without waiting for the definitive Treaty.

Mr. Otto has received notice that he will be sent as Minister Plenipotentiary to the United States, tho' in consequence of Mr. Jackson's appointment as Minister Plenipotentiary of England at Paris during the Congress at Amiens, Mr. Otto may receive a corresponding appointment here, so that neither he nor Mr. Jackson, who will probably succeed Mr. Liston in America, will be at liberty to leave Europe before the spring.

Nothing decisive has yet taken place respecting the 6th and 7th Articles of our Treaty with this Country ; I shall, however, be able to send you more explicit, and, I am willing to hope, more satisfactory information upon this subject, in the course of the next month.

I have called Lord Hawkesbury's attention to the subject of the Trade between the English West Indies and our Ports, which, without timely regulations, may be liable to great embarrassment upon the return of Peace ; but he is at present so engaged, that I have not yet been able to bring the subject fairly under consideration : I shall resume at the first moment I perceive a favorable opening to do so.

Notwithstanding the fine and abundant Harvests of this Country, Corn continues to be dear and in the opinion of all judges will so far maintain the high price that the ports will be open throughout the year.

With perfect Respect & Esteem, &c., &c.

RUFUS KING.

R. KING TO ROBERT R. LIVINGSTON, &C., &C.

LONDON, Dec. 3, 1801.

DEAR SIR :

The French papers having announced your arrival at L'Orient, in the early part of the last month, I conclude that you have before this time reached Paris, and therefore avail myself of the earliest opportunity to offer you my cordial congratulations on your mission, and to express my earnest hope that its success may in every respect correspond with the favourable anticipations, in which the public, as well as all those who have the satisfaction of knowing you, have beforehand indulged themselves.

The return of Peace will serve to render your residence in Europe more agreeable, not only by the good humour and politeness it may be expected to reestablish, but by relieving you from the endless detail of business, in which you would have unavoidably been engaged by a continuation of the war.

The distance between us is so inconsiderable, that I promise myself the pleasure of frequently hearing of your welfare ; and Mrs. King, who unites with me in sincere regards to Mrs. Livingston, likewise joins me in the offer of our services in any way in which they may be made useful to you or any part of your family.

With great Respect & Esteem, &c., &c.

RUFUS KING.

R. TROUP TO R. KING.

NEW YORK, 5th December, 1801.

DEAR SIR :

. . . We received the account of peace between Great Britain and France in this city on the 20th ulto, via Boston. It instantly operated almost like the hand of death upon all business. I had two auctions on that day on hand at the Coffee House : one of Sir Wm. (Pulteney's) real property in this city ;

the other of lands in my hands as an executor of an insolvent estate. There were several other auctions depending. All was knocked up, instead of being knocked down ! Not a bid was given ; every thing was buzz and confusion in the Coffee House. Ships have fallen. Wheat, corn and flour have been constantly on the fall ! In short all business dull and nearly at a stand. I hear however, of no bankruptcies, and much serious mischief does not seem to be apprehended. . . .

For twelve days past the city has been much agitated with a duel * between Hamilton's oldest son Philip and a Mr. Eacher—a brother lawyer of mine and a violent and bitter democrat. . . . Young Hamilton was mortally wounded and soon after died. Never did I see a man so completely overwhelmed with grief as Hamilton has been. The scene I was present at, when Mrs. Hamilton came to see her son on his deathbed (he died about a mile out of the city) and when she met her husband and son in one room, beggars all description ! Young Hamilton was very promising in genius and acquirements, and Hamilton formed high expectations of his future greatness ! . . . At present Hamilton is more composed and is able again to attend to business ; but his countenance is strongly stamped with grief. Eacher has not since made his appearance at the bar. There is a general current of opinion agt. him, except amongst the violent democrats.   Very truly yours,

R. T.

———

Talleyrand and La Forêt. †

London, Dec. 7, 1801.

Otto called upon me in the evening to mention that he had received credentials as Min. Plenip. to this Court, and to make inquiry respecting the mode of dress, presentation, &c. After going over this subject we talked of various others and among them I spoke of the reputation he had established by keeping his secret so well and not gambling in the Eng. funds during the negotiation, and then observed that tho' I understood him well enough and could account for his discretion, which was so very

---

* See vol. iii., p. 33.   † Memorandum Book.

commendable, I could not tell how Talleyrand & La Forêt, especially the first, were kept back and restrained, for they must have known all that was doing. Otto made no scruples about Talleyrand's character and likewise admitted that La Forêt was fond of money and liked speculation, &c. In America he was always engaged in little bargains and calculating. Indeed it must be owing to something of this sort that he had been sent to Munich as minister—a place no ways equal to that he held in the Post office. But he was Talleyrand's man and agent and very likely had been engaged in some affair wh. made it expedient to send him away from Paris. As to the negotiation here it was curious, early at the time of the proposed armistice. The first proposition which he received from France to be made to the Brit. Govt. arrived at 3 o'clock P.M.; before 8 o'clock it was known in the City, or rather he knew it was there known as soon as 8 o'clock, and might have been sooner known, & the purport of it appeared in the Morning Post ; all this before he had made his communication to the Brit. Govt. In his very next dispatch, Otto said, he took notice of this circumstance, justified himself and expressed surprise how the intelligence should have got air. In a future stage of the discussion, the purport of an important dispatch was actually known on the Exchange of London and produced a rise of 2 per cent in the funds before he, Mr. Otto, received it. In his next dispatch to his Govt. he stated this extraordinary fact and protested against the injury to his own character, wh. wd. immediately proceed from it. In reply he was told that there could have been no disclosure thro' any of the officers of the Bureau, as the dispatch was written by Mr. Talleyrand himself and not trusted to any of his Secretaries. After this complaint, Otto remarked, an attempt was immediately made and persisted in to take the business out of his hands, and that understanding the motive, he had to employ the best means in his power to prevent the success of the intrigue.

During the late negotiation the Parties were doubtless restrained by the resistance they had before met with ! ! ! Otto said he had been offered a share in a concern by wh. Talleyrand was to gain £200,000 Stg, himself £100,000 Stg, and the English concurred, he knew not how much, but he had peremptorily refused.

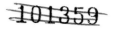

Genet.

Otto told me that Genet was the author of his own instructions, wh. he published in America ; being a favorite of Brissot, who with the Commee. of his day was engaged in a thousand affairs, he was desired to draw a sketch of his own Instructions, wh. were brought at a late hour of the day, read over with haste & signed. Besides Genet was a known Royalist and in all his conduct in America played a part ! ! !

Admiral Sir William Parker.

This Admiral was sent to Halifax, as Lord Spencer told me, because he was believed to be a prudent officer and would curb the plundering spirit of the squadron stationed on our coast.

Instead of his conduct corresponding with this character, he turned out to be an avaricious and disobedient Commander—and during his command increased, instead of curbing, the depredation on American trade.   Captain Pelew of the Cleopatra was one of the most vexatious of those under Parker's command.   On my complaint, Lord Spencer recalled Pelew, but Parker instead of obeying and sending him home, gave him leave to make a cruise after Spaniards in the West Indies and Gulf of Mexico, where he ran the Cleopatra ashore and was obliged to return to Halifax, where her repairs cost upwards of £8,000 Stg.

Parker also under the pretence of sending seven or eight refractory soldiers who were condemned at Halifax to serve in the fields as convicts or slaves in Jamaica, sent the America, a 74, with them to the West Indies with orders to cruize for Spaniards in the Gulf of Florida, where she was lost.   Parker for these instances of disobedience and for sending the America off her station, was lately brought to a Court Martial at Portsmouth and acquitted ; owing as Nepean told me to the base spirit of gain, with wh. the majority of the court was influenced—a spirit, said he, which has done us more mischief than can be imagined, wh. not only excited the resentment of for. and neutral States, but occasioned the Mutiny wh. well nigh ruined the Brit. Navy.

The system of secrecy as to the votes of the members of a Court Martial must be done away with as it serves to protect

base men and cover base principles.   An Act of Parliament
must be made for this purpose and Sir Wm. Scott had engaged to
go into a thorough reform of the Prize Courts in order thro' them
to check these depredations.

***

R. KING TO WILLIAM EATON, TUNIS.

LONDON, Dec. 10, 1801.

SIR :

The Jewels for the Bey being finished, and Mr. Hargraves purposing to embark in an English Frigate, which sails in a day or
two, for Algiers, I have concluded to send them to you by him,
without waiting for the arms, which, though in great forwardness,
will not be completed in less than two months.   Randall &
Bridge, the King's Jewellers, who have executed this commission,
have assured me that the Jewels should be most carefully and
securely packed, so that I hope you will receive them speedily,
and in good condition ; the invoice of these articles you have
enclosed.   As soon as the arms are finished, they shall likewise
be forwarded to you.   The Cloths, as I have before advised you,
have been shipped and will, I expect, reach you before Mr.
Hargrave's arrival.

The Cloths and Silks first sent, tho' unsuitable for the purpose
for which they were purchased, may sell for sufficient to reimburse
their cost and charge, especially as the silks were supplied at
reduced prices.

Mr. McDonough will no longer remain at Tripoli ; his successor will be instructed to observe in respect to the United States
and their affairs a conduct conformable to the good understanding and harmony subsisting between the United States and Great
Britain.   With great respect &c &c

RUFUS KING.

***

R. KING TO MR. ADDINGTON.

Private.

GR. CUMBERLAND PLACE, Dec. 11, 1801.

DEAR SIR :

Will you do me the favour to inform me whether the business,
concerning which I have but too perseveringly resorted to you,

has yet been decided by the Cabinet ? The delays which have so long prevailed, are doubtless such as belong to, and are usual in affairs of this nature. Experience has taught me that I had formed erroneous estimates of these matters, and I am now convinced of what I suspect others have long since been, that I consulted my zeal rather than my prudence, when I was prevailed upon to engage in a service, for which every day of my life shows me my own incapacity. I however console myself that a little more time and patience will bring me my relief. I entreat you, my dear Sir, to pardon these observations, which are by no means designed to draw from you the slightest notice of the occasion of them, but merely to excuse myself in your good opinion for the endless trouble that it has been my misfortune (for such I shall always think it) to give you.

I am, Dr. Sir, your obliged & faithful Svt.

R. K.

Note. Ansd. There had been a decision of the Cabinet, which Lord Hawkesbury would communicate.

J. Q. Adams to R. King.

QUINCY, 11 December, 1801.

DEAR SIR :

Since I wrote you last, (13 October) I have been to the city of Washington, and brought home my wife and child—We have spent a fortnight here with my father, and in a few days expect to get settled in Boston.

At New. York, on my return home, I first heard of the peace concluded between France and England, which was very unexpected here, as it appears to have been, even in London. Its influence upon our affairs public and private will no doubt be important and not in every respect favourable. Much partial inconvenience is to be foreseen ; but if the enterprise and industry of our country is checked in one quarter, I believe it will soon make its way in another. The prices of goods have generally fallen, and some unremunerative stagnation of commerce must ensue. Our merchants and ship-builders, however, anticipate a temporary advantage from the want of vessels in France, where they hope to find a good market for many of their supernumerary ships.

Our internal affairs continue to present an aspect of great tranquillity. The Session of Congress must have commenced, but we have not yet received the President's speech.

About a fortnight since, General Hamilton's eldest son was killed in a duel with a Mr. Eacker. He is said to have been a young man of great promise.*

Faithfully your's
JOHN QUINCY ADAMS.

The letter of condolence of Mr. King to his friend, General Hamilton, written on January 12, 1802, is here given, though out of date.

R. KING TO HAMILTON.

Both as a friend and a father I do most unfeignedly participate and condole with you in the heavy affliction that has fallen upon your family. It would be altogether vain for me to have recourse to the usual topics of consolation. In so severe a calamity it must be sought for among the treasures of your own mind, which nature has so eminently endowed ; and after a while it will likewise be found in the promising branches of your family which remain, to recall to your remembrance as well as to console you for the loss you have suffered.

With most faithful regard & attachment, &c.

T. SEDGWICK TO R. KING.

STOCKBRIDGE, 14 December, 1801.

MY DEAR SIR :

. . . I am retired to private life and as yet I am rejoiced that I am so. The little prospect of benefit which I saw from any thing that I could do, the injury which my private concerns

------

* In the *Life of Hamilton*, vol. vii., p. 499, an account of this duel, with the circumstances which led to it, is given. The young man was only nineteen years of age, but warmly interested in the political questions of the day, the discussion of which involved his father's name and character, and brought on the quarrel which resulted in his death.

sustained by my absence, and the importance of my presence to the welfare of my family, at the same time afforded cogent motives, & justified, in my opinion, a conformity of conduct to them.

I confess to you, my dear sir, that I have been disappointed in the effect produced in New England by the election of Mr. Jefferson. I did believe that his known hostility to the federal measures, which are essential to its prosperity, & not less so his enmity to those institutions which habit, and as I supposed principle had endeared to the people, would, at the same time, have checked the progress of democracy, lessened the number of its adherents, and infused into the well disposed a spirit of union among themselves, & of exertion against their adversaries ; but, instead of this, democratic influence has increased, as I believe, in every state.   This, as I think, is owing, more than to any other cause, to the spirit of avarice, which has been fostered not only by the general course of public events, but by the measures of the government, and the addresses which have openly & constantly been made to this odious, degrading & sordid passion. Every puny prater who talks much of the interest of the people, the necessity of public economy, and the importance of calculating every public measure on the principle of taking the least portion possible of " the fruits of labor from the mouth which earns it," is sure of an affectionate reception from the people. Even well meaning men, perceiving the effects of these delusive professions, have employed them, as instruments to acquire popularity.   Hence every warm, and generous, and manly sentiment is stifled ; and hence *national degradation* on one hand, and the *glory of our country*, on the other, have become unmeaning & unintelligible expressions.   The decrease of public burdens is represented, as certain, from the election of Mr. J.

There is another circumstance which is equally discouraging. The aristocracy of virtue is destroyed ; personal influence is at an end.   No length nor degree of popular service, neither the most shining talents, nor the most and disinterested conduct, give anything like weight and authority to character.   What means are there, then, of regaining power by the federalists ?   Whenever the federal systems shall be broken, and the feebleness which must result from a complete relaxation shall *be felt*, the people may remember those men whose wise counsels have once saved

them from ruin & again place the government in their hands. . . .
But should the blunders & folly of the Philosophers consign them
again to insignificance, how long will the federalists be able to
defend themselves against those means which have been found
sufficient for the destruction of their influence?   . . .

I do not think that Mr. J——n has lost any influence by his removals from office.   There is nothing more mischievous & mon-
strous than the principle, and it is avowed, on which this conduct
rests.   It is, palpably, rendering the aggregate of the emoluments
of all the offices, holden at the pleasure of the president, a mass
of electioneering corruption.   And yet there is a wonderful tranquillity prevailing on the avowal and practice of this conduct.
There was a time when the resentment of the people of Connecticut would have been roused, almost to frenzy, by removing such
men as Chester, Goodrich and Whittlesey, from important offices,
to fill them with such as Thirley, Bishop and Wolcott, let the
motive have been whatever it might ; but on this occasion, tho' a
most detestable motive is declared, no great degree of sensibility
seems to be excited among even good men ; and so far from
ruining the President's influence, the number of Jacobin voters at
the last congressional election, in that state, was greater than at
any former election.

Amidst all the unpleasing reflections which are presented to
the mind there is one which, to me, affords consolation.   You
will not be removed.   There is nothing, unless I am greatly deceived, that the leaders of that party, a certain little great man
excepted, view with more horror than a rupture with G. Britain.
Yet do they consider that dreaded event as not improbable.
They will, therefore, avoid everything that may furnish evidence
to charge them with an intention to produce it.   They will not,
therefore, remove a federalist from, to send a democrat to, the
court of London.   And I do most sincerely hope, tho' there is
not on earth a man whom I more wish to see, that it may not be
too disagreeable to you to continue there.

But what will be the course of conduct which this administration will pursue?   As I have told you heretofore it will be the
object of Mr. Jefferson's ambition to reduce in practice the
administration of this government to the principles of the confederation.   . . .

The revenue is so abundant that, even, should all our expenses be continued, it will probably be supposed that some of the most unpopular taxes may be repealed. Perhaps the salt duty will be considered as the most grateful sacrifice. . . .

There is nothing which the party more anxiously wish than the destruction of the judicial arrangements made during the last session, because of the impediments which that throws in the way of their rapid progress to the ultimate goal of democratic reform. It is certain that a demolition of this system is contemplated by the President; for the Secy. of state has written to the marshals or clerks of all the eastern districts, & I suppose of all the districts, to report to him, the number of actions which have been determined in those courts, & the number now depending—the object undoubtedly is to show how much money is paid for how little business. Yet it is said, with what truth I know not, that some of the party are of opinion that the Judges who are appointed cannot be displaced by a repeal of the law. This, I believe, is certain that a repeal will not be attempted, unless it can be assured beforehand that a majority in both houses can be obtained, in favor of the measure. I am not, myself, satisfied that a repeal of the law would be unconstitutional, for that would imply that a rational reform of the judicial, under circumstances which might reasonably be expected, would be impracticable; but I shall be happy if such doubts, however founded, shall prevent so inauspicious a procedure. . . .

What will be the result of peace in Europe I know not—in this country the effect must have a considerable influence on almost all descriptions of persons. Except those whose dependence for support is on salaries, there will be a general decrease of the means of expense, and a consequent reduction of the prices of all property. How far this will create discontent, and what will be the direction of it, you can conjecture.

I am ever sincerely yours.

R. KING TO LORD ELDON.

GREAT CUMBD. PLACE, Dec. 17, 1801.

MY LORD:

I take the liberty to send you enclosed a Draught of the proposed convention as it was settled in our former Conferences with the addition of a new article founded upon the demand that the payments on your side should be made by Installments corresponding with those to be made in America.

With perfect Respect &c.

R. K.

———

R. KING TO LORD ELDON.

GREAT CUMBD. PLACE, Dec. 21, 1801.

MY LORD :

I called in Downing Street today in hopes that Lord Hawkesbury would be prepared to give me a definitive answer concerning the Draught of the Convention which by your Lordship's permission I took the liberty to send you.   But as he had not seen it he could say nothing upon the subject.   Will you have the goodness to send the Draught to Lord Hawkesbury, with such alterations as you may think proper to make upon it.

Being desirous to finish this affair before the interruption of the Holidays, I pray you to pardon the solicitude with which I pursue it.

With great Respect & Esteem, &c., &c.

RUFUS KING.

CHAPTER III.

The two following letters will show the views of leading Federalists inspired by the Message of President Jefferson to Congress, and are therefore full of interest, conveying, as they did to Mr. King, the gloomy forebodings that filled their minds as to the future of the country under its new rulers.

JOSEPH HALE TO R. KING.

BOSTON, Dec. 19, 1801.

DEAR SIR :

We yesterday received the enclosed message. This mode of testifying his homage of respect to the National Legislature, the President has preferred to that which custom & habit had already sanctioned. Would to God ! that in this manner only his administration were distinguished from that of his predecessors !

38

The Genevan & American Philosophers you will find more bold in experiment than wise & intelligent as statesmen. In their visionary brains the amount of our revenue by import is calculated even to a cent for preceding years. Its surplus is to astonish the citizens. The armistice lately signed at London is to produce general & perpetual harmony between Nations. Our government is only to state its claims upon other nations to have them at once recognized & improved. The wild principles of uproar & misrule which have given elevation & political consequence to our existing administration are philosophically speaking to produce tranquillity & subordination in an inverse ratio to their tendency towards anarchy & confusion. Our nation is to derive consequence from being stript of every national attribute & from the sovereignty & independence of the several estates. Our National credit is to be supported by withdrawing the sources of revenue by which alone it can be maintained. The independence of our Judiciary is to be confirmed by being made wholly subservient to the will of the legislature & the caprice of Executive visions. The farmer at the toil of his ploughshare is to learn military tactics & when diking his meadows the principles of fortification. To crown all, a National character is to be derived from freely admitting to the rights of citizenship the " unhappy fugitives " from law & justice of every other nation upon earth. Such is my brief comment upon the inclosed text. Gloomy apprehensions may have rendered me unfit to give an opinion upon the subject. Your knowledge & experience will, I hope for the welfare of our country, enable you to entertain more agreeable reflections than at this moment irresistibly impress my mind. As under adverse prospects we are inclined to seek consolation, so in the present instance I am disposed to repose with a degree of confidence on the habits & principles of New England & the virtue, intelligence, & patriotism of men of talents & influence throughout our country. Their temperate, still voice may for a time be drowned in the clamours of democratic frenzy, but their energies must & will eventually impress & correct the public sentiment & acquire additional momentum from the unreasonable tho' natural checks & opposition of weak & unprincipled men.

Your friend & obed servt.

JOSEPH HALE.

F. Ames to R. King.

December 20th, 1801.

My dear Sir :

The new President's speech is out, he calls it a message. This difference is pretended to be important to save time, money and ceremony. Is not this philosophy, dignity &c &c. The message announces the downfall of the late revision of the Judiciary ; economy, the patriotism of the shallow and the trick of the ambitious—It proposes that Congress shall legislate in every case to the very rim and outside edge of its power—lest executive discretion should take its place and usurp its powers. Therefore the items for appropriation are to be designated specifically. Instead of laying down rules of conduct, Congress is to apply these rules in detail and is to be president, as to army, navy and taxes, the U. S. Gov't has little to do, and is to be dismantled like an old ship. For it is evident that the state gov'ts are to be exhibited as alone safe and salutary. Thus Congress is to do everything instead of the heads of departments. Committees instead of Cong. The sovereign people are to be excited to controul these and Virginia is to be as strong as the union is made weak.

I am full of commentary on this ample text, but you will not need my help to make your own. Those who lean for support on one state, and on exciting the passions of the people to weaken every obstacle to the domination of that state, will understand their part. You will see a broad hint about the *carrying Trade.* Expect Madison's resolutions over again and the pretty plan of the Report on the privileges and restrictions of our Commerce.

You will see perhaps by some of the Mass'tts papers that the Farmer, alias Atty General U. S., alias Lincoln is outrageously agt. the federalists and the whole body of the Clergy and denounces the wrath of The People unless they abstain from their evil ways. The peace (between France and England) will not calm the agitations of this country : its terms present France as an object both of terror & admiration. Unless Buonaparte shd. die, her exorbitant power will be consolidated so as to overturn Europe first, then the World. But his life is precarious. I am surprised at the kind of admiration lavished by wise men on this adventurer ; allow him heroism—allow him genius—yet his admirers invest him with qualities which he has given little evidence that he possesses. Political sagacity is ascribed to him as if he excelled Pitt and Thugut and all the old statesmen of old Govts. The vis major requires very little of it. . . . I cannot conceive of a long duration of peace, when all that exists is prodigious and out of nature. Ambition sees no obstacles and it's victims can have no shelter. Is not Europe as much a prey as Italy was to Rome after the war with Pyrrhus ? Spain, Portugal, Holland and Italy are so many provinces of France.

This state affords no matter of news. It is quiet, but soon to be agitated by the intrigues to bring in Gerry Governor. The National Egis, a paper at Worcester, is set up for that end. Lincoln is said to have formed, as well as promoted, the plan, but when there was a call for money, he was off. It is hoped by printing frothy nonsense in that county to revolutionize the state. What sense we have is no match for our prejudice and nonsense, and soon or late, the contest will turn against us. I omitted to say that the Farmer in his Egis modestly and consistently rails agt. the Palladium as a gazette that is supported by the Federalists, and the Clergy.

Yrs &c

R. KING TO SECRETARY OF STATE.

No. 45.

LONDON, Dec. 23, 1801.

SIR :

In consequence of a letter written by lord Hawkesbury to Sir John Nicholl, the King's Advocate, a copy of which is annexed, a sentence of restitution has been given by the High Court of Admiralty in favour of all the American Ships and Cargoes, detained on their passages to Havre de Grace, except the Ship Frederick and Cargo, of New York, whose Agents, contrary to my instructions, brought on her trial before the interference in her favour, which we had reason to expect on the part of this Government. As an appeal has been made in this case, perhaps the sentence of condemnation may be reversed in the Court of Appeals.

These cases are not more remarkable on account of the Executive intervention, by which a restitution has been attained, than for the singular circumstance that the Claimants' best interests and wishes have been against their own success; inasmuch as a recurrence to the insurance offices would have been a less loss than will now attend the adventures from the fall of markets in consequence of the Peace.

With perfect Respect & Esteem &c

RUFUS KING.

TO HIS MAJESTY'S ADVOCATE GENERAL.

Copy.

DOWNING STREET, November 23, 1801.

SIR :

Mr. King, the American Minister at this Court, having represented to me that several American Vessels, destined for the Port of Havre, have been recently captured off that Port, and that the Owners of these Vessels and their Cargoes were from special circumstances ignorant of the Blockade of the Port and of the notification thereof, at the period of their departure from the Ports of the United States, and of their respective captures; I have it in command to desire you to signify to the Judge of the High Court of Admiralty, that considering the ignorance of the Blockade of Havre de Grace (notwithstanding the notification thereof) under which the American Vessels lately taken, were going to that Port, and the special circumstances which have occasioned such ignorance; and considering also the communications which had passed upon the subject between Mr. King, the Minister of the United States and his Majesty's Servants previous to the capture of those Vessels, it is his Majesty's pleasure that all the Rights and Interests which may belong to him in such captured Vessels and their Cargoes shall be given up and released, and that the proprietors thereof, who were really so ignorant of the Blockade shall be relieved as far as by law they may from any penalties to which their property would otherwise be exposed on account of its being destined to a Blockaded Port.

I have the honour to be &c

HAWKESBURY.

LORD DUNMORE.*

Sir Andrew J. Hammond, who commanded the naval force on board of wh. Lord Dunmore, with Gov. Eden of Maryland, took refuge told me that not 4 Genn. of the Country joined Lord Dunmore, indeed he said he remembered none but Warmely ; that the negroes carried off were about 700 ; that those who adhered to Lord Dunmore were chiefly Scotchmen from the shores of Virginia.   When he left the Chesapeake on Sir Wm. and Lord Howe's arrival at N. York, he had near 150 transports with Lord Dunmore and his adherents on board ; that Dunmore wished to have burned and destroyed the country ; that he resisted it and proposed to him the plan to leave the Chesapeake and to send his Lps. adherents to St. Augustine, Bermudas & Halifax, wh. he did.

That owing to the attacks of the Provincials he cd. not water the Transports and was obliged to go up the Potomac with all the empty casks he cd. collect to take in fresh water.   It was on this expedition, which was solely for water, that Dunmore wanted to land and burn Brent or Brett's house on the Potomac.   This he, Hammond, resisted till the Provincials assembled on the shore and fired upon & wounded two or three of his men and killed one as they passed in their boats from ship to ship.   Dunmore then renewed the proposal of landing, to wh. he consented, & Lord Dunmore landed with about 1000 men, drove the Provincials killing 18 or 20, burned Brent or Brett's house, &c, and laid waste the country for five miles round, reembarking in the evg. with a trifling loss.   In the night a boat came to them from Alexandria, offering to pilot them and serve as guides to burn Alexandria & Gen. Washington's house.   Dunmore was eager to embark at 12 o'clock that night ; he opposed, said the burning of houses & towns wd. not serve to reconcile America & Engd., and to Dunmore's great mortification informed him that so far from permitting the expedition agt. Alexandria, he wd. the next morning weigh anchor and return down the Chesapeake, wh. he said he did tho' not more than $\frac{2}{3}$ of the water casks had been filled.

Afterwards he said that Genl. Washington whom he knew personally & had before passed a week or more with him at Mount Vernon, sent his Aid de Camp Hamilton to thank him for his forbearance and moderation when near Alexandria.

* Memorandum Book.

HAWKESBURY.*

Dec. 26, 1801.

Called on Ld. Hawkesbury and delivered to him the draught of a Convention including the articles before settled concerning the 6th. Article of the Treaty of 1794, & an addl. one respecting the Commission under the 7th. Article. I had before sent him this last article, but now delivered the entire draught. He said he wd. take the earliest opportunity to see Ld. Eldon, and on my explaining the objections to the awards being paid into the Bank &c., as had been proposed, he appeared to acquiesce and approve the modification I had suggested.

The conversation took a turn towards general politics. He asked my opinion of the success of the Fr. Exp. to St. Domingo, wh. gave me an opportunity to speak of the force sent; wh. he said they were told by the Fr. Govt. would be 15 ships of the line and 20,000 troops. I said the best hopes of success were placed in managing Toussaint, who was ignorant, superstitious and as far as one cd. judge a suitable character for the experiment; unless the Fr. went this way to work they wd. fail, &c. Lord H. said that there were difft. opinions among their best informed men; Maitland & he believed a majority of opinions inclined to this conclusion.

He asked me if I had heard any thing farther from Paris respecting Louisiana.—I answered in the negative, except that I had heard the Govt. had been offered to Massena at the same time that the Embassy to Petersburgh and Constantinople were offered to him.

Ld. H. said that the French wd. make great exertions to improve & extend their colonies; that during the negotiations they always insisted upon the necessity of their having extensive colonies at the close of the war, as Eng. had at the close of her civil war; and whither they might send their perturbed spirits, &c. Lannes had been sent to Portugal, Macdonald to Copenhagen and doubtless Massena wd. be persuaded to go to Constantinople, &c. Ld. H. then enquired if I thought Otto wd. remain here, adding if Bonaparte was sincere for peace, &c., it wd. be the best proof he cd. give to leave Otto here. Besides

* Memorandum Book.

London wd. not be a proper place to send Massena or any others of wh. he may be jealous, as from its proximity it wd. be convenient to carry on, and with the utmost safety, any conspiracy agt. him. It was impossible to say what the situation of France is to be; whether the old family would be restored or a new dynasty established. Bonaparte was as strong and as well prepared as he or any one could be. St. Cloud which was repairing was one of the strongest military posts about Paris. All Europe at present held the same language; all are rejoiced at peace; it is popular everywhere and the minds of men in every Cabinet and State, fatigued with the cares and efforts of war, are anxious for repose, so that from without Bonaparte has nothing to apprehend. . . .

Bonaparte was certainly an extraordinary character; he has satisfied his ambition as a warrior, and was now aiming at reputation as a statesman. His views were turned to commerce, manufactures, finance &c; success in these pursuits peace. At present he has great difficulties on acct. of the state of credit, public and private; and his most pressing labour must be to overcome these difficulties; they certainly were formidable and one must wait to see the effect of his plans.

WILLIAM PINKNEY TO R. KING.

BATH, Jany 9, 1802.

DEAR SIR:

I have had the pleasure to receive your letter of yesterday and have communicated the gratifying intelligence contained in it to Mr. Trumbull.

I offer you my sincere congratulations on the successful close of the business, the whole course of which must have been to you a trial of patience,* for which nothing but the actual issue could compensate.

* Mr. Gore, who was in Paris awaiting the decision as to the reassembling of the Commission under the 7th Article, had written to Mr. King, Oct. 15, 1801. I have known too intimately the trials which your patience has experienced in this unnecessarily protracted negotiation, and your repeated sacrifice of personal feeling to public duty, not to appreciate the weight of this new disappointment, the more aggravated as it could not have been suspected by the most jealous distrust. Should the business fail now, it will display such a character in one party as to leave no doubts in the other of its future conduct, & of the relation, which the two countries must ever bear to each other.

As it is stipulated that the Commission under the 7th Article is to recommence immediately, I presume that it will be proper that the absent members of the Board shd. repair with as little delay as possible to London. My own wish, indeed, wd. have been to remain here a few weeks longer for the benefit of the waters. . . .

Will you allow me to enquire whether it has been found practicable to introduce into the Convention a clause relative to the Bank Stock?

With unfeigned Esteem.

WM PINKNEY.

January (probably 8th) 1802.

* Ld. Hawkesbury, having notified Mr. King that the draught of the Convention, having been agreed upon, shd. be engrossed and ready for signature the next day, he desired him to meet him then at his office for the purpose of signature. Mr. King says:

On my arrival at the hour assigned, Mr. Hammond desired me to go into the room of Mr. Rolliston, the first Clerk, who had prepared two copies, & Lord Hawkesbury being engaged, I collated the copies with Mr. Rolliston, who put Lord Hawkesbury's & my seals to them. As he was about to affix the seals I asked him if he had received any instructions how to place them, he answered no, but that they should be placed on a line. I acquiesced and the seals were so placed. Mr. Hammond then joined us and we went into Lord Hawkesbury's room, where we signed in the presence of Hammond, his Lordship signing first. I then mentioned that it was of no consequence, but I was not sure that the signatures and seals had not, as on former occasions, been one above the other & not on a line. Hammond immediately turned to the Treaty of 1794 and found that such had been the mode of execn. Lord Hawkesbury did not appear to think the difference of consequence, & I immediately said it was an affair of no importance—as between us and them there cd. be no dispute about questions of this sort, any interference of Pretensions

* Memorandum Book.

wd. doubtless relate to more interesting concerns.   Lord Hawkesbury treated the subject as of no significance—and the third and
fourth copies, which were not signed until two or three days
afterwards, were executed in like manner as the first.

R. KING TO SECRETARY OF STATE.

No. 48.

LONDON January 9, 1802.

SIR :

At length I am able to send you a Convention which I yesterday signed with Lord Hawkesbury, respecting the 6th & 7th
Articles of our Treaty of 1794.   The Commutation of the 6th
article of the Treaty of 1794, and the confirmation so far as it
respects the future operation of the 4th Article of the Treaty of
Peace remain as they were settled in October last : and I have
nothing to add to my former reports upon these Points.   The
Claim upon us to consent to a commutation of the 7th Article
has been given up, and it is agreed that the Commissioners shall
reassemble and proceed in the execution of their duties, according to the provisions of the Article, except only that instead of
their demands being made payable at such times as they should
appoint, the same shall be payable in three equal instalments,
corresponding with those to be paid in America.

As our Claims are to be ascertained by the Board of Commissioners, which has heretofore added interest up to the day on
which its awards were made payable, and which is at liberty to
do so in respect to their future awards, the payment by instalment's may not be thought a material disadvantage, the main
point, that of ascertaining the amount of our claims being satisfactory secured.   Having already burdened my correspondence
with pieces and reports upon these Subjects, which I fear have
been thought both tedious and uninteresting, I do not add, by
way of supplement, a particular account of what has passed since
the date of my No. 40, especially as the discussion has related
solely to the Commission in London, the agreement respecting
which is too explicit to stand in need of explanation.

Two Copies of the Convention have been executed, one of which will be enclosed with the original of this Letter; two more copies are preparing and will in like manner be executed as originals, and endorsed with the Duplicate and Triplicate hereof. I shall likewise send you copies of Lord Hawkesbury's full powers as soon as they can be prepared; those which I made use of are dated June 10, 1796.

Lord Hawkesbury has agreed to send a copy of the third article of the Convention to the British Commissioners; in like manner, I shall send a copy of it to the American Commissioners; and as they are all upon the spot, they will be at liberty to resume their business without farther delay. It will perhaps be thought most convenient that the Ratifications should be exchanged here.

The Lord Chancellor has assured me that the Maryland Claim shall speedily be decided in his Court; a measure, it seems, deemed necessary to enable the Crown to signify its pleasure respecting the Bank Stock. Although the disappointments we have met with on this Subject must weaken our confidence in the course we have been pursuing, I think it would be impolitic at present to change it; the claim, which in my conviction is most just, shall continue to receive my unremitting attention.

With Perfect Respect & Esteem &c.

RUFUS KING.

R. KING TO JAMES MADISON, ESQ.

Private.

LONDON January 11, 1802.

DEAR SIR:

Although for the reason suggested in my official correspondence I have omitted to send you an account of what passed respecting the VI and VII Articles of the Treaty of 1794, subsequent to Mr. Dawson's departure, I have on reflection thought it might be satisfactory and perhaps useful that I should in this way supply the omission.

Lord Grenville on being consulted by Lord Hawkesbury having given an explicit opinion that he had in no respect pledged the Government concerning the settlement of the 6th & 7th Articles of the Treaty of 1794, and that the execution of the latter article according to its provisions would be a measure which ought to have a material influence on the ascertainment of the sum to be accepted for the abolition of the former, I prepared and sent to Mr. Addington a concise view of the origin, progress and present situation of the Negotiation, corresponding with a more detailed Statement which I likewise sent to the Lord Chancellor, and a copy of which is annexed. Special considerations induced me to prefer this manner of making the representation, to one that would have been more regular, and which I remained at liberty to make, should circumstances require it. In subsequent conversations with Mr. Addington, I had reason to be satisfied with the steps I had taken ; for he told me that he saw the subject in its true light and was ready to admit that to those who were ignorant of personal characters, the objection if persisted in, would unavoidably have the appearance of a mere expedient. To him as well as Lord Hawkesbury I took pains to explain the mutual advantages of a friendly settlement, and the impossibility that I could consent to change the footing upon which the question was now placed.

The business remained in this situation until the middle of December, when Lord Hawkesbury informed me that having again been considered by the Cabinet, it had been decided to close the affair of the Convention upon the Terms which had already been settled, and to agree that the Commissioners under the 7th Article should proceed, provided their awards instead of being payable as they should appoint should be payable by instalments corresponding with those to be paid in America ; and the money deposited in the Bank of England, to be applied on account of the American instalments, which, to an equal amount, should be converted into a fund to satisfy the awards in favor of American claimants.

After taking time to consider this communication, it appeared to me to offer the means of bringing the business to a conclusion ; taken together it amounted to this proposition, that they would accept £600,000 payable by instalments in lieu of the 6th Article, in the execution of which they had a majority of voices, and consent to the execution of the 7th Article according to its Provisions, in which we have a majority of voices ; provided the payments to be made by them should be at the same time as those to be made by us. The two Commissions having been considered as reciprocal checks upon each other in the hands of the respective Governments, the converse of this arrangement will test its merits and determine whether we ought to have rejected it. I thought not ; but disliked the mode in which the end aimed at was to be attained, and therefore prepared an article which, by making the awards payable by instalments to the Claimants, should attain the same end in a more convenient manner. The sum of the awards would be greater or less than £600,000 ; for it was not likely to be precisely that sum ; if less, a balance must still be remitted from America ; if more, in every instalment of every award, the American Claimant would have to receive part of his instalment in America and the balance in England. Besides the trouble of the accounts which must be kept upon this plan, it would create considerable inconvenience, and perhaps injustice ; for all the American Claimants had been called upon to execute Powers of Attorney and appoint Agents to conduct their claims in England, and with much trouble and some expence had complied with this demand. These Claimants, in some cases, had deceased ; in others, become insolvent ; and in not a few instances (including perhaps cases of insolvency) having anticipated the awards in their favour, had authorized their attornies to reimburse their advances out of the monies which might come into their hands from the awards ; besides the plan contained no provision in respect to awards in favour of British subjects.

Upon stating these objections to the Lord Chancellor, he expressed his preference of the article which I had prepared, and which was finally adopted. Another objection, which it was not necessary for me to mention to the Chancellor, had its influence upon my mind ; I mean the appearance which this arrangement would have produced, that the two countries had mutually released each other and had agreed to pay their own Sufferers, an appearance that might have encouraged the Sufferers by French Depredations to call upon Congress to indemnify their losses. What Congress would be inclined to do upon such application it is in every respect unfit for me to conjecture ; tho' in forming a contract in behalf of the public, it was my duty to take care that its deliberations should not be embarrassed by even the appearance of a Precedent, should the supposed case arise.

I take the liberty of adding a word or two to my former communications concerning the II. Article. What is to be deemed a
bona fide Debt, in the sense of the last clause of that Article, will
not depend upon a reference to what was once so, but is a judicial
question within the competence of our Tribunals to determine,
and which must consequently be decided by those general and
acknowledged Principles, by which the Decisions are in similar
cases uniformly governed. If I be not mistaken, it is here understood and expected that the affairs of the old Debts is finally
settled as between the two Governments, and with that share of
Prudence which it behooves the Tribunals of every country to
observe in questions affected by national stipulations, I am persuaded that we shall hear no more of them.

Having for many years thought the settlement now accomplished to be a measure of national importance, and one that had,
in some degree, become indispensable to do away prejudices that
interested and disappointed men had raised against our public
faith, I may, I hope, be permitted, in a private letter to you, to
observe that I have pursued this negotiation with zeal and perseverance, notwithstanding the mass of misrepresentation, prejudice and error with which it has been encumbered. I have done
so in circumstances often discouraging and sometimes apparently
desperate ; cheering myself always with these reflections, which I
have somewhere met with, that it is the duty of every one entrusted with what concerns the welfare of his country, in the
midst of Despair to perform all the offices of Hope. How far
what is done has been well done remains to be determined. If
the President and Senate approve, I shall have nothing to regret.

> With sincere regard and esteem &c. &c.
>
> RUFUS KING.

Mr. King, having finally accomplished the work which he
had so sedulously sought, under so many difficulties and dis-
couragements, to bring to an end, naturally closes his private
letter to Mr. Madison with a reference to these difficulties, in
the overcoming of which he had been so patient and had been
encouraged by a deep sense of duty. Those who have followed the correspondence on the subject will see how ably,
clearly, and yet courteously, Mr. King met and finally over-

came the studied delays interposed by the British Ministers, and the frivolous pretexts for postponing action. It cannot be doubted that the personal respect in which he was held contributed largely in bringing about the result.

––––––

R. King to Secretary of State.

No. 49.

London, Jan. 12, 1802.

SIR :

. . . There is reason to believe the business of the definitive Treaty is going on in a conciliatory way, and as soon as the variety of inferior points, brought forward by the Parties to the Preliminaries, shall have been discussed and decided, that the definitive Treaty will be completed. The consent of this Government to the sailing of the French expedition to St. Domingo is in itself a measure of such importance, as can leave no doubt of its opinion respecting the issue of the Congress at Amiens.

It is true that an English squadron of equal force to that of France was to have proceeded to the West Indies about the same time, that the French squadron sailed, and that it was prevented only by a Mutiny of the crews of several of the ships, which had been ordered upon the Service. This Squadron which had been collected upon the Western coast of Ireland, has returned to Portsmouth, where a Court Martial is now sitting for the trial of the Ringleaders of the Mutiny. These to the number of ten or twelve will probably suffer ; after which the Squadron will proceed to Jamaica whither a number of other ships have been sent in consequence of the Mutiny, and which will be relieved upon the arrival of those originally destined for that Station. The Mutiny is said to have arisen from an aversion to the West Indies, as an unhealthy service, joined to the desire of being paid off and discharged at the end of the war. It is somewhat remarkable that the Ringleaders in the revolt are all Englishmen, a distinction that in the former Mutinies, belonged as exclusively to the Irish. . . .

With perfect Respect & Esteem &c.

RUFUS KING.

CHAPTER IV.

R. King to James Madison.

Private.

London, January 12, 1802.

DEAR SIR :

From the month of May till September or October, including
what is here called the long vacation, very little business can be
done in London, it being the custom of almost all official characters to pass the Summer in the Country and to visit London as
seldom as they can.

I am not aware that anything very pressing will in the course
of the Summer, especially if the Peace be definitely settled, be
likely to require my Services ; and I should like, if I could do so
without interfering with my official duties, to employ the time in
seeing a little of France and some parts of the neighbouring

Countries. This I should not think of doing, if my visit to Washington shall be thought advantageous nor in any event without the permission of the President.

With Sincere Esteem, &c.

RUFUS KING.

R. KING TO HIS EXCELLENCY JOHN ADAMS.

LONDON, January 12, 1802.

SIR :

I have the honour to send you enclosed the copy of a Convention which I have signed with Lord Hawkesbury concerning the 6th & 7th Articles of the Treaty of 1794. As the discussions which have led to this result were begun and conducted under your instructions, I feel it to be my Duty, as well as a mark of Respect that is due to you, to send you this Copy by the same opportunity that I avail myself of to transmit the original to the Department of State.

No one knows more thoroughly than you do the source of those Difficulties, often discouraging, & sometimes disgusting, which continue to encumber our negotiations with this Government ; the affair of the Debts of all others was the most likely to revive feelings and prejudices not yet extinguished, and which have been suffered to do so much real disservice to both Countries ; I have notwithstanding persevered and waded through—whether meritoriously or otherwise, is a question that I must refer to those whose Province it is to decide.

With entire respect and the most sincere attachment &c.

RUFUS KING.

R. KING TO CHIEF-JUSTICE MARSHALL.

Private.

LONDON, Jany. 12, 1802.

DEAR SIR :

It was more than six months after you left the Department of State before I received your last official letter, which was accompanied by a private one of nearly the same date. I ought sooner to have acknowledged its receipt but I have been waiting in hopes that I should be enabled to inform you, which I have now the satisfaction of doing, that the difficulties respecting the execution of the 6th & 7th Articles of the Treaty of 1794 had been settled. I have signed a Convention with Lord Hawkesbury by which England agrees to accept £600,000 payable in three equal instalments of one, two and three years next after the date of the Exchange of Ratifications, in satisfaction of her claims under the 6th Article, which is abolished ; and moreover consents that the Commissioners under the 7th Article shall immediately reassemble and proceed in the discharge of their duties according to the Provisions of the Article, excepting that instead of the awards being made payable at such times as they might appoint, the same shall be payable in three equal instalments corresponding with those to be paid by the U. S.   The Second Art. of the Convention is in these words, "Whereas it is agreed by the 4th Article of the definitive Treaty of Peace, concluded at Paris on the 3d day of September, 1783, between his B. M. and the U. S. that creditors on either side should meet with no lawful impediments to the recovery of the full value in Sterling money of all bonafide Debts theretofore contracted, it is hereby declared that the said 4th Article, so far as it respects its future operation, is hereby recognized, confirmed and declared to be binding and obligatory on his B. M. & the said U. S., and the same shall be accordingly observed with punctuality and good faith, and so as that the said Creditors shall hereafter meet with no lawful impediment to the recovery of the full value in Sterling money of their bonafide Debts."

This Article was inserted for the purpose of enabling the English minister to meet the complaints of the creditors against the sum we are to pay, by referring them to their judicial remedies. We could have no objection to it, provided it was so drawn up as not to enlarge the legal operation of the Article it recognizes. Upon this point I have no doubt.   It confirms the future operation of the 4th Article, or in other words, limits its operation to what is now a legal subject for it to operate upon ; what is now a bona fide Debt, that is what is a legal subject, will not depend upon a reference to what once might have been so, but is a question of judicial competence, and must consequently be decided by those general and acknowledged Principles by which similar cases are decided.   Here it is understood and expected that the affair of the Debts is finally settled as between the two Governments ; and with that share of Prudence which the Tribunals of every country are disposed to observe in questions affected by National stipulations, I am persuaded we shall hear no more of them. Being pressed for time to complete my official Dispatches in season for the Packet, I will only add to this hasty communication the assurance of sincere regard & respect, with which &c.,

RUFUS KING.

P.S. I have sent to the S. of S. a full and exact report of every material occurrence which happened in the course of a difficult and tedious discussion respecting this settlement.

R. KING TO SECRETARY OF STATE.

No. 50.

LONDON, Jan. 15, 1802.

SIR :

I have before mentioned to you that the cession of Louisiana (of which it seems to me, we can have doubt, notwithstanding what may be said to amuse us) was not once a topic of Enquiry or discussion in the negotiation of the Preliminaries ; and for the same reason that it was not heard of on that occasion *Lord Hawkesbury has* * recently informed *me that it* had not been and could not be mentioned *at Amiens*. It is impossible for me to suspect collusion in this affair and my persuasion, after the most careful attention, is that England abstains from mixing herself in it, precisely from those considerations which have led her to acquiesce in others of great importance to the Balance of Europe, as well as her own repose, and upon which she has been altogether silent.

The expedition to St. Domingo did not sail without previous explanations between London and Paris ; its destination was understood to be exclusively to that colony ; at present it is conjectured should the situation of St. Domingo not require the whole force, that a part of it will be sent to take possession of New Orleans.

* Italics in cipher.

I have sent to Mr. Livingston a Copy of the Paper enclosed in my No. 42.,* and shall give to him whatever information upon this and other interesting subjects it may be in my power to do.

As the object and words of the 2nd Article of the Convention will be sought for and examined with care and attention, it occurs to me upon the revision of my former communications to suggest a single observation in addition to those heretofore made. If the second article of the Convention had been entirely omitted, the 4th Article of the Treaty of Peace would have remained in full force and operation ; the adoption of the second article of the Convention limits its force and operation in respect to subjects upon which it once might have so operated, but upon which from various causes it can and ought not in future to operate ; this reflection pursued in its detail will place the article in its true light.

With perfect Respect & Esteem &c.

RUFUS KING.

R. KING TO R. R. LIVINGSTON.

LONDON, Jan. 16, 1802.

DEAR SIR :

If you have received my letter of the 5th, the enclosure, the authenticity whereof I have no reason to doubt, will cast some light upon the subject of your last. During the negotiation of the Preliminaries, I conversed again and again *with the Prime Minister and Secretary of State for Foreign Affairs* concerning *the cession of Louisiana, who* † assured me that the measure was *in their* view of much importance, and one which they could not see but with great concern ; nevertheless that they were unable to interfere respecting it, for the same reason which compelled them to silence concerning other important objects, affecting the equi-

---

* Vol. iv., p. 15. The Copy of the Paper referred to was in some way omitted on page 15. The 5th article of that Treaty is in these words :

" Ce Traité étant en consequence de celui déja conclu entre Le Premier Consul et S. M. E. par lequel Le Roi cède à la France sa Possession de la Louisiane les Parties Contractantes conviennent d'effectuer le dit Traité et de s'arranger à l'égard de leurs Droits respectifs."

The previous treaty to which reference is made was signed Oct. 1, 1800.

† Italics in cipher.

librium of Europe, *and the* welfare *of Great Britain ;* and I am disposed to credit the assurances made to me *that the cession* was neither a subject of enquiry nor discussion during the negotiation of the Preliminaries.

I have since more than once conversed with the same Persons, with the view of impressing upon them the great importance in a variety of respects *of this cession,* especially as it will affect the security *of their colonies,* and offers the means of rearing up and extending the commercial marine *of France,* the only sure foundation upon which she can raise a navy that will be able to cope *with that of England.* Reflections and views of this sort have produced a revision of the Question, but with no other effect than to confirm the decision before made ; and you may infer with confidence that not a word has been *or will be said* upon the subject *at Amiens.*

In the explanations which took place concerning the Expedition that has lately sailed from *France,* it was *here* understood that it was to be wholly confined to the West Indies : the answer *to my* Enquiries was to this effect ; lately however an opinion gains strength that a part of the force, *should the* situation of *St. Domingo* permit, *will be sent to New Orleans. I have* been explicitly told that no such authentic iniormation has been *here* received, and that it is not likely to happen before the definitive Treaty is concluded. On the whole I am persuaded *that G. Britain will see with* much concern the accomplishment *of this cession ;* that it is her interest, and that therefore she will be disposed, to throw impediments in the way of its being completed, but that she will *use no* open measure of opposition, nor such as would afford a Pretence to involve her in new difficulties.

Unless *Spain* is besotted and blind indeed she must desire with anxiety to avail herself of every assistance to get rid of *the cession of Louisiana. Mr. P—y* has without doubt taken the earliest opportunity to explain the light in which the measure is viewed *by us and he* might with confidence infer the disinclination respecting *it of G. Britain.*

Whether it can now be prevented is a question of considerable difficulty ; but in whatever concerns the welfare of one's country, we are called upon even in circumstances of despair to perform the Duties of Hope. My principal reliance would, I confess, be placed upon a temperate, plain, and explicit representation *to the French* Government, which should expose without reserve, and, if the first essay should authorize it, in great detail the extent of the mischiefs, which *we* may be made to suffer from the completion *of the cession,* accompanying the same by assurances of our earnest desire to live in friendship and harmony with *France,* and to cultivate and extend commercial relations between the two Countries, and concluding with a direct insinuation that foreseeing as we do the pernicious influence of the measure upon our political and social happiness, it will be impossible for us to see it carried into operation with indifference ; or afterwards to preserve unimpaired the Confidence we wish to do, in the friendship of a Nation, towards which we cherish the grateful Remembrance of important services.

If *France* value our friendship, or if she care nothing about us, except as her own interest requires, to prevent our too intimate connection with her Rival, the development before hand, of what we believe will be the consequence of measures in the accomplishment of which she is engaged, may have the effect to prevent them.

But I have to entreat your Pardon for any suggestions on my part upon Subjects which your superior Judgment and experience are much more capable than mine to conduct.

With perfect Respect & Esteem &c.

RUFUS KING.

J. Q. ADAMS TO R. KING.

BOSTON, January 18, 1802.

DEAR SIR :

. . . Our political atmosphere still remains serene. Since the meeting of Congress, it appears there is a large majority in the House of Representatives, and a decided, though small one in the Senate, favourable to the views of the Executive. The measures recommended by the President at the opening of the Session, are all popular, in all parts of the union—But they are all undergoing a scrutiny in the public newspapers more able and more severe than they will probably meet in either house of Congress. A writer in the New-York evening post, said to be General Hamilton, has undertaken particularly to point out great and comprehensive errors of system in the message, and his doctrines find great approbation among the federalists, and among all those who consider themselves as the profound thinkers of the nation. These papers, will without doubt be transmitted to you by your friends at New York, and they, with the President's Message and the Report from the Secretary of the Treasury, will give you the fairest view of what our *Administration* and our *opposition* are at this time. As to Congress there has yet been no subject of debate before them, which has called forth any energy of opposition, The apparently leading ministerial members are General Smith, Mr. Giles and Mr. Randolph. The Vice-President has not yet made his appearance, being detained by necessary attention to his private concerns at New York.

The report from the Treasury exhibits a pleasing view of the present state of our finances. It is merely a statement, and avoids with caution the proposal of any measures. The President however has drawn from it the inference that our internal taxes ought to be repealed. This measure will probably be carried into effect. The established system of naturalization, and the judicial courts will have the same fate. Of all these changes the advantages are immediate, obvious, popular, and trifling. Their probable inconveniences are remote, are therefore not discernible to the short sight of the million ; and are of the most weighty consequence. As popularity is the fundamental principle both of our legislature and Executive, they will be satisfied to provide for the occasions of the day, and leave the future times to take care of themselves.

With the highest regard and esteem, I am, dear Sir, faithfully yours,

JOHN Q. ADAMS.

————

R. KING TO SECRETARY OF STATE.

NO. 51.

LONDON, Feb. 5, 1802.

SIR :

Having carefully examined what would be the footing of our Navigation with the British Dominions upon the return of Peace, I was quite prepared for, and indeed by several conversations with Mr. Addington, and other members of the Administration, had already brought under consideration, the subject of your Letter, of the 10th of December, which I received a few days ago.

Immediately after its receipt, I intimated to Lork Hawkesbury my desire to confer with him, respecting the points to which it relates, and upon his naming a day for this purpose, I prepared and sent him the paper a copy of which is annexed. Yesterday I received a duplicate of your letter of December 22nd, which has enabled me to be more explicit than I otherwise should have been, in my conference of this morning with Lord Hawkesbury. I began it by observing that during the continuance of the war, which had the effect to procure to our vessels some preference over others, we had not called their attention to the inequality of their Laws in respect to the Commercial intercourse between the two countries : but as the war was now at an end, we could not delay calling upon them to revise these Commercial Regulations, in order that they may be made comfortable to the respective Rights of the two Countries.

The revision of certain Branches of these Regulations being more urgent than that of others, and the countervailing Duties upon articles imported into Great Britain in American Vessels appearing to be the most urgent, I confined my observations chiefly to this point ; explaining to Lord Hawkesbury my motives for doing so, and after suggesting some further reflexions in addition to those contained in the paper I sent to him, I proposed that they should agree

either

To discontinue the countervailing Duties on Articles imported from the United States in American Vessels, as soon as the difference of Duties on articles imported into the United States in American and British Vessels shall be abolished,

or

To repeal the countervailing Duties upon imports and impose Duties upon all articles exported from Great Britain to the United States in American Vessels; corresponding with the difference of Duties, payable upon the importation of the like articles into the United States in American and British vessels.

Lord Hawkesbury admitted that the only legitimate purpose of the countervailing Right reserved to Great Britain, was to equalize the advantages and disadvantages of the vessels of the two countries in their commercial intercourse ; he said not a single word in vindication of the manner in which this right had been exercised ; and after intimating a preference of the first of the two propositions which I had made, he said he would submit the subject immediately to the Cabinet, and apprize me of its decision with as little delay as possible.

The American Mail was to have been despatched to-morrow, but upon my expressing to Lord Hawkesbury my hope that a few days only would be requisite to enable him to give me an answer upon the subject of our Conference, and my solicitude to transmit it to you by the Packet, he said he would order the Packet to be detained.

The few words which I said concerning the Tonnage Duty were in every respect conformable to the observations on that subject, in the paper sent to Lord Hawkesbury ; and the more I consider it, the more am I satisfied we shall find the advantage of establishing Light-house Duties so as to be distinct from the public Revenue.

Lord Hawkesbury assured me that the subject of the West India Trade should be immediately put in a train for examination.

I have but one observation to add ; it is this, that the return of Peace will not reestablish cordial harmony and good humour between this Country and the Maritime Nations of Europe, among which a general opinion prevails, whether correctly is another point, that the commercial and financial Prosperity of England is in too great a degree at the expence of her neighbours.

These sentiments may lead to restrictions and embarrassments upon the European commerce of this country, which will not fail to make its Trade with us an object of still greater value and importance than it is already known and confessed to be.

Difficulties of this sort are anticipated, and the Government consoles itself with the expectation of a progressive increase in the sale of its Manufactures in America.

The inference from these remarks is, that the present time is a favourable one to press for the consideration and admission of our past claims to a fair and equal share of the advantages to be derived from the Navigation and Trade between the two countries.

The Regulations upon this subject should in the first instance be temporary and ex parte ; in this way they may be adjusted to the reciprocal Rights of the Parties, and then become matter of national Stipulation.

With perfect Respect & Esteem &c

RUFUS KING.

R. KING TO LORD HAWKESBURY.

GREAT CUMBERLAND PLACE, Feby. 9, 1802.

MY LORD :

On revising my letter from the Secretary of State, I perceive that the same idea has suggested itself there, which your Lordship intimated to me yesterday, I mean the expediency of abolishing our Alien Tonnage Duty as well as 10 per cent upon our import Duties on goods imported in foreign vessels, the countervailing Duties here being likewise abolished ; and I therefore take the liberty of suggesting to your Lordship the expediency, that your act be so drawn up as to authorize the repeal of either or both of your countervailing Duties, upon due notice of a corresponding act on our part.

I have reason to conjecture that such has already been the tenour of the Act of Congress, and on the presumption that an entire abolition of all discrimination is mutually our true policy, I beg to express a wish that your Act may be prepared in conformity with the suggestion now made.

With perfect Respect &c

RUFUS KING.

R. KING TO SECRETARY OF STATE.

LONDON, Feb. 9, 1802.

SIR :

The definitive Treaty is not yet signed, but the preparations which are here making to reduce the war establishments, sufficiently evince the expectation of the Government upon this subject. The virtual annexation to France of the Italian Republic, notwithstanding the manner and character of the measure, will not be an impediment to the conclusion of Peace on the side of

England, and Austria and the residue of Italy have no voice at Amiens.

I do not learn what the Peace establishment of this country is likely to be ; the point can scarcely yet be decided, though every one agrees that it will be larger than formerly, and especially at Sea. There will be a squadron of from 20 to 25 Sail of the Line at Jamaica, during the continuance of the French land and naval forces in that quarter ; The expedition from Brest sailed on the 15 of Decr., and on the 28th it had encountered three successive Gales without being able to clear the Bay of Biscay. Admiral Gravina, who put into Ferrol, parted with the fleet on the 28th, when only 13 of 32 sail were together. Another ship has since reached Cadiz in distress, and the naval officers here believe that the expedition must have suffered very considerably.

The Fleet is said not to have been provisioned for more than four months, indeed considering the number of soldiers it carried, it could not well contain provisions for a longer period. Whether Toussaint submits or resists, it seems probable that the greater part of these Ships must proceed to the United States for repairs and provisions soon after they reach St. Domingo ; and possibly a detachment of the English Fleet may follow them ; of this you will before hand be able to judge from the preparations that will have been made for their reception.

Denmark, as I have already informed you, has acceded to the Convention of Petersburgh : Sweden at first hesitated, then ordered her Minister here to notify to this Court her intention to accede, afterwards hesitated again, and instructed her Minister to ask certain explanations of England in respect to the seizure of her Convoy, and the catalogue of Contraband ; and upon receiving for answer that her accession to the Convention of Petersburgh must precede all discussion upon these points, it is now said, she will accede. Prussia has not acceded ; and having nothing to gain by it, will not be likely to do so.

You may perhaps have observed in the late Continental, as well as in the English Papers, paragraphs stating a concert between England and France to repress the piratical practices of the Barbary Powers ; but there is not the smallest foundation for these reports, and I have reason to be satisfied that so far from a change of former views in this respect, not an intimation even upon this subject has been made by either Government to the other.

The rumours circulated in the English Papers, of another change of Ministers appear to be equally unfounded ; the present administration continues to be popular ; as yet they have imposed no new burthens upon the country, and although the ardour which was so general in favour of Peace has somewhat abated, and men begin to speak with freedom of the great uncertainty of its duration, still those, who made it, did so with honest views and in compliance with the public wishes, and on this account are thought deserving of applause and support. It is doubtless true that the Peace, joined to the prolonged negotiations at Amiens, has produced a great stagnation of business in all the commercial Towns of the Country, and it is said that the last Quarter's Revenue will fall considerably short of its former sum ; but these embarrassments may prove to be only temporary, and after a while men may resume and adjust their affairs, according to the new order of things which Peace may establish.

With perfect Respect & Esteem &c

RUFUS KING.

R. KING TO DANIEL PARKER, PARIS.

LONDON, Feby. 12, 1802.

DEAR SIR :

Our friend Mr. Gore having explained to you my desire to send one of my sons to a school in the neighbourhood of Paris, about which he took much pains to inform himself, I feel particularly grateful to you for the permission to place him under your immediate care. It has been my endeavour to impress upon his mind, that he is in every respect to regard you as he would me, and to use the same freedom in communicating to you whatever he ought and has been accustomed to communicate to me. My object is that he should obtain a solid education, and as I am pursuing the same plan with his two elder brothers here, I shall be enabled to compare and judge of their respective progress.

Mr. Des Cassaignes, who does me the favor to take the charge of my son in his journey to Paris, will conduct him to your house ; and it is my desire, after you shall have permitted him to go and pay his duty to Mr. Livingston and Family, that he may without loss of time be sent to school. As he knows but little French and his school fellows and masters may know as little English, he will for a few weeks suffer some embarrassment, and on this account I take the liberty of begging you occasionally to call & see him.

In respect to clothes, pocket money and whatever else regards the economy of the school, my wish is that he may be put upon a footing with his companions, and in no respect beneath them. . .

With unfeigned regards,

RUFUS KING.

It would appear that the journey to his school at Bagneux was a pleasant one and that he immediately determined to study his surroundings, for the following letter, the first he wrote to his father, shows that he certainly was curious. He was not then eleven years old.

BAGNEUX, CE 9 VENTOSE, 1802.

DEAR PAPA :

I hope you and Mamma are both pretty well, as I am.

I came here on Thursday and begin to like it very well. For the two first days we had but soup and eggs for dinner with some bread and wine and water, and after dinner five walnuts ; but to-day we had meat and eggs and after dinner we had each a cake. To-day we went to church (the protestants do not go). I turned myself catholic and in going into the church I dipped my finger in the Holy water, and touched my forehead and then my belly and then my two breasts, then I went into the church and the parson preached in French and Latin, and throwed frankincense about the church and the parson took a sponge upon a stick and throwd Holy water upon all in the church, and then on going out of the church we put our fingers in the Holy water, which was in a brass bowl in the beginning of the church. Give my love to Mamma (who I hope is well) and Edward and the little boy.

I remain, Dear Papa, your affectionate Son

JAMES KING.

The tone of his letters, of which many are preserved, give evidence that he at once entered cheerfully upon his new situation among strangers, whose language and habits were so different from those he had been accustomed to, and his father had the gratification to learn from friends in Paris and his teachers that his conduct and diligence were all that could be desired.

CHAPTER V.

King to Vansittart, Secretary of State, and Madison—Discriminating Duties on commercial Intercourse—England prepared to abolish them—Commission under 7th Article resumed their sittings—Sedgwick to King—Condition of Affairs in the U. S. as affected by Jefferson's Election—Ames to King—View of the Future not cheering—King to Madison—Delay of Negotiations at Amiens—Believes Peace will be concluded—Napoleon at Lyons appointed himself President of the Italian Republic—King to Secretary of State—McDonough, British Agent at Tripoli, exculpates himself from Charges against him—Debate on Bill to suspend Tonnage and countervailing Duties—Definitely settled by France to send a Colony to Louisiana, unless Affairs in St. Domingo prevent—King to Secretary of State—Ardour for Peace abating in England—Fleets to be put in Order.—Still believes there will be Peace chiefly advantageous to France—King to Secretary of State—Erving's Appointments—King to Secretary of State—Negotiations at Amiens still unsettled—Public Opinion in England seems to favor Rupture.

R. KING TO NICHOLAS VANSITTART, ESQ.

Private.

GREAT CUMBERLAND PLACE, Feb. 12, 1802.

SIR :

It will probably require three months to exchange the communications upon which our respective Governments can found their definite acts abolishing the discriminating Duties upon our commercial intercourse. It unfortunately so happens that these months will exclude the season, in which a considerable portion of our annual crops of Tobacco are shipped for a market ; and as a great number of our vessels are now out of employ, it will increase the embarrassments of their owners, if they are unable to engage in the carriage of Tobacco, as will be the case if your countervailing Duty upon this article be continued.

While the war lasted, we did not complain, although we enter-

tained the same opinion as I have expressed to you concerning
the inequality of these Duties. If our acquiescence has been in
some small degree beneficial to you, we have on that account no
motive to regret it ; but it would in return be a considerable
relief to us in the present situation of our navigation, if a clause
could be inserted in the Bill proposed to be brought into Parliament immediately repealing so much of the countervailing Duties
as regards the article of Tobacco. There can be no doubt that
the whole of these discriminating Duties upon our respective Imports will be done away, and I am persuaded that we shall
receive the anticipated repeal of the Duties on our Tobacco as
another and liberal proof of your disposition to promote a friendly
and harmonious intercourse between the two Countries. Should
any difficulties arise in the execution of our present views, of
which I have no apprehension, the subject will always remain
under your control.

With perfect Respect &c.,

RUFUS KING.

R. KING TO SECRETARY OF STATE.

No. 53.

LONDON, Feb. 13, 1802.

SIR :

I am authorized to inform you that the British Government
will without hesitation accede to a proposal for the abolition of
all discrimination of Duties, affecting the Navigation and commercial intercourse between our and their Territories, and in
consequence of what has passed upon this subject, a motion has
already been made in the House of Commons by Mr. Vansittart
of the Treasury to bring in a Bill authorizing his Majesty, at any
time after the passing of the act, by an order of Council, or by
Proclamation, to cause the countervailing Duties upon American
Vessels and upon Articles imported on American Vessels, or
either of them, or any part of the same, or of either of them,
wholly to cease, or to be suspended for such period or periods as
may be deemed expedient. We may count with certainty upon
the passage of the Bill to a Law, and that the extent of repeal
will be made to depend upon our own choice.

I have suggested the equity and importance of an immediate

suspension of the countervailing Duty upon Tobacco, and the Bill is so drawn up, as leaves the Government at liberty at any time to take it off, in particular cases by an order in Council, or to suspend it generally by proclamation. I have however received no assurance that this will be done, and we consequently must not be disappointed if it should be refused. I will resume the subject should a favourable occasion offer to do so ; in the meantime, individuals may, upon the circumstances of their cases, ask for a remission of this Duty.

Perhaps a future day will be named in our Law, or in the proclamation which the Law may authorize, upon which our discriminating Duties shall cease ; due notice of such measure would become the grounds for a correspondent abolition of the Duties here.

I annex the Copy of a Letter sent by Lord Hawkesbury to the British Commissioners under the 7th article of the Treaty of 1794. A copy of the Convention which I have lately signed with his Lordship, has in like manner been communicated by me to our Commissioners ; in consequence of these communications, the Board will immediately reassemble and proceed to business.

With perfect Respect & Esteem &c

RUFUS KING.

Copy.

DOWNING STREET, 11th Feby., 1802.

GENTLEMEN :

I herewith transmit to you the copy of a Convention concluded by me and Mr. King on the 8th of January last, explanatory of the 6th & 7th articles of the Treaty of Amity, Commerce and Navigation with the United States ; and I have to signify to you his Majesty's pleasure that you propose to the Commissioners on the part of the United States of the Board of which you are members, to reassemble and proceed with you in the execution of the Duties imposed upon you by the provisions of the 7th article of the said Treaty and by the third article of this Convention.

I am, &c

HAWKESBURY.

To MAURICE SWABEY, LL.D. }
 and JOHN ANSTEY, ESQ. }

R. KING TO JAMES MADISON.

Private.

LONDON, Feb. 13, 1802.

DEAR SIR :

I may and perhaps ought to say to you that I have found very proper dispositions in conversing with the different persons connected with the subject respecting the abolition of the discriminating Duties upon our Navigation and Commerce. No one defends the unequal operation of the present Law. All prefer abolition to revision. But the proposition to transfer their countervailing Duties from the imports from, to the exports to, the United States has no friends, notwithstanding the exact equality of the measure in reference to the object for which equality is sought ; if they impose the same discrimination upon the Exports as we place upon the Imports, the operation in regard to Navigation would be equal : if we carry, they would receive the Duty, if they carry, we should receive it. Two objections are made to this transfer : the first, that it is against their ordinary policy to impose Duties on their Manufactures ; the convoy Duty was an exception justified by peculiar circumstances and has ceased with the war ; the second, it would load their book of Rates with mere fractional proportions of a foreign Tariff, and moreover embarrass not only the business of the merchants, but that of the Custom house more than the sum of the Duties would justify. In respect to the abolition of discriminations on both sides, it will depend upon us whether it be complete or partial. Perhaps it will merit to be well considered whether we ought not to impose Light-house Duties according to the usage of other nations, and preserve our Tonnage Duties, at least until something shall be ascertained in respect to the West India Trade.* Of this, however, I flatter myself I need have no serious apprehension, since the more I have considered the Question, the more I am satisfied of the justice and ultimate success of our claim.

With sentiments of very sincere Respect &c

RUFUS KING.

* Upon this subject, I mean the West India Trade, I am solicitous to understand the views of the President, least I should happen to cross them by being ignorant of them.

R. KING TO SECRETARY OF STATE.

No. 54.

LONDON, Feb. 18, 1802.

SIR :

I annex a copy of the Bill which has been prepared and brought into Parliament by Mr. Vansittart concerning the countervailing Duties upon our Ships & Cargoes : and I now have reason to expect that the Privy Council will issue an order, suspending the countervailing Duty on Tobacco for six months as soon as the act is passed impowering them to do so. I shall not omit sending you the earliest information in my power of the decision of the Privy Council upon this point.

The Commissioners under the 7th article of the Treaty of 1794, have reassembled and are proceeding in business.

With perfect Respect &c

RUFUS KING.

———

T. SEDGWICK TO R. KING.

NEW YORK, 20th. Feby., 1802.

DEAR SIR :

. . . In the letter which I wrote you before the close of the last session I ventured to predict that you would not be recalled, partly because, I thought, and I do still think, that our rulers like you best at a distance, and partly because they deem your presence at the court of London a shield of the party, in the event of a rupture, which, I know, they, then, thought probable, and dreaded. The same motives, will, I think, continue to influence their conduct.

There are several of the measures of the administration which have been injurious to their influence, and, in fact stayed its progress in the eastern states, and I think have had, tho' in a less degree, a similar effect in this state. Among these are their removals from office which in some instances have been extremely injudicious. The officers removed in Connecticut were among the men the most popular and respectable in that state ; the substitutes had nothing to recommend them but a noisy activity against the federal administration.

. . . The repeal of the judicial act of the last session will, I am confident, have a more extensive effect. You know the character of Mr. Lansing & Mr. Lewis the chancellor & ch. Justice of this state. They are both zealous, and one, at least, a malignant supporter of Democracy. They have declared, and seem not to wish to have their opinions kept secret, that the repeal, without providing a substitute, is unconstitutional. The opinion of these gentlemen must have considerable influence. Indeed all men who have been misled by an attachment to refined theory, and who really wish a security of property and person, will be shocked by the establishment of a precedent which renders the judiciary, the only instrument of this security, dependent on, and subservient to, the prevailing faction in the legislature : and the more so when they reflect that this measure is in direct violation of the constitution, & not only so but establishes a principle of complete consolidation of all national & state authority. For if the legislature may do this there can be no *established* defence against legislative usurpation. Establish this *principle*, and at the same time an executive *practice* of rendering the emoluments of all the officers in the U. S. a mass of corruption at elections, and there is nothing left which can render the government an object of affection to virtuous and intelligent men.

The Democrats are in considerable degree indebted for their success to their address to the sordid & despicable passion of avarice ; and the President was not unmindful of his obligation to it, in his address to the legislature—to alleviate the burdens of his beloved constituents forms a prominent feature of his Message ; but he is rather unlucky in the means which he recommends for that purpose . . . In his desire to abolish the internal revenue he has two principal objects 1. a particular regard to the interest of the southern & western states, & 2. chiefly breaking down all the internal Machinery of the government, which, I presume, he considers as destroying the "lilliputian ties," as he predicted in that very decent letter which he wrote to his friend Mazzei. The cant expressions of the party now are the *external and mutual relations of the states*, which they seem to consider as the objects, exclusively, of national regard. This Theory will, I presume, decrease the number of their partizans in New England. I am persuaded, and, principally, from my knowledge of the people of that country, that Democracy will, there, become less and less powerful during the present administration.

I have the best evidence that Burr is completely an insulated man at Washington ; wholly without personal influence. Had he any influence it would be exerted to prevent a repeal of the internal taxes—an impoverished treasury is inconsistent with the vast objects which he has contemplated. It is a measure to which Gallatin, from his official situation, must be opposed, but he is too cunning to oppose, openly, the ardent wishes of his Master. The measure is hostile to the interests of the eastern states & I therefore doubt whether the repeal will take place, tho' our friends in Congress seem to entertain no doubt on the subject. I most sincerely wish the jacobins success, upon this occasion, because I am persuaded that it will prove injurious to their influence.

Should the internal revenues be repealed I am apprehensive that, under the present management, it will be found that the import and tonnage duties will be inadequate to the public exigencies. The value of exported produce must measure the amount of expenditure ; the pressure which will take place, resulting from the establishment of habits which can no longer be gratified, will increase emigration to the frontiers, and emigrants contribute almost nothing by the consumption of imports. Hence, I think, there will be some decrease of revenue, & if there be, a deficit is inevitable. Should this event happen I know *they* rely on obtaining loans which they suppose may be effected with great facility, by the accumulation of capital and the difficulty of employing it profitably. . . .

From the whole view which I am able to take of the political state of our country, and the past conjectures I can form of future probabilities, I am induced to believe that Mr. Jefferson will not be re-elected. But whether his successor will be a better or a worse man is to me doubtful. The popular tide as far as I am able to discern it, seems to set towards that description of men who have heretofore possessed the public confidence. Before the present rulers got into power, they and their adherents assured, with great confidence, the people, that the public records would afford complete evidence of the peculations of the federalists. *They* are now in possession of those records. Reports have been received, by the legislature, from the heads of all the departments, and not a single fact has been exhibited to ground a charge either of folly or wickedness, agt. their predecessors. As nothing of this sort has appeared it is concluded nothing will, because it is obvious that any pretext of this kind would have been seized on with avidity as well to justify their own malignant charges, as to ruin forever, their adversaries. . . .

I am sincerely & affectly. yours.

———

F. AMES TO R. KING.

BOSTON, February 23, 1802.

MY DEAR SIR:

. . . *That*, the ascendancy of France, we are told, is to be displayed on our borders, and that in exchange for $\frac{1}{2}$ St. Domingo, she is to have Louisiana. Our Southern brethren are expected to wince when this happens. I deduce no hopes from the event. Factions always hate & dread their domestic rivals more than foreign enemies. Virginia has the spirit of domestic restlessness and arrogance that abhors restraint, and of state ambition that wd. impose it, of laziness that will not earn, of luxury that will not retrench, of a debtor that will not pay. Great states are strong factions, and a feeble govt. is of course their victim and their instrument—at present their trophy.

To repeal the Judicial Law to save a small sum shocks many who could swallow the claim of a constitutional right to repeal it. It is understood to be the declaration of the bellum internecinum agt. the best institutions of the late administrations. Gouv. Morris's speeches are justly admired and have had effect on thinking men—i. e. on 600 of 6 millions.

Truth however filters through the stone & reaches the folks standing below, drop by drop. The mint is voted out. Govt. seems to be clearing the ships for action, by throwing every thing of value overboard——

Our General Court has rejected a motion in one house by Hichborn in the other by Morton for an address to the President. The majority was so small it shows an unsound state of the public opinion in this state. Still as it clearly proves the Jacobins to be a minority, this disclosure of their weakness tends to keep them weak. On inquiry I cannot find that they are gaining ground. Still it is to be supposed that those who address the popular passions will in the end prevail against those who presume on their sense & virtue. Gov. Strong's re-election is probable, though of course the virtuous Gerry will contest it. Robbins is the most conspicuous candidate for the Lt. Governor's place, vacant by the death of Mr Phillips. We make turnpikes and busy ourselves with local objects. Virginia rides the great horse. . . .

No doubt you are a watchful and anxious spectator of our affairs. It is beyond human foresight to predict the events that await us. We are hastening towards changes, which forebode other changes and so on to the end of the Chapter. We are not at present under a Theocracy, and if we were, our propensity to worship strange Gods would involve us in trouble.

I am with esteem & affection

Yrs

R. King to James Madison.

Private.

London, Feb. 27, 1802.

Dear Sir :

Hitherto it has been confidently asserted and generally believed that the Negotiations at Amiens would end in a definitive Treaty ; but within the last ten days some persons have imagined that they perceive symptoms of doubt and hesitation upon this subject. These however ought not to induce an opinion that the peace will fail to be concluded. The prolongation of the negotiation, besides being disadvantageous to this Country by retarding its plans of Finance, and creating embarrassments in its commercial affairs, expose it to all the casualties which may in the mean time happen, and which may be of a nature to have an influence upon its results. The News Papers which copy from each other, and propagate every sort of error, pretend to enlighten the Public in respect to the points which occasion this delay. Altho' I can do no more than deal in conjectures as to the discussions at Amiens, I feel pretty confident that I run no risque in assuring you that they bear no resemblance to the Reports of the News Papers. It is no more true that France has any thoughts of ceding Martinique for the advantage of Spain, than that England has acquiesced in, opposed, or said a word about the cession of Louisiana and the Floridas. My persuasion still is that the Treaty of Amiens will be concluded, tho' I am by no means confident that it can be of long duration.

It is time to have heard from Vienna concerning the late transactions at Lyons ; but probably they will wait till they have sounded the sentiments of Petersburgh before they disclose their own. A little Time must remove the Veil, which it has been attempted to throw over the proceedings at Lyons and, if what is confidently asserted to have passed there, be true, the whole is worthy only of the highest reprobation. For what other sentiments can we feel should it turn out, so far from Buonaparte having been chosen President of the Italian Republic, that he placed himself in that office as he had before done in another, by the use of his Bayonets. The Fact is believed to have been that the Italian Deputies proceeded to the election, and actually chose for their President their countryman Melzi and not Buonaparte, who so far from being the object of their preference had not as many votes by 30 as Berthier : the moment the scrutiny was finished, and the result pronounced within the Consulta, a body of Buonaparte's Guards, prepared for the occasion, marched into the Hall and remained there until this choice was annulled and Buonaparte appointed in the place of Melzi, who was then named and called upon to accept the office of Vice President !

With great esteem &c.,

RUFUS KING.

R. KING TO SECRETARY OF STATE.

NO. 55.

LONDON, March 5, 1802.

SIR :

.   .   . Lord Pelham a few days ago shewed me a letter from Mr. MacDonough, the British agent at Tripoli, exculpating himself from the charge of having excited the Bashaw of that Regency to make war upon the United States. He explicitly denies the charge and encloses a certificate to the same effect, signed by the Bashaw himself. Mr. MacDonough having thought it necessary to solicit this certificate from the Bashaw, will serve to shew him that his hostility to the United States may not be agreeable to Great Britain.

The Bill authorizing the Crown to suspend the Tonnage and Countervailing Duties upon American Ships & Cargoes is still before Parliament, but will without doubt pass in a few days. The Debate to which it has given rise, so far as regards General Gascoigne, one of the members from Liverpool, appears to have been for mere electioneering purposes ; and with respect to Dr. Laurence and Mr. Wyndham the occasion however unconnected was made use of as an opportunity to talk about the negotiation at Amiens and the dangerous Dominion of France.

I have seen a letter dated Paris, Feb. 26, which says it is definitively settled to send a colony to Louisiana and Florida. General Bernadotte is to have the direction and command of it ; preparations are making for the first expedition, whose departure will perhaps depend upon the accounts expected from St. Domingo. It is asserted that the Indian Nations adjoining to Florida have agents now here for the purpose of making Treaties with this Country to unite themselves with the troops and settlers that may be sent from hence. The Establishment of this Colony is a darling object and will be pursued with ardour and upon a great scale, unless the affairs of St. Domingo shall for the moment derange the plan. Louisiana, Guiana and the Desert Island of Tristan d'Acunha are each spoken of as places to which the rebellious and intractable Negroes and people of Color may be sent from St. Domingo and the other French Colonies.

With perfect Respect & Esteem &c.

RUFUS KING.

R. KING TO SECRETARY OF STATE.

No. 56.

LONDON, Mar. 8. 1802.

SIR :

It is ascertained that Austria is highly dissatisfied, as justly she may be, with the issue of the meeting at Lyons, where Buonaparte is said to have employed the same means to carry his purpose, as has before proved efficacious at St. Cloud.   Here too the ardour in favour of Peace has a great deal abated, and its security become the subject of increased solicitude and Doubt. The obstacles which have delayed the conclusion of the definitive Treaty, and which have been accompanied by an unexampled stagnation of the Trade of this Country, have much contributed to this temper of the public mind.   Every one ascribes these inconveniences to France, whose Chief is asserted daily to disclose views inconsistent with the repose and independence of every part of Europe.

In this state of dissatisfaction and uncertainty, instructions have been sent to all the Naval Arsenals to prepare the Ships of war for actual service ; the Channel Fleet will immediately sail, and in order to bring the Negotiation to an immediate issue, these demonstrations are accompanied by an explicit Demand on the part of England that the definitive Treaty on the Basis of the Preliminaries be signed without any further Delay ; if this be not done in a week, it is believed that Lord Cornwallis will leave Amiens & the war recommence.

I have all along believed, as even in the present critical posture of affairs I am still disposed to do, that Peace will be concluded ; because I have not supposed that England would depart from the Preliminaries ; and France, whatever may be her future views, has the most powerful inducement to conclude a Treaty that will require her to restore nothing; but will oblige England to evacuate Egypt and Malta, to make restrictions in Spain and Holland, and to give back to France all her colonies with 20.000 Seamen now in her possession.

The advantages seem indeed to be all on one side, and so considerable as to leave no doubt concerning the decision of France, unless the Tone and Circumstance of the Demand on the part of England shall be such as to put all consideration of interest out of the question.

With perfect Respect & Esteem &c.,

Rufus King.

R. KING TO SECRETARY OF STATE.

No. 57.

LONDON, Mar. 9, 1802.

SIR :

As your Letters * to me concerning Mr. Erving's appointments do not explicitly state the President's intention in respect to his being employed as an Assessor to the Commission under the Seventh Article of the Treaty with this Country, I desired him to send to the Board an Extract of his Instructions, which define his Duties ; and which would be sufficient to shew the President's expectations on this point. I at the same time wrote a letter to the Board copies of which and their answer you will find annexed.

With perfect Respect & Esteem &c

RUFUS KING.

These copies are omitted ; but the Commission declining with all proper respect to receive Mr. Erving as an assessor in their board, "the nature of that appointment and its Duties as prescribed and required by the Board" being incompatible, in their judgment, with "the office of agent for claims and that of their mercantile assessor," in answer to their notification of this decision, Mr. Erving replies: " I feel it proper, expressing an acquiescence in your deter-

* J. MADISON TO RUFUS KING.

DEPARTMENT OF STATE,
WASHINGTON, 27th July, 1801.

SIR :

G. W. Erving, Esquire, who will have the honour to hand you this Letter, is the Gentleman who, as I informed you sometime ago, has been appointed our Consul for London. The President has also assigned him to be the successor of Mr. Williams in the agency relative to claims and appeals, and to act in the character formerly filled by Mr. Cabot in connexion with the Board of Commissioners under the 7th Article of the British Treaty. For his services in those two agencies, with the eventual addition of that held by Mr. Lenox, in case it should become vacant, he will be allowed at the rate of two Thousand Dollars per annum after the resumption of business by the Board of Commissioners, and until that event happens, only half the sum. He will communicate his instructions to you, and I must request you to afford him such informatiou and advice to facilitate the execution of his various Trusts, as may be in your power.

With highest consideration &c

JAMES MADISON.

mination, to withdraw from your further consideration my Pretensions to the office in question."

R. KING TO SECRETARY OF STATE.

No. 58.

LONDON, Mar. 13, 1802.

SIR :

We have no farther intelligence concerning the Negotiations at Amiens since the date of my last. The same degree of uncertainty with the same apparent indifference, in respect to the issue of the discussion continues to exist. *Mr. Addington in a pretty free conversation told. me that* * during the last fortnight *his mind had* balanced whether *to wish the conclusion or rupture of the negotiation ; that he was* every day receiving *Letters* expressive of the same indecision *from* all parts *of the kingdom ; that they should* continue *to act* with good faith and *were ready to sign a* definitive Treaty, on the Basis of the Preliminaries, provided it be done without any further Delay.

The Fleets are prepared and preparing for sea, and if the negotiation fail, the war will on both sides be resumed with increased activity & zeal. I am not sure that my former reasoning in respect to the decision *of France* may not be in some degree erroneous. In ordinary times and in a more settled condition of things it would be correct, but it is quite possible, notwithstanding the advantageous terms of Peace upon the basis of the Preliminaries, *that the First Consul may believe*, that war will afford more efficacious means of promoting and securing *his personal views and authority* than can be derived from Peace. *This Country too may believe that war is* preferable *to the only Peace* now to be obtained. In either case there will be no Peace.

From the very great body of Forces both by Sea and Land in the West Indies, we may apprehend the most serious interruption of our Trade in those Seas, should the war be renewed. I have made this subject the topic of conversation with the Ministry, and should the negotiations fail, will do all in my power to procure to our Navigation a just and friendly treatment from this country.

With perfect Esteem & Respect &c

RUFUS KING.

* Italics in cipher.

CHAPTER VI.

Allusion has been made * to a treaty with the Bey of
Tunis which required certain presents to be given to him.
These, at the request of Mr. Eaton, the United States Agent
at Tunis, were procured in London by Mr. King, the Government having sanctioned his doing so. In a letter to Mr.
Eaton of March 12, 1802, notifying him that the presents
have been sent to him, Mr. King says they are

"of superior skill and richness . . . which Mortimer who is at
the head of the trade assures me are beyond any thing of the sort
ever before made ; and so indeed they ought to be considering
the sum of money which they cost us. You will doubtless be in-

* Vol. iii., pp. 246–52, 256, 329, 337, 355.

clined to allow us all the consideration and favour which the lustre and value of the presents give us a claim to expect ; at any rate these properties ought to have the effect to wipe away any suspicion, or unpleasant conjectures which the time required to prepare them may have excited."

It is of these articles that Mr. King writes in the following letter:

R. KING TO SECRETARY OF STATE.

No. 59.

LONDON, Mar. 20, 1802.

SIR :

Mess. Bird, Savage & Bird will send to the Department of the Treasury the several accounts of the Persons who have prepared the Present for Tunis, and in order that you may be fully apprized of the manner which I have adopted to forward the articles to Tunis I take the liberty of annexing copies of my letters upon the subject. We have no accounts from Mr. Hargraves since he left Algiers, where he arrived safe in the English Frigate which carried him from this Country. Early in February Mr. Eaton was at Leghorn, whither he had gone on account of his health, but he expected soon to return to Tunis.

Nothing decisive has occurred since the date of my last respecting the negotiations at Amiens ; it is however understood that the discussions are drawing to a close ; and the public opinion (especially since the arrival of the accounts of Toussaint's opposition in St. Domingo) seems to be that the definitive Treaty will be speedily concluded.

The Bill respecting the Countervailing Duties has passed the House of Commons in the shape in which it was introduced ; it is going through its stages in the other House, and will be completed in a few days.

With perfect Respect & Esteem, &c.,

RUFUS KING.

The rumors relative to the cession of Louisiana by Spain to France had been reported by Mr King, as has been seen, as early as March 29, 1801, to his Government in a letter in which he expressed his regret that the country had not in France " a minister of talents and entitled to confidence " to make "a plain and judicious representation on this subject to the French Government." From time to time more positive information was sent by him, and finally, on November 20, 1801, he transmitted to the Secretary of State the text of a secret treaty between France and Spain, made in March, 1801, and confirmatory of another secret one made on October 1, 1800, ceding Louisiana to France, and also the fact that the British Government objected for many reasons to such a transfer.

The appointment of Mr. R. R. Livingston as Minister to France, and the instructions given to him on September 28, 1801, before sailing for his post, indicated the anxiety of the Government to prevent, if possible, the consummation of this transfer, of which it was not yet certain; but saying, if the cession had been made, that

" sound policy will require, in that state of things, that nothing be said or done which will unnecessarily irritate our future neighbours, or check the liberality which they may be disposed to exercise in relation to the trade and navigation through the mouth of the Mississippi ; every thing being equally avoided, which may compromit the rights of the United States beyond those stipulated in the treaty between them and Spain."

Mr. Livingston, in writing to the Secretary of State, January 13, 1802, speaks of

" the secrecy and duplicity practised relative to this object (the French minister denied that the cession had been made) as an evidence to him that they apprehend some opposition, on the part of America, to their plans. I have, however, upon all occasions, declared that as long as France conforms to the existing treaty between us and Spain, the government of the United States does not consider herself as having any interest in opposing the exchange." *

---

* *Annals of Congress*, 1802–3, p. 1020. This whole correspondence relative to the Louisiana Treaty will be found in an Appendix to the *Annals of*

With such views, with the continued refusal on the part of France to declare herself upon the matter, and the silence of his own Government,* Mr. Livingston could not be expected to act with much vigor; and on March 24, 1802,† he writes to the Secretary of State that :

" I have but one hope left as to defeating this cession ; it consists in alarming Spain and England. The Spanish Minister is now absent ; but I have not failed to show, in the strongest light,

Congress, 1802–3, on p. 1003, and subsequent ones. It contains the President's message to the Senate, communicating the Convention with France and the accompanying correspondence.

* It may be interesting in this connection to see what were the views of the Government at Washington, July 24, 1801, as shown in the instructions of that date in the following letter to Mr. King, copied from the Instructions to Ministers.

DEPARTMENT OF STATE
WASHINGTON, 24th July, 1801.

RUFUS KING, ESQ.
    &c.

  SIR :

   .   .   .   .

The cession of Louisiana from Spain to France, as intimated in your letter of March 29 had been previously mentioned from several quarters, and has since been repeated from others as an arrangement believed to have taken place. Although no official or regulation confirmation of the fact has been received, it is more than a probability and has been the subject of instructions to Mr. Pinckney the Minister of the United States at Madrid, as it will also be to Mr Livingston the Minister going to Paris. They will both make use of the proper [*sic*] to prevent a change of our Southern and Southwestern neighbours, that is to say the means of peace and persuasion. Should Great Britain interpose her projects also in that quarter, the scene will become more interesting, and require still greater circumspection on the part of the United States. You will doubtless be always awake to circumstances which may indicate [*sic*] her views, and will lose no time in making them known to the President. Considering the facility with which her extensive Navy can present itself on our front, that she already flanks us on the North, and that if possessed of Spanish countries contiguous to us, she might soon have a range of settlements in our rear, as well as flank us on the South also, it is certainly not without reason that she is the last of Neighbours that would be agreeable to the United States.

   .   .   .   .

With sentiments etc.
JAMES MADISON.

† *Annals of Congress*, 1802–3, p. 1024.

to the Minister of Britain the danger that will result to them from the extension of the French possessions into Mexico, and the probable loss of Canada, if they are suffered to possess it. I have requested Mr. King to press this subject, also, as opportunity offers."

Mr. King had been fully possessed of the views of the British Ministry, which had never favored the cession, but yet had been unwilling to permit it to enter into the discussions at Amiens. Uninstructed as he had been by his own Government he had, however, formed positive opinions as to the complications which must arise under the changed condition of affairs, and in the following letter to Mr. Livingston, March 23d, expresses them clearly and with the firm conviction that in some way the threatened complication of our relations with France must be averted.

R. KING TO R. R. LIVINGSTON, PARIS.

LONDON, March 23, 1802.

SIR :

We cannot doubt that the acquisition of Louisiana has for a long time been an object with France, nor that the cession had been made, and the projected expedition resolved on before you left America. Supposing this to have been the case, without being quite sure that it was so, after again and again considering its injurious effects upon our political and social happiness, and how we ought to meet it, I long since satisfied my own mind of the course which I have ventured to suggest to you, believing that it would be alike suitable to either condition of the Business ; since, if undecided, it would be the most likely means to procure its announcement, and if resolved upon, the best calculation to lessen and defeat its mischiefs. It would be to little purpose that I should recapitulate the views in which I have seen the subject, and which have led me to the conclusion that I have embraced, especially as your mind seems to me to have taken the same range with my own. I prepared a letter to you upon this subject, which has lain by me some time for a convenient opportunity to Paris, but which on revision I do not now think worth the trouble of your perusal.

The sole questions which remain are, can the expedition be prevented and if not, how should we treat it ? Perhaps the only unconnected and ex parte means of Protection in our Power, are Iron and Gold. Notwithstanding the sanction to be derived from the example of almost every nation, as well as from justice and reason, which so far from refusing to States the faculty of inquiring concerning the dismemberment and increase of the Territories of their neighbours, make it their duty to do so, I suspect that the first of these means, if deemed even expedient, would be thought defensible only upon Principles too metaphysical and unascertained, and therefore, that it may be laid out of the question.

Although we may have no contemptible opinion of the efficacy of the latter means, there are considerable, and, perhaps, insuperable difficulties in the way of its employment. I should not approve, nor tolerate for a moment any underhand measure, or such as could not be openly avowed, and explained to our own people as well as to the rest of the world ; but we may, if we deem it our interest, without impropriety attempt to acquire the legitimate Title to Louisiana and the Floridas. If these belonged to us, we should, I hope, be as ready to defend them with arms in our hands, if necessary, as we should be to defend Charleston, New York, or Newport. But shall we be willing to pay down a sum of money large enough to acquire them ? For if the Title can be obtained in no other way than that of a direct purchase, a large sum of money will alone procure it. No set off of claims ; no balancing of accounts ; no prospect of future advantage will have any beneficial influence in our favour ; it must be actual money and a great deal of it which can serve our purpose. Great as the benefit would be to us of uniting to our Territories New Orleans with the entire left bank of the Mississippi and extending our Southern frontier to the ocean, I confess that I see little in the principles, to which we propose to devote ourselves, and by which our affairs are to be regulated, which authorises us to expect that a measure of such magnitude, and which would impose immediate and considerable Burthens upon our People, would be likely to be received with favour. It cannot be denied that economy is wisdom in States as well as individuals ; but by the former as well as the latter, it requires to be rightly understood, not to become a vice instead of a virtue.

If we can succeed by neither of these means, our Government may perhaps think it worth consideration, whether the new State of things in the West Indies may not lead to the accomplishment of its wishes. The settlement of Guadaloupe and St. Domingo seems likely to call for more men and money than were at first thought necessary, and may occasion the suspension of the expedition to Louisiana. France can more easily supply men than Money or Provisions ; the last must be purchased from the United States ; but how are they to be paid for ? I can imagine but two ways, either by the dollars accumulated in the Spanish Colonies, or by Bills upon France. Spain with great reluctance will open her coffers to her allies and will invent a thousand devices to avoid it ; tho' if no other resource exist she will be obliged to do so. Our merchants will not sell their Provisions for Bills on the French Treasury without a satisfactory Guarantee ; and our Government will not become the guaranty unless it promote our interest in doing so. Is it too visionary a speculation for us to think of obtaining the cession of New Orleans and the Floridas from France by assisting her to obtain the supplies she wants for her Fleet in the West Indies ? or is there any thing in the nature of the war that should restrain us from doing so ?

A Project of this sort would deserve to be received with favour at Madrid as it offers the only means of sparing the Spanish Treasure in America, and preventing what must there as elsewhere be the subject of apprehension. I mean the occupation of Louisiana by France. To the French too, it holds forth the means of immediate and important relief in circumstances of difficulty and without any other inconvenience than that of giving a new and different direction to their colonizing enterprizes.

I am obliged to you for your reflections upon the subject of Louisiana ; they ought to be received with all the consideration to which their justness and importance entitle them. But what I have before informed you upon this subject, and which I confirmed in a short letter of yesterday, I have no reason to believe has been in the least degree ill-founded. The consequences of the cession were fully explained before the signature of the Preliminaries ; and have been more than once restated and pressed since the meeting at Amiens, but the answer has been uniformly the same, and such as gives us not the slightest occasion to hope even that anything has been or will be done concerning it at Amiens. We must, therefore, depend upon ourselves and upon our own exertions, and in case they do not prevent the measure, the next enquiry, is how we should treat it.

On this subject, I have heretofore * expressed to you my opinion, which I do not perceive sufficient reason to induce me to change. France is one of the Great Powers which influence and in some sort control the affairs of the whole earth ; and on this account it seems to be the Duty of those, who have any part to act in the concerns of other States to study the Genius and endeavour to understand the character of this restless & powerful nation, which can only be opposed with success, when openly opposed. I do not mean an opposition of force, but that moral resistance which consists in the frank explanation of the injuries we foresee and apprehend, and the declaration beforehand of what we conceive to be our own Rights and Duties, should it become necessary to assert and perform them. No policy in my opinion has so often proved to be pernicious as that of shutting our eyes upon what we cannot avoid seeing, and of putting off exertions to prevent injury, and thereby leaving the public welfare either to the government of chance, or in the hands of the adversary ; a mode of administration which always amounts to a confession of weakness, and which places the public safety not in the safeguard of the public virtue and courage but in the moderation of ambition and power.

With this way of thinking, I would lose no time in telling France our apprehensions, at the same time that I assured her of our earnest desire to live in harmony and friendship ; I would inform our own People that I had done so ; and I would moreover endeavour by all suitable means to familiarize them with those measures to which the defence of the public welfare may compel us to resort. The Truth should not be disguised from ourselves or others ; that we are the first Power in our own hemisphere, and that we are disinclined to perform the part of the second. Sentiments of this sort openly and unostentatiously advanced and propagated would, if I mistake not, have the double effect to check measures to divide us, from whatever quarter they

* January 16, 1802, vol. iv., p. 59.

may proceed, and to enable us to defeat them, should they be attempted.

I have to crave your indulgence for this unreserved and confidential communication of opinions which are, I apprehend, somewhat at variance with those that are entitled to our respect and obedience. I should however add that I have been too often disappointed in things I have most firmly believed, to be over confident in my own opinions ; and I should rejoice should the course marked out to you, and from which I should not deviate, were I in your place, prove more advantageous than I can at present believe it will do.

With Perfect Respect & Esteem, &c.

RUFUS KING.

It will be seen that Mr. King in his free communication with Mr. Livingston had entered into a discussion of the methods by which the interests of the United States, resulting from this cession, could be secured either " by Iron or Gold," as the new arrangement must be broken up. But more important and noteworthy is the alternative he suggests as a method by which the French Government may be influenced to listen to our claims. Not a disposition to avoid offending them, but a positive declaration of a determination to prevent the dangers, not apprehended from Spain's possession of Louisiana, but probable from its transfer to a more active, enterprising, and restless country. In other words, a declaration of the principle upon which rests what is now called the Monroe doctrine. Upon a careful reading of the portion of the letter, beginning with the words, " On this subject I have heretofore expressed to you my opinion," etc., it will be found clearly and positively suggested that the French Government shall be told that the United States being

"the first power in our own hemisphere, we are disinclined to perform the part of the second. Sentiments of this sort openly and unostentatiously advanced and propagated would, if I mistake not, have the double effect to check measures to divide us, from whatever quarter they may proceed, and to enable us to defeat them, should they be attempted."

It does not appear that this view was taken either by the Minister or his Government, but it shows what Mr. King would have done had he been in the position to act, and the estimate he placed upon the bold assertion of the intrinsic power of the nation to make itself felt in the decision of questions relating to its own interests,—a power which he felt was stronger and better recognized than when he entered on his mission. Nor was he mistaken, though it took many years before Mr. Monroe distinctly avowed the principle on which the whole country now, in 1896, unanimously insists.

It is not a little curious, that Mr. Monroe was the negotiator with Mr. Livingston to make the Conventions with France for the purchase of Louisiana, and that the chief overt act to interfere with the principle was made in France's attempt to conquer Mexico, while the United States was engaged in the civil war of the Rebellion—an attempt nearly successful at the time, but checked and positively settled by the Mexicans themselves.

R. KING TO R. R. LIVINGSTON.

LONDON, Mar. 24, 1802.

DEAR SIR :

I have omitted to return you my thanks for your congratulations on the subject of the Convention concerning the Debts. Your construction of the II article is unquestionably the true one. As I am not aware that any opinion has prevailed that either the execution of the 6th article of the Treaty of 1794, according to its Provisions, or a commutation of our Engagements under it, (into a definite sum of money) would have exempted the Debtors from the suits of their Creditors, I cannot suppose that any disappointment can arise from the limited recognition of the IV article of the Treaty of Paris. The United States engaged to pay the Debts which could have been recovered at the close of the war had there been no lawful impediments, and which, by reason of such impediments, were not recoverable at the conclusion of the Treaty of 1794. In respect to all Debts recoverable at the conclusion of this Treaty, the Creditors were at liberty to pursue their judicial remedy, and had no Claim before the Commissioners, their cases being expressly excepted. In respect to these Creditors, therefore, it was no more than justice to declare that the Provisions of the Treaty of Peace in their favour, so far as regards their future operation, shall remain in force. The Terms of the recognition of the IV article of the Treaty of Peace, limits its operation so as to exclude all claims which once might, but now cannot according to the course of the Judiciary, be legally established ; for these claims, we make compensation, and for the others, leave the Creditors to their judicial Remedies.

This Government has communicated the Convention to the Creditors, who have met and, as I am informed by their Chairman, determined to petition Parliament for the difference between the £600,000 and the 5 millions which they assert to be the amount of their Claims ; and in order to pave the way for their Petition, they use no reserve in saying the settlement has been a political one on the part of Government and at their expense, and that they have a just demand to be indemnified out of the public Exchequer. I observe that meetings are held among our merchants to petition Congress for compensation for Losses by French Captures, and I conjecture that these Petitions will meet with much the same reception as those of the British Creditors to their Parliament.

I have lately learned, and from good authority, that the Spaniards have 15 Millions of Dollars embarked at the Havanna and Vera Cruz which I am inclined to conjecture will be ordered to St. Domingo, under the pretext of being sent to Europe with a detachment of the combined Fleet. When they reach St. Domingo such will be the necessities of the army and navy that the Dollars will be taken to buy Provisions and in lieu of their Draughts given upon the National Treasury. . . .

We are in expectation that the definitive Treaty will be completed in a very few days ; nobody seems now to apprehend its failure.

With perfect Respect & Esteem &c &c

R. K.

R. KING TO SECRETARY OF STATE.

No. 60.

LONDON, Mar. 29, 1802.
SIR :

I have the satisfaction to send you the annexed copy of Lord Hawkesbury's note announcing the Signature of the Definitive Treaty, and have the honour to be,

With perfect Respect & Esteem &c

R. K.

Copy.

Lord Hawkesbury presents his compliments to Mr. King, and has the honour to inform him that Mr. Moore is arrived with the Definitive Treaty of Peace, which was signed at Amiens at 4 o'clock on the 27th instant by his Majesty's Plenipotentiary and the French, Spanish and Batavian Plenipotentiaries.

DOWNING STREET, March 29, 1802.

———

LOUISIANA.*

March 26, 1802.

Lord Lansdowne, to whom I some days ago spoke concerning the cession of Louisiana & the Floridas, told me that it was his desire to have retained the Floridas and New Orleans : that with this view, in the preliminary articles first prepared in 1783, he agreed to give up Gibraltar and to receive in lieu of it Minorca, Martinique or Gaudaloupe and the Floridas ; that the stipulation in favour of Great Britain for the free navigation of the Mississippi was made in reference to the project of retaining the Floridas, but that a cry arose agt. the cession of Gibraltar, the King refused his sanction to it and it was therefore retained and the Floridas, Martinique and Minorca given up.

The stipulation about the Mississippi, being included in a different article, was retained when that to wh. it related was struck out.

Jay & Franklin wished Eng. to seize the Floridas after the signature of the Provisional Articles and before the Preliminaries ;

* Memorandum Book.

but objected to troops being sent from N. York on this service as Fr. & Spain would deem it collusive.

Franklin threatened Oswald to retain and sell the German prisoners unless the negroes were restored or paid for, saying they had carried off & sold the negroes we had bought and that it would be as just to sell the Germans they had bought.

Geo. Cabot to R. King.

March 27, 1802.

My dear Sir :

I have seldom received so much pleasure from news concerning you as that which is just now arrived. Your silence had been *un*-usually long & from various circumstances I was led to believe that you were in some sort of perplexity which prevented you from giving me the pleasure to which I was accustomed. As I am totally uninformed of the terms of your Convention & as I shou'd always desire to be informed of the instructions under which you acted I can make no observations of any worth on the subject ; yet I see much evidence that you have done what very few, *if any other man,* cou'd have done for us ; that you have done better than the Country had a right to expect after its ungenerous & capricious conduct ; that you have done so well as to gratify all your friends & confound all *our* Enemies. But will your Convention be ratified? this is a question my jealousy asks of me. I answer that *probably* it will, *notwithstanding* it *tends* to a final ex-tinction of all the animosities between the two Nations ; because at this moment our Master dreads & detests the Master of the French who despises him in turn & therefore no *business of fra-ternity* can proceed. Such at least is my opinion. It would be a useless labor for me to attempt giving you a minute account of our affairs—or indeed any account, for you probably know more of them than I do. We make a constant progress in the way we are destined to go, yet I must say that the Leaders outrun their Followers. The very able discussions of the Judiciary Question & great superiority of the Federalists in all the debates & public writings have manifestly checked the career of the *Revolutionists.* Six months ago I trembled for the coming Elections in N E—but it appears that N. H. has recovered a little of its old good politicks & chosen Gilman by a great majority, & *we think* in Massachusetts the public opinion is much meliorated.   These checks if only temporary are of great value.   .   .   .

I was in hopes that the blacks in St. Domingo wou'd long occupy & finally defeat the french arms, but appearances indicate that they will be beaten.   The armaments like all others from France must be supported by *other Nations.*   Force & Fraud will draw from Spaniards & Americans ¾th of the supplies.

Your faithful & affte friend

G. C.

WILLIAM VANS MURRAY TO R. KING.

CAMBRIDGE, E. S. MARYLAND, 5th April, 1802.

MY DEAR SIR :

.   .   .   We arrived after a passage of eleven weeks at Washington, where I was civilly & coldly received.   My outfit paid me & no questions asked me !   So the flutter which my intended Tableau de la negotiation had put me into was kindly spared. M. & G. behaved to me in all the business I had with them in a fair & candid way.

The principle of proscription goes on searching its game even in the smallest × road post offices.   The principle of depletion & disorganizing in all things connected with the most ancient opinions, the constitution & its out works & the well settled system of the past administrations goes on with a destructive zeal.   Internal Taxes—Judicial Sanctity—all are to be handled & overset, but as I write to you I ought to restrain myself from invective—whatever may be our opinions mutually.

There is an abundance of imitation, but it is in the small way & cannot afford a cure.   There is a hope & it seems to me the only one well founded, that they will divide & quarrel.   Already it is believed that B. gives umbrage to the Philosopher by his aspiring temper.   So we ought to expect a division in your State of which the Feds., if not themselves miserably divided, may avail themselves & the nation.   It may be hoped that the Feds. will gain wisdom by suffering.   To be in a minority is a new situation to them.   Hitherto they have been a majority & have had a Chief & that Chief in Power ; now in the minority.   I do not know that they, as a united party, acknowledge any Chief ; & yet have more need than ever of the energy which a Chief gives. It is true there are some strong men in Congress, but a chief should not be there—& there is none there.   I saw but few of the public men at W.   It is such a Town-in-country that there is not properly Society & contact ; but I assure you that I have not heard of any one man since my return as Chief.   It will always happen as it did after the death of Alexander among his Captains.   In fact we are in a strange situation.

It will give you pleasure to know that by allowing me my outfit to Paris (which I claimed) my situation is greatly bettered, as my estate is in land & bad rents & it would have been a terrible thing for me to sell near the whole to pay my debts, which the outfit nearly did.   I live with my brother in the Country & mean to build this autumn on a farm.   My friends of this county, which is Federal, wish me to go into public life.   This I decline : for I feel as if I had precisely escaped ruin ; and all my embarraisments were a suite of 13 year's public life, of one sort or other, in which my affairs became turned upside down.

What can you expect from a man placed in so very active a place as I am, but useless repinings at the present degraded state of public affairs ? and yet my dear Sir I wish to hold some little converse with you, & to show you by a letter that I am grateful for your remembrance of so sterile a correspondent.

We all rejoice that Govt. has, united with the claim your country has upon you, kept you at your post.   If I expect it, it is because they have great credit among all the enlightened men for this forbearance from the evil we believe they would do by your removal.   So I beg you—as I once before did, to stay where you are, at least for some few years.

Affectionately yrs.
W. V. MURRAY.

———

R. KING TO R. TROUP.

LONDON, April 6, 1802.

DEAR SIR :

. . . There is a rumour, may it prove to be well founded !, that a motion to repeal the internal taxes has been negatived in the H. of R.   Should they be continued and an independent judiciary preserved, I shall not despair of the public welfare. In four or five weeks we shall hear of the arrival of the Convention concerning the Br. debts, as well as whether the same be approved by Congress. In respect to the opinion of intelligent and reasonable men, I have no concern, but we cannot be sure that their opinion will be the general one, and I am therefore solicitous to hear how the settlement is thought of by those whose province it is to judge of its merits.

Peace is definitively made and will be ratified in a few weeks. The new ministers continue to stand well with Parliament and the country ; and such are the Resources, and confidence of monied men, that the new loan of 25 millions has been made on as low terms as the loans of the first year of the war, when enthusiasm was high, and the first Debt and Taxes not a moiety of their present amount. Singular indeed in this respect is the contrast between France and England : in one any considerable loan cannot be raised on any Terms, in the other the minister has but to ask and receive. In the former, mistress as she is of the greater part of Europe, the 5 pr. cents are at 55, while here after a long expensive and unsuccessful war the 3 per cents are at 75 and will probably soon reach 80.

Yrs. &c.,

R. KING.

P. S. Mrs. Ludlow's Baggage not having reached town I have not seen the opinions of Kent and her brother. I shall read them with attention before I say anything upon the subject, except that I have contended and with effect and advantage that the sentence of a foreign Tribunal in matters of Prize, is not in all cases conclusive.

———

R. KING TO SECRETARY OF STATE.

NO. 61.

LONDON April 7, 1802.

SIR :

The Moniteur of the 26th past contains the definitive Treaty dated the preceding day. Lord Hawkesbury's Letter to the Foreign Ministers says that it was signed on the evening of the 27th. By reason of the urgent manner in which the Negotiation was pressed to a conclusion by England, or some such cause, the several articles were settled on the 25th, and the respective Plenipotentiaries signed on that day an agreement that they would sign the Treaty, the articles whereof had been so agreed upon, as soon as copies could be prepared. The French Government has chosen to consider this first signature as the conclusion of the Treaty, and dated the copy inserted in the Moniteur accordingly.

In the main the definitive Treaty seems to adhere pretty closely to the Preliminaries ; in such articles as have undergone modifications, it is not obvious that the alteration is favourable to the views of this country. Malta, notwithstanding the string of propositions relative to its constitution, will be liable to the influence of France and open to her enterprize.   The clause which authorizes France to prefer a claim for the support of Italian, German and Russian Prisoners enables her to balance the claim of England for the maintainance of French Prisoners : this is however an article of form rather than of substance, as I do not find that there is any instance of money being paid or received on similar occasions.

If there be no separate article, which is not believed to be the case, designating the manner in which the Prince of Orange is to be indemnified, the article of the Definitive Treaty relating to that subject, differing as it does from the Treaty of Basis, seems more likely to prove prejudicial than advantageous to this country ; and the more so, as it is understood that in the very room where the Definitive Treaty was signed, and immediately afterwards, the French and the Dutch Minister signed a separate Convention by which the Batavian Republic is declared to be exempted from contributing anything towards the indemnities to be paid to the House of Orange.

But the principal objection which Lord Grenville, and those who think with him, will be likely to urge against the Definitive Treaty is the omission so contrary to former usage to recognize and confirm in a manner accommodated to the present state of Europe those antient Treaties which are asserted to be the Foundation of its public Law.

* 786 and others are likewise much dissatisfied with the cession

* Not deciphered.

of Louisiana to France ; speaking with me concerning it a day or two ago he said Ceylon, Trinidad and the Cape were as nothing in comparison to Louisiana and the Floridas ; and on my expressing my surprise that 128. 55. 28 should have known of the cession and yet advised the Peace, he said that 128. 55. 28 viewed the cession in the same light that he did, but that he knew nothing of it until after the conclusion of the Preliminaries.

The Minister lost no time, after the signature of the Definitive Treaty, in making his Loan and opening the Budget. 25 millions have been borrowed at the moderate interest of £3.18.2 per centum. The Income Tax, which with certain exceptions required the tenth of each man's income, is to be repealed, and the 56 millions for the redemption of which it stands pledged will be funded. The new Taxes, taken at Four Millions, are to be levied thus—an addition to the Duty on Malt, Hops and Beer of two millions : an addition to the assessed Taxes, one million ; and a Duty on the Imports and Exports of Great Britain of one million. Coupled with these measures are two others worthy of particular attention ; one a proposition to give a new shape and direction to the Sinking Fund of 1786, as well as to abandon the principle adopted during the late war, of providing a fund equal to the hundredth part of every new Debt, to be invariably applied in redeeming it ; the other, a motion by the Minister to continue the Law authorising the suspension of Cash payments by the Bank. The funds have risen considerably, and there seems to be very little opposition to the new Taxes. I shall not be inattentive to those which may affect our Trade ; tho' so far as regards the Tax on Exports our Treaty is entirely silent.

The Law respecting the Countervailing Duties received the King's assent on the 24th of last month ; as it finally passed in the form of the Bill of which I sent you a copy, it is not necessary that I should send you a copy of the Law. From the uncertainty whether Congress will be inclined to repeal the discriminating Duties paid in our Ports, I shall not press for the order of Council, taking off by way of anticipation and immediately the countervailing Duty on Tobacco, in the Ports of this country.

   With perfect Respect & Esteem

       Rufus King.

R. KING TO SECRETARY OF STATE.

No. 62.

LONDON, April 10, 1802.

SIR :

Some months ago I informed you that *Mr. Jackson** would probably be sent *to the United States as Mr. Liston's successor ;* *Mr. Merry* had been previously thought of and indeed named *for this mission.* As I have had the opportunity of knowing *both these Gentlemen* during *my residence here,* it was not without some regret that I heard of the intention to appoint *Mr. Jackson in lieu of Mr. Merry.* From this information I have been led to make further Enquiry respecting their reputation and the result has served rather to encrease than lessen my solicitude. *Mr. Jackson* is said to be positive, vain and intolerant ; he is moreover filled *with English prejudices* in respect to other countries, and as far as his opinions concerning the United States, seems more likely to disserve than benefit a liberal intercourse between them and his own country.

On the other hand, *Mr. Merry* appears to be a plain, unassuming and sensible man, having *lived* for many years *in Spain,* is in almost every point of character the reverse *of Mr. Jackson,* who were he to go *to America* would go for the sake of present employment, and with the hope of leaving it as soon as he could receive a similar appointment *in Europe* while *Mr. Merry* wishes for *the Mission* with the view of obtaining what he believes will prove to be an agreeable and permanent residence.

With these sentiments I have believed it to be proper to endeavour in every unexceptionable way in my power to discourage and throw impediments in the way of *the mission of Mr. Jackson,* and in a late conversation *with Lord Hawkesbury,* he offered me what I thought a fair occasion of expressing my sentiments upon this subject. His Lordship received my observations in good part and promised to consider what I had said to him before any definite step should be taken in the Business. I have followed up the opposition in other quarters which I thought likely to have an influence with decision, and am not without Expectation *that Mr. Jackson* will be relinquished.

* Italics in cipher.

As the explicit designation of a particular character, who would be agreeable, is matter of greater delicacy than to object to an Individual who might have been spoken of, I have rather confined myself to the latter course, in doing which, however, I was enabled indirectly and by way of contrast *to Mr. Jackson's* disqualifications to describe qualifications which seem to be almost peculiar *to Mr. Merry.*

Annexed I send you copies of my letter to Lord Hawkesbury, and of his answer declining to recognize Mr. Lewis as Consul of the United States at Calcutta. A like answer has in a similar case been lately given to the Envoy of Portugal. Conversing with one of the Directors of the East India Company concerning Mr. Lewis' appointment, he told me that before the late war France had been solicitous to place a Consul at Calcutta ; that from a persuasion that a Consul would be employed as a political instead of a commercial agent, they had declined his admission ; that the request would, however, probably be renewed, and in case an American Consul should be admitted, a French one could not be refused.

With perfect Respect & Esteem, &c

RUFUS KING.

CHAPTER VII.

R. Troup to R. King.

New York, 9th April, 1802.

My dear Sir :

. . . The federal party is still completely down ; though some think it in the attitude of rising. Every corner of the government has been ransacked to find out an officer to be removed in order that his place might be filled with one of Jefferson's sect ; and as things now stand that sect is in full possession of the government.

The repeal of the judicial bill, for the purpose of getting rid of our friend Judge Benson and others, has excited a very powerful sensation in the minds of the leading federalists throughout the union. . . Some of our friends in Congress have much distinguished themselves on this subject. Mr. Gouverneur Morris is much celebrated for his eloquence. The democratical paper at Washington pronounced his speech to be the grandest display of eloquence ever exhibited in a deliberative assembly ! Mr. Bayard of Delaware, Mr. Hemphill of Penna., Mr. Dana of Connecticut and several other federalists in the House of Representatives have also been much eulogized. Giles and Randolph of Virginia are the leaders of the House of Representatives, and their speeches develop the views and motives of Jefferson's sect more than any others. . . Congress are now engaged in repealing almost all the internal taxes, and the whiskey drinkers particularly will be in spirits. Virginia literally dominates. Jefferson is the supreme director of measures—he has no levee days—observes no ceremony—often sees company in an undress, sometimes with his slippers on—always accessible to, and very familiar with, the sovereign people. Madison is in a deep decline, and it is thought he will soon quit his office.

Burr has lost ground very much with Jefferson's sect during the present session of Congress. He played a cunning and ridiculous game whilst the repealing of the judicial bill was before the Senate. A few weeks ago whilst the federalists were at a public entertainment, celebrating General Washington's birthday, he made his appearance among them—asked whether he was an intruder—he was answered in the negative, and treated with becoming civility. Soon afterwards he asked for permission to give a toast—it was granted—and he gave " *The union of all honest men.*" This was generally received by the federalists as an offer on his part to coalesce. It has been attempted to be kept secret ; but it has got into circulation, and it has created heart burnings with some of Burr's party. Hamilton says there is a cabal going on at Washington between Burr and some of the federalists. Latterly it is represented that Burr has run to the other side again and is manifesting great violence. He has been not a little abused in the course of the winter in the democratic prints. It is said there is no cordiality or concert between him and Jefferson, and that they are not in the habit of approximating each other.

Jefferson is the idol to whom all devotion is paid ; and Burr will doubtless be dropped at another election, if they can do it without endangering Jefferson. In this state all power and all the offices are also engrossed by the democrats. No opposition is likely to be made for some time to come. Our system is just where it is by nature destined to be—in the hands of demagogues, and I think it will not be an easy work to rescue it from them. Hamilton is in utter despair of the system! and he looks forward to a serious commotion, and that at no very remote period! There is a deadly enmity between Burr and the Clintonians. If Burr should be taken up by the federalists, and brought forward for any conspicuous office, Hamilton and many of us will secede from the federal party and remain passive spectators. We think there can be no coalition with him without a desecration of all that is virtuous and all that is honorable in character. . . .

There is great complaint here of the dulness of all kinds of business, owing to the peace. We have had very considerable failures in Baltim., Philadelphia, and some not inconsiderable ones here. More are likely to follow. It is a consolation amidst the calamities that are befalling the merchants, the lawyers in the circle of your friends are doing well, altho' of late they have suffered, with other classes, a diminution of business. Hamilton is closely pursuing the law, and I have at length succeeded in making him somewhat mercenary. I have known him latterly to dun his clients for money, and in settling an account with me the other day, he reminded me that I had received a fee for him in settling a question referred to him and me jointly. These indications of regard to property give me hopes that we shall not be obliged to raise a subscription to pay for his funeral expenses. . .

R. T.

G. CABOT TO R. KING.

April 13, 1802.

MY DEAR SIR :

Our people distrust the French, & the Armament at St. Domingo will not be easily supplied by *fair* means ; still however they must be supplied as all french Armaments are by the people of the Countries to which they come & such of their Neighbours as dare not resist them ; they will get something by finesse & maneuvring, something by gross fraud & the remainder of their wants they will supply by force. Our intelligence has been generally that the Army of Le Clerc made progress, & was confident of success, but knowing as we do the policy of the French to put the best face on such affairs until they are obliged to abandon them, it is not impossible or improbable that the Blacks will maintain their liberty.

The meditated expedition to Louisiana causes some anxiety to the great men of the South who guide our national affairs, but after some thought I am of opinion that more good than evil will ultimately come of it.   Moral good & I may say political so often springs from physical evil & political troubles that these may be often ascribed without superstition to the kindness of a Guardian Providence   We must suffer all the miseries internal discord, disunion & anarchy inflict if we are not irresistibly combined by the superior iufluence of a common interest in repelling an external Enemy.   It may therefore be a blessing to the United States to have a french Establishment in Louisiana *as strong as France can make it*.   All the local & relative circumstances consider'd, it is demonstrable that we have nothing to fear from *mere force*.—I admit the *possibility* of another sort of influence which *might* work irreparable mischief, but on a calculation of chances I see such a preponderance of those which are favorable that I look to the end of this project with great confidence that it will (after much suffering perhaps) promote our permanent good.

You will see with pleasure the state of our Election in this Quarter.   I have no great reliance on a steady correctness of public opinion but undoubtedly Jacobinism has declined a little for the last six months.   The superiority of the Federal characters in Congress & the Newspapers evidently depresses & sometimes silences their opponents who have the national government absolutely in their hands.   How far those now in power will be able to carry the people is more doubtful than was thought a few months ago.   It is perfectly understood that the principle of the Admin. is *the popular passion ;* whatever mischief this will sanction may be expected ; but where this can not be had they will stop. We are men and acting on french principles, but as we are not french men, the French Philosophers make some mistakes concerning us.   .   .   .

Yours with aff & fidelity

G. C.

F. Ames to R. King.

DEDHEM, April 13, 1802.

DEAR SIR :

. . . I do not despair of G. B. and of course I trust somewhat in the chances of the world's escaping from the fangs of
french domination.   The ambitious project of getting Louisiana
can do nothing but good.   We need as all nations do the com-
pression on the outside of our circle of a formidable neighbor—
whose presence shall at all times excite stronger fears than demagogues can inspire the people with towards their govt.   The
object of popular aversion and dread has been only govt.   France
if she could float here and anchor on our coast has no terrors
equal to our near prospect of anarchy first and then Jacobin
despotism.   We ought to rejoice in a new position of things in
which courage toil and suffering might avail to extricate us from
imminent evils—instead of that smooth and swift descent down
the precipice that we have been making for a year past.   . . .

Great joy is felt here on occasion of the adjustment made with
G. Britain of the spoliation and treaty debts.   It is well known
and truly felt and acknowledged that your and Mr Gore's residence in London has been infinitely serviceable to the U. S.
This consideration ought to keep you both quiet a little longer in
a situation that the newspapers have said you were weary of and
about to quit.   God bless you when you return with the sight of
a country grateful, free and secure of it's freedom on fixed
principles.

With great regard &c

Yrs

FISHER AMES.

J. Hale to R. King.

BOSTON, 13 April, 1802.

DEAR SIR :

. . . In mine advising you of the *patriot* Erving's appointment I believe I indulged gloomy & indignant feelings &
even urged your return home.   My indignation at that & many
other measures of the philosopher is not & I hope never will be
abated.   Your continuance however in your present important
station for twelve or eighteen months to come, more mature
reflection induces me seriously to hope.   The London papers

advise of your determination to resign. The paragraphs upon this subject I feel confident have not been authorized by you. On the other hand my conjecture has fixed their source in the aforesaid *patriot* E.

The philosopher's message at the opening of the session I transmitted to you. His recommendations have been very implicitly followed. The results hitherto have been grateful to the feelings of the wise & virtuous. In New Hampshire & Massachusetts, particularly the latter, *the sect* have been utterly confounded by the emphatic voice of the people against them. Even the Chronicle after stating the votes (as far as ascertained) to be 20,000 for Strong & 13,000 for G., piously ejaculates, "the will of the people be done"! The confidence & impudence of the sect prior to the 1st Monday of this month you would scarcely credit. Their present chagrin & mortification you may easily conceive of. We are creditably informed that right principles & correspondent feelings are not confined to New England & that in Maryland a most happy change has taken place in the public mind. The Louisiana project must operate much good. If you see the federal papers at the northward handling that project as of little moment ; if you find them puffing Bonaparte & even the General Bernadotte, be not alarmed. Should matters come to a serious issue, upon yankees principally will the nation depend for its support, and you know they will not be wanting in spirit & energy. But when called upon for exertions in favor of the Nation, they expect to be treated in other respects as part of the Nation, whose rights & interest they are ever ready to maintain.

It is more to be hoped than expected that the delays attending the settlement of the definitive treaty will give more stability to the peace. The present state of the Continental powers however promise no more upon this head, than their suffering & exhausted state will necessarily induce. The sect & even the philosopher openly inveigh against Bonaparte. They are chagrined beyond measure that he shows so little gratitude for their past attachment. One source of apprehension is therefore removed, and at present there is not much reason to fear that we shall be thrown into the arms of France, should the present European armistice end.

Your friend & obed. Servt.

JOSEPH HALE.

R. King to Rt. Hon. Lord Hawkesbury.

Confidential.

LONDON, April 21, 1802.

My Lord :

By the Treaty of Alliance concluded at Paris in 1778, between the United States of America and France, the latter renounced forever the possession of every part of the Continent of America, lying to the East of the course of the Mississippi. This renunciation confirming that which had been previously made in the Treaty of 1763 between Great Britain and France, authorized the expectation that France, content with her widely spread dominions, would abstain from seeking an extension of them in this part of the American Continent : an expectation that appeared the more reasonable inasmuch as the motives to such extension could not be satisfactorily reconciled with a just regard to the Rights and security of those Powers between which this portion of America is divided, and by which the same is at present possessed.

Contrary nevertheless to expectations which have been entertained on this subject, if credit be due to uniform and uncontradicted Reports, the Government of France has prevailed upon his Catholic Majesty to cede to France both the Provinces of Louisiana and the Floridas, and having thus acquired a station at the mouth and on both sides of the Mississippi, may be inclined to interfere with and interrupt the open Navigation of the River.

By the Treaty of Peace concluded at Paris in 1783, between the United States of America and Great Britain, it is mutually stipulated that the Navigation of the River Mississippi, from its source to the ocean, shall forever remain free and open to the subjects of Great Britain and the citizens of the United States of America. Without enlarging upon the great and peculiar importance of this Navigation to the United States, a large and increasing portion of whose people can conveniently communicate with each other and with foreign countries by no other route, I take the liberty thro' your Lordship to request that the British Government will in confidence explain itself upon this subject ; and especially that it will explicitly declare whether any communication has been received by it from the Government of France or Spain respecting the said cession ; or whether his Britannic Majesty has in any manner acquiesced in, or sanctioned the same, so as to impair or affect the stipulations above referred to concerning the free navigation of the Mississippi ; In a word, I intreat your Lordship to open yourself on this occasion with that freedom which, in matters of weighty concern, is due from one friendly nation to another, and which in the present instance, will have the effect to do away all those misconceptions that may otherwise prevail in respect to the privity of Great Britain to the cession in question.

With the highest consideration and respect &c.,

RUFUS KING.

J. McHENRY TO R. KING.

BALTIMORE, April 27, 1802.

DEAR SIR :

Perhaps, for the present, it may be as well to suspend doing anything relative to the engravings of the Indian Medals, that I took the liberty to request you to have executed for me. My object was, to have used them in a collection of my own public papers, that I had contemplated throwing together, in a small volume. I have not relinquished this design, but as some of the pieces may require notes, and as the publication is intended more for private than public gratification, I am in no hurry to carry it into effect. Mr. Jefferson, I am told, ordered a new set of medals for the Indians, with new devices and emblems. Would to God that he had confined his revolutionary genius to things of no greater importance, we should have had less, to-day, to apprehend for the fate of the Constitution and our Country.

The ultimate effects of peace, upon our Merchants and the Country at large, are not yet fully developed. There have been several failures in most of our trading Cities, and there is a diminution of foreign trade everywhere visible. We calculate upon a decrease in our importations from the East Indies, proportionate to the articles we received from that quarter, and exported during the war. We calculate upon the total loss of that part of our trade, with the French and Spanish Islands and the Spanish main, which arose out of, and had its existence in, the late war. In short, we calculate upon the commerce of the U. S. rapidly and with few exceptions reverting to, and flowing only in those channels in which it flowed previous to the war ; of course the excess of our shipping, beyond what this trade will require, if not purchased by Europeans, must rot in our ports, and our commerce in foreign products and manufactures, be confined, principally if not wholly, to what we shall want for our own use or consumption, and our exports, to such part of our productions and industry as shall be wanted by foreign nations. If you can open new or other sources of trade to our merchants, you will be a greater benefactor to your Country, than were you to teach our farmers to raise two blades of grass from a stem which at present produces but one. Perhaps more correct reflections upon her interests may induce Great Britain to favor your operations, should they be directed (as I presume they are) to liberalize (if I may so express myself) the trade of this Country with her various foreign possessions. According to my humble conceptions, it would be wisdom in Great Britain, were she to open the doors of her Colonies, to our trade, much wider than her system of restraints and monopoly would advise or dictate. But no person understands this subject better than yourself, or is better qualified to make upon others, the proper impressions. I shall only observe, that a good commercial treaty, at this juncture, when our trade is either annihilated or stranded, in almost every quarter, in which it has so lately flourished, would come most opportunely to the American merchant and people.

I must refer you to your other correspondents for a general view of the state of politics, and complexion of public opinion as relative to the capacity of the existing administration, to manage wisely the affairs of this Country. Here and there, in this State, may be observed symptoms of incipient distrust in the administration, and disappointment of some of the acts and proceedings of Congress. I do not however augur, from these partial appearances, any sudden change for the better in the democratic part of our representation in Congress, or check to the career of the administration, altho' the probability is, that there will not be wanting matter, to encrease the bulk of these discontents until they become instrumental in the production of good.

Connecticut in this great and trying crisis has behaved nobly, both in and out of Congress. Massachusetts is slowly resuming her ancient consequence and imposing posture.   Rhode Island begins to inquire, whether she is in the right path.   Tho' little favourable to federalism can be predicted relative to New York and New Jersey, these states must not be considered as irretrievably lost.   Pennsylvania still clings to democracy ; she is said to be not quite content with some of her demagogues, but at the same time, not sufficiently dissatisfied with them, to dismiss them from her councils or confidence.   Of the Southern states, I can say little.   Accounts from them are various.   I believe the safest rule is to look to the Eastward.   .   .   .

Your faithful & humble servant

JAMES McHENRY.

R. KING TO NICHOLAS VANSITTART, ESQ.

GREAT CUMBERLAND PLACE, Ap. 29, 1802.

SIR :

As several points upon which we have touched in our conversations respecting the Bill before Parliament, imposing certain Duties upon Exports and Imports and the Tonnage of Vessels, were the subject of discussion when the Convoy Duties were imposed, I take the liberty to send you the copy of the Report which I made to my Government of the conference which on that occasion I had with Mr. Pitt, thinking this as satisfactory a mode, as any that I could adopt, of communicating to you the objections then made against certain of the Provisions of the Convoy Duty, and which so far as respects the Principle of the Export Duties, now proposed to be laid, are equally applicable to the present as to the former Bill.

Without repeating what has been already said, I will beg of you to give all the weight which it deserves to the obvious and just influence to be deduced from the Spirit and Tenor of our Treaty of Amity &c, and according to which, as we think, we are not liable to pay a higher Duty for Permission to export your manufactures than is paid by your other customers.   Agreeably to the proposed Tariff, the consumers of British manufactures, living in Europe, will pay only half per cent for permission to export the same, while we who live farther off, and who consequently pay higher freight and Insurance, are required to pay double that rate, or one per cent for the like Permission.

It is true that the difference will not be as considerable as under the Convoy Law; but it is not against the greater or less degree, but against discrimination altogether that we contend. When the objection was formerly pressed, it was replied, as you will perceive by the enclosed Report, that the Duty being taken in reference to Convoys, which would cost more in long than in short voyages, was for this reason not inequitable. Whatever force there might have been in this reply, it must be admitted to have no influence whatever in reference to the discrimination now proposed, the effect of which in regard to American and European Purchasers of British manufactures is, that each having purchased goods upon the same terms and of the same amount, the former is called upon before he leaves the Warehouse to pay for the Government Permission to carry away his Purchase, double the sum demanded of the latter for a like permission; and if the Americans be supposed to purchase British manufactures of the value of Six Millions annually, and it be likewise admitted that the Europeans purchase to the same amount, the former will annually pay according to the proposed discrimination £30,000 sterling more than the latter; or in other words, for permission to export the same quantity of Goods, the British Government will require the European purchaser to pay only £30,000, at the same time that it obliges the American Purchaser to pay Sixty Thousand.

This discrimination is at the same time too plain to leave any doubt of the sentiments which it must unavoidably excite; and I cannot but flatter myself that, upon a reconsideration of the subject, it will be thought both just and prudent that every sort of discrimination and preference should be abolished.

With great Consideration & Respect &c.

RUFUS KING.

R. KING TO SECRETARY OF STATE.

No. 63.

LONDON, Ap. 30, 1802.

SIR :

The definitive Treaty having been duly ratified, Peace was yesterday proclaimed with the accustomed formalities. Measures are already taken to reduce the Army and Navy to a peace establishment ; and as the warrants and orders to impress Seamen have been recalled, we may expect the discontinuance of farther applications from American Seamen, detained against their consent in the British Service.

Mr Lenox has closed his agency, and according to your instructions delivered over to Mr Erving the Papers of his office. As this Agency arose out of the Transactions of the war, it will, I presume, cease with the war. The Consuls being authorized to afford during Peace the Relief due to our deserted and distressed Seamen within their respective Consulate, a special Agency for the purpose will be unnecessary.

Sweden has finally acceded to the Convention concluded in June last between Great Britian and Russia. Lord St. Helens, the English Ambassador at St. Petersburgh, after communicating this intelligence in a letter to Lord Hawkesbury of the 2nd instant, an extract whereof has been published by this Government, adds, " I have moreover the satisfaction of being enabled to assure your Lordship that the Swedish Ambassador, Baron de Stedingk, has been distinctly informed by the Count de Kotschonbey, the Russian Minister for Foreign Affairs, that as the motives which had occasioned the late revival of the System of the Armed Neutrality were now happily done away with, that System is considered by this Court as completely annulled and abandoned, not only as a general code of maritime Law, but even in its more limited meaning of a specific engagement between Russia and other Confederates."

Lord Hawkesbury has recently informed me that Mr. Merry, and not Mr. Jackson, will be sent to the United States as Mr. Liston's Successor. Mr. Merry has taken Mr. Jackson's place as Minister Plenipotentiary at Paris for the purpose of exchanging the Ratifications of the Definitive Treaty ; and I understand that he will probably be sent to Madrid on a particular service before he embarks.

With perfect Respect & Esteem &c.

RUFUS KING.

R. KING TO SECRETARY OF STATE.

No. 64.

LONDON, May 3, 1802.

SIR :

In order that the pecuniary affairs of the United States might be managed with economy and that I myself might be free from unnecessary accountability in respect to the public money disbursed in this country, I settled an arrangement with Mess. Bird, Savage & Bird, who were recommended to me by my Predecessor, which I communicated to the Department of State immediately after my arrival here.

By this arrangement these Gentlemen agreed to receive all such public money, and to apply the same according to the directions which should from time to time be given to them. For the collection, custody and disbursement thereof, they were to charge no commission, but in case they should be occasionally called upon for advances, exceeding the money in hand, they were at liberty to charge interest at the rate of five per cent from the date of such advance till its reimbursement ; and in order that we might not be paying interest for advances in one branch of the public Expenditures, while another was in Cash, no loans were to be made, nor interest paid, except for such sum as the aggregate of the whole Expenditures exceeded the total amount of the money in hand. These loans were reimbursed as soon as farther remittances were received ; and by this course on the one hand the public service was liable to no disappointment from the failure or want of punctuality in Remittances, and on the other this security and accommodation were obtained upon terms both reasonable and convenient. No part of the public Funds, in any instances, remained in my possession, the Bills of exchange, as soon as received, having in all cases been sent to Mess. Bird, Savage & Bird for collection. According to my Instructions, as well as from the nature of the case, a superintendence and control over these Funds, were annexed to my office, and hitherto the duty has been duly discharged.

Although I have received no particular Instructions upon the subject, I had no sooner looked into the business of the Prize cases depending in the Tribunals of this country, and with the prosecution whereof the public had charged itself, than I perceived the expediency of adopting immediate measures for the purpose of securing the money which might be recovered for the several Claimants, and of obtaining a reimbursement of the Expenses, which the Government had already incurred, and would be liable to incur, in the prosecution of the claims.

With respect to the first ; as the public Agent received a salary it appeared to me unfit that he should charge the claimants with a Commission ; and as many disagreements existed not only in relation to the several proportions of claims belonging to more than one person, but disputes of a still more difficult nature in cases of Bankruptcy and Insolvency, and in which the money was liable to be, and in some instances had been, attached in the Agent's hand, to await the decisions of the English Tribunals, I instructed the Agent in no case to charge the Claimants a Commission and took measures that all monies recovered from the Captors or the British Government (after deducting the costs which had been advanced by the United States) should be paid directly into the Bank of England and placed to my credit in my official capacity. This precaution put an end to all further suits, as by reason of my office I could not be made a party to them. I executed a Power of Attorney authorizing the public Agent to draw for the money thus standing to my credit in the Bank of England in order that the same might be paid over to the claimants, and prepared and sent him special Instructions concerning the discharges which he should require of them.

In regard to money standing on account of Costs, which had been incurred by the public, I ordered that the same should in all cases be paid over to Bird, Savage & Bird, and credited to the funds for the prosecution of appeals.

This arrangement had the advantage of being a convenient check upon the important accounts of the public Agent. The Bank account will show that no part of the money thus placed to my credit has been drawn for except by the Agents, nor by them except in favour of the claimants. Messrs. Bird, Savage & Bird's accounts joined to that of the Agent will likewise shew the sums which have been detained on account of Costs incurred by the Public, as well as the manner in which such sums have afterwards been disposed of.

I have thought it proper to trouble you with this communication instead of referring you to my early correspondence with the Department of State upon this subject ; and I am led to do so principally in consequence of an embarrassment which has lately happened by the refusal of Messrs Bird, Savage & Bird to advance to Mr. Lenox the money requisite to enable him to reimburse the advances which have been made for the relief and protection of our Seamen up to the first day of this month. According to his Instructions, Mr. Lenox furnished me with a statement of the money wanted for this purpose ; and agreeably to my Instructions and the plan which had been settled with Messrs Bird, Savage & Bird, I wrote a letter to them requesting that they would pay to Mr. Lenox £800., the amount of his Estimate. These Gentlemen paid to Mr. Lenox £250., being the amount of the last year's Remittances for this service, but refused to advance the difference in pursuance, as they allege in their letter to me, of direct instructions from the Department of the Treasury, which require them to limit their disbursements, by the sums remitted to them, and forbid them on any occasion to make advances on the public credit.

As these Instructions have had the effect to transfer the superintendence and control of the public Expenditures in this country from the Minister to the Agents of the Treasury, without enquiring whether the reform is likely to prove advantageous to the public, there can be no hesitation on my part in acquiescing in it, and accordingly I shall not in future, without special instructions, regard our pecuniary affairs here, as in any sort under my control and direction.

With perfect Respect & Esteem &c.

Rufus King.

J. Marshall to R. King.

Richmond, May 5, 1802.

Dear Sir :

This fortunate accomplishment of the long & difficult negotiation with which you were charged, is peculiarly gratifying to those who unite a knowledge of the embarrassing circumstances attending it, to a real wish that your embassy may be as honorable to yourself as it has been useful to your country.

You have effected what, in America, has been heretofore deemed impracticable. You have made a treaty with one of the great rival Nations of Europe, which is not only acceptable to all, but the merit of which is claimed by both parties. The advocates of the present administration ascribe to it great praise, for having, with so much dexterity & so little loss, extricated our country from a debt of twenty-four million of dollars in which a former administration had involved it ; while the friends of the ancient state of things, are not slow in adding the present happy accomodation to the long list of their Merits.

Yet amidst this universal approbation so correctly given to an adjustment of differences which unquestionably deserve it, the mortifying reflection obtrudes itself, that the reputation of the most wise & skilful conduct depends, in this our capricious world, so much on accident. Had Mr. Adams been reelected President of the United States, or had his successor been a gentleman whose political opinions accorded with those held by the preceding executive, a very different reception, I still believe, would have been given to the same measure. The payment of a specific sum would then have been pronounced, by those who now take merit to themselves for it, a humiliating national degradation, an abandonment of national interest, a free will offering of millions to Britain for her grace & favor, by those who sought to engage in a war with France, rather than repay, in part, by a small loan to that republic, the immense debt of gratitude we owe her.

Such is, & such I fear will ever be human justice !

When I recollect the advantage actually gained by Great Britain, in having obtained the fifth commissioner, I am truly surprized at the sum agreed on. I believe it is as much, & not more than, in strict justice, ought to be paid, but, after the impressions made by the late board of commissioners I really apprehended strict justice to be unattainable ; & I think, not only, that great credit is due to the American Negotiator for having reduced this enormous claim to a reasonable amount, but that, all circumstances considered, some sentiment of respect should be felt for the moderation & equity of the English Minister.

The national tribunals, I hope will continue to manifest, in the exposition of the treaty of peace, " that share of prudence," which is required by justice, & which can alone preserve the reputation of the nation.

Public opinion in this quarter of the union has sustained no essential change. That disposition to coalesce with what is, now, the majority in America as well as in this state, which was strongly display'd by the minority twelve months past, exists no longer. It has expired. But the minority is only recovering its strength & firmness. It acquires nothing

Our political tempests will long, very long, exist, after those who are now toss'd about by them shall be at rest.

Your obedt. Servt.

J. Marshall.

CHAPTER VIII.

R. KING TO SECRETARY OF STATE.

No. 65.

LONDON, May 5, 1802.

SIR :

The Bill imposing Duties on Exports and Imports and the Tonnage Duties has passed the House of Commons, and will doubtless go through the House of Lords, and receive the Royal assent, without alteration : if it be yet printed, I will enclose a copy thereof with this Letter.

In respect to the Duties on Imports, the Bill, in effect, revives the correspondent Provisions of the Convoy Act, with the addition in most cases, of a fifth to the Duties imposed by that act. The Tonnage Duties as well as the Duties upon Goods exported to any part of Europe are the same as under the Convoy Act : the Duties upon Goods exported to America and other places out of Europe are reduced to half the rates imposed by the Convoy Act ; and with regard to articles excepted from the payment of Duties inwards and outwards, as well as to the regulations for warehousing certain Goods, and allowing Drawbacks in case of re-exportation, the like provisions are contained in the present Bill, as were inserted in the Convoy Act.

In consequence of the large quantity of Cotton lately imported from the United States and the superior quality of a portion of the Georgia Cotton, it was proposed to put a higher Duty upon our cotton than upon that of Turkey, which is of an inferior quality. But on conferring with the officers charged with the settlement of these Duties, the discrimination has been given up, and without distinguishing between Sea Island and other cotton of the United States, as had at first been proposed, the duty is reduced to the lowest rate or to that imposed upon the Cotton of Turkey : and as all other Cotton will pay higher Duties than that of the United States and Turkey, ours will stand upon a comparatively good footing in this market.

As the proposed Tonnage Duty upon our Vessels is as low as upon the Vessels of any other country, and applies to British equally with foreign Vessels, so far as respects discrimination there is nothing to complain of.

With regard to the proposed Export Duty, after several conferences with Mr. Vansittart of the Treasury, to whom I was referred by Lord Hawkesbury to discuss the subject, and in which I urged, but without success, the abolition of all discrimination between the Purchasers of British Manufactures, I thought it my duty to write him a letter * upon the subject, a copy whereof is annexed ; if his answer should be received in time, a copy of it shall also be subjoined.

With perfect Respect & Esteem &c

RUFUS KING.

R. TROUP TO R. KING.

NEW YORK, 6 May, 1802.

MY DEAR SIR :

. . . Burr has gone south on an ostensible visit to his daughter, who married a man named Alston, and is settled in Charleston. The real object of the visit is well understood, and it is supposed to occasion at least a sigh to Jefferson. I think,

* Letter 29th April, p. 111.

however, and such is the general opinion, that Jefferson has not
a formidable rival in Burr.   The Clintonian party, which is
warmly attached to Jefferson, in this State is much more influential than Burr's party ; and the Clintonian party hate Burr as
much as the Jacobins in France hate Bonaparte.   In this city the
Clintonians and Burrites are at dagger's points.   Their feuds at
our late election were a subject of no small gratification to our
zealous federalists.   The Clintonian and democratic printer in
this City during the winter has blackguarded Burr without reserve.   At Washington it is understood he has played a little
cunning and trimming game.   Jefferson and his friends think
they know him profoundly. . . .

In this State federalism begins to rise from its tomb, as evidenced by the recent election. . . .   The violence of Clinton
and his adherents and the violence also of Jefferson in removals
from office have excited a powerful public sentiment against their
administration.   By the bye, Mrs. Montgomery calls Jefferson's
administration a philosophical experiment. . . .

Your convention is ratified.   A few days ago Congress was
occupied with a bill to carry it into effect.   It is very grateful to
all parties.   Mrs. Montgomery says the chancellor writes in very
strong terms of approbation of your conduct.   There is not the
least probability of your recall.   The democrats are changing
their tone with respect to France, and particularly with respect
to Bonaparte.   It is certain that the chancellor has not been
pleased with his reception.   I should not be surprised if violent
hatred was to succeed the violent love for the Great Nation.
Bonaparte is universally cursed.   Louisiana and the Islands are
a subject of great heartburning with Jefferson and his adherents ;
at length their eyes are beginning to open.   Our captains of vessels and merchants have been most infamously treated by Le
Clerc at St. Domingo.   The general opinion here is that the conquest of Toussaint and his followers will be a lengthy, expensive
and bloody job.   If the war in Europe should recommence, Le
Clerc will be defeated, and probably compelled to quit St. Domingo, if he can.

Mr. Jay is in the deepest retirement and his name is scarcely
ever mentioned. . . .   Hamilton is devoted to the law—is
making money faster than ever. . . .   Mr. Rensselaer, the

Patroon, is to be married in the course of two or three weeks
to Miss Paterson, a daughter of Judge Paterson of New
Jersey. . . .

Yours

R. T.

R. KING TO SECRETARY OF STATE.

No. 66.

LONDON, May 7, 1802.

SIR :

Among the few great principles of national policy worthy
of fixing the attention of our Statesmen, I am willing to hope
there is not one, concerning which there is greater unanimity of
opinion than in that which enjoins upon us all to do our utmost
in every way and upon all occasions, to maintain and perpetuate
the union of our country.

With this persuasion, though the subject may not be thought
to be included among the duties of my mission, I have not been
able to remain inattentive or indifferent to the cession of Louisiana and the Floridas to France, because I have viewed it as a
measure calculated, and possibly intended, to weaken and divide
us, I have already communicated to you what passed between me
and the Ministers of this Country in relation to this cession, during the negotiation for Peace ; but as these communications were
merely verbal, and as it appeared to me to be of some importance
that they should be distinctly and formally confirmed, as well as
that they should be ascertained of the sentiments of this Government in respect to this cession, I prepared and sent to Lord
Hawkesbury a confidential Letter * upon the subject, a copy
whereof, together with a copy of his answer, is annexed. I will
only add that I have reason to be satisfied that the cession of
Louisania and the Floridas is considered by all the late Ministry,
as well as by all other men of influence in this country, as a
measure of the greatest consequence, and which must have an
unavoidable influence upon the duration of Peace.

With perfect Respect & Esteem &c

RUFUS KING.

* April 21, 1802, page 108.

LORD HAWKESBURY TO RUFUS KING, ESQ.

Confidential.

DOWNING STREET, 7th May, 1802.

SIR :

I have the honor to acknowledge the receipt of your confidential Letter of 21st ultimo.

It is impossible that so important an Event, as the cession of Louisiana by Spain to France, should be regarded by the King in any other light than as highly interesting to his Majesty and to the United States ; and should render it more necessary than ever that there should subsist between the two Governments that spirit of confidence which is become so essential to the security of their respective Territories and Possessions.

With regard to the free Navigation of the Mississippi, I conceive that it is perfectly clear, according to the Law of Nations, that in the event of the District of Louisiana being ceded to France, that Country would come into the possession of it, subject to all the engagements which appertained to it at the time of cession, and that the French Government could consequently allege no colourable pretext for excluding his Majesty's subjects, or the citizens of the United States from the navigation of the River Mississippi.

With regard to the second Question in your Letter, I can have no difficulty in informing you, that no communication whatever has been received by his Majesty from the Government of France or Spain, relative to any Convention or Treaty for the cession of Louisiana or the Floridas, and I can at the same time most truly assure you that his Majesty has not in any manner, directly or indirectly acquiesced in or sanctioned this cession.

In making this communication to you for the information of the Government of the United States, I think it right to acquaint you that his Majesty will be anxious to learn their sentiments on every part of this subject, and the line of policy which they will be induced to adopt in the event of this arrangement being carried into effect.

I have the honor to be with great consideration

HAWKESBURY.

R. King to General Hamilton.

Secret and confidential.

London, May 7, 1802.

Dear Sir :

As I know of no measure from abroad which is capable of such extensive and injurious effects as the cession of Louisiana and the Floridas to France it has been a subject of my unremitting solicitude and attention from the moment of our first suspicions concerning it. Its importance was fully and frequently developed to the ministers of this country before the conclusion of the Preliminaries and during the negotiation at Amiens ; but no explanation was demanded of France, lest it should embarrass the conclusion of Peace.

Mr. Pinckney absurdly enough is *offering* to purchase the Floridas of Spain, which has already disposed of them. Mr. Livingston can obtain no answer whatever to his repeated notes on this subject at Paris, while we learn for a certainty that an Expedition to be commanded by Bernadotte is already prepared in the Ports of France, and will go directly to the Mississippi unless the bad state of the affairs of St. Domingo should alter its destination.

In these circumstances I have thought it prudent to ask this Government to explain itself upon this important measure, and I send you in entire confidence Copies of my Letter and of the answer which I have received and transmitted to the Department of State.

In Thornton's last Dispatches which I have seen, he repeats a conversation between him and the President, in which the latter is represented to have said that this cession would inevitably change the political System of the United States in respect to their foreign Relations ; inasmuch as it would lead to jealousies, irritation and hostility ; and, alluding to the northwest boundary of the United States, suggested the expediency of an immediate settlement of it by an agreement to close the boundary by taking for that purpose the shortest line between Lake Superior and any part of the Mississippi.

With sincere regards &c.

Rufus King.

G. Cabot to R. King.

May 11, 1802.

My dear Friend :

I congratulate you on the success of your Convention which is approved by men of all parties. We are this moment told that the Definitive Treaty is signed at Amiens but many of us see as much danger in the peace as we apprehended in the war ; for myself I decided early that there cou'd be no security in paper promises against a nation of conquerors—with the power which France possesses *she cannot possibly be at rest ;* all experience of human nature forbids the expectation that she will cease from her exertions until she is compelled by force or shall conquer the remains of civilized States. It might be very troublesome to us but wou'd probably be happy for other nations if France shou'd assail *us* so rudely as to unite us internally in a determined resistance—we cou'd not injure her by any force of our own but we cou'd defend ourselves with certainty if united & cou'd do so much toward sustaining those who are able to injure her that she cou'd have no hope of success.

" The Sect " which now governs has lost much reputation since the meeting of Congress ; the want of principle has not been more manifest than the want of talents & weight of character. So much time & labor has been employed in search of faults without finding any in the Members of the old administrations that men are irresistibly led to the conclusion that the charges against them were false which were circulated while they were in power.—From Maryland to New Hampshire inclusively the career of Jacobinism is arrested & in most places the tide of opinion sets the other way. You know we were all deteriorating last year, the progress is everywhere checked, in most places stopped, & in many the course changed. There has never been a period when the Federal Cause was maintained with more good sense and dignity than since its leaders & advocates have been in the minority. I am fully persuaded that the Federalists have a more salutary influence than they cou'd have had if the Presidential Election had issued according to their wishes—they cannot effect a positive act but they prevent *almost* every bad one that is meditated & those which pass in spite of opposition still have one good effect that of strengthening the federal cause—all this needs no further explanation, so I pray God to preserve you many years !

G. C.

R. KING TO N. LOW.

LONDON, May 15, 1802.

DEAR SIR :

. . . I am glad you happened to ask my opinion respecting Mr. Samuel Williams, who has been removed from the offices of Consul and Agent for the prosecution of claims and appeals. Indeed I almost reproach myself for not having mentioned him to you after I heard of his removal. I am inclined to hope that the public as well as individuals, whose concerns were entrusted to Mr. Williams, may be faithfully served by his successor ; but sure I am they are not likely to be better served : for I am convinced the public has not had in its employ a more attentive, intelligent and faithful Officer than Mr. Williams. I have known him well for more than twenty years (or, as our friend Genl. Knox would say, upwards of a quarter of a century). He was my contemporary at College, has been known to me ever since, and was removed from Hamburgh to London at my request, on account of his peculiar fitness for the employ, and I would confide my business and property to him, as I am persuaded you and others may do, with the most unreserved confidence in his Integrity and Talents.

He is a man of property, has been regularly bred to business and is established in London. I may add that he has the unanimous testimony of the Board of Commissioners, which his late colleague, Mr. Cabot, also possessed, of having neglected nothing in performing his duties in connection with them. I think it no more than mere justice to Mr. Williams to say thus much, and to add my consent that you should communicate the same to any person who may desire to be acquainted with his reputation.

With perfect Regard & Esteem

RUFUS KING.

R. King to Secretary of State.

No. 67.

London, May 17, 1802.

Sir :

As Lord Grenville's speech against the Definitive Treaty of Peace, and Lord Hawkesbury's in vindication of it, will both be printed under their respective correction, and as these will contain more exactly than I could give them the arguments made use of in the two Houses of Parliament when the Treaty was under consideration, it is unnecessary that I should do more than state the division which was strong in both Houses in support of the Treaty ; the opposition had only 16 in the Lords, and 20 in the Commons.   As soon as these discourses are published I will take care to send you copies of them.

Herewith you will receive a copy of the Convention and additional articles between Great Britain and Russia, together with the acts of accession of Denmark and Sweden.   The explanatory article, concerning the Colony Trade, taken in connection with Lord Grenville's speech, which I formerly sent you, on the Russian Convention, is worthy of attention ; as the article consenting to as free a Trade between the Colonies and the North of Europe as may be carried on between them and the United States, is a departure from a contrary system which it has been the view of the past administration to establish and may become the foundation of doing away the discrimination in favour of direct trade between the United States and Great Britain, sanctioned by the last Treaty between Great Britain and Russia.

I likewise enclose a copy of the Law just passed, imposing Duties upon Imports and Exports, and upon the Tonnage of Vessels.

Mr. Eaton, who returned to Tunis on the 1st of March, informs me that the Tagan, cloths and Jewels had all arrived in safety, and proved highly acceptable to the Bey ; and Mr. Gavino in a letter dated on the 5th ultimo, acknowledges the receipt of the arms prepared by Mortimer and Company, which arrived at Gibraltar on the second of the same month, and were to be put on board the first American Frigate touching there and bound up the Mediterranean.

With perfect Respect & Esteem &c.

Rufus King.

R. King to Secretary of State.

No. 68.

London, May 26, 1802.

Sir :

Considerable solicitude has prevailed among the British manufacturers and merchants concerning their Trade with France, and her late Allies, founded upon the Belief that France would exclude either wholly, or in a very great degree, the Manufactures of this country. The prohibitory laws of France, passed during the war, have been declared to be in force, and were it not for a recent and extraordinary Law, which puts into the hands of the Chief Consul, provisionally, the whole Regulation of Commerce, as well in respect to the Imports, as to the admission and exclusion of foreign Manufacturers, no English Fabrics could be, as at present very few are, imported into France ; the want of something ascertained and uniform upon this subject has operated to discourage all regular and advantageous Commerce between the two Countries.

This inconvenience has without doubt been already felt on both sides, and in consequence thereof we are told that France has made an overture, not to enter into a commercial Treaty, but to digest and agree in certain understood and reciprocal Regulations to be established by Law, and according to which the Trade between the two countries should be carried on for a limited time. A Proposition of this sort is under consideration here, and seems likely to become the foundation of a new experiment to regulate the mutual Dealings of these Rival Countries. Unless, however, a Law be immediately passed vesting in the Executive here, as has been done in France, the power of regulating the commercial intercourse between France and Great Britain, the subject must be referred to a new Parliament, as it is believed that the present Parliament will be dissolved in the course of three weeks, in order that the General Election may take place without interfering with the Harvests.

Circumstances have lately occurred in addition to the refusal of Bird, Savage and Bird to advance to Mr. Lenox the money to enable him to clear off his public accounts, which have created in my mind a suspicion that their affairs may not be altogether free of embarrassment, altho' their fortune may turn out to be solid and ample, and the disappointments, incurred at the close of the war, may not ultimately and materially affect them, I think it my duty to apprize you in confidence of my apprehensions that possibly this may not be the case.

With perfect Respect and Esteem,

RUFUS KING.

R. KING TO DR. DRURY.

LONDON, June 3, 1802.

DEAR SIR :

My confidence in the discipline and course of education observed at Harrow leaves me nothing to desire in this respect, and I ought perhaps to beg your excuses in expressing to you a wish that may possibly appear to interfere with the regularity of this course ; but as my sons are advancing towards an age in which it would suit my views in respect to the completion of their education, that they should advance in the school as fast as their acquirements will permit (to hurry them faster, I know would be disadvantageous), I have thought I might without impropriety take the liberty of intimating this reflection to you, in doing which I persuade myself that I shall not be understood, either as supposing my sons to have more pretensions than their companions in general, or as being behind where they might have been expected to be. My wish is that they should receive all the advantages to be received from going through Harrow previously to their leaving England, which it is my intention that they shall do when they separate from your instruction.

Whether they will then be sent to a University upon the Continent,* or only pass a year or two abroad and afterwards return to America to complete their education, will depend upon circum-

---

* The following from a note book, with extracts from Gibbon's *Memoirs*, shows Mr. King's views about the English Universities of that day :

" Mr. Gibbon has written much to prove the danger, as well as the inutility of sending young men to the English Universities. His sentiments, joined to the opinion of Knox, which agree with my own reflections, have decided me against sending any of my children there. I must make diligent enquiry concerning the Universities upon the continent." See also vol. iii., p. 550.

stances of which I am not at present master. As they are Americans, their education must not be entirely abroad, and were I not desirous of giving them an opportunity to obtain the modern languages at an age most convenient and safe for this acquisition, I should send them home immediately from Harrow.

With most perfect respect

Your obliged & obedt. Servt.

RUFUS KING.

DR. DRURY TO R. KING.

HARROW, 4th June, 1802.

DEAR SIR :

It will always afford me the sincerest pleasure to fulfil the wishes of those parents, who honour me with their confidence, to the utmost of my power and to take care that their children have that degree of attention to their morals and improvement, which duty prescribes ; and a sufficient stimulus to industry and competition to call forth the powers of their minds. But we must be cautious how we push them beyond their strength. Your sons possess most amiable and docile minds, their understandings are sound and good, but neither of them have shown as yet that superiority of genius wh. would allow me to place them higher in the school with any probable advantage to themselves. The younger is more forward for his age than many who are below him, and it is fortunate that his apprehension is so far quicker than his brother's as to enable him to proceed with him in the same class, [there was only little more than one year between them] and of course of the same employments. At Xmas next they will be in the same remove in which most of those authors are read, which are used in the sixth or head Form. If I could carry my own ideas always into execution, no boy should attain this situation before the age of fourteen [they were 14 & 13]. But this I have found impossible, the different ages at which the young people are sent to Harrow and the very different state of their proficiency, when they come, as well as the variety of their capacities have proved obstacles to my design ; but the experience of more than thirty years has convinced me that this rule, as a general one, would prove more safe than an earlier elevation to the higher Forms of the school. . . . With regard to your sons, I could wish when they leave Harrow, if they choose to pursue classical studies, they may want no aid beyond their own industry to perfect this branch of study, and this they will accomplish if your convenience and engagement will allow them to conclude their school education at Harrow.

Most respectfully and faithfully yours
JOSEPH DRURY.

On April 8, 1802, Mr. King wrote to his friend General Hamilton a letter, of which the following is the concluding portion, showing at that time his desire to return home.* This letter is here given in connection with the answer.

R KING TO A. HAMILTON.

LONDON, April 8, 1802.

DEAR SIR :

. . . I do not enter upon the situation of Europe since the peace. It would be too long a labor to do so. While the war lasted, constant and endless occasions presented themselves to employ myself here in the benefit of our countrymen, and I flatter myself for the public advantage.

The revision of our commercial treaty has been a service to which I have all along looked as the conclusion of my mission. † As, however, I have no reason to suppose it likely soon to take place, I am not much inclined to remain here a mere figurant, and am therefore seriously thinking of my return. Without deciding anything on this point, I confidentially ask your opinion

---

* *Works of A. Hamilton*, vol. vi., p. 538.

† In a private letter to Mr. Madison, Secretary of State, Oct. 8, 1801 (vol. iii., p. 522), Mr. King had expressed his desire " to assist in the revision of our treaty with this country" and said, as it might require conference, with reference to treaties with France also, "should the President confide the negotiation here to me, might there not be considerable advantage in my receiving permission to pass a fortnight with you at the Seat of Government or with Mr. Livingston here or at Paris ? "

To this suggestion, no answer had been sent to him, indicating clearly that it was not the President's intention to confide the negotiation to him.

respecting it. This I have not done except in the present instance.

Very faithfully

RUFUS KING.

Before returning, I am desirous to pass a few months upon the continent.

A. HAMILTON TO R. KING.

NEW YORK, June 3, 1802.

MY DEAR SIR :

I have been long very delinquent towards you, as a correspondent, and am to thank you that you have not cast me off altogether as an irretrievable reprobate. But you know how to appreciate the causes, and you have made a construction equally just and indulgent.

In your last you ask my opinion about a matter delicate and important both in a public and in a personal view. I shall give it with the frankness to which you have a right, and I may add that the impressions of your other friends, so far as they have fallen under my observation, do not differ from my own. While you were in the midst of a negotiation interesting to your country, it was your duty to keep your post. You have now accomplished the object and with the good fortune not very common of having the universal plaudit. This done, it seems to me most advisable that you return home. There is little probability that your continuance in your present station will be productive of much positive good. Nor are circumstances such as to give reason to apprehend that the substitute for you, whoever he may be, can do much harm. Your stay or return therefore, as it regards our transatlantic concerns, is probably not material : while your presence at home may be useful in ways which it is not necessary to particularise. Besides it is questionable whether you can continue longer in the service of the present administration with what is due as well to your own character as to the common cause. I am far from thinking that a man is bound to quit a public office merely because the administration of the Government may have changed hands. But when those who have come into power are undisguised persecutors of the party to which he has been attached and study with ostentation to heap upon it every indignity and injury—he ought not in my opinion to permit himself to make an exception or to lend his talents to the support of such characters. If in addition to this, it be true that the principles and plans of the men at the head of affairs tend to the degradation of the Government and to their own disgrace, it will hardly be possible to be in any way connected with them without sharing in the disrepute which they may be destined to experience.

I wish I had time to give you a comprehensive & particular map of our political situation. But more than a rude outline is beyond my leisure, devoted as I am more than ever to my professional pursuits.

You have seen the course of the Administration hitherto, especially during the last session of Congress, and I am persuaded you will agree in opinion with me that it could hardly have been more diligent—in mischief. What you will ask has been and is likely to be the effect on the public mind?

Our friends are sanguine that a great change for the better has been wrought and is progressive. I suppose good has been done —that the Federalists have been reunited and cemented— have been awakened and alarmed. Perhaps too there may be some sensible and moderate men of the adverse party who are beginning to doubt. But I as yet discover no satisfactory symptoms of a revolution of opinion in the *mass.*

Nor do I look with much expectation to any serious alteration until inconveniences are extensively felt or until time has produced a disposition to coquet with new lovers—Vibrations of power, you are aware, are the genius of our Government.

There is however a circumstance which may accelerate the fall of the party. There is certainly a most serious scism between the Chief and his heir apparent; a scism absolutely incurable, because founded in the breasts of both in the rivalship of an insatiable and unprincipled ambition. The effects are already apparent and are ripening into a more bitter animosity between the partizans of the two men than ever existed between the Federalists and Antifederalists.

Unluckily we are not as neutral to the quarrel as we ought to be—You saw how far our friends in Congress went in polluting themselves with the support of the second personage for the presidency. The Cabal did not terminate there. Several men, of no inconsiderable importance among us, like the enterprising and adventurous character of this man, and hope to soar with him to power. Many more through hatred to the Chief and through an impatience to recover the reins are linking themselves with the Vice-Chief, almost without perceiving it and professing to have no other object than to make use of him ; while he knows that he is making use of them. What this may end in, it is difficult to foresee.

Of one thing only I am sure, that in no event will I be directly or indirectly implicated in a responsibility for the elevation or support of either of two men, who in different senses, are in my eyes equally unworthy of the confidence of intelligent or honest men.

Truly, my dear Sir, the prospects of our Country are not bril. liant. The mass is far from sound. At headquarters a most visionary theory presides. Depend upon it this is the fact to a great extreme. No army, no navy, no *active* commerce—natural defence, not by arms but by embargoes, prohibitions of trade, &c. —as little government as possible within—these are the pernicious dreams which as far and as fast as possible will be attempted to be realized. Mr. Jefferson is distressed at the codfish having latterly emigrated to the southern Coast lest the people there should be tempted to catch them ! and commerce of which we have already too much, receive an accession. Be assured this is no pleasantry, but a very sober anecdote.

Among Federalists old errors are not cured. They also continue to dream though not so preposterously as their opponent. All will be very well (say they) when the power once more gets back into Federal hands. The people convinced by experience of their error will repose a *permanent* confidence in good men. *Risum teneatis ?* Adieu.

Yrs. ever—

A. H.

P. S. The bearer our acquaintance—Wm. Bayard continues worthy of high esteem & regard.

A. H.

R. Troup to R. King.

NEW YORK, June 6, 1802.

DEAR SIR :

. . . The fatigue occasioned by the constant sitting of our courts exhausted us all very much.   I find that Hamilton's health, notwithstanding the quickness and enormous strength of his mind, is impairing, as well as mine.   This man's mind, by the by, seems to be progressing to greater and greater maturity ; such is the common opinion of our bar ; and I may say with truth that his powers are now enormous ! and the only chance we have of success is now and then when he happens to be on the weaker side : and yet he is always complaining that he does not get his share of judgments and decrees !   Our new Chancellor (Lansing) is attentive and honest, but his mind is narrow and piddling ; and he is utterly destitute of those liberal and comprehensive views, which are suited to the Court over which he presides.   It is a great source of consolation, however, to such as do not admire (and I confess myself of this number) the republican system, that our Supreme Court and Court of Chancery *respect the rights of property.*

We are now in profound tranquillity.   The peace has drawn after it a diminution of business of all sorts. . . The fall of our produce and our late open water have not affected the prices of lands, but they have materially injured payments. . . .

We poor fallen federalists are indulging our expectation that the sun of federalism is beginning to rise again.   In Massachusetts and Connecticut larger majorities for the federalists appeared at the State elections than in those of last year.   In this State we have also gained—but in my opinion not more has appeared than demonstrates the existence of life ; what two or three years will produce is beyond conjecture. . . .

The Clintonians and Jeffersonians are at open hostility with the Burrites.   This will be evident from the pamphlet accompanying this letter.   Burr is now at Savannah doing what he can *to render Jefferson more popular and promote his re-election.*   That you may understand the pamphlet better, I have also sent you herewith the history of Adams' administration.   The rancour between these parties is indescribable.   The cant of the Clintonians and Jeffersonians is that we have coalesced with Burr—which is an infamous falsehood—as far as our friends in this State are concerned ; though we have reason to think that Burr has been caballing with some of our friends to the southward. The high probability is that Burr is a gone man, and that all his cunning, enterprise and industry will not save him. The pamphlet exhibits a just picture of Burr's character. The history of Adams' administration is a paltry and rascally thing ; the author is a British renegade. . . .

Coleman is very zealous and devoted to the federal cause ; but his paper is that of the scholar and the gentleman. . . .

Yours

Rob. Troup.

CHAPTER IX.

R. KING TO SECRETARY OF STATE.

No. 69.

LONDON, June 10, 1802.

SIR :

I have duly received your Letter of Ap. 7th, communicating the President's approbation of the Convention respecting the 6th and 7th Articles of the Treaty of 1794 ; and by private accounts of a later date, we have the farther satisfaction to hear that the Senate has likewise added its sanction.

In respect to the Countervailing Duties, I have nothing to add

137

to my former communication ; their continuance or repeal is a question submitted to the decision of Congress. The press of Business towards the close of the Session of Parliament employs the whole time of the Ministers ; at present therefore I do not think it expedient to resume the subject of our West India Trade. As soon as a convenient opening offers I will recall it to Lord Hawkesbury's attention.

By this opportunity I send you a copy of the Report of the Committee of the House of Commons, respecting the vaccine inoculation, a discovery of the highest interest to humanity ; also a statement of the national Debt together with the calculations concerning the late modification of the Sinking Fund. By the first ship bound to the Chesapeake, I will send you a copy of the late Enumeration of this Country, so far as it has been completed ; the Supplement shall be forwarded as soon as it is printed. As our Census is a subject of much enquiry, I shall be obliged to you to send me a dozen copies of the former as well as of the late Census, some of which I wish to deposit in the public Museums and Libraries.

　　　　　With perfect Respect & Esteem &c.

　　　　　　　　　　　　　　　　　Rufus King.

————

T. Sedgwick to R. King.

Wiscasset, in Maine, 15 June, 1802.

My dear Sir :

I have just now had the pleasure to receive your letter of the 6th of April for which I am much obliged to you. No part of it has given me more pleasure than the intimation it gave of your intended return. As the convention you made is ratified, I am of opinion your presence will be more useful here than in England. Strange as it might appear to a superficial observer, it is nevertheless true that an adjustment of all differences with G. B. was ardently desired by J——n and his friends, even before the cession of Louisiana afforded additional motives to it. I never had a doubt, therefore, that any reasonable terms would be accepted.

In my last letter, as well as I can recollect, I predicted that the policy of the President would weaken his adherents in New England. This prediction is verified by the elections, at least in this state ; our legislature being more federal than it has been since the adoption of the constitution, and as far as I am informed composed of better materials.   In New Hampshire, it is true that Governor Gilman was elected by a smaller majority than this the preceeding year, but I am assured that the defection was owing more to local than national causes.

Till now I have never been in this district, and have been astonished at the progress of improvement which is everywhere apparent.   The increase of population has everywhere been considerable, but the accumulation of wealth incomparably greater. Portland, Bath, this place, & several others, have become flourishing trading places, but none more so than the village of Kennebunk.   I have indeed been astonished at the appearance which every part of the country that I have seen exhibits.   But among all that I have seen here none has been more pleasing than two of your nieces ; of the name of Southgate, whom I saw at Portland, and one of whom is now here.

I would never have abandoned the govt. personally but from the most complete conviction that the people would make an experiment of democracy.   Under this conviction I could perceive no reason for sacrificing my comfort to objects of the attainment of which I despaired.   On my retiring I was certain that inaction would render me unhappy, and therefore began anew the practice in my profession.   This soon became disgusting to me, and I was inclined to accept the office of Judge merely to avoid the evils of idleness.   Whether I shall continue in it is as yet uncertain.   Should I quit it I shall never again return to the bar but try what I can do in the cultivation of land.

Farewell,

THEODORE SEDGWICK.

R. KING TO N. LOW.

LONDON, June 15, 1802.

DEAR SIR :

. . . I observe your doubts in respect to the funds : but my confidence is not yet lost and I therefore desire you to continue your investments on my account.   The funds may be less secure than they ought to be, and the prices such as to yield but little

more than 6 per cent.   Nevertheless Property invested in the funds
requires so little trouble and the annuity is paid with so much
regularity, and the capital is at all times so easily converted into
money, and in portions suiting one's convenience, that to people
disliking business and the care of managing property, the funds
will with us, as everywhere else, in general be preferred to other
property. . . .

R. KING.

R. KING TO JAMES MADISON, ESQ.

Private.

LONDON, June 16, 1802.

DEAR SIR :

I am much obliged to you for your Letter of Ap. 7. and beg of
you to present my respectful acknowledgments to the President
for the permission he has given me to visit France and some of
the neighbouring Countries.

As yet I have not formed any plan upon this subject, and shall
wait for the return of the Convention before I do so ; perhaps I
may pass a few weeks at Paris, in July or August, but do not
think it probable that I shall go farther from my post.

It is some months since the return home of my Secretary Mr.
John Pickering ; I have expected as his successor my nephew
Mr. H. Southgate, who will probably arrive in the course of the
summer.   Since Mr. Pickering left me, Mr. John Munro of Scotland, who has been employed in my office for several years, has
done the duties of my Secretary ; and as I have been fully satisfied with his fidelity and attention, I have allowed him the pay.
If I avail myself of the President's permission to extend my
voyage beyond Paris, or for more than three or four weeks, I
shall leave my friend Mr. Gore, (one of the Commissioners under
the 7th Article of the Treaty of 1794) Chargé des affaires during
my absence ; in this case you will understand that his agency
will be attended with no expence to the public.

With very great Respect & Esteem &c.

RUFUS KING.

R. King to Secretary of State.

No. 70.

London, June 20, 1802.

Sir :

I have duly received the duplicate of your Letter of May the first ; the original has not yet reached me, owing probably to the Packet's detention at Halifax on her way to Falmouth. As soon as she arrives, I will take immediate measures to complete the Convention by exchanging the Ratifications.

The Commission under the 7th Article of the Treaty of 1794, is proceeding in a satisfactory manner ; upwards of fifty cases which were prepared for hearing soon after the suspension of the Commission, have been so far decided since the recommencement of its business that they wait only for the date of the Exchange of the Ratifications of the Convention in order that their respective Sums may be computed and fixed. The question of Interest, about which nothing has been said since the reassembling of the Board, will occur when these computations are to be made. As the claims preferred by British Subjects for captures alleged to have been illegal amount altogether to a considerable sum, and as it is conjectured that many of these claims are destitute of any just foundation, it is desirable that they should receive an early consideration and decision : this will also happen as soon as the Ratifications are exchanged.

Mr. Cabot's assistance will, I am persuaded, prove a material advantage to the American Claimants, and, at the same time, no small relief to the Commissioners ; as his knowledge of the course of our Trade, and of the peculiar manner in which certain portions of it are carried on, enable him to give explanations that are familiar to mercantile men, but without which there would be some difficulties in deciding many of the cases before the commission.

Although I understand that the Board has been apprized of the annual allowance to be received by Mr. Cabot, during his service in connexion with the Commission, I purpose to write a letter to the Commissioners communicating to them agreeably to your letter to me, that to induce Mr. Cabot to return and resume his functions in this country, the President has been pleased to allow him an annual salary of 1500 Dollars.

In respect to the Countervailing Duties upon our ships and Cargoes entering the Ports of Great Britain, I can only repeat what I have already remarked to you that their discontinuance partially or wholly having been entirely, and as I thought liberally submitted to the decision of Congress, I do not perceive that I can with propriety resume the subject until Congress shall have come to some decision concerning it. The intention of suspending immediately the countervailing Duty on Tobacco was upon the idea that the discriminating Duties had been or certainly would be repealed in America : but as soon as I perceived that such repeal had become doubtful on account of the unexpected opposition the proposal met with, I thought it due to a candid course of Proceeding, to intimate my doubts upon this point to the British Minister ; and in consequence thereof it was determined by the Treasury to postpone the suspension until more precise information of the views of Congress should be received.

With Perfect Respect and Esteem,

Rufus King.

R. King to George W. Erving, Esq.

Great Cumberland Place, June 21, 1802.

Sir :

As the answer invariably given to former applications respecting Seamen, representing themselves to be American Citizens, but who have no document to prove their citizenship, would without doubt be repeated in answer to any further and formal demands in their favour, I doubt of the expediency of making the application suggested by you in favour of the seamen, whose discharge as Americans has been refused, but who have been released in consequence of the late reduction of the naval forces of this country.

Mr. Lenox informed me that he delivered to you a List of detained Seamen of this description ; by comparing the names of those who have applied to you for succour with the List, you will be enabled to ascertain how many of the applicants are of this class. I request you to make the comparison, and inform me of the result : as in case the number is very considerable, I would take an opportunity of informally speaking to Lord St. Vincent upon the subject. I am, Sir,

Your obedient Servant,

Rufus King.

R. King to G. W. Erving, Esq.

RANDELLS, SURRY, July 1, 1802.

SIR :

To guard against unfounded claims for relief, as well as to check the Repetition of those which are correct, it has heretofore been deemed indispensable to keep an alphabetical and descriptive list of all seamen representing themselves to be Americans and claiming succour from the U. S.   The Description should at least express the town and State, and if foreign born, the place of their nativity, together with the proof of Citizenship, and the name of the man of war from which they have been discharged. Such a list, if collated with that left with you by Mr. Lenox, would without trouble and immediately supply the information I wished for, to enable me to determine upon the expediency of the application you have advised to be made to the Admiralty ; and I request that you will in future keep such a list.   Without greater precision in respect to the number and national character of the persons, representing themselves to be American Seamen, lately discharged from the naval service of this Country, I am not inclined to apply to the admiralty for the purpose of engaging it to defray the expence of their passage to America ; but if you should continue to be satisfied of the citizenship of these persons, and the means designated for their return home be insufficient, I recommend to you to call upon Mr. Nepean and confer with him upon the subject ; this being in my opinion a better course, whether we regard the success or failure of the attempt, than to make the application in writing.   It will however be advantageous that you should ascertain, as far as practicable, the number of American Seamen who have been lately discharged and who desire to return home ; and if you could make out, even with a little trouble, a List of their names, I am persuaded it might promote the accomplishment of your object.

With due respect &c.,

RUFUS KING.

R. King to Lord Hawkesbury.

LEATHERHEAD, SURRY, July 5, 1802.

MY LORD :

I have the Satisfaction to inform your Lordship, that I have just received the Convention, which we signed in January last, duly ratified on the part of the President of the United States, together with Instructions to exchange the same for the like Ratification on the part of his Majesty.

It affords me additional pleasure to be authorized to add, that although the Subject might have been deferred to a future Session of Congress, the President conceiving that its immediate Consideration would be a satisfactory Evidence of the disposition of our public Councils, lost no time in laying the Convention before Congress, which has made the requisite appropriations to carry the same into effect. Whenever it shall be convenient to your Lordship, I will wait upon you to complete this Business by exchanging the Ratifications.

With perfect Consideration, &c.,

RUFUS KING.

R. KING TO SECRETARY OF STATE.

NO. 71.

LONDON, July 5, 1802.

SIR :

The loan lately obtained by the Dutch Government, and for which a rate of profit is secured to the Lenders hitherto unknown in that frugal and industrious Country, and which it is thought may have a disadvantageous effect upon its money operations in future, has for some time past excited a good deal of curiosity, the public being at a loss to conjecture the purpose to which so considerable a sum could be destined. It is now believed that Fifteen Millions of Guilders, part of this loan, have been paid to procure from France a release of the claims of the Prince of Orange, which he himself would have given up for half the sum : this payment explains the separate engagement signed at Amiens by the French and Dutch ambassadors relative to these Claims.

The plan of indemnities about which the Princes of Germany have been so long amused, is supposed to be settled, between France, Russia and Prussia, and without the assistance of Austria. We are told that the Prince of Orange is to receive his indemnity in Germany, and that Austria will consult her prudence and acquiesce in a statement made under the influence of France, and sanctioned by her most powerful neighbours.

The commercial Negotiation between this country and France has hitherto made very little, if any, progress, and at present it seems altogether uncertain whether any arrangement upon this subject will be completed. In the meantime France is active in extending and strengthening her influence in every quarter, as well as in concerting projects, and executing plans both at home and abroad, which do not seem capable of being explained in a manner consistent with the sincerity of her professions concerning the Peace of Europe.

Mr. Otto is still here, waiting for his successor, who is not expected to arrive before the middle of September : this delay will probably operate to postpone Mr. Otto's journey to America till the ensuing Spring.

With perfect Respect & Esteem, &c.,

RUFUS KING.

R. KING TO LORD HAWKESBURY.

GREAT CUMBERLAND PLACE, July 12, 1802.

MY LORD :

I have received the orders of the President of the United States to lay before your Lordship the enclosed Evidence of the misconduct of ——— O'Brien, Esq., Commander of His Majesty's Frigate Emerald, in the impressment on board the American Schooner Sea-flower, of Philadelphia, and upon the high seas, of William Munro and Lindsay Addison, Citizens and Seamen of the United States. Referring to the reflexions upon the Subject, which I have heretofore submitted to your Lordship's consideration, and which derive new force from the reestablishment of a general peace, I take the liberty to request your Lordship's immediate interference in order that the said Munro and Addison may be forthwith discharged, and orders given to the said ——— O'Brien, Esq., as well as to all others, his Majesty's Naval Officers, carefully to abstain from the like irregularities in future.

Acknowledging, as I am instructed to do, the equitable and friendly sentiments of his Majesty's Government towards that of the United States, and which are fully and sincerely reciprocated by the latter, I flatter myself that your Lordship's influence will not be wanting in favour of a regulation which, without injury to Great Britain, is due to the rights of the United States as well as essential to the Security of their Commerce.

With great Consideration & Respect, &c.,

RUFUS KING.

R. KING TO ROBERT R. LIVINGSTON, ESQ.

LONDON, July 12, 1802.

DEAR SIR :

I have had the honour to receive your letter of June 30th. Whether either or both the Floridas have been ceded seems altogether matter of inference and conjecture, as no document we have seen offers any direct evidence upon the subject. The same reasons which have led me to suppose it probable that the Floridas would not be reserved by Spain after Louisania passed into the hands of France, induce me to think that West Florida would not be kept if East Florida be ceded with Louisiana. The chief object, and almost the only one, which has made the Floridas of any value to Spain, must cease with the cession of Louisiana, and as the Floridas in themselves are rather a burthen than a benefit to Spain, I cannot but think, whether they have or have not been ceded, that France, being mistress of Louisiana, will acquire, whenever she chooses to do so, a Title to the Floridas also. If so France, and not Spain, is the Power with which every efficient discussion should be made concerning these Provinces. As the free Navigation and use of the Mississippi is a Right above all computation to the United States, New Orleans and the Floridas would on this account, as well as others, prove a most valuable acquisition ; and according to my creed they must and will ultimately belong to us. If so, every step we take should have a reference to this negotiation, and notwithstanding we cannot at all times advance towards the attainment of our object, Prudence should restrain us from whatever may serve to obstruct or defeat the accomplishment of our purpose. Upon these principles we ought to give no explicit sanction to the transfer of these Provinces from Spain to any other Power, nor enter into any engagements jointly with others concerning them ; for altho' we may at present be content that they should remain in the possession of Spain, it is by no means plain that it would be consistent with sound policy for us to give money in order that they may be left in this situation. If doubts may however exist upon this point, there surely can be none that it would be repugnant to every principle of policy which might, or is likely to, influence our Government to form a Guaranty jointly with France or any other Power, to secure the possession of these Provinces to Spain or any other Nation, inasmuch as such Guaranty might not only prove an impediment to our acquiring them ourselves, but probably would involve us in a disadvantageous war on that account. If these Provinces remain in the possession of Spain, as we wish they may, it cannot be long before all the continental Colonies of that nation will imitate the example we have given them. Having had the means of a good deal of information upon this subject, concerning which so little is known, and so much concealed, I feel confident that this crisis cannot be at a great distance. Aware that such is the situation of the Colonies, Spain has been solicitous and pressed the point with zeal, tho' unsuccessfully, upon Mr. Pinckney in the year 1795 to procure from us a Guaranty of her American Possessions. Should another war break out between England and France, as we cannot doubt will be the case in the course of a few years, Spain as heretofore will become a party of it, and it is quite probable that England may succeed in the attempt to take possession of New Orleans and the Floridas ; either of these events would constitute the casus fœderis, and we should consequently be called upon to fulfil our Guaranty.

On account of the peculiar situation of these Provinces, and independent of our views as to the acquisition of them, we should therefore abstain from entering into any Guaranty concerning them ; a species of stipulation it can never be our interest to enter into with any of the great commercial Powers of Europe, since it is one rarely, if ever, to be formed except by a Power in a condition not only to construe, but to enforce the observance of her construction of the engagement.

From the tenor of these observations, which, tho' hastily written, are so far as regards their principal object the fruit of much consideration, you will infer my dislike of a purchase, except for ourselves, as well as my repugnance to a Guaranty under any circumstances. As I write to you without any reserve and upon a subject whose limits are not yet fully explored, and concerning which opinions may therefore be supposed to vary, you will I am sure excuse the little ceremony which I have observed in the expression of my sentiments, the justness whereof, I shall on all occasions be inclined to distrust, if they happen to be in opposition to your more weighty opinion.

With great and sincere Respect, &c.

RUFUS KING.

R. KING TO SECRETARY OF STATE.

No. 72.

LONDON, July 16, 1802.

SIR :

As soon as I received from Mr. Fenwick the President's Ratification of the Convention, I gave notice thereof to Lord Hawkesbury, and we yesterday exchanged the Ratifications, and mutually executed the usual Certificates thereof. Two original Copies of the British Ratification have been delivered to me together with duplicate Certificates of the exchange. I shall commit them to the charge of Mr. Christie, late a Representative in Congress from Maryland, who will deliver them to you in Washington. The duplicate Ratification and Certificate of Exchange shall be forwarded by the next good opportunity. I have taken the liberty to ensure Mr. Christie that whatever expence he may incur in the performance of this service will be readily reimbursed by you.

With perfect respect and esteem, &c,

RUFUS KING.

R. KING TO SECRETARY OF STATE.

No. 73.

LONDON, July 19, 1802.

SIR :

I yesterday received a letter from Commodore Morris, dated United States frigate Chesapeake, Gibraltar Bay, June 25, announcing the unexpected declaration of war against the United

States by the Emperor of Morocco. I have given notice of the event to our Consuls in this country, to the end that all American Vessels in the Ports thereof may make use of such precautions in favour of their security, as those having the charge of them may deem expedient. Whether this unjust Proceeding has arisen out of the civil commotions which for some time past are understood to have prevailed in Morocco, or from some other cause, I am altogether ignorant, having no exact information either concerning the internal condition of Morocco, or of the State of our Relations with this Power. The declaration, however, will serve as another proof, if another be wanting, that our security against the Barbary Powers must depend upon Force and not upon Treaties, upon Ships of war instead of presents and subsidies.

The early part of the Summer having been uncommonly dry, the crop of Hay will be very short ; and the weather during the last four weeks (the Hay season for the South of England) having been cloudy and wet, the Crop which has been cut is not only short in quantity but ill cured. Old Hay has in consequence thereof risen in the London market from five to eight Guineas the load of eighteen hundred ; and altho' the Wheat and other Grain have promised a plentiful Harvest, the continuance of rainy weather begins to excite serious concern lest the Corn should suffer from mildew and other injuries to which it is exposed.

With perfect Respect and Esteem, &c.

RUFUS KING.

R. KING TO R. TROUP.

LONDON, July 19, 1802.

DEAR SIR :

. . . Mrs. King and I think of going for a few weeks to France. . . Though I have not fixed upon any precise time, I am much inclined to return home. My children too are growing too old to remain abroad. After visiting Paris, I must come to a decision on this subject.

Adieu, yours &c..,

RUFUS KING.

R. King to James Madison, Esq.
Private.

London, July 21, 1802.

Dear Sir :

As an item in my contingent account relates to the Publication of Robinson's Admiralty Reports, it may be thought proper that I should say a word or two in explanation of this expense.

It has not, as you may well know, been the practice of this country to publish Reports of the decisions of its prize Tribunals ; and while a pretty general opinion has prevailed that England administers the Law of Nations in matters of prize with great rigour, Englishmen have uniformly asserted that these Tribunals have manifested greater moderation in that respect than those of any other Nation. So long as the decisions of the English prize Courts remained unpublished, this Disagreement would continue to exist, and so long likewise foreign States would remain without precise notion of the maxims of Public Law by which these Tribunals profess to regulate their Decisions.

Upon Sir William Scott's appointment as Judge of the High Court of Admiralty, being alike distinguished for Learning and Integrity, and desirous of extending his reputation beyond the limits of his own country, it occurred to me that the opportunity was a favourable one to endeavour to promote the publication of the Reports of his Court, the natural effect whereof upon such a mind as Sir William Scott's seemed likely to be in favour of a mild interpretation of the Laws of War and Peace, and what appeared to me of much importance, such a publication would have a Tendency to procure for this important branch of public Law a fixed character in place of the uncertain and contentious Reputation it has hitherto possessed : by going into the hands of merchants and men of business, these Reports would moreover enable them to avoid such adventures as might be liable to interruption.

I accordingly conversed with Sir William Scott upon the subject ; at first the proposal encountered difficulty chiefly on account of the contrary usage ; this objection was finally yielded, and Sir William Scott acquiesced, provided Government would consent and a suitable Reporter could be found to undertake the work. I then applied to the Minister and suggested such arguments as seemed to me likely to engage his attention, and, after a time, the

Government gave its consent and nothing remained but to find a Reporter.

As these Reports were not expected to be called for by professional men, who are the principal purchasers of the Common Law Reports, it was apprehended that the demand might not be sufficient to reimburse the expenses of publication, and to obviate this objection, recourse was had as usual in cases of this character to last subscriptions. Considering the utility of the publication and the part I had taken to promote it, I thought it expedient to subscribe for Fifty Copies. These have been sent from time to time, and in the order of their publication, to the Department of State, except the five copies which I have distributed among the American Ministers in Europe and some other public Characters.

Upon this explanation which ought to have been, and I believe was, given to your Predecessor at the time of the subscription, I flatter myself the President will not disapprove of this small Expense. As but few cases remain undecided in the High Court of Admiralty, which expects, as I hear, to get through the whole of its Business in the course of a few weeks even, I presume that these Reports will not be extended far beyond their present size. I have suggested the advantage of adding to them an appendix, containing the Form of all Instruments used in the process of the Prize Courts ; and as Sir William Scott has given Direction to the Registrar to supply Doctor Robinson with all such copies as he may require for this purpose, I am in hopes this useful addition will be made.

These Reports are supposed to undergo the revision and correction of the Judge before they are put to press.

With Sentiments of Sincere Respect & Esteem &c.

RUFUS KING.

CHAPTER X.

K. KING TO R. R. LIVINGSTON.

Private and personal.

LONDON, Aug. 4, 1802.

DEAR SIR :

Although I had nothing of interest to say, I should have written to you by Mr. V. R. Livingston had he not left us a day or
two sooner than he expected. Having ever since the conclusion
of the war thought seriously of returning home, I have lately decided to do so, and in my official letter of this date, have resigned
my office, and requested to be relieved in season to embark early
next Spring. As I think it possible that you may be inclined to
pass some time in this country before you return to America, and
in that case might consent to be transferred from your present
Residence to this country, I take the earliest moment to inform
you of my determination to return home, in order that you may
be apprized of the vacancy, which my resignation will create.
Mrs. King and I availing ourselves of the leave of temporary
absence which I have received, propose in the course of next
week to embark for Holland, from whence we may pass entirely

thro' the Low Countries on our way to Paris, where we think of spending five or six weeks in September and October.

    With Sentiments of great Regard & Esteem &c.

                                        RUFUS KING.

R. KING TO JOHN MARSHALL, ESQ.

Private.

                        LONDON, Aug. 5, 1802.

DEAR SIR :

I have duly received and beg you to accept my acknowledgements for your obliging Letter of May 4. Notwithstanding I do think the settlement of the British Claims, circumstanced as they were, honourable and advantageous to us, as well as the evidence of a conciliatory disposition on the part of the English administration, I am with you entirely persuaded that it would have met with a different reception at home, had the administration remained in the hands of those from whom it has been lately removed.

In a private letter to you, connected and influential as you have been in the promotion of this adjustment, I may without impropriety say that if there be any merit in this settlement, it is in every respect due to those who projected and approved the plan which led to it. For not only every material point of the negotiation was completed, but the precise form finally accepted had been offered as an ultimatum before I had any knowledge of the opinion of the present Administration. I would not insinuate that any sentiments, unfavourable to the settlement which has been made, were entertained by the present Administration ; on the contrary, it approved of what had been done here, and I think sincerely desired to see the Business closed upon the terms which had been offered. I earnestly wish that on other and still more important concerns, its sentiments had been equally correct, as they have been in respect to this Business ; but I must disregard opinions formed with solicitude, and after careful reflexion, not to hesitate in believing this to have been the case ; and it is for this reason, among others, that upon mature consideration of my duty to the public, as well as of what I owe to myself, I have thought it incumbent upon me to resign my Mission and ask leave to return home.

Although I am quite sensible that this is a measure of no sort of importance in a public view, the interest which you have so kindly taken in what personally concerns me, induces me to make you this communication and not without the hope that it will receive your approbation.

With Sentiments of the highest Respect & Esteem &c.

RUFUS KING.

R. KING TO ROBERT SOUTHGATE, ESQ.

LONDON, August 5, 1802.

MY DEAR SIR :

. . . I had continued to expect the arrival of my nephew Horatio. I rather inferred from what he (Mr. Boyd) told us, that both he and you had relinquished the plan of his coming to England.

I engaged only a temporary secretary, and now shall not think of looking for another, as I have in my official letter of this date resigned my mission and requested to be relieved in season to return home early next Spring.

It was my wish to have returned some time ago, but being engaged in a negotiation of considerable difficulty and importance, I have not been able until now to do so with propriety. The negotiation which detained me being completed, and nothing of importance remaining in the discussion whereof I can hope to be useful, I think myself free to resign my office ; a measure that will I hope receive the approbation of my friends. . . .

I remain with Sincere Esteem &c.

RUFUS KING.

R. KING TO SECRETARY OF STATE.

NO. 74.

LONDON, Aug. 5, 1802.

SIR :

It is now six years that I have resided in this country. When I left America it was not my expectation to be absent more than four years. So long as the war continued I did not think of returning home, believing that my residence here might be of some public advantage.   When the preliminaries of peace were signed, I found myself engaged in a negotiation of considerable Difficulty and importance which restrained me from asking the President's leave to resign my mission.   The negotiation being since completed, and nothing very material remaining to be discussed in which I can flatter myself with being able to render any important service, I have to request that the President would be pleased to accept the resignation of my office and permit me to return home.

The season is already too far advanced to leave time to receive the President's permission before the commencement of the long nights and stormy season of the present year.   I am not therefore solicitous to be relieved before the month of April next as my family is large and I am moreover desirous to carry home with me my library, furniture, carriages and other bulky articles, it would be a great accommodation to me if the President would allow me a passage in a frigate or other national vessel, which at the same time would relieve my family from any concern in respect to the cruizers of Morocco, or any other piratical state, and save me from the heavy charges which I must otherwise incur in returning home after seven years' residence in the most expensive Country of Europe.

With perfect Respect & Esteem,

RUFUS KING.

R. KING TO JAMES MADISON, ESQ.

Private.

LONDON, August 5, 1802.

DEAR SIR :

In my official letter of this date, I have taken the liberty to ask the accommodation of a passage home for myself and family in one of the public ships.   Should the President consent, the same Vessel might bring out my successor, and carry me back. At first I thought, that a frigate returning home from the Mediterranean might without inconvenience receive orders to touch here and take me on board ; but upon inquiry I find, that, coming from that quarter, she might be liable to perform quarantine, which would occasion a long detention, as well as great expence. The chief purpose of this letter is to request the favour of you, to inform me, as early as you can with convenience, of the President's determination in order that I may be able seasonably to make my arrangements concerning my baggage, which I must endeavour to diminish in case I shall be obliged to hire a vessel to carry me home. I have likewise to ask the additional favour of you, to apprize my Agent, Mr. Nicholas Low of New York, of the President's decision, so that in case I cannot be accommodated by a Passage in a public ship, he may execute a provisional order I have given him to prepare and send from New York a Vessel to carry me and my family home.

With Sentiments of great Respect and Esteem,

RUFUS KING.

P. S. In case I go home in a public ship, I should like to be allowed to carry in her a few sheep of the Breeds most esteemed here, and perhaps my carriage and horses ; the latter are free and I have reason to believe that I should find no difficulty in obtaining permission to export a small number of the former whose properties are certainly superior to those of our country.

R. KING TO SECRETARY OF STATE.

No. 75.

LONDON, Aug. 10, 1802.

SIR :

As I am about to avail myself of the President's permission to pass a few weeks upon the Continent, I have thought it expedient to endeavour previously to ascertain the sentiments of this Government concerning the Trade and Navigation between the United States and the British Colonies in the West Indies, as well as to press for a final decision respecting the Maryland Bank Stock. For these purposes I asked a conference of Lord Hawkesbury in a note, the copy whereof is annexed. His Lordship received me at the time I had proposed, but I regret that I am not able to send you a more satisfactory Report of what passed on this occasion.

In respect to the Bank Stock Lord Hawkesbury said he had lately received a communication from the Chancellor concerning it, and that measures should be taken to effect a transfer of the

Stock to the Crown, when it would be in a situation that would enable him to receive the King's pleasure respecting it. He intimated that he had understood there were other claims beside that of the State of Maryland, but so far as he expressed any opinion, it seemed to be that there would be no difficulty of importance in the way of a satisfactory settlement; after the Stock had been transferred to the Crown. I repeated to his Lordship arguments which had been urged upon his Predecessor, and tried, tho' without success, to obtain from him an explicit engagement, that the Stock should be transferred to me after its transfer to the Crown.

Respecting the West India Trade, his Lordship said after a short conversation explanatory of our expectations, that he could give me no explicit information whether, or how far, they should be able to accede to our claims ; the fact being, as he observed, that not only on account of the constant succession of more pressing concerns, which his Majesty's Ministers had been called upon to decide, but from the unsettled as well as uncertain Condition of the West India Colonies, they had not been able to go into the consideration of the Regulations which it might be deemed expedient to adopt ; that they were yet also to learn the real Situation of Saint Domingo, as well as of some other important Colonies ; and that as any change in their former system would in some sort depend upon the probable condition not only of their own but of other Colonies, they must wait a little longer before they could form a safe opinion upon this important subject.

I remarked to Lord Hawkesbury, that on account of our just claim to an equal participation in a Trade as necessary to them as to us, as well as from the tenor of the article agreed to by England, but refused by America in the Treaty of 1794, we had not expected that a recurrence would be had at the end of the war to the exclusive system which had prevailed before ; that any considerable delay in the decision of this point would operate in the same way as a decision in favour of the old system, which, as his Lordship must know, we considered as unequal and injurious ; that my apprehension, therefore, was in case of such delay, we should think ourselves obliged to meet the disadvantages to which our Navigation is liable under the former System by Regulations which would impose the like Disadvantages upon the British Navigation : these Countervailing Regulations would prove mutually, tho' I could not admit that they would be equally, inconvenient, and might moreover have the effect to disturb the harmonious and beneficial intercourse it was the common interest of the two Countries to promote.

His Lordship made no distinct answer to these Remarks, contenting himself to repeat in substance what he had before observed, concerning the pressure of affairs of greater Interest, and the uncertain Situation of the West India Colonies.

As I found that I had not obtained any precise assurance upon the subject, which probably has not yet been discussed in the Cabinet, I observed that notwithstanding the question might not appear to be of equal importance with others which continue to engage the attention of the English Ministry, it nevertheless had excited, and might again excite, a lively interest in the United States ; that the subject had employed much of my attention ; and I had sometimes flattered myself with the hope that I should during my residence here, be enabled to assist in the equitable and satisfactory settlement of it ; that I expected to terminate my mission and return to America early in the next Spring and that it would afford me some satisfaction to be authorized to inform you that both this Business and the other regarding the Maryland Bank Stock should be decided before my departure.

Lord Hawkesbury replied that he could not officially assure me that this should be done ; but that according to his personal view of the subjects, he foresaw no reason likely to delay the Decision of them beyond the time I had mentioned. This vague reply, and which binds to nothing, ended our Conference upon these Topics.

Lord Hawkesbury then enquired of me if I had received any late intelligence concerning the Expedition to Louisiana ; on my answering in the Negative, he said, according to their advices the French Expedition was in preparation and that it would certainly proceed. I, in turn, asked his Lordship, how far he gave credit to the rumour which had of late been circulated that France was preparing a formidable Expedition against Algiers ; he answered, that the project existed, and that the army would be marched into Spain, and embarked in the Spanish Ports, and that Spain, tho' it was understood that she has recently concluded Peace with Algiers, would nevertheless be expected to aid the French with Provisions, Ships and perhaps money. I did not ask whether England was likely also to be embroiled with Algiers in consequence of the late capture of one or two English Vessels by the Cruizers of this Regency; having understood that it is here admitted that the Papers of these Vessels were irregular, and that the demand of England would be confined to the liberation of the Crew, leaving the Vessels as forfeited to the Captors.

Before leaving Lord Hawkesbury, I took occasion to observe that although my absence would be only for a short time, to guard against any inconvenience which it might possibly occasion, I would take the liberty before my departure of introducing to him, Mr. Gore, one of the Commissioners under the 7th Article of the Treaty, who wd. act as our Chargé des affaires during my absence. His Lordship replied that he should be happy to receive Mr. Gore, and I shall accordingly present him in that character to Lord Hawkesbury before I leave town. My plan is to embark at Harwich about the 15th instant for Holland, from thence to go to Brussels, and then either directly to Paris, or turning to my left and travelling a few days on the Borders of the Rhine, to proceed to Paris thro' some of the more Eastern Provinces of France. As it is the invaluable Specimens of the fine arts more than the men and manners of Paris, which I am desirous to see, a few weeks residence there will satisfy my curiosity. I do not therefore think of prolonging my absence beyond the middle of November, when the New Parliament will meet, and my return hither may be a fortnight sooner.

With perfect Respect & Esteem,
RUFUS KING.

C. GORE TO LORD HAWKESBURY.

GREAT CUMBERLAND PLACE, Aug. 24, 1802.

SIR :

Mr. Gore presents his compliments to Lord Hawkesbury, and has the honour to inform him, that since the departure of Mr. King, he has received for this Gentleman Instructions and a full power from the President of the United States to adjust by amicable Negotiation with the Government of his Britannic Majesty whatever remains unsettled as to the Boundaries between the Territories of the two Nations.

Mr. Gore takes the liberty of proposing to his Lordship to communicate to him, whenever he shall be at leisure to attend thereto, the views of the President of the United States, in order that his Lordship may give to the subject such consideration as he may think its importance requires, and that having a distinct knowledge thereof, his Lordship may, on the return of Mr. King, be enabled to concur in such measures for defining and settling the Boundary lines between the two countries, as shall appear most conducive to their mutual interests and future harmony.

Mr. Gore flatters himself that Lord Hawkesbury will see, in this Proposal of the President, a new Proof of the sincere and earnest desire of the Government of the United States to live in friendship with that of his Majesty, inasmuch as it invites to an adjustment by amicable negotiation of not only whatever may now be the occasion of inquietude between the Parties, but also of everything, as far as can be foreseen, which may interrupt in future that good understanding so essential to the interests and happiness of both Nations.

R. TROUP TO R. KING.

NEW YORK, Aug. 24, 1802.

DEAR SIR :

. . . Burr in my opinion is acting a little and skulking part. Although Jefferson hates him as much as one demagogue can possibly hate another who is aiming to rival him, yet Burr does not come forward in an open and manly way agt. him. On the contrary Burr still attempts to cause it to be believed that he is a sincere supporter of Jefferson and administration ; and this we are told is to be the complexion of Burr's intended paper. The duel between Clinton and Swartout has been a precious morsel to us poor fallen—and hungry federalists.*

We calculate generally that Burr is ruined in politics as well as in fortune. Saving a few particulars not interesting, the view of

* See Hildreth's *Hist. of United States,* 2d ser., vol. ii., p. 468.

his political conduct is a just one. His manœuvering for the Presidency is past a doubt with us all ; and was so before the view made its appearance. Hamilton has often said he could prove it to the satisfaction of any court and jury. No mortal can yet calculate the present state of public opinion. Federalism is looking up. At the last 4th of July the toasts everywhere given prove that Hamilton is regaining that general esteem and confidence, which he seems to have lost, and his standing is very much our political thermometer. Was an election now to be held either for Governor or President, it is my opinion we should lose. What may be the progress of opinion towards a new order of things, it is impossible to calculate with even tolerable precision. . . .

Yours,

Robt. Troup.

T. Sedgwick to R. King.

Stockbridge, 24 Aug., 1802.

Dear Sir :

. . . The last letter which I addressed to you was from Wiscasset. Maine has improved, is improving, and will, I think, continue to improve, beyond what you can easily imagine. The gentlemen of that country may be compared, without disgracing them, to those of any other part of New England. In politics they have good principles and a good spirit. In Massachusetts, generally, the political tide, is setting, strongly, in a right direction, and I have no doubt will, for some time, continue and increase. . . .

As well as I can conjecture from the best information I have been able to obtain, the measures of the administration have not increased, but, on the whole, impaired the popularity of the President and his friends. With the better part—those whom we esteem—from facts, which you understand, there exists a most profound contempt of his understanding and a perfect abhorrence and detestation of his morals. The opinion which, among this class of people universally prevails, that he is hostile to the christian religion has produced a firm union among the clergy, who possess an influence in New England that will be felt. In this part of the U. S. it is not to be feared that either democracy or

Jacobinism will prevail. In New York, I am inclined to believe, that, at least, the progress of Clintonianism, for as far as that faction prevails it is neither democracy nor jacobinism, is brought to a stand. But the great line of division by which parties are separated in other states is more obscurely marked there than anywhere else—the people are more under the dominion of personal influence. And it is impossible at present to predict in what the rupture between Burr and the Clintons will ultimately terminate. Burr's intentions, the means he possesses, and the instruments which he will employ are at present unknown. But it is known that many active and ardent spirits are enlisted in his service, and servilely devoted to him ; and that his party comprises in it nearly all the needy and desperate adventurers in the community. Such a party, so united, and with such a leader, is not to be despised, however inconsiderable the number at present. The breach between Burr, the Clintonians & the Livingstons, is, in all probability, irreparable. What direction Burr will take will depend, wholly, on the opinion he shall form of the means of promoting his present aggrandizement . . . You will receive a warm welcome from your friends, and from no one more than myself. I am sensible that your residence where you are may be of much benefit to our country. I know, too, that your presence here would be of immense importance. Where you will render the best service, you are the most competent judge. Of this, I think, you may be certain that your return will depend on your own pleasure. You will not be recalled. . . .

Your sincere friend,
THEODORE SEDGWICK.

CHAPTER XI.

Availing himself of the permission granted to him by the
President, Mr. King prepared to visit the Continent of Europe and pass through its western portions until he reached
Paris. At no other period during his residence abroad as
Minister to Great Britain could he have left his post in London, for the state of war between that country and France,
and the hostile aspect of the latter towards the United
States, would have prevented his visiting those States
which were more or less involved in the active operations of
the war. Peace had now, however, been declared between
the rival nations and intercourse was again free. His pressing work in England had been accomplished to the satisfaction of his government; and although there was much to be
done to arrange the still unsettled questions between the
United States and Great Britain and to strengthen the good
feeling between the two countries, it was not probable that
for some months anything could be effected, for the public

men of England were accustomed at that time of the year to take a period of rest and relaxation from business. Besides these considerations, the relations between France and the United States were on a better footing, although France had recently consummated what seemed an unfriendly act, and one by which the future welfare of the United States might be endangered, in accepting the cession of Louisiana from Spain.

Under these circumstances Mr. King felt that he could properly and satisfactorily carry out his wish to see the western countries of Europe before his return home, and enjoy the pleasure he was so fitted to receive of spending a few months in lands celebrated for their beautiful scenery, in studying the habits of the people with whose history he was so familiar, and in examining the works of art and monuments in their cities, terminating his journey by a short sojourn in Paris, where so much was to be seen, so many distinguished men were assembled, and where the First Consul had firmly established himself.

He first provided for the conduct of the business of the United States in London by appointing his friend Christopher Gore, one of the Commissioners under the 7th Article of the Treaty of 1794, as Chargé d'Affaires during his absence, having notified the Secretary of State that this " would be without expense to the public." Having thus arranged his affairs, he started from London and embarked at Harwich on August 15th, in a vessel for Helviotsluys, which place he reached the next day after a short and comfortable passage. His party consisted of " Mrs. King, Smith and Ingersoll,* with two servants and travelling carriage," as he says

---

* Mr. Charles J. Ingersoll of Philadelphia, then a young man, had for some time been on intimate terms with Mr. King and his family in London. A warm attachment sprang up among them, due largely to Mr. Ingersoll's brightness of manner, intelligence, and at that time congeniality of views with those of Mr. King, who had a sincere regard for him. These kind feelings continued during Mr. King's life, of which there are many evidences in his Correspondence. In his *Recollections*, p. 16, in the prefatory chapter, Mr. Ingersoll says : " After Rufus King, American Minister in England, performed his initiatory

in a Diary which, though meagre in details, was kept only until he left Brussels. Though it records little that would be particularly interesting to reproduce here, the pages show the interest he took in the new scenes, in habits so different from those of his own country and of the English people whom he had so recently left, and in the buildings and works of art in Holland, with the latter of which he was not much impressed. We have nothing of the Rhine along which he travelled, nor of Switzerland with its alpine scenery and its sturdy liberty-loving people, nor of Eastern France through which he journeyed to Paris, where he arrived about the 15th of October and which he left in the middle of November, reaching London on the 17th. He and his party seem to have enjoyed their tour, to have met with no interruptions or mishaps, and to have returned to England in health.

During the whole period of his absence a constant correspondence was maintained between Mr. Gore and himself, but unfortunately few of Mr. Gore's letters are preserved and none of Mr. King's. The former kept him informed about the business of the Legation, consisting of communications with the British Ministry, especially relative to the boundaries of the United States, for the adjustment of which a commission was sent to Mr. King during his absence, and for the early settlement of which Mr. Gore made an earnest plea, as likely to promote mutual benefit and the future peace of the two countries.

But the most interesting portions of his letters to Mr. and Mrs. King were those relating to the boys, whom they had left in England at school and under the loving care of Mr. and Mrs. Gore. They had not been blessed with children, but they always seemed to look upon the children of their old friends as if they were their own and took them to their

and important accessorial part in the attainment of Louisiana, I went in his diplomatic family from London to Paris in 1802, . . . returned with Mr. King from England to America, with the first intelligence of its (Louisiana's) acquisition."

hearts as they had taken their parents before them. Nothing that interested the boys escaped their care and attention and every little incident of their lives at school or during the holidays, which were passed with Mr. Gore, was treasured up to be reported to their absent friends as accounts they would be anxious to receive and which would cheer them during the separation.

Writing of the Harrow boys, who were with him, he says:

"They recite sixty or seventy lines of Virgil every morning—billiards, shooting and riding occupy the residue of the day. Their health is perfectly right, & both à la physique & à la morale they are in every respect, as we or you would desire them to be. . . . Frederick (the baby) whom I have just been tossing in the air and spanking, for he is literally a sans-culotte, daily improves in strength, good humour and smiles."

In a note to one of Mr. Gore's letters the Harrow boys say:

"We have been out to day shooting Moor Hens; we killed three and by the first of September, if we had dogs, we should be able to shoot even partridges."

Having procured a dog, Mr. Gore writes that on their first going out for game, September 2d:

"John shot a partridge & a pigeon & Charles a partridge & pigeon; there seems some question whether the latter's partridge had not been dropped before, but on the whole, after fair discussion & mature deliberation it is concluded that Charles is justly entitled to the merit of having killed a partridge & pigeon."

The following quotations will show the way in which Mr. Gore continued to write about the children and to comfort their parents:

"The children are all well. Mrs. Gore who came to town last night (Oct. 15th) saw Edward, en passant, and takes him to Randalls (their country place) to-day. Frederick's teeth in front, that is to say two, are very distinct & apparent. His health is firm & he will soon walk. He is quite an aspiring youth, for he is ever on tiptoe to attain a commanding view—to humble himself to the level of his feet is all that is necessary for him to move like other boys.   If you do not return soon it is not absolutely certain that we shall not have him in jacket and breeches.   John & Charles say they study hard and expect to be in the Shell at Christmas when they shall have a fag.   I doubt whether enough has been said to convince you how very properly the boys conducted during the vacation.   They are entitled to every mark of remembrance which their mother promised & she will not, I am sure, forget to bring all and more than they expected, as tokens of her regard and satisfaction in their good behaviour."

The object in giving these extracts is to show that the home life of Mr. and Mrs. King was one which manifested an affectionate and cheerful intercourse, that showed itself in the manner in which their children were taught obedience to them, confidence in their parents, and respect to those about them.   It could, therefore, and must have been a source of satisfaction to know that their absence produced no change, and that the same docile and winning manners won the warm commendation of their friends as they had among their teachers.

It has been said that there are no letters of Mr. King's during his tour on the Continent giving an account of his journey.   There are, however, two which, though a little out of date here, and written while in Paris, relate to public matters, and are here given.

R. KING TO MR. CAZENOVE, PARIS.

PARIS, Oct. 23, 1802.

SIR :

It was my purpose to have gone last evening with Mrs. King to pay our Compliments to Mr. and Mrs. Talleyrand, and at the same time to have said a word or two to you concerning the affair you communicated to me on the part of Mr. T.   Unfortunately we were detained till too late an hour by some friends who called upon us in the early part of the evening.

I have just been at Mr. Talleyrand's office, but he has not arrived in town, and I must therefore send you this note to say in regard to the communication you made to me on Thursday, that as I do not perceive that my interference would be likely to prove beneficial, I must ask the favor of you to regard what has passed between us as though it had never happened.

With unvaried Sentiments of Esteem &c. yours

R. K.

At the head of this letter Mr. King writes as follows, to explain the matter to which the letter refers:

" Mr. Livingston being twice postponed, and others who came later to the audience chamber of Talleyrand received before him, wrote a note complaining of this indignity and notifying his determination to confine himself to written communications with the Department of for. affairs. Talleyrand draughted an answer in wh. he complains of the captious compt. of Livingston, wh. he ascribes to his want of Experience and having begun late in life the diplomic. career, and expresses a hope that the Pr., whose knowledge of diplomacy he foresees, wd. see no reason to justify his minr. This letter Talleyrand gave to Cazenove to show to me, with a request that I wd. interfere to persuade Livingston to recall his complt. &c. I communicated this overture to Mr. L., and it was our joint opinion that I should decline any interference."

R. KING TO G. W. ERVING, ESQ., CONSUL OF THE UNITED STATES AT LONDON.

PARIS, Oct. 17, 1802.

SIR :

I have just received your Letter of the 19th instant and lose no time in sending you my reply, to say that you appeared to have misconceived the nature and object of your Correspondence with the Alien office, which neither required, nor gave to you any, much less the exclusive, faculty of granting Passports to American Citizens upon their entry, and residence within, or their departure from the limits of your Consulship. Indeed the late modification of the Alien Law, the purport whereof was communicated to the several American Consuls, especially changed the measures of Police respecting Aliens which had before existed, and in a great measure, if not altogether, dispensed with your farther interference. It will doubtless be sufficient to prevent the steps you have supposed yourself authorized to adopt in respect to the Passports which may have been granted by Mr. Gore, that you should know that Mr. Gore is charged with the affairs of the United States in England during my absence, and that he finds of course among the ordinary authorities of this character that of granting Passports to American Citizens.

I am, Sir, with due respect &c.

R. K.

The admirable letters of Mr. Gore to Mr. King and his communications with Lord Hawkesbury and Mr. Madison might well find a place here, but as they are long, and generally relate to matters which, though then brought into notice, were not settled at that time, they must be passed over. There was, however, one subject of deep interest with reference to which, during Mr. King's absence, he had to take an active part. Mr. Jefferson, in a letter to Dr. Rush, September 23, 1800,* had written, "you will hear of an attempt at insurrection in this State (Virginia). I am looking with anxiety to see what will be its effect in our State. We are truly to be pitied." The insurrection was put down, and the leaders were captured and imprisoned. A question arose as to what should be done to them, and the Legislature had brought before them some resolutions relative to the matter, but postponed them until a future time. They were, however, referred to Gov. Monroe, who, on June 15, 1801, communicated them to the President, Mr. Jefferson, and again, on November 17, called his attention to them. In the answer to this letter, Mr. Jefferson, November 24, 1801, wrote: †

"That the publication of these resolutions might have an ill effect in more than one quarter. In confidence of attention to this I shall indulge greater freedom in writing. Common male-

---

* *Jefferson's Works*, vol. iv., p. 336.
† *Ibid.*, vol. iv., p. 419.

factors, I presume, make no part of the object of that resolution. Neither their numbers, nor the nature of their offences, seem to require any provisions beyond those practised heretofore, and found adequate to the suppression of ordinary crime. Conspiracy, insurgency, treason, rebellion, (among the description of persons who brought on thus the alarm, and on themselves the tragedy of 1800) were doubtless in the view of everyone; but many perhaps contemplated, and one expression of the resolution might comprehend, a much larger scope. Respect to both opinions makes it my duty to understand the resolution in all the extent of which it is possible."

Without following him in the details of the letter, it may be stated that he suggests that in some way these persons might be placed in colonies in lands at home, or even abroad, and discusses various plans by which they might be removed, with the objections that might be urged against them. Among places proposed, he writes: *

"On our western and southern frontiers Spain holds an immense country, the occupancy of which, however, is in the Indian natives, except, a few insulated spots, possessed by Spanish subjects. It is very questionable, indeed, whether the Indians would sell? Whether Spain would be willing to receive these people? and nearly certain that she would not alienate the sovereignty, &c." †

He speaks also of the West Indies, and finally says that "Africa would offer a last and undoubted resort, if all others more desirable should fail us."

With this statement of the serious question which was troubling the people of Virginia, and incidentally the other States where slaves abounded, we are prepared for the following letter, which the President wrote to Mr. King on

---

* *Jefferson's Works*, vol. iv., p. 420.

† Mr. Jefferson, at this time, evidently ignored or thought little of the information of the reported cession of Louisiana and, as it was supposed, of the Floridas to France, sent to him by Mr. King on June 1 and August 24 of 1801. —*Editor*.

July 13, 1802, asking his co-operation in obtaining from the Sierra Leone Company permission to transport " the slaves guilty of insurgency " to their colony, and giving his views upon this interesting matter; at the same time, affording him an opportunity " to assure you (Mr. King) of his perfect satisfaction with the manner in which you have conducted the several matters confided to you by us." *

T. Jefferson to R. King.

WASHINGTON, July 13, 1802.

DEAR SIR :

The course of things in the neighboring islands of the West Indies appear to have given a considerable impulse to the minds of slaves in different parts of the United States. A great disposition to insurgency has manifested itself among them, which, in one instance, in the State of Virginia, broke out into actual insurrection. This was easily suppressed ; but many of those concerned (between twenty and thirty, I believe) fell victims to the law. So extensive an execution could not but excite sensibility in the public mind and begat a regret that the laws had not provided, for such cases, some alternative combining more mildness with equal efficacy. The Legislature of the State at a subsequent meeting took the subject into consideration, and have communicated to me through the Governor of the State, their wish that some place could be provided, out of the limits of the United States, to which slaves guilty of insurgency might be transported ; and they have particularly looked to Africa as offering the most desirable receptacle. We might, for instance, enter into negotiations with the natives, on some part of the coast, to obtain a settlement ; and, by establishing an African Company, combine with it commercial operations, which might not only reimburse expenses, but procure profit also. But there being already such an establishment on that coast by the English Sierra Leone company, made for the express purpose of colonizing civilized blacks to that country, it would seem better, by incorporating our emigrants with theirs, to make one strong, rather than two weak colonies. This would be more desirable because

* *Jefferson's Works*, vol. iv., pp. 442-44.

the blacks settled at Sierra Leone having chiefly gone from the States, would often receive among those we should send, their acquaintances and relatives.

The object of this letter therefore is to ask the favor of you to enter into conference with such persons private and public as would be necessary to give us permission to send thither the persons under contemplation. It is material to observe that they are not felons, or common malefactors, but persons guilty of what the Safety of Society, under actual circumstances, obliges us to treat as a crime, but which their feelings may represent in a far different shape. They are such as will be a valuable acquisition to the settlement already existing there, and well calculated to co-operate in the plan of civilization.

As the expense of so distant a transportation would be very heavy, and might weigh unfavorably in deciding between the modes of punishment, it is very desirable that it should be lessened as much as practicable. If the regulations of the place would permit these emigrants to dispose of themselves, as the Germans and others do who come to this country poor, by giving their labor for a certain time to some one who will pay their passage ; and if the master of the vessel could be permitted to carry articles of commerce from this country and take back others from that, which might yield a mercantile profit sufficient to cover the expenses of the voyage, a serious difficulty would be removed. I will ask your attention therefore to arrangements necessary for this purpose.

The consequences of permitting emancipations to become extensive, unless the condition of emigration be annexed to them, furnish also matter of solicitation to the Legislature of Virginia, as you will perceive by their resolution enclosed to you. Although provision for the settlement of emancipated negroes might perhaps be obtainable nearer home than Africa, yet it is desirable that we should be free to expatriate this description of people to the Colony of Sierra Leone, if considerations respecting either themselves or us should render it more expedient. I will pray you therefore to get the same permission extended to the reception of these as well as the first mentioned. Nor will there be a selection of bad subjects ; the emancipations, for the most part, being either of the whole slaves of the master, or of such individuals as have particularly deserved well ; the latter is most frequent.

The request of the Legislature of Virginia having produced to me the occasion of addressing you, I avail myself of it to assure you of my perfect satisfaction with the manner in which you have conducted the several matters confided to you by us ; and to express my hope that through your agency we may be able to remove everything inauspicious to a cordial friendship between this country and the one in which you are stationed ; a friendship dictated by too many considerations not to be felt by the wise and the dispassionate of both nations. It is therefore with the sincerest pleasure I have observed on the part of the British government various manifestations of just and friendly disposition towards us. We wish to cultivate peace and friendship with all nations, believing that course most conducive to the welfare of our own. It is natural that these friendships should bear some proportion to the common interests of the parties. The interesting relations between Great Britain and the United States are certainly of the first order ; and as such are estimated and will be faithfully cultivated by us. These sentiments have been communicated to you from time to time in the official correspondence of the Secretary of State ; but I have thought it might not be unacceptable to be assured that they perfectly concur with my own personal convictions both in relation to yourself and the country in which you are. I pray you to accept assurances of my high consideration and respect.

This letter of the President was received by Mr. Gore, who upon ascertaining its contents, under his authority as Chargé d'Affaires during Mr. King's absence, immediately took steps to obtain the information asked for in it, and in a letter to the President explains the result of his investigations.

C. GORE TO HIS EXCELLENCY THOMAS JEFFERSON.

LONDON, 10 Oct. 1802.

SIR :

In consequence of being left by Mr. King in charge with the affairs of the United States, and of his desire that I should inspect all letters directed to him, I opened that from yourself under date of the 13 of July, and which was received on the 13th ultimo.

This, sir, I must pray you to accept as an apology for having broken its seal, and if my subsequent conduct shall appear an intrusion, you will do me the justice, to impute it to the most respectful motives, combined with an earnest desire to promote the object of the Letter, if in no other way, at least in obtaining and forwarding all such information as could be procured here, and might help to advance the wise and humane plan, you have so benevolently contemplated of opening a path for the emancipation of the Blacks, on such terms as may prove beneficial to themselves and not injurious to others. I was the more induced to act in this business from the belief that Mr. King would not be here to attain any information in season to reach the United States until late in the winter.

Lord Hawkesbury, to whom I thought proper first to mention the subject, professed a warm desire to do everything in his power to promote your views, but at the same time the affair must rest entirely with the Directors of the Sierra Leone Company and that he was really fearful their late experience had been such as to deter them from the admission of characters like those alluded to.

I then took an opportunity of conferring with Mr. Thornton, Chairman of the Court of Directors, and stated to him the Resolution of the Legislature of Virginia, and your idea of the best mode of carrying the same into effect with such arguments, so far as I could think of any, in addition to those contained in your letter, to show that the admission of the Blacks from the United States might under such regulations as wisdom and prudence should prescribe, prove an addition and strength and benefit to their colony. But the establishment has suffered much from the maroons, who have been permitted to go there from Jamaica, and the Directors consider that the rise of their colony has been rather impeded than advanced by the Blacks from Nova Scotia. They have been lately obliged to apply to Parliament for pecuniary aid, and to ask assistance of troops, to keep in check the restless and disturbed spirits already there. The military force is not so great as they wish for, and they entertain serious apprehensions if it be sufficient to protect the well disposed, and repress the constant disposition manifested in many of the Colonists to revolt and overturn the existing Government.

These reasons appear to have great weight in Mr. Thornton's mind against the policy of admitting such settlers, as would be most likely to come from the United States. He has however come to no determination against the measure, but promises to advise with his friends and see if any expedient can be devised by which the danger to be feared from acceding to the proposal may be guarded against.

It is possible that on Mr. King's return he may be able to suggest such reasons as shall induce the Directors to lend a favourable ear to the plan. He is intimate with some of the most influential of them, and if aught can be added to the strong motives they profess, and I have no doubt sincerely, to do every thing acceptable to the exalted character, at whose instance the proposition has been made, it may be expected from the personal influences of this gentleman. Although from the considerations mentioned, which with others are to be seen in the State of the Colony, as described in the memorial to Parliament, and the report of the Committee, I do not think there is much reason to hope, that an incorporation of the Blacks of the United States with those of Sierra Leone, can be reconciled in the minds of the Directors to the Safety and prosperity of the Establishment.

I am indebted to Mr. Thornton for the Papers referred to, and which you will find gave an accurate statement of that colony, the evils most to be guarded against, with the means thought necessary for its security, and the expenses of the Establishment. As these Papers are scarce and contain information which may be valuable on this subject, I have taken the liberty to enclose them with this letter.

Should an occasion occur which may promise advantage to the proposal from any endeavours of mine, you may rely on their being cheerfully and faithfully exerted to that end, and if farther information can be procured which in my judgment may be useful in this interesting business before the arrival of Mr. King, I pray you, sir, to be assured that I shall derive great pleasure in forwarding it.

I have the honour to be with perfect Respect,

C. GORE.

J. Q. ADAMS TO R. KING.

BOSTON, 8 October, 1802.

DEAR SIR :

We have enjoyed during the summer an extraordinary degree of tranquility, and since the session of Congress terminated in May, no public event of material importance has happened. The newspapers have been chiefly filled with personal attacks upon the President and Vice-President, coming from different and perhaps opposite quarters ; all arising originally from divisions in their own party. These divisions have occasioned animosities of no small inveteracy between individuals. You have doubtless been better informed of the transactions at New York than it would be in my power to inform you. The warfare there has been between the friends of Mr. Burr, and those of the Clinton family. In Virginia the principal batteries have been pointed at Mr. Jefferson, by a Scotsman, named Callender, of whom you have probably heard heretofore.* He writes under the influence of personal resentment and revenge, but the effect of his publications upon the reputation of the President has been considerable.

What the consequence of these internal feuds in the ruling party will be is not yet apparent. But independent of them and considered as a single party in opposition to the federalists, the strength of the present administration is continually increasing. It has obtained and preserves an irresistible preponderance in thirteen of the sixteen State legislatures, and the resistence in the three others scarcely maintains its ground. In both houses of Congress the majority is already decisive, but at the ensuing Congress, will be much larger. The division in the Senate is now nearly equal. But for the next two years, there will be nearly two thirds of the partizans of the present government. In the State of Pennsylvania their ascendancy is so great that the federalists have scarcely dared to name a candidate in opposition to Governor McKean's re-election ; federalism is indeed in that state so completely palsied, that scarcely a trace of it is to be discovered except in here and there a newspaper edited by New England men.

This party triumph is not enjoyed with moderation. The basis

* For an account of Callender and his work see Hildreth's *Hist. of the United States*, 2d ser., vol. ii., p. 453 *et seq.*

of it all is democratic popularity, and the leaders are all sensible how sandy a foundation it is. Strong as the fabric appears they are constantly trembling lest its corner stones should fail : and as their principal alarm is lest the old administration should recover favour in the eyes of the people, the great engine of party, with which they endeavour to fortify themselves, is slander upon their predecessors. This they continue under every shape and on all occasions. Nor are these exertions unsuccessful. They carried the system to such a pitch that even a Committee of the National house of Representatives, called a committee of Investigation, at the close of the session made a report, the manner and form of which were both highly exceptionable to every maxim of common justice and honour. This report was hurried through the house with as little regard to decorum as it was made. It has since been analysed and refuted by several publications in various parts of the Union, but most effectually by a pamphlet of Mr. Wolcott, which will doubtless be sent you by some of your friends ; and which will shew you a fair specimen both of our Administration and its Opposition.

The concern of the *Republicans*, as they stile themselves, is the result of consciousness, rather than of real dangers. The power of the Administration rests upon a support of a much stronger majority of the people throughout the Union than the former administrations ever possessed since the first establishment of the Constitution. Whatever the merits or the demerits of the former administrations may have been, there never was a system of measures more completely and irrevocably abandoned and rejected by the popular voice. It never can and never will be revived. The experiment, such as it was, has failed, and to attempt its restoration would be as absurd, as to undertake the resurrection of a carcass seven years in its grave. The alarm of the pilots at the helm is therefore without cause. What they take for breakers are mere clouds of unsubstantial vapour. The only risque to which they are exposed is the shallowness of their waters. Their system is so short sighted, and so contracted, that it will never stand a popular test even of twelve years, and the people whom almost unbounded prosperity could not attach to their predecessors, will not learn from adversity to be better pleased with them.

VOL IV—12

The yellow fever made its appearance at an earlier period than usual, in many of our cities. It has not hitherto spread so extensively, as upon former occasions ; but it has been as malignant in the cases which have happened as it was ever known. A Dysentery of extreme violence has likewise prevailed in the western part of this Commonwealth and the neighbouring part of Connecticut. The approach of the Winter season gives us hopes of relief from these scourges. But the summer has been so long protracted that at the moment I write this, Fahrenheit's thermometer stands at 82 and has been higher in the course of the day. The harvests throughout the Country have been plentiful.

Your very obedt. Servt.

JOHN QUINCY ADAMS.

CHAPTER XII.

In Dr. Lieber's *Letters* there is an anecdote about Mr. King, which indicates his prudence during his stay in Paris. His journey to the Continent, and Paris particularly, was not, as he tells us, to see men and manners but to enjoy the invaluable specimens of the fine arts collected in that city. It is evident, however, that the high position he held as the representative of his country in England, opened to him an entrance to the society of the most distingushed men in France, of which his correspondence gives us no hint, farther than that he and his wife were guests at Talleyrand's house and that he met Lafayette while in Paris. There is nothing to show the conferences which he must have had with Mr. Livingston, especially relative to the cession of Louisiana— which was a matter of deep interest and anxious consideration, and which must have been discussed between them. He did not seek to come in contact with the First Consul, and indeed, as the anecdote here given shows, declined to be presented to him.

Dr. Lieber says:*

"I give you an anecdote which will be interesting to the Chairman of Foreign Affairs. President King tells me that when his father Rufus King was American Minister in London, he paid a visit to Paris after the peace of Amiens, where Fox likewise went. Fox went to see Consul Bonaparte. The latter desired that King would have himself presented, or the Chief Officers of the Consul told King that they would gladly present him. King, who was then engaged in making a treaty with England, declined because he knew that Bonaparte was very disagreeable to George III. and he thought he had no right to do anything that could interfere with his relation to the British court or ministry. When he returned to England and went to court, George III. went up to him and said, 'Mr. King I am very much obliged to you; you have treated me like a gentleman, which is more than I can say of all my subjects.'

"I give the words exactly as President King gave them to me, and he says he gave the words to me exactly as he could remember them, the anecdote being in lively remembrance in the family. He thinks he can now repeat the very words in which his father told the affair immediately after his return from court and that they are the *ipsissima Verba* of George III."

It will not be out of place to reproduce here another anecdote of George III. which was often spoken of in Mr. King's family. It was more particularly mentioned by his son, Gov. John A. King when on a very cold day on November 25th he had come from Albany to New York to review the troops there. He had been out all the morning in his uniform without an overcoat, and when one of his aides expressed his astonishment at this, he said to him, "I remembered King George's advice to my father and have put on an extra shirt," as he was accustomed to do when he went out on horseback on cold days.

---

* Extract from a letter from Dr. Lieber to Charles Sumner upon a diplomatic question in 1863,—Dr. Lieber's *Letters.*

G. Cabot to R. King.

Nov. 6, 1802.

My dear Sir :

The failure of the Federalists in the Election of J. Q. Adams may be attributed to negligence or rather weariness. They were sufficiently numerous in the District to have given 500 majority : but the failure of Mr. Pickering proves the decline of good influence in that district. On the whole I think it certain that Democracy gains strength in number & loses or rather has lost much among the sensible.

. . . Some of our Jacobin writers have abused you & charged you with avowing monarchical sentiments in letters to me : they are systematic in all these labors to render odious every man who they foresee may rise to important stations & *is not of their sect.* . . .

I am glad you concluded to pass over to France & see for yourself what remains to be seen. I want you to see the disgust which must prevail there at everything Democratic after having made the world mad with the love of it. I want to see if weary of Bonaparte's power they are ripe for new changes : tell me what you see & think on these subjects when you return to England.

Ever faithfully yours,

G. C.

Wm. V. Murray to R. King.

Baltimore, 12 Nov., 1802.

Dear Sir :

We know of your intention of returning—of the policy of that I say nothing. Your last negociation on the debts gave a satisfaction which had nothing surprising in it but that it should please both parties. The leading Demos. even spoke, I learn, in high terms of it. For some time the Feds. have talked of running you & Genl. Pinckney as P. & V. P. fairly & side by side. It is believed that this has alarmed the Demos. : for lately at Annapolis, where our Legislature is now in Session, some of the subalterns, echoes of the chiefs, have undertaken to blame you on account of the Bank Stock which they say you neglect. We know better. Their object is to prejudice you I presume in this state, where I may be allow'd to assure you that you are in great esteem. As this letter may reach you before your taking of Leave I thought it right to tell you this, that no formality of proof on your part which wd. enable the Feds. to give an answer to such a report, shd. it be stirred next election, might be omitted and out of reach.

Our papers will show you to what an excess abuse runs—The Louisiana affair staggers many of the more thinking Demos. & materials seem to accumulate in favour of the Fed. Side.

Smith lately informed me that you were on your way to Paris —I rejoice that before you return you will have seen that singular people at home—I am too unwell & weak to write to G. by this ship which sails I learn early in the morning.

Tom Paine arrived here 12 days since—few of the respectable Demos. visited him—He was arrested for 50 Louis lent him by a very respectable Irish gentleman (O'Mealy) of this place while Tom was confined by Robespierre—He went on a week since to the Fed. city where the boarders of the Tavern where he alighted refused to remain in the house if Tom were admitted to the public table. The Tavern where I am, Evans, the best in Town I hear, refused to admit him because the frequenters of it manifested the same spirit—He will do no harm—& perhaps some *good.*

He was I learn civilly received by the P. whom I suspect he will much embarass.*

Yours respectfully,
Wm. V. Murray.

Wm. Hindman to R. King.

Baltimore, Nov. 21, 1802.

My Dear Sir:

Inclosed is the Speech of our Governor to the Legislature in which You will discover Yourself implicated—From the Information I have collected, it appears to Me that the present ruling

---

* One of the first acts of the President is the permission given to Paine in a letter to him, March 18, 1801. He writes: " You expressed a wish to get a passage to this country in a public vessel. Mr. Dawson is charged with orders to the captain of the *Maryland* (which had carried Mr. Dawson to Havre with the newly signed Convention with France) to receive and accommodate you with a passage back."—Jefferson's *Works*, vol. iv., p. 371.

Party in the United States, dreading your Return before the ensuing presidential Election (altho some Time ago lavish in your Praises, & highly approbating your ministerial Conduct) are determined as far as in their Power to destroy You in the good Opinion of your Countrymen, and particularly in the State of Maryland, (which may hold the Balance at the next Election for President,) where You heretofore stood very high, & in which I hope there will be no Change ; for the Purpose of accomplishing their diabolical Purpose, They are now industriously circulating a Report, " That You have not exerted Yourself to procure the Bank Stock for the State of Maryland, that You have neglected its Interest, & if You had used Your Endeavors the Stock would have been secured long ago."—This I am persuaded is not true— It would be extremely desirable to your Friends, who are anxious that you should be the next President, & at the same Time greatly promote the Federal Interest, if this Party could be put down by a Communication to the Secretary of State proving this Report to be altogether without Foundation either by obtaining the Stock or making it appear that every Exertion had been made by You for that Purpose.

I hope You will excuse the Liberty I have taken in this Business, I have been actuated by a Love to my Country & Yourself.

I wish You and your Family a happy Return to your native Country.

Yr. very Hble. Servt.
WM. HINDMAN.

R. KING TO HIS EXCELLENCY MR. LIVINGSTON.

LONDON, Nov. 24, 1802.

DEAR SIR :

I cannot write to you with confidence respecting the critical state of public affairs ; in a few days I may be able to do so. The speech and addresses of the two Houses pledge the country to nothing precise, tho' they are sufficient evidence of the insecurity of Peace ; if to these be added the orders which have been sent in every direction to retain such of the Conquests made during the late war, as have not been surrendered, and the military and naval preparations making throughout the country, the probabilities seem to be greater in favour of War than Peace.

In relation to our affairs, so far as we may suppose the war would affect them, the chance in favour of its happening is such as should lead us to suspend all measures, the conclusion of which might be advisable upon the supposition of the continuance of Peace.   I shall repeat the observation with which I began, that I have not yet had sufficient opportunities to form as correct an opinion upon this most interesting and important subject as I hope to be able to do very shortly.   Knowing your solicitude, I have, however, thought it prudent to send you these observations together with the renewal of the assurances of

Esteem and Respect with which, &c.

RUFUS KING.

R. KING TO SECRETARY OF STATE.

No. 76.

LONDON, Nov. 26, 1802.

SIR :

Mr. Gore has acknowledged the receipt of such letters from the Department of State as have been received during my absence, and his correspondence will have given you exact information of all that has hitherto been done towards the accomplishment of the several objects of the President's instructions. I shall immediately resume the business that has been so well commenced, and as well from the nature of the subject as from the temper and disposition that are understood to prevail in respect to America, I am inclined to hope that we shall experience no material difficulty in effecting a final and satisfactory adjustment of our Boundaries.

At the date of Mr. Gore's last letter there seems to have been much solicitude on the subject of Peace ; the sympathy of the nation was at that time strongly excited by the conduct of France toward Switzerland, and a verbal insinuation was made by the English Minister at Paris, that the King would not see with indifference the interference of France in the internal affairs of that country.   This step was accompanied by orders to stop the farther reduction of the land and naval forces, and, as is believed, to retain provisionally instead of giving up, according to the Treaty of Amiens, the conquests which England had made during the war. These measures, which little pains were taken to conceal or explain, were supposed both at Paris and London to have been adopted in consequence of a concert formed with the two Imperial Courts, and therefore occasioned serious apprehensions lest Europe should again and immediately be involved in a new and disastrous war.

Things remained in this situation till the meeting of Parliament, and the King's Speech, which it was expected would remove or confirm these apprehensions, was waited for with much impatience. On the one hand it offers no assurance of the continuance of Peace, while on the other it is too vague to authorize a conclusion that England desires or may expect an early renewal of the war. Neither the speech nor the addresses give any satisfactory explanation of the measures which had been adopted ; but the Debates of Parliament, which I attended, though cautiously managed by the Ministers, cast some light on the subject ; and from them combined with other circumstances, it appears that no concert has been established either with Austria or Russia ; that although the State of the Swiss is matter of deep regret, it will not influence England, unsupported as she is by a single ally, to engage in a war that could not rescue the Swiss from the power of France ; and that moreover no such material change has, in the opinion of the Cabinet, taken place in the relative condition and strength of the Powers of the Continent since the Treaty of Amiens as would justify England in renewing the war.

Upon the supposition that such are the opinions of the Cabinet, it is to the Treaty of Amiens, and not to certain political events that have since occurred, that we must seek for an explanation of the conduct of England in the increase of her Forces and in the orders which she is said to have dispatched to retain such of her Conquests as have not been surrendered.

There are several points connected with the Treaty of Amiens, some or all of which may have had an influence in producing the measures alluded to ; these are the Government of Malta, the commercial intercourse which it was expected the peace would restore between Great Britain and France, and the indemnity promised to the Prince of Orange.

As the difficulties which have arisen independent both of France and England in carrying into effect the Article respecting Malta, are such as to render farther time or stipulations necessary to secure the purpose aimed at by the parties, it is natural that things should remain as they are until these difficulties can be adjusted ; there is therefore nothing extraordinary in England continuing to occupy Malta ; still, however, France may press for a literal performance of the engagement of England, and this joined to other motives may induce England to increase rather than diminish her Forces.

Though the Definitive Treaty did no more than restore peace, it was generally expected, as incident to a state of peace, that a commercial intercourse would be opened between the two countries subject to duties as well as partial exclusions. So far as regards the Trade from France to Great Britain, peace has replaced the same upon the footing it stood before the last commercial Treaty, while in France the Laws passed during the War, prohibiting the importation of every sort of Goods of the Growth or Fabric of the British dominions, and making them liable to confiscation if found within the French Territories, are not only maintained, but enforced with so much Rigour that a number of British Vessels, driven into the Ports of France in distress and to escape the perils of the Ocean (such is the English account) have been confiscated together with their Cargoes ; and the only answer given to the complaints of the English Minister at Paris has been that in these, as in other cases of Judicial cognizance, the Laws must have their course. This evidence of the views of France, whose interference has produced a similar, tho' not equally extensive, prohibition of English Manufactures in Spain, has excited much discontent ; and in a Nation so highly commercial as England, cannot fail of having an effect upon its public councils : yet neither these tokens of inhospitality, nor the business of Malta would justify the provisional Detention of the Conquests which England had agreed to surrender.

The preliminaries were severely censured by the Grenville opposition, as in no respect more deficient than in the entire omission of a Proviso for the Prince of Orange. The Definitive Treaty contains an express stipulation in his favour ; and the honour of England is perhaps bound to enforce its due observance.

It will be remembered that France entered into an engagement, (as it is believed for a sum of money received from Holland) on the very day of the conclusion of the Definitive Treaty to release the Dutch from contributing towards the indemnities of the Prince of Orange. England, without doubt, remonstrated against the bad faith of this Transaction and probably was assured that ample Indemnities would be found in Germany ; instead whereof the Compensation that has been offered by the Diet, under the recommendation of the initiating Powers, falls far beneath the just claims of the Prince of Orange, and, in the opinion of most persons, does not exceed a tenth even of their amount. It is therefore natural enough to conjecture that seeing the inexecution of the Treaty in a point of much importance to an ancient and fallen Friend, as well as material to her own honour, England may have given notice of her having resolved to suspend the farther execution of the Treaty on her part, until she sees a just and faithful performance of it on the part of France and her allies ; a Supposition the more probable by the orders being made to exclude the Dutch colonies, which alone were likely to be affected—Martinique and St. Lucie being already surrendered.

You will perceive that this Speculation goes upon the idea that orders have really been given to arrest the farther execution on the side of England—a fact tho' generally believed, not yet acknowledged. If the manifest ill-humour that exists, arises alone or principally from this cause, well grounded hopes ought to be entertained that Justice will be rendered to the Prince of Orange, and the Treaty of Peace suffered to go into complete operation.

With perfect Respect and Esteem &c.

RUFUS KING.

R. KING TO HIS EXCELLENCY MR. LIVINGSTON.

LONDON, Nov. 29, 1802.

DEAR SIR :

I have duly received your Letter of the 17th ; a Note I wrote to you from Calais will have acknowledged the receipt of your Letter dated the day after we left Paris.

My sentiments in regard to the continuance of Peace are somewhat changed since my Letter of the 24th, which went by a

Messenger ; and notwithstanding I still find it difficult to reconcile the Discourses of Ministers with the Fact mentioned in that
Letter I am more inclined than I was to believe that the views
here are pacific. . . .

I have seen and conversed with the Bearer of your Letter of
the 17th ; the situation of St. Domingo may give us farther time ;
nothing else seems likely to delay the measure we have so much
at heart to promote.

Faithfully & with great Esteem &c.,

RUFUS KING.

R. KING TO MR. WILLIAM EATON, TUNIS.

LONDON, November 29, 1802.

SIR :

My absence from England for the last three months has delayed
my answer of your letter of July 6, respecting Mr. Hargraves'
claim of a commission upon the cost of the articles prepared in
this country, and sent as a Present to the Bey of Tunis. So far
as relates to the personal care and assistance of Mr. Hargraves in
the transportation of the Jewellery from Algiers to Tunis, he has
undoubtedly a claim to be compensated ; for the transportation
of the cloths and arms, the residue, and by far the greatest portion
of the present he can have no such claim. In regard to the order-
ing the articles here, and the superintending their execution, I am
not a little surprized at Mr. Hargraves' pretension, which most
certainly he never could have thought of making to me, who had
put the whole business in Train, under the most exact Instructions, before his arrival in England. It is true, on the refusal of
the Bey to accept the cloths first sent by Mawhood & Co., and
our determination to send cloths of the first instead of inferior
quality (which was likewise resolved upon before Mr. Hargraves'
arrival) I desired Mr. Hargraves to call at the Store of Mawhood
& Co, and give his advice in the choice of the cloths ; as these
were to be superfine, this advice could be of no service, except in
the selection of colours, a matter of some though not of great
importance. He did, I believe, occasionally visit Mortimer and
Rundell and Bridge, who prepared the arms and Jewels, but I

think you may with safety refer to Mr. Hargraves for the fact, that his advice and instructions were in no sense of any importance. Mr. Hargraves certainly manifested a disposition to be useful to us in any way that his knowledge and aid should be wanted ; but I really never had a notion that he thought himself entrusted by you or me with the superintendence or charge of this business ; and my finally entrusting him with the Jewels, was on his repeated solicitations and an alteration of my first intentions.

On the whole if Mr. Hargraves receives one hundred Guineas, I should think him liberally paid ; had he intimated to me his expectation of being paid for his advice and assistance, I should have entirely excluded him from any concern in the Business ; the Jewels might have been sent by a different route, and with very little, if any, addition to the premium of Insurance.

With much Respect &c.

RUFUS KING.

W. WILBERFORCE TO R. KING.

BROMFD., Tuesday, Dec. 6, 1802.

MY DEAR SIR :

I believe you are an early man (which my Health does not suffer me to be) & perhaps you would breakfast with me some morning on your way to town.   I never breakfast before ¼ after 10, and seldom go from home before 12.   So that if you should do me the favor of calling on Wednesday morning, you would find me here. . . .   I but too much concur with you concerning ye probability of the renewal of ye war, & for that very reason am anxious that preparations should be made for it.   It is *here* (to speak openly) that I distrust our Minrs.   I fear they are not acting up to the gt. exigencies of our situatn.   It may be strong language ; but if they were I should have no great fears as to the Issue—as it is, my Expectations are very gloomy.

Believe me always, my dear Sir, with cordial esteem & regard,

Yours very sincerely,

W. WILBERFORCE.

RIGHT HONOURABLE H. ADDINGTON.

Private.

RANDALLS NEAR LEATHERHEAD, SURRY, Dec. 7, 1802.

DEAR SIR :

Upon the Experience I have had of the Efficacy of your interference of bringing to a decision Questions which had been long depending, I may I hope be allowed to ask your assistance to hasten the conclusion of an unsettled affair, that justice, and, if I may be permitted to say so, good policy require should be finished without farther delay.

I refer to our claim of the Maryland Bank Stock, a subject with which you are not wholly unacquainted, and which has been depending, sometimes as a judicial and at others as a diplomatic question ever since the year 1783. The title to the stock may be stated in a few words : it was purchased by the Colony of Maryland with money levied by a tax upon its inhabitants, and placed in the names of agents in London, who before the American war received and applied the Dividends according to the instructions of the Colony : the war interrupted the correspondence between Maryland and its Agents ; in the Treaty of Peace, by which the Independence of Maryland and the other colonies, the King " relinquished all claims to the Government, *Property* and territorial Rights of the same (i.e. the Colonies) and every part thereof." Before the Treaty the stock was the Property of Maryland, and by the Treaty, which consents to the dissolution of the Colony Corporation, or in other words to the Independence of Maryland, the King in express words relinquished all claims to whatever was the Property of Maryland, and consequently to the stock in question. How it has ever been supposed that this stock accrued to the King upon the Dissolution of the Corporation of Maryland, when he not only consented to this Dissolution, but in the act of consent transferred to Maryland any claim he had to the stock, is to me utterly incomprehensible.

I have thought, sir, that you would excuse me for troubling you in this business, especially when I assure you that it has been the occasion of Dissatisfaction in an important part of my country, as well as the subject of such reiterated application on my part, as I never could have reconciled with my respect for others or myself,

to have made, but from a strong conviction of its peculiar importance. I expect soon to return to America, and it is no
affectation on my part, when I tell you that I shall feel some
embarrassment with the sentiments and opinions which I have
sent before me, if this stock should not be transferred before
my Departure.

With sincere Respect and Esteem &c.

RUFUS KING.

R. KING TO SECRETARY OF STATE.

No. 77.

LONDON, Dec. 18, 1802.

From whatever cause the Language and measures of the English Ministers in the month of October proceed, it is now evident
that they produced no beneficial effect upon the Government of
France, and that the Temper then manifested, had it been persisted in, would have involved the Nation in a new War. But
the tone was soon lowered ; the orders supposed to have been
given to retain certain possessions that were to be surrendered
have been recalled, and with the exception of Malta, concerning
which farther negotiations are said to be requisite to give effect
to former Stipulations, every thing will be delivered up according
to the Provisions of the Treaty of Peace. The Discourses of the
Ministers, together with all that has transpired in the Debates in
Parliament manifest the pacific wishes of the Nation, and France,
in regard to this country, continues to be as exclusively the Arbiter
of Peace, as she was of the continuance of War. The augmentation of the land and naval forces of Great Britain will not regain
her influence upon the Continent, and the measure has probably
been adopted to secure the Dominion of Ireland, which recent
information proves to be as extensively disaffected as at any
period of the war, rather than to promote the object referred to in
my last Dispatch.

With perfect Respect & Esteem &c.

RUFUS KING.

CHAPTER XIII.

R. Troup to R. King.

New York, 12 Dec. 1802.

Dear Sir :

. . . The papers contain proofs thus far exhibited of Burr's manœuvres for the Presidency. A new pamphlet containing farther proofs against him is on the tapis and will be out as soon as Burr turns his back on this city on his way to Washington. . . . The democratical party is gaining strength through the Union generally. The late election for members of Congress in Massachusetts shows an evident growth of democracy. . . . In Pennsylvania federalism seems to be annihilated. In Jersey the parties in the Legislature are upon a tie. . . . In this State, it appears to me, that democracy since the last election has not decreased. The quarrel between Clinton and Burr will not materially divide the party. Burr is a gone man ; he is expelled from the Jeffersonian party, and I believe he never will possess any material weight in the political scale. Jefferson is really in the dust in point of character, but notwithstanding this, he is looked up to and venerated as the Gog and Magog of his party. Things are according to the natural destiny of the government and I see no reason to suppose they will alter. . . .

The project on foot here seems to be to run you at the next election for Vice-President or President—which of the two is not determined. You will therefore have to prepare yourself for further political contests. . . .

I delivered your message to Benson, but he declines visiting Paris till Bonaparte is made either King or Emperor. He does not like the democratical title of First Consul.

God bless you.

R. King to Dan'l Parker, Paris.

London, Dec. 13, 1802.

Dear Sir :

As you will naturally suppose that I am solicitous concerning the education of my children, you will, I am persuaded, excuse the trouble I am about to give in requesting that you will have the goodness to pursue the enquiries we proposed to make respecting the plan of education lately submitted to the public by M. Thurot and associates. . . . My object is to endeavour to unite as far as practicable the peculiar advantages of English and French education, each good as well as deficient, but united probably nearer than anything else is a perfect system ; and the enquiries I am now making are for the purpose of enabling me to decide whether such an establishment exists at Paris as would be likely to fulfill my expectations in regard to French instruction, and as would moreover consent to receive my two elder sons upon the terms on which alone I should be willing to send them there.

In a few months they will respectively have completed their 15th and 14th years. Their standing at Harrow, a public school near London, corresponds with their ages, and in about two and a half or three years, they will probably be at or near the end of the school, or in other words will have laid the foundation of a classical education. My belief is that they would be able to attain this station by being at Harrow only one half of each of these years ; that is to say, during the two terms which include the six months commencing the middle of January ; the remaining six months from the middle of July to the middle of January, of which fourteen weeks are included in two vacations at midsummer and Christmas, I could send them to Paris. Although they have some knowledge of French and can read it without much difficulty, they would require the first half year to become sufficiently familiar with the language to proceed with ease and advantage in some branches of instruction ; in the meantime, however, they would be taught music, drawing, and, what is more important, mathematics ; they could likewise continue their Greek and Latin exercises and might begin with Spanish, which I wish them to know early and thoroughly.

Not only the instruction but the discipline is an object of much importance, both as regards the cultivation of morals and the protection of the pupils from the vices and habits to which their age exposes them. With this explanation of my views, will you confer with Mr. Barlow and ask him to unite with you in making such enquiries of M. Thurot or any better establishment, as will enable you to give me your opinion and advice. I would send my sons in July next.

With sincere regards, &c., I am yours,

RUFUS KING.

———

R. KING TO SECRETARY OF STATE.

No. 78.

LONDON, Dec. 19, 1802.

SIR :

In the Bill that after the holidays will be brought into Parliament for the consideration of the Customs, the Duties upon articles imported from the United States will stand nearly as they do at present, except that it has been proposed to raise the Duty upon Oil coming from any foreign Country from £28.3.1 to £31.10. I have had one or two Conferences upon the subject with the Department of the Treasury, and am now preparing a Representation upon which their Lordships will decide before the Draught of the Bill is completed. The British St. Malo fishery produces more oil than is consumed in the country, and the proposed augmentation of duty is vindicated by alleging that Spermaceti oil having of late years considerably receded in price, it has become requisite to raise the Duty upon it in order that it may be, according to its first intention, prohibitory.

Until recently there has been no discrimination of Duties upon foreign fish oils ; notwithstanding the Spermaceti Oil is so much better and dearer than the brown oil, the duty has operated to exclude the latter, while the former, by reason of its superior quality and price has found here a precarious market. Foreign Oils are not only meant to be excluded from the British Market, but the Bounties given to the British whale Fisheries must likewise secure them a preference in the foreign Markets. The conferences with the Treasury have therefore embraced these several Regulations ; and tho' I have not much expectation of any such reduction of the Duties as will allow our Oils, except in extraordinary circumstances, to be consumed in Great Britain, I have the satisfaction to inform you that foreign Oils of every sort will hereafter be allowed to be deposited here under similar Regulations to those which regard our Rice and Tobacco. This system will likewise be made to comprehend our Flour, wheat and other species of corn, as well as some other articles, such as Furs, Lumber &c. of inferior importance. The deposit of the chief articles of our Exports upon safe and convenient Terms in the Ports of this country, a system altogether different from that of Importation and Exportation under Duties and Drawbacks, will afford a considerable advantage to our Merchants, who may, thro' their correspondents here, distribute as before their Cargoes throughout the different markets of the continent ; and if the state of the English market admit it, they may on payment of the Duties, likewise dispose of them for the consumption of this country.

The new regulation of the Corn Trade, which is connected with this system, will likewise merit our attention. When wheat is under 5 % the quarter, the duty on Importation will be 24/3. When 5 % and under 54, the duty will be 2/6 ; and when 54 and upwards, the duty will be /6d. If the Foreigner does not choose to import and pay the duty, he may deposit his wheat in the public Warehouses for exportation or home consumption ; in the latter case it will be liable to pay the second rate of duties, altho' the price may be 54/, or above, unless the King, by Proclamation permits the same to be taken out of the Warehouses and sold on payment of the lowest Duty.

As yet the notice specifying the countervailing Duties upon goods imported in American vessels, has not been formed, and is, I understand, delayed to learn whether it is likely that our discriminating Duties will be repealed. There has been no intimation of an intention to extend the countervailing Duties to the System of Deposits. I have not yet examined, tho' you may think it worthy of consideration, how far the extension of this plan of depositing instead of importing our Productions may have an influence upon the question of the Expediency of the repeal of the discriminating Duties on our side and the countervailing Duties on the side of this country.

With great Respect & Esteem &c.

Rufus King.

R. King to Geo. W. Erving, Esq.

Randall's, Surry, Dec. 20, 1802.

Sir :

As I shall stay in town on Tuesday night, I request that you will call upon me between 9 and 10 o'clock on Wednesday morning, in order that I may understand with precision what proportion of the money received by Mr. Williams in the Mart'que Cases you think yourself authorized according to former usage to claim for the United States. My Letter to you on this subject was founded upon the representation you had made to me that the deductions, according to former usage, ought to exceed 1 per centum ; but as Mr. Williams states explicitly that it was not the usage to deduct more than one per centum in addition to the taxed costs and average sum allowed by the Board of Commissioners, I desire you will furnish me with Evidence that a larger proportion was retained by your Predecessor.

I am, sir, your ob. St.

R. K.

R. King to His Excellency, the President of the U. S.

London, Dec. 20, 1802.
Sir :

Mr. Gore having during my absence acknowledged the receipt of your letter to me, and at the same time transmitted to you copies of his Correspondence with the President of the Sierra Leone Company, I have only to resume the subject where he left it.

The idle and disorderly character of the slaves, who deserted their Masters and joined the British army in America, and who constitute the greater part of the Inhabitants of Sierra Leone, has produced an unfavorable opinion of our slaves in general, which it is not easy to correct, and which unfortunately operates against the adoption of the Plan we have offered to the African Company.

Hitherto the colony has done but little towards defraying the Expenses of its Protection, which are so considerable that the Company feels the burthen and is unwilling to consent to any measure that may chance to increase it.   I have taken some pains, but hitherto without success, to do away what has appeared to me an unfounded apprehension on this subject and to engage the company to adopt our Proposition.   I have not yet pressed for a decision, having reason to believe that it might be in the negative. At present I am recommending a modification of the plan to be tried in the first instance as an experiment and upon a small scale, and ultimately adopted upon a larger one, if found to be free from the inconveniences that are apprehended.   Though I cannot encourage the expectation that the Company will agree to the Proposal upon any terms, I am not without hope that it may consent to receive a limited number of our negroes by way of experiment.

There is no prospect whatever of our being able to combine the Transportation of these slaves with any beneficial plan of Trade.   It would be an important point gained could we obtain permission to send them to Sierra Leone, and the Expense of their passage would be small in comparision with the advantage of their banishment.

I cannot close this Letter without begging you to be assured that I am truly sensible of your obliging appreciation of the manner in which I have performed the Duties of my office in this Country. The like zeal and industry will continue to be employed during the residue of my mission, and I shall, moreover, be ready after my return home to give to the Department of State any such information as it may be supposed my residence here has enabled me to acquire.

With distinguished consideration &c.

RUFUS KING.

R. KING TO GEO. W. ERVING, ESQ.

GREAT CUMBERLAND PLACE, Dec. 22, 1802.

SIR :

It having been the practice of your Predecessor to retain only one percentum of the sums recovered in the Martinique cases, there seems to be no good reason for claiming more, and I therefore recommend to you to receive from Mr. Williams at this rate in the Martinique Cases referred to in your Letters of the 13 and 20. instant.

In regard to the ascertainment of the former usage in reimbursing the Public advances in these and other Cases, concerning which you repeat your apprehension that Mr. Williams may, as the private agent of the claimants, pursue a course embarrassing to you, and injurious to the public, it does not appear to me that the public interest is in any degree likely to be disregarded by the American Commissioners with whose assistance the measures to procure this reimbursement were concerted and who will have it in their power to enforce their observance. I think it moreover due to Mr. Williams to add, what a knowledge of the capacity and zeal with which he served the public as your Predecessor authorizes me to do, my full persuasion that so far from embarrassing your agency, he will continue to afford you such information and aid as his Experience and knowledge of the business enable him to do, and as will materially contribute to the discharge of your agency with satisfaction to yourself, and advantage to the public.

With much respect &c.

RUFUS KING.

R. King to James Madison, Esq.

Private.

LONDON, Dec. 31, 1802.

DEAR SIR :

I have duly recd. your letter of Oct. 9. and am obliged to you for the early reply you have sent me, as well as for the like communication you were good enough to make to my agent in New York. As I expect the Vessel coming to me from America, will be here and ready for me and my family to embark by the 10th. of April, I am making the requisite preparations, and hope I may not be disappointed in receiving my Letters of Recall in season, to enable me to leave England immediately after that date.

With sentiments of Respect & Esteem &c.

R. K.

———

On January 3, 1803, to anticipate a little, Mr. Low writes that he has made an arrangement for a ship of which the captain is to provide such provisions and stores as may be required, with the permission, if Mr. King desires it, for other passengers than his family. The contract was that the vessel shall be ready on the 10th of April, " to receive his family and servants with his furniture, carriages, horses, sheep, cow and other articles."

On August 5, 1802, Mr. King wrote to Mr. Madison a private letter saying that in his official letter to the Secretary of State of the same date, resigning his office and requesting permission from the President to return home, he had asked for the accommodation of a passage home for himself and family in one of the public ships, which might be returning home or which might bring out his successor and carry him back. It is to the answer to that letter, by Mr. Madison, privately, on October 9, 1802, which contains the refusal to grant this request of a public conveyance that Mr. King refers above. Mr. Livingston * had been sent out recently in the Boston Frigate to Havre, and it was natural for Mr. King to think that a similar privilege might be ex-

* See letter of R. Troup, vol. iii., p. 526, for the reasons.

tended to him, who had so long and satisfactorily served his country and who supposed that his successor would be appointed before the next April, the time he named for the termination of his embassy. What reasons were assigned in this letter for the refusal of the request cannot be here given, for the letter cannot be found. But in the official files of the Department of State there is a letter from the Secretary of State, which follows, and gives the reasons.

WASHINGTON, DEPARTMENT OF STATE, Dec. 16, 1802.

RUFUS KING, ESQ.:

Having in a private letter under cover of one to Mr. N. Low of New York * communicated the result of yours on the subject of your return to the United States in a national ship and having had nothing to add to my last several letters on other subjects, I have thus long delayed an official answer to your letters numbered from 64 to 75 inclusive, I now acknowledge the receipt of them and inclose the permission which you ask to return to the United States. Your successor is not yet named.

The satisfaction which the President has derived from the manner in which you have pursued the several objects committed to you, and which I am authorized to repeat to you on this occasion, makes him the more regret that the particular accommodation you wished for the repassage of your family could not be afforded. Considering the actual situation and calls for the public vessels not laid up, the only chance of such an arrangement lay in the returns from the Mediterranean and that chance is frustrated by the Quarantine regulations in Great Britain to which vessels from that quarter are subject. . . .

With Great Respect &c.

JAMES MADISON.

* " Mr. N. Low, Mr. King's Agent in New York, writes to him on Oct. 23, 1802, that, having been absent from New York, he finds on his return a letter from Mr. Madison of 9th inst. with one inclosed for you (which you have herewith) from which I learn that a Government ship will not be sent for you ; and as you depend in this event upon one being sent for you from hence, you may be assured that it shall be done upon the best terms that may be, . . . to be ready to receive you and your baggage at London on the 10th of April next."

The appointment of a successor to Mr. King * was not made, as stated above, or even suggested during this year, and thus the contingency of one being sent out in a public ship, on which Mr. King might return, did not occur. But the President's own views of such an employment of a public ship may be learned from a letter † addressed by him to Gov. Monroe, January 13, 1803, informing him of his

---

* Mr. C. J. Ingersoll, in his *Recollections*, p. 353, writing of the appointments of foreign Ministers under Mr. Jefferson, says :

"But no step was taken for the appointment of another Minister to England, superseding Rufus King, although differing entirely from the President's politics, and having been six years resident in London as American Minister. I believe Mr. Jefferson has left, now published, his opinion that four years is about the proper duration of an American Mission in Europe ; with Mr. King's, when his had lasted six years and he considered seven a reasonable period, President Jefferson never interfered to put an end to it, but left the time to Mr. King, whose valuable services, particularly in the Louisiana acquisition, were officially avowed by Mr. Livingston in his correspondence with their government."

† "I am particularly concerned that, in the present case, you have more than one sacrifice to make. To reform the prodigalities of our predecessors is understood to be peculiarly our duty, and to bring the government to a simple and economical course. They, in order to increase expense, debt, taxation and patronage, tried always how much they could give. The outfit given to ministers resident to enable them to furnish their house, but given by no nation to a temporary minister, who is never expected to take a house or to entertain, but considered on the footing of a *voyageur*, they gave to their extraordinary ministers by wholesale. In the beginning of our administration, among other articles of reformation in expense, it was determined not to give an outfit to ministers extraordinary, and not to incur the expense with any minister of sending a frigate to carry or bring him. The Boston happened to be going to the Mediterranean, and was permitted, therefore, to take up Mr. Livingston and touch in a port of France. A frigate was denied to Charles Pinckney, and has been refused to Mr. King for his return. Mr. Madison's friendship and mine to you being so well known, the public will have eagle eyes to watch, if we grant you any indulgences out of the general rule : and on the other hand, the example set in your case will be more cogent on future ones, and produce greater approbation to our conduct."—Jefferson's *Works*, vol. iv., p. 455.

That the decision of the President was a correct one, though not for the reasons given in this letter, can hardly be questioned : the Government was relieved from the necessity and embarrassment of deciding such a question in the future, and left it to those appointed to make such arrangements as each might desire.

nomination and confirmation of it by the Senate, as Envoy Extraordinary and Minister Plenipotentiary to France and Spain to assist Messrs. Livingston and Pinckney in their negotiations about Louisiana. He earnestly pressed his acceptance of the mission, and deprecated his refusal, telling him at the same time that he could not send him in a public ship.

CHAPTER XIV.

R. TROUP TO R. KING.

NEW YORK Jan. 8, 1803.

DEAR SIR :

. . . Congress have not yet engaged, so far as the papers inform us, in any important measures. It is said that a few days ago they were deliberating with close doors, and it is conjectured that the violation of our Spanish Treaty by the Spanish officers at New Orleans was the subject.* Jefferson's milk and water communication on this subject is not generally liked. From appearances the nation would not be opposed, and particularly the

---

* See Hildreth's *Hist. of U. S.*, 2d Ser., v. ii., p. 471.

Kentuckians and Tennesseans, to prompt and strong measures. What the government will do is a problem.

Jefferson's message to Congress at the opening of the session is an opiate to the nation. There is as yet no promising appearance of his declension in popularity; and as he and all his satellites continue in their demagoguish career I have little doubt that they will retain their places; and there seems to be little reason to conclude that it will be wise at the next election to attempt to disturb them. By the by, they begin openly to avow that it will probably be our interest to draw still closer our ties of amity with Great Britain.

Our merchants are rising up pretty generally against our meeting Great Britain on the ground of abolishing the countervailing duties; and it is said that remonstrances will go to Congress against the measure. . . .

God bless you and grant you and your family a short and pleasant passage home, where your friends will be very happy to meet you again, and amongst them none will be happier than, Dear Sir,

Your very humble servt.
Robt. Troup.

R. King to Nicholas Vansittart Esq.

Randalls, Surrey, Jan. 8, 1803.

Sir :

After the conversation we lately had upon the subject, I will not trouble you at much length respecting the proposed augmentation of Duty upon foreign Spermaceti Oil. Under the Old System of Duties our whale fishery has not increased, while yours has extended itself so as to be able to supply more than your own consumption, which our united fisheries a few years back were unable to do. Under these Circumstances it is proposed to raise the duty on foreign Spermaceti Oil from £22.3.1. to £31.10 the Ton. The obvious effect of this measure will be to depress our whale fishery by the entire exclusion of our Spermaceti Oil from your market, where it sometimes finds in small quantities a precarious sale : the proceeds of these sales are laid out in the purchase of British manufactures.   Live and let live is a maxim in Trade, and in the present case may mean a little more than it usually does, for I cannot persuade myself, with the connexion that naturally exists between us, and seeing as we must the efforts that France is making to acquire a control over the maritime strength of the North of Europe, as she already has done over the South, that the Decrease of American Seamen can be indifferent to Great Britain ; and if it be not, I should hope for the sake of a common interest that you would not from light motives be willing to sanction any measure that would produce this effect.

I will not recall to your recollection by way of complaint, the various modes of encouraging your whale fishery, which, with whatever views adopted, have had the effect to withdraw from our service numbers of our most intelligent and useful adventurers.

As we have no laws prohibiting the transfer of their skill and persons to a foreign State, they were free to accept your invitation and we could only regret their preference.

But it would be matter of greater concern, should these measures be followed up by a Regulation which would still farther depress our whale fishery, that cannot be beneficial to your Revenue, and which is not wanted as a Protection to a Branch of Industry, that has already not only established itself, but continues to thrive under an encouragement that has brought it to maturity.

With sentiments of Respect & Esteem &c.

RUFUS KING.

R. KING TO WILLIAM WILBERFORCE, ESQ.

RANDALLS, Jan. 8, 1803.

DEAR SIR :

Will you give me leave to recall to your recollection my request that you would converse with your neighbor, Mr. Thornton, concerning the permission we have applied for to send certain of our negroes to Sierra Leone.   Although I really cannot suppose the plan in its full extent liable to the objections that I understand have been made to it, and which are founded upon the presumption that our negroes are all of the same idle and disorderly character as those who joined the English army in America, and who were afterwards abandoned to, and infested by, the vices of a succession of garrison towns, yet I am not disposed to urge a project upon merely speculative reasons. Instead therefore of the first proposal, suppose the Company should consent to our sending to its colony a limited number of negroes by way of experiment. If benefit instead of injury should be the result of the Experiment, the Permission would be continued ; if otherwise, it would be refused. The Negroes we may send are only such as may hereafter be manumitted by their Masters, and those who shall be detected in attempting to excite Insurrections among their fellow slaves. The former will include our most meritorious slaves, and the latter will not be the idle and the vicious, and these would not possess sufficient influence over their associates to become Leaders in Schemes of Insurrection.

I don't think it requisite, since I know your way of thinking in this respect, to enlarge upon the advantages to our respective Countries that may be derived from those occasional good offices and tokens of regard which, in small as well as important concerns, have so much influence in extending the intercourse and strengthening the friendship of Nations ; these are reflexions with which your mind is familiar and which I am persuaded you will apply as far as may be reasonable to the object of this letter.

With great truth and regard &c.

RUFUS KING.

W. WILBERFORCE TO R. KING.

Private.

BROOMFIELD, Tuesday, 11th Jan., 1803.

MY DEAR SIR :

Your letter having been written on *Saturday*, did not reach London until yesterday, and owing to a mistake, I have only this day received my letters of yesterday. I lose no time in assuring you that I will not fail to impress in the strongest manner I am able on Mr. A. the extreme Importance of cultivating that friendship betwn. the two countries so desirable, on all accounts, for both. I will endeavour to enforce the same consideration on Lord H.y, but I am not on the same *confidential* terms with him as with Mr. A, and cannot so easily create an opportunity for full and unreserved Discussion. I have a natural and fair plea to urge in vindication of my Solicitude on this Subject besides the Interest I take in it on general grounds as an English M. of Parlt. anxious abt. the welfare of his country. The commercial connection betn. the American and Yorke. merchts. has long called my particular attention to the state of America and to whatever may tend to cement our union with her.

Before I heard from you I had been thinkg. of requestg. you to refresh my Memory on the affair you mentioned to me in wh. the State of Maryland was principally concerned. In the multitude of topics we discussed during your kind Visit, I did not recollect what you stated on that Head with sufficient distinctness to enable me to reason from it satisfactorily—at ye same time being a matter in its nature public, it furnishes on that account a peculiarly fit instance of the course of proceeding which ought to be pursued by our Govt. with a view to the effect before stated as so desirable. May I beg you to let me have a Statement of the Maryland case either in writing or verbally. . . .

I cannot conclude without assuring you that I am gratified by every mark of your confidence and that you may be assured of my bearing in mind the Secresy and ye Discretion which that confidence may justly claim & of my endeavouring to turn it to good account by promoting that end which in common we have in view. . . .

With cordial Esteem and Regard, yours very sincerely,

W. WILBERFORCE.

R. KING TO THE DUKE OF PORTLAND.

GREAT CUMBERLAND PLACE, Jan. 12, 1803.

MY LORD:

I lose no time in making my acknowledgments to your Grace for the Communication that I have just received thro' Sir Stephen Cottrell concerning the vessel employed to carry a number of American Seamen to the United States, and which has been for some time detained at Falmouth on account of a contagious fever that broke out among the Passengers. Sir Stephen has engaged to send me Copies of the Report of the Physician, together with such other Papers as will explain the malignant character of the Disease : these being forwarded to the U. S. will enable the Government to adopt timely precautions against the Contagion, should the fever again break out during the Passage.

With Sentiments of the highest Respect &c.

RUFUS KING.

R. KING TO SIR STEPHEN COTTRELL.

GREAT CUMBERLAND PLACE, January 13, 1803.

SIR :

I have the honour to acknowledge the receipt of your Letter of yesterday, respecting the Ship Mary employed to carry American Seamen to the United States, and at present under quarantine at Falmouth. In addition to the Reports of the quarantine Physician, I have endeavoured to inform myself of the actual condition of this Vessel, as well in respect to her ability to perform the voyage, as to the quantity of Provisions remaining for the subsistence of the Passengers and Crew ; and am sorry to learn from Mr. Erving, the American Consul in London, and who engaged the Vessel to perform this Service, that although he has doubts of the sea-worthiness of the Ship, as well as of the sufficiency of the Provisions, he is unable, by reason of the present situation of the Vessel, to obtain such information on these points as both humanity and justice seem to require. In these circumstances I take the liberty to request thro' you the interference of his Majesty's Council for the purpose of obtaining exact information upon these two points, so necessary to be ascertained previously to the Mary's being permitted to proceed on her Voyage. The same motives which recommended the communication on this subject that his Grace the Lord President so obligingly directed to be made to me, will I am persuaded approve the measure it is the aim of this application to accomplish.

With perfect Respect &c.

RUFUS KING.

R. KING TO GEO. W. ERVING, ESQ., AGENT FOR SEAMEN.

GREAT CUMBERLAND PLACE, January 13, 1803.

SIR :

Pursuant of our conversation of last Evening, I have sent a letter to Sir Stephen Cottrell, for the purpose of obtaining an order of Council to prevent the Ship sailing until her sea-worthiness and the sufficiency of her Provisions can be ascertained ; this will without doubt be done.

But I infer from a conversation I have had with Sir Stephen Cottrell that the Council will be likely to do no more than to give orders to the Quarantine Officers at Falmouth to allow the Ship to be visited by such persons as shall be employed to make the proposed Survey ; and that it will be expedient that Mr. Fox should engage a suitable person to perform this service. I apprise you of this circumstance, in order that you may write to Mr. Fox to have the Survey made.

I am, Sir, your obedt. servt.

R. K.

R. KING TO ALBERT GALLATIN, ESQ., SECRETARY OF THE TREASURY, U. S.

LONDON, Jan. 13, 1803.

SIR :

I have duly received your Letter of Nov. 16, together with one from the Treasurer of the 18. of the same month, enclosing Mr. Glassford's Bill of Exchange upon the Lords Commissioners of the Treasury of this Country for Seventy thousand Pounds Sterling. The Bill was presented on the 10th instant, has been duly accepted, and shall be disposed of according to your direction.

The Exchange between London and Amsterdam has for some time been growing more favourable to the former, and bills on the latter, as you will perceive by the annexed note of the rate of Exchange, are at this time above par.

In addition to the ordinary Remittances from Holland to England, in payment of the manufactures of the latter, considerable sums are, and will continue to be, remitted to the English Proprietors of Estates in the Dutch Colonies ; the produce whereof is now obliged to go to Holland, and this circumstance among others has had its effect in turning the Exchange in favour of England.

I shall have sufficient time before the Bill upon the Treasury falls due to make such enquiries as may be requisite to enable me to engage a House of Reputation to transact our money concerns in this country. In doing this it will be my aim to reduce the compensation to the lowest rate at which we can expect our business to be done, by a House whose solidity and credit are above all doubt.

You are doubtless apprised of the embarrassments of the Bank of Amsterdam during the late war, whose stock in consequence thereof suffered great depreciation : that all foreign Bills of Exchange were acquitted in current Guilders instead of Bank money as had been the usage. Towards the close of last September the city of Amsterdam published a Paper founded upon a Report of the commissaires of the Bank, announcing that the deficit had been entirely supplied by a Tax for this purpose paid by the city of Amsterdam ; that the Guaranty of the city being thus satisfied and the Bank completely re-established, it had become expedient to re-establish the ancient Law respecting the acquittance of Bills of Exchange and therefore that it had been resolved :

" Art. I. That the value of every Bill of Exchange which shall be drawn or negotiated in this city of the 30th of the month of October approaching, upon places situated out of the Republic, and the amount of which shall be 300 florins and upwards shall be acquitted in the Bank of this city.

" II. That all Bills of Exchange upon, or payable in this City of the value of 300 florins and upwards, drawn from places situated in the French Republic, Great Britain, Spain, Portugal and Italy, shall be paid in Bank after the 31st Jany, 1803.

" III. That every Bill of Exchange which conformably to the Articles I. and II., is to be acquitted in Bank, and shall be proved to have been done so in any other manner, shall be held to be accepted, and each of the two contravening Persons shall pay a fine of 3 per cent. upon the total sum of these payments made out of the Bank.

" IV. That payments of Bills of Exchange will not be considered good but conformably to the 1st and 2d Articles, the usage introduced for some time of writing in Bank to oneself for another, as well as that of regulating the payment of it in current money, shall cease at the periods mentioned in the said Articles : the Resolution of the Council of Commerce of the 6th of October 1796 being in that respect revoked by the present."

The Bank florins in which Bills from this Country are now payable have risen and are now 5 per cent. above the current money.

With great Respect,&c.,

RUFUS KING.

R. KING TO LORD HAWKESBURY.

GREAT CUMBERLAND PLACE, Jan'y. 18, 1803.

MY LORD :

Referring to the observations transmitted to your Lordship in my Letter of the 3d of Feb'y past, explanatory of the principle upon which we claim an equal participation of the Trade between the United States and the British West Indies, I take the liberty to recall the subject to your Lordship's recollection as one that has been long under consideration, and upon which I have received orders to require the Decision of his Majesty's Government.

If contrary to the maxims by which the Trade of the Colonies was formerly regulated, new circumstances have rendered it expedient to open an intercourse between them and foreign States, it is this measure and not the admission of such foreign States to a share in the Trade, which breaks in upon a system that could no longer be maintained with advantage.

Such intercourse being opened, each party is alike competent to make Laws for its Regulation, and as neither can claim or expect to do so exclusively of the other, such Regulation becomes fit matter for mutual Explanation and agreement.

In conformity with this principle, an Article respecting this Trade was prepared and inserted in the Treaty of 1794, although afterwards excluded at the instance of the United States by reason of its inequality.

Should the United States in imitation of the example set them by Great Britain pass a Law applying the same rule to British Vessels, which the law of Great Britain applies to those of the United States, the effect would be that neither British nor American vessels could carry on the Trade : but on Flour, Corn, Timber, Staves and other articles, of first necessity to the Colonies, which must be received from the United States, the American vessels would carry them to some Port or Island in the West Indies, belonging to a third Power, whither the British vessels would go to receive the same ; carrying thither to purchase them such articles of Colonial produce as are allowed to be exported to the United States. In this way an Entrepôt would be established in the West Indies for the mutual sale and purchase of these commodities, and as the Question principally regards the Navigation of the two Countries, it is evident that the effect of these exclusive Regulations would be more beneficial to the United States than to Great Britain, inasmuch as the voyage from the United States to the Place of Deposit in the West Indies would be longer and consequently would afford more employment than between the said place of Deposit and the British West Indies.

Notwithstanding the Equity of such a Law on the part of the United States and the probable advantage it would secure to their navigation we have no hesitation in preferring an amicable and equal participation of the Trade, to the certainty of even acquiring an unequal share of it, by a measure of retaliation, which being resorted to in one branch of Trade, may by one or both sides be extended to others, and in the end might have the effect to disturb the harmony, as well as the extensive and mutually beneficial intercourse between the two countries.

Whether it may be deemed more convenient to alter the existing Law on the part of Great Britain, so as to allow the Trade in question to be carried on equally by American and British Vessels, or to enter into a compact for this purpose, as was intended by the Treaty of 1794, is not a point of material difficulty ; tho' in the nature of the subject, a preference seems due to an adjustment by mutual stipulation : in either mode as a security against the Extension of this Trade beyond the Limits, which it may be desired to give it, it might be provided that the return Cargoes of American vessels should be carried directly to the United States, and that they should moreover be purchased as well as limited by the proceeds of Cargoes imported in American Vessels.

With distinguished Consideration &c.

RUFUS KING.

R. KING TO HIS EXCELLENCY, THE GOVERNOR OF MARYLAND.

LONDON, Jan. 18, 1803.

SIR :

Having lately seen your Excellency's Message of November last to the General Assembly of Maryland, I was a little surprised at that part of it which refers to a verbal message stated to have been delivered by Mr. Christie from me to the Executive of Maryland ; and I think it alike due to your Excellency and myself to take the earliest opportunity to correct a representation that has arisen without doubt from a misapprehension of the object and perhaps the tenour of the communication that I made to Mr. Christie.   Not having had the honour of a direct correspondence with the Executive of Maryland concerning the State interest in the Bank of England, I might have doubted the propriety of my commencing it, especially as the subject had been repeatedly given me in charge by the President, and my communications respecting it had been regularly made to the Department of State, and, I presume, thro' it to the Executive of Maryland. Knowing however the solicitude which existed in Maryland respecting this property, so long, and I may add, so unreasonably detained, I thought it probable that Mr. Christie's friends, upon his return from England, would make enquiries of him concerning it, and therefore took an opportunity before he left London to explain to him its precise situation ; but without any expectation that the explanation would or could assume the shape of an official communication to the Executive of Maryland.   Being unacquainted with the purport of Mr. Christie's communication, I can say nothing of its accuracy, and the sole object of this Letter is to beg you to be assured that I should have made a direct and written communication to the Executive of Maryland, had it been my intention to have made any direct and written communication whatever.   With great Respect &c.

RUFUS KING.

———

JOHN JAY TO R. KING.

BEDFORD, 20 Jany, 1803.

DEAR SIR :

I ought to have written to you long ago, but a series of occurrences have for two years past left me little Leisure for epistolary correspondence.   I allude to Mrs. Jay's long and painful Illness, and (when she appeared to be fast recovering) her unexpected Death. The Vicissitudes in my own Health, the Removal of my Family to this place, and the many things to be done for their Accommodation, the gradually increasing Indisposition of my Son, who is now on the Ocean going to Italy to avoid the Winter here, &c., these are afflicting Circumstances ; but considering where and what we are, Troubles of one kind or other are to be expected and to be borne with Patience and Resignation.

My Expectations from Retirement have not been disappointed ; and had Mrs. Jay continued with me, I should deem this the most agreeable part of my life.

The post once a week brings me our Newspapers, which, with those you are so kind as to send me, furnish a History of the Times. By this History, as well as those of former times, we are taught the Vanity of expecting that, from the Perfectibility of human nature and the Lights of Philosophy, the Multitude will become virtuous & wise, or their Demagogues candid and honest. As G. Morris says " what is, is " and we must make the best of it. For the present they probably reason so in France. It would not however surprize me if future Irruptions from that Volcano should again desolate some of the neighbouring Countries. Viewing the French Revolution as a Tragedy I am inclined to think, that we have only seen the *first* act concluded. You may live to see the *next ;* but I shall doubtless by that time be removed to a Theatre of a different kind.

Not having had leisure to visit New York since my Removal from Albany to this place, I cannot give you any particular Information relative to our mutual Friends there. Judge Benson is again at the Bar, and I regret it. If these are not upside down Times, they certainly are up and down Times—but Athens the City of Philosophers, and Rome the City of everything, saw and felt much worse. With great Esteem and Regard I am

Dear Sir

Your most obt. Servt.

JOHN JAY.

Mr. Sedgwick, January 27, 1803,* writes to General Hamilton among other things :

* *Hamilton's Works*, vol. vi., p. 553.

It is very important that the federalists should retain and acquire the possession of the State governments wherever in their power.   For this reason, and indeed for many others, I am glad Mr. King is about to return home.   With wisdom and prudence, I think it is probable that he may be placed at the head of the government of New York.   He may there do infinitely more good than in the inefficient office of Vice-President.   General Pinckney must in all events be considered as our candidate for the first office.   I have been inexpressibly disgusted with some of our friends who have suggested that we ought to consider him only as designed for the second.   There is, however, another consideration on the subject which ought to be considered as conclusive.   We shall most certainly not succeed at the next election, nor is it, in my mind, desirable that we should.   Should Mr. King be holden up for this office, it would lessen at least the probability of his success for the government of New York.

R. KING TO SECRETARY OF STATE.

No. 79.

LONDON, Jany. 28, 1803.

SIR :

No farther progress has yet been made in the discussion of the Boundaries : from one or two conversations that I have had with Col. Barclay, who has returned to town, I perceive that his opinion, whatever influence it may have, will be favourable to such a settlement of the Eastern Boundary as would be satisfactory to us : the chief difficulty in the Settlement that I foresee at present, respects the Island of Campo Bello which to avoid questions of interfering jurisdiction arising from its being Westward of the suitable Boundary-Line, should belong to Massachusetts.   If it should be ceded, I shall have no hesitation to agree to a confirmation of the Titles of the Settlers, derived from Nova Scotia.   But the Minister may hesitate about a cession.   Lord Hawkesbury some weeks ago sent an Instruction to the Attorney General to take measures to effect the Transfer of the Maryland Bank Stock to the King, in order that his majesty might be enabled to dispose of it in such a way as he should think fit ; and as Hilary Term has commenced, I presume the transfer will shortly be made to the Crown. On this subject I have lately seen in the News Papers the Message of the Governor of Maryland to the General Assembly of that State, and take the liberty to annex to this Letter the copy of one that I thought myself called upon, in consequence of this Message, to write to Governor Mercer.

In my last conversation with Lord Hawkesbury respecting the intercourse between the United States and the British Colonies in the West Indies, he desired me to write him a Letter upon that subject, in order that he might submit it to the consideration of the Cabinet, and I accordingly sent him the Letter, a copy of which is adjoined.*

Although I have received no answer to the Letter to Mr. Vansittart, a copy whereof is likewise annexed,* respecting the proposed augmentation of Duty upon Spermaceti Oil, he told me a few days ago that unless they found stronger opposition from the Board of Trade than was expected, the Treasury would be disposed to abandon the proposed increase of Duty. . . .

With perfect Respect & Esteem &c.

R. K.

P. S. At Paris, they say Victor will proceed with his troops directly to Louisiana ; here it is believed that the General with the Etat Major and a few troops may go to Louisiana, but that the greater part of the forces will be landed in St. Domingo.

R. KING TO LORD HAWKESBURY.

Private.

LONDON, Feby. 1, 1803.

MY LORD :

There are three subjects upon which I have received orders to press for the final determination of his Majesty's Government before I leave England. These are the Maryland Bank Stock, the Boundaries and the Intercourse between the U. S. and the British Colonies in the West Indies. As I expect to embark in

* The length of these letters prevents their insertion here.—ED.

the Month of April, your Lordship must be sensible that no further time is to be lost in taking measures to bring these points to a decision, if it be intended that they shall be adjusted before my departure.

With perfect Respect &c.

R. K.

R. KING TO MESSRS. BIRD, SAVAGE, AND BIRD.

LONDON, Feby. 7, 1803.

GENTLEMEN :

I received at a late hour last Evening a Letter from your Mr. H. M. Bird, communicating the information that your House will be obliged to stop payment this morning and that the U. S. are your Creditors for a considerable sum.

Having casually heard from the late American Consul, Mr. Williams, that he had lately accepted Bills for several Thousand Pounds payable to your House on account of the U. S., I cannot doubt that you will be of opinion with me that these Bills, being held in Trust, should be delivered to me in order that they may be collected and applied to the Service of the U. S. and I therefore request you to deliver the same to the Bearer, John Munro.

With due Respect &c.

RUFUS KING.

R. KING TO SECRETARY OF STATE.

NO. 80.

LONDON, Feby. 7, 1803.

SIR :

Last Evening (Tuesday) I received a note from Mr. Bird, informing me that his House would be obliged to stop payment this morning, and that the United States are Creditors for a considerable sum. The former Consul, Mr. Williams, having casually informed me that he had lately accepted Bills for several Thousand Pounds, payable to Bird, Savage & Bird, for the service of the United States, I have written them a Letter requiring that they would deliver up to me all Bills of Exchange that have been remitted to them and which they hold in trust for the United States. I have not yet received their answer but as they have without doubt been pressed in their affairs, I fear there is little probability of recovering these Draughts, which may have been already discounted.

In consequence of this failure, I shall be under the necessity of making the best arrangement in my Power with some other House for the payment of the appointments of the several agents of the United States in this country.

Mr. Livingston in a Letter dated at Paris the 3rd instant, informs me that he had just received accounts from Mr. Graham at Madrid that the Spanish Government has passed a most extraordinary decree by which all American Vessels coming from the United States are denied entry into any of the Ports of Spain until they shall have duly performed Quarantine in some foreign Port.

With perfect Respect & Esteem &c.

RUFUS KING.

R. KING TO SECRETARY OF STATE.

No. 81.

LONDON, Feb. 9, 1803.

SIR :

As I apprehended might be the case, Bird, Savage & Bird have answered my demand for the surrender of the Bills of Exchange lately remitted to them, by saying they were unable to deliver them up, as they had been discounted before their failure. I have requested them to prepare and send me their accounts, including all receipts and payments up to the day on which they stopped, and I hope to receive them in season to forward by the mail of this month which will not be dispatched before the 12th.

Having understood the assigned reason for the failure to be the delay that has attended the Remittances on account of large debts due in America, I shall direct Mr. Erving, the Consul to attend the first meeting of the Creditors, when a State of the affairs of the House is to be exhibited. By this means we may ascertain the names and debts of the American Debtors, and by the priority due to the United States, I presume the Treasury will be able to secure the speedy and full recovery of the Debt due from this House.

With great Respect & Esteem &c.

RUFUS KING.

R. KING TO A. GALLATIN, ESQ.

LONDON, Feb. 9, 1803.

SIR :

My Letters to the Secretary of State will apprise you of the failure of the House of Bird, Savage & Bird, and their accounts which I expect to forward by the mail of this month, will enable you to take immediate measures for the recovery in America of the considerable balance that I understand to be due to the United States.

It is fortunate that the large Bill upon the English Treasury was sent to me instead of this House. The Bankers in Holland recommend to me to invest its amount when received in a Bill at 3 months. I am making inquiries here upon this subject and shall adopt what may appear to me the most advantageous mode of remittance.

I have had several conversations with Sir Francis Baring with the view of settling the Terms upon which his House (which is perhaps the most solid House in England) would undertake our money agency in this Country. He will receive and collect Bills of Exchange and remit the proceeds to Holland for one half per centum ; this is as low as the Business could be done by inferior Houses. I have pressed him to receive and sell our funded stock and to remit its proceeds upon the same Terms. This he declines doing, but would transact this part of the Business for one per centum. The proposition I last made him, and which he has under consideration, is to allow one per centum on the sale of stocks and the remitting of the proceeds, including the Brokerage upon the sale of the Stocks, which I understand to be as much as a quarter per centum.

With great Respect &c.

RUFUS KING.

CHAPTER XV.

Mr. King, in anticipation of his return home had written
to Mr. N. Low to procure for him a ready furnished house
in the country to which he might go on his arrival at New
York.   He had received an answer, that one *ready furnished*
was out of the question.   "You seem to have forgotten the
state of things in this country, when you direct a ready
furnished house to be engaged."   Search, however, was
made and on Feb. 2, 1803, Mr. Low wrote to him.

" I have succeeded beyond all calculation in obtaining for you
a ready furnished country house   .   .   .   with the privilege of
making it your first winter residence, which it is mine and the
opinion of your friends here that you will do."

The house was situated in Greenwich about two miles and a half from the City Hall, belonging to a Mr. Andrew Smith, who was about to make a voyage, with his family, to India.

R. King to Nicholas Vansittart, Esq.

Great Cumberland Place, Feb. 16, 1803.

Sir :

I take the liberty to sd. you enclosed a letter that I have received from the Master of the American Ship *Iris*, a regular Trader between New York and London, complaining of the seizure of several small quantities of wine and spirits, being the remains of Sea-stores provided for the use of the passengers and crew. I likewise enclose the copy of a letter which I wrote to Mr. Rose in the year 1799 upon this subject ; on this occasion Mr. Rose assured me that he would either by a clause to be inserted in an Act of Parliament, or in some other way take measures to prevent a repetition of their Proceedings. The ships employed as regular Traders between the United States and Great Britain, derive no small portion of their earnings from the passengers who pass and repass in the prosecution of their commercial concerns ; and it seems as reasonable that the requisite stores for their accommodation should be provided in America where they are cheaper than in England, as that the Provisions for the crew should be there laid in.

If the captains be held to report all such stores, the quantity of which may be limited and to deposit them on his arrival at the Custom House, they might be delivered back previous to his sailing and the Revenue thereby secured against fraud.

I ask the favour of you to give an order for the restoration of the Stores of the *Iris*, and moreover to procure the establishment of some safe and convenient Regulations upon this subject, applicable to further cases, not only in the Port of London, but in that of Liverpool and others with which we have frequent intercourse.

With great respect, &c.

R. K.

P.S.—Since writing the above I have received a second letter from the Captain of the *Iris*, asking my interference to relieve

him from the embarrassment to which he may be liable in consequence of the discovery of some Chocolate and other articles in
the possession of the Ship's Steward.   On this subject I can say
no more than that I have reason from the good character of the
Master to believe him ignorant and innocent of this transaction,
and therefore flatter myself that he may not be made liable to expense or embarrassment.

R. KING TO MESSRS. BIRD, SAVAGE, AND BIRD.

GREAT CUMBERLAND PLACE, Feby. 13, 1803.

GENTLEMEN :

It is quite indifferent to me whether you balance my private
account by a transfer from the Diplomatic Fund on account of
the current quarter's salary, or allow me to pay you the Balance
in Cash, which I am ready to do.   Perhaps it will be most correct, because it will correspond with the fact, that you should
balance my account as well as those of the other agents of the
United States by suitable transfers for this purpose from the public accounts to which they respectively belong.

In regard to Mawhood & Co's claims, as you took no discharge
from them (which if you were in Cash, I think you ought to have
done) it remains to be paid : but the transaction should appear
by proper entries in the Debtor and Creditor sides of the account.

I agree with you in opinion that it will be proper to bring the
balances of the several accounts into a general account which may
show the real Balance due to the United States.

Be good enough to send me my Book with these accounts duly
entered, in order that I may be able to examine them before they
are finally made up.

I remain, Gentlemen, your obed. servt.

RUFUS KING.

R. KING TO R. R. LIVINGSTON.

LONDON, 23 Feb. 1803.

DEAR SIR :

Having just seen a Letter from Mr. Thornton, the British
chargé des affaires at Washington dated January 11, which states

that *the President had just nominated Mr. Monroe, Envoy Extra. and Minister Plenipotentiary to France and Spain to treat with either or both concerning the Mississippi.* No mention is made of my Successor.

Yours faithfully

RUFUS KING.

R. KING TO ALBERT GALLATIN, ESQ.

LONDON, Feb. 25, 1803.

SIR :

The annexed copy of my correspondence with Sir Francis Baring & Co., will sufficiently explain the Terms upon which I have in your behalf agreed with this House to transact such Business as may be committed to it by the Department of the Treasury or any other Branch of the Government of the United States.

My Letter of the 9th instant is erroneous in stating that this House would consent both to sell the funded Debt and remit the Proceeds for a commission of one per cent. This error arose from a misconception, on my part, of the tenour of a conversation on this subject that I had with Sir Francis Baring, and which was corrected by subsequent conferences ; the offer having been confined to the mere Sale of the funded Debt, exclusive of Brokerage and the Commission for remitting the Proceeds to the Continent.

I have taken pains to inform myself of the Terms upon which similar Business is done between our Merchants and those of this Country ; and the result is a persuasion that this arrangement is not only safe and reputable, as it regards the solidity and character of the agents (points of considerable importance) but moreover that the Terms are as low as the like Business has been done between individuals ; the more general custom appearing to have been a charge of half per cent on remittances from America and half per cent more on remitting the Proceeds to any part of the Continent ; and in respect to the Sale of Stocks, I have not found that it has in any instance been done for less Commission than one per cent, exclusive of Brokerage, and in most cases the Commission has been from two to two and a half per cent. One half per cent is understood to be the regular and common charge for making remittances from this Country to the Continent.

The failure of Mess. Bird, Savage and Bird made it requisite to have recourse to some other House to receive and pay the appointments of the public agents of the United States in this Country. I received offers from several respectable Commercial and Banking Houses to transact the Business on the same Terms as had been done by Bird, Savage and Bird ; but as Sir Francis Baring & Co were willing to do it upon the like Terms, and were moreover to be employed as the Bankers of the United States in a more important concern, I had no hesitation in giving them a preference. . . .

With great respect &c.

RUFUS KING.

R. KING TO SECRETARY OF STATE.

No. 82.

LONDON, Feb. 28, 1803.

SIR :

I have duly received your Letters of the 16 and 23 December. By Lord Hawkesbury's desire I have conferred with Col. Barclay respecting the continuation of the Boundary thro' the Bay of Passamaquoddy, who has made no objection to the line we have proposed, tho' he appears to think that it would be improper to cede to us the Island of Campo Bello unless the cession should be desired by the Inhabitants. No objection has been made to our Title to Moose Island and at present I foresee nothing to impede a settlement of this Boundary, except the difficulty of engaging the Ministers to bestow upon the Subject sufficient time to understand it. With regard to the line between the Source of the St. Croix and the North West corner of Nova Scotia, I have no reason to suppose there will be any objection to its being ascertained in the way we have proposed.

Not having been able to fix the attention of Lord Hawkesbury upon the Subject, I am not able to give you any information concerning the line between the North West corner of Nova Scotia and the head of the Connecticut River, or between the Lake of the Woods and the Mississippi.

As soon as I have informed myself of the practical interpretation of the Law, which it is supposed impedes the importation of the cotton and other produce of the Western Country, I will make such application to the Government as may be proper to remove the impediments. . . . General Victor is still detained in Holland, and it is said the Expedition will proceed to Louisiana in a few weeks.

With perfect Respect & Esteem &c.

RUFUS KING.

R. KING TO R. R. LIVINGSTON.

LONDON, Mar. 4, 1803.

DR. SIR:

I have seen a letter from one of the Senators, dated Washington Jan'y 10, that says a message had been sent to the H. of Reps., but not to the Senate, which was received with closed doors, and was understood to communicate the answer of the Gov'r of New Orleans to Gov. Claiborne's Letter.

The answer insinuates that the shutting of the Port by the intendant was not in compliance with an express order of the King of Spain, but a measure resulting from general Instructions for the Government of the Colonies on the return of Peace ; that being shut, it would not be proper, nor in his power, to open the Port without the express orders of the Crown ; and as the deposit would be *inconvenient to the Colony*, that it would be *unjust* to construe the Treaty so vigorously as to claim it as a Right. The writer observes that he has not seen the letter which is kept secret, but that he has rec'd good information as to its purport.

I do not learn that any communication has been made to Congress of the Representations or Exertions you have made upon this Subject, an omission that seems to me, in several respects, to be of much importance.

We have newspapers from New York to the 28 Jan'y. The enclosed scraps were sent me in a letter ; when I receive my Papers, I will forward them to you. A Gentleman of New York in a letter to his correspondent here, says the Vice President will visit the western country and the Mississippi Territory next Spring, and insinuates that it is not improbable that he may hereafter reside there. Yrs. most sincerely,

R. KING.

R. KING TO R. R. LIVINGSTON, ESQ.

LONDON, March 11, 1803.

DEAR SIR :

The Newspapers will have given you the message of Tuesday from the King to Parliament ; the two Houses have without dissent offered in reply the usual assurances of support which are made at the commencement of a war. I attended the House of Commons, but the conversation which passed, for there was no debate, cast no light upon the discussion depending with France. The Mins'r merely said that a full disclosure shd be made in case no satisfactory settlement shd not be attained. The Message has been followed by a general Impress of Seamen, the calling out of the Militia, and by Proclamation recalling all Br. Seamen in for. service, and offering bounties to such as shall voluntarily enter into the Navy.

Without puzzling oneself to discover the exact points in discussion, the temper manifested on both sides, and the Eclat which each has chosen to give to its measures, will make it difficult to accomplish a Reconciliation. It seems to me that the Ministry here cannot go back, if so the decision rests with Bonaparte. From the reference which the message has made to the armaments in Holland, it is pretty natural to conclude that a fleet of observation will immediately appear in the Channel, and that detachments, or small squadrons will watch the arsenal Ports of both France and Holland ; if so, the Expedition to Louisiana must remain in Port, until the questions in discussion are decided. How far our affairs will be beneficially effected by this unexpected, tho' very natural course of things, is more than I am able to determine, and I shd be thankful for the assistance of your Sentiments to enable me to form a satisfactory opinion respecting this Point. Should we like to see the English in N. O. not with the view of keeping it, but to prevent its going into the hands of France ; or perhaps to assist us in acquiring a title to, and the possession of it ? If you are authorized to negotiate a purchase, would not the occupation by the English benefit your bargain, it being well and previously understood, that if we obtain the Title, they would give us the Possession ?   All this is mere speculation, and more, it is very hasty and occurs as I write.   But crude as it is, it may be worth consideration.   You see I write in confidence and without the least reserve ; I need not say that it is merely between you and me.   Most faithfully,

R. K.

R. King to Rt. Honorable Lord Hawkesbury.

Great Cumberland Place, Mar. 12, 1803.

My Lord :

The Cotton, Flour, and other Articles, the produce of the Western States of America, and which are brought down the Mississippi, are according to a Treaty between the United States and his Catholic Majesty, deposited at New Orleans from whence the vessels of the United States receive and carry the Same to the Ports of America or to those of some foreign State. American Vessels laden with Cotton, and other Articles, the produce of these Western States, and which were taken on board at New Orleans have of late, upon their arrival in this Country, been denied an Entry upon the ground that they came from a Spanish Port.

Without objection to the Law, which forbids a foreign Ship to import into Great Britain the produce even of her own country except the same be brought directly from the Ports of the country to which she belongs, it is evident that the Prohibition does not in its principle or object apply to the Case of Vessels in the circumstances of those just mentioned ; and without detaining your Lordship with Reflexions to elucidate this truth, I take the liberty of submitting the case to your Lordship's consideration and of requesting your interference in such way as may be proper for the purpose of removing the Impediments which prevent the entry of American Vessels coming from New Orleans and laden with Articles of the growth and manufacture of the United States.

With great consideration, &c.

Rufus King.

R. KING TO SECRETARY OF STATE.

No. 84.

LONDON, Mar. 16, 1803.

SIR :

Couriers last evening arrived at the French Ambassador's from Paris, and at the same time a Messenger from Lord Whitworth ; they left Paris after the communication of the King's Message to Parliament of the 8th inst. had been received there. General Andreossi and the Dutch Ambassador both told me to-day that for the purpose of taking away the pretext of war (as they expressed themselves) arising out of the Colonial Expeditions, prepared in the Dutch and French Ports, the Expedition to Louisiana has been countermanded and will not now proceed.

The answer from Paris, it is understood, possesses a sincere desire of Peace, demands the immediate fulfilment of the Stipulations of the Treaty of Amiens, and precise explanations why the Evacuation of Malta has been hitherto delayed. It likewise alludes to the King's Message, and insinuates that it is impossible to imagine that it can be here believed that the proposed armaments can have any influence upon the determination of France.

With perfect Respect & Esteem, &c.

RUFUS KING.

———

G. CABOT TO R. KING.

BOSTON, March 10, 1803.

MY DEAR SIR :

My spirits sink when I look upon the picture you have given of Europe in your several letters of 3d & 4th January. I scarcely recollect a period in the course of the war when the destructive power of France was so much to be feared. It seems to me that only two nations remain whose aid would be effectual if it cou'd be directed to the support of the British Empire against the dangers that assail it. I mean Russia & the U. S.; the former has less powerful motives for giving it than the latter, for Russia is not only invincible but almost invulnerable from the want of Civilization.

It ought to be the policy of England to refrain from the Combat (*if she can safely*) until some substantial cooperation can be secured. I hope you won't think me extravagant if I say that this Country wou'd be a competent ally if we were once fully engaged ; but we shall not engage if we can avoid it : we shall rather pay tribute for being permitted to remain neutral while others are destroyed whose safety is necessary to our own. Such at least must be the conclusions which every man will draw from the measures of our Govt. & especially the mission of the french hearted Monroe.

All good men regret that you are about to leave the place you have filled so well for seven critical years ; few however wonder at it & not many can disapprove your determination. From something you said I infer that you contemplate a visit to this part of the Country after your arrival ; I pray ardently that this may be realized as I am persuaded you will receive some pleasure & communicate a great deal ; I hope you will come early & allow yourself ample time to see your well-ripened friends leisurely. The Louisiana business interests the public very much but I have long ago settled my opinion upon it & endeavored to propagate it, which is that " *France will not push us to a war at this time.*" I ground this upon the obvious policy of avoiding to create for G. B. the only important ally she needs & can hope for, & on the other side the certainty that we shall take no part against France if we can avoid it, but may be foolish & even base enough to favor the views of France against the only power in the World able &, from interest, necessarily disposed to assist in defending us. If however it shou'd happen that France has grown too arrogant to make these calculations & shou'd treat us as she does her neighbours, she may provoke us to a resistance which wou'd be happy for this Country & perhaps for many others. I pray you to receive my best wishes for a favorable passage home. I remain always your sincere friend

GEORGE CABOT.

R. KING TO SECRETARY OF STATE.

No. 85.

LONDON, Mar. 17, 1803.

SIR :

War seems more and more probable, and it appears to me inevitable. Holland will be immediately involved, and Spain and Portugal must obey the commands of France. The day after the

King's Message to Parliament was communicated to the French Government, Bonaparte delivered to Lord Whitworth a Paper (a copy of which I have seen) stating

1st. That the Expedition preparing in the Dutch Ports was, as all the world knew, destined for America, but, in consequence of the Message, that it had been recalled and would not proceed.

2d. That if the armament announced in the Message be not satisfactorily explained, or if it take place, that France would march 20,000 men into Holland.

3d. That the forces debarked in the Ports of Holland would be reinforced and assembled on the coast of Flandres.

4th. That the French army will be immediately put on a war establishment.

5th. That camps will be formed on the coasts of France between Dunkirk and Boulogne.

6th. That an army would enter Switzerland.

7th. That an army would march into Italy and occupy Tarento.

8th. That England must not expect, under the cover of an armament, to avoid the execution of the Treaty of Amiens.

The greatest activity continues to prevail in the military and naval Departments ; it is understood that the Squadrons in the West and East Indies & in the Mediterranean will not immediately require reinforcement, and that a respectable fleet will soon appear in the Channel and on the Coast of Ireland. The regular Army on foot in Great Britain (exclusive of the forces in Ireland, Egypt, Malta, Gibraltar and the Colonies) consists of 27,000 Infantry and 12,000 Cavalry, and it will be reinforced immediately by 37,000 of the militia which have been called out.

I don't yet hear of Mr. Monroe's arrival, tho' I learn from Mr. Livingston that he is daily expected in France. Mr. Merry is preparing to embark for the U. S. and is pressed by his Government to be ready to leave England the first week in April.

With perfect Respect. R. K.

R. KING TO SECRETARY OF STATE.

No. 86.

LONDON, Mar. 19, 1803.

SIR :

Orders are sometime past given to evacuate Egypt and the English forces have at this time probably left that Country. The independence of Malta, by the Treaty of Amiens is placed under the protection and guarantee of Great Britain, France, Spain, Austria, Russia and Prussia. Austria has acceded, Russia consents to accede, provided the Maltese language be abolished, to which France agrees, and Prussia is ready to assume the guarantee, when that alone is wanted to give effect to the Stipulation respecting Malta. This view is necessary to enable you to form a correct opinion of the demand which the French Ambassador has just made for the Evacuation of Malta, and of Lord Hawkesbury's answer which was received by the French Ambassador on the 15th, and as soon as it could be translated sent to Paris, where it is expected to have arrived last evening or this morning.

The answer begins by laying down the maxim of the Law of Nations that " Conventio omnis intelligitur rebus sic stantibus," and after declaring that the consideration of things, as settled by the public Treaties of Europe, and the restitutions to be made pursuant to the Treaty of Amiens, was a principal and essential reason with his Britannic Majesty for entering into that Treaty, and without which it would not have been made, it enumerates the changes that have since happened without the privity and consent of Great Britain, and which have so materially altered the relative condition of the Powers that are Parties to the Treaty of Amiens : this recapitulation is followed by a reference to the publication of Sebastiani's Report of his Mission to the Barbary Powers, Egypt & Syria as well as to the Exposition of the affairs of France, sent by Bonaparte to the Legislative Body, both of which are stated to contain sentiments injurious to the Reputation and Honour of the British Nation. The answer concludes by insinuating that Great Britain, in these circumstances, might justly refuse to proceed in the farther execution of the Treaty of Amiens, instead whereof his Majesty desirous of the continuance of Peace, and willing to offer to France still farther proofs of his moderation, is ready to enter into such mutual discussions and explanations with France, as in the present posture of affairs may be calculated to secure the just Rights of the two Nations and to maintain the Repose of Europe.

Instead of a mere discussion, respecting the interpretation of the Treaty of peace of Amiens, or the execution of any of its articles, this answer renders the subject so intricate that even in a different Temper from that which now exists, the Parties would find great

difficulty in adjusting their respective Pretensions.   The French
Ambassador expects to receive the Reply of his Government on
the 22.   The military preparations proceed here without the
smallest relaxation, and every appearance indicates to my mind
the Expectation of War.

I have the honour to be &c.

R. K.

CHAPTER XVI.

R. King to R. R. Livingston, Esq., Paris.

LONDON, Mar. 23, 1803.

DEAR SIR :

I have received your Letters of Feb. 24 and March 8 & 15. Except the last I think I have written to you by every Messenger, since my Letter of the 11th the words of the Communication respecting the Expedition for Louisiana were, " the message (of the King) speaks of the expedition of Helveotsluys ; all the world knows it was destined for America, and about proceeding to its Destination, mais d'apres le message de S. M. l'embarquement et le depart vont être contremandés."

Bonaparte gave Lord Whitworth the alternative of war or the Evacuation of Malta on the 13th instant. I refer to the scene at the Drawing Room.* Lord Hawkesbury's note of the 15 in answer to General Andreossi's demand of the Evacuation of Malta, states that Sebastiani's Report and other information disclose the views of France upon the Turkish Empire and "that the King cannot consent to evacuate Malta unless substantial security be provided for those Objects which in present circumstances would be endangered by that measure"—in other words the King will evacuate on the provision of such security ; if the Turkish Empire be those objects which wd. be endangered by the Evacuation of Malta and the possession of this Island . . . by G. Britain be deemed security against the danger, would not the possession of it by some other Power who would be able to defend it, and be likely to resist the views of France, afford the substantial security that the note requires ? if so, would not the possession by Russia fulfil this purpose ? The only material doubt which offers, arises from the presumed fact that France would at Amiens have agreed to this arrangements had England proposed it. Still as the holding of Malta by England is thought a security against the views of France upon Turkey, and the note in effect offers to evacuate upon the provision of substantial security against the dangers with which the Turkish Empire is threatened, it is difficult to imagine any other security than that of giving Malta to Russia and obtaining her Guarantee of the Integrity of the Dominion of the Turk.

The tenour of the note as here cited may be depended upon ; the reflexions which follow are of less importance, and I have submitted them to you, as the grounds upon which I am less sanguine than I have been that the present discussion would end in war.

With great Truth &c.

RUFUS KING.

I have a letter from the Secy. of State of Jany. 29, which informs me my successor had not then been named and that the time fixed for my leaving England might arrive before any arrangements for the vacancy can have their effect !

* See letter of R. R. Livingston to the President, March 12, 1803. *Annals of Congress*, 1802–3, App. p. 1115.

R. King to Secretary of State.

No. 87.

London, Mar. 25, 1803.

Sir :

It is now nearly a fortnight since Lord Hawkesbury informed me that he had lately ascertained that the American Commissioners under the 7th article of the Treaty of Amity and Commerce, with the concurrence of the 3d Commissioner, conceived themselves authorized to allow Interest upon the Claims before them for the time during which the Proceedings of the Comn. had been suspended ; that as the Suspension had taken place in consequence of that of the Commission in America, it did not appear to him that the Board here had authority to allow Interest for this portion of time ; that he made me this Communication in hopes that we might agree in the just interpretation of the Powers of the Commissioners, as it would be disagreeable particularly at the juncture of affairs when he was speaking, again to arrest the Proceedings of the Commissioners. I replied that the Subject was both unexpected and new ; that it should receive my immediate consideration, and that I would take the earliest opportunity in my power of conversing with him respecting it.

After maturely reflecting upon the objection which originates with and was entertained by Dr. Swabey before the conclusion of the Convention, in virtue of which the Board has resumed its Proceedings, I informed Lord Hawkesbury that I was ready to meet him ; but owing to the discussions going on with France he has not yet appointed a day to receive me : in the mean time the Commission proceeds in examining and deciding the cases before it, leaving open the ascertainment of the amount of the respective Claims. As the first instalment of the £600,000 to be received by Great Britain is payable in July, and as from the nature of the Negotiation with France I may not be able to meet Lord Hawkesbury soon, it has appeared to me proper to apprise you of this objection to the Powers of the Commissioners which may be followed up by a suspension of the Proceedings.

With perfect Respect &c.

R. K.

R. King to Philip Sansom, Esq.

GREAT CUMBERLAND PLACE, Mar. 28, 1803.

SIR :

Being much pressed for time between my public engagements and the objects to which I am obliged to attend before I leave this country, I am afraid it may not be in my power immediately to wait upon all the members of the Committee of American merchants ; tho' I shall endeavour to do so before my departure.

In the mean time I take the liberty of presenting to you and them my respectful acknowledgments for the distinguished kindness and honour the Committee have conferred upon me, and I avail myself of the opportunity likewise to thank them for the information and assistance that on various occasions I have received from them during my residence in this country.

With sentiments of great personal Esteem and Respect, &c.

RUFUS KING.

R. King to Secretary of State.

No. 88.

LONDON, Mar. 28, 1803.

SIR :

My No. 86 communicated the tenour of Lord Hawkesbury's note of the 15th to the French Ambassador : the conclusion of the note refers to the demand of France for the Evacuation of Malta and declares " that the King cannot consent to its Evacuation unless substantial security be provided for those objects which in present circumstances would be endangered by that measure."

Yesterday morning the French Ambassador received a Courier with the answer of his Government which was delivered to Lord Hawkesbury in the course of the day. It contrasts the blessings of Peace with the miseries of war, and professes on the side of France a sincere desire to maintain the enjoyment of the former ; it denies the existence of any such naval and military preparations as are spoken of in the King's Message to Parliament, and in respect to the changes which are said to have taken place in the relative condition of France since the Treaty of Amiens, it affirms that the Forces and influence of France have not been increased. With regard to Sebastiani's Report, the answer justifies its publication as a necessary vindication of the reputation of the First Consul against the false and criminal imputation cast upon it in the History of the Campaign of Egypt published in London by Sir Robert Wilson, an officer in the service of his Britannic Majesty.

The answer seeks no Explanation of the substantial security upon the provision of which Lord Hawkesbury's note offers by implication to Evacuate Malta, but concludes with saying the first Consul does not take up the Gauntlet thrown down by his Britannic Majesty, and in respect to Malta, the Treaty of Amiens has definitely provided for its Evacuation by England and its Restitution to the Order of St. John.

It is natural to infer from this conclusion that the French Ambassador has orders to reiterate his demand upon this point ; the English Cabinet will refuse as before ; and as the English Forces occupy Malta, the war will probably be declared and commenced on the side of France.

The first Consul has given notice at Berlin, in case of war with Great Britain, that he shall take possession of Hanover, occupy Hamburgh and close the Elbe.

With perfect Respect, &c.

R. K.

R. KING TO R. R. LIVINGSTON, ESQ.

LONDON, Mar. 29, 1803.

DEAR SIR :

The essential clause of Lord Hawkesbury's Note of the 15, and which is cited in my last Letter, by implication declares that England is ready to evacuate Malta upon certain conditions, which are not however explained ; in other words the Note insinuates that altho' it has become impossible to execute the Provisions of the Treaty of Amiens, England is nevertheless willing to discuss with France the Terms upon which the Evacuation shall be made.

Whether the Reflexions contained in my last letter are well founded in respect to the Terms must now remain matter of mere conjecture, inasmuch as the answer of the French Government which has been just delivered, declines all inquiry and discussion concerning them and refers itself to the Treaty of Amiens, as marking out the only course to be pursued on that subject.

The Parties seem therefore to be at issue ; but as England possesses the object of disagreement will France follow up her demand that it should be surrendered by a declaration of war to enforce it ?   If not, will England do more than continue to retain Malta and go on with preparations to meet the consequences. This doubt suggests a curious state of things, but one that could not be of long duration : both Parties would expect War while each would prefer to receive rather than to give the assault ; in this situation the commencement of the war would be an affair of accident, as well as Malta of mutual recrimination.

I am not sure that it may not now be the Intention of France to proceed as tho' the armament of England had not been made. The first Consul is not obliged to renew or enforce his demand respecting Malta.   The English armament may proceed without danger to France, which may continue to dispatch Expeditions to the Colonies, leaving it to England to begin the war, should she choose to do so by interrupting them.

This speculation, for it is no more, agrees with the Rumour of yesterday and to-day from Holland, that the Expedition for Louisiana is again resumed, notwithstanding it was declared, as I have explained to you, that it was countermanded in consequence of the King's Message.

Yours faithfully,

R. K.

P. S.   I entreat you to observe great caution on this subject, as a conjecture that your information comes from me would place me in delicate circumstances.

———

R. KING TO RIGHT HONBLE. CHARLES ABBOT.

GREAT CUMBERLAND PLACE, March 31, 1803.

SIR :

Enquiring of Mr. Planta of the British Museum the best mode of preserving public Records, he gave me the first information I had received of the Report on this subject drawn up under your direction and lately printed by order of the House of Commons. As we are beginning already to suffer in America from negligence and want of care in preserving our Records and public Reports, and as the subject at this Time engages the attention of our Government, it would be of great advantage to us to possess the information contained in this Report : but as it is not published, I hope you will pardon my taking the liberty of asking you to permit me to receive two copies of this Report.

I have to make you my best acknowledgments for the Pieces respecting the population act, with which you were kind enough to supply me. Unfortunately during my absence last summer my Secretary sent some of these pieces to America, so that my set wants the Enumeration of Scotland, the Parish Registers, and the observations on the Result of the Population act.

I am almost ashamed to trouble you again upon this subject and the more so as it is out of my power to make you a return of equivalent value. I take the lib'ty, however, to send you a copy of the last census. I hope to receive in a more convenient form a few copies of this and the former census, one of which, by your permission, I will send to you.

P. S. I have found and added the first census.

With great Respect & Esteem, &c.

Rufus King.

R. King to Secretary of State.

No. 89.

London, April 2, 1803.

Sir :

Nothing farther has occurred since the date of my last ; no answer has yet been given to the note of the French Ambassador, whic hdeclines all discussion respecting Malta. Lord Hawkesbury's answer will probably be delivered to-day ; it will without doubt persist in the Determination communicated in his first note, and may disclose new and additional reasons in its support. If, as is said to be the case, the First Consul has lately made an overture to Russia for a partition of the Turkish Empire, the facts may be urged on this occasion notwithstanding the refusal of Russia to listen to the Proposal.

I still continue to believe the war unavoidable, in which England can have no expectation of a single ally. The System of Russia is pacific with less attachment, however, to France than to England. Austria is not yet recovered from the blows by which she was driven from the contest ; and Prussia will be inclined to adhere to her past Policy. Although Denmark and Sweden have been much dissatisfied with England, France contrary to her usual policy, has done nothing to secure their confidence ; while England has been endeavouring to reestablish her ancient friendship with these States ; for this purpose, she has given assurances that what is called the two Swedish Convoys shall be restored or paid for. The first which consisted of 17 Vessels was condemned, and the Envoy of Sweden has given in his claim for compensation, which amounts to sixty thousand pounds sterling ; the claim for the second consisting of 21 Vessels, and which I think is not yet presented, will be about ninety thousand pounds sterling. By cultivating the friendship of these Powers, England expects with the good will of Russia to keep the Baltic open, against the efforts that France will again make to close it. Portugal will be compelled to exclude the English trade, and Spain with all Italy must obey the orders that shall be given her.

I have sought occasion both with ministers and other leading men, since the discussion with France, to indicate the disadvantage which England has heretofore brought upon herself by the system of warfare she has been accustomed to pursue, and which has been chiefly directed against the Colonies of her enemy, which after being acquired at the expense of much blood and treasure in addition to the vexation of the commerce of Neutral Nations, have been commonly restored, enriched by English capital, at the conclusion of Peace. Instead of a warfare, liable to these objections, and which has moreover furnished an opportunity to France to appear as the friend and Protector of Neutral States, a system might be suggested that would not only avoid these disadvantages, but would materially contribute to the future prosperity of Great Britain. No Neutral Commerce would be interrupted by it, on the contrary it would serve to encrease and extend it, and when the object was once obtained, no Treaty of

Peace could restore things to their former state.   This conversation has been everywhere understood and well received, and it is my firm belief, if the war break out, that Great Britain will immediately attempt the emancipation and independence of South America.

In a late conversation with *Mr. Addington,** he observed to me, if the war happen, it would perhaps be one of their first attempts to occupy New Orleans.   I interrupted him by saying, I hoped the measure would be well weighed before it should be attempted ; that true it was we could not see with indifference that Country in the hands of France, but it was equally true that it would be contrary to our views, and with much concern that we should see it in the possession of England.   We had no objection to Spain continuing to possess it ; they were quiet neighbours, and we looked forward without impatience to events which, in the ordinary course of things, must, at no distant day, annex this Country to the United States.   Mr. Addington desired me to be assured, that England would not accept the Country, were all agreed to give it up to her ; that were she to occupy it, it would not be to keep it, but to prevent another power from obtaining it, and in his opinion, that this end would be best effected by its belonging to the United States.   I expressed my acquiescence in the last part of his remark, but observed that if the country should be occupied by England, it would be suspected to be in concert with the United States, and might involve us in misunderstandings with another Power with which we desired to live in Peace ; he said if you can obtain it well, but if not, we ought to prevent its going into the hands of France, tho' you may be assured, continued Mr. Addington, that nothing shall be done injurious to the interest of the United States.   Here the conversation ended.

I have lately received your letter of January 29th, and as soon as Lord Hawkesbury shall have named a time to receive me, which I have requested him to do, I will explain to him, in conversation, the President's views relative to the *Mississippi.*

Considering the critical state of affairs, it is much to be wished that my successor may arrive before my departure.   I shall delay taking my leave to the last moment ; and should the posture of

* Italics in cipher.

affairs in my opinion require it, I will risk the expense of detaining my vessel beyond the time in which I have engaged to embark ; in any event, I shall not leave London before the last week of the present month.

With perfect Respect,
R. K.

R. KING TO HIS EXCELLY. R. R. LIVINGSTON.

LONDON, Ap. 8, 1803.

DEAR SIR :

I have duly received your letter of the first instant. Notwithstanding the vagueness of Lord H's note of the 15th, a defect sometimes received as proof of diplomatic prudence, the result will probably shew that the note contained a fixed determination not to execute the Treaty of Amiens, so far as respects Malta ; for I am more and more persuaded that in the opinion of the Cabinet, Malta itself is the only security for those objects that would be endangered by the evacuation. In my last letter, I alluded to a verbal communication which has been probably succeeded by a written one to the same effect, and there is reason to think, that in the conversation it was plainly insinuated that the keeping of Malta by England was the only security she would receive for the objects of her solicitude. If so, and Bonaparte adhere, as you suppose he will, to his purpose not *to permit any discussion respecting Malta*, " puisque la Traité d' Amiens a pourvue á tout," the die may be regarded as thrown, and the results cannot be delayed many days. The reply of Bonaparte may be war, if it be to gain time, it will be war from hence. Liston writes that in his opinion, the Expedition for Louisiana will not proceed in the present uncertain state of affairs ; and I am inclined to believe, should it attempt to proceed, that it might meet with opposition ; England would interrupt the expedition to Louisiana, if she believe the war inevitable : and if instead of Louisiana it should be bound to Martinique, the garrison whereof is too weak to defend it, she ought likewise to stop it.

I have sent frequent and, as far as I have been able, faithful and full accounts to our Govrt. of the tenour and probable issue of the discussions between this Country and France, and shall continue to do so until my departure, respecting which I am a little embarrassed, as I have broken up my establishment, shipped my effects, and in a few days shall be under a heavy demurrage if I detain my ship.   On the whole so critical and important is the state of affairs that I shall probably detain my vessel a short time in hopes my successor may arrive, or in the interim that Reconciliation or war may put an end to the present uncertainty.*

It is much to be regretted that my successor has not been more seasonably named and at his post, as it would have been more easy to have entered upon the duties while I remained, than after my departure.   Besides the commencement of a new war is most important in respect to our Trade which shd be the object of earnest attention by our Minister here in order to prevent the mistakes which interest or omission may supply in the orders & instructions to the naval officers.

Faithfully yrs.
R. K.

P.S.—I think you may with confidence act upon the opinion that England will not evacuate Malta.   I am deceived, or their point is decided ; all must therefore depend on the First Consul who must abandon the Treaty of Amiens so far as respects Malta, or take war.   Respecting the change of Ministers, which is spoken of as ignorantly and inconsistently as the question of War and Peace, I don't think anything has been settled ; if it be war, I am of opinion that Pitt, perhaps Lord Melville, but neither Grenville nor Windham, will be employed.   Addington and Hawkesbury will remain, and who also may be more of a Problem : that is a mere personal speculation, as I really have no clue, if one even exist, to lead me to the last.

I wish to explain to you an interesting conversation I have lately had respecting New Orleans, but I am really pushed by so many personal concerns, joined to some few of a public nature,

---

* Mr. Livingston in a letter to the Secretary of State of April 11, 1803, writing of the probability of the renewal of the war and of the possible effect upon the negotiation relating to Louisiana of the interference of Great Britain, says : " I have written to Mr. King, pressing him to stay until a successor is appointed.   The moment is so critical that we cannot justify being without a Minister in England, and he is a very useful one." *Annals of Congress,* 1802-3, Appendix, p. 1127.

that I scarce find time to write to you the scraps, which always in haste I send to you, but with which I should not embarrass you, except that from all I know and conjecture, it is of considerable importance that you should know all that is passing.

R. King to Secretary of State.

No. 90.

LONDON, April 9, 1803.

SIR :

The Question of Peace or War may at this moment be decided. Lord Hawkesbury's note in reply to the refusal of France to admit of any discussion respecting Malta, is dated the 3d & was dispatched the 4th instant.

It expresses the King's regret that the French Government had declined giving the satisfaction and explanation he had demanded, and that it had accompanied *this Evasion* by a renewed demand of the Evacuation of Malta. In these circumstances, the note states that the King had deemed it expedient to order his Ambassador at Paris to ascertain whether the French Government persists in its refusal, or whether it will without delay give the satisfaction and explanation that may be calculated to maintain Peace between the two Nations.

Lord Whitworth's note to Mr. Talleyrand is probably now before the First Consul, who must recede from the ground he has taken with so much eclat, or receive a declaration of war.

With perfect respect, etc.,

R. K.

CHAPTER XVII.

R. KING TO RT. HON. LORD HAWKESBURY.

GREAT CUMBERLAND PLACE, April 10, 1803.

MY LORD :

I have the honour to send you enclosed the Draught of a Convention concerning the Boundaries of the United States, drawn up
according to the Tenour of our Conferences on this subject, and am

With great consideration &c.

R. KING.

The Draught covers nine pages of foolscap paper.

R. KING TO R. R. LIVINGSTON.

LONDON, April 12, 1803.

DEAR SIR:

I have before communicated to you the two last notes exchanged between France and this country ; the French note dated Mar. 29. concludes en resumé, "que le premier Consul ne veut pas rétirer le defit de la guerre fait par l'Angleterre (referring to the armament) et qu'il ne peut y avoir discussion sur Malte, puis que la traité d'Amiens a pourvu á tout." The English Reply dated the 3d instant declares "that his Majesty perceives with great regret that the French Govt. continues to withhold all satisfaction and explanation on the points respecting which he had complained, and at the same time it evades all discussion concerning the same, that it repeats the requisition that Malta be forthwith evacuated by his forces. In duty to himself and to the interest of his People, his M. has in these circumstances deemed it expedient to give Instructions to his Ambassador at Paris to ascertain distinctly whether the fr. Gov. is determined to withhold all satisfaction and explanation on the subject of his Complaints, or whether it is disposed without delay to give the satisfaction and explanation that in the present state of affairs shall be calculated to lead to an arrangement in respect to the disagreements subsisting between the two countries." Possessing these extracts, you will judge as well as I am able to do of the probable issue. General Andreossi last evening received a courier with Dispatches acknowledging the receipt of L. H's. note of the 3d, and saying only that they were dans un pourparler with Lord Whitworth for the purpose of hearing what he had to say.

Should the war take place, as I still think it must if the first Consul persist in respect to Malta, it is to be hoped you will have authority to assume a principle in regard to Louisiana which at all times, but more easily in time of war between England and France, we can and ought to assert and maintain. To the country West of the Mississippi we have no claim ; from the country East of it, in virtue of the irrevocable renunciation of France and the duty we owe to ourselves and posterity, we have the Right to exclude her forever ; and it is only by adhering to this principle, that we shall be able to preserve the Union and protect the Independence of our Country. Yours &c.

R. KING.

ALBERT GALLATIN TO RUFUS KING.

TREASURY DEPARTMENT, WASHINGTON, April 28, 1803.

SIR :

I have the honor to acknowledge the receipt of your favors dated 9th & 25th Feby. & 4th March 1803.

The terms upon which the House of Sir Francis Baring & Co. have consented to transact the business of this Department in London, as stated in your correspondence with them, annexed to your letter of February 25, are satisfactory ; and I fully approve of the agreement made by you in my behalf, and communicated to them in your letter of 23. February.

Permit me to express my acknowledgments for the trouble you have taken in effecting this negotiation, and for the favorable issue which has resulted from your attention to the remittance of the £70,000 to Holland. . . .

With great respect your obed. Servt.

ALBERT GALLATIN.

On May 1, 1803, Mr. King addressed a letter to the Secretary of State [1] giving an account of the state of the Negotiation relative to Bank of England stock, belonging to the State of Maryland, and which he said at that time, with accrued interest, amounted to £187,507.12.   He writes :

" I have now the satisfaction to send you the copy of a letter that I have received from Lord Hawkesbury, in which the King engages, in the event of its being decided that the title to this stock has accrued and belongs to the Crown, that the same shall be transferred to the State of Maryland, together with the accumulations proceeding from the re-investment of the dividends."

He states, however, that as late as the 27th April, though all the other claims had been settled, objections still were maintained by Mr. " Harford, devisee of Lord Baltimore, claiming as Lord Proprietor of the Province of Maryland, and, as such, entitled to all forfeitures." Mr. King says that

[1] *Annals of Congress*, 1802-3, App. p. 999.

a settlement might then have been made had he been willing
to have " engaged to transfer to Mr. Harford ten thousand
pounds bank stock." This, for reasons he gives, he declined
to do, and therefore suggests that Mr. Chase, the agent of
Maryland, be instructed how to proceed to settle all the
claims,

though it may require some time to complete the business ; but
it is a satisfaction that we hitherto have not enjoyed, that no
future change in the Court of Chancery, or in the Ministry can
alter the decision of the one or precise engagement of the other.
It would have given me great pleasure to have seen the close
of a business that is of great importance to the State of Maryland, and which has so constantly as well as zealously engaged my
attention ; but the entanglements of an intricate suit in chancery,
early and unfortunately thrown into an embarrassing situation, are
reached with difficulty by diplomatic means ; there have, moreover, been some difficulties in our way which neither patience nor
industry has hitherto been able to surmount. We may now, I think,
put our opponents at defiance, as we at length stand on secure
ground, and with a little more patience may reckon with confidence upon the attainment of the object. I shall leave with the
papers of the Legation such a view of the subject as I hope may
enable my successor with little trouble to hasten the conclusion
of this long protracted business.

There is here an interruption of the correspondence of Mr.
King, but a memorandum book supplies much interesting
matter during the closing days of his mission, which is here
given as it was written from day to day.

LONDON, May 4, 1803.

Taking Leave.

Having sent a copy of my letter of recall to Lord Hawkesbury
and requested him to apprize the King of my intention to take
my leave ; and Sr. Stephen Cottrell having by direction of Lord
Hawkesbury waited upon me to settle the mode of my going to
St. James, I had my audience of leave after the levee of to-day—
The Spanish Envoy had his audience to deliver his credentials
before my audience.

The Ceremony on entering the King's closet was the same as at my first audience. My harangue was in these words :

"Sir, Having received the permission of my Govt. to return home, as will be confirmed to your Majesty by my letter of recall, I am instructed to avail myself of this occasion to renew to your Majesty the assurance of the continued and sincere disposition of the U. S. to cherish and perpetuate the good understanding and harmony happily subsisting between your Majesty and them.

"It is the purpose of my Govt. to continue the residence of a Min. Plenipotentiary near your Majesty, whose arrival may soon be expected, and who will confirm to your Majesty the assurance that I have just now repeated.

"Accustomed as I had been to view with respect the British nation, its laws and its monarchy, my residence here has served to enlarge and strengthen this sentiment, and I shall return to my country with increased veneration for a Government which, under your Majesty's guidance, fulfills the obligations of good faith and justice towards other nations, while it secures in the highest degree to your Majesty's people those civil and moral advantages, the enjoyment of which constitutes the chief end of human society.

"I have a word more to add, which so far as regards myself requires your Majesty's indulgence, I have to offer your Majesty my respectful acknowledgments for the manner in which on all occasions you have received and considered me : and I should be unwilling to omit the opportunity of expressing to your Majesty my obligations to the noble personage (Lord Hawkesbury) who is present as well as to his noble and honourable colleagues for the candour, good faith and liberality with which they have discussed and decided whatever has concerned the interest of my country."

The King heard me with attention and replied :

"I must say, Mr. King, that I am sorry for your departure. I know nothing of the character, indeed I do not know the name, of your successor ; but be he who he may, I fear I shall have reason to regret your absence ; for your conduct here has been so entirely proper, both as it regarded the interest of your own Country and of this, as to have given me perfect satisfaction. In regard to the assurance you make me in behalf of the States, I receive it in good part ; and declare to you in return that on my side I wish for friendship and a constant good understanding with America. I have never had but one opinion on this subject since the event which separated us and I assure you now, that I will never change it. It is to our mutual advantage to be friends, and I foresee nothing that is likely to make us otherwise."

The conversation which followed was relative to the present critical posture of affairs with France. The King showed great firmness as well as confidence ; said that his first duty was to ascertain the justice of his cause; and being satisfied on this point, he should have no uneasiness for the event.

It may have been during this conversation or some other about this time, that the king, in speaking with Mr. King relative to his return home, asked him what he intended to do with his boys, who were at Harrow ? The answer must have been one stating the course he adopted of leaving them to finish their studies at Harrow, and then send them to Paris to learn French, mathematics, etc., for the king answered him, "All wrong, Mr. King; boys should be educated in the country in which they are to live."

Mr. King reports the following conversation as having occurred on May 4, 1803:

Conversing with Lord Hawkesbury respecting the Swedish Convoy and the Treaty between Sweden and Great Britain, Lord Hawkesbury said it was certainly expedient to revise the article concerning contraband, which as it now stands makes naval Stores and Provisions contraband.

In respect to naval Stores he certainly did think them contraband, while he was clearly convinced that Provisions were not so, except in case of blockade or siege, when they became with all other goods contraband. But though he considered naval Stores contraband, still in a case like that of Sweden, whose staple articles were naval Stores it was a rigorous interpretation to confiscate naval Stores and he sh^d therefore think it a reasonable practise to make use of the milder doctrine of pre-emption. I expressed my approbation of his opinions and remarked that what created the greatest embarrassment, in Treaties relative to

contraband, was their want of precision : the description should
be minute and every article should be named, as the rule is one
of practise among unlearned men, who should be under no difficulty in distinguishing the lawful from the unlawful or contraband
goods. Lord H. assented.

MEMORANDUM, May 6, 1803.

The ultimatum delivered by Lord Whitworth required him to
leave Paris on Tuesday evening May 2d, unless France should
have signed a minute by which she agreed :

1. To the military possession of Malta for 10 years by England ;

2. To the cession to England of the Island of Lampedosa ;

3. To the complete evacuation of Holland by the French
forces.

On Tuesday forenoon Talleyrand answered Lord Whitworth's
demand by a note declaring :

1. That the Island of Lampedosa not belonging to France,
the First Consul could neither object nor consent to the cession
of it to England.

2. That the occupation of Malta for 10 years being contrary to
the Treaty of Amiens was inadmissible. Were it not so, the consent of Holland and Spain, parties to the Treaty of Amiens, would
be requisite ; and even after they should have consented that the
guarantying Powers should be consulted.

3. Holland would be evacuated as soon as England shall have
executed the Treaty of Amiens, &c.

Before this answer of Talleyrand was delivered, a messenger
was dispatched to Andreossi the French Ambassador in London
for the purpose of apprizing him of its purport, and moreover to
state, if Lord Whitworth should not be satisfied, as it was supposed he would not be, with the answer, that at the last hour and
when according to his Ldp's. previous demands his passports
would be delivered to him, Talleyrand would send him a note
requesting a meeting on the next (Wednesday) morning, when
Talleyrand would offer the First Consul's consent that the military possession of Malta (notwithstanding the departure from the

Treaty of Amiens) should be given either to Russia, Austria or Prussia at the choice of England. The same messenger brought orders to Andreossi to demand his Passports grounding the demand upon Lord Whitworth's having done so at Paris ; but to say he should not use them unless Lord Whitworth quitted Paris, as he had intimated his intention of doing on the evening of the 2d ; in that case Andreossi was instructed to leave London and be at Dover by the time Lord Whitworth should reach Calais.

After Andreossi had received the Messenger which was on Friday morning he sent a note demanding his Passports and explaining the occasion as well as the manner in which he should obey them. The note stated also that Portalis, the Secy. of Legation, would remain to assist the French in returning to their country and in taking the charge of the Ambassador's effects.

At 4 o'clock I called in Downing Street, where a Cabinet council was sitting in consequence of Andreossi's note. Hammond, whom I saw, told me they had received no messenger from Lord Whitworth and were ignorant whether any answer has been given to their ultimatum, having no dispatch from him later than Monday. I then communicated to them the purport of the answer as well as the intention of detaining Lord Whitworth with a new proposition. He assured me they were entirely ignorant of these transactions and views, and then asked me to allow him to communicate in confidence to Lord Hawkesbury what I had communicated to him to which I consented. This he did and afterwards brought me Lord H's thanks, saying I had done him the greatest kindness that it was possible for him to have received. The opinion manifestly as regarded the new proposition was, that Lord W. would follow his orders and disregard it. Both Andreossi and Schimmelpenninck thought so and regarded the proposition as an indescretion useless and destructive of the principle upon which until now the Treaty of Amiens had been maintained.

Mr. Addington's communication to Parliament on Friday evening of Andreossi's having demanded his Passports and of his expectation that he should make them a communication respecting the negotiation on the following Monday (May 9.) was accompanied with a manner which proved his expectation that the war had been decided upon.

Mr. Addington moved an adjournment on Friday, May 6th, over Saturday to Monday, May 9, when he expected to make his communication.   This was opposed by the old opposition, as well as the new, and the House divided 185 for and 95 against the adjournment.

On Saturday, May 7, a messenger arrived at 4 o'clock A.M., with Lord Whitworth's dispatch, communicating Talleyrand's last proposition, which Lord W. had thought sufficient to divert him from the execution of his orders to leave Paris on Tuesday evening.   A Cabinet council was held immediately, and another messenger dispatched with the result—which was an adherance to the former demand, except that instead of requiring the explicit consent of France that England should keep Malta 10 years, the stipulation should be that she should keep it till measures should be concerted for its complete independence, with a limitation in a secret article that this possession should not exceed 10 years.

Lord Whitworth was ordered to leave Paris in 36 hours after receiving this dispatch, unless the terms were complied with.

DUKE OF PORTLAND'S DINNER.

May 8, 1803.

The Duke, Mr. Addington, Lord Pelham, Lord Hawkesbury, Lord Eldon, Lord Rosselyn, Sir Wm. Scott, Mr. King, Mr. Hammond, Young Mr. Ingersoll & myself and Mr. Merry.

Mr. Addington & Lord Hawkesbury both told me that in the event of war, instead of exposing the King to the charge of bad faith, they should be able to show that Bonaparte had resolved to break his engagements made at Amiens, and that their demands were justified as the necessary means of compelling him to observe his stipulations.

They should be able to prove, on their side, a sincere and solicitous disposition, as well as corresponding endeavours, to execute the stipulations respecting Malta, and on the side of Bonaparte not only a disinclination, but a series of efforts by dispersing the langues,* sequestering their property in France and promoting its

-----

* One of the conditions of Russia under which she would consent to a joint occupation of Malta was " provided the Maltese language be abolished, to which France agrees.—*Life and Correspondence of Rufus King* in his letter to the Secretary of State, March 19, 1803, vol. iv., p. 231.

sequestration elsewhere effectually to defeat and render of no importance the execution of this article of the Treaty. Not only these facts would be fixed upon him, but their aim and object would be demonstrated, for Bonaparte himself, in a conference he had demanded and held with Lord Whitworth, had observed to him that he judged it proper himself, in order that he might not hear the same thing from any other, to state to him that France must have Egypt ; that he had no wish nor hope to go to war to obtain it, preferring a peaceable acquisition of it ; but that Egypt must be acquired by France was not to be disguised. He should hope that England would not renew the war, but in case she did, that nothing short of invasion would be resorted to ; that undoubtedly the chances were against success—they might fail 99 times in a hundred, but the last would be fatal.

This avowal coupled with the opposition given to the execution of the Treaty of Malta (Amiens, relative to Malta ?) by endeavouring to defeat the end of the stipulations, coupled with the practices which could be fastened on Bonaparte in respect to the Ionian Islands, and coupled with Sebastiani's Report, demonstrated a settled intention and plan of bad faith, already begun to be put in execution, not less dangerous to the repose of Europe and the essential interest of England than it is calculated to depreciate and degrade the character and station of England in the face of the rest of Europe.

Both H. & A. intimated an opinion that Lord Whitworth ought to have left Paris on the preceding Tuesday. Hawkesbury was more reserved than Addington on this point : the latter said the true course for Lord Whitworth would have been to have answered Mr. Talleyrand's proposition by saying, your courier, sir, will travel faster than I shall be able to do, I therefore propose to you to forward your new proposal to your Ambassador at London ; it not being a compliance with our demands I must obey my orders and leave Paris.

RUSSIAN MEDIATION.

May 10, 1803, Tuesday.

A Russian messenger arrived today—also an English messenger from Petersburgh.

May 11, 1803, Wednesday.

The Russian Ambassador had to-day a long conference with Lord Hawkesbury. The object was to offer the mediation of his court between England and France. Ld. Hawkesbury replied that England having taken precise ground in the negotiations, which upon a well considered view had appeared essential to the national honour and interest to be maintained, in this state of affairs there seemed little prospect of any advantage to be expected from the interference of any other Power, though it would be satisfactory if such interference would have the effect to engage France to yield to those terms without which there would be no security for the continuance of peace.

CONFERENCE WITH ADDINGTON.

May 12, Thursday.

Met Mr. Addington by appointment : who after disclosing the state of the negotiation (a messenger having arrived, who left Paris on Tuesday, the day after Ld. W. had received his last instructions) and expressing his surprise that Ld. W. had not left Paris in the first instance on the 2d of May, said he would positively leave it in 36 hours after the delivery of his note unless their terms were yielded.

I then spoke to him respecting the probable cession of Louisiana by France to the U. S. He declared his hope that it had been done. I alluded to the provisional expedition to occupy N. Orleans. He said that would be wholly out of view if we acquired it, and on this point was very explicit that England would be satisfied if the U. S. obtained Louisiana.

I mentioned the embarrassment of our navigation arising out of the want of sufficient clearness and precision in the orders given to the Br. men of war and privateers, as well as from the incapacity of the W. India Courts of Prize. He replied that both these subjects should be carefully attended to in case of war. I discussed fully the subject of the impressment of seamen on the high seas. He seemed to agree with me and said he would confer again with Lord St. Vincent who hesitated in agreeing to my proposal that no such impressment should be made by either side.

Conference with Lord Hawkesbury.

12th May, 1803.

Most of the points discussed with Mr. Addington were touched upon with Lord Hawkesbury, who expressed similar opinions concerning them which were entertained by Mr. Addington. Signed with L. H. the Convention relating to the Boundaries of the U. S. L. H. seemed pleased with the prospect I held out to him that Louisiana would be ceded to the U. S.

May 13th, Friday.

Conference with Lord St. Vincent respecting the impressment of seamen on the high seas ; went over the various topics calculated to shew to him first the little importance of the principle as not more men than would man a single ship are procured in this way during a war, and the practice is one which creates irritation and bad humour in the U. S. and tends to indispose them towards England, &c. &c.

He stated various qualifications and among others that the search and impressment should be made only when a vessel last sailed from a Br. Port.

I replied that they might make such laws as they liked and institute the means of enforcing these laws, to prevent their seamen being carried out of their country by for. vessels, and if so it would not be requisite to search for them on the ocean ; they might forbid any seaman to be shipped in the Br. Dominions by a foreign vessel except with the privity and consent of some proper officer, who might be charged to prevent the shipping of Br. subjects. The officers of a forn merchant might be liable to penalty and the ship herself infected by taking away Br. seamen. In a word so far as respects their being carried away they might become prohibited like certain goods, &c.

Lord St. Vincent promised to think further on the subject and to confer with Lord Hawkesbury again. He assured me no new prize commissions should be issued to the W. Ind. judges and that measures should be taken without delay to organize the two new courts. He also promised to watch over the new orders for the purpose of rendering them as clear and precise as possible. He expressed his satisfaction at the probability that Louisiana has been or will be ceded to the U. S.

WAR.

May 14, 1803, Saturday.

At xii o'ck to-day a messenger arrived in 40 hours from Paris with dispatches from Lord Whitworth, who had on the evening of the 12th received his Passports and was to leave Paris immediately after the messenger.

The French Ambassador likewise received a courier and will probably leave London to-morrow.

Sunday, May 15, 1803.

The messenger dispatched by Lord Whitworth on the day he left Paris was charged with the communication of the Russian mediation which had been before announced here.

In the course of the day Andreossi received two or three couriers. One of them was charged with a dispatch instructing Andreossi, in case no act of hostility had taken place to insinuate thro' the Batavian Ambassador, who might make the suggestion as merely a speculation of his own, that the First Consul might perhaps leave Malta in the hands of the English for 10 years provided France should be permitted to occupy Tarento, Otranto, and such positions in the Kingdom of Naples as she possessed at the signature of the Treaty of Amiens.

If Hawkesbury listened to the overture, Andreossi was to then appear, and, not as instructed to do so, but presuming on the desire of the First Consul to avoid the war, to take on himself to sign a convention the draught whereof was sent him and which corresponded with the insinuation to be made by the Dutch Minister—but in case Ld. Hawkesbury rejected the overture, no trace was to remain of the overture.

Schimmelpenninck (the Batav. Ambass.) accordingly opened the subject under the strictest engagements of privacy to Ld. Hawkesbury, who said it was nothing new, having before been insinuated to Ld. Whitworth by Jos. Bonaparte, and that it was quite inadmissible : that he would, however, communicate with Addington, and in case he differed from him, it should be laid before the Cabinet ; in which event Schimmelpenninck was to be informed of it. As he received no such information, it is presumed that Addington and Hawkesbury agreed and no reference was made to the Cabinet. The last French courier that arrived to-day brought a letter from Ld. Whitworth who was on his journey and intended to reach Calais to-night—where he will probably await for Andreossi's arrival at Dover, in order that they might both cross the channel at the same time.

Monday, May 16, 1803.

Andreossi left London this morning at 5 o'clock. At midnight last night a messenger arrived from Lord Whitworth with a note sent after his departure from Paris and received on his route offering Malta on the same terms which the Dutch Ambassador had insinuated as his own suggestions. A Cabinet council was assembled to-day, which refused the offer on the same ground which France had done in respect to Lampedosa, and a messenger was dispatched to meet L. W. either at Calais or this side with the answer.

R. KING TO EARL ST. VINCENT.

Private.

GREAT CUMBERLAND PLACE, May 15, 1803.

MY LORD :

It seems that the die is cast ; and as the war is now unavoidable, I should return to my country with additional satisfaction could I carry with me the proposed Agreement of England relative to the impressment of Seamen on the High Seas. Did I not know that the object in itself is of small, very small importance to this Country, I should hesitate in urging it, notwithstanding the great embarrassment it has produced, and will continue to create in America.

It would be indiscreet in me to press these Reflexions in favour of a liberal policy between two countries, whose best Interests, like their Language and Laws, are the same : but as I must leave London on Tuesday, I take the liberty to ask your Lordship in a private Note, to inform me whether it be probable that the arrangement I have so much at heart can be made ?

With sentiments of the most sincere respect & Esteem

I have the honour to be &c.

RUFUS KING.

C. GORE TO R. KING.

LONDON, GREAT CUMBERLAND PLACE,
20 May, 1803.

DEAR FRIEND:

We have nothing new in London. Hammond says he is in hourly expectation of hearing of some captures, and that nothing can be done at present relative to the Convention about Seamen. This he told me yesterday afternoon. He thinks the Government here has not made so strong a case as he expected, but when questioned as to the defects of the case he could not specify them : he will doubtless be more precise after he has seen his noble neighbour. He does all that belongs to his political character in not siding with the Administn. On Monday night we (R. Pinkney & myself) go to the House, where it is presumed the debate will occupy two nights. But before then I hope and trust you will be on your way rejoicing with a fair wind & safe ship. . . .   Yours ever,

C. GORE.

The following letter, though written in New York at a later date than those among which it is placed, relates to events which occurred before Mr. King sailed, and therefore properly belongs here.

R. KING TO SECRETARY OF STATE.

NEW YORK, July, 1803.

SIR :

I take the liberty to add a few miscellaneous articles by way of supplement to my last dispatch.

As soon as war appeared to me inevitable, I thought it advisable to renew the attempt to form an arrangement with the British Government for the protection of our seamen ; with this view I had several conferences both with Lord Hawkesbury and Mr. Addington, who avowed a sincere disposition to do whatever might be in their power to prevent the dissatisfaction on this subject that had so frequently manifested itself during the late war. With very candid professions, I, however, found several objections in discussing the subject with the first Lord of the Admiralty. Lord Hawkesbury having promised to sign any agreement upon the subject that I should conclude with Lord St. Vincent, I endeavored to qualify and remove the objections he offered to our project : and finally the day before I left London, Lord St. Vincent consented to the following regulations :

1. No seaman nor seafaring person shall, upon the high seas and without the jurisdiction of either party, be demanded or taken out of any vessel belonging to the citizens or subjects of one of the parties, by the public or private armed vessels or men of war belonging to, or in the navy of the other party ; and strict orders shall be given for the due observance of this engagement.

2. Each party will prohibit its citizens or subjects from clandestinely concealing or carrying away from the territories or colonial possessions of the other, any seamen belonging to such other ports.

3. These regulations shall be in force for five years and no longer.

On parting with his Lordship I engaged to draw up, in the form of a convention, and send him these articles in the course of the evening, who promised to forward them, with his approbation, to Lord Hawkesbury. I accordingly prepared and sent the draught to his Lordship, who sent me a letter in the course of the night, stating that on further reflection he was of opinion that the narrow seas ought to be excepted, they having been as his Lordship remarked, immemorially considered to be within the dominions of Great Britain ; that with this correction, he had sent the proposed convention to Lord Hawkesbury, who, his Lordship presumed, would not sign it before he should have consulted the Judge of the High Court of Admiralty, Sir William Scott.

As I had supposed from the tenor of my conferences with Lord St. Vincent, that the doctrine of *mare clausum* would not be revived against us on this occasion, but that England would be content with the limited jurisdiction or dominion over the seas adjacent to her territories, which is assigned by the law of nations to other States, I was not a little disappointed on receiving this communication : and, after weighing well the nature of the principle and the disadvantage of its admission, I concluded to abandon the negotiation, rather than to acquiesce in the doctrine it proposed to establish.

I regret not to have been able to put this business on a satisfactory footing, knowing as I do its very great importance to both parties ; but I flatter myself that I have not misjudged the interests of our own country, in refusing to sanction a principle that might be productive of more extensive evils than those it was our aim to prevent.

Neutral Flag.

As it is possible that another attempt will be made during the present war to establish the rule that free bottoms make free goods, I ought not to omit the communication of the following anecdote :

Soon after the British armament in March past, Bonaparte sent his aid-de-camp-du-roi to Berlin, to announce his determination to occupy Hanover, and close the Elbe against England, in the event of war.   The Prussian Cabinet, a thing very rarely done, immediately dispatched a courier with orders to Baron Jacobi, the Prussian Ambassador at London, to apprize the English Government of the views of France, to impress the dissatisfaction with which Prussia had learned them, and to offer to protect Hanover and the North of Germany, provided England would give her consent to the principle that free ships should make free goods.   The English Cabinet immediately replied, that the German Empire is bound to protect the rights of its several members ; that Hanover must therefore look to Germany, and not to England, for support ; and, in respect to the proposed rule that free ships should make free goods, that no advantage nor service could be named which would be sufficient to engage England to give it her sanction.   In any circumstances this would be the opinion of England ; in the present instance, if I mistake not, the proposition was believed to have come, indirectly, from Paris.

Colony Trade.

In a very late conversation with Mr. Addington respecting the colony trade, he insinuated the probability that events might happen in the course of the present war, alluding, as I understood, to South America, that would enable England to form with us such commercial arrangements as would be satisfactory.   As

Mr. Addington meant to be obscure, I could only conjecture his meaning ; and my inference was, in case of the independence of South America, that the colony system must everywhere be abandoned—an opinion not peculiar to Mr. Addington, but one that is entertained by the principal members of the late English Ministry.

South America.

When the preliminaries of the late peace were signed, an expedition, fully prepared, was in readiness to set sail for the purpose of assisting the inhabitants of the province of Caraccas in throwing off obedience to Spain. Trinidad was retained by England, chiefly with the view of furthering this revolt ; and if Spain be drawn into the war, which she will be unable to avoid, the expedition to the Caraccas will be revived. No probable change of the Ministry of England will change this intention, for it is known to be the opinion of the first men of the nation that the secondary object of the present war, and one that must give England courage as well as resources to go on with the struggle, is the entire independence of South America.

With perfect Respect & Esteem &c.

RUFUS KING.

R. KING TO LORD HAWKESBURY.

LONDON, May 15, 1803.

MY LORD :

In the present critical posture of affairs, I lose no time in communicating to your Lordship, for his Majesty's information, that a treaty was signed at Paris on the 30th of April past, by the Plenipotentiaries of America and France, by which the complete sovereignty of the town and territory of New Orleans, as well as of all Louisiana, as the same was heretofore possessed by Spain, has been acquired by the United States of America.

In drawing up this treaty, care has been taken so to frame the same as not to infringe any right of Great Britain in the navigation of the river Mississippi.

I flatter myself that this communication will be received with satisfaction, and regarded as a new proof of the disposition of the

United States to observe towards His Majesty a spirit of amity and confidence, important at all times, and more especially so in present circumstances, to the harmony and mutual prosperity of the two countries.*

LORD HAWKESBURY TO MR. KING.

DOWNING STREET, May 19, 1803.

SIR :

Having laid before the King your letter of the 15th of this month, in which you inform me that a treaty was signed at Paris on the 10th of last month by the plenipotentiaries of America and France, by which the complete Sovereignty of the Town & Territory of New Orleans, as well as of all Louisiana has been acquired by the U. S., I have received his Majesty's commands to express to you the pleasure with which his Majesty has received this intelligence, and to add that his Majesty regards the care which has been taken so to frame this Treaty as not to infringe any right of Gr. Britain in the Navigation of the Mississippi as the most satisfactory evidence of the disposition on the part of the Government of the U. S., correspondent to that which his Majesty entertains to promote and improve the harmony and good understanding which so happily subsists between the two countries and which are so conducive to their mutual benefit.

I have it also in command to assure you, Sir, that the sentiments which you have expressed in making this communication are considered by his Majesty' Government as the additional proof of the cordiality and confidence which you have uniformly manifested in the whole course of your public mission, and which have so justly entitled you to the Esteem and Regard of his Majesty's Government. I desire you to accept of the assurances of distinguished consideration with which I have the honour to be, Sir, yr. mo. ob. Servt.

(Signed)

HAWKESBURY.

* *Annals of Congress*, 1802–3, App., p. 1150.

CHAPTER XVIII.

The following brief memorandum records the close of
Mr. King's mission to England, though he did not sail until
the 21st of May.

"May 18th. Left London for Cowes this morning. Lord
Whitworth arrived at Dover and Andreossi crossed from there to
Calais."

It was a momentous date in the history of Europe, marking as it did the absolute rupture of the peace of Amiens by
the return of the Ambassadors of England and France to
their respective countries, an event in which the United
States were deeply interested in many ways. France had
just sold Louisiana to them, and England was to renew her
commercial Treaties with a power which was not only her
rival but had shown, even under adverse circumstances, a

determination to demand for herself a fair share of the commerce of the world, and especially of the islands of the West Indies, which lay so near to her.   How earnestly and in many respects successfully Mr. King had exerted himself to establish the rights and claims of his country the correspondence which has been given will clearly show.   But it may not be amiss here to review somewhat the work he had done and to advert to the reasons which led him to ask for permission to return home at a time when his country seemed most to want the services of an able and experienced Minister.

Having served in several capacities in the early history of his country after the establishment of its Independence, in the Continental Congress, the Convention for the formation of the Federal Constitution, and the Senate after the formation of the Government, by which services he became thoroughly informed as to the history of his country, and was largely instrumental in establishing the Government on a firm basis, Mr. King felt a desire to employ his talents on another field in which he believed that he might benefit his country.   The Treaty made by Mr. Jay with Great Britain, excellent as under the circumstances it was, had defects which it was felt and decided must be met and removed, and other questions which must necessarily arise between two commercial nations, one of which had long enjoyed almost absolute control and the other seeking for its own people to share some of the profits of commerce, had to be discussed and placed upon an amicable footing.

Under the circumstances, Mr. King intimated to his friend General Hamilton that he thought he could be of use to his country in a Mission to Great Britain if the President should see fit to appoint him Minister.   President Washington, though at first objecting, not on account of any doubt as to his qualifications for the position, but because he was unwilling to name one who had been accused of holding what were called monarchical opinions, finally made the appointment of Mr. King as Envoy Extraordinary and Minister

Plenipotentiary to Great Britain. It is only necessary, as has been said here, to recall the zeal, ability, and firmness with which he performed the duties of his office to the entire satisfaction of Presidents Washington, Adams, and Jefferson, to the great advantage of his country, and with the confidence and respect of the Government of Great Britain for the courtesy and great ability with which he discussed the serious questions that constantly presented themselves. Conscious that he would be able to meet intelligently the new aspects of international relations, and perhaps to settle for many years the policy of the two countries in their commercial intercourse, he had, at an early date, reminded the adminstration of Mr. Jefferson of the approaching time for a revision of the Commercial Treaty between the two countries.

On October 8, 1801, he wrote a private letter to Mr. Madison, then Secretary of State,* saying among other things:

"It was my earnest hope, when I came hither, that I should have had, before this period, an opportunity to assist in the revision of our treaty with this country. We have sufficiently seen, and become acquainted with its operation during war; and the time is come when it is to be tried as a rule of mutual conduct in peace. If I be not mistaken, it will be found our interest on every account to aim at its revision as soon as possible. The Treaty with France may also require to be revised: ought we not to lay down a common basis for these Treaties and endeavour to form them so as to act upon common and not interfering Principles? To do so will require concert in the projects, as well as in the negotiations. Should the President confide the negotiation here to me, might there not be a considerable advantage in my receiving his permission to pass a fortnight with you at the seat of Government, or with Mr Livingston here or at Paris? If the subject have not been fully discussed with Mr. L. before his embarkation, the conferences in America would be most useful. Upon the supposition that our affairs still depending here be satisfactorily closed, I might embark in March directly for the

* *Rufus King's Life*, etc., vol. iii., p. 522.

Chesapeake, pass a fortnight in Washington, and returning by New York be here again in July."

It does not appear that any answer was ever sent to this suggestion, and therefore Mr. King must have been satisfied that, with the exception of pending questions, his services would not be called for. As an evidence of this he wrote to his friend, General Hamilton, on April 8, 1802 * :

" The Revision of our commercial treaty has been a service to which I have along looked as the conclusion of my mission. As however I have no reason to suppose it likely soon to take place, I am not much inclined to remain here a mere figurant and am therefore thinking seriously of my return. Without deciding anything on this point, I confidently ask your opinion respecting it. This I have not done except in the present instance."

This opinion General Hamilton gives on June 3, 1802,† as follows :

" In your last, you ask my opinion about a matter delicate and important, both in a public and in a personal view. I shall give it with a frankness to which you have a right ; and I may add, that the impressions of your other friends, so far as they have fallen under my observation, do not differ from my own. While you were in the midst of a negotiation, interesting to your country, it was your duty to keep your post. You have now accomplished the object and with the good fortune, not very common, of having the universal plaudit. This done, it seems to me, most advisable that you return home. There is little probability that your continuance in your present station will be productive of much positive good. Nor are circumstances such as to give reason to apprehend that the substitute for you, whoever he may be, can do much harm. Your stay or return, therefore, as it regards our transatlantic concerns, is probably not material ; while your presence at home may be useful in many ways which it is not necessary to particularize. Besides it is questionable whether you can long continue in the service of the present administration, consistent with what is due as well to your own character, as to

* *R. King's Life*, etc., iv., p. 135.　　† *Ibid.*, iv., p. 136.

the common cause. I am far from thinking that a man is bound to quit a public office merely because the administration of the Government may have changed hands. But, when those who have come into power are undisguised persecutors of the party to which he has been attached and study with ostentation to heap upon it every indignity and injury, he ought not, in my opinion, to permit himself to be made an exception or to lend his talents to the support of such characters. If, in addition to this, it be true that principles and plans of the men at the head of affairs tend to the degradation of the Government and to their own disgrace, it will hardly be possible to be in any way connected with them, without sharing in the disrepute which they may be destined to experience."

He was thus confirmed in the decision, which he had announced to Mr. Sedgwick on April 6, 1802, but he does not appear to have taken any steps to make it known until in his official letter to the Secretary of State on August 5th. In this he says * :

"It is now six years that I have resided in this country. When I left America it was not my expectation to be absent more than four years. So long as the war continued I did not think of returning home, believing that my residence here might be of some public advantage. When the preliminaries of peace were signed, I found myself engaged in a negotiation of considerable difficulty and importance, which restrained me from asking the President's leave to resign my mission. The negotiation being since completed and nothing very material remaining to be discussed in which I can flatter myself with being able to render any important service, I have to request the President to accept the resignation of my office and permit me to return home."

On the same date, August 5, 1802,† Mr. King wrote to John Marshall that though the present administration approved and desired the business settled by the convention closed upon the terms which had been offered, and of which every material point was completed before he knew the opinion of the present administration,

* *R. King's Life*, etc., iv., p. 155.　　　† *Ibid.*, iv., p. 153.

" I earnestly wish that on other and still more important concerns, its sentiments had been equally correct, as they have been
in respect to this business ; but I must disregard opinions formed
with solicitude, and after careful reflection, not to hesitate in believing this to be the case ; and it is for this reason, among others,
that upon mature consideration of my duty to the public, as well
as of what I owe to myself, I have thought it incumbent on me to
resign my Mission and ask leave to return home,"

an action which he hopes will receive Mr. M.'s approbation.

To Dr. Southgate, his brother-in-law,* August 5, 1802, he
also communicates his decision :

" It was my wish to have returned some time ago, but being
engaged in a negotiation of considerable difficulty and importance,
I have not been able until now to do so with propriety. The
negotiation which detained me being completed, and nothing of
importance remaining in the discussion whereof I can hope to be
useful, I think myself free to resign my office."

In all of the letters the same reason is given by Mr. King,
showing that though not now recalled, as the President's
advisers † had urged that he should be, he understood that

---

* *R. King's Life*, etc., iv., p. 144.

† Mr. J. C. Hamilton in his *Life of Alexander Hamilton*, vol. vii., p. 584,
makes the following note :

" Monroe to Jefferson, Richmond, April 30, 1801. 'On my return I found
Col. Taylor and some other respectable characters attending the Courts, and
from him and one or two others, who spoke of it, I understood it was in their
opinion generally expected and wished, that our present Envoy at London should
be withdrawn. *They think nothing is done unless that is done ;* that as every
calamity foreign and domestic we have experienced from Great Britain, a person known to be friendly to her interests, acquainted with our interior, able to
guide her councils and *plan her measures against us* ought *not to be left there*
under the present Administration.' This letter, in Monroe's autograph, is
stated not to have been sent. Giles also wrote to Jefferson from the same place,
June 1, 1801. 'The ejected party is now almost universally considered as
having been employed in conjunction with Great Britain, in a scheme for the
total destruction of the liberties of the people. . . . The continuation of
Mr. King in London, it is apprehended, may be attended with unpleasant
effects.' He then urged an absolute repeal of the whole judiciary system, terminating the present officers, and creating an entire new system."

the administration of Mr. Jefferson did not intend to confide to him the discussion or settlement of any other questions between the two countries than those already pending, and that, therefore, he not only could be of no further service abroad, but felt that he was not in harmony with the President and his advisers, and, therefore, he resigned his position.

It may be said, however, that as he had promised in his letter to the President, expressing his sensibility of the President's "obliging appreciation of the manner in which I have performed the duties of my office in this country," "that the like zeal and industry will continue to be employed during the residue of my mission," Mr. King continued to be actively engaged in bringing to a conclusion the matters entrusted to him. Among others was the business of endeavoring to determine with the British Government the Boundaries of the Northeastern and Northwestern parts of the United States. After many conferences with Lord Hawkesbury, he sent him a draught of a convention on the subject, which was signed by him and Lord Hawkesbury on May 12, 1803, and communicated by the President to the Senate on Oct. 24th, with the papers relating to it, for their advice and consent as to its ratification. This was not given until February 9, 1804, excepting, however, the 5th Article.* They refused to remove the injunction of secresy, as to its publication.

The most serious question remaining open was that of the Impressment of American seamen by authority of the Brit-

---

* The 5th Article related to the Northwest point of separation between the two countries. By the Treaty of Peace this was agreed to be the northwest corner of the Lake of the Woods. In the official despatch, No. 98, May 15th, 1803, communicating to the Secretary of State the fact of the Signature of the Boundaries' Convention, Mr. King says relative to the 5th Article :

"The Source of the River Mississippi nearest to the Lake of the Woods, according to Mackenzies' Report, will be found twenty nine Miles to the Westward of any part of that Lake, which is represented to be nearly circular. Hence a direct line between the North Westernmost part of the Lake and the nearest source of the Mississippi, which is preferred by this Government, has appeared to me equally advantageous with the Lines we had proposed."

ish Government in the ports of Great Britain and from vessels on the high seas. From the first day of his entering upon his mission, Mr. King, under his instructions, had urged the removal of this serious grievance and had at various times earnestly, but unavailingly, pressed the British Ministry to put a stop to these proceedings, which threatened to destroy the harmony and good-will between the two nations. Upon the establishment of peace between England and France, by the Treaty of Amiens, the demand for seamen to man the British navy being less pressing, there had been less complaint made of this unwarrantable action. But Mr. King, ever alive to the interests of his country and fearing that a renewal of the war between England and France might be attended with a repetition of those outrageous proceedings, determined to endeavor, before he sailed for home, to make a convention with Great Britain by which she might renounce the claim she made to search for and take her native citizens and those she claimed to be such, wherever she might find them, whether in the commercial or naval service of the United States.

He accordingly, as has been seen, called the attention of Lord St. Vincent to a careful consideration of the subject and seemed to have brought it to a satisfactory conclusion, for a period of five years at least, believing firmly that his mission would be crowned with this most gratifying result. But at the last moment before he sailed, his lordship interposed an objection to even that settlement by claiming that there should still be a right of search " in the narrow seas " about Great Britain. With this restriction, Mr. King preferred to abandon further proceedings as his own judgment was opposed to such a partial settlement.* Indeed, though

* Mr. Jefferson in a letter to the Secretary of State says : " With respect to the impressment of our seamen I think we had better propose to Great Britain to act on the stipulations which had been agreed to between that Government and Mr. King, as if they had been signed ; I think they were, that they would forbid impressments at sea, and that we should acquiesce in the search of their harbors necessary to prevent concealments of their citizens. Mr. Thornton's attempt to justify his nation in using our ports as cruizing stations on our

several years after, the exercise of this claim was the main ostensible cause of the War of 1812 with Great Britain, peace was made without obtaining the abandonment of the alleged right by that Government although the practice was discontinued and finally abandoned.

Mr. King had made frequent and persistent demands upon the British Government for the surrender to the State of Maryland certain shares of the Bank of England, which had belonged to that Colony before the War of the Revolution, which had been held by trustees in England, but which were finally claimed to belong to the crown, escheated when the charter of the Colony was dissolved by the war. He obtained from Lord Hawkesbury the promise that they should be paid over to the State of Maryland as soon as certain claims of Lord Baltimore's trustees were settled by law. Mr. King sailed before the decision, declaring them to be invalid, was rendered, after which the Government paid the money to the State of Maryland.

Not having been instructed by his Government, and in daily expectation of the arrival of his successor as minister, Mr. King made no appointment of a Chargé d'Affaires, so that until the arrival of Mr. Monroe, there was really no official representative of the Government in London except the Consul who had received no authority to perform other than the ordinary duties of his office. Mr. Gore explains this action in a letter to Mr. Madison, the Secretary of State.

LONDON, June 4, 1803.

SIR :

Your letter of the 6th April last came to hand on the 26th instant, a few days after the departure of Mr. King, who, you will have learnt, not conceiving it to be the intention of the President, did not name any chargé d'affaires on leaving the court.

friends and ourselves, renders the matter so serious as to call, I think, for an answer. That we ought in courtesy and friendship to extend to them all the rights of hospitality is certain, that they should not use our hospitality to injure our friends or ourselves, is equally enjoined by morality and honor."—*Jefferson's Works*, iv., p. 501, August 25, 1803.

Perceiving however from the estimate of expenses that it was possible several months might elapse before the arrival of a Minister, I thought it suitable to mention to Lord Hawkesbury, that it was to be inferred from your communication to me, that the President had contemplated Mr. King's naming some person to take charge of our affairs here, and that I feared a longer time might pass before the United States would be represented than was expected by their government.   This I did with a view of preventing any misconception that otherwise might, by possibility, arise from the absence of the usual Representative of our Government in this country, and also to inform him that under these circumstances, I should, until the arrival of a person authorised to act in a character of a Minister, take the liberty of making to him such Representations in behalf of our Government, or citizens, as the affairs might require, in cases where delay would be materially inconvenient.

To which he replied in terms of great civility and professed a perfect readiness to receive every communication I should make on these subjects and to give the same all the attention that their nature and importance might require.   .   .   .

The salary of Mr. Munro and the contingent charges incident to the business, will be all the Expense to which the U. States will be liable ; these I flatter myself will be approved by the President, whom, Sir, I pray you to assure that my Endeavours will be faithfully exerted to diminish as much as possible the inconvenience to the Government and Citizens of the United States, arising from this vacancy in the legation, which it would seem, by your letter, was not contemplated by the Government.

With perfect respect &c.

C. Gore.

C. Gore to R. King.

London, June 5, 1803.

My Dear Friend :

A few days after your departure, I received a letter of the 6th April from Mr. Madison, directed *to myself*, relative to measures adopted by himself and Mr. Gallatin to supply the deficiency in the diplomatic fund occasioned by the failure of Bird's house ;

and enclosing an estimate of the expenses &c, under the following head, " Remittances to be made to London computed for 9 months" (here followed the details). In part of the letter he says " to enable the person left in charge of our affairs on the departure of Mr. King to apply to the British Government for reimbursement of what we paid towards the expenses of the late Board at Philadelphia beyond our proportion I enclose," etc.   .   .   .

Several letters also on the subject of these remittances came from Mr. Gallatin and one from Mr. Madison on the 19th of April, directed to you, and in case of your absence to me. This latter one from M. also contained the estimate before referred to. I enclose you a copy of my letter to Mr. M., which will explain to you the course I concluded, after some reflection, to pursue. My brother Pinkney from whom as you know I had something to apprehend, had it been thought advisable to accede to your proposal, was consulted and he approves of the conduct thought proper to adopt. He imputes this *façon*, as the french would say, of acting in the Government to a promise either express, or so strongly implied as to amount to the same thing, from the President, or Mr. M., or both, to name Erving chargé here, on your taking leave ; which, on more mature consideration, they had thought proper to abandon, and thus have involved themselves in a dilemma, that possibly they had hoped might have been avoided by your naming me ; though this event they certainly had no reason to expect. I learn from another quarter that E., in contemplation of your naming me and my undertaking to act, had prepared a regular protest, which he had intended to publish against such unwarrantable assumption of a character by you and me contrary to the will and disposition of the Government of the U. S.

The course I have adopted appears to me under all the existing circumstances it was my duty to pursue, and which I do not think the Government or my friends can censure. If they do, I feel justified myself, and that is a consolation to be secured at all events. It was stated to me that if I chose to assume the character, there would be no objection here. But I absolutely declined, and prayed it to be so distinctly understood. This forms no part of my communication to Mr. M., and you will of course suffer it to rest with you, who know all my feelings and inclina-

tions on this and every other subject. Lord Hawkesbury invited
me to his dinner yesterday and I attended that after having first
paid my respects at court. In the line of etiquette and ceremony,
this is all I shall probably ever feel it necessary to do. To some
people it might be matter of great importance to know that the
King and Queen made very particular enquiries after them and
professions of good will ; you may estimate them at what rate you
please, but this was the fact.

Pinkney and myself heard the debate on the proposed address
in answer to the King's message informing the house of the
departure of L^d. W. from Paris. Mr. Pitt was brilliant and exceedingly delighted the house. Hammond thought if you could have
entertained an idea how great it was, you certainly would have
remained to hear it. Fox did not speak till the second night,
and it was by far the best speech I ever heard him deliver, and in
my opinion the most pernicious that he or any other man could
have uttered. No doubt remains that the Doctor intends to carry
on the Government without Mr. Pitt, who, as far as I can judge,
does not seem to me to have injured the present administration,
or to have benefitted his own party by the debate on Friday
night. Lord H. evidently advanced himself in the public opinion
by his reply. . . .

The following extracts from a letter from Mr. Gore to his
friend Mr. King will show something of the condition of
affairs in London after his departure and before the arrival
of a successor.

C. GORE TO R. KING.

LONDON, July 2, 1803.

. . . We have nearly finished our awards ; I mean all that
will be ready for us before the 15th of July ; which will comprise
the whole of the cases, except about 20., and I do not yet despair
of completing these and returning this autumn. Eustis has given
me to understand that my character has been culumniated at
Washington for the disposition I have manifested to protract the
commission ; that it would have been earlier closed had it not

been for me, and that Pinkney was determined to get through the Southern cases & return home. In some philippic, which he made at the Board, I did say that I felt it my duty to remain & close the commission, at the same time saying that it was unnecessary for me to remark that no diligence or exertion of mine would be wanting to bring the business to as speedy a termination as possible. I do not believe that such a base and unfounded slander as this could have intentionally originated in him. You know better than any man, but no one can tell all the contest I have had in my own mind for the last five years, between a sense of duty which, according to my judgment, constrained me to remain and endeavour to perfect what I had undertaken, and a desire to return, a desire prompted by the strongest interests, which called me home, and rendered extremely ardent by constantly experiencing the mortification and disgust of so inglorious a station. I do not know on reflection, a single thing I could have attempted, which has not been to expedite the business, & least of all did I expect such an imputation; however it gives me no pain, so perfectly satisfied am I not only of its falsehood, but also that no man of common honesty will ever give it currency & that none of common sense can give it credit. . . .

Lord H. sent me notice some time since that passports would be granted at the alien office to such of our citizens as desired to go to France, on receiving one from me. On this I requested Hammond that the alien office might be directed to grant them on Erving's, & informed him, H, explicitly that I could not and should not grant any. When Lord H. sent me notice of the blockade of the Elbe, he included a desire that I would notify the same to our consuls, which I accordingly did. Erving replied to me that he should receive no official communication whatever from me, & that he had written to Lord H. requesting his Lordship to signify to him if this was a communication from his Majesty's Govt. I understand from P. that such was his determination, had I been left chargé d'affaires by you.

Young Mercer informs me he has a letter from Govr. Monroe, informing him that the Governor has received his commission as Minister &c. to this court, and that he will be here in a few days; and that Livingston is also about to pay a visit to this country. . . .

The boys from whom I received letters yesterday, are perfectly well. We shall go to their Speechday, which is next Thursday. James, from whom we heard about ten days since, was then in good health & spirits. London is become quite empty ; to us it has been so ever since your departure. My wife writes to Mrs. King, and I pray you to offer to her and Edward my affectionate regards & to believe me

Ever your assured friend

C. GORE.

R. KING TO JOHN ADAMS.

AT SEA, 22 June, 1803.

SIR—

On the 16th of last month the King of Great Britain sent a message to Parliament announcing the termination of the discussions with France, and calling on them to support him in his determination to employ the power & resources of the nation in opposing the spirit of ambition and encroachments of the Government of France. Letters of marque had been issued against France, and I conjecture that orders have likewise been given to detain the Ships of Spain & Holland, until it be ascertained whether these powers would be able to maintain their neutrality. The King's Message was ordered to be taken into consideration on the 23d. We sailed from Cowes on the 21st so that I can give no account of the sense of Parliament. I take the liberty to send you the English declaration and a copy of the correspondence which was laid before Parliament.

With great respect I remain &c

RUFUS KING.

P. S. The English Ambassador had returned to London from Paris, & the French Ambassador had left England before we did

CHAPTER XIX.

Mr. King reached New York after a long voyage on the last day of June, as we are informed by the announcement in the *Evening Post* of Friday, July 1, 1803.

" The honourable Rufus King, our late Minister to the Court of Great Britain, arrived yesterday with his family in the John Morgan from London. He came on shore in the afternoon and was met, on landing, by a large number of our most respectable citizens, who had assembled to welcome his safe return to his native country. No expressions of respect towards this gentleman can do justice to his eminent talents and the unremitted attention with which he has so assiduously guarded the rights and watched over the interests of our nation.   May he long enjoy in the gratitude of his fellow citizens the reward of his great and useful services."

Among the gratifying evidences of welcome to America, none could have given Mr. King more pleasure than the following from his old friend and constant correspondent:

GEORGE CABOT TO RUFUS KING.

BOSTON, July 1, 1803.

MY DEAR FRIEND :

We hear from New York that Mr. King is arrived and confirms our accounts of war ; the first gives me unmingled pleasure—the last excites a mixed sentiment of joy and anxiety.   I have constantly believed that the struggle between France and England must continue until the power of the former is effectually abridged, *or the latter falls.*

You can judge best of the issue, but after every allowance for the immense advantages of force on the side of France, with all continental Europe at her disposal, and the wishes of all the fools and knaves throughout the universe on her side, I entertain great hopes and confidence in the final success of England.   She has means and motives sufficient which I trust will not be unavailing for want of talents to employ them. . . .   The cession of Louisiana is an excellent thing for France.   It is like selling us a Ship after she is surrounded by a British Fleet : it puts into safe-keeping what she could not keep herself, for England could take Louisiana in the first moment of war without the loss of a man. France could neither settle it nor protect it ; she is therefore rid of an encumbrance that wounded her pride, receives money and regains the friendship of our populace.

I pray you to make my best regards acceptable to Mrs. King. I think you too wise to seek public honors, & I hope you are too patriotic to shun them if they seek you.

Your faithful and affectionate friend

GEORGE CABOT.

P. S. An expression which I well remember in a letter from you after your visit to Paris, leads me to expect the pleasure of seeing you here—I know nothing of the objection which may exist to your executing such an intention, and I can assure you it would give infinite pleasure to a great many people here & especially to me.

Mr. King, as a letter to Mr. Gore informs us, wrote on July 2d to Mr. Madison, the Secretary of State, informing him of his arrival and offering to go to Washington if required to report to the Government. He received a reply which is here given and in consequence of it did not make a visit to the capital. It is quite probable that he did not particularly desire, under all the circumstances, to go to Washington, and he certainly felt relieved when he found that he was not required to make the visit there.

JAS. MADISON TO R. KING.

Private.

WASHINGTON, July 5, 1803.

DEAR SIR :

I recd. by the mail of last evening yours of the 2d instant. I do not know that any rule has been established which requires public ministers on their return to the U. States, to repair to the seat of Government. Where no public considerations make such a visit important, and it would be inconvenient to the individual, it could not reasonably be exacted as a mere tribute of respect. In your case it is readily conceived that your time must be claimed by private arrangements ; and altho' personal explanation might not be without a value, it does not occur that they would turn on any points, on which your written communications are not, or will not be sufficient. The ideas of the President on the subject accord with those here expressed, and I have the pleasure to add that he appears to be too well satisfied of your respectful dispositions, by manifestations already given, to need any farther testimony which might be afforded by a trip to the seat of Government.

I have seen the Secretary of the Treasury as you wished. He will take into consideration the subject referred to him, with every favorable disposition, which his construction of the law will permit.

Very Sincerely & respectfully I remain Dr. Sir
yr. most obedt. hble. servt.
JAMES MADISON.

Your letter of June 22, with the several other letters & papers forwarded at the time have been duly recd. A letter from Havre of May 15, promises, by a vessel which was to sail for N. York a few days after, despatches from our Minister at Paris, by a confidential Bearer. The 19th of April is the date of the last which have yet come to hand.

It is evident from this that Mr. King prepared, while on board ship, a report of the final days of his mission, which he forwarded to Washington at once upon his landing in New York, and to which on the ——— July he added the supplement which appears on the 259–262 pages of this volume.

ALBERT GALLATIN TO R. KING.

TREASURY DEPARTMENT, July 6th, 1803.

SIR :

I had the honor to receive your letter of the 2nd instant, and have directed the Collector to permit the entry of your baggage &c., as free from duty. Although some doubt was at first entertained on that subject, I feel a conviction that this decision is consistent with the spirit, & not forbidden by the letter, of the law.

Permit me to embrace this opportunity of returning my sincere thanks for the manner in which you transacted the business of this Department, with which, foreign as it was to the duties of your mission, I was obliged to trouble you.

I have the honor to be with great respect
Sir, your obedt. Servt.
ALBERT GALLATIN.

THE HONBLE. RUFUS KING
NEW YORK.

John Jay to R. King.

BEDFORD, July 6, 1803.

DEAR SIR :

By the last post we were informed that you and your family had arrived at New York in good Health. I congratulate you very sincerely on this agreeable Termination of a long absence from your country. From the Recommencement of Hostilities in Europe, I fear you have left London too soon ; but that consideration loses a part of its weight from the Reflection that if proper counsels prevail, your Presence here will not be unproductive of advantages.

A series of circumstances, not very important and yet not uninteresting, have ever since my Removal to this place, made it inconvenient for me to leave it. Many inducements urge me to visit New York & the pleasure of seeing you is now added to the number. I hope and expect the circumstances alluded to will not be of much longer duration.

Be pleased to present my best Compts. to Mrs. King.

With great Esteem & Regard I am, &c.

JOHN JAY.

Joseph Hale to R. King, N. Y.

BOSTON, July 7, 1803.

DEAR SIR :

Permit me to congratulate you on your safe return to New York ; although the existing state of Europe requires on our part a different representation at the Court of St. James than I apprehend we shall possess, presuming upon the probable character of your successor there. In wealth & in various improvements you will find the U. S. to have made great advances since you left us. I wish it could be added that they had equally advanced in political wisdom. Our retrograde movements in that respect are the more to be regretted when we contemplate the actual state of Europe.

By this Post you will receive from me our Anniversary Oration by a Son of Judge Sullivan. We think well of the performance, although it recommends uniting with England against France ; it is even in that view more correct than the memorial imputed to our Minister at St. Cloud. If the Oration reaches you, the postage will not be expensive, as one side of the package is left open. Its sentiments in general you will not disapprove.

Be pleased to present my best respects to Mrs. K., and believe me, Dear Sir,

With the highest respect and attachment &c.

JOSEPH HALE.

Mr. Payne is married & gone with his Lady to Balls-town Springs.

J. Q. ADAMS TO R. KING.

DEAR SIR: BOSTON, 8 July, 1803.

I have just received your favour of the 5th inst., inclosing two letters from Lord & Lady Carysfort, for your care of which and the parcels which accompanied them, please to accept my best thanks. The parcels may wait for a convenient and safe opportunity ; and one of them being a brittle article, will require care in the conveyance.

I enclosed some weeks since, a letter from you enclosing a list of the debtors to Bird, Savage & Bird, in this country ; and information of the great obligation for which I was indebted to you, with Mr. Gore and Mr. Williams, in taking up for my honour the bills I had drawn upon that house. About two months ago, I made a remittance to Mr. Williams, adequate to discharge the whole of his advances for me on that occasion. Whether it will ever be in my power to repay his and your act of friendship, in taking the heavy charge of the bills, and saving me from the additional burthen of protest damages I know not ; but that I shall ever retain a grateful sense of your kindness I do know, and hope you will never have reason to doubt.

I am happy to have this occasion of congratulating you upon your return to our native country, where I hope you will find a residence still more agreeable and satisfactory than that of the period you have past in Europe. With my best regards to Mrs. King, I remain,

Dear Sir, faithfully yours

JOHN QUINCY ADAMS.

G. Cabot to R. King.

Boston, July 9, 1803.

My dear Sir :

I received from you at the beginning of this week, the Declaration of the British Government & their correspondence with France, and I take great pleasure in observing that so much dignity & firmness as well as moderation, has been displayed by the British Ministry. Had I known the secrets however I shou'd have trembled lest matters shou'd have been given up, which would have been of more consequence than all the conquests of Great Britain and 20 sail of the line besides. Malta is the spot *intended by Providence*, for G. B. to enable her to cover Egypt, the Levant and Adriatic—to watch Toulon and observe the whole Mediterranean. Nothing should tempt G. B. to yield it to France, while France remains so formidable. . . .

Our jacobins have already indulged their French feelings—they allow that the success of England—at least in defending herself—is necessary to keep France from troubling us ; yet such is their profligacy and their hatred that they would rather risk the liberty of our country, than see the English beat the French.

I hear very seldom lately from our friend Hamilton, whom you know I love *excessively ;* when you see him, I pray you tender him my affectionate regards, & believe me ever with sincere attachment

Your faithful,

George Cabot.

John Adams to R. King.

Quincy, July 10, 1803.

Dear Sir :

I duly received his Britannic Majesty's Declaration and a List of Papers presented to Parliament, with the kind Letter you did me the Honor to write me on the twenty-second of same. With great sincerity, I thank you, Sir, for this instance of your polite attention to me, and for a great number of others of a like kind during your Embassy in England. I was so situated that I could not acknowledge the Receipt of many Pamphlets of an interesting nature, which you were so good as to send me.

Your conduct during your whole residence in England, so far as it ever came to my Knowledge, was so entirely satisfactory to me and so highly honorable and beneficial to your Country, that I cannot but regret the necessity you found yourself under to return. This however does not prevent Mrs. Adams from joining with me in most cordial Congratulations with you and Mrs. King on your fortunate voyage and perfect health.

I ought not to conclude this Letter without expressing to you my most hearty Thanks for your Friendship to my son. With great Esteem,

I am, Dear Sir, your obliged Friend &c.

JOHN ADAMS.

R. KING TO C. GORE, LONDON.

NEW YORK, July 10, 1803.

MY DEAR FRIEND :

We are not yet removed to our own house owing to the difficulty and delay in receiving our baggage, &c. from the ship ; but as Mr. Gallatin has given an order that all our effects shall be delivered free of duty, and we expect the ship will be discharged of her cargo tomorrow, we shall in a few days, as we expect, be in our own house. I regret to have sold my house in town, as I cannot buy a smaller and less convenient one for the money I received and as I want it to put my furniture in ; we have put every thing in a fire proof store, where it must remain till I settle myself. I adhere to the project of a country establishment and a small house in town ; but I will not be in a hurry about either.

The glass is above 80, and we are very sensible to the heat, more so than formerly. . . . As yet the city is healthy and we hear nothing of yellow fever here or elsewhere.

Govt. has not yet received any despatches from Paris relative to Louisiana—the last dates from thence are April 19. My imperfect Report is all they know of the Business in this Country.

As far as I learn the opin. of our friends here, they regard the Cession as an event of gt. importance, especially as it gives us the control of the Mississippi. I don't perceive that any importance is annexed to the acquisition west of the River ; the subject is little understood and the pour and the contre not yet discussed

—on the whole it seems agreed on all sides that the measure will operate in favour of the present administration; whose authority and popularity extend themselves in every quarter. In this State, I understand that the federalists failed everywhere in the late Election; and even in Connecticut & Massachusetts they are gradually losing credit—at least such is here the opinion among even our friends. . . .

I offered to go on to Washington if required, and I received a civil answer wh. leaves me at liberty to stay at home. So far as regards myself personally they are desirous to receive and treat me with kindness and even distinction.

Once more yrs.

RUFUS KING.

T. SEDGWICK TO R. KING.

BOSTON, July 12, 1803.

MY DEAR SIR:

Among the congratulations which you will receive, on your arrival, none are more sincere than those I have the pleasure to give you. Many public as well as private considerations conduce to render this a pleasing event; and among them the expectation, and I am confident it is well founded, that I shall enjoy the satisfaction, within twelve months, of saluting you as Governor of New York. However improbable this event may appear to you, I have no doubt that it is in the power of your friends, or in other words the friends of sound principles, to secure it; and to men of that description, there is nothing which they ought to deem more desirable. Perhaps the station may not be an object of your wishes, tho' I think there is none in our country which can afford to a disposition such as yours so many sources of gratification. Whatever may be your own feelings, I hope you will think that you are so much of public property that your friends have a right to dispose of you at their pleasure.

When I began this letter, I had intended only to have given you, what indeed you cannot want, assurances of the continuance of my esteem & friendship, and I insensibly expressed my sentiments on a subject, on which I have long & anxiously reflected. I am now on my way from the eastward where I saw two of your brothers, and was much pleased with both. Assure Mrs. King that I cordially sympathize with her in the pleasure she enjoys in returning to her native city & in seeing the improvements which have taken place in her absence.

I am sincerely & affectly. yours

THEODORE SEDGWICK.

GOV. JOHN T. MERCER TO R. KING.

IN COUNCIL CHAMBER, ANNAPOLIS,
July 12, 1803.

SIR :

The Letter you did me the honor to address to me of the 10th of May last, enclosing a Copy of your Communications to the Secretary of State, under the 1st of May, has been duly received and communicated to the Council ; and permit me to offer to you my sincere thanks for the zeal, ability and perseverance which you have manifested in prosecuting the just claims of the State.

Your communication will be submitted to the Legislature at the commencement of their next Session—from the expression of their sentiments, those acknowledgments can only be derived, which coming from the immediate Representatives of the People, must prove most satisfactory to yourself.

I have the honor to be with much respect

Your obedient Servant

JOHN T. MERCER.

C. GORE TO R. KING.

LONDON, July 13, 1803.

MY DEAR FRIEND :

. . . We were at Harrow on the 7th, Speech day, and found the boys in perfect health & spirits. They come to London a fortnight hence. I have not heard from James for a long time. Barlow, whose cause is now decided and favourably for him, will go for Paris shortly, that is to say, when he receives his award, which may be within ten days, & by him we shall write.

Our awards are made to the number of 291, and to-morrow we shall execute those that are ready, which are 13 more. These will bring the amount of *cases* awarded on beyond 300. The number of awards will be about 500 ; and the remaining cases will be about thirty : of these all are decided by the Board and referred to the merchants excepting eight. Some of them, though only provisionally, not being yet reported on by the Registrar and merchants. The aforementioned eight will be referred within a few days. The British cases are to be acted on next week. We want about seven or eight reports from the Courts, and there are five or six cases only pending. The money will be ready & paid at the treasury either on the 15th, or within a day or two after. I sometimes have strong hopes of being able to quit this autumn, and have bespoke the refusal of the Galen's cabin ; but the objection to closing are in reality considerable, and there is not everywhere a strong disposition to remove them.

Monroe is expected here daily as your successor. Pinkney has received instructions and authority to act as agent of the Maryland Bank Stock Concern, from the State of Maryland, and credentials from the Prest. of the U. States to act also in his name on this behalf. P. tells me as his belief, that M. is to come here, be received, appoint a chargé d'affaires & then go to Spain. The papers tell you all, at least as much as I could about the Russian mediation &c. The Spirit of the country is evidently and generally rising ; and it is already much beyond the temper of the administration—Mrs. Gore enjoys her health tolerably considering that we are confined to London. We miss you and Mrs. King more and more every day. We are in many respects alone—I can truly say that in many things & on many topics I have none to communicate with, for though with these that are here I agree in part, yet not in all, & for a free communication on many subjects this is necessary. I am heartily tired, and never felt more anxiety to be away than at this moment. My wife desires her affectionate regards, and I pray you present mine and hers to yours & Edward.

Yrs. truly

C. G.

Miss Burnley is dead.

The expression of welcome made to Mr. King on his arrival at New York was renewed some days afterwards by a public dinner in his honor, of which the following account was given at the time :

New York, July 13, 1803.*

A select company of the most respectable citizens, without regard to political distinctions, principally merchants, amounting to about 200, gave a public dinner to our late Ambassador at the Court of Great Britain as a mark of respect.

Mr. King gave as a Toast " The City of New York—Prosperity and harmony to its citizens."—After his retiring, Mr. Varick offered the following toast, which was drunk with six cheers.

Rufus King—May foreign nations ever recognize in the American Envoy the firm Patriot, the able and dignified Statesman.

R. King, New York, to C. Gore, London.

July 22, 1803.

Dr. Sir :

To day & yesterday the heat, which has been excessive since the beginning of the month, has moderated and we cease to be in the fluid state in wh. we have been during the last fortnight. Although we have been a week at housekeeping, we are not yet settled, and another week will be requisite before we shall begin to feel at home. As the coloured woman we brought with us, and who was to cook for us, very soon rebelled, and has been dismissed, we have taken a French cook, who is to go to market and cook our dinners. His soups are good and should no grave objections on the score of finance arise, we may do very well with him, we give him $20. a month &c.—Every one tells us that the real difficulty proceeds from the ill manner in which you are served by your servants, and from what I have already seen it is plain that servants are not only worse here than with you, but much worse than 10 years ago here.

Edward & Frederick are well ; the latter has suffered a little from the heat, but is now recovered. Mrs. K. also is well and already growing fat. I have been very sensible to the heat, but by keeping at home and quiet as much as possible, I have been well.

* *The Evening Post*, July 13, 1803

I find a little embarrassment for the want of my books, &c. and as my term where I am is short, I think it not prudent to open my trunks, and the more so, as I have no room or place to put my books up, and looking round for houses and enquiring their prices and rents, I feel sorry that I sold my house ; tho' I did not like it, yet it would have been very convenient for me on my first return and until I could have actually set myself down more to my mind.

I can send you no news, except that it is known that the Louisiana purchase is to cost us 15. mill. Dol.—3,750,000 whereof is to be paid to our own people. Our friends say the money is no object. But I am sure that the Govt. may feel not a little embarrassed with this part of the Business—the view we entertained of the acquisition in England seems to be that wh. our friends here have adopted ; that we do not want Territory over the River & that the Floridas and New Orleans ought to satisfy us. . . .

Gen. Smith of Baltimore was here a few days ago, and assured me that he had no knowledge who is to be my successor at London : This is the case with all those I meet with. But a common persuasion seems to destine Mr. Livingston or Mr. Monroe for the Mission to London. I hear nothing further of our friend Pinkney's appointment. . . . I wrote a private letter to Madison saying I did not know the usage, whether our Minstrs. were expected to visit the seat of Gov. on their return, intimated that I desired not to be deficient in respect, and that I wd. cheerfully proceed to Washington, if he was of opinion that my omitting to do so wd. be thought in the slightest degree disrespectful —I recd. a very satisfactory answer, which dispensed with my journey.

Yrs.

R. K.

C. Gore to R. King.

London, July 29, 1803.

My dear Friend :

It is with real sorrow that I have to inform you of the rebellion breaking out in Ireland, and at a time the most unexpected. All persons had flatter'd themselves, that the country was radically mended ; even the old opposition, that was fond of exaggerating rather than diminishing the evils England had to contend with, was constrained from the evidence of their friends, who visited that island, to believe that Irishmen were gratified with the change, and were sincerely & heartily disposed to resist the common enemy. The newspapers give you the particulars of the tragical scene of Dublin, and rumour leaves no room to doubt, that the first accounts will be found short of the real horrors, that disgrace these wretched people.

The true English spirit continues to rise, and I have a confidence that this and their resources will prove equal to the tremendous conflict they are entering upon. The northern powers are remonstrating with acrimony, as I learn, against the shutting of the Elbe, and Monroe told me yesterday that the Weser was also blockaded, but I see no account of it in the papers, neither do I learn that it is true from others.

This gentleman arrived here about a week since. Before his arrival I received a letter from Parker, saying M. had a strong wish to live in the house you occupied, that he might be near us, and of his great respect and warm desire to live on the most cordial terms &c., &c., &c. All this I trust was duly estimated. The day after I learnt that he was in town, I paid him my respects, stated to him what I knew of the business of the Legation &c., and the next day sent him the letters, which had been received since your absence, and apprized him that all the papers belonging to the embassy, and left by you, were here. The day before yesterday he returned the visit, & on the same day we dined together at Mr. Hope's. Sir T. B. was there. He said that Bingham, who was at Tunbridge Wells, had written to desire that they would be particularly attentive to M. An answer was returned that they always were to Americans of distinguished character, whatever was their party. B. came to town yesterday to pay his respects. He did not, till he met M. in Paris, know he was so able & so moderate a man. I cannot waste a sheet of paper on this son of Wealth, but suffice it to say, he admires France & Frenchmen, thinks England weak and foolish in the extreme in going to war, and that nothing but the earnest desire of the present administration to unsheath the sword, occasioned the contest.

The boys are here in perfect health & good spirits. They are not yet absolutely settled at the Abbé's,* but will be next week ; they have already slept there and will take their beds with him to-night. We wrote to James today—Mrs. Gore sends to Mrs. King his last letter.

I ought to have told you what you will know without, though, that if Mr. M. asks for any information which I can afford, it will be cheerfully given—if not, I shall by no means intrude myself, or my opinions upon him. I most seriously feel your absence. There is not in England a man with whom I can talk confidentially, and even on subjects that perhaps do not admit of any great difference of opinion, one is obliged to be on their guard, lest misconstructions should be made. Our board must adjourn to the first Monday of December. There are a few cases yet before the courts ; and our brethren will not consent to act on them until that process is ended. We have sent a list of the awards to the Govt., and every individual in whose favor they are made, and submitted to them the propriety of printing it. The number of awards is 467—of cases 300. The amount of these is £1.083.990. 3.8. ; forty two cases remain to be acted upon, all of which, except about half a dozen have been referred to C. & P. for report : such as are perfect in relation to the judicial remedy, absolutely ; and such as are not, provisionally.

I may possibly go to France. After the motive of gratifying my wife, I have very few to go there, but then none exist to detain me here, and many make me desire to be absent. The British treasury paid on the day, viz. 15. July, and the few we have to make I entertain no doubt will be paid, the first instalment on presentation & the others when due.

My affectionate regards to Mrs. King & the children, ever Sincerely yours

                                        C. G.

R. King to C. Gore, London.

Dear Sir :   New York, Aug. 12, 1803.

. . . I have satisfactorily ascertained that Mr. Livingston or Mr. Monroe, as may be settled between themselves is to succeed

* They were here during the vacation to study French.

me at London. . . .   Monroe is authorized to buy the Floridas of Spain or whoever is the owner, provided he can make the purchase in a certain sum in 6 pr cents.   It is expected as I hear that the Impost will be sufficient to pay the Interest of this adn. to the public Debt without new Taxes.—A loan will be made to raise the money to pay the Debt owed by France to our own people and which we have assumed.   It is matter of speculation why this Debt was not payable in 6 pr cent stock instead of money. It was without doubt the expectation of Govt. here that such would have been the arrangement, and the creditors would have had no ground of complaint.

I am so little in the way of hearing what pub. opinion is that I can tell you nothing precise respecting the Purchase of Louisiana. In the papers that I see, I observe some doubts are beginning to arise both as to the utility and prudence of the measure, and it would not surprise me if a considerable difference of opinion should exist in the Senate & H. of Reps.

The measure must be the subject of very extensive future examination, provided, as I understand to be the case, an amendment of the Constitution will be requisite to enable Congress to receive the ceded territory into the Union. . . .

R. K.

RUFUS KING TO C. GORE, LONDON.

NEW YORK, Aug. 20, 1803.

MY DEAR SIR :

. . . I do not think you could, without impropriety, certainly not without public inconvenience, have declined to act as far as you have consented to do—if your own feelings had not forbidden it, I should have seen nothing remiss in your assuming the character which the Gov. supposed you to fill.   I hear nothing more of my successor *—tho' as I have before informed you, I do conclude that Livingston or Monroe will go to London. Since the indiscreet publication of the unsound as well as unwise and impolitic memorial of the former (I allude to the memorial respecting Louisiana presented to Bonaparte in September

* This seems very extraordinary, as Mr. Monroe was actually in London, acting as Minister, on the 18th of July. See Mr. Gore's letter, August 24, 1803.

last) his situation there will be less agreeable than otherwise it might have been; and in regard to Monroe, P. Porcupine will make him uneasy & in some degree put him out of good company, by republishing with comments an article from his unwise and stupid performances. If Mr. Jefferson would do as he ought, he would appoint you as my successsor. . . .

Washington is at this season deserted—from the fixed opinion that no one from the North or from the high country of the South, can pass the months of August and September there without intermittent or bilious fever. Mr. Gallatin informs me that no considerable progress is made in building the City, and were the Govt. in New York or Phil. it would not think of moving to Washington. To leave it, however, is another matter. Our City continues to be scourged with the yellow fever : it is probable that upwards of 20.000 of the Inhabitants have retired to the country & the quarters of the city, where the influence is supposed to have most prevailed, are evacuated, and in consequence of their Removal, fewer cases happen than otherwise wd. take place—hitherto not more than 18 new cases, nor more than 9 deaths have taken place any one day ; but from the severity of the attack in a plurality of cases, the Effects of the Disease are more and more alarming than formerly. Men in perfect health to all appearance, and who are engaged in their business as usual, are seized and die in the course of 40 hours. The same disagreement & hesitation, as to the mode of treatment which have heretofore existed among our physicians, continue to prevail, & the patients unhappily have less confidence of recovery in consequence of this bad state of things. I have no hope of the fever ceasing before the frost ; but as the City will daily become less populous, I am in hopes that the total mortality may not be very great, tho' we have many weeks of suffering to endure before the setting in of the frost. Our other cities are healthy and free from fever. . . .

R. KING.

P. S. So far as I hear little is said abt. Louisiana. The article wh. secures to French & Spanish produce & manufactures arriving in French or Span. Bottoms the Privilege of paying no higher Duties than the like Articles wd. pay, if imported in Amer. Bot-

toms, confirms the Privilege to the Ports within the ceded country, and limits its duration to twelve years ; it moreover restrains
the U. S. from giving the same advantages during the twelve
years to any other Country.   Perhaps the article is as impolitic,
as I believe it to have been an unnecessary, one, but I cannot
think an unjustifiable one, since the Treaty with Eng. must be
supposed to refer to the Territories of the U. S. at its date, and
since, moreover, the Privilege must be regarded as a part of the
Price to obtain the cession ; it wd. have been more wise to have
communicated the article to G. B. in the first instance, but I am
persuaded she will see it in its true light.   .   .   .

CHAPER XX.

C. GORE TO R. KING.

LONDON, August 24, 1803.

MY DEAR FRIEND :

We rejoice sincerely that you arrived safely and in so short a
passage. From the winds here, apprehensions were entertained
that your patience would have been put to a greater trial. Our
weather has been extremely hot, and since the middle of June, we
have had scarcely any rain. The Boys are quite well ; they are
at the Abbé Ruffini's. They with Williams & Cabot dine here to-
day, and Cabot sails in the morning. They do perfectly well, and
really merit the esteem & regard of all who know them. They
dined here in company with Monroe & his family a few days
since, and afterwards accompanied us to Vauxhall.

M., you will see, is determined to quit this country. I think
there can be no doubt that Spain & France completely dupe this
wise administration. Bernadotte is assembling troops on the

frontiers of Spain, & this latter power announces that unless France arrests these measures, she will raise 80,000 men, and formal notice of this threat is given here. The Spanish money arrives, and Mr. Addington really fears that some portion of it finds its way into France. A Fleet is said to be fitting out at Ferrol, supposed to be destined to Ireland. Yet England is desirous to keep Spain neutral, who lulls this Government by saying, if she is compelled by Bonaparte to furnish the succours contracted for by treaty, she will do that & nothing more ; and that she will not commute this obligation for money, which has been requested ; so I presume she will have the ships, men and money. We hear that Spain has sold Porto Rico to Denmark ; doubtless with the consent, if not at the instance, of France. Hopes are indulged that Russia may be induced to take a part against France, but whether on good grounds I do not know. France is preparing to seize the Grecian isles and Turkey is her object. Austria has hitherto refused to lend herself to the views & desires of the Consul, in respect to her ports in the Adriatic ; but whether she will be able to persist in her refusal is quite uncertain. If she do, it may serve as a pretence for the withdrawal of the French army from the channel and the coasts on the North Seas ; and it is not impossible that this mighty chief may need some apology for such a measure, considering the force and front that G. Britain is determined to display. The insurrection in Ireland was undoubtedly of French manufacture, and there are great causes for alarm in that quarter. There are some accounts to-day of a new plotting discovered in Paris,—you have the story in the papers.

Our Board has decided all the British Complaints except one, which is continued for evidence. What we have awarded against the U. S. will amount to about 100,000 dollars. There are about 8 or 9 cases, waiting for exports from the Admiralty, & three depending in the courts. These will be awarded on, or dismissed in December, and in February or March, the Commission will be finally closed, and we shall return home in the Spring and my most earnest wishes would be gratified if we were to live within a dozen miles, if not in the same town with you & Mrs. King. You can have no conception how much we miss your society, and how completely insulated I am becoming, if nothing worse. The

Monroes receive our civilities & he appears, when in his company, disposed to be attentive and kind. We dined yesterday at Pinkney's, but the Minister's connections will be entirely different from ours. He has seen Hawkesbury twice, once on his arrival and on his introduction to the King. He has also seen Hammond once. His arrival here was 18th July, I suspect he knows nothing that passes here, and appears to have a sort of creed that it is improper to know what is passing in relation to the European powers, unless the U. S. are directly interested. He will therefore have a quiet time in England, for you know they do not press their knowledge, no more than their civility on any man. Bidwell saw James well a few days since. The obstacles to quitting France & coming to England are so many, that I think we shall remain in London until we embark for Boston. Mrs. Gore unites with me in affectionate regards to Mrs. King & the boys.

Ever yours
C. GORE.

C. GORE TO R. KING.

LONDON, Aug. 30, 1803.

MY DEAR FRIEND :

Hammond, whom I saw yesterday, tells me it is not true that Porto Rico has been ceded to Denmark, that a negotiation was on foot between Spain and another northern power for such a cession, but it is now at an end. He thinks that Bonaparte is bad with most of his Generals, and that his opponents increase upon him. But as you know, incredulity on some subjects is not the greatest defect of certain men, you may judge what weight to give to such accounts, they doubtless have their emissaries in all parts of France, and some who are very obnoxious to Bonaparte, even in Paris ; and they believe that his efforts to prepare for the invasion are much slackened. Spain convinces England, that she intends to remain neuter & endeavours, perhaps not without effect, to produce a belief that she is capable of maintaining this character against France. Miranda saw Vansittart and H. Addington yesterday, and it was agreed then that the former should write a letter, merely professing his desire to quit England on their paying him five years pension, which, for that consideration,

is to be renounced forever.   Some Captain of a frigate is to offer
him a passage for himself, & two friends to be landed at Trinidad, where he is to take his people and go wherever he pleases.
He hopes to find two vessels from the U. S. with musquets &c.
&c.   I told him that to procure the men he talks of will not be
easy, to obtain the articles is very sensible, provided he has some
mercantile friends there to make the speculation.   He writes you
again having already written by our friend Cabot.   When he was
yesterday with Vansittart & Healy, they had received the extract
from Mr. Livingston's memorial, which speaks of the tyranny of
G. B., and the union of France and America to form a maritime
code, which should depress this evil spirit of England.   They were
outrageous, according to his account, against the U. S. for giving
vent to so odious a sentiment.   But he had in his pocket the
Philadelphia Gazette, containing the memorial and some strictures
on this offensive paragraph, & availed himself of the occasion,
which it proffered, of showing that the same opinion was entertained in America, as in England, of what they complained—and
this, as he thinks, much abated their wrath.   So he believes that
his having borrowed from me this paper and making such use of
it, has really done great good to the U. S.   H. on Saturday, mentioned it to me, and we read the paper together.   His expressions
of the writer were such as you would suppose, but he very wisely
refrained from attributing any importance to it, & I assured him
it would be as unpopular with us as here.   I must tell you one
anecdote, though you will be careful not to mention it,—Fulton wrote to Boulton & Watts for one or two steam engines to be
shipped to Brockholst Livingston in New York, who would pay
for them, the engines to be made according to directions of *Joel
Barlow*.   The Government here took it into their heads to believe,
these were intended for Fulton's diving machines, that are to blow
up the British Navy, the dockyard &c. &c. at Portsmouth of which
they have some, *certainly not strong*, apprehensions ; and Boulton
& Watts do not ship the machines, lest the destination of N.
York should be only a trick, and so soon as the vessel carrying
them should be in the channel, they might be transhipped for
France and affixed to these terrible instruments of destruction.
I told him that L. & Fulton were jointly concerned in the construction and patent for constructing and using a boat, that was

designed to work against the stream, and I entertained no doubt that this was the real purpose of the engines desired. He said, however, B. & W. had orders not to ship them. Their suspicions will be increased on reading the memorial. Barlow sailed for France about a week since & carried some letters for James.

A gentleman told me to-day he had seen a letter from Gentz, the author, now at Vienna, which says that if E. had had a skilful man at Berlin, when the French troops marched for Hanover, they might have been stopt by Prussia ; that in the Cabinet it was absolutely decided one evening to resist the French by an army of 50,000 men, that the King went in the night to some chateau to sleep and altered his disposition before morning ; that a clever Englishman at that court might have prevailed on this power to have interfered in the preservation of Hanover. Gentz says that he has travelled over all the northern parts of Europe ; that England is every where unpopular ; and an universal stupor prevails among all the powers of the continent, which is created by the vigour and quickness of the Consul's motions. The spirit which is awakened in the people at large will do much agt. the imbecility of the ministry. Dumourier and Pichegru are here ; & there is some reason to believe an attempt will be made to invade France. Dumourier, I learn, is disgusted with the want of spirit in the administration, and I think whatever may have been their original intention, it would be so unpopular that they will not dare to employ him. Miranda declines to see Dumourier.

I enclose you herewith a statement which in a great measure explains itself. My principal reason for troubling you with it is that it is not improbable that Erving may, among his friends at least, circulate some stories about this business. You will readily conceive that my wish is only to correct any false impressions he may attempt to impose, & will of course never make any other use, than to such ends, of this statement.* . . .

Truly, & ever yours
C. GORE.

* The statement written by William Pinkney, the associate of Mr. Gore in the Commission of claims under the 7th Article of the Treaty with Great Britain, is a long one, and although in some points other than those immediately referring to Mr. Gore it also concerns Mr. King's relations with Mr. Erving, it is not possible to print it here, nor even that furnished in the letter of Mr. Gore himself, which covers many pages. They were sent to Mr. King by his

C. Gore to R. King.

LONDON, August 31, 1803.

MY DEAR FRIEND :

Since writing the letter that accompanies this I have thought you would expect a more detailed account of the affair, to which the inclosure alludes, than is contained therein.   Notwithstanding the reflection that this is due from me to you, and that I am sure you take a deep interest in whatever concerns my character & conduct, it is not without some pain I again bring this loathsome subject to my mind, as it presents to me the Maryland worthies and Captain Lewis, who it seems are the advisers of this man & by whose advice, contrary to that of Monroe & Pinkney, he thought himself bound to act.   .   .   .

friend not to vindicate the line of conduct he had adopted, but to give him a true statement of the facts and of what he had done, of the correctness and propriety of which Mr. Gore had no doubt, nor did he suppose his friend would have, as he was well aware of the animus of Mr. Erving towards him and others. Mr. Erving, disappointed in not receiving the consideration and influence which upon his arrival in England he had expected, had shown himself antagonistic to Messrs. King, Williams, and Gore, whom he had not been able to make to yield to his pretensions—possibly warranted on his part by the belief that the administration would look favourably on his pretensions and acts.

With Mr. Gore in particular he had reason to feel himself somewhat aggrieved, who, with the other members of the Commission, had refused to allow him to interfere, in a way which his instructions from home would seem to warrant ; and because that gentleman had been appointed chargé des affaires during Mr. King's absence on the continent, when he asserted his right to act for the U. S., he being Consul in London ; and now that Mr. King had left England without appointing a chargé des affaires, as it afterwards appeared that the Government at home expected him to do, he was ready to take umbrage at any act of Mr. Gore's indicating a desire to look after the interests of the country in England and to give to or receive information from the ministry which might under the circumstances seem proper. Mr. Erving having received some communications from friends in the U. S., stating that Mr. Gore had calumniated him in letters written to his correspondents in America, was greatly incensed, demanded an explanation, and finally sent a challenge to Mr. Gore through the parties named in Mr. G.'s letter, contrary to the advice of Messrs. Pinkney & Monroe, which he promptly declined under the obligation of the position he held, as well as for other reasons.   This is an outline of the matter which is given here chiefly as due to Mr. Gore's high character and as calling forth from Mr. King, as will be seen in his letter, high encomiums as to his integrity, ability and manliness.

R. King to C. Gore, London.

NEW YORK, Sept. 6, 1803.

MY DEAR SIR :

.   .   .   We have papers to the 22d July, which announce Mr. Monroe's arrival in London : I make you my compliments on being relieved from the employment which might have detained you in London more constantly and longer than you would have desired.

.   .   .   I am staggered with the general arming which appears to be making in England. I don't see clearly that this mob of an army will be able to resist the enemy agt. whom it is to be put in motion ; a regular army of 200,000 or 150,000 wd. in my poor opinion be more to be relied upon than the nation en masse : in point of economy the army would likewise be preferable, for if all the men of the nation are to be drilled and trained, as the newspapers state it to be the project that they shall be, I should apprehend the manufacturers would suffer and the agriculture be neglected. In so complicated a machine, its ordinary movements should be changed with infinite caution, since what may seem the remedy of one inconvenience, may become the cause of a still greater and more alarming one. There may be a militia, including the whole people in America and I believe such to have been once the situation of Switzerland ; but these would be no authorities to justify a universal militia in England : and my greatest fear is, if the nation be armed, that the unavoidable consequence will be the change of the monarchy for a Republic—two armies of 60,000 each, with an army of Reserve of 30,000 would defeat and destroy any body of French that can be landed in England ; and were I responsible, I shd. feel more safe with this force than with the whole nation in arms. We here wish the attempt to invade may be made, because we believe it will certainly fail, and that the failure will increase the confidence, reputation and security of England.

Owing to the continuance of the fever which continues to prevail in our unfortunate city, we are cut off from the usual intercourse with our neighbours, so that I see but few persons & those my neighbours. Hence I cannot send you any opinion wh. can be relied upon respecting the probable sentiments of Congress concerning the Louisiana cession. An intelligent Connecticut man told me some time since that the cession would be disliked by New England, and I shall not be surprised if the Eastern Delegates or Senators oppose the Ratification. I understand that the President has no thoughts of opening the western side of the River for settlement, tho' past experience has taught us, that nothing but a cordon of troops will restrain our people from going over the River and settling themselves down upon the western bank. This has, as I hear, been already done, there being as many as 4,000 Inhabitants settled upon the Missouri 40 or 50 miles west of the Mississippi. These will increase and after a while set up a new State. The Plan is to persuade the Indians which remain within the U. S. to exchange their present territories for Lands to be assigned to them over the Mississippi, and perhaps a suitable spot may be marked out as the Sierra Leone for the negroes. Notwithstanding the satisfaction of the negotiators with their performance, I believe the Govt. is and will be embarrassed with the cession, which may become the immediate cause of very important political events among the states.

I don't make much progress in the purchase of a farm. The fever has turned the attention of many persons toward the neighbouring country and the farmers who are in easy circumstances raise the price of their lands—a farm of 270 acres, of which 200 are ploughed land and meadow, & the residue woodland, with such buildings as wd. be sufficient for a farmer, but upon which I should be obliged to build for my family residence &c., is valued at 30,000 dol. ; three years ago it might have been purchased for 25000, or 22500 dols. The situation is good,* being on the Sound 19 miles from New York on the Postroad, which is but a short mile from the Farm house. I have not been to see it, and considering the price do not know that I shall. . . .

I am not only unsuccessful in finding a farm or wintry retreat, but have equal difficulty to obtain a house to suit us, tho' to say the truth this is a moment quite unfavourable to search for one. . . .

Yours very truly,

R. K.

* Hunter's Island on Long Island Sound.

Mr. King wrote a letter to Mr. Vansittart in London, Sept. 8, 1803, which gives his opinions on several topics among which in his memorandum Book are the following.

U. S. will be neutral and impartial—no doubts of this policy— Eng. an interesting spectacle—an invasion desirable, as its defeat will give confidence and reputation at home and abroad.

C. Gore to R. King.

London, Sept. 6, 1803.

My dear Friend :

We yesterday received yours of the 22d July, whereby we learnt you were at housekeeping, and meeting the usual troubles of all countries, but probably much greater with us than in any other, where there is equal wealth and luxury—I mean that of servants. It is clear that I shall regret having sold my house, for not only it will be difficult to purchase to my mind, but by what they write me from Boston, building is nearly double what it was in 1800, when I was there. My intention is to take nothing home, but what is absolutely necessary, and which will form part of my baggage. . . .

The boys are perfectly well & happy & behave well. The Abbé goes with them to plays, to the circus, &c. & amuses himself as well as them. They were with us on Saturday, and we took them to the little theatre in the Haymarket that evening. The rule is that they dine here on Saturday, stay that night & Sunday to dinner, & return to Holborn in the evening, on Wednesdays, also dining with us, and whenever else we have any company, as I wish to mix them in good society, as much as is convenient with their studies ; though I consider the great object of their being at the Abbé's in the holidays is that they may be amused, if not profitably, at least without injury. The project will attain this end and probably give them some taste for French & Spanish, and drawing. Williams is affectionate towards them, and treats them with attention, and I have a firm persuasion that their morals will remain pure & their minds be improved. I am sorry to be confirmed in my opinions of the education of our youth. The only chance for a happy result to the political conflicts our country is destined to undergo, before she settles down into a permanent government & established character, is in the moral habits, sober & just views of the rising generation—and unless the basis of these be laid in early youth, they are scarcely ever attained.

Livingston's memorial occasions much disgust here : but possibly this may be received with pleasure by, at least, one man, and I am told he will be given up by the adminis'n, but it is difficult for me to see whom they intend to set up as V. P. unless it be him.   Sumpter acts as Secretary to the minister—of course any cause of difference between these wise negotiators is not likely to be allayed.   I learn through —— that Livingston made another memorial, wherein he proposed a scheme by which the U. S. should provide a certain number of ships of the Line, to be under the control of France and fight for the freedom of the seas.   This may be the mere creature of S's imagination, or it may have been an indiscretion of L.   It is, however pretty evident that a portion of the followers of the present Government intend to ruin L. The gentleman here assumes no merit to himself, but ascribes all to the superior wisdom and discernment of the President, whose plans they very humbly executed.   I have thought that this admin. will endeavour to bargain away the lands west of the Mississippi for those which Spain holds east of that river, and obtain some money also.   This would certainly free them from the evils of this purchase both as respects the lands owned & the cash to be paid, and give to the U. States all they want.   I thought the other day to sound M. as to S. A. and observed to him that it could not be long before that country would throw off the yoke of Spain.   He considers this not improbable, but seems impressed with the idea, that they have not sense enough to form a free government, and thinks Spain will be quite willing to grant us exclusive privileges in trade to her settlements, and prepare herself by degrees for the dropping of S. A. from her dominions.   Perhaps one may conjecture from these hints the views of the Govn. in this respect, and how easily some men may be duped.

I could not refrain from conversing with him on the new state of things, which the possession of St. Domingo by the Blacks would produce in the U. States, and suggested to him whether it would not be wise that there should be a concurrent effort on this subject, so important to both. He received my remarks, or appeared to receive them with some interest, but from what I perceive and hear of him, and what we know of the English character, there is no great probability of their conferring much together. You understand, for I think I before told you, that our negotiators consider Louisiana as running E. of the River M. to the Rio Perdido, and so taking all the coast from that E. boundary to the river M., and of this they notified Spain. From what I learn the Government is more in fear for Ireland than of an invasion here. All the French, Italian, and Swiss are to be sent off according to the proclamation of the King. You will see a curious paragraph by the printers of the London Courier, in which it is stated that some person offered to become a fellow labourer, provided Bonaparte's character could be supported.

My affectionate regards to Mrs. King and the boys. I am purchasing books & preparing to return home—and this is all my occupation. I have done walking & in this great city am almost literally without society & certainly without friends.

Yours,

C. G.

C. Gore to R. King.

London, Sept. 18, 1803.

My dear Friend :

The boys went to Harrow on Thursday morning in good health and spirits, having passed their holidays very much to their own & our satisfaction. Their behaviour has been altogether such as we could have wished. I shall consider it due to the friendship that subsists between us, to give you information, if I observe anything amiss or of a wrong tendency in them ; so that you may rest perfectly satisfied with the truth of my report. They have promised that should any misfortune occur, of any sort or kind, the same shall be communicated to me directly, and I have the pleasure of believing that they will in any event, have an entire confidence in me. We are (now the boys have gone to Harrow) literally alone. Sometimes we see the Pinkneys. Mrs. Gore has been unwell and confined to the house for ten days past with a cold, that has affected her like the influenza. The M.s are in Wigmere street, and them we never see except by an accidental meeting. The Trumbulls are at Brighton or Worthing. If Mrs. Gore can muster strength and spirits enough, we shall probably make an excursion, for some days, into the country, before the winter sets in. This will, I am sure, be the most unpleasant & gloomy season that we have ever passed in Europe, and I every day regret more & more that we could not return this autumn. On ten thousand occasions we shall miss you & Mrs. King, and we shall be continually reminded of the happiness we enjoyed, by feeling the want of your society and the utter impossibility of indemnifying ourselves by any new connections. My great occupation now is in increasing my library, and rendering it as complete as my means will allow.

'It is generally believed, and by the Government, that an attempt will be made to invade this country and at no very distant day. Any diversion in favour of England, on the part of any of the Continental powers, is not expected. Great apprehensions are entertained for the safety of Portugal, and the ministry here probably begin to feel that that they have been duped by Spain. . . . The Spanish messenger, that went from hence with some new project, was not permitted to pass through France. He landed at Calais but was ordered to reimbark & was relanded in England. So that if the declaration of war is to depend on the return of this messenger, a considerable time must yet elapse, before that event takes place. But it is hardly possible that B. should refrain from compelling S., even if she be indisposed, to take some step directly & openly hostile, before the delivery of any project from this Government.

. . . Mr. Monroe has received no dispatches from Washington since his arrival here;* and I learn through P. that he has seen Lord H. only at his first visit, when presented to the King, and at the Levée, and when he wanted to introduce him (Pinkney) to his Lordship, as agent for the Maryland Bank Stock. Questions relative to the impress of our seamen constantly arise, and, it is said, some violences have been committed on our citizens in the Thames. How they intend to regulate the commerce between the two Countries after October does not appear. One would

* He arrived in London July 18th.

think there should be a harmony as to the measures to be pursued by G. B. in relation to St. Domingo, but no doubt our Government will be indisposed to take any step in concert with G. B., lest it should give umbrage to France—although their own safety is directly concerned in the manner in which E. shall arrange with the Blacks on the Island. Mr. M. will probably be instructed to ask some explanation of our admin. on the offensive paragraphs of L's memorial.

Our affectionate regards to Mrs. K.

C. GORE TO R. KING.

LONDON, Sept. 22, 1803.

MY DEAR FRIEND :

I yesterday received your favour to 2nd August, and though I do not see the probability of our living so near together, as I trust would conduce to the mutual happiness of ourselves & family, I do assure you that your wishes to that end afford me the highest gratification, and there is no object to attain which I would sacrifice so much. The little I saw when at home—my knowledge of the pursuits and occupations, the attainments and objects of ambition of those with whom I must be associated on my return, afford me some idea of the reflections, which cannot fail to crowd on my mind. While I have not the means, I assure you, I have as little desire to vie with my neighbours in their modes of ennobling themselves, or pursuing enjoyment. The great eating parties with all the accompaniments of conversation & amusement, that attend them in any great town, never had, at least since I was thirty years of age, any charm for me ; and now they would be a task, at which I am very unwilling to labour. On the other hand, the society of a few friends, who have had considerable converse, both with the world and with books, is the most enviable pleasure of life. Had other men filled the chair of government, I should have been gratified to have represented it at this court for a few years, at the end of which term, I could have retired to my farm at Waltham, with what would to me have been an independence, though very far from what our monied aristocracy deem a competence. As the case is, I shall take my place at the Bar for a few years in the expectation of maintaining myself, while I am building my house at Waltham, and procuring one at Boston, which shall be small. This does not suit all my feelings, but on the whole I believe it the best course for me to pursue. My Library will be rather more than double what it was when you left us, and with such additions as I shall make during my practice for four or five years, I hope to have a comfortable resource for age. Now we have land in plenty, and rather reasonable in the neighbourhood of Boston & in my neighbourhood, and did not political considerations, and what I know is more, considerations in regard to your children, fix you immovably in N. York, I should hope to prevail on you to remove to us, before you purchase. You should have any of my lands and we could be within a quarter of an hour's walk of each other, and the education of your younger children would be better in Massachusetts, I trust, than in N. York. The Commission being closed, and as I never shall undertake another business with such a variety of embarrassments, & where the certainty of being responsible only for evils & disappointments, and of deriving no credit from success was so clear, I shall in future be without solemn looks or depressed feelings.   .   .   .

Portugal bends to France, as does every part of the Continent, and you may be assured the Govt. here expects to have the contest singly to bear against the accumulating power of Bonaparte & that they also believe an attempt at invasion will soon be made. M.[iranda], who writes you by this oppor'y has renewed assurances from Govt., that he shall go out in a frigate within a month, and have advanced to him cash to prepare himself ; before that time they expect to be at war with S.

Mrs. Gore who is yet quite indisposed unites with me in affectionate regards to Mrs. K. & the children. You say nothing of Hamilton, Jay or Benson. Are they yet in your vicinity ?

Yours truly &c. &c.   C. GORE.

―――――

C. GORE TO R. KING.

LONDON, Sept. 30th, 1803.

MY DEAR FRIEND :

Mr. Merry sailed from Portsmouth on the 28th instant, and my letters by him you will probably receive before this. I sometime since suggested to him the propriety of his knowing the views and intentions of the administration in regard to St. Domingo, and whether the measures they might adopt for the purpose of restraining or limiting the evils that threaten'd their colonies from the existence of a settlement of free blacks near them, would not be most likely to produce the effect desired by the concurrence of our Government, so far as it could concur. He opened the subject to Lord H. who told him that he thought it important now it was suggested, but really it never before entered his mind. Monroe, as I believe I mentioned to you, told me in a conversation I made with him, that he thought it would be a good place for the Southern States to send their free negroes, and those whom they thought fit not to punish capitally. This latter gentleman has received no letters from the Government since his arrival here ; and of course has no instructions relative to the renewal of the treaty or proposing any substitute. Merry goes out without any instructions on the subject, but is directed to ask of our Government some explanation of Livingston's memorial, so far as it relates to checking their tyranny on the seas. For two days past a squadron of small ships have been bombarding Calais and attempting to destroy some boats which are there, or are endeavouring to pass to Boulogne, but with what success we do not learn. It is certain, in the mind of all persons, that Bonaparte will make an attempt to throw a body of troops on this Island, but the nation is so well prepared, that perhaps it might be advantageous not only for G. B., but for the world, that he should succeed in debarking 30 or 40,000 men, especially if a like number were destroyed in the channel. The nations of the Continent seem to view the struggle without interest, certainly without any on the part of this Kingdom. The changes that have been made in Portugal, have all been in favour of France ; and little doubt is now affected by any that all the resources of Spain & Portugal in Europe will soon be at the command of Bonaparte. An expedition is believed to be fitting at Ferrol for Ireland, & it is supposed that Augereau will have the command. It is said that there is a general expectation on the Continent that England will be conquer'd—and yet they expect to preserve their independence ! It is certainly a time when bravery and wisdom seem to have deserted all cabinets but the French.

You observe I am speaking of Europe—what you say is reported
of Bonaparte's making grants prior to the cession, is certainly
very much in character.

Yours affectionately,   C. Gore.

Robt. R. Livingston to R. King, New York.

Paris, 14th Oct., 1803.

Dear Sir :

I did not receive your last letter from England till about one
month ago ; the receipt of it gave me the more pleasure as I was
somewhat hurt that you should quit your harbour without giving
me a farewell shot.   You know that Mr. Monroe has taken your
station ; the intercourse being interrupted I hear very little from
him & I am sorry to add that I hear as little from the United
States.   The high opinion that is here entertained of our treaty,
& the compts. I receive would make me vain enough to believe
that silence at home gave consent, were I not happily roused from
my golden dream, by the kind offices of the Boston floppers (for
their's are the only papers I have lately recd.) who tell me that I
am a fool, a lunatic, a minion & a great many other things equally
well calculated to cure me of vanity, & to raise the reputation of
the country which has for upward of thirty years successively
employed me in high and confidential offices.   I am sorry the
sense of the country in their legislature has not been taken upon
this important question of the treaty at a much earlier day ; for
such are the fluctuations of European politicks, that if the treaty
secures advantages, which I trust it does, the sooner we put
ourselves in possession of them the better.   Things remain here
much as you left them ; the most active preparations still go on
for the attack on England and Ireland & there is every reason to
believe that they are sincerely intended, with whatever hazard
they may be attended.   Perhaps prudence would direct this
government to content themselves with appearances, since the
expenses to which England puts herself in preparation are immense & must be ruinous in the long run ; but on the other hand
France has to fear changes in the state of Europe—for no nation
can be indifferent to the fate of England in which that of many

others must be involved. Russia has renewed her proffered mediation ; the Court of St. James say they are ready to accept it, but that no mediation founded on the basis of the treaty at Amiens can be admitted. France is more moderate in her reply and appears disposed to accept any reasonable modifications of it.

From Mr. Gelston, to whom I have written, you will learn that we are at war with the Emperor of Morocco, & that Capt. Bainbridge has taken one of his corsairs of 22 guns. The Turkish Empire seems crumbling into dust, the mamlukes have driven the crescent out of all Egypt except Alexandria, & they are in their turn likely to be driven out by Abd-el-hahal, who is at the head of 400,000 men overrunning Asia and alike destroying Jews and Mahometans & Christians in the name of the one living God, whom alone he professes to worship, independent of all forms or creeds heretofore received. As he makes converts wherever he goes, either by the word or by the sword, there is no calculating the extent of his powers.

This, my dear Sir, is an eventful age, and I think we are very ungrateful if we do not thank God for having placed us out of the reach of fires that are scorching and consuming the rest of the world. But man is not perhaps made to be perfectly happy here, & for this reason where he has no real evils, he has the address to form imaginary ones, in which, I think, our countrymen are not behindhand with the rest of the world. . . . I have not yet obtained my congé, but as an office forms a contrast to hell, at least in one point, I presume I shall find no difficulty in getting out of it.

With much esteem & regard &c,
Rob. R. Livingston.

CHAPTER XXI.

C. GORE TO R. KING.

LONDON, 21st Octr., 1803.

MY DEAR FRIEND :

. . . Our acounts from N. York, which are to the 8th September, painfully convince us of the ravages of the yellow fever, and that no abatement can be expected during the coming season. I have heard that some hopes were entertained of a return of Congress to N. York or Philadelphia. Should such an event have been calculated on, the sickness of your city at the present will be a powerful argument against the choice of that. The acquisition of Louisiana takes from Washington its character of central, and probably the Southern gentlemen may carry us deeper into the ancient dominion ; though I confess it is not very important to my mind, for at the rate we are proceeding it is not certain we shall remain united much longer.

It is said an Embargo is imposed on all vessels bound to Portugal or Spain, and I presume the ministry is at length driven to the necessity of accepting the war against the latter of these powers. *M*[iranda] has absolute assurances from the Government that he shall be dispatched shortly to Trinidad. I saw a note from Vansittart to M; saying that they only waited for Nepean to recover a little strength (he is quite sick) *pour vaquer vos affaires.* The administration has applied to Sir Francis Baring to be the medium, thro' whom every thing is to be arranged, prepared & shipt for the expedition. Fullarton is here. *M.* was to see him again last evening; he has already had one conversation with him, F. visiting him before he saw the ministers. When every thing is settled, *M.* will write you, and this will be in a few days.

The breach, I think, widens between Monroe & Livingston. The former supposes the latter detains his letters in Paris and assumes all the merit of the Louisiana Convention, while he humbly refrains from appropriating any to himself, but every thing to the superior wisdom, determined yet prudent conduct of the President. He however is said to deny that any other causes than these had the least influence on Bonaparte and that peace or war in Europe, the result would have been the same!! Hammond, whom I see frequently, and who always receives me kindly and confidentially, told me a few days since that neither he nor Ld. H. had seen Monroe, but twice since his arrival in England, except at the Levee, and that all his time was passed in sucking in wisdom from Consul E., and a few other democrats. He has no secretary now. Alston, the young painter, visited him for a passport: he replied that being without a secretary & so extremely pressed for time, he could not conveniently attend to making out one, and desired him to go to the Consul. But as the young man is going on the continent, he is informed that one from the Minister is at least more useful, if not absolutely necessary to his safety. Indeed I believe they take & detain the Consular certificate at the Alien office on embarking. So far as I learn any thing of M., I am satisfied he has neither the inclination, nor capacity to do the smallest good here; neither do I believe it consistent with his idea of propriety that he should even know what is passing in E. or on the Continent. I do not express these opinions to any one else, for besides it being otherwise improper, they would be imputed to very different motives than the real ones.

I think Hammond has some very odd fears relative to Fulton's boat & its power of blowing up the British Navy. H. says he has learned from several quarters that L. and his family received very large grants of land prior to the sale, but I do not believe it. Bingham (who, by the way, thinks his conversations with Talleyrand effected the Convention) does not suppose that conveyances of land were made to any individuals prior to the cession, but you know he gives himself credit for full as much knowledge as the world thinks him entitled to. Alexr. Baring, who is now with you, will be more likely to know than any one here. The Commission at Paris is at a stand, the Commissioners not being able to construe the convention, and waiting for instructions from the Government. The cause why our citizens are to be paid in specie rather than in stock, may be found in the character & connections of the creditors—at least a censorious world will say so.

I am now filing my opinion on the colony trade, and having come across an old paper of yours with some remarks on this subject, I shall take the liberty to offer them as my own, they concurring with my sentiments & better expressed than I could expect to do myself. I sent you the Times by a ship lately bound for N. York, and when opport. offers, will send you a further file. The Editors of this paper have become outrageously ministerial. The pieces on the late negotiations shall likewise be forwarded. With affectionate attachment to Mrs. King & the children, I

Remain faithfully yours.

C. Gore.

R. King to C. Gore, London.

New York, Oct. 24, 1803.

My dear Friend :

. . . I congratulate you that your Business is so nearly finished that you are able to look forward with confidence to your return early in the Spring. . . . In regard to the insinuation that it seems has been made at Washington, that you were inclined to prolong your residence unnecessarily in England, and wh. could have proceeded only from the malignity and envy of some falsehearted Jacobin, I wonder that you suffered it to engage a second thought. The truth is, my Dr. Sir, that you are too honest & too virtuous, that you have too much regard for your own reputation and your duty to the Public, not to be the object of Jacobin hatred and persecution ; and I am only surprized that you do not consider the proofs of this hatred, as the highest evidence of your own integrity rather than as that sort of attack agt. which a good man feels impelled to defend himself. Be persuaded that we live in times, when it behooves a man to make his election between the upright performance of his duty to God & his Country, with the persecution of triumphant Jacobinism, and the corrupt and degrading violation of these sacred duties, with the Hosannas of this abominable sect. No man who knows you or whose good opinion is an object of desire, wd. believe this insinuation.

Here as far as I am able to judge, those who know anything of the Proceedings of your Board, consider them as highly honourable to yr. character and, except that your prudence has naturally contributed to remove Jacobin complaints agt. England, even the privileged cast do not revile you in my hearing. . . .

I don't enclose the President's message, as it will have reached Engd. before my letter. The prominent point respects Louisiana ; the cession whereof is ascribed to "the just Discernment of the Enlightened Government of France" instead of that posture of things which wd. have prevented its occupation by France until she shd. have first acquired the consent of England. As $\frac{2}{3}$ of the Senate are of the faithful sect, there can be no question abt. the Ratification, unless some scruple shd. arise abt. the constitutional powers of Congress to admit a new State (which the Treaty re-requires) including territory not within the limits of the U. S. But this scruple, if it exists, will be so managed that France may have no occasion to be dissatisfied. As the Treaty has not been published, the Public know little of its Provisions, and hence the newspapers have (as I am informed for I see but one or two) been on all sides pretty silent. Little and indeed less has been said in its favor than agt. it. I believe that I have before insinuated a doubt whether the Govt. has seen this treaty in the advantageous light in which it has been regarded by the Envoys ; tho' this hesitation will not prevent its acceptance, any more than the claim of merit that will be bottomed upon its being concluded. There is no doubt that parts of the Govt., if not the whole, think a better bargain might and ought under existing Circumstances to, have been made, and it is quite possible that the chief agt. on our part may not receive those testimonies of satisfaction that he may think his almost exclusive due. Whether this may be so or not, it is understood that he has asked leave to come home next spring and from the manner in which the family here is treated by their chiefs, it wd. not be surprizing shd. he return dissatisfied and that he and his name might shew a disposition to return to their former Party. Should this be the case, if I mistake not, the ruling party wd. give them up willingly, feeling themselves strong enow to shake them off ; and rid themselves of their numerous claims for office.

I don't know what important object, if any, is to engage the attention of Congress during the present Session. It seems that the proposition to amend the Constitution so as that the votes for President & Vice President may be distinguished, is to be submitted to the several State Legislatures without delay, and I am told that such is the composition of these Legislatures that it is likely that this alteration will be approved by the constitutional proportion of them. . . .

The memorial to which you refer in a late letter, was to say the least, a most indiscreet effusion—and considering the avowed opinion of our own Govt. relative to the principles of the Northern confederation as well as the decision wh. G. Britain has shown in opposition to these pretended Rules or Principles, prudence must condemn the utterance of sentiments so false and obnoxious as some of those contained in Mr. Ls. memorial.

If Monroe has done his duty, he has anticipated all complaint by such observations, authorized by the tenour of the instructions of the *Present Govt.* to the Legation at London, as would without a formal disavowal, satisfy the Eng. Cabinet that these exceptionable expressions and sentiments were not dictated by his Govt. If he has not done this, it wd. not surprise me if our Gt. were called upon for an explanation upon that head. I hope this may not happen, as it wd. involve the Govt. in a dilemma from which it wd. be extremely difficult to extricate itself, and shd. the subject be pushed too briskly, it is possible that the Govt. might think itself forced to avoid what it wd. never attempt to enforce, if left to itself.

I have some thoughts of going on to Washington this autumn, but shall know so few people there, and have so little pleasure in hearing the croakings of those I do know, that I think it probable that my natural indolence will prevail. Were you snug at Waltham, I do really believe that the earnest desire we have to see you and Mrs. Gore would overcome all my indolence and that we should post off without a week's delay to embrace you. Our family is well and we all write in affectionate regards to you and yours.

Faithfully and always yr.

R. K.

C. GORE TO R. KING.

LONDON, Nov. 1, 1803.

MY DEAR FRIEND :

Our last letters from you are of the 6th Sept., and then the yellow fever was continuing its ravages. Since then we learn of it at Philadelphia and Alexandria. You will see by the papers that the vaccine inoculation is supposed by some to prevent any one taking the plague. For this year I hope the country by the present day is free. Here the weather is extremely cold & without rain. We have scarcely known twenty-four hours rain since July came in, & some accounts say the wheat is light, which certainly was to be expected from the dryness of the season. . . .

The Volunteers are training and those of London have been reviewed, as P. Porcupine says by the King & *Mr. Sheridan.* They amounted to upwards of 30,000, and I have no doubt that these and the other volunteers about the country, should Bonaparte be enabled to execute his threats of invasion, would fight well and bravely for their King & their own independence : but should he not soon come, the spirit will flag & they become sick of their new trade. Ulterior consequences, and certainly of a very serious nature are to be apprehended, as you justly remark from such an immense body, though the system, you will see, is materially changed from what it was on Mr. Addington's introduction.   There are now probably somewhere about 400,000 volunteers in this Kingdom, and of this number it is not impossible many may have, on some future day, very different views from the Monarch, the Nobles & the rich commoners.   This is an evil, however, entirely overlooked at the present day in the extreme hour of a French invasion.   Yet, I think the temper of the nation is now sanguine & confident of success.   The merchants here are really, I believe, desirous of the attempt being made, but it is very much, I fear, in the mercantile idea—horœ momento cita mors venit aut victoria læta.   They are uneasy at the embarrassments thrown in the way of their commerce, and think that, should Bonaparte be defeated in his projected invasion, their manufactures & the produce of their colonies would find a sure market, & the returns flow regularly back.   When we calculate the chances against him, it is scarcely possible to believe he will attempt crossing the channel, yet every thing indicates this to be his intention.   From Brest & Ferrol it is expected he will make the attempt to throw a large force into Ireland.

Vessels were prohibited sailing to Portugal & Spain for some days.   It was then said, this was merely to prevent their sailing without convoy, & the restriction has been taken off.   Probably on reflection it was found nothing Spanish or Portuguese could be detained here, while the measure would be ground of a retaliation, that would be extremely injurious to the British subjects, who have considerable property there.   I rather suspect there was some gaucherie in the business.   Accounts are daily expected from Spain & Portugal which will no longer leave to England an option in her relative state to these two powers.   The papers this evening, just come in & which you will have, seem to render it possible that Russia may interfere in behalf of Spain.   If so, I pity M. [iranda], for in such case my belief is this Govt. could do nought.   .   .   .

Our friends are now busy on the great subject of Louisiana; a subject which I am sure will soon change, and in a very material view, the relations of the different States.   I have already understood, that the Eastern States are now contemplated as of no weight in the scale, and of course not entitled to any influence. Every thing that the present administration wishes to effect may be done through the Western States, now fast bound by the ties of gratitude. The wealth of the Southern & Western States will soon leave us far in the rear on that score, as we already are on that of population.

A deep misfortune undoubtedly will be felt from the rude & uncultivated minds of those, who will soon have such a preponderating influence in our federal politics. Wise men should turn their thoughts to what is to be the next chapter in our ever varying systems : for I really believe that the present is nearly read through, a few, but very few verses remain ; and those, probably like some of the old testament ones, full of hard names. Mr. Monroe, I hear for I never see him, is without a Secretary. Your former Sec. has much leisure now and could assist the Minister & himself too, but nothing I presume would induce him to take the man you or I employed. I frequently am told of the complaints he makes at being obliged to fill a few passports—it is only a few, for most of those who require them, unless going on the continent, are taught to confide in the Consuls.

Notwithstanding I wrote Mr. Madison several letters, giving to the Government an exact state of what was passing here & on the continent, so far as I knew, which accounts have all proved true, also in answer to several things committed by them to my charge, yet I have received not a line from any member of the administration. This was in some measure the more necessary, as Erving here wrote me an impertinent letter on my communicating to him, by desire of Lord Hawkesbury, the blockade of the Elbe, and also one to L⁴ H. to know whether he might rely on the information which Mr. Gore had pleased to communicate. A copy of this letter, as well as those impudent notes he wrote you & me, last autumn, on the subject of passports, I am told, he sent to the Government. Civility, I think, would have dictated to the Secry. the fitness of some reply to my letters, all these circumstances considered ; I am further told that he was prepared, had you left any person chargé d' affaires, to have made a formal & public protest against the act, and against the pretension of such chargé. These are trifles, but among friends, they are interesting. They show the impudence of some men & the strange opinions of others, for P. told me he thought the minister on quitting had no authority to name a chargé d' affaires ; so it is presumable this intention was

duly reflected on, advised and determined.   The Govt. of the
United S. & of Maryland have united in empowering P. to negotiate & settle the Bank Stock business, leaving him no discretion
to offer more for the settlement of the claim of the man who refuses to acquiesce, than the amount of Russel's demand, which
sum the State is willing should be appropriated to this object, as
it is relieved from that.   No answer has yet been obtained from
the discontented man—I forget his name—and they have not
been able to see the Atty. Genl.   P. in his new character has been
formally introduced to Lord Hawkesbury by Monroe.   His
powers were received before M's arrival.   I trust he will see
reason, why greater progress has not been made in the business
in time past.   .   .   .

Yours ever & faithfully,

C. GORE.

Trumbull has returned to Bath, where he purposes remaining
until Dec.   He has written me, making very affectionate enquiries
after your health, &c.   He is a good fellow & worthy of a better
fate, but when a man arrives at years of discretion, & chooses for
himself, he can blame no one.

21st Nov.   Mr. Addington declines, for the present, giving his
permission to the expedition of M., but promises that so soon as
Spain makes the war, it shall proceed.   Nepean shews him letters
by which it appears, that several ships of the Line are fitting out
at Carthagena, for the purpose of joining the French at Toulon ;
and others, from whence it amounts to an high probability, that
an armament is preparing at Ferrol to make the attempt from
thence for the invasion of Ireland.   But he, A., mistrusts all information from the admiralty relative to Spain, because the Navy
is anxious for a Spanish war.   Things therefore are at a stand
in regard to S. A.   .   .   .   Davidson prepares all that is necessary
for the expedition & Nepean says in a very few weeks after
Mr. A. shall give his sanction, the business shall proceed, and
news is anxiously looked for from Spain, which shall even convince the incredulous Doctor.   It is understood that a large
sum was raised in Lisbon, and chiefly from British Merchants
there, by which Lannes was induced to pledge his master's word
that Portugal should not be invaded for six months.   Miranda

desires me to say to you that he has agreed to the suspension of his project ; and remains here, because he supposes such a de-rangement has taken place in N. York, owing to the yellow fever, that no dependance can be made on anything from thence ; and that he hopes to hear from you.   On the whole I think he can depend on no effort in his behalf here until Spain makes the war, or some opposition shall drive the minister from his pacific pur-poses.   Spain has sent 1600 men to reinforce her troops either at Carthagena or La Vera Cruz.

You will see Cobbett in his last paper goes upon the idea that there was some foundation for the communication in some of the papers relative to the discussion on the subject of a new treaty between the U. S. & G. B. . . . I saw H. on Saturday ; he says they never see or hear of M., & so far as regards their office, he might as well be in Virginia.   He thinks that if our Govt. have any wishes relative to the commercial relations of the two countries, it becomes them to make the proposal.   Every one must know that E. is now too much occupied with what is much more inter-esting, to advance any propositions.   He supposes some Jacobin made those insertions in the newspapers to answer some purpose. Cobbett, you see, presumes that this Govt. did for the purpose of preparing the country for great sacrifices or a rupture.   I under-stand from another quarter, that it is supposed to be exceeding wise policy, to let France see that we suffer our treaty with G. B. to die, & that we have no wish of making another, so we may attain favour in the eyes of Bonaparte.   H. has information that Hayley is about sailing from N. York with a vessel, fitted for a privateer, with guns in her hold, and, after she is out, to place her guns on deck & cruize against the English.   As he is going to France, Tom Paine is to be his passenger.   They are in great hopes of taking him in which all good men will wish them success. English goods now find a market on the Continent, & large quan-tities are shipt thither.   Many Frenchmen come to London & purchase largely with cash.   Mrs. Mallet yesterday informed Mrs. Gore that the *minister* was certainly going home this ensuing Spring.   He will not come here previous to his embarking, I pre-sume.   Some person reports from Paris, that he denies all merit in the gentleman here in obtaining the late convention, and this very publickly, & assumes the whole to himself, imputing it entirely in his superior address and wisdom.   Merry, as I told you, had orders to remonstrate against his famous memoire. Lord H. directed him to communicate the reply to you.   . . .

My affectionate regards to Mrs. King.

Yrs. truly & ever,

C. GORE.

R. KING TO C. GORE, LONDON.

NEW YORK, Nov. 1, 1803.

MY DR. SIR :

There being a large and willing majority of both Houses of Congress of the true sect, the measures of the Ex. will receive no impediment.   Great is the Prophet, and in the whole earth there is none to be likened unto him, is the language of the faithful !

The Louisiana Treaty has been ratified and the H. of R. is engaged in preparing such laws respecting it as are called for by the President, and this in contempt of the Remonstrance of the Spanish Minister, who declares that the Conditions on wh. Spain promised to cede not having been performed, the Country is still her property.

The Conduct of Spain is the occasion of various and unsatisfactory speculations.   Some believe that France having the offer of a better price from Spain is at the bottom of the Opposition ; others allege that Spain is encouraged by G. Br., while the majority, not regarding Spain as an independent power and looking on the French Govt. as enlightened, honest & powerful, rely upon it that the opposition will not be persisted in.

As I know nothing about it, the subject engages no part of my attention ; and, to say the truth, I consider the state and tendency of the Country such that an upright and prudent man, to be happy, shd. know little of our public affairs.   You and I cannot alter certain opinions which we entertain and wh. are confirmed by experience, as well as by those authorities which our education and habits enable us to consult.   With those opinions we are proscribed by those whose best interests and happiness wd. be promoted by their observance ; hence the course which a wise man shd. in these circumstances pursue is too clearly marked out to be neglected.

It is our Duty to seek those models with which past time abounds, and to imitate their Conduct in retirement, rather than to engage in the desperate strife of factions. . . .

Our fever is nearly or quite over. The Bankers, public officers, &c., are returning to town, and in the course of the week the town will be full again. We remain where we are some weeks longer, and until we can open and put up our furniture.

Yr. assured Friend,
RUFUS KING.

R. KING PROBABLY TO COL. PICKERING.

NEW YORK, Nov. 4, 1803.

DEAR SIR :

Congress may admit new States, but can the Executive by treaty admit them, or, what is equivalent, enter into engagements binding Congress to do so? As by the Louisiana Treaty, the ceded territory must be formed into States, & admitted into the Union, is it understood that Congress can annex any condition to their admission? if not, as Slavery is authorized & exists in Louisiana, and the treaty engages to protect the Property of the inhabitants, will not the present inequality, arising from the Representation of Slaves, be increased?

As the provision of the Constitution on this subject may be regarded as one of its greatest blemishes, it would be with reluctance that one could consent to its being extended to the Louisiana States; and provided any act of Congress or of the several states should be deemed requisite to give validity to the stipulation of the treaty on this subject, ought not an effort to be made to limit the Representation to the free inhabitants only? Had it been foreseen that we could raise revenue to the extent we have done, from indirect taxes, the Representation of Slaves wd. never have been admitted; but going upon the maxim that taxation and Representation are inseparable, and that the Genl. Govt. must resort to direct taxes, the States in which Slavery does not exist, were injudiciously led to concede to this unreasonable provision of the Constitution. On account of the effect upon the public opinion, produced by alterations of the fundamental Laws of a Country, we should hesitate in proposing what may appear to be beneficial ; but I know no one alteration of the Constitution of the U. S. which I would so readily propose, as to confine representation and taxation to the free inhabitants. . . .

Yr. obt. & faithful Servt.

RUFUS KING.

R. KING TO C. GORE, LONDON.

NEW YORK, Nov. 20, 1803.

MY DEAR FRIEND :

. . . A day or two since I saw one of the members of the H. of R. who is here on leave of absence ; he is of the ruling sect, and says all is going on well, that the Spanish Ambassador's remonstrance will retard nothing in the measures for occupying Louisiana, and that the Ambassador himself says no opposition will be made by the Govt. ; if so this business will produce no immediate Embarrassment.

We yesterday had a Rumour that *Mr. Dawson* is named Govr. of the new acquisition ; but whether this be so, I know not. Already as I hear in Connecticut as well as the upper part of this State, they are beginning to talk of *moving* to Louisiana, the country which will produce sugar & cotton & corn, &c. &c. ! ! ! and there can be no doubt that the project of reserving the Lands west of the Mississippi for posterity will be defeated by the Emigrants of the Eastern and Western States.

The proposed amendment to the Constitution respecting the Election of President & Vice President has passed the House, and is before the Senate where its fate is sd. to be doubtful. Mr. Adams is supposed to approve the alteration, with an alteration the purport whereof is not mentioned. Mr. Dayton proposes to abolish the office of V. President, & what other schemes may be proposed is more than I know.

In the order of important communications I shd. inform you that citizen Jerome Bonaparte arrived here last Evening : he has passed some months at Baltimore, a fortnight at Philadelphia, and how long he is to honour us with his residence is not foretold. At Baltimore he was on the point of being married to a daughter of Mr. W. Patterson, but fortunately the young lady was persuaded to make a visit to Virginia. The young Prince is said to spend a great deal of money which the Span. ambassador is good enough to supply.

To pass from trifles to what is really interesting, I have a word to say respecting some of our friends, Mr. Jay lives retired upon his farm at Bedford, W. Chester, 50 miles from Town, which he has not visited these last two years. We expect to see him here this winter. Excepting the solitude of his situation I hear he lives much at his ease and enjoys tolerable health. . . .

Benson is the same man I left him, except a little older, he has been at Boston during the fever, says all our friends are well there except Ames, of whom he gives but an indifferent acct. Having himself formerly recd. advantage by a voyage to Amsterdam, he recommends to Ames to go to the E. Indies for his health !

Hamilton is at the head of his profession, and in the annual rect. of a handsome income. He lives wholly at his house 9. miles from town so that on an average he must spend three hours a day on the road going and returning between his house and town, which he performs four or five days each week. I don't perceive that he meddles or feels much concerning Politics. He has formed very decided opinions of our System as well as of our administration, and as the one and the other has the voice of the country, he has nothing to do but to prophecy !

G. Morris, who has laid out over 50 or 60 *M* Dollars in buildings and alterations at Morrisania lives much to his own taste *en garçon*, receives his friends on Sundays, keeps a good look and can talk as decidedly and agreeably, provided you have no theory to defend or suggest, as anyone. . . .

Owing to the fever, which has wholly disappeared, we have seen very little of the manners and society of our city since our return ; but I think I have such a glimpse already as by a sort of anticipation enables one to form a pretty correct opinion of them. Jay is a recluse, a rigorous one, and tho' not precisely from the same motives, I am not sure that I shd. not prefer the like Retreat in preference to *the enjoyment* of our City Society. . . .

With affectionate regards &c

R. K.

R. King to C. Gore, London.

NEW YORK, Dec. 7, 1803.

MY DR. SIR :

Our last letters from you were by Mr. Merry, who after a rough passage over the ocean and a tedious one up the Chesapeake, reached Washington last week. I wish he may find himself tolerably comfortable there, as otherwise his reports will be shaded with the discontents he may himself feel.

The Spanish minister delivered a memorial respecting the surrender of Louisiana, expressing the disinclination of his court to comply. The Govt. has notwithstanding determined to take possession and a force sufft. to do so, even in case of opposition, is ordered to march. I, however, understand that it is not probable that any opposition will be made. Except the occasion and conversation that one hears respecting this cession, we have no domestic object which engages the pub. attention. Whether you are invaded in Engd., or will be invaded during the Winter, is a fruitful source of dispute. I am a believer that you have not been invaded, and that it is not the purpose of Bonaparte to invade England, but that his real object is Ireland.

Our commerce and navigation are checked rather than increased by the war. The shutting up of Hamburgh and the Regulations of France abt. Eng. Man^{ures} & Produce, are embarrassments to our trade. Freights are very low. . . .

Your faithful friend

R. K.

_____

C. Gore to R. King.

LONDON, December 7, 1803.

MY DEAR FRIEND :

. . . I have a friendly letter from Col. Pickering, in answer to one written him on the subject of our outfit * and it has relieved my mind from the only anxiety it has suffered, on that subject;

* In a previous letter Mr. Gore had written that at the instigation of Mr. Pinkney an application would be made to the Government by the Commissioners under the 7th Article of the Treaty of Peace for the payment to them of an outfit. He had joined in this particularly because of the wants of Mr. P. who "had been encouraged to believe the Government would acknowledge its propriety and accede to the request." Mr. G. would of course benefit by it if granted.

for all my fears were, that our own friends might disapprove of the application. As to the final issue of the claim, or the manner in which the Government & its friends shall please to regard and treat it, I have not the smallest concern. Pinkney would never have forgiven me, had I not joined in the request, and thinking as he did upon the subject, he might have had just cause to blame my declining to submit the justice of the claim to the Government. I enquired of Mr. Hammond to-day, if there were any reason to believe that Russia was about to change her politics? His reply was that they had not the least intelligence from which they could draw any inference. The alarm of invasion seems fast subsiding, though no doubt is entertained of the intention to invade Ireland from Brest, should Admiral Cornwallis be blown off. The manner in which this Admiral has kept his station does not afford Bonaparte a very good prospect, and perhaps he is now raising a pretext by the levy of contributions in the Northern States and petty powers, for the diversion of his forces from the sea. . . .

Mr. Monroe has lately presented a very temperate memorial on the subject of seamen impressed. Not a word has ever passed relative to a renewal of the old treaty, or the making of a new one. This I understand not from M., whom I have seen only once, though we are on very good terms these three months. *M* was here this morning, and desired Mrs. G. to tell me that his affairs were in good train, but I know nothing further—undoubtedly everything depends on the determination that may be made, whether peace shall continue to subsist between the two countries. . . .

Ever yours

C. GORE.

CHAPTER XXII.

The Convention for the eastern and northwestern boundaries which had been negotiated by Mr. King with the
British Government, was laid before the Senate for advice
and consent as to its ratification. Some doubt was felt in
that body as to whether it conflicted with the Louisiana
treaty, the signature of which was of an earlier date than
that of the Boundary Convention. Mr. Henry Adams gives
an account of the facts concerning this hesitation which the
following letters will show to be incorrect so far as Mr. King
is concerned. Speaking of Mr. Merry, he says:

"At the moment when he was, as he thought, socially mal-
treated, and when he was told by Madison that America meant
to insist on her neutral rights, he learned that the Government
did not intend to ratify Rufus King's boundary convention. The
Senate held that the stipulations of its fifth article respecting the
Mississippi might embarrass the new territory west of the river.
King knew of the Louisiana cession when he signed the treaty;

but the Senate had its own views on the subject, and under the lead of General Smith preferred to follow them, as it had done in regard to the second article of the treaty with France, Sept. 30, 1800, and as it was about to do in regard to Pinckney's claims convention, Aug. 11, 1802, with Spain. Merry was surprised to find Madison, instead of explaining the grounds of the Senate's hesitation, or entering into a discussion of the precise geographical difficulty, contented himself with a bald statement of the fact. The British Minister thought this was not the most courteous way of dealing with a treaty negotiated after a full acquaintance with all the circumstances, and he wrote to his government to be on its guard, &c., &c."

Mr. Madison could not give the reasons why the Senate refused to ratify the Convention, because that body refused to withdraw the injunction of secrecy, and therefore they were unknown to him. As regards Mr. King's knowledge of the cession of Louisiana at the time when he signed the Convention, his answer to the Committee of the Senate, of which John Quincy Adams was Chairman, inquiring about the fact, explicitly denied it and thus removed that objection to its ratification.

JAMES MADISON TO R. KING.

WASHINGTON, Dec. 4, 1803.

DEAR SIR:

I cannot better fulfill the object of the Committee of which Mr. Adams is chairman, than by enclosing you his letter to me accompanying it. Writing from my house, where a copy cannot be conveniently taken, I am induced to avoid delay by sending you the original which I ask the favor of you to return with your answer.

With great esteem I remain

Your most obedt. servt.

JAMES MADISON.

[Endorsed by R. King.]

Copy of letter referred to:

SIR:

Some difficulty having arisen in the Senate, in considering the expediency of advising and consenting to the ratification of the Treaty of limits, between the U. S. & G. B., signed on the 12th of May, 1803, a comtee. of that body has been appointed to enquire and report upon the subject.

The difficulty arises from the circumstance that the Treaty with the French republic, containing the cession of Louisiana, was signed on the 30th of April twelve days earlier than that with G. Br. and some apprehension is entertained that the Boundary line contemplated in the 3rd art. of ye. latter, may by a possible future construction be pretended to operate as a limitation to the claims of territory acquired by the U. S. in the former of these Instruments.

But as the Ratification, if it can be effected, without unnecessary delay is a desirable object, it has occurred to the committee that Mr. King, may possibly have it in his power to give information which might remove the obstacle ; I have therefore in behalf of the comtee. to ask whether from any information in possession of your Department, or wh. may be obtained, in such manner as you may deem expedient, it can be ascertained whether the 3rd art. of the Treaty with G. Br. was concluded with any reference whatsoever to that with the Fr. Rep., or with any Right or claim wh. the U. S. have acquired by it.

I am, etc.,

[Signed.]   J. Q. ADAMS.

Copy of a letter from Mr. King :

NEW YORK, Dec. 9, 1803.

SIR :

The draft of the convention with Great Britain respecting boundaries, having been settled in previous conferences, was drawn up and sent by me to Lord Hawkesbury on the 11th of April ; on the 12th of May the convention was signed without the alteration of a word of the original draft ; and on the 15 of May the letter of Messrs. Livingston & Monroe (a copy of which was annexed to my No. 100) announcing the treaty of cession with France, was received and communicated by me to Lord Hawkesbury. At the date of the signature of the convention with Great Britain, I had no knowledge of the Treaty with France and have reason to be satisfied, that Lord Hawkesbury was equally uninformed of it. It results that the Convention was concluded without any reference whatsoever to the Treaty of Cession with France. With much respect &c.

[Signed.] Rufus King,
Secretary of State.

JAMES MADISON TO R. KING.
Private.

WASHINGTON, Dec. 18, 1803.

DEAR SIR :

I have recd. and communicated to the Committee of the Senate the information contained in your favor of the 9th which clearly shows that the Convention of May 12, with G. Br. is not to be construed by any reference to that of April 30, with France.

I am mortified at troubling you on a subject which more than any other is in itself unworthy the attention of either of us, but which is obtruded on mine by sensibilities in others which neither public prudence nor social considerations will allow to be disregarded. Since the arrival of Mr. Merry & his lady,* several points of ceremony have started up, with respect to which it will be convenient to learn the usage abroad, particularly in England, where your station must have involved some acquaintance with it. Will you allow me then to ask the following questions :

1. On the arrival of a foreign minister, is the first visit paid by him or the ministers of the country ? 2. To which is the precedence given in scenes of a more public ceremony and of ordinary hospitalities ? 3. Is the order of attention precisely the same in the case of ladies, as of their husbands ?

* " The President's contempt of courtly niceties caused some trouble in diplomatic circles. Merry, the new British Minister, took deep offense at the President's republican humors. Proceeding in full dress at an appointed hour to make his first official call, in company with the Secretary of State, he found the hall of audience empty, and instead, came upon the President in a narrow entry, from which he had to back out in order to get introduced ; Jefferson, appearing, to his amazement, in a slovenly undress, with slippers down at the heel and Connemara stockings. When he and his wife dined afterwards at the White House Jefferson took to the table, not Mrs. Merry, but the lady nearest him, the wife of the Secretary of State. This he conceived to be a new insult and, notwithstanding Monroe's wife was similarly treated at London, he declined further social hospitalities from the President, and when the latter made

Our wish would be to unfetter social intercourse as well as public business as much as possible from ceremonious clogs, by substituting the pell mell ; but this may be rendered difficult by the pretentions & expectations opposed to it.   And as it is proper that we should not be behind other nations either in civility or self-respect, it is well to know the manner in which other nations respect both us and themselves.   This information will be pertinent, whether a reciprocity in the object, or the right possessed in every country be exercised of establishing a practice for itself.

To enable you to give the apter shape to your answer to the third enquiry, it may be proper to remark, that it refers among other particulars to that long used at the President's as well as elsewhere, of selecting the lady first handed to the table.   In general this mark of civility has been shown to the ladies of foreign Ministers ; but was it seems disapproved of and at one time varied by the last President.   The practice of the present has been different, without however adverting to precedents, or rather supposing it to be conformable to them, and without an intimation of discontent anywhere, till the late occasion, which has produced it from several quarters.

I will thank you not to delay your answer longer than you conveniently may require.   I would have preferred waiting till I have the promised pleasure of seeing you here, but that you make the weather a condition of your visit, and that some occasion may in the mean time arise, on which the information asked may be apropos.   With great respect & esteem I am, Dear Sir,

yr. mo. obedt. Servt.

JAMES MADISON.

overtures to arrange the difficulty administered an airy rebuke.   D'Yrujo, who had acquiesced nearly three years in the President's practice, made common cause with Merry on this point.   An explanation to the British Ministry followed.   Merry's wife was thought to be the chief agent in producing what was a mere misunderstanding."—Note in Schouler, *Hist. of U. States*, vol. ii., p. 81.

Mr. Henry Adams, *Hist. of U. S.*, vol. ii., pp. 360 *et seq.*, gives a full account of these matters and of the effect of his treatment on Mr. Merry, who deeply resented the slight which he considered had been put upon him, and it will be seen that his dispatches to his government reflected his feelings and gave an idea that the administration of Mr. Jefferson was determined to make more decided demands upon England for the settlement of pending questions.

See also Mr. Madison's letters to Mr. Monroe, *Letters, &c., of James Madison*, vol. ii., pp. 188, 195.

Mr. Henry Adams, *Hist. of U. States*, vol. ii., p. 365, after quoting Mr. Jefferson's " Canons of Etiquette to be observed by the Executive," says: " Such according to Rufus King, whose aid was invoked on this occasion, was the usage in London." It is hardly probable that this is correct, and the Editor is at a loss to know from what source Mr. A. derived his information. A careful search for an answer by Mr. King to the letter of Mr. Madison, has been made but none can be found in the public correspondence or in that in the Editor's possession. As Mr. Madison's letter is marked private, the answer was probably also private.

C. Gore to R. King.

LONDON, December 20, 1803.

MY DEAR FRIEND :

. . . The Minerva arrived from Boston about a week since, and it is almost settled that we embark in her. She will probably quit this the beginning of March. . . . We exceedingly rejoice at your promise of visiting us next summer, and be assured we shall not rest satisfied without a performance. There are no persons whom it would afford us such sincere pleasure again to meet, and my own affairs & professional pursuits will not permit me for a year or two to move far from town. It is unnecessary for me to say that nothing would tempt me to engage in public life, under those who now rule our country, for nothing is more certain than that they would not employ me. Yet I may be permitted to remark, that so different are all their notions & conduct from what I conceive wise & honest, that were their dispositions towards me exactly the reverse of what I know them to be, mine could not change, and of course I could not move in their train. . . .

It is to me inconceivable how men, entertaining a proper sense of duty, could proceed with such intemperate haste in ratifying the Louisiana treaty. That with Spain was, without any question, executory, so far as related to the cession of the country to France, and surely, they, who were about to oblige the U. S. to the payment of a large sum & the performance of other stipulations, ought to see that France had the right to convey. One would expect that such rash & imprudent measures could not fail to discover to the people, whose affairs they thus mismanage, their utter incapacity to preside over the concerns of a great nation.

The expectation of Bonaparte's attempt to invade England daily lessens. The papers, which I send by this ship will (besides showing you, in the Courier, the opinion entertained of the President's message) communicate the intelligence of a misunderstanding between Bavaria & Austria. Nothing more is yet known than the simple fact, as related in the papers. Whether it proceeds from the hasty & imprudent temper of the Elector, or from the intrigues of France to occasion a quarrel between those powers, and avail herself of this occasion to find plunder for her troops on the continent, and an apology for quitting the coast, is all matter of conjecture. It is said by some who pretend to know, that the character of England is rising and that of France falling in the eyes of Europe ; that these nations begin to see the justice of the British cause, and that the war is entirely owing to the ambition of the Consul. If such an alteration of sentiment has really been produced, in my opinion it is owing to a conviction on the part of those, who have changed their judgment, that Bonaparte can not execute his threats on England, & is therefore determined to turn his arms on them. . . .

A letter came here a few days ago from Swan to young Mr. Higginson whom you know, saying that the Virginia faction thwarted all Mr. L's views ; that never was anything more abominable than the attempt of M. to assume any share of the merit in gaining Louisiana ; that the Government only supported the claim of the latter to avoid the charge of misspending the public money in sending him out ; and, finally, that the Federalists ought to support him L. as Vice President at the next election, and begging him H. to write out so to his friends in America. From what is said in another quarter here, I have little doubt but the present administn. intend to discard him & his connections. It will rely entirely on Southern & Western influences for continuing in power and leave the Northern & Eastern States to perish for their ingratitude in poverty & disgrace. . . .

Truly yours C. GORE.

A letter from Mr. Charles J. Ingersoll, who had been on very intimate social relations with Mr. King and his family in London during the former's residence in Europe, shows that he had not forgotten those from whom he had received much kindness. It is dated Dec. 6, 1803.

"I am told you have bo't a house and are settling down in the Broadway. As you may suppose I often look towards you with pleasure and gratitude ; and for some weeks past I have been about enquiring of you and yours.

"J'espére que madame se trouve à son aise dans la nouvelle maison, et qu'elle l'a meublé et garni à son goût. I tender the homage of my most respectful consideration to Edward who I hope has found a Vauxhall in New York. Little Master Gore by this time, *I guess*, can ask for his bread and butter.

"I am jogging along my professional path ; my father nudges me along, and the Governor has given me a publick room adjoining the Court, where I have established my desk and armchair ; so that they say I do tolerably well. The U. S. Government looks to me like a salt monster, 180 miles too big ; * if it don't vanish I flatter myself it must dissolve.

"Our State rulers threaten to toss away that excrescence on civilization, the bar ; and Counsellor Ingersoll declares he'll go to New York—all the eminent lawyers have their eyes on one city or another to remove to in case of extremes." . . .

R. KING TO CHAS. J. INGERSOLL.

NEW YORK, December 21, 1803.

DEAR SIR :

When we have but little to do, we are prone to lose our habits of regularity, and I can offer you no better excuse for my delay in replying to the obliging letter that I lately received from you. I am glad to hear that you have seriously taken an office and engaged in business, as I am firmly persuaded you will succeed to

----

* A thought probably prompted by the publication by the President about this time of the existence of a mountain of pure rock-salt in Louisiana " 180 miles long & 45 wide and 400 feet high," as one of the precious benefits derived by the purchase of that Province.

your satisfaction and acquire distinction, if you have patience and will persevere.

During our fever, we resided at Greenwich : about three weeks ago I gave up my house there and removed to town, having taken, not purchased as you had heard, Mr. Peter Livingston's house in Broadway.   My lease will expire on May day, before which I must seek another habitation.   Mrs. K. enjoys her health as she was accustomed to do before we went abroad, and better than at any period during our absence.   Little Fritz bore the summer well and will, we hope, carry his rosy cheeks thro' the winter. Edward, who has for want of something better been a day scholar in a French school near my house in the country, is just preparing to go to Mr. Harris, a clergyman of good education and accustomed to the instruction of boys, who will receive him into his family.   He lives a few miles out of town, so that I should have no apprehension in his remaining with him in the event of another fever.

We often hear from our sons in England, who are, I flatter myself, doing as well as I have any right to expect.   From James (in Paris) we do not receive frequent accounts ; our last letter was written in September when he was well and happy.   I had thought of bringing him home next spring, but I am so little satisfied with our academies here, that I have determined to leave him abroad some time longer.

As no one is more out of politics than I am, you must expect nothing from me on this interesting topic : I have talked about going to Washington in the course of the winter, but as I am snug by my fire side, with my books about me, I suspect my voyage will begin and end in talk.

With sincere regard &c &c

RUFUS KING.

C. GORE TO R. KING.

LONDON, December 23, 1803.

MY DEAR FRIEND :

.   .   .   Col. Livingston left there (Paris) but not having given his address, it is very probable I may not see him.   Notwithstanding what the papers chose to say on the subject, there is no probability that Talleyrand has confided anything to him.   On

Wednesday, Hammond did not believe that he was in England; the papers said he arrived on Monday. The Courier will announce the arrangement of the misunderstanding between Austria & Bavaria. Some of the gales have been tremendous, but, with the persevering spirit of a true Eng. Bull-dog, Cornwallis keeps his station off Brest. An idea is entertained that should the fleet come out, the British will waste their time and powder on the armed ships & that in the mean while the transports will be able to proceed with their troops. It is, however, said, that the intention is to pay the principal, if not their whole, attention to destruction of the transports. Occurrences daily happen, which go far to support an idea of the utter impracticability of crossing the channel hostilely in these flat bottom boats.

Affectionately yours

C. GORE.

Dec. 29. . . . It is understood that some of Cornwallis' squadron have been obliged to come into port. The storm on Christmas day was extremely violent. I do not know the grounds, but by the appearances abroad, it would seem that the Admin. really expect the attempt at invasion will be shortly hazarded.

yours as ever

C. G.

With this letter of Mr. Gore's, the correspondence for the year 1803 closes. Mr. King, as he says, was out of politics and was quietly enjoying the pleasure of social intercourse among the friends about him and the company of his books. But he seems to have been interested in the discussion of the different points suggested by the acquisition of Louisiana. Several papers are found among his manuscripts, which are given in an appendix. They appear to have been written for publication, but if they were published, they cannot be traced. As however they present his views relative to the extent of the Territory purchased, based upon a critical examination of its history, and to the question of the wisdom of the purchase, they will be given as they are found.

R. KING TO C. GORE.

LONDON, Jany. 4, 1804.

MY DEAR FRIEND:

. . . I am a little sceptical concerning the invasion of England although Bonaparte would play a deep game by doing nothing except to garnish the coast with his Battalions, & to build flat bottom Boats. I do not think this Fabian mode of war is in his character, and therefore conclude that a grand Project will somewhere be attempted. Perhaps when the Eng. fleets are driven off the Enemy coasts, the Dutch & French & Ferrol fleets will attempt a combined operation by the invasion of Ireland. Perhaps the show is in the West, and the real efforts are making in the East to pass an army into the Morea by crossing the Adriatic . . . These are however mere Speculations and of the worst sort as they are not founded upon any kind of information. . . . I can only hope as I earnestly do, that no sinister Event may endanger the security of the nation where you are, which may be regarded as the principal and almost the sole Barrier agt. an Evil that menaces every Country.

Things here go on in the order which those who direct them wish, and are pleased with. The Louisiana Business will be carried into effect according to the provisions of the Treaty. Already we have accounts of the delivery of the Colony to the French Prefect, who has notified the inhabitants that he expects the American Commissioners at N. Orleans and shall surrender the Country to the U. S. This will be done and we shall enter peaceably into the Possession & Government.

You will see in the news papers the debates respecting the Constitutionality of certain of the Articles of the Treaty. Whether the Govt. will admit the force of the objections, and submit an amendment to the States, by which Congress may be authorized to carry the Treaty into effect or recommend to Congress to do so as the Constitution stands, is more than I am able to decide, and is a question if I mistake not with which those who have to determine it are not a little embarrassed.

In our quarter, the western acquisition, by which I mean the Territory over the River, is not liked and I think it seems to be pretty generally wished that the Govt. would exchange it for the Floridas. This in my view would be the best mode of avoiding the otherwise great Difficulties of various kinds which will be sure to arise. From the tenor of the President's message at the opening of Congress, this will not be done, as he talks of the uses of this Region to which our Posterity are to apply it. If our Govt. be even willing, the consent of France must be had, before we can make this Exchange, or in any way dispose of this Country; a Right inconvenient to us and of no honest value to France, and reserved therefore for mischievous ends.

As to the next Election, there can be no doubt that the Pr. will be re-elected—a Vice President of the same Politics is also sure to be chosen, if the amendment of the Constitution takes Place of wh. there can scarcely be doubt. Whether it will be Col. Burr or some other Person is not mentioned. The former Genan. is in a deep minority with his Party here, and is making considerable efforts to better his situation, as the London servants say; but if the Federalists are steady he must fail; on this point however after what happened at the election at Washington one can never feel at ease. I sent you the Examination: the object of which is to repel the charge that Col. Burr intrigued with the Federalists to become President—or in other words to reconcile himself to the Democrats who have suspected him. It is curious that at the moment of this publication, and ever since, the friends of Col. Burr are making overtures to the Federalists to elect him Governor of this state in opposition to Gov. Clinton. Such are the inconsistencies that some men can practice and such the intellect of the Community which they must despise. . . .

We hear that there is some Buzz at Washington concerning Merry's Reception. The day and hour were appointed for his first audience, and he was attended by the Sec'y of State. Mr. Jefferson rec'd him in his slippers, and altogether in an undress! —at least such is our report. . . .

I write to the boys, who are now at the Abbé's, and shall again propose to them to talk with you concerning their future professions. I should like, were it practicable, to decide immediately which of the three boys I shall put into the House of Sir F. Baring, as in this case I should wish you to converse with Sir Francis respecting the subject before your embarkation. Genl. M (iranda) has I conclude left England before this date. If the question is at length settled with Spain, as it shd. have been months ago, he may yet see his wishes accomplished.   He & you know my sentiments on this subject, which nothing can alter.   I do not write to the Genl., because I am expecting to hear of him in another quarter.   Should he make a beginning, the news wd. electrify this country, which contains an immense number of individuals who would be ready to take up their Bed and walk.

Yrs. affectionately,

R. K.

C. GORE TO R. KING.

LONDON, February 8, 1804.

MY DEAR FRIEND :

Since I last wrote we have received your favours of Nov. 20 & Dec. 7 and January. 4.   The boys left us about a fortnight ago for Harrow.   They were perfectly well, and so conducted themselves during the vacation.   John at present seems inclined to the profession of law, & Charles, so far as he has any predilections, to that of a merchant.   .   .   .

What you feared has certainly come to pass.   M's dispatches are truly of a very sombre hue.   The reception of the Prest., the details of leading into dinner, &c. &c. were as particularly recounted, as the wounded pride of the Lady, or the injured dignity of the Minister could possibly require.   The want of accommodation there, high prices, bad or rather no markets, lead them to view the seat of our philosophic empire, if not the philosophers themselves, with great disgust.   The Convention you subscribed here, the President declined for a time to ratify, making a reservation of Louisiana.   Now it is said, he will ratify, making a reservation of any rights that may have accrued to us, by the cession of this country.   H. says he hopes to God the admin. here will not take the ratification so made.   It is further believed, that Monroe has orders to propose an arrangement of the business of seamen, by a convention, in which G. B. shall agree, that the American Flag shall protect all persons who sail under it.   The Under-Sec. is outrageous, but his superiors, operated upon much as are some other great men in the West, may act according to existing circumstances, though my persuasion is that they will not yield that point.

Feb'y 9. Yesterday Pinkney & myself dined at Ld. Hawkesbury's. His Lordship there took me aside & mentioned the unpleasant accounts they had received from Washington. I declared my regrets that anything should arise to afford occasion therefor, that it would be a pity if circumstances, in themselves really trifling & of no public consequence, should be suffered to produce a coolness between the Govt. of the U. S. and the Rep. of his Majesty ; that without pretending to judge as to the real weight or importance, that should be ascribed to what he alluded, I was sure he would concur with me in the opinion, that wisdom dictated a total disregard of personal considerations & trivial circumstances in weighing the just and important relations of two countries situated as were the U. S. & G. B., especially at this highly interesting & convulsed state of Europe. While he agreed with me in these reflections, he said Mr. M. (erry) had taken particular pains to enquire of Mr. Liston & Mr. Hammond, what was the etiquette observed when they were in the U. S., that he might neither claim nor expect more respect or attention than was the custom. I only replied that surely Mr. M. did appear to me to go out with a disposition favourable to the harmony & interests of the two nations, and that I hoped that if Mr. M. saw that whatever course had been adopted was alike to all the foreign ministers, both himself & his Majesty's Govt. would not feel in it any particular cause of dissatisfaction, & at least not to suffer it to have more influence than its intrinsic importance demanded. I was sorry to find however that it has & will have considerable weight in the minds of this Govt. Without particularising, it is certain he principally referred to the leading into dinner & seating at table. In this silly business, they probably see here a disposition to affront England, and it will with others, increase a growing discontent with us. He then remarked to me about your convention, and said explicitly that the Government, if it came back as they had reason to fear, would not consent to a ratification. Dinner was announced and we parted, he saying that he would ask another opportunity of conferring further on these subjects before my departure. If he should I will surely do everything in my power to soften & diminish the growing prejudice against our Government, the effects whereof we shall feel whenever G. B. is more at her ease in her European relations. After dinner, at which were several of the foreign Ministers, and two or three of the nobility, he called on me to take some wine & said he would give one toast, by my consent, which was Mr. King. This was drunk & such remarks made afterwards on the subject of it, as were gratifying to all (how relished by P. I cannot say) but they were such as would insure your condemnation by all the Democrats of our country.

Some few weeks ago, Erving, as Consul, sent a memorial to Lord Hawksbury relative to a vessel that was here in distress, with a request that the cargo, which was oil & in a leaky state, might be unladen &c, &c, and saying that the parties had applied to Mr. Monroe for his interference, who after examining the subject & finding it purely commercial, referred them to the Consul. A note was returned saying that it was the invariable usage of the office to receive no memorials from Consuls, that if Mr. Monroe would make any application relative to the interests of his Government, or its citizens, it would be attended to with all the promptness that its nature required, and especially in the case alluded to. Monroe made no application, and the man's oil, I presume, goes on wasting. They conceive here that it is Jefferson's intention to disgust all foreign ministers at Washington, and by degrees insinuate Consuls into the business at foreign courts, and when these Genln. shall retire from our Government, leave all affairs to be transacted by Commercial Agents. This may be his scheme, especially as it would be cheaper & by multiplying certifs., he might impose all the expense on the merchants trading to the different countries.

Genl. M. is still here, waiting the decision of the Government in relation to Spain. Possibly an original error in not considering it as a party in the war, is the cause of the present delay & of all the subsequent errors.

. . . We shall probably sail in the beginning of March. We are to execute our last awards on Saturday next. Two cases yet hang in the Courts, one in the admir'ty, & the other before the Lords : these Swaby has consented to decide that I may not lose my passage. . . .

Ever & affectionately yours

C. GORE.

Thomas Jefferson to R. King.

WASHINGTON, Feby 17, 1804.

Sir :

I now return you the M.S. History of Bacon's rebellion with many thanks for the communication. It is really a valuable morsel in the history of Virginia. That transaction is the more marked as it was the only rebellion or insurrection which had ever taken place in the colony before the American revolution. Neither its cause nor course have been well understood, the public records containing little on the subject. It is very long since I read the several histories of Virginia, but the impression remaining in my mind was not at all that which this writer gives ; and it is impossible to refuse assent to the candor & simplicity of his story. I have taken the liberty of copying it, which has been the reason for the detention of it. I had an opportunity of communicating it to a person who was just putting into the press a history of Virginia, but still in a situation to be corrected. I think it possible that among the antient MSS. I possess at Monticello, I may be able to trace the author. I shall endeavour to do it the first visit I make to that place ; and if with success, I will do myself the pleasure of communicating it to you ; from the public records there is no hope, as they were destroyed by the British, I believe, very completely, during their invasion of Virginia. Accept my salutations and assurances of high consideration and respect.

TH. JEFFERSON.

C. Gore to R. King.

LONDON, February 19, 1804.

My dear Sir :

By the newspapers which I have put on board the Oneida Chief you will see that the King is seriously indisposed. I learn that the stories about his having the dropsy are altogether untrue, but he is violently mad. It has been coming on for some time, and said to have been occasioned at first by drinking cold water, when very warm. The night before last he slept seven hours, awoke perfectly collected, took his medicines & eat his food as he should do. From this some hopes are entertained that he may recover, but I doubt if they be very strong. . . .

The Maryland Bank Stock is through the Chancery & the costs adjusted. So it only remains to pass from the crown, which will be impeded by the King's malady. We execute our last awards to-day & close next week. . . .

Yours ever & affectionately

C. GORE.

C. GORE TO R. KING.

LONDON, February 29, 1804.

MY DEAR FRIEND :

I have only time to say that we expect to leave town on Saturday for Gravesend, where we embark. Our commission closed with perfect harmony on the 23d inst. I can only say that personally I have been treated by Ld. H. & Hammond with great kindness & attention. The King is better ; this, I understand from those who wish it, and those who think the public good may be promoted by a different dispensation of Providence. . . .

C. GORE.

CHAPTER XXIII.

At the close of a letter from Mr. King to Mr. Gore, September 6, 1803, p. 303 in this volume, he remarks: " Notwithstanding the satisfaction of the negotiators with their performance, I believe that Govt. is and will be embarrassed with the cession [of Louisiana], which may become the immediate cause of very important political events among the States." It was not long before the correctness of this opinion was manifested by the debates in the Senate and House on the provisions for carrying out the Conventions and by subsequent events.

The constant troubles with the Spanish authorities at New Orleans, interfering with the navigation of the Mississippi and the commerce of the western portions of the United States, induced Mr. Jefferson to endeavor by purchase to become possessed of New Orleans and the adjacent districts, and thus secure the free navigation of the river. Mr. Livingston, who was sent to France as Minister, when he found that Louisiana had been transferred to that country, endeavored to accomplish the purchase ; but to his astonishment he was in the end offered the whole of Louisiana, with

346

New Orleans, at a price which seemed not too large. The First Consul's necessities suggested the offer, the treaty of purchase was made and, when received in the United States, was accepted by the President and ratified by the Senate. So far all seemed well, although the objections made to the ratification by the Federalists showed that the action was hasty and that the provisions of the Conventions were such as involved serious constitutional questions. The President himself had believed that an amendment to the Constitution would be required to make this addition, with its peculiar provisions, to the territory of the United States; but his friends in the Senate had set aside the scruples and ratified the agreement.

When, however, it became necessary to make the appropriations for the payment and to provide a government for the new territory, the objections to the Conventions were again brought forward, and a stern opposition was made by the Federalists on the broad constitutional question, and especially upon the clause in the Convention that " the inhabitants of the ceded territory should be incorporated in the Union of the United States" with all the rights and privileges of the citizens of the United States. They contended that there was no power which " was competent to such an act of incorporation "; that therefore " this could not be effected without an amendment of the Constitution," an amendment which would require " the assent of each individual State and all of them to admit " a foreign country as an associate in the Union." Besides they contended that the New England States by the admission of this territory, with the government of it in the control of the administration and its friends, chiefly in Virginia, would be cut off from their proper influence in the affairs of the nation. Their opposition was of no avail; the money was appropriated, the territorial government established, no constitutional amendment was adopted, and Virginia and the republican party carried their measures.

But the end was not here. Another amendment to the

Constitution had been passed through the same Congress, providing for a change in the manner of electing the President and Vice-President. Two candidates for the office of President had hitherto been voted for : the one receiving the highest vote was to be President and the other Vice-President. The election of Mr. Jefferson had been placed in jeopardy by this provision, and his friends, who had decided upon his re-election and a possible succession of other Virginians, determined, if possible, to prevent any interference with their plans, and brought forward the amendment by which the candidates for each office should be designated and the choice of President could only be made from among those voted for as such.

To this strong and earnest objections were made by the Federalists, who contended that by this provision it would be impossible ever to elect a Federal president,* as by a combination of the larger States, they could control the election and thus the smaller States would have their privileges curtailed, privileges which under the existing balances of the Constitution they might enjoy. This and other reasons were ably presented as objections to the proposed change, but it was passed by the same dominant party through Congress, and was ratified by a sufficient number of the States to make it valid. Its wisdom has not yet been proved though it still continues to be the law.

As if to rouse the Federalists still more and to make them afraid that every balance of the Constitution might be destroyed, the attempt to tamper with the judiciary and to reduce it also to a political machine was the next step adopted by the friends of the administration. In the debates which took place in the impeachment of two of the judges of the U. States Courts, it was openly suggested that even the

---

* Indeed, Mr. Cooke of Tennessee avowed that this was one of their objects. He said "that the majority of the Republicans might obtain the man of their choice, and, with certainty, prevent the election of either a President or Vice President from the Federalists." Mr. Taylor of Virginia suggested that the proposed amendment would finally destroy the minority.

Supreme Court, the only department the administration could not control, the buttress of the Constitution, should be subjected to the power of Congress, by changing the tenure of office which made the judges independent of the other departments. Happily the threatened change was averted and that court still maintains its high and independent character.

A considerable number of the leading Federalists, Messrs. Pickering,* Tracy, Griswold, and others, who had already been outraged by the removal of their friends from office, saw danger in these various movements and endeavored to arouse their friends to resist further encroachments upon the Constitution by the party which now dominated the country. They truly loved their country, and were among those who had laid its foundations so as to secure, as they believed, its prosperity, but they thought it best that the New England States, to which they belonged, should, for self-protection, separate themselves from those who were threatening, by other measures also, to destroy their proper share in the benefits of the Union. They, therefore, took measures, by correspondence and concert of action, to endeavor to bring about a separation, but felt that without the assistance of New York, they could not hope to succeed. They, therefore, sought the assistance of Aaron Burr, who had been rejected by his party † and offered himself to them, to accomplish their object. He had been nominated as a candidate for the office of Governor of New York and it was hoped by many Federalists, that with their help he might be elected and thus be ready to forward their schemes, which he seemed

---

* See T. Pickering's letter, March 4, 1804, R. King's *Life*, p. 363.

† Schouler, *Hist. of U. S.*, vol. ii., p. 59, says: " At a dinner in honor of the event [the peaceful acquisition of Louisiana] on January 27, 1804, at Stelle's Hotel, Capitol Hill, which the Republican Members of Congress and high officials generally attended, ' the general applause indicated that Jefferson would be put forward for a second term, while Burr, who was one of the guests, would be dropped. Not long after, at a caucus of the Republican Senators and Representatives (February 28th), Jefferson was nominated for President unanimously, with George Clinton as his associate for Vice-President."

inclined to do. Happily he was defeated and the hope of assistance through him by the plotters was destroyed.

But this was not the only drawback to the success of their plans. They found positive objections and a refusal to entertain their propositions by those Federalists, Messrs. Hamilton, King, Cabot, and others, whom they looked upon as the head of that party, and whose assistance it was necessary to obtain, and as a consequence the whole scheme fell through.

Before proceeding with the correspondence relative to the details of the proposed separation of certain States from the Union, it may be well to bring forward the narrative of certain events, which, to a certain extent, have been hinted at. In a letter of January 27, 1803,* addressed by Mr. Sedgwick to General Hamilton, in anticipation of Mr. King's return home, he spoke strongly of the advisability of holding the Federal control of the State governments and recommended the nomination of Mr. King to the office of Governor of the State of New York, to which he thought it possible he might be elected, and in which he might "do infinitely more good than in the inefficient office of Vice-President. General Pinckney must in all events be considered the candidate for the first office. . . . Should Mr. King be holden up for this office (the Vice-Presidency), it would lessen, at least, the probability of success for the government of New York."

The friends of Mr. King continued, however, to desire his election to the office of Vice-President, for at a public dinner of the Federalists in Washington on February 22, 1804, at which Mr. Pickering presided, Messrs. Pinckney and King were by consent nominated as their candidates for the Presidency and Vice-Presidency, but without designation as to which should have the precedence; though at a subsequent and much later meeting Mr. Pinckney was named for the first office.

In the meantime, Mr. Clinton having been chosen as the Republican candidate for the Vice-Presidency, Mr. Burr was

* R. King's *Life*, vol. iv., p. 215.

left out in the cold.   The New York Governorship was still unsettled, and he hoped, as had been said, by the help of the dissatisfied Federalists, to succeed in reaching it.   The Federalists who remained loyal to their party views desired, as had been suggested by Mr. Sedgwick a year before, a candidate upon whom they could unite and bring back those who were wandering away to the support of Mr. Burr.   It would appear from the two following letters, that Mr. King, unconsulted, was proposed as their candidate.

The letter of General Hamilton was written from Albany, where he was engaged in defending the liberty of the press against the construction of the judge that he alone could decide whether an article was libellous or not, and the jury could only determine the question of publication.   He contended that the dictum "the greater the truth, the greater the libel," was contrary to the "genius of our civil institutions and manifestly a palpable outrage on human rights, common justice, and even common sense, . . . that the liberty of the Press consists in publishing with impunity the Truth with good motives and for justified ends, whether it related to men or measures. . . . If the intent be a subject of enquiry, the giving of the Truth in evidence is requisite as a means to determine the intent."

While this important trial of an editor was going on, the canvass for candidates for Governor occupied the minds of those assembled in Albany and it was carried on with great warmth: the letter given shows how earnestly Hamilton sought to avert the calamity which was threatening in the nomination of Burr by the aid of the Federalists.

A. HAMILTON TO R. KING.*

ALBANY, February 24, 1804.

MY DEAR SIR :

You will have heard before this reaches you of the fluctuations and changes which have taken place in the measures of the reigning party, as to a candidate for Governor ; and you will probably also have been informed that pursuant to the opinions expressed

* See also Hamilton's *Works*, vi., 559.

by our friends before I left New York, I had taken an open part in favour of Mr. Lansing.

It is a fact to be regretted, though anticipated, that the federalists, very extensively, had embarked with zeal in the support of Mr. Burr ; yet an impression to the contrary and in favour of Mr. Lansing had been made & there was good ground to hope that a proper direction, in the main, might have been given to the current of federalism. The substitution of Mr. Lewis has essentially varied the prospect ; and the best informed among us here agree that the Federalists as a body could not be diverted from Mr. Burr to Mr. Lewis by any efforts of leading characters, if they should ever deem the support of the latter expedient.

Though I have no reason to think that my original calculation was wrong, while the competition was between *Clinton* & *Burr,* yet from the moment the former declined, I began to consider the latter as having a chance of success. It was still however my reliance that *Lansing* would outrun him ; but now that Chief Justice Lewis is the competitor, the probability of success in my judgment inclines to Mr. Burr.

Thus situated two questions have arisen ; 1st, whether a federal candidate ought not to be run as a means of defeating Mr. Burr, and of keeping the federalists from becoming a personal faction allied to him ; 2nd, whether in the conflict of parties as they now stand, the strongest of them disconcerted and disjointed, there would not be a considerable hope of success for a Federal candidate.

These questions have received no solution in scarcely any one's mind ; but it is agreed that if an attempt is to be made, you must be the candidate. There is no other man among us, under whose standard either fragment of the democratic party could as easily rally. It is enough to say, you have been absent during the time in which party animosities have become matured and fixed, and therefore are much less than any other distinguished federalist an object of them.

To detach the Federalists from Burr, they must believe two things—one, that we are in earnest as to our candidate, and that it is not a mere diversion ; the other, that there is some chance of success. All believe, & some leading democrats admit, that if either of the two democratic rival parties should come to expect a defeat, they would arrange themselves under your banners.

Reflect well on all these things and make up your mind, in case
you should be invited to consent.   I have not time to enlarge.

Yrs very truly

A. HAMILTON.

Mr. King's letter was written on the same day as the above
in New York, and explains itself.*

R. KING TO GENL. HAMILTON, ALBANY.

Feby. 24, 1804.

DR. SIR :

Mr. D. B. Ogden called upon me a few minutes past, and as I
understood from him that he purposes writing to you by the mail
of this Evening, I think it proper, in order to avoid any misconceptions of the tenour of our conversation, to repeat to you the
purport of what I said to him, viz—" Whether it will be expedient
to offer a federal candidate for the Govr. is a point upon which,
from the want of information concerning the relative strength
and disposition of parties, and the consequent probability of success, I professed myself (to Mr. D.) quite unable to judge.

" With respect to my being the fedl. candidate, altho' I would
not say that my mind was absolutely decided, as I had never considered the subject, the objections to my consenting appeared to
me to be unsurmountable."

faithfully &c.

RUFUS KING.

In resuming the consideration of the plan proposed by
some of the leading Federalists in Congress to bring about
the making of a northern Confederacy, the intention is to
state only the facts which connect the name of Mr. King
with it and to show that he would have nothing to do with
the movement for a separation of the States.

* Mr. J. C. Hamilton in Hamilton's *Life*, vii., 778, with his usual unwillingness to give Mr. King credit where he can avoid it, says—" the nomination of
a federal candidate, in the person of King, was thought of, but the idea was
not pursued." He does not say that he declined allowing his name to be used
notwithstanding the strong appeal made to him.

It would seem that the first knowledge of it was from a letter of Timothy Pickering, March 4, 1804,* in which after showing that the acquisition of Louisiana and the legislation consequent upon it, would throw the power of the Government forever in the control of the Southern and slave-holding States and thus shut out New England from its proper influence in the Union, he therefore urged that steps be taken without delay to counteract this danger and form, with the addition of New York and New Jersey, a separate government.

Without expressing any opinion as to the wisdom or feasibility of the measure, Mr. King on March 9th, † acknowledged the receipt of his letters with the remark that " the views they disclose ought to fix the attention of the real friends of liberty in this quarter of the Union, and the more so as things seem to be fast advancing to a crisis."

In a letter from Mr. Cabot, Boston, March 17, 1804, ‡ to Mr. King, he says :

" An *experiment* has been suggested by some of your friends to which I object that it is impracticable, and, if practicable, would be ineffectual. The thing proposed is obvious and natural, but it would now be thought too bold and would be fatal to the advocates as public men : yet the time *may* soon come, when it will be demanded by the people of the N. & East, and then it will un-

---

* R. King's *Life*, iv., p. 363 ; given also in Lodge's *Cabot*, p. 447. See also letter of Pickering to King, March 3d, p. 359.

† R. King's *Life*, iv., p. 366.

Henry Adams, *History of the United States*, ii., p. 178, says : " Of all Federalist leaders, moderate and extreme, Rufus King, who had recently returned from London, stood highest in the confidence of his party. He was to be the Federalist candidate for Vice-President ; he had mixed in none of the feuds which made Hamilton obnoxious to his former friends, and while King's manners were conciliatory, his opinions were more moderate than those of other party leaders. . . ." Rufus King was as cautious as Pickering. He acknowledged this letter in vague terms of compliment, saying that Pickering's views "ought to fix the attention of the real friends of liberty in this quarter of the Union, and the more so as things seem to be fast advancing to a crisis."

‡ R. King's *Life*, iv., p. 369.

avoidably take place. I am not satisfied that the thing itself is to be desired. My habitual opinions have been always strongly against it and I don't see in the present mismanagement motives for changing my opinion."

There does not appear that any answer was given or preserved to this letter, but on March 19, 1804, the following papers are found in the handwriting of Mr. King, endorsed "O. Wolcott, Conversation Spring 1804."

"March 19, 1804.

"The opposition or at least the dissimilitude of Interests between the Northern & Southern States is such, and the present and increasing preponderance of the power of those of the South is such that the balance between North and South, which secured to the former an equal share of influence & honours, an equal encouragement of industry, and the like Protection of Property, with the latter, is altered and permanently settled in favour of the Southern States. As in all similar cases power will be increased for the benefit of the Possessors, and the Northern States are destined to be ruled, and not only so but ruled unjustly and for the advantage of the Southern States.

"Hence the necessity of a division of the confederacy. Patience wd. lead to delay—the mercenary character of the Northern People, fearful for their commerce, timid for their money in the funds, recommend Procrastination. In the mean time Jacobinism extends itself and the means of successful opposition to Virginia is lessened. Commerce wd. be equally successful & the pub. Creditors wd. be equally secure. In July 1803 the public Debt due east of Pennsylvania amounted to $32,160,000 & to this a proper proportion of the Dutch Dt. shd. be added, & assumed. The Louisiana Dbt. shd. be left to those for wh. benefit it was made.

"Means have been taken to rouse the three N. En. States M., N. H. & Conn, to begin—but they are slow, cautious &c. ; the Demos. in Cong. from the North are dissatisfied but obedient to Virginia, and so they will be until they are from home told to do otherwise. They are also destitute of Talents, and incapable of influence. Eustis & Bradbury may be attached to Burr ; but both of them more attached to their own projects. Eustis has lost reputation with all sides : his object is to be collector of Boston

Bradley profligate &c.—Burr's views unknown—believed to be supported in N. Yk. by Persons hostile to Virginia : if so, and he becomes Govr., N. Yk. may be united with the Northern States in the Project of Separation : his sentiments on this point unknown (met him accidentally in the Nat. Library, an interview proposed by him at N. Yk.) altho' a bad man perhaps the Federalists shd. support him, as the evil daily extends itself & his Election seems the only chance of rescuing N. Yk. from Virginia—but if Burr gains N. Yk. merely to gain the Presidency—the support and success wd. be subject of Regret for the southern power being as stated, the occasional possession of the Presidency wd. do no good, might do harm.

" The only remedy is separation—will Burr agree and pledge himself to this object.

" April 5

" According to the proposal of the Library *Mr. Griswold* visited Burr April 4 : the purport of the Conversation was that he must go on democratically to obtain the Govt.—that if he succeeded, he shd. administer the Govt. in a manner that wd. be satisfactory to the Federalists—no particular explanation was made on this head—in respect to the affairs of the Nation, Burr said that the Northern States must be governed by Virginia, or govern Virginia, and that there was no middle mode—that the Democratical members of Congress from the East were in this sentiment, some of those from N. York (Phelps, Thomas, Paterson & Root) and some of the Leaders in Jersey and likewise in Pennsylvania.

" Griswold said the Federalists to the Eastward would be solicitous to understand the policy of N. Yk, they might be active or passive according to the opinion they should form on this point—it was to this enquiry, that Burr replied, that he shd. administer the govt. in a manner satisfactory to the Federalists ! I could not learn that Griswold engaged anything on his side, limiting himself as I was given to understand, to mere enquiry : but according to what has been told me, I conclude that Griswold wishes Burr success agt. Lewis, believing by his means to rescue N. Yk. from the Jeffersonian Politicks ! ! ! "

" April. 5. 1804

" Informant. O. W. Before Congress adjourned Phelps and one or two other of the democratical members of Congress from

N. Yk went to the President to know of him whether he regarded
Burr as a Republican ; & referring to the pending Election of
N. Yk for Govr., whether the Presidt. wd. disapprove of Col.
Burr's being supported by the Republicans ; or in other words
whether those who shd. support Col. Burr for Govr. wd. be regarded favourably ; or entitled to the favour of the President ?
Jefferson replied that he considered Burr to be a Republican, that
it was a division among republicans and that therefore Republicans
might with Equal Propriety support or vote for either Candidate.

" Yesterday, Ap. 4, an interview took Place between Phelps and
DeWitt Clinton ; Phelps recited the opinion of Jefferson respecting the candidates for Govr. Clinton stated that Gen. Jno. Smith
having heard of the interview between Phelps and Jefferson, had
gone to require a farther Explanation—that Jefferson in this interview admitted that in substance he had stated what Phelps had
reported ; but added that this Opinion was given upon the idea
of a mere division among the Republicans—that if the federalists
took a part, it wd. materially alter the case and that the candidate
opposed by the Feds shd. be supported by the Republicans ! ! !

" The interview between Phelps & DeW. C. broke up with
mutual recriminations and dissatisfaction."

Informt. O. W.

" Ap. 5.

" Genl. Varnum, one of the Demo. members of Cong. from Virginia has been surrounded by the Burrites on his way thro' N. Yk
to Mass. Concerning the caucus held at Washington to agree on a
Vice President, the Genl. stated that during the session a correspondence was opened between Dawson and another member
from Virginia and DeWitt Clinton—that one or two of the New
York members were privy to this correspondence—the object
whereof was to engage Gov. Clinton to become the Vice President—his consent was in this way obtained, without any previous
communication with the Eastern demo. members ; when a meeting of all the demo. members was called to agree in the Choice of
a V. Pr.—when met this consent of Gov. Clinton was announced,
—the Eastern members complained that the business had gone
thus far without their having been consulted, and moved to adjourn the meeting. The Virginians opposed it, and the assembly
took a Ballot ; the result whereof has been published.

"Some days after the Eastern Demo. members (those East of N. Yk) met and deputed Varnum to the Virginians to express their disapprobation of the Proceedings which had taken place without their privity, and to declare that as the Engagement had been made without their consent, they left the contract to be fulfilled by the Virginians who had formed it."

In the reply of Mr. J. Quincy Adams to thirteen citizens of Massachusetts, in 1829, the following remarks are found : *

"The information concerning the project communicated to me at Washington, in the spring of 1804, corresponded in the main with that detailed by Mr. Plumer. . . . The session closed on the 4th of March, 1804, and I shortly afterwards returned to spend the summer at Quincy. On my way thither, I was detained several days at New York, during which I frequently visited Mr. Rufus King, who had recently returned from his first mission to England. On the 8th day of April, I called and passed great part of the evening with him in his Library. I found there, sitting with him, Mr. Timothy Pickering, who shortly after I went in, took leave and withdrew. As he left the house, Mr. King said to me, ' Colonel Pickering has been talking to me about a project they have for a separation of the States and a Northern Confederacy : and he has also been this day talking of it with General Hamilton. Have you heard anything of it at Washington ?' I said I had, much, but not from Colonel Pickering. 'Well,' said Mr. King, 'I disapprove entirely of the project ; and so, I am happy to tell you, does General Hamilton.' I told Mr. King that I rejoiced to hear that this was his opinion, and was equally gratified to learn it was that of General Hamilton,—that I was utterly averse to the project myself and much concerned at the countenance I had heard it was receiving at Connecticut and at Boston. It was the acquisition of Louisiana which had been the immediate incentive to the plan. I had much conversation with Mr. King on that subject ; and I found his opinions concerning it concurring with my own ; and, I understood from him, not differing from those of General Hamilton. We agreed, and lamented that one inevitable consequence of the annexation of Louisiana to the

* *New England Federalism*, by H. Adams, p. 147.

Union would be to diminish the relative weight and influence of the Northern section ; that it would aggravate the evil of the slave representation, and endanger the Union itself, by the expansion of its bulk and the enfeebling extension of its line of defence against foreign invasion. But the alternative was—Louisiana and the mouths of the Mississippi in the possession of France, under Napoleon Bonaparte. The loss of sectional influence, we hoped and believed, would be more than compensated by the extension of national power and security. A fearful cause of war with France was removed. From a formidable and ambitious neighbor, she would be turned, by her altered and steadily operating interests, into a natural ally. Should ever these anticipations fail, we considered a severance of the Union as a remedy more desperate than any possible disease." *

Such was the position of affairs, when the New York election took place on April 25th and Burr was defeated. Henry Adams says : †

" Pickering & Griswold saw their hopes shattered by the New York election. They gained at the utmost only an agreement to hold a private meeting of leading Federalists at Boston in the following autumn ‡ ; and as Hamilton was to be present, he probably intended to take part only in order to stop once for all the intrigues of these two men. Such an assemblage under the combined authority of Cabot, King, and Hamilton could not have failed to restore discipline."

The history of this unwise project, so far as General Hamilton is concerned, is summed up in a conversation, five days

---

* Mr. John Quincy Adams (p. 227, *New England Federalism*) further says : " So secret was it (the project) that, although during that session of Congress I was sitting at the side of Mr. Plumer in the Senate of the United States and contracted with him an intimate friendship which continues to this day, yet I never knew that he had been made acquainted with the project at the time, far less that he had favored it, until after the note of preparation sounded last autumn in the Boston newspapers, preliminary to the summons of the Confederates addressed to me."

† *Hist. U. S.*, ii., p. 186.
‡ *Life of Plumer*, p. 299.

before his duel, with Colonel Trumbull, who had been dining with him. Mr. J. C. Hamilton * says :

" After dinner, when they were alone, Hamilton turned to Trumbull, and, looking at him with deep meaning, said: ' You are going to Boston. You will see the principal men there. Tell them from ME as MY request, for God's sake, to cease these conversations and threatenings about a separation of the Union. It must hang together as long as it can be made to.' "

In his celebrated letter to Sedgwick, written on the eve of his duel, Hamilton says :

" I will here express but one sentiment, which is that DISMEMBERMENT OF OUR EMPIRE will be a clear sacrifice of great positive advantages, without any counterbalancing good ; administering no relief to our real disease which is DEMOCRACY ; the poison of which, by a subdivision, will only be more concentrated in each part, and consequently the more virulent.

" King is on his way to Boston, where you may chance to see him, and hear from himself his sentiments."

The death of General Hamilton seems to have arrested further attempts to enlist the sympathy of leading Federalists. There is no report of what took place during Mr. King's visit to Boston, nor whether any general conference was held there as had been proposed.

T. PICKERING TO R. KING.

WASHINGTON, March 3, 1804.

DEAR SIR :

As long ago as the 4th of November last, you were so obliging as to notice my Letter concerning Louisiana. The ruling party do not *now* pretend that the Louisianians are *Citizens* of the U. States. They do not venture to say—they have never said—that the Government had a Constitutional power to incorporate that new & immense Country into the Union ; yet they will not give

* *Life of Hamilton*, vii., 822.

themselves the trouble to alter the Constitution for that purpose. It appears very evident that in a few years, when their power shall be more confirmed, and the implicit obedience of the people has been habitual, they will erect States in that Territory and incorporate them into the Union. Mr. Adams had not arrived when the Treaty was ratified, but he approved of it and of the consequent appropriation for the purchase-money; fondly believing that an amendment to the Constitution, to embrace that new object, would have been a mighty easy thing. He presented a Resolution really for that purpose; but after lying some time, it was called up and even contemptuously rejected; his own, Mr. Hillhouse's and mine being the only votes in its favour. It is further evident, that the Constitution will henceforward be only a convenient instrument, to be shaped, by construction, into any form that will best promote the views of the operators. In the name of the Constitution they will commit every arbitrary act which their projects may require; or they will alter it to suit their purposes. I begin to think it would be better if we had none. The leaders of the populace wanting the sanction of a constitutional power might then be more cautious in their measures.

We have commenced the consideration of the Impeachment of Judge Pickering of Portsmouth (I presume you know that he is not a relative of mine) for high crimes and misdemeanors. Process was served upon him in January and he was summoned to appear at the bar of the Senate yesterday. Mr. Harper delivered to the President (Mr. Burr) a letter from himself, and a petition (admirably drawn) from Jacob L. Pickering the Judge's son. In his letter Mr. Harper suggested Judge Pickering's insanity, and that he appeared not as his attorney, and could not enter an appearance for him, but at his son's request, to support the facts stated in his petition; which described Judge Pickering to have been insane at the times when he held the district courts mentioned in the articles of impeachment; and as still insane and so infirm in body as to be utterly incapable of being brought at this time, in person, to the Bar of the Senate, and tendered affidavits to substantiate these facts: praying also that the trial of the impeachment might be postponed. Mr. Harper asked if he might be permitted to speak in support of the petition.

The managers on the part of the House of Representatives objected. They wished the non-appearance of the Judge might be recorded as a *default*. The Senate retired (conformably to a previous arrangement) to an adjoining room to consider this point. After near an hour spent in loose debate, they came to this conclusion only, that they would return to their Chamber, and that the President should inform the managers, that the Senate had not come to a determination ; and that when they had they would give due notice thereof to the House of Representatives.

To-day we met again, and *with closed doors*, discussed the question. All the Jeffersonians who spoke were for denying the prayer of the petition and the hearing of counsel in support of it, declaring that Judge Pickering ought to plead, or that his friends should put in a plea for him, if not guilty ; and that under this plea, all the evidence they proposed to offer, to prove his insanity, might be given. Some of them supposed, or pretended to think, that if he was proved to be insane, he might be found guilty. Mr. Tracy replied, with a poignancy which would have excited a proper feeling in men unhackneyed in the measures of a party malignant and cruel as death. He remarked that *intelligence* was essential to the commission of a *crime*, and that no court would pronounce an insane person guilty of high crimes and misdemeanors, who were not themselves insane. Still, however, they all persisted to argue against the hearing of counsel on the petition until near four o'clock when the court adjourned.

In this debate (I am sorry it was not public) there were manifested a virulence and rancour which shocked every man, who had any feelings of justice or humanity. Let this party progress in the course they have travelled for two years past, and before Mr. Jefferson's second Presidency expires, I shall not be surprised, if I live so long, to see bloody victims of their ambition, inexorable malice and revenge. One or two Marats or Robespierres, with half a dozen congenial spirits, would carry along enough of the half moderates to make a majority in the Senate to concur in any measures ; and by similar means they would be forced through the House of Representatives. Could Senators vote by *ballot*, Judge Pickering would not, being proved insane, be convicted of any crime ; but voting viva voce, many have not honest fortitude enough to say *nay* to any measure which is supposed to involve popularity, and I do not know what will be the result. The late amendment to the Constitution would hardly have been adopted by a *majority ;* much less by *two thirds* of the Senate, if their votes had been given by ballots.

The British Convention for settling Boundaries, which you took some pains to negotiate, and which was signed the 12th of May, you would naturally suppose must have been readily approved by the Senate ; seeing it conformed to your instruction ; and was, in fact, made by our own Government ; and especially after the President, in his message at the opening of the Session, had informed Congress and the world, that the terms of the Convention were entirely satisfactory to both parties. But the President altered his mind ; the Senate followed of course ; and the advice to ratify was, with the exception of the fifth article, which, you will recollect, respected the Northwestern boundary. And yet in a paper which he sent me, (occasioned with an accidental written correspondence between us) speaking of the Treaty of Cession of Louisiana, to the U. States, he said expressly " But this Treaty was not known to the negotiators of either party at London nor could the rights acquired by it be affected by arrangements instituted and compleated there merely for the purpose of explaining and supplying provisions in the Treaty of 1783." Why then suspend the 5th Article ? why not ratify absolutely ? Mr. Jefferson is not contented with the immense extent of Louisiana as held by the French. Its northern boundary not having been explicitly defined (tho' undoubtedly it reached to the utmost range of the Mississippi and Missouri) he wants to carry it to the parallel of the 49° of North Latitude. To effect this end, he certainly supposes the suppression of the 5th Article will contribute. For this object your *entirely satisfactory* convention is put in jeopardy. He thinks, however, or pretends to think, that G. Britain will readily agree to the other articles ; and he doubtless supposes they will negotiate to his wishes relative to the northern boundary of Louisiana. Some of his *magnanimous* partisans in the Senate have openly avowed the propriety of pushing G. Britain *now* on any points we desire to gain ; because her present critical situation will dispose her to yield (as they imagine) what in a time of peace she might refuse ! This avowal was made this week, when we were discussing Sam. Smith's *wise* bill *for the protection of the seamen of the U. States ;* and which the Senate (doubtless on the hint from the *oracle*) had the grace to reject, by postponing it to next December. A like bill before the House of Repres. must meet the like fate. It is understood the President is negotiating on this Subject.

In this debate S. Smith told us that you were once on the point of signing a convention relative to American seamen—or rather seamen on board of American vessels ; when it was suddenly declined by the British Ministry. In a former debate, he said that the British Ministry had consented to renounce all impressments from our vessels, except within the *narrow seas.* Apropos. What do the British mean by the words "narrow seas " ?

I shall be much obliged by your giving me any information which it may not be improper to communicate on the subject of impressing our seamen ; or, if any part be confidential, you will so mark it. The Act of Congress, presenting the certificates to be given to seamen, is defective. I have had some thoughts of offering a bill for amending it ; and to introduce some guards to prevent the disreputable modes of obtaining proofs of citizenship, whereby all certificates, even of our native seamen, are rendered suspicious. Any hints on this head will be gratefully received.

Faithfully yours

T. PICKERING.

T. PICKERING TO R. KING.

DEAR SIR :   WASHINGTON, March 4, 1804.

I must request you to consider this as a continuation of my letter yesterday.

I am disgusted with the men who now rule us and with their measures. At some manifestations of their malignancy I am shocked. The coward wretch at the head, while, like a Parisian revolutionary monster, prating about humanity, could feel an infernal pleasure in the utter destruction of his opponents. We have too long witnessed his general turpitude—his cruel removals of faithful officers, and the substitution of corruption and baseness for integrity and worth. We have now before the Senate a nomination of Meriweather Jones of Richmond, Editor of the Examiner, a paper devoted to Jefferson and Jacobinism ; and he is now to be rewarded. Mr. Hopkins, Commissioner of Loans, a man of property and integrity, is to give room to this Jones. The

Commissioner may have at once in his hands thirty thousand dollars, to pay the public creditors in Virginia. He is required by law to give bond only in a sum of from five to ten thousand dollars ; and Jones' character is so notoriously bad, that, we have satisfactory evidence, he could not now get credit at any store in Richmond for a suit of clothes ! Yet, I am far from thinking if this evidence were laid before the Senate, that his nomination will be rejected ! I am therefore ready to say "come out from among them and be ye separate." Corruption is the object and instrument of the Chief, and the tendency of his administration, for the purpose of maintaining himself in power & for the accomplishment of his infidel and visionary schemes. The corrupt portion of the people are the agents of his misrule ; corruption is the recommendation to office ; and many of some pretentions to character, but too feeble to resist temptation, become apostates. Virtue and worth are his enemies, and therefore he would overwhelm them.

The collision of democrats in your State promises some amendment. The administration of your Government cannot possibly be worse. The federalists here in general, anxiously desire the election of Mr. Burr to the chair of New York ; for they despair of a present ascendency of the federal party. Mr. Burr alone, we think, can break your democratic phalanx, and we anticipate much good from his success. Were New York detached (as under his administration it would be) from the Virginia influence, the whole Union should be benefited. Jefferson would then be forced to observe some caution and forbearance in his measures. And if a *separation* should be deemed proper, the five New England States, New York and New Jersey would naturally be united. Among those seven States there is a sufficient congeniality of character to authorize the expectation of practicable harmony and a permanent union ; New York the centre. Without a separation, can those States ever rid themselves of negro Presidents and negro Congresses, and regain their just weight in the political balance ? At this moment the Slaves of the middle and southern States have fifteen Representatives in Congress ; and they will appoint 15. Electors of the next President & Vice President ; and the number of slaves is continually increasing. You know this evil. But will the Slave States ever renounce this advantage ?

As population is *in fact* no rule of taxation, the negro representation ought to be given up. If refused, it would be a strong ground of separation ; tho' perhaps an earlier occasion may occur to declare it. How many Indian wars, excited by the avidity of the western and southern States for Indian Lands, shall we have to encounter ? and who will pay the millions to support them ? The Atlantic States. Yet the first moment we ourselves need assistance and call on the western States for Taxes, they will declare off, or at any rate refuse to obey the call. Kentucky effectually resisted the collection of the excise ; and of the $37,-000 direct tax assessed upon her so many years ago, she has paid only $4,000, & probably will never pay the residue. In the mean time we are maintaining their representatives in Congress for governing us, who surely can much better govern ourselves. Whenever the Western States detach themselves they will take Louisiana with them. In thirty years, the white population in the Western States will equal that of the 13 States, when they declared themselves independent of G. Britain. On the Census of 1790, Kentucky was entitled to *two* Representatives ; under that of 1800 she sends *six*.

The facility with which we have seen an essential change in the Constitution, proposed and generally adopted, will perhaps remove your scruples about proposing what you intimate respecting Negro representation. But I begin to doubt whether that or any other change we could propose, with a chance of adoption, would be worth the breath, paper and ink, which would be expended in the acquisition. Some think Congress will rise in 15 or 20 days * * *

Ever your faithful and obedient

T. PICKERING.

I do not know *one reflecting* Nov. Anglian, who is not anxious for the GREAT EVENT at which I have glanced. They fear, *they dread* the effects of the corruption so rapidly extending ; and that if a decision be long delayed, it will be in vain to attempt it. If there be no improper delay, we have not any doubt but that the *great measure* may be taken without the smallest hazard to private property or the public funds ; the revenues of the Northern States being equal to their portion of the public debt. Leaving that for Louisiana on those who incurred it.

R. King to T. Pickering.

New York, Mar. 9, 1804.

Dear Sir :

I have duly received, & beg you to accept my acknowledgments for your letters of the 3d & 4th instant—the views which they disclose ought to fix the attention of the real friends of Liberty in this quarter of the Union, & the more so as things seem to be fast advancing to a crisis—to save the post I can do little more than acknowledge the receipt of your letters—by the mail of tomorrow or Monday I will send you a copy of my Despatch to the Sec'y of State respecting the effort I made to conclude a convention concerning seamen.

Perhaps you will recollect a long letter from Lord Grenville to me, pointing out the defects of our Law for granting Protection to seamen : it was sent to the Dept. of State while you were in it, and according to my Recollection, was so very particular as to shew the only ex parte regulations that the Br. Govt. would be likely to respect.

As to our native seaman, there would I suspect, be little difficulty in framing such rules as might effectually protect them—and if nations alone were in question, the Northern States would find little embarrassment, as they do not depend upon foreign seamen to carry on their trade.

But the Southern States could not carry on their trade without the aid of foreign seamen ; and Great Britain will not consent that our naturalization of her seamen shall exempt them from being recalled & obliged to serve & defend their native country.

Were I in your place, I should leave it to the friends of the present Govt. to do what they can to obtain what we were unable to accomplish—it is perhaps all that the federalists can do, to oppose improper acts ; leaving the origination of all Laws, especially those which affect the Executive Power & Responsibility to the Legislative Agents of the President—The packet brings us no news from Engd. Monroe, towards the close of Novr. presented a *temperate memorial* on the subject of seamen : no answer has been given : except this Comn. the Department for For. affairs knew nothing of Monroe—no negotiation is on foot respecting the old treaty, and I conjecture that this memorial about the impressment of seamen is the only act of our minister at London since his arrival.

faithfully yr. obt. ser^t

RUFUS KING.

P. S.   I am unable to give you any correct opinion respecting the election of Govr.   The Federalists with the exception of certain individuals, will pretty generally vote for Burr—this will not be enough—and what portion of *Demos* will join him, I know not —pray how did it happen that he had not a single vote at Washington for Vice President.

———

R. KING TO T. PICKERING.

NEW YORK, MAR. 10, 1804.

DEAR SIR :

Enclosed I send you the extract promised in my last, and I likewise add copies of my letters to the Secy of State in answer to an enquiry that your colleague Mr. Adams in behalf of a Com^{ee}. of the senate requested Mr. Madison to make of me.   The project of a Convention respecting seamen had it taken effect, would have been beneficial but less extensively so than we may be apt to suppose ; inasmuch as a large, by far the larger proportion of seamen taken out of our employ, are impressed within the territorial Limits of G. Br.—which instead of being restrained by the convention wd. have rec'd an implied sanction.

That allegiance is unalienable, and seamen liable to impressment are two points about which English Lawyers & Statesmen entertain no doubt—and I shall be disappointed if the Eng. Govt. even consent to limit its authority, or tie up its hands in these respects, within its own proper jurisdiction.

The late Bill will I fear have a mischievous instead of a beneficial effect : and joined to other circumstances may produce to our trade greater embarrassment than of late it has suffered. Very much depends upon the existence of good humour between G. Br. & the U. S.   Many hundred naval officers are intrusted with the power of the nation ; these all look for favor & promotion, and are careful to find out the sentiments & temper of their government towards Foreign Nations—& the opinions they form in this respect have a material influence in the exercise of their several powers. Circumstances therefore of apparently small importance, but which are of a nature to produce irritation or disturb a satisfactory state of things, may lead to mischievous consequences—and tho' England has too powerful an interest to involve herself seriously with the U. S. yet the difference between a favourable & temperate exercise of her Rights as a Belligerent, and a vigorous and harsh one, would be most terribly felt throughout our Commercial Cities. Nothing will be obtained by menacing because nothing ought so to be obtained from a great Nation. I have somewhere seen a very precise definition of what the English mean by the narrow seas, at this moment I do not recollect the exact limits—they include however the sea according to my memory, between the Continent and Great Britain, and the claim is, I think, extended north almost, or quite to the northern point of Norway—St. George's channel which is carried far southward is likewise within the narrow seas, so that a vessel arriving from America with the purpose of entering the Baltic by the route of the Br. Channel, would be within the narrow seas, according to the Eng. construction of their limits, from the time of her making soundings till she reached the Categat. When Ld St Vincent proposed to me the addition by which the narrow seas should be excepted so as that within these limits our vessels might be visited & searched for British seamen, I remarked to him that all parts of the high seas within the territorial jurisdiction of G. Br. had been excepted in the proposed article, and that the narrow seas were or were not within their jurisdiction ; if they were not, the exception ought not to be made. His reply was that the express exception of them would remove doubts which might otherwise be raised.

As this exception would have subjected our vessels trading with the North of Europe as well as those trading with Holland & some parts of France to the most embarrassing visits in search of British seamen, I preferred leaving the subject on its present footing to a Convention which wd have afforded no little protection to our seamen.

Very faithfully yr obtd sert.

Rufus King.

G. Cabot to R. King, New York.

BOSTON, March 17, 1804.

My dear Sir :

In reply to your inquiry respecting the opinion of our Legislature on the subject of Louisiana, I cou'd only speculate. The session is ended & no one attempted to discover what was thought or what might be done. We add thousands to our possessions, but have long since discarded the idea of *security*. *The many* do not think at all, and the *few* think only to despond. Indeed most men are compelled to admit that *our evils must be borne until their intolerability generates their cure.* Most of those which we fear must therefore happen before a remedy can be prescribed. *An experiment* has been suggested by some of our friends to which I object that it is impracticable, and, if practicable, wou'd be ineffectual. The thing proposed is obvious and natural, but it would now be thought too bold and would be fatal to the advocates as public men ; yet the time *may* soon come when it will be demanded by the people of N. & East, and then it will unavoidably take place. I am not satisfied that the thing itself is to be desired. My habitual opinions have been always strongly against it, and I do not see in the present mismanagement motives for changing my opinion.

It is doubtless true that we are not so perfectly mad in N. E. as the people in some other States, especially those of the South ; but here we are altogether democratic in our principles ; and those principles of necessity place power in the worst hands. If the favourable aspect of our State Politics seems to contradict my opinion, I confess that those principles have not *yet* produced all the mischief to which they tend ; but at the same time I insist that our appearance is deceptive, being better than the reality and the reality better than can be well maintained. You see good men in high office here contrary to the natural operation of democratic elections ; but those men hold their powers upon the sole condition that they will not use them, and the moment they shall dare to exercise them with vigor, they will cease to be popular, and of course cease to fill the high offices they now hold.

There is an unusual apathy among the Federalists here. They have lost more of their vivacity than of their numbers ; I fear they lose some of these. Our national admintn. may destroy

Judiciaries and Constitutions and make new ones without exciting much sensibility ; but if they had involved us by their folly and baseness in a war with G. B. I believe N. E. might be roused to do *anything* which her leading men shou'd recommend. Some distinct general cause of evil like this and fairly imputable to the wickedness or ignorance of those who govern wou'd be fatal to their power or to the Union of the States. We are loyal to the National Govt., and can bear every species of public dishonor, but the moment our loyalty appears to be made the instrument of our *impoverishment,* we shall be disposed to act with effect in defence of *all that is dear to us.* . . .

We are now going on according to the course of nature and shall follow those who have gone before us from bad to worse 'till suffering or the fear of suffering, *generally and deeply felt,* stimulate us to do better. Indeed I expect no essential improvement in our systems, but from suffering, from fear, or from force. I think no material change can be made, except by those whom we call Jacobins. Good men wou'd not, if they had opportunity, establish any system of sufficient force to protect itself : the violent and unprincipled are more likely to make a govt. independent of popular consent than their betters.

I beg you however not to infer that because I think we cannot do things impossible, that I would not attempt every possible good, or that I do not think any great good can be accomplished. So far would that be from the truth, that I firmly believe we owe much of what we enjoy and of what we hope for, to the influence of the federal party. We are a minority and unable to conquer the vast body which keeps the field, but we are so powerful, that he is compelled to confine his movements to a narrow compass, lest he should give us an advantage over him. We have therefore the most commanding motive to preserve to our party all the weight we can by adhering to the principles on which it is formed and keep it well combined and well informed ; prepare to think and act alike on every important occasion. In this way we prevent some mischief entirely and mitigate what we cannot wholly avert, and shall be able to soften every catastrophe in the political Drama, which must happen, and turn them to the best account. . . .

Your faithful & affec. friend.

G. C.

CHAPTER XXIV.

On March 11, 1804, Mr. King wrote the following letter to the Secretary of State, which explains itself.

R. KING TO SECRETARY OF STATE.

NEW YORK.

SIR :

As my mission abroad had no other connection with the money department of our Government than what arose from the payment and receipt of my annual appointments, I made it a point, carefully, not to have the custody or to become accountable for any money belonging to the public. Hence I have concluded that I have no accounts to settle with the Treasury. As, however, this Department keeps its accounts in such manner as it may deem expedient, I am not sure that it may not have accounts with my name. On this subject I took the liberty to speak to the Secretary of the Treasury, when he was in this quarter during the last summer, and he was so obliging as to say that he would look into the question on his return to Washington. From the variety of his engagements I apprehend the subject has escaped his recollection, and I am therefore under the necessity of begging you to inform yourself and me whether there is any unclosed account with me, either in your Department or that of the Treasury.

With sentiments &c.

RUFUS KING.

The Secretary, on March 29, 1804, writes that this letter was received and sent to Mr. Gallatin, who promised to attend to the matter, and communicated the result of his examination as follows :

A. GALLATIN TO R. KING.

TREASURY DEPARTMENT, April 20, 1804.

DEAR SIR :

I did not forget that I had promised to attend to the situation of your public account, if, upon enquiry I found that any charges existed on the Treasury books against you. But the pressure of business during the session of Congress and a wish to obtain Mr. Baring's accounts which were necessary to give a full view of the subject have prevented an investigation until this time.

It appears that there are two accounts opened against you ; one, called the general account, includes all the payments made to you or on your account either at the Treasury or by Messrs. Bird, Savage and Bird, and by Sir Francis Baring and Co. ; the other relates to the payments to or on account of Major General Lafayette.* . . . You have, as yet, received no credit on either of those two heads, it being the usage that the party should state an account and transmit it to the Auditor with such vouchers and explanations as he may possess and think necessary. The items of salary need only be stated and the Secretary of State will inform whether the dates and allowances claimed are the proper ones. In respect to the items of postages, stationery or other contingencies each should strictly be accompanied with receipts or other vouchers, but Mr. Harrison informs me that they are not very strict on that subject with foreign Ministers, from the impracticability in most cases to obtain on their return home those receipts, &c, which are demanded in the settlement of domestic accounts. Such as you may have you will of course transmit ; but I apprehend no difficulty whatever in the immediate settlement of that first branch of the account as soon as you shall have stated and transmitted it.

In respect to the second division of that general account, and

---

* Mr. Gallatin here gives the items of these two accounts, upon which he comments in the letter. The first amounted to $78,978.32, and the second to $2698.18. Two of these items—the payments to Wilson and Chisholme—he does not see " to what appropriation to charge them." They amount to £102.7 sterling.

which consists of payments made by your order, it appears to me that from the face of the accounts it results that the money did not go through your hands, unless it be for the first item, . . . and even in these it is probable that it did not. If so, no receipts are necessary nor any other voucher, but to show the authority under which, or the reason why you directed the payment. All the items composing that branch of the account are charged provisionally, as requiring explanation. . . .

The other account of disbursements for Lafayette is settled and you stand charged with $4,895.09, being the amount paid, by your orders, beyond the sum granted by Congress. You may on that subject give any explanation you may think proper : but I do not perceive the possibility of giving you credit for the sum without the special interference of Congress. Whether or how an application should be made for that purpose will be a matter of future consideration. . . .

With sincere Respect & Esteem &c.

ALBERT GALLATIN.

In the course of the letter, Mr. Gallatin says :

" I only mean to point out the manner in which you should state your account and claim credit ; the receipts and vouchers should be transmitted to the Auditor, with such explanations as may be wanted, but in the course of the settlement I will with great cheerfulness assist in removing difficulties and in explaining to you what objections are made, and what may be required from you to remove them."

In accordance with the suggestions of this letter Mr. King transmitted, May 1, 1804, to the Auditor of the Treasury an account specifying the items due to him and claimed by him—amounting in all to $94,136 (being £18,981.15.4,) in dollars at 4.44 cents to the pound sterling " according to which he received and paid out." By this account he claimed as due to him $856.30.

On the original paper, retained by Mr. King (a copy he says was sent to the Auditor) is the following *Remark*, sent most probably as an explanation :

" Remark—By turning to the accounts of Messrs. Bird, Savage
and Bird and of Sir Francis Baring and Co, it will be perceived
that the credit side of this accouut (with the exception of nine
thousand dollars received from Mr. Pickering *) is wholly taken
from a transcript of these accounts ; the same is likewise the fact
in respect to the whole contingent account on the Debtor side :
the fact being that the only account which Mr. King has, either
of the contingent account or of the payments made to him by the
Bankers, is his Bankers' book."

There is a letter to the Auditor of the Treasury (in the
copy of which the date is not given), in which Mr. King explains his mode of providing for the care of the public
money during his mission in England :

SIR :

The Secretary of the Treasury has been good enough at my request to furnish me with copies of several accounts in my name
from the Books of your Department. Before I submit to your
consideration any observations upon the items of these accounts
it may be proper that I should state to you how far I consider
myself personally accountable in respect to the public money expended in England during my mission to that country. As the
custody of public money formed no part of my official duty, and
as for this reason, as well as others, I was unwilling to be its
keeper, my earliest attention after my arrival in England was
directed to the choice of a Banker, who would receive, keep and
disburse whatever money should be remitted for the public service in that country.

Messrs. Bird, Savage and Bird having been employed as Bankers of the United States during the time of my Predecessor, Mr.
Pinckney, upon his recommendation I settled with them the terms
upon which their agency should be continued. This agreement
was reported by me to the Secretary of State in my dispatch No.
4, Sept. 7, 1796, and sanctioned by letters to me dated Sept. 30
and Oct. 26, 1796.

According to this arrangement all remittances on account of
the public service in England were immediately upon the receipt
of the Bills put into the hands of the Bankers for collection, who

* His outfit.

kept and paid out the money so collected to the persons authorized to receive the same. On the failure of Bird, Savage and Bird, the house of Sir Francis Baring and Company, with the approbation of the Secretary of the Treasury, was substituted in their place ; and by strictly adhering to this system, I myself never had the custody of a shilling of public money during my residence abroad. In common with the Commissioners under the seventh article of the British Treaty, and other persons in the public employ, I applied for, and received from the Bankers, my quarterly appointments, and for these receipts and these only can I with any justice admit myself to be personally responsible.

By my direction money was advanced by the Bankers for the prosecution of appeals in the Prize Courts, for the purchase of presents to the Barbary Powers, in payment for military stores, Military Books, and Indian Medals, for copper supplied to the mint, for the support of General Lafayette and for other public purposes. In some cases these disbursements were made pursuant to express instructions, in others by virtue of the discretion which was supposed to appertain to my office.

At the same time that with all deference to the opinion of others I think myself bound to decline all accountability for money that I never received. I am ready to afford every explanation in my power concerning any payment made by the Bankers upon my recommendation. . . .

In carrying this out, Mr. King then enters upon a consideration of certain specific charges made by him and of which he claims the payment.*

* Payments to General Lafayette.

It will probably be recollected that General Lafayette, after being imprisoned by the Prussians at Magdeburgh, was turned over to the imperialists and confined in an Austrian dungeon. As soon as this information reached America the President General Washington wrote a letter to the Emperor of Germany (which was sent to the American Minister in London, and delivered to the Imperial Ambassador there, who forwarded it to the Emperor) soliciting that Lafayette should be released and allowed to come to the U. S. Toward the autumn of 1797 the Imperial Minister at Hamburg by order of his Court, gave notice to Mr. Williams, the American Consul there, that Lafayette would be released, that he would be escorted to Hamburg and delivered over to the American Consul, on condition of his embarking for America in eight days. Coming out of prison and being wholly destitute of means to provide for him-

After examining the account, the Auditor of the Treasury sent a communication to the Secretary of State, Mr. Madison, specifying certain charges made by Mr. King, and asking whether or not they were to be allowed. The Secretary, on June 20th, answered the inquiry, saying that certain of these were to be admitted as proper, but that others could not be admitted to his credit. Among them was the payment of money to Genl. Lafayette beyond the appropriation by Congress, one to Philip Wilson to enable him to return home, and certain payments for contingencies, postages, &c., and a change of a few days relating to the term on which his mission expired. The letter says:

self and family a passage to America, the General ordered his aide-de-camp Cardignan to apprize me of his situation, and to ask for money to enable him to convey himself and family to the United States.

Considering the General's connexion with the U.S., the application of the President to the Emperor for his release, and his discharge and delivery to the American Consul on condition of his proceeding to America, I did not hesitate in consenting to give orders to the Bankers of the U.S., to advance the sum requisite for this purpose. When General Lafayette arrived at Hamburg, the season was so far advanced that he concluded to remain with his family during the winter in Holstein, and Cardignan in his behalf applied to me that the proposed advance to enable Lafayette to proceed to America should be made and applied for his subsistence in Holstein during the winter. This was agreed to with an intimation that the whole sum to be advanced would not exceed a thousand or twelve hundred pounds sterling.

Lest I might act under an erroneous impression in respect to the proper limits of discretion on this occasion, my dispatch no. 47 dated Sep. 5, 1797, nearly four months before the first advance was made to Lafayette, I acquainted the Secretary of State with my intention and after it was decided that the General and family would pass the winter in Holstein, I wrote a private letter to the Secretary of State, of which the following is an extract:

"There remains only about £200, of the fund destined for the use of Lafayette: this is already called for, and the necessities of this unfortunate character will require advances (to what extent I cannot ascertain) for the subsistence of himself and family during the winter. I have before mentioned to you that I should, if required, make such advances as may be requisite for this purpose, as well as to enable him to remove to America; and I think I am not mistaken in my belief that the President will approve this exercise of discretion."

Receiving no instructions upon the subject between Christmas 1797 and the middle of May 1798, several advances were made by the bankers to General Lafayette, amounting to about £1200. sterling. The paper marked D. is a Voucher for these advances—General Lafayette's receipt.—See R. King's *Life*, ii., 223 *et seq.*

"From the above it follows that some of the charges under the head of contingencies are inadmissible and it will therefore be necessary to specify the latter so as to exclude the inadmissible charges. Mr. King may also be requested to specify them with as much more minuteness as he finds it in his power to do."

R. HARRISON TO R. KING.

TREASURY DEPARTMENT, Auditor's Office,
June 22, 1804.

SIR :

In order that you may be fully informed of the present situation of your accounts which were returned to me yesterday, I have now the honor to enclose three papers marked A, B, & C. The first contains a statement of the points it was judged proper to refer to the Secretary of State. The second his decision on these points, and by the last you will perceive that, before a settlement can be effected, it has become necessary that you furnish another account of your *contingent* expenses with all the minuteness your materials will permit, and, more especially, so as to exhibit distinctly the amount of each payment for Stationery, Presentation fees and Christmas presents ; or so as to exclude, in a word, everything except Postage, Newspapers, Pamphlets and. the printing of necessary papers ; these being the only charges which can be allowed consistently with the regulations long since established.

With respect to the overpayment to General La fayette, it is totally unconnected with the accounts now under consideration ; and I presume it must stand as it does until relief shall be afforded by an Act of Congress.

Expecting to hear from you as soon as your convenience will permit, I have the honor to remain with sentiments of high consideration &c. &c. R. HARRISON.

R. KING TO SECRETARY OF STATE.

NEW YORK, June 27, 1804.

SIR :

The auditor of the Treasury has sent me a copy of your opinion concerning several questions, which it seems have arisen in the examination of my account with the United States, and I take the liberty of enclosing to you my answer to the auditor with a request that you will be so obliging as to send it to him after you have read it. I must and do feel real concern in dissenting from your sentiments on this occasion, especially as my own may be thought liable to the influence of personal interest. But as we form as well as act upon our opinions respecting our own affairs, equally as concerning those of others, and as it is within the President's competence to allow the charge, I flatter myself that I may rely upon his and your impartiality to give to the following observations respecting the presents made to the under Officers and Servants of the Court the weight to which they may be entitled.

It is the custom at the Court of London, on the first presentation of a foreign Minister, as well as at every Christmas during his residence, to make presents in money to the amount of about £30 sterling on each occasion to the under Officers and Servants of the Court. This contribution no foreign Minister declines giving ; and it is not a personal, but official tribute, on the payment whereof there is no option as in the case of ordinary expenses ; I may safely add my conviction that there is not a single foreign Minister to whom this extra charge is not allowed by his Government. I enclose a list * of these Pensioners of the Corps diplomatique in London and submit it to the President's equity to determine, whether I shall be required to reimburse to the Public the payments which I made to them.

Whether these charges were made by my Predecessor is more

* List of persons to whom the present against their respective names is given by all foreign Ministers on their first presentation at St. James.

The King's Valets de chambre, in the Levée rooms, 4 Guineas. The King's footman, 2 do.—The Sergeant porter of the Court. 1. do.—The 7 Gentlemen porters-1. do—The six Marshalmen, 1 do—The underporters at St. James, 1. do—The yeomen of the Guards 2. do.—The Queens porter and underporter. 1½ do.—The Queen's footman 2. do.—The Prince of Wales porter and footman 2½ do.—The Grooms of the King's bedchamber, who give notice of Court mournings, 1. do—The chamberkeepers at the Secretary's office 2. do—The porter at do. 1 do—The servants of the Master of Ceremonies 1. do—The servants of the assistant Master 1. do—in all, £26.5.

The same persons receive Christmas presents in one or two instances less than those named on the presentation, but Christmas presents are given to the servants of the Prime Minister, and of the Secretary of State, so that the Christmas present exceeds by 2 or 3 Guineas the present on presentation.

than I know, but admitting they were not, his omission should not prejudice his Successors. It may be recollected Mr. Pinckney was absent on a mission to Spain, during which his expenses were paid and his regular appointments as Minister at London continued. Besides the expenses of the Mission during my time were increased at least by a quarter beyond what they were in the time of my Predecessor. These reflexions are made not solely for my own sake, but for the sake of any gentlemen, who with the present salary may be my Successor, and their object is to establish the just distinction that exists between official and personal expenses, and to prevail upon the President to free me and my Successors from the former.

With perfect Consideration & Respect &c, &c,

RUFUS KING.

R. KING TO R. HARRISON, AUDITOR.

NEW YORK, June 27, 1804.

SIR :

I have had the honour to receive your letter of the 22nd instant, together with the opinion of the Secretary of State concerning the several points which were referred to his consideration. As I am to infer from the tenour of your letters that your Department possesses no discretionary power in respect to these points, I ought not to waste your time by any observations concerning them. I may however be permitted to observe that the diplomatic account, which always included my contingent account, was every year, according to my instructions, transmitted by the Bankers to the Secretary of State, and for the purpose, as I always supposed, of being annually examined and settled. No observation was ever made to me concerning the items of, or manner of stating this account, and I therefore concluded, especially as every item is within the President's competence to allow, that from year to year it had received the approbation of those whose province it was to judge of it.

Had the slightest intimation been given to me that the particulars now asked for would be expected, I should have endeavoured, however inconvenient, to obtain and preserve as far as practicable the means of enabling myself to comply with the demand. As I have before stated to you this account was faithfully made out and examined by me once in every year, but as no care was taken to preserve the memoranda from which the same was drawn up, it is not now in my power to specify the amount of each particular article, or to furnish a separate statement of my yearly expense for copy-books, paper, pens, wax, wafers &c included under the name of stationery.

The charges for presentation and Christmas presents to the under officers and servants of the Court, which are official expenses, that no foreign minister can with credit decline, are already separately stated in the account transmitted to you. If it be deemed fit that I should put my hand into my own pocket to reimburse to the public money that without advantage to me has gone into the pockets of others, there will be no difficulty in ascertaining the amount. As the money advanced for poor Wilson's passage has no relation to my private account, I will only add that since the allowance of Wilson's expenses from Lisbon to Norfolk, for he was obliged to put into Lisbon on his passage, it may seem that this change should be disallowed.

Very faithfully and with great Respect &c
RUFUS KING.

To finish this subject the following letters, though somewhat out of sequence as to date, will show that a settlement of Mr. King's accounts was reached without any material change.

J. MADISON TO R. KING.

DEPARTMENT OF STATE, July 13, 1804.
SIR :

I have had the honor to receive your letter of the 29th ult., enclosing one to the Auditor which was handed to him. The President having directed that your charges for presentation and Christmas presents and for stationery be admitted to your credit in the books of the Treasury, the letter of which a copy is enclosed was transmitted to the Auditor as his guide. The enclosed extract from the accounts of Messrs. Bulkleys, late Bankers at Lisbon, will evince that no charge for the relief afforded to Philip

Wilson and his family was admitted to their credit, for the same reason which operates against that claimed by you.*

I have the honor to be &c &c

JAMES MADISON.

As stated in the letter, the auditor was directed to allow these claims. The Secretary's letter was answered by Mr. King as below.

R. KING TO SECRETARY OF STATE.

WALTHAM NEAR BOSTON, July 24, 1804.

SIR :

Owing to my absence from New York, I had not the honour of receiving your letter of the 13th before yesterday. Although the suspended items in my account are in my judgment equitable charges, yet as they seem not to be included within the contingent expenses heretofore allowed, I feel myself duly sensible of the President's liberality in the direction which he has authorized to be sent to the Treasury Department on this subject, and beg the favour of you, Sir, to present to him my respectful acknowledgements.   In regard to the allowance that I supposed to have been made at the Treasury on account of Ph. Wilson's expenses, I have probably misapplied the information given to me by the late Secretary of the Treasury, Mr. W. who, on my speaking to him respecting the advance made for Wilson in London, told me that there was a precedent for its payment, as he well remembered that on Wilson's arrival at Norfolk, certain expenses attending his passage were allowed and paid.   Whether this payment was to the Master of the ship, or to enable Wilson to get on from Norfolk to Philadelphia, or on some other account, I am ignorant.   Knowing of the Lisbon expenses, I concluded it was to them Mr. Wolcott referred.

But I have already given you too much trouble on this unim-

---

* " That there is no existing provision in America by which our advances can be reimbursed."   This claim for £52. was based upon a subscription to a fund to enable Philip Wilson & family, who had been impoverished in unsuccessfully prosecuting a claim in London, to return home.   The minister, as such, subscribed the above amount for that purpose.   His vessel was driven into Lisbon.

portant point. I will only add that should this small disbursement, as well as the more considerable one to General Lafayette appear to the President to have been made from motives that merit his approbation, I should hope that he will not think it inexpedient to recommend to Congress to cover the same by a suitable appropriation.

In cases of private persons, it behoves them to petition Congress for relief ; but officers of the United States and accountable to and removable by the President naturally look to him for protection in all cases of expense, when without authority they may, nevertheless, have exercised a sound discretion.

Yours &c

RUFUS KING.

THOS. T. TUCKER, TREASURER UNITED STATES, TO R. KING.

TREASURY OF THE UNITED STATES, WASHINGTON, October 6, 1804.

SIR :

Enclosed you will find my Draft No. 7138, on Jonathan Burrall Esq for $339.\frac{51}{100}$ Dollars, being the amount of Warrant No. 32, Issued by the Secretary of the Treasury, on receipt of which be pleased to favor me with an acknowledgment.

I am with great respect Sir, your Obedt. Servt.

TH. T. TUCKER, Treasurer Un. States.

RUFUS KING ESQ.

BOSTON, Oct. 17, 1804.

SIR :

I have duly received your Letter of Octr. 6 enclosing your Draft No. 7138 on Jonathan Burrall Esq for $339\frac{51}{100}$ Dollars payable to my order, stated to be the amount of Warrant No. 32, issued by the Secretary of the Treasury, and being I presume a Balance due to me upon the settlement of my accounts in the Department of the Treasury.

I have the honour to be with great Respt.

Sir, your ob. Servt.

RUFUS KING.

TH. T. TUCKER, Treasurer U. S.

On the original account sent to the Auditor of the Treasury, there is the following in R. King's handwriting :

Nov. 7, 1804—Allowed balance .	$339.51	
Suppd. deduction P. Wilson . .	233.32	
Salary from 23d inst of 20th May to		
18th ins of 20th say 5 days a 24.65	123.25	696.08
Unknown disallowances . . .		160.72

The amount sent to him by draft is thus accounted for. It is therefore probable that the disbursement to Lafayette was allowed by the President.

The three letters which follow, though somewhat out of their order as to dates, are in several ways interesting and are here inserted :

F. BARING TO R. KING.

LONDON, 1 March, 1804.

MY DEAR SIR :

I cannot suffer our friend Mr. Gore to leave the country without conversing with you by the only means in my power ; indeed I have long felt a propensity to begin a correspondence which was in a great measure superfluous whilst Mr. Gore remained. I am just returned from Bath & from paying my last respects & duty to our friend Bingham ; a melancholy task & still more melancholy reflexion that such a man should be cut off in the prime of life. I never saw a more firm manly mind, nor (if I may use the word) more stern integrity ; solely occupied with the consideration of what was correctly right, without suffering the slightest bias or partiality to operate upon his mind. And though my sons do not enjoy some advantages which the Customs both of America & of England sanction, yet I can say most sincerely that they as well as myself are perfectly satisfied and that we shall ever hold his memory in the highest respect & reverence. He was surrounded by the families of his two daughters & Lord Lansdowne, whose attentions to him were incessant ; indeed nothing was omitted that could have been supplied.

I am returned to a most busy, anxious, I may say a most gloomy scene both at home & abroad—both indeed are so bad that it is with reluctance I touch upon either. You know perfectly well the carte du pays of things as they are, or rather were. Some, who were tired of the system of divide et impera, formed a coalition upon general principles of opposition to the Minister, but of equal reserve as to the consequences. Windham & Grenville, who are for war, unite with Fox & Grey, who are for peace. Windham, whatever we may think of his head, has character. But we now find the stern, austere Grenville will bend to anything for the sake of peace. Every man must lament that Fox with the best talents should yield so easily to a connexion which can neither be satisfactory nor reputable to himself. Grey embarks from friendship for Fox, for every great pugilist must have his bottle-holder. Sheridan is at sea & I fear his necessities, more than anything else, have governed his conduct. The Prince has given him a place which is about a single drop of water, in the ocean. I have no confidence in this union ; it will neither do for the Court or people, and cannot stand alone.

In what manner this junto will try their strength remains to be ascertained, as existing circumstances will shut many mouths, most probably will prevent any distinct plan from being formed. Pitt keeps aloof of connection, but is always on the ground and is much beyond the other competitors in sagacity. Since the King's illness the prince has only consulted with Thurlow, whose rough outside may easily be mistaken for what it is not : he will make no such mistakes as Roslyn did on a former occasion, which is so far safe. L. Moira commands in Scotland where he has distinguished himself by talents both civil and military ; he will no doubt act a conspicuous part under a new head. L. Lansdowne is on his road from Bath, but will not arrive till the end of the week ; of course he has not made up his mind. In 2 or 3 days the whole must develop itself, but I must write en avance or I shall lose the opportunity.

With regard to Invasion, I cannot think it will pass away & under such tremendous preparation guided by such a Man ; it is folly to be presumptuous. It is true the french will have great, very great obstacles to encounter ; but it is too much to say these obstacles will not be forced ; it is equally so to say they may not be evaded under a combination of favorable winds & circumstances. If you think I am nervous, I will freely confess to you that I wish the attempt should be made ; for if it shall not be made, the military force assembled is so enormous that the whole of the North of Europe is in danger, & I think it essential for the *safety of the World*, that Europe should enjoy more repose & have longer time to recruit before the flame burst out on the Continent, & which it must do ere long. When I urged the safety of the world to Bingham, he never would admit that America under any circumstances could possibly be in danger ; my opinion is, as it always has been, that Britain was the bulwark to America, & that the downfall of one would be followed by the destruction of the other. Indeed I cannot discover in what manner Universal Empire is to be prevented, if the power of France, say the unity of that power, remains intact, for its impulse is irresistible.

You will perceive what interesting events are on the point of developing themselves at the moment I write.—The internal government of this Country—Invasion or no Invasion—& on the latter circumstance depends continental war. In every event I hope we shall remain at peace with America. I shudder as much at a war with Scotland or Ireland, as with America. I only fear too much influence on the part of the people, whose passions constantly absorb & make them forget their interest, or even common sense. I am thoroughly confident in the pacific disposition of the rulers on your side, but in America, as well as in England, our Sovereign Lords & Masters, the Mob, must be obeyed. I could travel over much more ground with you, but I think to have stated the multum in parvo in times so pregnant with events, & yet at the moment so completely uncertain in every description or point of view whatever, I therefore shall conclude with the assurance of my being with great regard

My dear Sir, your most truly faithful humble Servant,

F. BARING.

———

C. GORE TO R. KING.

BOSTON, April 17, 1804.

MY DEAR FRIEND :

L'd. H., I mentioned to you before had invited me to a conference previous to my departure, proposed by a note to me to call at his office one day.   As he said nothing further of Merry's rank &c., I was of course silent.   It is their determination to keep things on the same footing with us, as the Treaty placed them, unless any commercial regulations of ours should render a different account necessary on their part, which I think they apprehend more than they have reason for.   As to the war, he seemed to think it was impossible for Bonaparte to avoid making an attempt to invade England after the immense means he had collected, and the enormous expence he had incurr'd, although he believed that his only hopes of success were in Ireland, and to that end probably were intended his preparations ag't. England.   It is thought (said by him to be known) that no powers on the continent would engage in the contest, unless France should make an attempt on the Morea, or on Egypt, in which case Russia had declared she would resist with all her force—and in this declaration & a conduct conformable thereto G. B. confided.   I passed an hour & a half with him, and at the latter part of the time, the L'd. Chancellor entered, who assisted at the conversation.   By them I was treated with great kindness and apparent confidence. The latter gentleman visited me before I quitted.   They both desired their Regards & Respects to you.   A coalition has been formed between Mr. Fox, L'd. Grenville, Windham, &c., which, however, does not embrace Mr. Pitt.   The only object of this coalition, as I was told by Mr. Coke, was to oppose the present administration & to endeavour to attain their dismissal from office.   .   .   .

J. Madison to R. King.

DEPARTMENT OF STATE, WASHINGTON, 24 May, 1804.

SIR :

An occasion has occurred, in relation to a demand set up by the proctors, who have conducted the American suits, in London, on account of captures, to request the favour of your stating how far they are supported in it by any promise made by you.   It seems that suitors in the Prize court have a right to cause their proctor's bill to be taxed, which produces a deduction, supposed to average about fifteen per cent ; but they allege that by way of encouragement to their attentions, you promised them that they should be paid the full amount of their bills in the American causes, in which the Government of the U. States are responsible to pay them, without resorting to taxation. Mr. Ewing being about to make a final settlement with them has referred the determination of this part of their claims to instructions from the Department of State. Requesting an answer as soon as your convenience will admit. I have the honor to remain Sir your most obed't Serv't,

JAMES MADISON.

R. KING TO J. MADISON.

NEW YORK, May 29, 1804.

SIR :

In answer to your letter of the 24inst, I have the honour to state that no engagement was ever made by me that the long bills of the Proctors' should be paid. In consequence of an instruction that I gave to the agent Mr. Bayard to require that the Proctors' bills should be regularly taxed, several of them came to me to represent what they called the usage on this subject, and to urge me to authorize or promise them payment on their long or untaxed bills. My answer was explicit that I could make no engagement to this effect, but that the demand must be referred to the Govt. of the U. States, whose decision would perhaps be influenced by the satisfactory or unsatisfactory adjustment of the American Claims.

With great Respect &c.

RUFUS KING.

P. S. The payments from time to time made to the Proctors were on account, leaving the question concerning their long bills open for the President's decision. I do not recollect whether the taxed or long bills were admitted by the Commissioners. My impression is that the taxed bills only were received. Mr Gore or Mr. Cabot can ascertain this point.

CHAPTER XXV.

Burr disappointed—Sought Revenge by Death of Hamilton—King's Connection with the Duel between them—Charges against him of Coldness of Heart and of not endeavoring to prevent the Duel examined and disproved —King to C. King, denying a Statement by Dr. Mason—C. King to R. King—Interview with Dr. Mason—Report Incorrect—W. Wallace to King —Result of the Duel—Pendleton to King—Hamilton mortally wounded— Correspondence with Gen. Clarkson relative to the Duel—Pitcairn to King —Deplores the Death of Hamilton.

Aaron Burr, who had been the recipient of his party's favors, and had nearly reached the office of President, found himself deserted, as has been seen, by his former friends, and moved by his ruling passion, ambition, sought to obtain through the agency of a large portion of the federalists, who believed themselves outraged by the acts of the President and his friends, a return to that power from which he hoped much in the future. It was very evident to him, when again defeated, that the leading opponent he had was Alexander Hamilton. There can be no doubt that he felt that he could not overcome or destroy his influence and that he stood in the way of any political advancement. There was but one way in which he could get rid of this obstacle to his success and that was to remove it by a duel, which would put an end to one or the other, and as history records he took means to insure the death of his adversary by careful practice.

Mr. Jabez Hammond in his *History of Political Parties in New York* (i., 210), presents very clearly the effect upon Mr. Burr of the result in the election of Governor in that State.*

* " The result of the New York election [that of Mr. Lewis by a very large majority] had entirely prostrated the political prospects of Col. Burr. He was

It is not proposed to present a full and particular account of the circumstances and correspondence relative to the duel which removed the leading statesman of the day from the sphere of usefulness in which his energy and consummate ability had so long benefited his country, and which brought upon his adversary the universal scorn of all parties and a bitter retribution which he little looked for. As the name of Rufus King, the warm and trusted friend of Hamilton, has been connected with history of this event, and at times with a criticism which he did not deserve, it is due to him that a true statement of his position should be given.

irrevocably cast off from the republican party in the nation ; and the event of the contest in this State had proved that his friends were not sufficiently numerous when connected with the federalists, or so many of them as would join his standard, to sustain him here. Should the federalists as a party ever gain the ascendency, the prospect of which was extremely unpromising, he knew by what had recently occurred, that *he* would have no hopes of promotion from that party. His political fortunes therefore seemed totally wrecked and irretrievably ruined. In reflecting upon the cause of that ruin, he undoubtedly regarded Gen. Hamilton as the principal agent. If at any time he had expected the aid of the federal members of congress to elect him president in preference to Mr. Jefferson, he had there met the opposition of Mr. Hamilton ; for on that occasion Mr. Bayard of Delaware and Mr. Morris of Vermont, two of Mr. H's friends, had given the election to Mr. Jefferson. In the late contest when his political life was at stake, the same opponent had there stood in his way ; and to his denunciation and great and commanding influence, Mr. Burr charged the defection and desertion of so large a portion of federalists from their party. These considerations must have produced in the gloomy and despairing mind of Mr. Burr a settled determination that he would have revenge—a revenge that nothing short of the life of Hamilton would satiate. It is impossible for me to account for the duel which took place after this election, between Burr and Hamilton, upon any other principle. It is true, that had the answer of Gen. Hamilton to the first communication of Burr been more guarded and more conciliatory in its tone and manner, it might have put Burr more clearly in the wrong, and furnished positive and decisive evidence that from the commencement he premeditated and determined on a mortal contest. But he knew that Gen. Hamilton from youth had been a military man, and that he was sensitively alive to his honor as a soldier ; and a careful review of the correspondence as it was actually conducted will convince all candid men that Burr, when he wrote the first note, was resolved that the issue should be nothing less than the death of one of the parties."

In the *Life of Josiah Quincy* by his son Edmund Quincy, published in 1868, p. 84, there is given an extract from a Journal of Mr. J. Quincy while in New York in November, 1805, on his way to Washington to take his seat in Congress. He mentions the hospitable entertainment he received there and speaks of a number of eminent men he met. Among them was Mr. Pendleton, who was General Hamilton's second in the duel, and whom he questioned about it:

"I asked Mr. Pendleton * whether in the opinion of Mr. Hamilton's friends Mr. King had conducted with propriety in leaving New York, previous to the duel, after having been particularly consulted by Hamilton on the subject. Mr. Pendleton answered that the facts were that Hamilton did consult King and that early. He was that 'judicious friend,' of whom Hamilton speaks in one of his letters. After having thus been consulted some time previously to the time fixed for the duel, King commenced a journey. I know that this conduct of King has been considered as indicating *great coldness of heart* in King. It certainly does nothing else. A man who had felt deeply the public and private stake which was put at risk, could not, it has been said, have left the vicinity until the final decision, particularly after the marks of confidence he had received from Hamilton. On the contrary, Mr. King says he could have done nothing by staying—that the duel was inevitable. From political considerations, he might wish to be at a distance from the scene."

In this statement, published sixty-three years after it was recorded, it would seem as if the family of General Hamilton censured Mr. King for taking his journey, arranged for some time before the duel, and that Mr. Pendleton remarked that it " has been considered as indicating great coldness of heart. It certainly does nothing else," because he left the vicinity while the affair was still pending. It does

---

* " I was led to this inquiry because a brother-in-law of mine, Washington Morton, a young man of strong passions, who had married Miss Schuyler (sister of Mrs. Hamilton) had spoken very indignantly of the conduct of King, giving the impression that such was the feeling of his wife's family."

not appear that the feelings of the family upon the matter
were indicated by anything but the opinion of his brother-
in-law, who had married Mrs. Hamilton's sister, "a young
man of strong passions, who had spoken very indignantly
of the conduct of King." It may have been true, and yet
what constitutes "coldness of heart" is a matter of opinion ;
and the fact might have been that Mr. King, finding his
remonstrances could have no effect, preferred not being
present—but not, as Mr. Pendleton suggested, that he might
"from political considerations, wish to be at a distance
from the scene" Mr. King never showed an unwillingness
to meet any responsibility, and no personal or political considerations as to the future would have been entertained
for a moment.

The facts are that Mr. King, who had not visited his
friends and family in Massachusetts since his return from
Europe, had decided to do so in the summer of that year,
and to follow out a suggestion made to him on April 22d
by Mr. Gore.

"We sincerely regret your suffering under the ague and fever,
and most truly hope it has now left you. We shall anxiously
await your coming hither, which we pray you not to delay longer
than the season renders necessary. June and July are pleasant
months here. In August you can visit your family and friends
at the Eastward and return to us in September and to New York
in November."

There can be no doubt that his arrangements, when
travelling was not so expeditious or comfortable as in these
days, had been somewhat in accordance with this plan,
which he carried out. In the meantime the trouble arose
in which he was consulted by General Hamilton. The decision to accept a challenge was made by the latter, and
when it was given on the 27th June and accepted on the
28th the time for the duel was not fixed. In the *Remarks*, which were offered by Mr. Pendleton to Mr. Van
Ness as from General Hamilton, but not accepted by him,
the closing paragraph is in the following words :

"If the alternative alluded to in the close of the letter (of the 27th) is definitely tendered, it must be accepted ; the time, place and manner, to be afterwards regulated : I should not think it right in the midst of a Circuit Court to withdraw my services from those who may have confided important interests to me, and expose them to the embarrassment of seeking other counsel, who may not have time to be sufficiently instructed in their cases. I shall also want a little time to make some arrangements respecting my own affairs." *

There was, therefore, as this condition was explained by Mr. Pendleton and accepted, no certainty when the duel would take place. In fact it did not occur until the 11th of July. With this uncertainty before him, having it is presumed arranged his journey, and with the feeling that nothing more could be done to avert what he deprecated, it is not necessary to believe that there was no anxiety on the part of Mr. King, or unconcern as to the result that would warrant the accusation of "great coldness of heart." It cannot be supposed that there was not entire sympathy and understanding between the two men, for Hamilton in his last letter to Sedgwick speaks of King as on his way to Boston.

But whatever some may think about his absence from New York at the time of the duel, there is another charge against Mr. King, "that he was blamed for not endeavoring to prevent this fatal duel," made in the Autobiography of Charles Biddle, published in 1883.† It may be said that Mr. Biddle held Aaron Burr in high regard, as this record shows, while on the other hand he had few kind words to say of his political opponent, Alexander Hamilton, except as to his great abilities. He says, p. 309 :

"If General Hamilton had not opposed Colonel Burr, I have very little doubt he would have been elected Governor of New York, and if he had it would have been a fortunate circumstance for the country, as well as for themselves and their families.

* *Life of Hamilton*, vii., 815.

† An examination of this charge and refutation of it were made and published by the Editor of the present *Life*, in the *Magazine of American History*, vol. xi., p. 212. This account will be freely used here.—Ed.

"In this unfortunate affair, Mr. Rufus King was blamed, I think deservedly, for not endeavoring to prevent this fatal duel. He is the moderate judicious friend General Hamilton alludes to in the paper enclosed in his will."

This was not written at the time of the duel, "but some years after, when time had softened bitter feelings," manifesting that there were even then some who still entertained the opinion that Mr. King might have prevented the duel, that he did not exert his influence with General Hamilton, and that he suffered in the minds of honorable men in consequence.

As this was the first publication, in a work of acknowledged character, of the charge, it is due to Mr. King that it should be corrected and refuted. He certainly was the warm and faithful friend of General Hamilton, a friendship dating from before the days when they sat together in the Convention for the formation of the Constitution of the United States, and, apart from personal esteem and friendship, he too well knew and prized the valuable services and the ability of that distinguished man to leave unused any influence he might have to avert the calamity, which he must have anticipated as the result of a hostile meeting; and it is known that he had been consulted. General Hamilton has stated this fact in the paper left by him.

Happily Mr. King has, in a paper which will be found below, made a statement, in his own handwriting and signed by him, which gives an account of his agency in the matter and shows how shocked he was, at the time it was written in 1819, that the charge above referred to was made — a charge he appears never before to have heard.

R. KING TO CHARLES KING.*

JAMAICA, L. I., Ap. 2, 1819.

DEAR SIR:

To my surprise and regret, I have been informed that Dr. Mason in a late conversation at a dinner table stated in reference

* His son.

to the duel between Genl. Hamilton and Colonel Burr, in which the former was mortally wounded, that it was in my power to have prevented the duel, and that evidence of this fact could be produced ; a statement which had the effect of creating the belief that I approved of and promoted the duel.

I request that you will take an early opportunity of calling on Doctor Mason and in my behalf assuring him that the reverse of the alleged fact is the truth, and that so far from approving and promoting the duel, I disapproved of it and endeavoured to prevail on Genl. Hamilton not to meet Col. Burr.

Ask Doctor Mason to furnish you with the evidence to which he referred and upon which he thought himself justified in making the foregoing statement. Say to him, moreover, on my part, that I willingly believe, after receiving this communication, that he will take greater pleasure in correcting than he could have experienced in stating a charge that is wholly unfounded.

With affectionate Regards, I am faithfully yrs.

RUFUS KING.

On the margin of a copy of the letter given above is written by Mr. King :

" Remark. Mr. Bogert gave me this information, which he received from a gentleman present at this dinner, who was impressed by Dr. M.'s statement that I encouraged the duel. Mr. Bogert more than once conferred with this person, in order accurately to understand the tenor of Dr. M.'s charge, and the impression of it upon the person in question. Mr. Bogert has seen and approves of this letter as correct in its recital of what was communicated to him.   R. K."

On the reverse of the original letter appears the following :

C. KING TO R. KING.

WEDNESDAY EV'G, April 7, 1819.

I received this letter on the 5th of April and in the course of that day called at Dr. Mason's house and was informed by Mrs.

Mason that the Dr. was in the country, arranging his library. Being engaged on the 6th, I deferred repeating the call 'till this afternoon (the 7th) when I saw Dr. Mason, and informing him that I called on the part of my father, who had heard a report which was very unpleasant to him, presented him with this letter, as the best mode of explaining the object of my visit. He read it attentively and returned it to me with the observation, "that there was no truth at all in the report to which it referred." He then went on to explain "that at the dinner table of Mr. Richards, Mr. H. W. Warner alluding to the duel of Genl. Hamilton and Col. Burr mentioned Mr. Pendleton as *the calm and judicious friend*, to whom Genl. Hamilton referred, as having taken his advice previous to the duel. Dr. Mason remarked hereupon that he understood that friend to be Mr. King—but that this remark was unaccompanied with any other, or any comment —that Mr. Warner had within a day or two called upon him in much agitation, that they had talked over the subject, and Mr. Warner had left him prepared to give Mr. Bogert such an explanation of what really passed at the dinner already alluded to, as would do away the unjust inferences that appeared to have been drawn from it. I expressed the pleasure I felt at this statement and entered into a detail of what really took place between my father and Genl. Hamilton at their interview on the subject of this unfortunate duel, specifying particularly that the *only point*, upon which Genl. Hamilton asked my father's opinion was whether he, Genl. Hamilton, was bound to give a definite answer to Burr's enquiry, as to whether he, Hamilton, had at any time or in any place expressed opinions unfavourable or derogatory to Col. Burr; to which my father answered decidedly, No; that if Mr. Burr would specify any particular fact, then and then only, it would be proper for Genl. Hamilton to deny or affirm it—that such should be the tenor of Genl. Hamilton's reply to Burr. That preparatory to and during the discussion of this question, the main one, of whether Genl. Hamilton should under any circumstances accept a challenge from Mr. Burr arose, and that my father *decidedly advised that he should not ;* but that Genl. Hamilton having stated that his mind was made up on this subject, as also to throw away his fire, if they should meet, my father then endeavoured to prove to him, that if he, Mr. H., would persist in fighting, he owed to his family and the rights of self-defence to fire at his antagonist.

Dr. Mason replied that these circumstances were new to him, but that the letter I had shewn to him, communicated what he did not know, but what he was rejoiced to find, that my father dissuaded Genl. Hamilton from fighting—as his letter stated he did. I hereupon rose, to take my leave, expressing the pleasure I felt that a report which could not but be disagreeable to my father and unjust to Dr. Mason, had been so satisfactorily explained—to which Dr. Mason rejoined that he was also well pleased at it ; and that no man in the country would rejoice more than himself to see my father occupying that station in the country which was justly due to him.

I immediately returned home (about half past six o'clk P.M.) and committed the result of this interview to writing.

CHAS. KING.

On the back of the rough copy of a letter to General Clarkson, p. 399, is the following, either sent or proposed to be sent, to some intimate friend and in R. King's handwriting :

" You cannot my Dr. Sir, hold in greater abhorrence than I do the Practice of Duelling. Our lamented friend was not unacquainted with my opinion on the subject, but with a mind the most capacious and discriminating that I ever knew, he had laid down for the gov. of himself certain rules upon the subj. of Duels, the fallacy of which wd. not fail to be seen by any man of ordinary understanding ; with these Guides, it is my deliberate opinion, that he could not have avoided a meeting with Col. Burr, had he even declined the first Challenge."

On the same page also in R. King's handwriting is the following :

I regard it as a violation of our civil, our moral and our religious Duty. I go farther and do not consider it as even proof of Courage.

It cannot be necessary to search for other proof of the falseness of the charge, to which allusion has above been made, of indifference to the welfare of his friend, and that at the solemn moment of deciding what course should be pursued, Mr. King, when friendship could speak with such commanding voice, was wanting in the counsel he should give.

There are several other letters, bearing upon the subject of the duel, which will present some interesting features and are given below.

WM. WALLACE, NEW YORK, TO R. KING, HARTFORD, CONN.

July 11, 5 P. M., 1804.

MY DEAR SIR :

This morng. we were all alarmed at a report of Col. Hamilton's being killed in a duel with Col. Burr. Knowing that such a report would interest you, I seize the present opportunity to say "a meeting took place between those gentlemen this morng., the cause said to be political, the consequence a wound (supposed mortal) on Col. Hamilton. He received the shot of his antagonist, it is said with the determination of not returning the first fire. He was brought to Mr. Bayard's at Greenwich, where Mr. Low and I were at 12 o'clock. He was still alive but I conceive there is nothing further than a possibility of his recovery. We have not heard from him since that time. A general sense of regret prevails. We have nothing else since your departure.

Yours &c &c,

WM. WALLACE.

NATH. PENDLETON TO R. KING, BOSTON.

N. Y., Thursday, July—1804.

MY DEAR SIR :

Before you receive this our dear and excellent friend Hamilton will be no more. He & Col. B. met yesterday morning at seven o'clock on the Jersey shore. Genl. H. persisted in the resolution he had taken before you left us to receive & not return the first shot. Unhappily Mr. B's first shot was fatal. It passed between the two lower ribs of the right side, and lodged near the spine, and in its passage, the surgeons say, it must have passed through the lungs or the liver. He was brought over to Mr. Bayard's where he continues. I have just left him, and the Doctors say he cannot outlive the day.

I have not time now to communicate any of the reflections that crowd upon my mind on this most extensive public and private calamity. It has occasioned a strong public sensation which will be much increased when he is dead.

I am my dear Sir with esteem

your obedient servant,

NATH. PENDLETON.

GEN. M. CLARKSON TO R. KING.

NEW YORK, August 20, 1804.

MY DEAR SIR :

Since the late melancholy event which has deprived us of our friend Hamilton, a report has reached me, that yourself in conjunction with Mr. Pendleton and myself had given it as an opinion that a duel was unavoidable ; a report of this nature (as I abhor the practice) has occasioned me great uneasiness, and as I was only a hearer of what you related to me and had no other agency in the business, you will much oblige me by a line to this effect. I promise you that no other use shall be made of the letter but only to show it to two persons from whom I received the information—who I am very solicitous should be rightly informed on the subject. Previous to the fatal event the silence you imposed on me was most scrupulously attended to ; but which agitated my mind exceedingly ; immediately upon my hearing of its having taken place, I directly went to our friend, who I found had already requested that I should be sent for. The scene which I witnessed has almost been too much for me, and the idea now suggested has not contributed to my repose. Let me request, my dear Sir, to hear from you as soon as possible.

Your sincere friend & obedt. Servt.,

M. CLARKSON.

P. S. We are endeavoring to obtain by subscription some property for the children of our friend ; is anything of a similar nature likely to be done in Boston ?

R. KING TO GEN. CLARKSON.

WALTHAM NEAR BOSTON, Aug. 24, 1804.

MY DEAR SIR :

I lose no time in replying to yr. letter of the 20th which I received last Evening—considering the reserve that I have observed on this subject of national affliction, I was truly surprized that any such Rumour as that you mention should have got into circulation upon my authority. No persons can be justified by any observation that you ever made to me, or that I ever made to another, in reporting that you had given an opinion that a Duel between our lamented friend and Col. Burr was unavoidable.

It was not until the challenge had been given and accepted, that I mentioned the affair to you and that under an injunction of secrecy. Knowing our friend's determination to be passive, my mind was agitated with strong forebodings of what has happened, and tho' the Correspondence was closed by an agreement of the Parties to meet each other, I nevertheless mentioned the subject to you, and asked if you could perceive any mode of interference. Your answer, expressive of much sorrow, was in the negative. I did not however, infer from this answer that in yr. opinion our friend might not have declined a meeting with Col. Burr, but merely by the acceptance of his adversary's challenge, that the interference of third persons was precluded.

With sentiments of Resp. & Esteem &c.

(Signed)   R. KING.

P. S. You are at liberty to make any use of the above that you may deem proper.

2nd P. S. There exists in this quarter a difficulty that may disappoint our hopes of pecuniary succour for the family of our lamented friend. I allude to the misunderstanding that existed between him and Mr. Adams. Should we fail in procuring money, I understood that certain persons who purchased a tract of land in Pennsylvania of Col. Pickering and for which they paid him $25,000, will be disposed to convey the lands to the family of the deceased. This would be a valuable property at a distant day, but cash only will pay debts.

This letter, of which only a copy is preserved, was probably written to Genl. Clarkson, as it refers to Mr. King's letter to him of Aug. 24.

DEAR SIR :

Mrs. Hamilton having written to Mr. Cabot to endeavour to procure for Alexander a situation in a respectable commercial house, Mr. Higginson has readily consented to take him ; and until a suitable family can be found to take Alexander as a boarder, Mr. Higginson will receive him into his own family. This will give to the young man an opportunity of becoming acquainted with the respectable persons of the town, and with such young men as are of the best reputation.

In my answer to your letter of the 20th, I omitted to say anything concerning either Mr. Pendleton or myself in respect to the report to which your letter alludes. I have no recollection that Mr. Pendleton ever expressed to me any opinion whether General H. could, or ought to, decline a meeting with Col. Burr. I very well remember that he entirely agreed with me of the inconsistency of the General's determination to receive the fire of his adversary and to throw away his own.

No person can view with deeper abhorrence than I do the practice of duelling, and our lamented friend was not unacquainted with my opinion upon this subject.

With sincere Regards yr. ob. & faithful Servt.

(Signed)   RUFUS KING.

J. PITCAIRN * TO R. KING.

HAMBURG, Sept. 25, 1804.

We hear from America, that Genl. Armstrong succeeds Mr. Livingston, so that in pleasing the Virginians, the family may be preserved to the party. All men acquainted with America learned with sorrow & indignation the death of General Hamilton—few in any age had richer gifts from nature, and none ever made a more diligent & effectual use of them for the benefit of his Country. Times were favourable ; they showed his manly integrity, his disinterested character, and various Genius, in fair

* Mr. Pitcairn had been for many years U. S. Consul at Hamburg.

views, and considering him as an important labourer in rearing the new Constitution and in founding public credit, he takes high rank among the ornaments and benefactors of mankind. His murderer must be wretched ; no civilized land is to him an asylum ; should the laws hunt him from America, he would find abhorrence & Contempt meet him on every European shore.

.   .   .

Your very obedient Servant

Jos. PITCAIRN.

CHAPTER XXVI.

The last years of the life of General Hamilton had been devoted to the more diligent pursuit of his profession, in order that he might be able to make provision for his family. And yet when an examination into his affairs was made after his death, it was found that his estate was seriously embarrassed. In the *Diary and Letters of Gouverneur Morris*, vol. ii., pp. 458–9, he writes, July 14, 1804:

"Mr. Hammond, who dined with us, desired me to think of some means to provide for poor Hamilton's family. Mr. Gracie and Mr. Wolcott called for the same purpose. I had already mentioned the matter to Mr. Low, who seems to think a subscription will not go down well, because the children have a rich grandfather. . . ."

Together with others of General Hamilton's friends, Morris spent much time endeavoring to arrange his affairs, which were in sad disorder:

"Our friend Hamilton [he wrote to Robert Morris] has been suddenly cut off in the midst of embarrassments which would have required years of professional industry to set straight : a debt of between fifty thousand and sixty thousand dollars hanging over him, a property which in time may sell for seventy thousand or eighty thousand, but which, if brought to the hammer, would not, in all probability, fetch forty ; a family of seven young children. We have opened a subscription to provide for these orphans, and his warm-hearted friends, judging of others by themselves, expect more from it than I do."

M. CLARKSON TO R. KING.

" NEW YORK, Aug. 20, 1804.

" . . . P. S. We are endeavoring to obtain by subscription some property for the children of our friend. Is any thing of a similar nature likely to be done at Boston ? "

Whether or not this intimation was the first that Mr. King received of the purpose of General Hamilton's friends, he writes as follows to some friend in New York asking him to act for him :

R. KING TO ———.

(Copy of a Letter.)

" WALTHAM NEAR BOSTON, July 23, 1804.

" MY DEAR SIR :

" Being detained on the road, we did not reach this place till yesterday. The same cause that retarded our journey prevents my proceeding at present on a visit to Boston ; having been severely attacked by an intermittent, I am compelled to give an exact attention to the restoration of my health. I hope however in three or four days that I shall be able to venture into town. In the mean time I have delivered your letter to me to my friend Mr. Gore, who has gone this morning to town with Judge Benson. They will confer with Cabot, Higginson and Otis upon the subject. At present I can give no opinion concerning the benevolent object that is aimed at. It is, however, on every account fit that I should authorize you, as I now do, to do in my behalf at New York as you may think suitable and to this I give you carte blanche. "

It is altogether probable that when he was able to go to Boston and during the month or more he remained there,

Mr. King took occasion to speak of, and urge a co-operation of the Boston friends of General Hamilton in, raising money for the benefit of the children of one whom they all loved. There is in the postscript of the letter to General Clarkson, of the 24th August, an evidence of this, and of the generous gift of lands by Mr. Cabot and other citizens of Boston, should it be impossible to raise money.

" .   .   .   2d P. S.   There exists in this quarter a difficulty that may disappoint our hopes of pecuniary succours for the family of our lamented friend.   I allude to the misunderstanding that existed between him and Mr. Adams.   Should we fail in procuring money, I understand that certain persons who purchased a tract of land in Pennsylvania of Col. Pickering, and for which they paid him $25,000, will be disposed to convey the lands to the family of the deceased.   This would be a valuable property at a distant day, but cash only will pay debts."

Not long after this Mr. King left Boston for a visit to his family in Maine, and during the time he passed with them the suggestion of the gift of lands was acted upon.   The history of this gift is connected with a previous act of esteem for a political as well as personal friend.   Mr. Timothy Pickering had become interested in certain lands in Pennsylvania, and not very long before, in 1801, had determined to go and live upon them, having little or no other means of support. Gratitude for the work he had done in connection with the early years of the Government of the United States, the desire to enable him to continue his services, instead of burying himself in the wild lands, and personal regard and esteem led a number of his friends in Boston to buy his lands for a fair price and thus enable him to live where he could still exert his influence.   The consequence was that a subscription was opened and funds in shares of $100 each were taken by some thirty or more persons to the amount of $25,000, for which the lands were to be conveyed to them. The deeds for these lands had not been made out; and all those who had contributed the money "engaged to pay into the hands of the Honorable George Cabot, Thomas Davis and Theodore Lyman, Esqrs., the sums of money set against our respective names to be by them applied to the benefit of the children or family of General Hamilton in any manner they shall judge proper . . . and authorize the said Timothy Pickering Esq. to convey by a quit-claim deed to such person or persons as shall be named to him for that purpose, by the aforementioned gentlemen."

This was stated to be done "in remembrance of the exalted worth and pre-eminent services of the late General Hamilton— his extraordinary and truly patriotic exertions, which contributed so much to save our country from the greatest impending calamities; his able, disinterested and successful efforts to inculcate the wisdom, justice and advantage of all those maxims of jurisprudence, which render sacred the rights of property and which are inseparable from true liberty, and especially recollecting that the devotion of his time and talents to these public interests has operated to deprive his family of a common share of those pecuniary advantages, which his labors, if applied to them, would have easily made abundant; we, therefore, whose names are subscribed, do testify in some degree our sense of departed excellence and our gratitude for benefits conferred on our country."

Mr. King evidently received particular information in reference to the action of gentlemen in New York, for on his return to Waltham he wrote to Mr. Cabot:

R. KING TO GEORGE CABOT.

"Oct. 10th, 1804.

"According to the schedule of General Hamilton's estate, drawn up by himself a few days before his death, it appears that his property consists altogether of new lands, situate in the western part of New York, and of a house, nine miles from the city. The new lands cost fifty-five thousand dollars and the country house and grounds about twenty-five thousand. The General's debts amount to fifty-five thousand dollars; and as the estate is unproductive, and the debts bear interest, it is the opinion of judicious persons that, with the most prudent management, the estate will be barely sufficient to pay the debts. Mrs. Hamilton is a daughter of General Schuyler, who has a family of eight or nine children.   The General is supposed to have a good real estate, but not much personal property : so that little expectation can be entertained of any considerable succor from this quarter, either for the maintenance of General Hamilton's family or for the education and advancement of his children.   To the sorrow that every virtuous mind has felt for this distinguished patriot, it is painful to add the reflection that his young and helpless family must depend for their support, not upon the earnings of their father—for he served the public—but upon the contributions of a few individuals who admired his unequalled worth.   The subscription for this purpose at New York amounted to upwards of sixteen thousand dollars when I last heard from thence (which was before my journey to the eastward) and it was expected that a considerable addition would be made to this fund."*

* Mr. James A. Hamilton in his *Reminiscences*, published in 1869, makes the following statement on p. 78 :

" At a dinner party in New York, shortly after the close of the Revolutionary War, at which were present Messrs. G. Morris, John Jay, R. Harrison, John Delafield, Robert Lenox, Nicholas Low, I. O. Hoffman, and Alexander Hamilton, the question was discussed whether the purchase of wild lands or of lots in the suburbs of the city would be the more profitable investment.   John Jay was in favor of New York, and made purchases there, and as his means enabled him to hold his lots, his speculation made him rich.   Hoffman also bought land in the vicinity of the city.   Some of the others, including my father, took the opposite view, and invested in the lands in the northern counties of the State. The wild lands were purchased at a few cents the acre, but they were not settled very rapidly.   After the death of Hamilton, it was found, as I have already said, his means were not equal to the payment of his debts, and several of his friends advanced money for that purpose, taking those lands in payment.

" Having learned that Major William Popham, one of the gentlemen who had shown that kindness to my father, was at an advanced period of life in poor circumstances, I addressed him the following letter : "

NEW YORK, October 14, 1824.

My DEAR SIR,

I was this day for the first time informed by a person, who became acquainted with the circumstance at the time it occurred, that you advanced one hundred dollars to pay my father's debts.   The gratitude that is due to you from every member of his family for this generous act can never be effaced.   You must, therefore, believe that I do not send you the enclosed cheque for the same sum in the hope of cancelling what is due to you, but in obedience to the sacred injunction of my father, and because under present circumstances it may promote your convenience.

I requested Mr. Pendleton, one of my father's executors, to inform me of the

On the 10th of November a letter was addressed to Colonel Pickering, by the trustees appointed above, stating that

"the design which was formed to transfer to the heirs of General Hamilton the lands purchased of you in 1801 is now accomplished, so far as depended on the acts of those purchasers,"

and that it only remained to make out the conveyances to the executors of General Hamilton's will or to other persons, as might be agreed on.

C. Gore to R. King, New York.

"Boston, November 25th, 1804.

"The papers that respect the transfer of property to poor Hamilton's heirs went on yesterday. After this land was conveyed, Lyman and Davis thought proper to propose to some others to subscribe Cash; I mean those who were not interested in the land. Our friend Cabot objected because he thought it would be unavailing: but the former gentlemen, thinking it right

arrangements made to pay my father's debts, for at that time I was young [he was 16 years old]. He informed me with reluctance that my father's lands in Scriba's Patent had been taken by certain gentlemen in this city, whose names he would not mention, at prices which, he said, were perhaps more than they were worth at the time. These gentlemen hoped with the amount thus raised and the sums due my father, to pay his debts and leave the Grange clear to his family.

I mention this to show you that I have not been indifferent to this very delicate matter, and that if in my course through life, I should come in collision with any of these persons (with you, I am happy to say, I am sure I have not) to whom I am indebted for these or similar acts of generous devotion to my father's memory, it has been in ignorance, and must always be to me a subject of deep and mortifying regret.

With great regard, your friend and obedient servant,

James A. Hamilton.

It cannot be that this is an account of the same transaction which has been recorded; there is not even a suggestion in it of any security or equivalent for the money subscribed to pay the debts: it was a free gift so far as can be ascertained. That there may also have been a transfer to others of the Scriba patent lands, which cost General Hamilton "fifty-five thousand dollars," is possible, but no account of it appears—unless in the public records, where the names of the parties to whom the lands were transferred, could have been found.

that these should be applied to made their address to —— and
——, both of whom refused to give a farthing. Lloyd who
offered the subscription paper says he is sure that he made such
remarks to M., as will render his journey to —— rather unpleasant ; —— agreed to the merits of the deceased Statesman
and his claims on the public, but observed his children needed
his money as much."

The Trustees on November 26, 1804, addressed a letter to
the executors of the last will and testament of General
Hamilton in which they state the circumstances under
which the conveyance of lands at their disposal was to
be made, and say,

"As we are entrusted with the nomination of the persons to
whom the property shall be conveyed, we cannot hesitate to
name the Executors of General Hamilton's will, leaving it with
them to name others, if they thing it expedient, and also to arrange with Col. Pickering the time and circumstances of making
the conveyance."

The communication closed with an expression of their
"poignant sorrow" for the death of General Hamilton, and
their "strong sympathy for those who were by nature
attached to him."

The Executors answered in a letter dated November 29,
1804, accepting the trust committed to them, with expressions of their high appreciation of "their act of muni-
ficence." *

As a result, the lands were secured to the children of
General Hamilton, and as Mr. Charles W. Upham in his
Life of Timothy Pickering says in closing the account of
this transaction, "the act itself and all the parties to it,
deserve to be kept in perpetual remembrance."

The following portion of a letter, though a little out of
date, speaks of the purchase of the Estate of General Hamilton in the City of New York.

* Vol. iv., pp. 36 to 41.—*Life and Letters of George Cabot*, by Henry Cabot
Lodge, pp. 304–310.

R. King to C. Gore.

New York, Jany 10, 1808.

. . . I believe that I some time since mentioned to you the plan we had set on foot to purchase at its cost Genl. Hamilton's estate. As we have been solicitous to confine the purchase to this City, the time that has elapsed without completing it, has been longer than we expected. It is, however, nearly completed and so far as to be beyond the chance of failure. By this measure his family will secure abt. 20.000 Dol., that would have been lost without it. The Estate from Genl. Schuyler is less than the public expected. From what I hear Mrs. H's share will not in its present state yield her an annuity of more than 750 Dols; whether it can be converted into a more productive fund is matter for enquiry. After Hamilton's death, Gen. Schuyler (having before made his will) executed a Deed of gift, which purports to have been signed, sealed and *delivered* before the subscribing witnesses of about 7 acres of his homestead to Mrs. Hamilton. The Deed was not given to Mrs. Hamilton, but remained in the Genl.'s possession, and was found among his papers. The Exec'rs have examined the witnesses, who say they were requested to be witnesses of the execution of the Deed in question, that they were so, but that they were not informed of the purport of the Deed, and did not see it delivered.—Upon this evidence one or two lawyers at Albany have given an opinion that the instrument is a nullity. The property is worth 18 or 20 thousand Dollars. The Eldest son has informed Mrs. H. that he will release any claim on his part to the 7 acres, Mr. Rensselaer will do the same in behalf of his son. What the other heirs will do is unknown.

That the delivery of a Deed is essential to its validity, will not be contradicted, but what amounts to a delivery is the question. Without much confidence in my own opinion, I am inclined to think that a deed executed as this has been, is well executed and that it will pass the Estate ; its remaining in the possession of the Grantor is immaterial, provided it was duly executed by him. Farewell & always affectionately, Rufus King.

An article appeared in the *Alexandria Expositor* on 19th March, 1804, making a statement from an English correspondent of certain opinions expressed by Mr. King shortly before his return home from England. The letters which follow will show how utterly unfounded it was.

R. KING TO EDITOR OF "ALEXANDRIA EXPOSITOR."

WALTHAM NEAR BOSTON, Aug. 22, 1804.

SIR :

By turning to your paper of the 19th of March past, you will find the publication to my disadvantage, which was the occasion of a letter which I wrote to Mr. Crowe, and to which I have lately received the enclosed answer. Being absent from home, it is not in my power to send you a copy of my letter, which however merely covered the Editorial Article of your paper of Mar. 19, and claimed of Mr. Crowe's justice an explicit denial of the Comn. I am represented to have made to him. It cannot be my desire to draw Mr. Crowe's or any other Gentleman's name before the public, nor to give to this affair an air of importance that does not on any acct. belong to it, but as men of exact notions may have thought unfavorably of me, in consequence of this publication, I am persuaded that you will not hesitate, as far as may be in your power, to correct the misrepresentation.

With sentiments of respect, I am, Sir, yr. obedt. Servt.

RUFUS KING.

P.S. Mr. King leaves it altogether to the choice of the Editor of the Expositor, to make the correction by an Editorial Article, or the publication of this and Mr. Crowe's letter.

The letter from Mr. King was dated March 29th, 1804.

R. KING TO JAMES CROWE—NEAR NORWICH, ENGLAND.

SIR :

I take the liberty to send you inclosed the Extract of a letter said to have been received in this country from a person in the neighbourhood of Norwich, and which has been recently published in the Expositor, a newspaper printed at Alexandria, Virginia.

The object of this publication, so far as regards me will not be misunderstood by men of correct sentiments, and I owe it equally to them and to myself, to remove the impression to my disadvantage it is calculated to produce.

As the observation, said to have been made to you, was never made by me to you, or to any other person, I am confident that you will take pleasure in doing me the justice to declare that I never made to you the observation ascribed to me in this publication, nor any other of like import. To guard against accident I send you this letter in duplicate ; and request the favour of you, for the same reason, to return me duplicates of your answer, addressed to Mr. Samuel Williams, 13 Finsbury Square, London, who will without delay forward the same to me.

With sentiments of Esteem and Respect, &c.

RUFUS KING.

———

Copy of the editorial article of the newspaper called the "*Alexandria Expositor* (for the Country) March 19, 1804."

"While the United States, under the fostering influence of a democratic Administration, are hastily progressing to a state of Prosperity and happiness the world never before witnessed, G. Britain is feeling the greatest distress. It would seem almost impossible for a native citizen of this country to form a correct idea of the wretchedness of her state, or the manifold evils arising from the profligate frame of her Government. It is the nature of evil to increase itself until the mass overcomes human forbearance ; the violent passions are let loose, and all the ties of civil society are for a period dissolved. Happy will it be for Great Britain, if she profits by the examples afforded by the last thirty years, now that so large a proportion of her subjects are in arms. She certainly may be free the moment she wills it ; and it is not impossible but the ebullitions of a moment may annihilate her kings and her Nobles, her unfrocked and her ermined oppressors, and elevate her people into men, who having rights, "know, and knowing, dare maintain them." Anxiously we wish for so great, so glorious an event. This wish seldom absent, is now more deeply impressed, in consequence of letters we received by the Princess Augusta Packet ; they are dated the latter end of November, some extracts from which we shall lay before our readers ; they will pretty plainly exhibit the state of the public mind in England. It will also be seen that Mr. King was a little sanguine in his expectations when there. We imagine he is not quite so much so now. Mr. Crowe, the gentleman to whom he expressed them, is a man of large fortune, who resides within two miles of the City of Norwich, and of a family intimately connected with that of the Editor of the *Expositor's.*

First Extract.

(After mentioning the price of corn, the situation of the volunteers, and other particulars relating to England, the extract finishes in these words.)

" In such calamitous times, I have thought it best to have all my children around me, that they may want no protection I can give them. The scarcity of money is another evil. In taking a hundred pounds a man does not receive a single guinea, and to crown the whole, the wheat crops were much injured by the mildew. I hope Mr. Jefferson continues to possess the confidence he so justly merits in your nation, though I was a little alarmed at hearing that Mr. King, your late Ambassador here, told Mr. James Crowe that he was going back to America in hopes of being elected President. I understood he spoke as if he was sure of his election. I hope, however, he will be disappointed."

Part of 2. Extract to designate the writer.

" No place is more inconvenient than Norwich by the present state of things. The volunteers seem to feel themselves the tools of their officers, who expect by their excessive zeal to earn some of the good things which Government has to bestow : nor do they like to be paraded about for the amusement of the Ladies, or to gratify the vanity of their new made Colonels, who never shot anything but Partridges ; and at London I assure you they do not like to be marched about at 6 o'clock in a morning and late at night. Some time since they refused the services of many they would now accept. I had that honor when at Norwich, for declining which I heartily thanked them many times since, and I assure them that I never will be so foolish again as to offer my services."

JAS. CROWE TO R. KING.

LAKENHAM NEAR NORWICH 9th May 1804.

SIR :

I have the honor of your letter of 29th March last enclosing an Extract of a letter published at Alexandria in the newspaper called the Expositor of 19th same month. I have had them some days by me, wishing before I should send you an answer, to ascertain, if possible, the means by which the Editor made so strange a mistake, and as the printed letter pointed at the person from whom it appeared to be derived, I went to him yesterday and he readly acknowledged sending occasionally to the Editor, intelligence from which sometimes articles had been inserted in his paper ; but that he thinks he could not have insinuated anything which could have conveyed the Idea " that I had heard you say, you were going to America in hopes of being elected President " nor did he understand from me I ever had any conversation with you on the subject.

About the time, Sir, you were leaving England, it was reported, that on your return from your Embassy, you would probably be appointed to a high situation in your own Country, and I remember observing to the person above alluded to—that I was glad to hear it, for I thought you worthy even of being elected President of the United States, or words to that effect. Nothing else passed and certainly I never said to him, nor to any other person, that *you* told me you had any hopes of being President ; and I do solemnly and in the most unequivocal manner declare, that so far from your having told me you had any expectations of being chosen President, I don't recollect ever having heard you say one word respecting American affairs ; either as they concerned yourself, or any other individual, or any party in that State, or anything relative to the Government or political views of that Country.

I beg, Sir, you will make any use you think proper of this letter and believe me to be with the highest respect and regard
Your most obedient humble Servt.

JAS. CROWE.

R. Dinmore to R. King.

ALEXANDRIA, 31 Aug. 1804.

Sir :

Your communication enclosing Mr. Crowe's letter of 9th May last, I had the honor of receiving this morning. The justice you require shall be immediately rendered and the Correspondence published in an early Expositor, of which I will send you a Copy.

I sincerely wish, Sir, you had either written me previous to your letter to Mr. Crowe, or sent that Gentleman the entire Expositor of the 19th March last. It would have prevented an application I see Mr. Crowe made to my father, under the impression that I received the information from him ; for Mr. C. says " as the printed letter pointed at the Person from whom it appeared to be derived, *I went to him yesterday.*" The letter, Sir, from which the extract was given, was not from my father but from a relation who lives 21 miles from Mr. Crowe. Consequently no information relative to the report could be procured by Mr. C.'s enquiry.

Had you, Sir, first honored me with a line on the subject, I would at once have given up my authority which would have directed Mr. Crowe's enquiry, had you then thought it necessary to write to him ; and as the report was published here during the Session of Congress, I would have laid the letter itself before any of your friends then in this Neighbourbood. This I shall always be willing to do, as I have the letter now by me from which the Extract was made.

Had Mr. C. received the whole article, he would have seen that it contained Extracts from letters from three different Correspondents, & I think from the internal evidence, would have known the quarter from whence it was derived ; as he only received the Editorial Article, his application was misapplied.

I am satisfied, Sir, you will expect no apology from me, for the insertion into the Expositor, of the Extract alluded to. I conceived my information correct, tho' I have now no doubt of its originating in mistake ; I therefore published it, nor believing, as I do, that the welfare and happiness of the Citizens of the U.S. are essentially dependent on the re-election of Mr. Jefferson, should I have felt justified in concealing Intelligence I deemed so important.

I remain, Sir, with sentiments of respect &c., &c.

R. DINMORE.

P. S. As it is my intention to publish the above with your & Mr. Crowe's letters, I have not identified my authority, which I shall now do. The letter was written by my Brother, at whose house Mr. C. generally resides, when he visits his Taham Estate. As it might injure my Brother in England, was I to publish him as my Authority, I prefer doing it in a part of my address to you, which I shall not insert in the Expositor ; but I conceive you will admit that I had some grounds for supposing my information Correct.

Should not the above letter prove satisfactory, I will readily give you any other which you may think more so.

R. KING TO R. DINMORE, ALEXANDRIA.

PORTLAND, DISTRICT OF MAINE, Sep. 16, 1804.

SIR :

I have duly received your letter of the 31st past. My sole aim has been to effect the refutation of the publication to my prejudice contained in your paper of the 19th March, and as this will be done by the publication of Mr. Crowe's letter to me, I can have no motive to expect an apology from you or the publication of anything that might prove injurious to any other person.

It is however proper that I should correct the error into which you have fallen in supposing that only the Editorial remarks of your paper of March 19th were sent to Mr. Crowe ; the fact being that the entire article, including the whole of the extracts of your correspondent's letter, was transmitted ; and the paragraph of Mr. Crowe's letter that you have cited shows that these extracts were before him.

As the observation, ascribed to me, is stated by your correspondent to have been made to Mr. Crowe, it seemed to me that it was to him, and to him only, that I could with fitness apply for the disavowal that he has so fully supplied.

I am, Sir, with Respect, &c.

RUFUS KING.

CHAPTER XXVII.

Allusion has been made to a journey by Mr. King to New
England in the summer of 1804. After many years of absence
in England, he desired to renew his former relations with
his friends, especially in Boston, and to visit his family, all
of whom lived in the District of Maine. He had given an
intimation of his intention to Mr. Gore, who had recently
returned from England, and whom he looked upon, justly, as
his warmest and most confidential friend, as the correspondence with that gentleman so clearly shows. Mr. Gore had
suggested to him at what season such a visit could be made
most agreeably :

" June & July are pleasant months here (in Boston) ; in August
you can visit your family and friends at the Eastward, and return
to us in September, and to New York in November."

Following these suggestions, he appears to have made his
arrangements to start on his journey, with his friend Judge
Egbert Benson, early in July. He passed some days in
Hartford, Connecticut, where the members of the Alsop
family, his wife's relations, lived, and he also had many
political and personal friends. No record of his visit there
is found ; nor of his arrival in Massachusetts, until we learn

through a letter, July 23d, from Waltham, Mr. Gore's home, to a friend in New York, that,

" being detained on the road, we did not reach this place till yesterday. The same cause that retarded our journey prevents my proceeding at present on a visit to Boston ; having been severely attacked by an intermittent, I am compelled to give an exact attention to the restoration of my health."

He is announced in the *Columbian Centinel* as having arrived in Boston on July 25th, with Judge Benson ; and by a correspondent of the *Gazette of the United States*, from Boston, on July 27th, as having been, with Judge Benson, present at the demonstration of respect to Alexander Hamilton, when Harrison Gray Otis delivered a memorial address. Again, on August 18th, the *Centinel* says :

" The School Committee visited the Public Schools of Boston, accompanied by Hon. Mr. King, Mr. Gore and a number of official characters ; all of whom were gratified with the exercises. Afterwards they were refreshed at an elegant dinner at Fanueil Hall."

These are the only facts connected with this first visit to Boston which are recorded, though there were many subjects to be talked about of the deepest interest. An account to interested friends of his life and mission abroad, the very serious questions which had been started by former associates relative to the outrageous acts of Jefferson's administration, with the threat that these could be counteracted in their influence only by a separation of the Northern and Southern States for self-preservation ; the steps to be taken to relieve the children of their acknowledged leader, General Hamilton, from the pecuniary embarrassment consequent upon his death in the midst of his active professional career,—these and other topics would occupy many days of earnest conversation, and enable those with whom he was brought in contact to feel the influence of his calm judgment and clear foresight. It was well known that General Hamilton and he were both earnestly opposed to even the thought of a disruption of the Union as a remedy for the evil effects of a rampant democracy, but with many warm and able federalists deprecated a resort to such an extreme measure; and when it is remembered that a large portion of the federalists were for other reasons alienated from the extreme men by personal hostility, the task of counteracting a decided though ill-considered plan was at the same time one which required firmness and prudence, which Mr. King would exercise the more positively, as he had been put forward as the head of the party by his nomination as their candidate for the Vice-Presidency,—an office for which at that time leading men were named.

Besides, he was passing his time at Waltham, the home of those to whom he was sincerely attached, Mr. and Mrs. C. Gore; an attachment to the former dating from the beginning of his professional career, and which had been strengthened as they grew older by constant and confidential intercourse, recognizing, as both did, in each other, the purity of character, the correct lives, the perfect harmony in their political views, the love of the country they both represented at home and abroad, an instinctive unity of high motives in the conduct of their public and private affairs, and the love of a domestic and quiet and family life, where affection ruled, and where example influenced. Both, too, had loving assistants in their wives to brighten their homes, to welcome their friends, and, in Mr. King's case, to help him to bring up their children in obedient and willing recognition of a parent's love and guardianship. To Mr. and Mrs. Gore there had not been granted the blessing of children; but their warm hearts adopted those of their lifelong friends, and whenever the opportunity occurred, to the end of their lives, they never failed to show to these children, even when grown to manhood, the same tender care, earnest sympathy, and warm attachment, that they began to exercise in their childhood.

Much, therefore, these friends had in common to enable them to enjoy the recalling of the persons they had met, and of the events which occurred during their residence in London, both in important official positions, often embarrassed by circumstances which they could not control, but with the consciousness that they had both contributed to sustain the dignity of their country and raise it to a higher plane by a conscientious and faithful and able performance of the duties laid upon them.   They had with them also a friend in Judge Benson, into whose willing ears and appreciative mind they could pour out the reminiscences and suggestions of bright and accurate observers.

Leaving the hospitable home of Mr. Gore, Mr. King appears to have made a visit to Salem, for on September 3d,

"the Hon. Mr. King, late Minister to the Court of St. James . . . dined at General Derby's in company with a number of respectable public and private characters." *

On August 29th, the following letter had been addressed to Mr. King:

NEWBURYPORT, Aug. 29, 1804.

DEAR SIR

The citizens of Newburyport learn with great satisfaction that you are now on a visit to this your native State, while they have a lively conviction of your eminent public services, they cherish the most affectionate remembrance of you as their Fellow Townsman.   Having learned that you are about passing to the Eastward, they solicit the honour of your company at a publick Dinner and ask you to name a day for that purpose which shall be most accommodated to your convenience.   In their behalf,
    Dear Sir, your faithful & affectionate servants,
                                MOSES BROWN,
                                DUDLEY A. TYNG,
                                EDWARD RAND,
                                EBENEZER STOCKER,
                                WILLIAM FARIS.

* *Columbian Centinel*, September 4, 1804.

It cannot be doubted that Mr. King, touched by the tone
of tender remembrance, gladly accepted this invitation to
meet the old friends, among whom his professional studies
were made under Theophilus Parsons, his first causes were
tried, and by whom he had been sent, his first political employment, to the General Court of Massachusetts. It was
the city which, when undecided as to his removal from the
State to New York, he said he loved better than any spot
on the earth.

The dinner took place on Tuesday, September 5th, 1804,
and is thus noticed in the *Newburyport Herald* of September 7th.

" On Tuesday last arrived in town, the Hon. Rufus King, Esq.,
on a journey to the eastward, and on Wednesday the gentlemen
of the town provided for him an elegant entertainment at Washington Hall, where sociality and good humor attended, and
where a number of patriotic toasts and enlivening songs crowned
the repast with the most refined and unlimited enjoyment. Far
is it from us to delineate the virtues of the man, to honor whom
this entertainment was given ; it would be weakness to attempt
it, but the love and respect which his presence inspired was so
great, that every tongue was ready to exclaim, as Franklin observed
of Washington,—If my country bestowed a sceptre he is worthy
of it."

Though evidently on his way to Maine, there cannot be
found any facts to show how Mr. King passed his time
among his friends there, until he returned to Boston, a period
of more than a month, except the following account of a
reception at Portland : *

" The Hon. Mr. King in company with the Hon. Egbert Benson, has been received at Portland, in his native district, with the
most expressive marks of affection and esteem. The inhabitants
on Saturday last gave an entertainment in honor of these eminent
Statesmen."

                * *The Centinel*, October 6, 1804.

On his arrival at Boston, his friends welcomed him with what the papers announce as a " Tribute of Respect," a public dinner.

TRIBUTE OF RESPECT.*

We are happy to learn, that the gentlemen of this town intend giving a Public Dinner to the Hon. RUFUS KING, Esq., late American Minister at the Court of London, in testimony of their esteem for his exalted talents, and public and private worth. It has been inquired why this step was not taken previous to his visit to the District of Maine? We can answer, there was no place, either suitable or convenient for such a purpose—The capacious Rooms at Concert Hall, where Entertainments of the kind, can alone be given, were in a state of repair at that time, and are now but just compleated.

The *Dinner*, we understand, will be given tomorrow.

A detailed account of this dinner is given in *The Repertory*, from which the following is copied. The toasts, † which are

* *New England Palladium*, Tuesday, October 16, 1804.

† 1. *Our Publick Ministers.* In future as formerly, may our first interests be confided to our first characters.

2. *The Administration of* WASHINGTON *and* ADAMS. The Morning and Evening Stars of our national glory.

(*After his Excellency had retired.*)

3. Governour STRONG. May the excellence of his character silence the malice which it cannot appease.

4. *The State of New York.* Too respectable to be the *Dupe of Virginia*, may she again associate with those who are faithful to the publick liberty.

5. The CLERGY. Devoted to the best interests of humanity—may they ever feel the calumnies of the impious to be their proudest eulogy.

6. *Our Navy.* May its strength protect our Commerce and its glory confound its enemies *at Washington* and Tripoli.

7. *Our little Army.* May it never have to bear reproach from the brave, nor always to take it from the base.

8. HAMILTON. May our Country find indemnity for his loss, in the value of his Counsels.

9. *Union among honest Men.* If it cannot *displace* Knaves, may it *disarm* them.

here presented in the note, clearly show the tone of opinion upon the current events, among a large proportion of the old Federalists.

TRIBUTE OF RESPECT.

On Wednesday last a sumptuous and elegant publick dinner was given at Concert Hall to the honourable Rufus King, our late minister to the Court of Great Britain—This welcome to a distinguished citizen was manifested in a style of unusual cordiality and splendour.

The company consisted of about two hundred. Among the guests were his Excellency the Governor (who arrived in town

10. *The Country of our Fathers.* May its Spirit keep it safe and its justice keep it free.

11. *The Press.* May it always *correct* publick opinion, never *corrupt* it.

12. *Publick Opinion.* May it be sufficient shield for Honest men and a scourge for knaves.

13. May those Yankees who cannot endure Federal *sunshine*, go to Louisiana for MOONSHINE.

14. May Slaves cease to be represented by freeman and may the Representatives of freemen never act the part of Slaves.

15. The liberty that men *seek* when they are *wise*, and *respect* when they are *honest*.

16. *Gun Boat No. 1.* If our gun boats are of no use upon the water, may they at least be the *best upon earth.*

17. May we cultivate and defend the soil we *already possess*, without paying or fighting for what we can *neither cultivate nor defend.*

VOLUNTEERS.

By the Hon. Mr. KING. The town of Boston, first to assert, may it be the last to surrender the rights of freemen.

By Judge BENSON. The approbation of the *worthy*, the testimonial of *worth.*

(After Mr. KING had retired.)

The Hon. RUFUS KING—whose eminent services have contributed to preserve peace and amity between Countries naturally allied by sentiment and interest.

(After Judge BENSON had retired.)

The Hon. Judge BENSON—*once* the ornament of the bench and always the delight of his friends.

The *Louisiana Jubilee.* May it not prove to be the celebration of *all fool's* day.

that morning,) his Honour the Lieut. Governour and other publick characters. Judge Benson and other strangers of distinction and the reverend Clergy—The hon. Stephenson Higginson Esq. was president, and the hon. J. C. Jones, Samuel Parkman and J. Lyman Vice Presidents—The Hall which has been enlarged and repaired was furnished with the most brilliant decorations, and the whole entertainment was conducted with a sympathy of sentiment and "flow of soul" worthy "of men" who are conscious that the object of their politicks and principles has ever been

> "When leagu'd together, to maintain the cause
> Of true religion, liberty and laws."

The bitterness of party feeling was shown in the opposition papers in Boston, and especially in the *Independent Chronicle*, which on October 22d contained the following:

"As the Junto cry out 'Washington and Adams,' how comes it about that neither Mr. Adams nor his son dined at Mr. King's entertainments? The fact is the old gentleman begins to find out how far he has been duped by the Junto." *

The Yankee section of the Union. May those who *began the battle* guard against being cheated out of the fruits of the Victory.

British Influence. May those who seek that secret find it, where it alone exists—*In the Ancient Dominion.*

Mountains of Salt—to pickle Mammoths, and catch gulls in our new Empire.

The remedy of impeachment, for obstinate Judges who will neither "die nor resign." May the Inventors be obliged to swallow their own Medicine.

JAMES A. BAYARD. When men in power declare that such worth and talents *shalt not have place,* may the people indignantly respond THEY SHALL!!

Our Farmers, on the Sea Coast, may their Cornfields be defended against Gun boat No. 3.

May the grass, on WASHINGTON'S grave never again be blighted with hypocritick tears.

Our brave tars suffering in Tripoli—Alas! we fear that in the *honey moon* of our connection with Louisiana, our Captive brethren are forgotten.

BONAPARTE. May he learn *justice* from the British Government, and *meekness* from ours.[1]

* Schouler, in his *History of the United States,* vol. ii., p. 60, says, "King on his return from Europe was honored in Boston by a banquet decidedly Anti-administration in character, from which the Adamses took care to absent themselves."

[1] *The Repertory,* Boston, Friday, October 19, 1804.

Mr. Adams felt himself called upon to deny that his absence was intentional, and the answer he had given to the
Committee who had invited him to be present was published in the *Columbian Centinel.*

" J. Adams presents his compliments to the Committee of arrangements—Friendship for Mr. King and respect for the Company would have been more than sufficient to have induced him
to have accepted with pleasure the obliging invitation to the dinner in honor of a gentleman whose wisdom, independence and
integrity have done so much honor and real service to his Country ; but the present ill state of his health constrains him to deny
himself and to entreat the gentlemen to accept of his apology."

With respect to John Quincy Adams he set out for Washington on the evening previous to the dinner, for the meeting of Congress early in November.

A *Kingly* FESTIVAL.

It is a singular apology, that in the whole town of Boston there was no room
elegant enough to entertain Mr. KING, and that the federalists had to wait 3
or 4 months after his arrival before they could give him a dinner. The truth
is, when Mr. King visited the place of his nativity ; a few federalists thought
fit to honor him with a social festival, and this little *domestic circle* was noticed
in the papers, as a *reprimand,* to the " Junto " for suffering him to remain so
long in Boston without public notice. The Junto felt the " rap over the
knuckles," and on his return had no other way to *get off,* than depreciating the
town of Boston, by declaring to the world, there was no hall elegant enough to
entertain him. Now be it known, that in the town of Boston, there is a large
and commodious Hall, well known by the name of " FANEUIL HALL "—A
hall sacred to liberty ! The hall in which the constituted authorities of the
town give their annual entertainment—The hall in which the Governor, Council, and House of Representatives formerly dined on an election day—The hall
in which WASHINGTON was entertained when he visited Boston. But it
seems, the Essex-Junto, (who stile themselves *Washington federalists,*) thought
that Faneuil Hall was not elegant enough to introduce a man whose appellation
had any analogy to the title of KING ; a Hall whose walls had often resounded
in detestation of monarchy, was degrading to the character they were entertaining. Or rather the Junto were sensible, that their toasts were so different from
the sentiments inculcated by John Hancock and Samuel Adams, they were
afraid the very stones and bricks of the building would rise up in judgment
against them. They were conscious of their apostacy, from first principles,
and dreaded lest the portrait of FANEUIL should resume a bodily vigor, and
with a patriotic ire drive from the sanctuary of liberty, the revilers of those sen-

timents which added to the REVERENCE *of the* EDIFICE'——— It is with regret we observe, that Mr. King and Mr. Gore have been, through the subtlety of the Junto, the vehicles to abuse the present administration. These gentlemen it might be supposed, would have seen through the design of this insidious party. *

A public dinner was given at Faneuil Hall in honor of Mr. John Adams on October 31st, his seventieth birthday, and Mr. King was one of the invited guests. Among the volunteer toasts offered was the following:

"The Hon. Rufus King, whose talents and prudence have preserved the best interests of his country. May he receive ample reward in the confidence of its best citizens."

Such are the only accessible memoranda of the visit to the eastward, from which he soon after returned to New York. The Legislature of that State met early in November, for the purpose of choosing electors for the Presidential election, and a Senator of the United States to fill a vacancy caused by the appointment of General Armstrong as Minister to France. The electors chosen were persons representing the friends of Messrs. Jefferson and Clinton; and the votes for Senator were given to Mr. Samuel L. Mitchell, the Federalists supporting Mr. King as the opposing but unsuccessful candidate. Thus in the same year he was suggested as the best and most available candidate of the Federal party for Governor of the State of New York, for the Senate of the United States, and for the Vice-Presidency. The additional fact that his long absence from the country had kept him aloof from personal engagement in the factional strifes of the time, and his known moderate and conservative views, rendered him more likely to be a successful candidate for those high offices than any other Federalist who could be named; but they had lost their power, and other men and other measures prevailed.

* The *Independent Chronicle*, Boston, October 22, 1804.

Wm. Loughton Smith to R. King.

PHILAD., Oct. 18, 1804.

DEAR SIR

. . . (Referring to his brother, J. A. Smith, then abroad in Europe) He will be much disappointed in learning the real state of our politics, and the little prospect of an early change ; still, little congenial as I am on this head, I am not without hopes of one day witnessing the event he so fondly anticipated, & the realizing of which will not only afford the greatest joy to my brother & myself, but to every true and unprejudiced American.

In the mean time, we must continue to cherish and inculcate good principles, &, while we endeavour to tolerate the present things, say meliora spero. The loss of Washington, Hamilton, and, I must add, my respected friend, Mr. Izard, endears to me still more the few real worthies, who remain. You cannot be ignorant that all the respectable men throughout the Continent look to you & Genl. Pinckney as their political saviours, and that all their measures are predicated on a wish of, and directed to, the attainment of your future elevation to the Chief Magistr. Great public considerations are thus superadded to those of personal regard which have bound me to you ever since I had an opportunity of knowing you, and impel me to request you to take good care of yourself and keep out of all those scrapes which may endanger a life so precious to us. I am glad to find that our friend Pinckney is at the head of the Anti-Ludling Memorialists, and I trust that your sentimts are equally pacific. It was my intention to have progressed further north this summer, at least as far as New York, but Hamilton's death & your absence, with other causes, contributed to change my design.

With my best respects to Mrs. King and renewal of my warmest wishes for your happiness, . . .

Your affectionate frd.
Wm. Loughton Smith.

R. R. Livingston to R. King, N. Y.

PARIS. 22 Oct. 1804

DEAR SIR

. . . When I come out, which will not be till the next Spring as I propose to spend the winter in Italy and shall leave this as soon as I can resign our business to Genl. Armstrong, who has arrived at Nantz but is not come up to Paris, . . . I hope to close my mission with an important concession on the part of this government, which has always hitherto been refused, that of having consuls in their Islands. Mr. Talleyrand & two other of the ministers have promised me to use their influence that it be granted by the Emperor, and I doubt not that it will be done. This will be a great check upon their West India pirates.

Mr. Monroe was in Holland, & I expect him here today on his way to Spain, where I believe our affairs do not stand so well as might be wished, but as they will not quarrel with us I think that by a little firmness & address they may be re-established. There will probably be a change in the Batavian Republick : my friend Shimelpenninck will be placed at the head of it. The preparations for the coronation are immense ; it will, perhaps be the most superb festival that Europe has ever seen. The Pope sets out on the 3d. Nov. to perform the ceremony. . . .

Your most obd. hum. servt.

R. R. LIVINGSTON.

GEN. LAFAYETTE TO R. KING.

LA GRANGE 26 November 1804

MY DEAR SIR

While on your European Embassy you were admiring the prodigies of General Moreau, or feeling for His Virtues, you could neither fear for France the Misfortune, nor expect for the United States the Honor of his present Situation. My Sentiments on the Occasion with Respect to Both Countries and to Him, I leave you to judge, and I know you will consider these few lines By Him as a welcome Expression of the grateful Affectionate Regard of

Your Sincere Friend

LAFAYETTE.

The probable breaking-out of war between England and Spain suggested to Miranda, who was ever hopeful of accomplishing the freedom of the American Colonies from the Spanish yoke, that an opportunity was now presented for him to engage the assistance of Great Britain in his work. That country was always ready to use any method of crippling an enemy, but, as the letter from Miranda shows, was not inclined to take many risks in doing so. Mr. King had evidently been to a certain extent cognizant of Miranda's plans, as the following letter will show :

R. King to C. Gore.

Jany 4, 1804

"Genl. M (iranda) has I conclude left England before this date. If the question is at length settled with Spain, as it sh^d have been months ago, he may yet see his wishes accomplished. He & you know my sentiments on this subject, which nothing can alter. I do not write to the General, because I am expecting to hear of him in another quarter. Should he make a beginning, the news w^d. electrify this country, which contains an immense number of individuals, who would be ready to take up their bed and walk."

Mr. Gore writes to Mr. King from London, February 10, 1804 :

"Genl. M. is still here waiting the decision of this government in relation to Spain—Possibly an original error in not considering it as a party to the war is the cause of the present delay and of all the subsequent errors."

Miranda to R. King.*

Tres reservé.

Londres *30* (sic) Feb^r. 1804

Mon digne et cher ami

C'est avec un plaisir infini que je reçois votre Paragraphe dans la Lettre de M^r. Gore daté a New York le 4 Janv^r. dernier. Ma Lettre du 21. Sept. passé est la derniere que je vous ai écrit ; et comme ni la rupture avec l'Espagne a eu lieu encore, ni j'avois

---

Very Confidential.

* My worthy and dear Friend

It has given me infinite pleasure to receive your paragraph in the letter from Mr. Gore, dated the 4th of January last. My letter of 21st of Sept. past, is the last that I have written to you ; and as neither the rupture with Spain has yet

reçu aucune nouvelle de votre part, Je n'ai pas crû ápropos de faire mon mouvement encore. Je n'ai pas besoin de vous dire les sotises que M^r. A.—a fait depuis cette epoque, vous en aurez jugé mieux que personne.—Venons à ce qui nous regarde plus de près.

Voici l'arrangement que nous avons conclû ce matin avec M^r. Vansittart. Vargas (qui est ici) doit partir sous 15 jours pour *la Trinidad* afin de preparer les choses &c et je dois le suivre un mois après, dans un Batiment armé, portant en même tems les munitions, armes et habillemens qui seront necessaires pour commencer par nous-mêmes ; ce pays-ci se reservant de venir à notre secours après. C'est tout ce qu'on peut faire avec des pareilles gens, et a moins que nous ne soyons pas bouleversés dans l'intermede, par l'invasion dont nous sommes menacés.

Je compte en tout cas avec vos secours ; et dans cette supposition J'ai dressi *la note jointe*, afin que M^r. Gore á Boston, et vous a New York puissent nos envoyer ce qui est le plus essentiel dans le commencement, et selon les stipulations qui nous paraitront plus raisonables. La Maison de Brown et Cie a Trinidad, m'à écrit se chargeant de tout volontier, enfin selon les choses progressent vous aurez de mes nouvelles. L'ami G— vous remettra deux Livres de ma part, qui ont paru, depuis votre depart ; l'un par Volney concernant les E. U d' Amerique 2. v. 8 vo., l'autre avec de très belles *vues* de Paris, qui amuseront peutêtre Mad. King, 2 v. 4to par Holcroft.

Vale,

M——.

taken place, nor have I received any news from you, I have not deemed it fitting to make as yet my movement. I need not speak to you of the sottises that Mr. A—— has made since that period ; you can understand them better than any one else. Let us consider what concerns us more immediately.

The following arrangement was concluded this morning with Mr. Vansittart. Vargas, who is here, is to leave in 15 days for *Trinidad* in order to prepare things &c, and I am to follow him a month afterwards in an armed vessel, carrying at the same time the munitions, arms and equipments which will be necessary to commence by ourselves ; this country reserving to itself to come to our assistance afterwards. This is all we can do with such people, and provided we should not be overwhelmed by the invasion with which we are now threatened.

I count in all events upon your help, and in this expectation I have written *the joint note*, in order that Mr. Gore at Boston and you in New York may send

Mr. Gore wrote on April 17, 1804:

"Boston.

" As to Miranda's affair, I shall not mention a word of it until I learn that his friend is gone out, for I think it would be premature, and I will thank you not to say anything unless, or before, you hear from me again.   He ought to have sent another letter to me in the Downs, and from his not doing it, I fear some new difficulty occurred with the Brit. Gov^t.   From what I wrote you last autumn * you will see how he was deceived ; but as I never told him, it could not be reasoned upon."

Again on April 20th Mr. Gore encloses in a letter to Mr. King one from M. Vargas, in which, after wishing Mr. Gore a pleasant voyage home, he requests him to send a letter which he encloses to a M. Bonaventure Sire, a mer-

us whatever may be most essential in the beginning, and according to such stipulations as may appear to us most reasonable.   The house of Brown and Co. at Trinidad has written to me as willing to take charge of every thing.   Finally as matters progress you shall hear from me.   L'ami G. will deliver to you two books from me, which have appeared since you left ; one by Volney concerning the U. S. of America 2. v. 8vo ; the other with very beautiful views of Paris, which will perhaps amuse Mrs. King, par Holcroft.

Vale,   M——

The articles wanted are the following—20,000 good Muskets with Bayonets ; gun powder and ammunition for ditto in superabundance—Cast iron Artillery & ammunition for ditto, Bar Iron and Sheet Lead and a proportion of steel side arms.   For which articles payment will be given when landed on the Coast at the rate of one hundred or one hundred and fifty per cent over and above prime cost, of those articles in the United States of America.

Advantages offered to the Trade—Every Vessel bringing in the proportion of one thousand muskets, (or other of the above articles in lieu thereof) for every hundred Tons burthen, shall be entitled to the benefit of paying only one half the customary duties on the cargoes they may bring for sale into the country— with the advantage also of a deduction of one half the usual exportation duties, upon all the articles, the produce of the country, which they may choose to carry away.

All descriptions of Goods to be equally admissible into the country.

M——A.

London 12 March 1804.

N. B.   The Vessels to be directed to call upon the House of Mess Wm. *Brown & Co.*, at Puerto *d'Espagne*, on the Island of Trinidad for instruction.

* R. King's *Life*, iv., pp. 298, 299, 305, 314, 319, 321.

chant in New York, who was also to receive certain letters, books, and linen articles, and deliver them to Mr. Gore, who is requested by M. Vargas to send them à l'Isle de la Trinité, addressed to Mr. Vargas, to the care of Colonel Rutherford, Surveyor-General of that island.

Mr. Vargas also says that he had passed in New York, where he had been, under the name of Fermin Sarmiento, by which name he is to be spoken of there, especially in case that it may be necessary to ascertain the address of M. Sire through the Spanish Consul, who is under no circumstances to be informed of the place of residence of M. Vargas, but to be led to believe he is still in London.

In his letter Mr. Gore says:

"Vargas said they (the papers) were very interesting documents relating to S. America. Should any be procured, pray forward them as desired."

C. GORE TO R. KING.

BOSTON May 3, 1804

MY DEAR SIR

The particular object of this Letter is to enquire, if you have chosen to say, or propose to any person, to do anything relative to the Business on which M. wrote you. My reason for enquiring is that I have a prospect of doing somewhat here and possibly advantageous to myself. And the Manner or Extent, at least, will depend on knowing whether any thing, or what may be undertaken from another Quarter. Pray have the goodness to answer me by return of Post, and believe me truly & ever yours

C. GORE.

C. GORE TO R. KING.

BOSTON May 15, 1804

MY DEAR SIR

The most that has passed here, relative to the subject of my last letter, has been like what you state to have taken place in New York. Mr. S. H. is disposed to enter upon the Business, so soon as anything shall have been done to render it certain that they, who have so long fed our Friend with Hopes, intend to promote his Wishes by a Conduct suitable to their own Interest, & promising an Attainment of the Object. The sailing of V. with the promised Supplies would, in my mind be strong, if not conclusive Evidence of this Intention ; but I do not know, that this would be satisfactory to S. H. ; yet my opinion would probably have weight with him. I have an intention, in some degree, to be interested in the adventure, though without incurring much Risque. I will, however, come to no conclusion, on any part of the subject, without consulting with you.

Williams has sent me Duplicate of some Letters, originals whereof he has forwarded, under cover to you, by the Juliana. When received, you will please to open them & retain for yourself all that relate to this Concern. . . .

With affectionate Regards &c.

C. GORE.

There is an intermission of correspondence on this matter until the autumn of 1804, when Mr. Gore writes :

C. GORE TO R. KING.

BOSTON, Nov. 25, 1804.

MY DEAR FRIEND :

. . . I was rejoiced to read the account of the Spanish war, and immediately renewed my conversation with those Friends I had before spoken to on the business, and as formerly, they were disposed to undertake it with Spirit, and were willing to pay to me 25 or 20 per cent of the net Profits, if any should be made on the adventure : and I had contemplated making a journey to N. Y., if you thought it adviseable, with the view of attempting a similar arrangement there. If I could assure myself, free from all hazard, enough to build me two Houses, say 50,000 Dollars I would go there with the Cargoes, should that be deemed necessary ; but this I would not attempt, except on the condition that such a sum was secured to me before my Departure. However all this for the present, at least, is passed by. A Letter which was in our paper yesterday and dated in London, says that a Merchant told—the Letter writer—that Lord Hawkesbury recommended to him a Caution in trading to Spain, as the future relations between G. B. & S. were very uncertain. The writer of this letter was S. Williams. . . .

Ever,

C. G.

In a letter of January 10, 1805, Mr. King writes this post-script in answer to Mr. Gore's letter of November 25, 1804, not having written during the interval, as he says:

P. S. As I must take a second sheet for a cover, I may as well say a word or two on a subject touched upon in a former letter from you. I refer to the Spanish war and the measures that may grow out of it. You have seen the Eng. accounts of the capture of the Span. Frigates : since the date of that acc^t. we have no news from Eng^d. Unless Spain be advised by Bonaparte to subscribe to her own disgrace, which would not surprize me, the war at this moment exists.

I will suppose it so ; and that the Expedition has actually sailed for Trinidad, of which we must receive the earliest accounts. Yet I do not foresee an immediate state of things that promises a golden shower to those who become adventurers. If war has been declared, it will have been first known in London, where there are individuals ready to accompany and who will be engaged to accompany the Expedition with a supply of every thing, except perhaps provisions, that will be wanted. If so supplies of the same sort from this country will be late, and in competition with those from England. Besides it seems to me that something must be begun before any steps that are not those of hazard, that are not parts of the enterprize, can be undertaken. As to arms, ammunition and military stores, if the Expedition be set forward in time of war, as seems to be the probable case, there will be no motive on the part of England to stint supplies of this sort, any more than of goods of an innocent character. Any supplies, therefore, that in the present want of exact information, may be sent from this country, will be sent at a considerable risque of loss, instead of gain. From this little sketch you will discern the state of my opinions respecting this subject ; but admitting, as I am ready to do, that I see the business not in its true light, and that great advantages will be gained by the first supplies sent from hence, I feel too clearly convinced of the justness of my decision in another part of your letter, to express an equal deference for even your dissent from me. I allude to your going personally, with the supplies that may be sent.

On no consideration that could be promised, should you consent to go. But I am satisfied that you have, even before now, discarded the thought, if it has occurred since it first presented itself to you. If, however, you should seriously think of it again, before you decide give me an opportunity of being more full in support of my opinion.

Adieu.

Such, up to the above date, are some of the facts concerning Miranda's efforts, which indicate Mr. King's interest in this plan to revolutionize the Spanish colonies in South and Central America, and how little dependence could be placed on the promises of Great Britain ; the Ministers holding out hopes and arranging plans, but putting off their execution.

CHAPTER XXVIII.

C. GORE TO R. KING.

BOSTON, January 1, 1805.

MY DEAR FRIEND :

It is long time since I heard from you by letter, though we learn
through Mr. Wallace that you & yours enjoy good health. Mrs.
Gore is as well as I have known her for many years ; & for myself,
I am more like to die of a plethora than any other disorder. For
this is quite the season of feasting, and a man, who has his living
to obtain, cannot refuse the intended kindnesses of his friends,
although he may perish in the acceptance. As for exercise, that
is for the present out of the question. The streets and roads are
covered with ice, and a man walks at the hazard of his limbs and
perhaps of never walking again.

. . . Pinkney* sent me the newspapers, which contain the

---

* William Pinkney had been his associate on the Commission for the settlement
of American Claims under Jay's Treaty, and afterwards appointed by the State
of Maryland to look after its claims for the Maryland Bank Stock, which, after
many efforts for a settlement made by Mr. King, still remained undecided
when he left England.

Compliments of Language & Substance, wherewith his Country-men regaled his ears & purse.   It is impossible to avoid observ-ing the studied silence as to him, who really obtained the Boon for Maryland and as to everything relative to our Commission. The latter, if brought into view, might have reflected honour on the last Administration, and to have given the due acknowledge-ment, to the Former, might have rendered justice to a Character, whom they wished to keep out of sight.   .   .   .

Affectionately yours,

C. Gore.

R. King to C. Gore.

New York, Jany. 10, 1805.

My dear Friend :

Having nothing either personal or public to say, I have for several weeks omitted to write to you ; we are happy to know from your letter that Wallace brought us that Mrs. Gore enjoys such excellent health, and that yours also is better than while you were in the course of violent exercise.   With the exception of Frederick (his youngest son) and myself who have heavy colds, we are all well.   Mrs. King was never better, notwithstanding the inclemency of the season prevents her accustomed exercise.   The Frost has prevented me from riding, and I begin, or fancy I do, to feel the want of exercise.   .   .   . *

I. Allen Smith to R. King.

Constantinople, January 22^d, 1805.

My dear Sir :

I have just been favoured with your letters and duplicates of the 10th and 22^d of August & regret that I was so unfortunate as to lose that of April to which you allude.   The President's resolu-tion respecting a mission to Russia is what I always expected ; but I should have reproached myself had I neglected in writing

---

* The concluding portions of this letter, except some information as to his views relative to the education of his younger sons, will be found on p. 410 rel-ative to the Hamilton affairs and p. 434 relative to Miranda.

to you to touch on a subject, which appeared to me of importance to my country or to have satisfied, within myself, a sentiment of gratitude which I had so much reason to feel. Although persuaded that the Court of Russia would receive with pleasure a minister from the U. States, and that no period could be more favourable for such a mission than that of the administration of the Chancellor Vorontion, I studiously avoided ever expressing myself on this subject to any one, until my arrival at Astracan, resolving to return through Russia, I took the liberty of mentioning it in a letter to you, & afterwards to my Brother, on my arrival at Constantinople. I have therefore the satisfaction of having done nothing more than what appeared to me to be my duty & of having been ready to sacrifice my own pursuits and pleasures to the service of my Country. . . .

I read with infinite regret the report you give me of the condition of our public affairs. I consoled myself, after having been so long a witness of the Evils which reign in Europe, with the idea that I should find reason and moderation in America ; and I see with great disappointment & sorrow, that a people whom I thought the most capable of forming accurate notions on the important subject of liberty, have not yet been convinced, even after the experience of the French Revolution, that the shortest and beaten road of Tyranny, is that which leads through Democracy. I perfectly agree with you, that, however gloomy the prospect, we ought not to despair ; but that men of honesty and energy of character should redouble their exertions to stem the current of revolutionary principles in a country, which above all others has enjoyed most the blessings of Justice & of equal laws. We received them by inheritance from England, the only country in Europe that possessed them, we had the courage to maintain them and it would be folly, wickedness, and absurdity to infringe them.

I cannot too earnestly intreat you, my dear Sir, to continue to me the advantage & pleasure of hearing from you, for I have lost nothing of that interest which I ought to feel for the welfare of our Common Country, or of that profound respect & sincere attachment with which I have the honour to be

Your most obliged Humb^l Servt

I. ALLEN SMITH.

T. Pickering to R. King.

WASHINGTON, Feby. 15, 1805.

DEAR SIR :

I think I lately inclosed to you Judge Chase's answer to the articles of impeachment. In that he referred, as you will have seen, to several documents. These were this morning laid on our tables. In this and one other packet, I enclose a copy.

The virulence of the party prosecuting and the aggravated evidence of angry irritated opponents, had thrown some light clouds over the Judge's character ; but in the course of the trial, I am inclined to think that these will be dissipated. I am now disposed to believe after hearing the testimony of the witnesses for the prosecution, and some of those produced by the Judge, that they will not find 23 senators hardy enough to condemn him.

I think John Randolph's opening Speech, as given in the Washington Federalist, is substantially correct. But the words concerning the four district Judges (Peters, Bedford, Winchester and Griffin) were more opprobrious than they appear in that paper. Those Judges, he said, were "men of weak and feeble temper, and of intellects" (making a considerable pause) "perhaps as feeble." And that by pardoning John Fries, Mr. Adams "had atoned for many failings ; for mercy, like charity, covered a multitude of sins."

With great respect & esteem I am yours

T. PICKERING.

RUFUS KING, ESQ.

Cyrus King to R. King.

PEPPERELLVILLE, Feby. 17, 1805.

MY DEAR BROTHER :

*.   .   .   The distresses which you mention of the Poor from the severity of the winter must be great and afflicting, especially in a part of the country where hard winters are not frequent. In this inhospitable region (as to Climate), where we are accustomed

---

* The blank refers to the receipt of a sum of money, sent by Mr. King to his brother Richard. C. King had been educated by his brother Rufus, and was his first secretary during the latter's mission to England.

to a much greater severity of weather, but few ever experienced so hard a winter as the present ; storms of snow have been unusually frequent and the frost intense.

I am happy to learn from you the health and welfare of your amiable family which will always be dear to me. Our friends in this part of the country are in general well. . . .

In gratitude and affection, I am dear Brother

CYRUS KING.

RUFUS KING TO T. PICKERING.

N. YORK, Feby. 18, 1805.

DEAR SIR :

I give you many thanks for the copy of Judge Chase's reply, which you were good enough to send to me. I have read it with great interest and attention ; and I may add with equal satisfaction. I am gratified that the Judge has prepared his answer in the manner he has done, as whatever may be the result of his trial, impartial men both now and hereafter will possess the authentic means of deciding for themselves. We have heard of a rude and disorderly debate in the H. of R. concerning the Georgia Claim ; & some persons have conjectured that a serious division would arise among the Democrats—nay, that it already exists, and that Judge Chase's best hope of acquittal proceeds from it. Who is to be the Attorney General & what delays his appointment ? does this indirectly wait for the conclusion of Chase's trial ? What has been the fate of the convention concerning boundaries made with England ? has she consented to our proposed omission, or does the business rest in the same state, as when the Senate dismissed it ? What is likely to become of your St. Domingo Bill ; concerning which trade I am sorry to see that Mr. Merry has intimated even opinions, that the laws & usages of nations do not in my belief authorize. England seems to be doing for you your business with Spain ; as in case of a war between those two nations, we shall have little trouble to adjust our demands with the latter.

With truth & attachment

I remain, dear Sir, yr. obed^t. Servt.

RUFUS KING.

T. Pickering to R. King.

Washington, Feby. 24, 1805.

Dear Sir :

I have received your letter of the 18th. The trial of Judge Chase has progressed so far, that his counsel will finish his defence tomorrow ; Mr. Harper closes. Luther Martin, in behalf of his "honourable friend" the Judge, occupied the whole of yesterday, 5½ hours ; and then told the court he was too much exhausted to conclude his argument ; assuring them, if the indulgence were granted, he would take up but little of their time on Monday. The Court (*Senate* I ought to call it ; Mr. Giles having, in our preliminary proceedings, banished the word Court) the Senate granted Mr. Martin's request. I regretted very much the apparent necessity of this indulgence ; fearing he would occupy so much of our time on Monday as to mar the defence of Mr. Harper, addressed to a court and audience (I mention the Audience, because a numerous body of respectable people may have an influence on judges, some of whom, tho' they have not the fear of God, yet have the fear of man before their eyes) half-exhausted. But I understand that Mr. Martin is enjoined, and has engaged, positively to conclude by noon. Mr. Harper, I am told, will speak not more than three hours ; but I much doubt the possibility of his compressing within that space all he will deem important on so copious a theme. The two last Articles of the impeachment are reserved for him (the proceedings at Newcastle & Baltimore) and he will notice any points which in the discourses of the other counsel on the six first articles were either omitted or too lightly touched.

There was on the part of John Randolph uncommon rudeness in the H. of R., in the debate on the Georgia claims ; but that will not have the smallest influence on the impeachment. The indecent replication of the H. of R. to Judge Chase's answer was subsequent to the abusive, impudent speech of Randolph on the Georgia claim ; and in that replication the whole pack united as usual. However, I am persuaded they sincerely wish they had not meddled with Judge Chase. The testimony of the multitude of witnesses has placed the Judge's judicial acts in a fair and *legal* point of view. The managers, with a better cause, would contend but feebly with such able counsel as appear for Judge Chase, and with so paltry an one, you may rely upon it, they make a very shabby figure. For the points of law, Rodney is their Goliath. The managers, I learn, expect to make all their speeches in one day—say Tuesday ; or at farthest to finish on Wednesday morning. I expect the decision of the Senate will immediately follow without any discussion.

We know not who is to be the attorney General, nor why the appointment is delayed ; unless it be the difficulty of finding one of the orthodox sect of competent abilities. John Thompson Mason of Georgetown (brother of Stephens Thompson Mason) might have received the appointment, I have heard ; but an uncle, without a child, lately deceased, has left him a very large estate ; and not enjoying very good health, he declines the office.

The British Convention is where the Senate were last year told it would be, if they persisted in their idle amendment. Even its name has not been lisped during the whole session, either by President or Senator.

The St. Domingo Bill—that is the bill for clearing armed merchant vessels, passed the Senate last Friday. The first section is all that resembles the original bill, which came up from the H. of R., and that is ameliorated. The master and owner are to give bonds with sureties, in double the value of the vessel and her tackle, that her arms shall not be used in any unlawful act, but merely in self defence in case of involuntary hostility. The penal section, for punishing offences committed abroad, as if committed at home, is struck out ; and its continuance is limited to the end of the next session of Congress. Samuel Smith introduced a section requiring bonds of the master and owner, that a vessel armed & cleared for any other port than the West Indies, should not proceed thither unless from stress of weather. We endeavoured to get this expunged, but failed. The Bill passed by a great majority—20 to 8—. I remarked to S. Smith that the bill did not reach the complaint of the French Minister, which went to a total discontinuance of the trade to St. Domingo. The French (he answered) do not now desire it ; the French Minister has told me so ; it was only a point of honour !—

Your two Senators voted for the bill. I also was very sorry to see Mr. Merry's letter on this subject ; and not a little surprized at its apparent imbecillity.

Your Senator Smith has presented a bill to grant to Aaron Burr the privilege of franking letters for the rest of his life.*

With very great regard, &c.

TIMOTHY PICKERING.

T. PICKERING TO R. KING.

WASHINGTON, March 1, 1805.

DEAR SIR :

I have much pleasure in announcing to you the acquittal of Judge Chase, this day. The Senators were called, alphabetically, by the President, on which each rose, when the President propounded the question, on each article in the forms following. " How say you ? Is Samuel Chase guilty or not guilty of a high crime or misdemeanour as charged in the article of impeachment now (or last read) ? " The Senator answered guilty or not guilty.†

Your two Senators uniformly said *not guilty.*

In great haste adieu

T. PICKERING.

T. PICKERING TO R. KING, N. YORK.

WASHINGTON, March 2, 1805.

DEAR SIR :

In your late letter, I think you asked me why the nomination of an Attorney General was delayed ? I could not then tell ; now it seems apparent. Yesterday, you will find by my letter of that date, Judge Chase was acquitted, and at the moment I began this letter, Robert Smith was nominated to be attorney general. Had Judge Chase been convicted on the articles of impeachment, doubtless Smith was to have been placed on the Bench. Crowninshield of Salem was at the same time nominated to be Secretary of the Navy.

The House of Representatives made short work with the *Burr-postage-Bill*—they yesterday postponed it to the first day of December next.

The Vice-President just now took leave of the Senate, in a concise & apparently extempore speech, marked by that good

---

* This was granted by Congress, after some hesitation in the H. of Reps.

† The detail of the votes, given in this letter, will be found in the Annals of Congress, 1804–5, pp. 665–669.

sense which you know he possesses. The Senate have unanimously passed a vote of thanks, in perfectly appropriate terms, testifying the impartiality, dignity and ability with which he has presided over their deliberations. I presume the Committee who are to present the vote of thanks, will ask for his address, and that both will be published.

Very truly yours,

T. PICKERING.

R. KING TO SAM. CHASE.

Copy.

N. YORK, March 6, 1805.

SIR :

We have this morning been made acquainted with the issue of the prosecution agt. you by the H. of R., and I cannot suffer a mail to be despatched witht. offerg. you my sincere and cordl. congrats, upon the decision wh. has been pronounced. Whatever may be due to the zeal and abilities of yr. Counsel, who without doubt have acquitted themselves in a manner worthy of the gt. charge they were bound to protect, I shall always believe that much very much of that influence and authority wh. have overawed and confounded the settled purpose of yr. Enemies, must be ascribed to the courageous, able, and convincing ansr. you yourself gave to the charges preferred agt. you ; an answer wh. not only possesses the highest merit, as a learned and satisfactory vindication of the just and necessary power of the judiciary, but which must remain an everlasting Record of the unworthy motives of yr. Persecutors.

Accept with my Congrats., the assurance of the distingd. considn. & Respect with which I have the honour to be, Sir, your most ob. & faith. ser

R. K.

SAM. CHASE, BALT., TO R. KING.

13th March, 1805.

MY DEAR SIR :

I am honored and gratified by your Congratulations on my acquittal by the Senate of the Impeachment by the House of Representatives. It has ever been my wish to obtain and preserve the

Esteem & Confidence of the virtuous and sensible part of my Fellow-Citizens. The approbation of characters like you, Sir, affords me peculiar Pleasure and is a great Consolation to Me, under the cruel persecution I have suffered. My answer was principally intended as a *Justification* of my official Conduct to judicial and professional Gentlemen. I can assure you that the Evidence produced on the trial fully supported my answer in all its parts ; and disclosed many facts that had escaped my Memory, and will, I expect, convince every impartial man of the Rectitude and propriety of my conduct, in the very instances charged to be criminal. It was not alleged in any article of Impeachment, that I had attempted to pack a Jury on the trial of Callender ; but the Managers calling a witness for this Purpose, I consented to the Inquiry, although I have no doubt the Senate would not have admitted such evidence without my Consent. You will find on perusing the trial, that this base attempt was entirely repelled.

In support of the 8th Article the Managers examined a Witness to prove that in my Charge to the Grand-Jury at Baltimore, I made a direct attack upon the present Executive, for Imbecility in office ; for, promoting his own Interest in preference to that of the public ; and for obtaining his Election by undue means—no such fact was stated ; nor had I any notice of it ; but I made no objection ; if I had, it would have been said that I was afraid of it. I proved that the evidence was not *true* by a Dozen of Witnesses of the very first Reputation. The name of the Managers' Witness is John Montgomery, a democrat, a leading member of the House of Delegates of this State. To my counsel I am greatly obliged for the very able legal and constitutional Defence they made for me ; for the whole labor rested on them, as I was unable from indisposition to take any Part ; and to the Justice of my Case and their abilities I impute my acquittal. I am in a peculiar Manner indebted to my Friend Mr. Harper for his professional assistance in preparing my answer, and for his Conduct of my defence. It affords me great Pleasure to add, that a more fair and impartial trial, conducted with greater Dignity, never took place in any country. The trial is now in the press in this City, & I expect will be the most accurate. I am sure you will receive great Pleasure from the perusal of it.

The conduct of my *accusers*, in refusing to pay the Expenses of the Witnesses summoned by my Direction, you will observe in the votes of the House of Representatives 60 agt. and only 18 for payment of them.

You will see by the amendment proposed by Mr. Randolph, to the Constitution, that an attempt will be made to make the Judiciary altogether dependent on a *Majority* of the two Branches of the Legislature ; and by the amendment proposed by Mr. Nicholson, that the Senate are to become a mere diplomatic Corps, dependant on the several State Legislatures. I can conceive no two measures more radically destructive of our Constitution. I can only oppose them by my Wishes ; my age, infirmities & the wicked Prosecution I have suffered, have determined me never to take any Part in any public Measure whatsoever.

I pray you, Sir, to accept my best Wishes for your Health and prosperity & believe, that I am with every sentiment of Respect & Esteem

Your affectionate & most obedient Servant,

Samuel Chase.

It was a matter of much anxiety to Mr. King to make such an arrangement for the future education of his two sons, who had now passed eight years at Harrow, and were then in Paris, at the school of M. Thurot, engaged in studying mathematics, French, and Spanish. The younger son, Charles, had decided that he would prefer the life of a merchant ; the older one, John, selecting that of a lawyer. The first suggestion was to place Charles in the house and under the care of his friend Sir Francis Baring ; but, as will be seen, though this gentleman had willingly consented to receive him, Mr. King had thought it better for such reasons as he deemed wise, to send him to Amsterdam, under the care of Messrs. Hope, and for this purpose he wrote directly to Mr. Labouchere in London, asking him to take an interest in the arrangement and in the care of his son, and to Mr. W. Hope—

R. KING TO W. HOPE.

NEW YORK, March 9, 1805.

DEAR SIR :

Before as well as since I left England, I have had communication with our friend, Sir Francis Baring, concerning my second son, who has now nearly completed his 16th year, and whom I propose to educate a merchant.   At first I thought of placing him in London, and Sir Francis consented to receive him into his house.   But such are the amusements and vices of that great metropolis, that I have hesitated in leaving him there, remote as he would be from my Superintendence, and by the advice of Sir Francis I am led to prefer placing him at Amsterdam, where there are fewer amusements, more industry and firmer habits of Business, provided I can there meet with a suitable situation for him. In a late letter from Sir Francis, he informs me thro' Mrs. Labouchére, he would consult you and her husband upon this subject : but as the intercourse between Holland and England is interrupted, and considerable time may elapse before I can learn your opinion thro' that channel, I have presumed upon our former acquaintance to address myself directly to you.

The chief objects of my solicitude are the promotion of the health and morals of my son and his education as a merchant. Should you consent to receive him into your house, he would be where I wish him to be educated, and could I indulge the hope that he might be so associated with your sons, as to be admitted also into your family, I should think I had attained for him the advantage and security which a good father must be sedulously anxious to provide.

In case it should be inconvenient for you to gratify my wishes on either or both these points, I am persuaded of your disposition to assist me with your friendly opinion and advice concerning the best means of attaining my object.   My case differs essentially from what it would be were I an inhabitant of your City ; for altho' the education of my son would then depend on his connection with some commercial House, he would live in my family and be under my observation and control ; and it is an arrangement that shall supply this constant care and superintendence about which I am most embarrassed.   Perhaps Messrs. Willinks, or Van Stopworts, whom I know, or some other respectable

House would consent to receive my son ; but even then I should be at a loss where to find that care and protection without which a youth is liable to fall into error and misfortune.

Hitherto I have made no application to any other people on this subject, preferring first to receive your answer, which I beg the favor of you to send me as early as shall be convenient. Be pleased to present my respectful compliments to Mrs. Hope, in which Mrs. King desires to unite hers, and be assured that I am with sentiments of great Respect and Esteem &c

RUFUS KING.

C. GORE TO R. KING.

BOSTON, March 10, 1805.

MY DEAR FRIEND :

. . . Our election has begun, or rather the preparations for it, and an unusual degree of Heat seems to be excited, more especially as the moral & official character of one of the Candidates is most vehemently attacked, which occasioned a cudgelling between the son of the Judge & the Printer ; and this Rencounter seems to have demanded from the latter a reiteration and justification of what had been before asserted. We have hopes that Strong may be again elected ; but this is by no means certain. Our House will be probably democratic, and I do not believe the Senate will be any better ; and They, who are Federalists, are not very skilful or able in supporting their cause. Probably a great mistake was made last autumn in changing our Rep. to Congress, for although it would not have been proper for the Federalists to have supported the existing Member, yet their success has sent one, who cannot render any service to the cause, & brought one here, who can afford much support to his own Party, and taken Him from a scene, where He could not fail of becoming an Opponent to the Administration, although not a convert to those who formerly held their Places. We appear to me to be changing very fast, & the little Federalism that is left, will soon be no more. We may rise to something else, but not to that. I had a letter the other day from Pinkney, who says that He is almost determined to settle in Annapolis, that He may be elected into their State Legislature, and endeavour to stop the Torrent. From this and other Parts of his Letter, it is probable he does not side with the present Administration. We hear nothing of Trumbull; Does He proceed successfully ? . . .

We have been somewhat alarmed here the last week at the Possibility of a Peace. Our Merchants are very anxious that Great Britain should not impair her Dignity, or hazard her security, by any pacific negotiations for the Present

As ever yours

C. GORE.

R. R. LIVINGSTON TO R. KING.

PARIS, 7th April, 1805.

DEAR SIR :

I have the pleasure to enclose to you an extract of a letter from the Minister of foreign affairs written to me by order of the Emperor & King just as he was about leaving Paris for Milan. This was accompanied by the work he mentions, and which I shall bring with me and deposit in the gallery of the Society for fine arts. You will find this a very princely present, which will be from its nature I hope not only useful to our young painters and sculptors, but to such other of our fellow citizens as are occupied in works of taste. The architect, the silversmith, the cabinet maker &c. will find models in their respective professions that cannot fail to impress their taste. It consists in twenty four volumes in fol. of prints & a number of portfols. containing paintings in oil & water colours, most of them copies from antiques & from Raphael ; several views of Constantinople, Cairo, &c. I shall have them carefully packed & hope they may arrive safe. If this extract, which is inclosed, should find its way into the paper, which it probably will, I pray you not to suffer it to be perverted & mutilated, as everything relative to me from here has been by false translations, but to have the goodness to anticipate these by publishing the original with such a translation as you shall find accurate. Though this present together with a portrait of the Emperor very richly set with diamonds was made me on my return from Italy, and six months after I had taken leave formally, and of course held no office, I have thought myself bound to send a copy of the letter (which contains no reference to my former public character) to Mr. Madison & to submit the disposition of these gifts to the Government, if they should suppose they come within the spirit, tho' they are certainly not within the letter of the constitution. It is under this restriction that you must receive that part of it which is d esignedorthe society.

I hope to sail about the 10th of May & to bring James with me. We all beg to be presented to Mrs. King. I am Dear Sir with much esteem & regard &c.

Rob. R. Livingston.

Extract accompanying this letter :

" Extract of a letter from his excellency Monsieur de Talleyrand 11ᵉ. Germinal, au 13.

* J'ai cru qu'il vous serait particulierement agréable de pouvoir favoriser dans votre pays le gout des arts, et dans cette vue, J'ai l'honneur de vous envoyer une collection de l'ancienne et de la nouvelle calcographie des Péres et Fréres Piranesi. Les desseins gravés et colorés seront convenablement placés au Muséum de New York et attesteront l'interêt que vous nous avez inspiré pour tout ce qui peut contribuer á l'instruction et á l'agrément de vos jeunes compatriotes.

Je vous prie Monsieur de recevoir l'assurance de ma haute consideration.   Signé,

C. M. Talleyrand.

Son Excellence Monsieur Livingston.

The Evening Post, June 22d, 1805, gives the following account of this collection :

" This rare and valuable collection, which Mr. Livingston brings with him consists of 24 vols. with folios of prints, together with several Portfolios containing copies in oil and water colours from Raphael and from antiques, Views from Constantinople, Cairo, &c. &c. The work will not only be useful to painters and sculptors, to many others.

---

* I have thought that it would be particularly agreeable to you to be able to promote the taste for arts in your country, and with that view I have the honour to send you a collection of the ancient and the new *calcographie* of the Péres et Fréres Piranesi. The engraved and coloured designs will be most properly placed in the Museum of New York, and will shew the interest you have manifested to us for everything that might contribute to the instruction and gratification of your young compatriots.

R. KING TO C. GORE.

NEW YORK, May 2, 1805.

MY DEAR FRIEND :

. . . I cannot help regretting that Robbins and Cobb are likely to fail in yr. election, in part on their accounts personally, but chiefly as their failure may be recd. as certain evidence that Strong will follow them into retirement. To you who think and feel as I do, it wd. be superfluous to express my sentiments on this most interesting subject. I will only say that it wd. be an honest consolation to hope even that an amendment is likely to happen ; but to do so would be folly.

I do not very well understand the state of Parties in England, still less the views of the Northern Powers ; as to Peace, it cannot take place at present, without humiliation to France or England ; and neither is in a disposition to submit to it. I can well enough comprehend the views of Bonaparte in making the overture ; and the answer of England was both discreet and, as I suppose, decisive. But the affair continues to be talked of, and the politics of Russia are to me mysterious ; still I do not believe there can be peace in the present relative condition of the Parties.

Where the secret Expedn. is bound I can't divine ; perhaps to So. Amer. ; but from the tenour of the debates in Parliament, I hesitate in believing so, tho' where else unless to the Cape of Good Hope I cannot conjecture.

Pray are you about to engage in any venture abroad ? tell me your projects, perhaps I may solicit a concern. I must endeavour to do something wh. shall help my Revenue, so fast do the disbursements increase. We are here very expensive and the passion grows stronger, as well as becomes more diffused. In Boston too I suspect you find a difference between the present and past times.

We have no letters from the boys since they arrived at Rotterdam (on their way to Paris), but hope soon to hear that they are safe and settled with Thurôt. Livingston intended to embark in Apl., but as he was at Rome late in Jan'y, I think he will not leave France before May, so that we shall not see James earlier than June. I am greatly at a loss what to do with Edward, there being no good school near here, and I don't much like to send all my children so far from us as we may be forced to do. . . .

Always yours   R. K.

C. Gore to R. King.

My dear Friend :

I had still some intention of hazarding some adventure abroad. My expenses here are considerably greater than the same comforts would have cost me a few years since. . . . With this view (to increase his means) I have contemplated making some shipments . . . to Holland or England. The last year most of the articles shipt from hence, either of West India or E India produce, netted a profit of 25 per cent ; and it is not improbable that I may embark in some project of this sort in the course of the present or next month. Should this or any other scheme have the appearance of being successful, I will communicate it and shall be happy in your taking any share or part. . . .

Yours truly
C. Gore.

Lord Suffolk to R. King.

Dear Sir :

Indisposition for a considerable time, and a wish to have addressed my answer to you in that Rank and Station, which I hope you will one day fill, have hitherto prevented my answering your obliging letter, for the contents of which I was prepaid from an answer given by Gen'l Washington on the same subject some years since ; for though the Validity of a part of the claim was acknowledged by him, he was of opinion that Restitution could never be obtained. I was willing to make one more effort for the sake of two natural children, whom my brother left behind him, to whom a considerable share was left by will, if any part of the property could have been recovered, but which I shall now consider as entirely out of the question.

In this country we have had a very warm political session with most of the great Talents on the side of opposition ; which you will be convinced of when I mention the names of Mr. Fox, Mr. Grey, Sheridan, Whithead, and a young man who has greatly distinguished himself Ld. Henry Petty, and of Irish members Mr. Grattan and Mr. Ponsonby. These are oppos'd by the single

Talent of Mr. Pitt, for as to his coadjutors (such as Ld. Castlereagh and Mr. Canning) they as frequently hurt as benefit his cause.   In the House of Lords there is equal deficiency, now that Ld. Melville is, I believe, on the Eve of Impeachment, he has no one that can be compar'd to Ld. Grenville.   But political Talent seems to me out of the question.   I believe it to be the wish of Mr. Pitt only to make use of minor characters whom he can easily rule and direct.   This may go on for some time, but it is in my opinion not a system to be permanent.   Much will depend on the health of the King, who certainly looks extremely well, but is now so lethargick, that at a review of near 2000 artillery a few days since, notwithstanding all the noise of cannon, &c., he was frequently asleep, and cou'd with some difficulty be rous'd.

Such our internal situation ; as to the external, you are much better acquainted with and can much better appreciate it than I can pretend to form a Judgment of what will be the Result of this eventful war in which we are engag'd.   Shall not therefore hazard any sentiment how soon, or in what manner it is likely to terminate ; but with many thanks for the trouble I have given you and many wishes for your welfare & happiness

I remain, Dear Sir, your oblig'd & faithful servant,

SUFFOLK.

All my family join in kind remembrance to you & Mrs. King.

CHAPTER XXIX.

R. King to C. Gore.

ROCKAWAY, Sept. 15, 1805.

MY DEAR FRIEND :

Yesterday I received a letter from M—— dated . . . July 13. "Apres des inconsequences et des retards inconcevables et insupportables, nous voila sur le point de partir—je compte de m'embarquer dans le courant de ce mois, et de vous envoyer quelqu'un, ou de vous voir moimême, &c., J'envoye ce même avis á notre ami G——"

Probably you have a letter by the same conveyance. Lest this should not be the fact, I send you the above extract. I apprehend from the earnestness with which succour is urged, that the means with wh. he is furnished are most inconsiderable,—perhaps he is merely sent out in a ship going to the Island of Tr., and that his chief hopes of assistance are derived from the posture of our affairs with Spain. It will soon be better understood, by the further communication that is promised, till when, though the affair may be matter of reflexion, nothing can be done. We know nothing

454

except what the News Papers tell us concerning our relations with Spain. Monroe has returned to England, his mission having totally failed. The objects of negotiation were the enlargement of C. Pinckney's Spanish Convention, so that it might include the cases of French captures, the sale and condemnation of which were had in Spanish ports and the settlement of the limits of Louisiana.

To the first Spain is understood to have answered that she could not interfere with proceedings had under the authority of France, and to the latter that we had possession of Louisiana already, its limits westerly being the ancient French Possessions and easterly the Mississippi and eastern shore of New Orleans—backing this reply with extracts of dispatches from Talleyrand to Cevallos, which show that France agrees with Spain on both points.

It is likely that Monroe held a lofty language in his communications with the Span. Court, but supported as they are by France, he has been treated with contempt. What will be the conduct of our magnanimous administration remains to be seen. My own belief is, notwithstanding the superior value of West Florida, and the time that has been made use of, that our present cabinet will do nothing. If so, and M. be without adequate succour from England, he will do nothing.

Our afflicted city is nearly depopulated, and we are aprehensive that we shall not be able to visit our homes until the 10th of Novr. Until yesterday McIntyre and our other servant have been in town ; He is now with us together with our other servants except the Cook, who is a frenchman, not much apprehensive of the fever, and who, moreover, has some connexion in the City that he does not like to have known. We are all well, and what Mrs. G. will think wonderful, Mrs. K. has become a bather ; she has bathed three mornings and intends going on. I think it will be of service to her general health, especially after the alarm that has attended her first attempts has entirely subsided—in a great measure it has already left her.

We received yesterday a well expressed and satisfactory letter from James, dated at Dr. Gardiner's.* He seems well pleased, and assures me that he is duly sensible of diligence and attention. I need not express to you, my dear friends, how anxious we natur-

* In Boston.

ally are concerning the success of our children ; you, who more than any others, know our way of thinking, our hopes, and our solicitudes, will enter into our views and feelings, and do whatever may best conduce to the education of the child we have placed near you. He is at present without vice and, with a fine temper, is not deficient in understanding. Treat him in every respect as your friendship for us may recommend. He will be sensible to your kindness ; as well as obedient and respectful to your control. We feel none of the anxiety arising from absence, since we are convinced that James is in every respect as safe and as advantageously placed under your observation and instruction as he would be under our own. With affectionate regards in which Mrs. K. joins me to Mrs. G., I am most faithfully yours,

R. K.

Jos. Pitcairn to R. King.

Hamburg, 25th Sept., 1805.

Dear Sir :

The French Minister, de Bourienne, formerly Secretary of State and still friend of Bonaparte, has since June ruled here with unlimited sway ; he lately caused a ship belonging to Mr. Keith of Virginia to be seized and obtained an order from Bernadotte to sell her, alleging that she belonged to Reuben Smith, another American, whom he accused of enlisting men for the British foreign troops. He rejects all proof that the vessel belongs to Keith, and has brought her under French colours from Cuxhaven to Hamburg, at the time the French evacuated that place. Mr. Forbes our consul here has endeavoured to get possession of her by the ordinary course of Law, and by demand as American Agent. To this moment he has not succeeded ; but no one will buy her, and they will on the final leaving of Hanover be obliged to let her go, or destroy her. As 't is probable this matter will come before our Government I thought you would be glad to know the particulars. . . .

With perfect esteem and gratitude, dear sir
Your obed. Servant
Jos. Pitcairn.

C. GORE TO R. KING.

BOSTON, October 7, 1805.

MY DEAR FRIEND :

. . . The Galen has arrived here from England, and confirms the accounts heretofore received of the Disposition of the Brit. Ministry to limit our Trade within very narrow Bounds. Indeed the Spirit that was evidenced in the capture of the Essex, Orne, with the natural consequences of her condemnation, ought to lead our merchants to expect the sending in for Examination all their vessels having on board the Colonial Produce of the Enemies of England. I do not see that any evidence on board the ship can show what the British Courts demand to be proved, viz, that it was not the intention of the Importer from the Colony to ship the article to Europe.

Before a Decision had taken place on the Essex's cargo, it is possible the thing might have been placed in such lights by an intelligent Minister, as to have prevented the Decree. Mr. Monroe was not in England then.

Our Merchants are anxious for their Property, and irritated at a Conduct in the British, which they think not only unjust, but perfidious. They believe if you had been in London, a different State of things would have existed : and they are now sagaciously asking if Mr. J. would ask you to go there, and if he did, whether you would consent. Perhaps there is a like probability of either.

Yours truly

C. G.

———

WILLIAM VAUGHAN TO R. KING.

LONDON, Oct. 9, 1805.

DEAR SIR :

. . . . I beg your acceptance of a pamphlet that has just made its appearance here, that will from its subject and the part you took on the question while minister from the United States, prove more interesting to you. It is entitled War in Disguise or the frauds of the neutral flags. It is attributed to a Mr. Stevens, a lawyer of some repute and ability, who has been in the West

Indies and who has considerable practice in Appeal Causes. It may perhaps be rather considered as the brief of an advocate than as the decision of a Judge. I do not conceive that Sir Wm. Scott will adopt it indiscriminately as his model either as to its Temper or its conclusions, though it is probable that the Question about the Rights of Navigation of Neutrals in war to do what they cannot do in peace will be more narrowed in its principles in this war than in the last.

Though you are removed from the theatre of war and of information, you will not remain an uninterested spectator as to what is going forward on the Continent respecting the new war & new coalition. The proclamation of the different powers will show their creed or intentions, and may be considered as the articles of an immense partnership with the heads at an immense distance from each other, and where their capital and enterprize must depend on minor agents. All parties are rushing to one point rather more equipped for a march than for an engagement as yet until every man is at his post. Success will be various, but the result is yet to be known. Great hopes are entertained about Russia. . . .

With great respect your mo. ob. humb. servt.

WM. VAUGHAN.

R. KING TO C. GORE.

JAMAICA, L. I., OCT. 28, 1805.

MY DEAR FRIEND :

We came hither about a week since, and as the weather has been favourable and the health Comtee. have invited us all back, have sent a servant or two to town to prepare our house. . . .

Our latest News from Europe makes it probable that a new Coalition has been formed ; it is to be hoped the allies have been secret as well as active, for unless Austria be herself well prepared, and moreover seasonably as well as vigorously supported by Russia & England, she will be sure to suffer severely by the irruption of the French Armies. Recollecting the separate views of the former Coalition, the want of common object, honourable to the Allies, and not humiliating to France, we may expect a manifesto from the new Coalition, correcting the former Error and such as shall deserve the approbation & good wishes of all other nations. If the Coalition are successful this autumn or make any serious impressions on the Power of Bonaparte, England will become haughty and elated, and in this temper I shall fear most serious depredations on our Trade. In respect to the late decision of the Court of Appeals I have not yet seen so correct a Report of it as enables me to form a precise opinion of its Extent ; if it go no further than to restrain the Exportation of Colonial Produce in the vessel in which the same was imported, unless an intermediate voyage shall have been performed by her, the abridgement wd. not be very important ; but if the negative proof, which you mention be demanded, there can be no security in sending Colonial Produce from the U. S. to Europe ; this wd. be so extravagant and so unjust that I cannot suppose the Principle is, has been, or will be insisted upon. Another reason why I discredit the operation of this Doctrine is derived from the disjointed and feeble condition of the Br. Cabinet at the date of the Decision : a new Principle of this comprehensive nature w^d not be adopted by feeble, ill-assorted and recently connected men—and my present persuasion is that the mere touching, and passing a Colonial Cargo thro' our Custom House, and then proceeding with the same ship & Cargo to Europe, has been considered as too slight a security ag^t Fraud, and that the decision has been such as to put an end to this particular mode of trade. . . .

Always & faithfully yrs.

R. K.

MR. WILBERFORCE TO R. KING.

UMDON HOUSE, NEW BIRMINGHAM, Nov. 7, 1805.

MY DEAR SIR :

Before I enter upon the Subject, which gives occasion for my now addressing you, let me assure you, with perfect sincerity, that I retain a lively sense of the pleasure & advantage I have often derived from your Society, during your too short residence in this country, and that I shall ever continue to feel a warm interest in your happiness & welfare. I heartily wish this letter may find you in fl. enjoyment of domestic comfort, the best of this world's blessings, and of good health ; and while I am on this head, let me beg my best respects to Mrs. King and any of your younger ones who may remember me.

The object of my now writing to you, is to recommend to your serious perusal a pamphlet lately published in this country entitled War in disguise, or ye frauds of ye Neutral Flags. To you, who from personal experience as well as general knowledge, are so thoroughly versed in all that concerns this subject, I scarcely need go on to state the general tenor of the Pamphlet, its very title will make that sufficiently clear. Neither will I anticipate any of its contents. I will however state what I know will convey to your mind an impression of its being a work of ability, and allowing for the bias, to which we are all liable from self interest, of its sound principles also, that it has received the warm approbation of Sir Wm. Scott. I will frankly confess to you that I was strongly prejudiced against the conclusions which I understood it was the author's object to establish, from a fear lest their practical adoption might at least weaken that cordiality between our country & yours, which to you, who know my moral as well as my political principles & feelings, I need scarcely say, it has been ever, & still is, my earnest wish to cultivate and improve. But serious Reflection has forced on me the persuasion, that our acting (I will not affirm too hastily to what precise extent) on the system recommended by the work in question, is, according to all human appearances, indispensable & necessary not only to our interest, but to our very existence. I happen to know that the Pamphlet was written rapidly, tho' by a man long & familiarly acquainted with his subject, & the part in which it appears to me the most defective, is that wherein it states the consequences of ye continuance of ye present system, to our maritime greatness. Much more might have been said on that head ; which however your acquaintance with History will readily supply. I shall be very anxious to hear what reception the Doctrine meets with on your side of the Atlantic. The self-interested will of course endeavour to raise a cry ; but if men of sound principles and deeper views, men of Judgment, Equity & Impartiality admit that Justice warrants and Self Defence enforces our Govt's adopting the measures (in ye. main) prescribed by ye writer in question, their opinion will more, I trust, than counterbalance the sentiments & efforts of men of a different description.   But how does this very state of things bring to my recollection & enforce on my feelings the important truth, on which you & I have often expressed our concurrence that Govts. which wish to cultivate a friendly connection between the countries to which they respectively belong, would do well to be assiduous in embracing every fair opportunity of testifying this Disposition.   They would meet with more ready & implicit credit when they affirm that they are actuated by similar Inclinations, on occasions which are less clear, and where they may be supposed to be more likely to be under the influence of Self Interest.

But, my dear Sir, you know us Englishmen, such as we are, our good qualities and our bad ones, & I would venture to affirm that your Residence in this Country may have produced impressions concerning the personal character of my countrymen which Books alone never would supply & thereby enable you to account for instances of conduct otherwise inexplicable.   It will give me pleasure to hear of your welfare, & if any of your friends should visit this country, I should feel a gratification in rendering them any good offices in my power & doing any thing I might be able to make their stay among us agreeable.   Once more I remain, my dear sir, with great esteem and Regard, &c.

W. WILBERFORCE.

P. S. You will, I am persuaded, be glad to hear that I have the happiness (I thank God) to enjoy great domestic comfort.   I have now 5 children, but Mrs. W.'s health is but very indifft. since her last confinement.   Our friend Montague & his nums. flock are all well.   Lord Harrowby has taken his eldest son with him to Berlin as an introduction to business.   He does great credit to his domestic education in every way.   .   .   .

C. GORE TO R. KING.

BOSTON, 9 Nov., 1805.

MY DEAR FRIEND :

I received from you Extracts of two letters of Genl. M., who, I fear, would not find any so well disposed to promote his views now, as last year.   Losses & Disappointments render our mer-

chants more cautious & timid & their Sanguine Expectations, in
the year past, have probably much diminished their means.

Our last accounts from Europe would incline us to hope that
Great Britain had foreseen & in some measure prepared for the
state of things that now exists on the Continent. How far Austria
may have provided to meet or divert the Forces of France is left
altogether to Conjecture.   Should the Coalition be successful, our
Trade would undoubtedly feel the depredating Spirit of the
British Cruizers, and the Fears of our merchants will be dread-
fully realized.   Judge Croke, at Halifax, seems disposed to catch
at the smallest Pretence, for passing Decrees of Condemnation :
and many of the Decisions in England go but too far in counte-
nancing the Rules he seems to have adopted.   The Case of the
Essex was a vessel loaded with the Produce of old Spain, bound
from the U. States to Havannah.   It seemed that she went from
Salem to Barcelona & bound thence to the E. Indies, meeting
some accident, or not being able to procure Dollars, she returned to Salem, landed her Cargo, which was on Shore for
several months, but not finding a market, the owners shipt it in
the same ship for the Havannah. Vessel & Cargo condemned
on the ground, that it was all one voyage, the foregoing circumstances notwithstanding,   To say the least, they manifestly require
different Evidence of the Intentions of the Owner, relating to
Colonial Produce, shipt from the U. S. in its original Importation
than formerely—and in case of the Importer into the U. S.,
transhipping it to Europe, they demand Evidence of his Intention which, it would seem to me, cannot be on board the Vessel ;
and I should fear that every Ship having on board Colonial Produce, might be lawfully seized by British Cruizers—and indeed
we have a case stated, if correctly, that confirms this Idea.   A
vessel, bound from Norfolk with Sugars, whh. her owners purchased there, was seized in the Channel & ordered for London ;
after she was in Possession of her Captors, she ran against Dover
Pier & bilged, so that the sugars were all lost.   The Vessel was
tried and acquitted, but no Damages given ;   There might have
been other circumstances in the Case, not related, which may
have justified the Denial of Damages, but as reported it goes the
Length I have mentioned.

Our Government, with the various Claimants on their Spirit

and their negotiating Talents, will have a plentiful Source of Embarrassment.   If they could only use some of the Complaints to excite and keep up an irritable State of the public mind against G. B., it would (be) an excellent medicine for their political Purposes.   But I think the Administration will be fearful of encouraging this Temper, lest it should go beyond their Views, and carry them into Scenes, to which their Talents and pecuniary Resources, as they have lowered and cramped the latter, should prove incompetent.   . . .

Ever truly yours,

C. Gore.

The following letter, though out of place as to date, from Octavia Southgate, niece of Mr. King, gives her impressions of him on July 1st, 1804.*

"The family I am now in, however have reconciled me very much to this place.   I am about 4 miles from New York, at Mr. Murray's.   You heard me mention this family as uncommonly amiable.   To me they supply in a great measure the loss of my own.   I am delighted at having an opportunity of spending a week with them in this way.   Aunt (King) has been drinking tea with us this evening.   She tells me they commence their journey this week.   They are very solicitous for me to go with them ; but Elisa will so soon follow them, that I don't think it will be so pleasant.   . . .   Aunt King will suit you exactly.   She is a charming, easy soul and I am sure she will be your favorite among your Aunts.   Uncle pleases me more every day.   He has laid by his accustomed majesty—to tell you the truth, for a long time I looked up to him as a superior being ; his presence awed and charmed me.   I gloried in him and felt a sensible pride

---

* The editor is indebted for this letter to Mrs. Emily E. Ford, of Brooklyn, N. Y., who thus writes : "In a letter from Octavia Southgate to her brother Horatio, who married for his second wife Mary Webster, my aunt and fourth daughter of Noah Webster, I found this passage, relating to her uncle." The journey, to which reference is made above, is that which was taken by Mr. King to New England and to visit his relatives there. This is another evidence of the fact that it was planned before the duel of Hamilton was decided upon. See *R. King's Life*, vol. iv., p. 390.

whenever I looked at him, but the idea of loving him never entered my head ; He always was attentive to me and appeared to be pleased to see me ; but he always called me *Miss South-gate ;* but since I went to Long Island with them he is totally changed. He speaks to me in the most affectionate terms, calls me his *daughter* and introduces me to all strangers as his *niece.* I now confess him to be when he pleases, a man of the most in-sinuating manner I ever knew."

Mr. King, who had long desired to make his permanent residence in the country, near New York, bought, on the 20th November, 1805, from Mr. Christopher Smith's estate, a farm of about sixty acres of arable land with about 30 additional acres of woodland near by, at Jamaica, Long Island, fronting on the main road between Brooklyn and Jamaica, to which he removed with his family on May 20, 1806. It is probable that his attention was drawn to this place by the fact that Mr. Alsop's estate held a mortgage upon the property, and also because of the proximity to a village where the Episcopal church, good schools, and a post office were of easy access and in a healthy part of the country. He speaks of these things in his letter to his sons, alluding also to the advantages afforded on Long Island for those who loved, as he did, hunting and game. It has al-ways been believed that his wife's instance decided him in making the purchase and residing there permanently.

It may here be said, though a little before the time, that he immediately began to make improvements in the house, and in the autumn of the following year to plant trees, fruit and ornamental, and shrubs. The pine and fir trees were sent to him through his friend Mr. Sheaffe, of Portsmouth, from New Hampshire, and are said to be among the first planted in that part of Long Island.*

* Mr. King, as his eldest son wrote of him, was a careful, and therefore a successful planter of trees and shrubs, in both of which he took great delight. He was also a good botanist, and loved the song of birds, which soon began to frequent his thrifty plantation, where they ever found shelter and protection. Some large oaks now stand near the house, the acorns of which he planted.

R. KING TO HIS SONS, PARIS.

NEW YORK, Nov. 24, 1805.

MY DEAR SONS:

Within a few days past we have recd. your letters of the beginning of Sept. : John's letter is dated before the distribution of Prizes, Charles' the day after.   Today Mr. LeRoy, father of the young gentleman of this name, who is with you, sent me the following extract of a letter from Mr. Cazenove, who resided with M. Talleyrand when we were in Paris—viz.

6. Septembre, 1805.

" J'ai assisté hier a la distribution des prix á la pension de Mons. Thurot : la compagnie etait trés nombreuse, presidée par un Senateur qui a remis les couronnes aux vainquers, et composèe des Parens et des amis de cette belle jeunesse, qui etait assise en Amphitheatre au fond de la salle.   Ceux qui avaint gagné des prix sortaient des rangs, et au son de la musique s'avançaient vers l'Estrade ou les Maitres et les Professeurs plaçaient les couronnes.   Cette Cerémonie trés solenelle et attendrissante éveille à un haut dégré l'emulation des Etudians.   Dites a Mons. King (en me rappelent á son souvener) que j'ai eu grand plaisir de voir ses fils s'avancer á plusieurs réprises pour recevoir des palmes qu'ils avaient merité ; leur noble & agréable figure et maintien étaient remarqués de toute l'assemblée : ils joignaient au regard assuré et la tête elevée d'un être qui se sent, la modestie et la douceur que caracterisent tant leur pêre.   Sans exageration le genie et la probité leur sortaient de tous les Pores."

I am really unable to describe to you the Emotions of Pride & satisfaction, which I have received from your letters and the Report of Mr. Cazenove.   We have read them over and over again ; and mother wears them in her Bosom !   Go on my deserving and beloved Sons, continue to excel, and you will thereby not only give to your Parents the richest and best reward of their tender and affectionate Cares, but be sure to obtain the success and applause among your Countrymen, which good and great men so ardently desire.   I have communicated to Mr. & Mrs. Gore, and to some other of our intimate friends the distinction you have acquired, and as Mr. Le Roy will show Mr. Cazenove's letter to his friends, I anticipate the Congratulations of my friends and acquaintance on the reputation you have gained.

Within a few days past I have purchased a place in the Country. It is about 12 miles from town, at Jamaica on Long Island. The house is not fashionable, but convenient, the outhouse good, and the Grounds consisting of about 50 Acres, sufficient to give me Pasture for my Cows and hay for my Horses. In addition there is at half a miles distance between thirty and forty acres of Woodland. In the village of Jamaica is a Church & Post Office, and family supplies are plentiful, good and various. A Stage goes & returns every day between Jamaica & Brookline, the town on Long Island opposite to New York, between which there is a Ferry. Long Island is the finest sporting country perhaps in America ; besides which the roads are good & the Rides pleasant, & numerous.

How happy shall we be when the Time arrives of the reunion of our family ; how greatly will the pleasure be enhanced, should our Sons return with pure morals, cultivated minds and polished manners !

I shall write to Mr. Parker in a day or two ; in the mean time present to him my Regards—if I can find any one going to Paris, I will send you such of the vols (I believe 3) of Washington's Life as are published.

Adieu my dear sons,

(signature burnt).

P. S. The fever disappeared early in this month—not more than 254 died this year of this malady. We returned to town about the 10th. having passed almost 4 months on Long Island. My new house is well forward and will be finished so that we may occupy it next autumn, during the winter we suspend the work. Mr. Chs. Williams called on us as he passed thro' town. It was a satisfaction to see him, as he had so lately seen you.

———

RUFUS KING TO GOUVERNEUR MORRIS.

Sunday, 1 o'clk, Nov. 24, 1805.

DEAR SIR :

I have received and will immediately forward your notes to the Mayor & Genl. Morton. The military will be disappointed that we have not given their invitation a preference ; they say they shd. not have made a dinner but on the appearance that the

Corporation wd. this year decline giving one, and it being probable that others have decided as we have, I have intimated to
Genl. Stevens, who has just left me, that we may, perhaps, have
it in our power to make him a visit after leaving the Hall * ;
Moreau is expected this evening, will stay with Genl. Stevens,
who desires that you & I will dine with him on Tuesday.

faithfully yrs

RUFUS KING.

P. S. Gore is not returned, I have no room unoccupied, but
we shall find one for you. Another year we will order things
better.

E. GORE TO R. KING.

BOSTON, 25 Nov., 1805.

MY DEAR FRIEND :

. . . I am afraid that Miranda will meet with Disappointment, if He expect much Assistance from this Quarter. Had he
been associated, as he hoped, considerable aid might have been
counted upon here. In addition to the natural want of Confidence, that arises from his Exertions being single & unsupported,
there is a general Gloom among mercantile men & indisposition
to adventurous Speculation, from the severe Losses they are daily
experiencing by the British Captures. The last accounts from
England bring accounts of the Condemnation of Property where
the only Grounds could have been that it had been imported &
exported by the same Persons ; for the Vessel was changed. The
goods had been ashore several months, and advertised for sale in
this Market, and there was not the smallest Pretence that the
Property was other than neutral. In the Gazette of this Day,
you will see a statement of the Principles said to have been
adopted in the Admiralty Court, under an account of the Capture
& Release of the Ship Three Thomas. This was written by
Samuel Cabot's son, & is noted in the Letter as a Quotation ; we
suppose it to have been so stated by S. Williams.

* *Diary and Letters of Gouverneur Morris,* ii., 470, November 25, 1805.

" After dinner, Mr. King and I visit a party to which we were invited—a
large dinner given to General Moreau.

" Miranda has been down, and, as we expected, met with no encouragement.
He is now engaged in a project which would be wise if backed by this country,
but appears wild in its present form."—*Diary and Letters of Gouverneur
Morris,* ii., 470, November 25, 1805.

Some of our coolest men, such as William Gray of Salem, David Sears & the like of this Town, are extremely violent. The times are becoming as portentous in our Relations with Great Britain, as when Mr. Jay went to England. However, They, one & all, say if you were to go there, you could arrange every thing satisfactorily. I mention this, for I should not be surprized if the Voice were so loud & so general as to impose on Mr. J. the necessity of naming you, and on yourself an irresistible Duty of complying. It has been suggested here to send on a Deputation of Merchants to Washington, for the Purpose of inducing the Government to adopt some rational measures of securing our Rights, and preventing National Disgrace by the measures, which some will be disposed to resort to with the real or pretended view of attaining our Ends. If such a Deputation should be determined on, the Merchants have requested me to make one to represent their case, &c. &c. I have declined and shall continue to decline such an Errand, for reasons which must be obvious to you ; and I am not aware that any personal considerations can be suggested to my mind, or any Prospect of rendering public Service, that will or ought to induce me to alter my opinion. I offer them, & sincerely, to afford all the Aid in my Power to enlighten their minds, or direct their Views, should the measure of sending the Deputation be persisted in. Something must be attempted here, otherwise the Violence of some of our best men will lead them into courses, productive of incalculable Evils to the country, and especially to themselves. They will afford a Handle to others to do that, which will disgrace our national character, offer an apology to G. B. to possess herself of our unprotected Property, & Seamen, and finally involve us in War, or base and unworthy Concessions. . . .

faithfully & ever yours

C. GORE.

T. PICKERING TO R. KING.

WASHINGTON, Dec. 5, 1805.

DEAR SIR :

. . . I am told that the President talks boldly ; yet it seems to me the expression "which party can do the other the most *harm*" does not look extremely warlike.

We have not yet had any treaties laid before us.   That with Tripoli must of course be ratified ; yet considering the high probability that the operations of Eaton & the Ex-Bashaw would, if pursued, have placed the U. States on elevated ground, I am inclined to think that the administration *now* wish that Mr. Lear, by an untimely negotiation, had not stopped their progress.   But Lear's conduct appears to me perfectly of a piece with the spirit of the administration, who tho' not desirous of benefiting by Hamet Bashaw's interest and efforts among his countrymen, were evidently ready to abandon him to his fate, if the support of his claims to the throne of Tripoli, should be found inconvenient.   .   .   .

With respect & esteem &c
T. Pickering.

C. Gore to R. King.

Boston, Decr. 10, 1805.

My dear Friend :

.   .   .   We rejoice that you have a Place in the Country, which, to the citizens of N. York, seems now a necessary accommodation.   Had it been consistent with the Interest of your Family to have been this way, it would more have gratified us.   .   .   .

Your letter of the 29th came a Day or two after the arrival of the Genl's (Miranda) Friend.   I introduced him to those most likely to enter into his views, and most capable of promoting them.   He had several meetings with them, but they declined doing any thing, and were probably more averse from reflecting on some of the Genl.'s Associates, than even the Hazard of the Enterprise.

We, this Day, have the President's Message, and while some of our Friends conclude, He pledges Himself to the attempt of obtaining, by all means, a disavowal of the Principles, on which G. B. interrupts our Trade, others suppose, that He merely intends to insist on G. B.'s allowing us to do that which she herself does, and that as G. B. will accede to this, He will appear with a great Parade of compulsory measures to have forced a compliance with his own Propositions from England.   They suppose that he limits the Grievance to our not being permitted to carry, to the Spanish Possessions, that which she suffers to be transported from New Providence, Jamaica or Trinidad.

I cannot but think He has committed Himself further, and brings forward what is alluded to, merely as instances of the Inconsistency & absurdity of the new Principles, as he calls them, *"founded neither in Justice, nor the Usage or acknowledgment of Nations."* The avowal & Practice whereof *impose on us the obligation of providing an effectual & determined Opposition, by a peaceable Remedy, which may lead to Force.*

As to the Spanish affair, it would seem to me, that being well assured from the situation of his Cab. & his allies, that some terms will be offered, whh. He can accept. He was desirous of having it appear that his own Conduct, and not his other Relations produced the result He foresees.

Our merchants are evidently anxious & alarmed ; for they have immense Property afloat, and the late Decisions in England afford them no grounds of Tranquillity ; although the Gentlemen there report from Mr. Monroe, as is said, that Great Britain will not go beyond what she did the last War. The Condemnations, however, speak a very different Language, & the Insurance offices in this Town, suffer heavy losses in consequence of these Decisions. I think the sufferers are not so vociferous or wild in their Projects of compelling a compliance from G. B. as they were. I am more afraid of what the Southern Merchants may wish done, than of our People, yet we are not entirely free of those Errors which would involve us in Loss, Disgrace, War or mean Submission, or both. . . .

Yours ever & faithfully,
C. GORE.

There is no copy of the letter below alluded to. It is to be regretted for it would have shown what was the current opinion relative to the subject of the Management of the Bank.

SAM. BRECK TO R. KING.

PHILADELPHIA, Dec. 16, 1805.

DEAR SIR :

The letter that you was so obliging as to write to me on the 12th inst. I duly received, and to which I now, with pleasure, return an answer. The opinion you offer respecting the Parent Bank here, and the Branch at New York, is similar to those which have been expressed by other gents. of your City and therefore leave no doubt of *the necessity of a change ;* indeed, as it regards the former, it has been a rule of the Stockholders in order to strengthen the Bank here, to leave out annually the greater part of the Directors required by our charter, that live at a distance, & to fill vacancies with others not Inhabitants of this City ; of course, at the ensuing election nearly all the Gentn. Directors of the Parent Bank, who reside in New York, will be changed for others of the City ; a measure that has been found necessary to pursue in order to secure a competent number of Directors here at all times, but particularly during the summer months, when our citizens are so unhappy as to be afflicted with sickness and to avoid which many of them retire to their country houses ; thus you see from the small number of Stockholders within the United States, it will often happen that men out of business, and but little acquainted with Bank concerns, are chosen Directors and, however unpleasant this circumstance may be, we are positively without a remedy !

But as it respects Branch Directors, the same necessity does not exist ; yet, even there, we have to encounter another difficulty not easily surmounted ; for who will inform the Directors of the Parent Bank of the individual that ought to be displaced at the Branch ? indeed that is a point of such delicacy as to deter any Gentn. from involving himself in a dispute with another ; but, under the rotation system, I have been told, the Directors were named by those of the Parent Bank residing in New York, and by our Board generally adopted.   How far under present circumstances, they may choose to recommend a change the Gentn. soon to be elected will decide.   Yet I cannot but be anxious lest a serious misunderstanding should take place that may excite an opposition to the renewal of our charter, soon to be required of the Government, *the chief of which*, I believe, has not the most cordial regard for the Institution, and, therefore, may be influenced by its enemies.   It is fortunate however, that except at New York the greatest harmony prevails & the affairs of all the offices of Discount & Deposit are perfectly well managed.

As our mutual friend Mr. Wolcott has expressed sentiments on this subject similar to yours I wish, *if you think proper*, that the contents of this letter may be communicated to him.

With Sincere regards,

SAM. BRECK.

T. PICKERING TO R. KING.

WASHINGTON, Dec. 18, 1805.

DEAR SIR :

. . . No great measure has yet been proposed in Congress, or even intimated ; & I am pretty well satisfied that none is intended ; the *supposed* strong language of the President, & the vapouring of his Gazette notwithstanding. If Bonaparte's success continue, nothing certainly will be attempted against Spain ; and if the latter yield any of her pretensions, it will be by command of the former, for an *adequate consideration* to be paid by the U. S.

Very truly yours
T. PICKERING.

RUFUS KING ESQ.

RUFUS KING TO C. GORE.

Secret.

NEW YORK, Dec. 25, 1805.

MY DEAR FRIEND :

The same commercial solicitude and alarm that sometime since manifested themselves with you, have lately taken Possession of the body of Merchants here. A memorial is preparing to be signed by Merchants of all Persuasions, and which is to be presented by a Deputation to the President and the two houses of Congress.

The object, as I understand, is negotation—some of our friends have expressed their wishes to me that I would not decline, if asked, to go to England. I have suggested to them the Difficulty that *now* would probably attend my negotiation, and the little Hopes that a satisfactory Result could be obtained—that independent of these considerations it was not likely that the Extive would adopt any measure which wd. imply a deficiency in its own Party : or that should admit that any Person could anywhere do more or better than the Gentleman now in England.

Tho' I have not either assented or dissented, I should feel very great hesitation were the measure proposed to me in a manner in other respects free from difficulty (a thing that seems to me very improbable) in consenting to accept the mission. The question involves interests difficult to be reconciled, if not in direct opposition. However possible it might have been at a period of Peace when these Interests were less visible, and the Passions less likely to be influenced by them, to have marked out and settled a Rule that might have been satisfactory ; the situation is totally changed, and we must encounter every disadvantage that is incident to the subject, in now attempting to effect an arrangement that would satisfy us. I have thought I ought to apprize you of what is here doing, as well as of the impression of my own mind. The last accounts from Washington confirm my first Belief that as nothing was intended to be done, so nothing will be done concerning the subjects about wh. the message was supposed to say, & mean, so much. The Confidential Communication related wholly to Mr. Monroe's fruitless negotiations in Spain. Not a word has been said, and no communication made, respecting England.

Very faithfully & always yours,

R. K.

G. (ouveneur) M. (orris) is here, having just returned from W.— "be ye fed, and be ye clothed," for you are Hungry & Naked— was the language used to him, but good wishes and their realization are not the same thing.

R. KING TO T. PICKERING.

NEW YORK, Dec. 26, 1805.

DEAR SIR :

I duly received your kind letters of the 5th & 18th together with the pieces which accompanied them. Your opinion agrees with my first impressions on reading the message, which seems to say much without binding to anything.

The change that occurred after Mr. Monroe quitted Madrid, has without doubt influenced Spain to give way in some important point, preserving her adherence to the chief ones. If the Policy succeeds, she will lose nothing, but gain time, which is all in present circumstances that she desires. How much of Policy and national Reputation there may be in acquiescing in this course is a Question that you, who have the whole subject before you, are best able to determine.

I am somewhat surprized that you have had no communication concerning England ; since it is not to be supposed that our minister there has been silent, when Doctrines have been promulgated and acted on, which unavoidably lead to the Prostration of our foreign commerce and the revenue we derive from it.

Should any communication be made to you on this subject, I should be particularly obliged to you to know it, provided the same can be done without impropriety. Our merchants are becoming very uneasy in respect to these Pretensions of England ; which are of a nature to render insecure our valuable trade in colonial Productions. A pamphlet * lately recd. here from England (a copy of which I have heard was forwarded to Mr. Madison) the object of which, I cannot doubt, has tended very much to increase our commercial solicitude.

Yours most faithfully
RUFUS KING.

* Entitled " War in disguise."

CHAPTER XXX.

C. GORE TO R. KING.

BOSTON, January, 13, 1806.

MY DEAR FRIEND :

. . . We have had the New York Memorial, which is variously thought of by our Friends : some of whom are not very discreet, even if their opinions are correct—to which I am not inclined to subscribe. All desire that a negotiation should be attempted, and many believe it would succed, if confided to, and undertaken by the only man in whom all Parties would be satisfied. Though I think it not probable such a measure will even be proposed under circumstances that will render it acceptable, I have a feeling that it would be successful. It is almost certain that in a Coalition formed of such various materials, joined to the common accidents of War, many months cannot pass in which a wise, discreet and vigilant minister would not find an opportunity of pressing American Claims with Effect. . . . Our friend Ames, you have seen, was appointed President of Harvard College, but notwithstanding the Corporation agreed that the Professor of Divinity should offer all the prayers, he declines the duties and the honour.

Faithfully & always yours, C. GORE.

T. PICKERING TO R. KING.

CITY OF WASHINGTON, Jan. 13, 1806.

DEAR SIR :

You will have noticed in the papers Dr. Logan's motion for interdicting the trade to St. Domingo. This occasioned a call (made, if I do not forget, by him) for documents on the Subject. This morning the inclosed communication from the President was laid on our tables, printed by order of the Senate : whether the presentation and short debate on Logan's original motion excited Genl. Turreau's attention, or that a hint was given him by Logan, I know not ; but the General's second letter is of a date subsequent to the call for papers. The style of his letter as well as Talleyrand's, is sufficiently *Bonapartean ;* and I apprehend there is here sufficient pliability to yield whatever the " master " of our sister Republic shall demand.

As the President must have received Talleyrand's letters long ago, & Turreau's by the middle of October, why did he not bring the subject before Congress ? Why was no answer sent to Turreau during a period of two months & a half ? Did he wait for such a man as Logan to bring forward a measure that might be unpopular with the general mercantile interest ? Or had he instructed Armstrong to represent to the French Government that the *interest* of *France* required a continuance of our commercial intercourse with St. Domingo ? concluding to wait the result, before he made any communication to Congress, should the latter be found necessary ?

Congress have yet *absolutely done nothing;* the House of Representative are again sitting with closed doors. I find that *federal* members have every day listened to *John Randolph* with unmixed pleasure, in opposition to the mean dastardly democrats of N. England ! This will furnish our interpretation of a declaration in the Aurora, which arrived here last evening : That a man high in office was in conflict with Randolph, and that one or the other must fall—or words to this effect. Jefferson certainly must wish for a supple leader in the House. Randolph has too much pride to follow implicitly his dictates. But no one yet appears with abilities to take his place.

Very truly yours,

T. PICKERING.

D. Parker to R. King

Dear Sir :

In my letter of the 15 Oct I informed you of the disaffection of both John and Charles to the Pension of M. Thurot, and I found from the information of M. Thurot that it had become absolutely necessary to remove them.   Their great dissatisfaction arose from the regulations of the school, finding themselves obliged to conform to rules which they thought suitable to children and not to young men, who in England had *great latitude* both in time and expences.   They became not only dissatisfied, but disgusted, and notwithstanding my intreaties and their profession to comply with them, I found it was not in their power, and that no progress whatever was to be expected from them in any branch. Under these circumstances I was extremely perplexed and embarrassed.   Your letter of Aug. 10., which I received through Mess. Hope & Co on the 10th Decr greatly relieved me. . . . Charles arrived in Amsterdam in the beginning of January. . . I found John averse to enter any Pension whatever, and he communicated to me your letters to him, in which you informed him, that he must enter and pass thro' a College in America previous to his entering on the study of the Law.   This information decided me to recommend his returning immediately to New York.   I hope you will approve of this determination. . . . I hope that under your own eye, both John and James will become all you can wish.   They have talents to fit them for the first employments.   Charles has a fine genuis, great spirit and activity, and will make a fine man.   Thus you have everything to hope for from your sons, to whom you have been the best of fathers.

The great Political events that have been crowded within the compass of four months, have filled Europe with amazement. By the *Moniteurs* which I send by your son for your use and that of Mr. Livingston, you will find an historical account of these events.   Mr. Haugwitz, the Prussian Minister, is expected in Paris this day ; the Emperor and Mr. Talleyrand in the course of 4 or 5 days ; it is expected that negotiations of great moment will be immediately opened in Paris & many well informed persons expect a general Peace ; I have not these expectations ; I cannot see any probability of a peace between England and France at present ; if England can secure the continuance of her connections with Russia, she will, perhaps wish to continue the War, and seek an indemnity by capturing the Spanish Colonies. She must lose her influence on the continent of Europe, except with Russia & Sweden. This Government will, in all probability control the remainder. The Electors of Bavaria & Wirtemberg are made kings, & their Territories much increased. Eugene Beauharnois is declared Successor to the Crown of Italy, & has married the eldest daughter of the King of Bavaria. It is reported that Joseph Bonaparte will be made King of Naples, that Lucien Bonaparte has divorced from his wife, & will marry the Queen of Etruria, that his brother Louis will be chief magistrate of Holland, that Madame Bonaparte, the mother of the Emperor, is made a Souverain Princess, & is to receive the Duchies of Parma, Placentia & Guastella in Italy, with remainder to the Prince & Princess Borghese. Thus Europe is parcelled out, as a private man would divide his own inheritance. Such is the astonishing power & greatness of one man. . . .

With assurance of constant attachment and Respect,

DAN PARKER.

R. KING TO C. GORE.

NEW YORK, January 26, 1806.
MY DEAR SIR :

The dissatisfaction here & South of us in respect to G. Br, increases rather than abates : the losses already sustained are considerable, but without a new shape of the Rule, few new losses will hereafter occur, as the Business is fitted to the Rule. But unless the political Situation of England restrain her Gov. the Rule will be new modified and extended so as in effect to put an end to a Trade in Colonial Articles between the U. S. and Europe. On this subject I had no Opinion to form, having several years ago convinced myself that the Pretension of England is not justifiable. If it be put on the Ground of self Defence, or strict necessity (which consistently with the conduct of G. Britain in trading herself with her Enemies cannot be done) even this Law is no justification, since it does not authorize the confiscation of a Friend's Goods—on the contrary, whenever it allows the

Seizure, it enjoins the taker to make restitution or indemnification. But you understand the Question as well as my Sentiments concerning it, so that I omit any further observations, except to say that I have of late revised my former Reflexions, which has in manner changed them ; and being impartial, I the more wonder that some of our friends with you, whose Judgments are worthy of all respect, should so materially differ from us.

The Pamphlet printed at Washington, said to be Mr. Madison's, shews the unsoundness of the Eng. Doctrine. A reply is here nearly finished to " War in Disguise " which has the same object in view. The late messages of the Pr. to Congress, disclosing the Instructions &c to Mr. Monroe, seems to be a throwing up of his hand, and a reference of the Business to Congress. This is the more likely to be the real Purpose, as it will shift the Responsibility from the Ex. to Congress. The House has been in conclave a fortnight and sent the Result to the Senate as a Secret. Tho' we do not know what this measure is, we know what it is not, and that it does not concern G. Britain. The mandate from France to interdict the St. Domingo Trade will be obeyed ; tho' the Law will be nugatory unless more efficient than the Bill. Spanh. affairs remain as at the beginning of the Session ; and the Success of Bonaparte will render the settlement more difficult.

A Petition is going round the town to the Pr., calling on him to disavow the Principal, laid down by Genl. Armstrong in the case of Nicklin & Griffith. I hear that all parties sign it. The Bill respecting Amer. seamen introduced into the Senate by Mr. Wright is too contemptible to pass into a Law, be the Resentment what it may. . . .

Always yrs. R. K.

R. Troup to R. King.

ALBANY, 3 Feb., 1806.

DEAR SIR :

. . . Our State concerns continue to be an object of content with the demagogues of the day. Demagogues Clinton & Co. by the superiority of their manœuvres, have carried a council of appointment against the wishes & efforts of Demagogues Lewis & Co. This council, the partizans of Clinton say, will be a club of Hercules in his hands and will enable him to break in pieces the Livingston faction. At present, appearances indicate a ma-

jority in the Senate for Lewis.   No doubt is entertained that
Nicholas has set himself in decided opposition to Clinton ; and
I have it from private but authentic source that Nicholas has
given Clinton a severe reprimand for his cabals.   Can we be
otherwise than in the most prosperous and happy condition when
the patriotism of a Virginia demagogue induces him to attempt
cooling the ardor of a Northern demagogue whose incessant
labors are exclusively directed to the public good ?

With the most sincere regard &c

ROBT. TROUP.

URIAH TRACY TO R. KING.

WASHINGTON, 6th Feby, 1806.

SIR :

Inclosed is a paper,* which you will peruse with interest, because of its intrinsic importance & because it has had the sanction of a Com.tee of the Senate.

I make no comments upon any part of the paper, excepting the
last † containing the non-importation part.   This I voted against
in Com.tee and am most decidedly opposed to its principles.   I
wish to *treat* with G. Britain, & not to throw any nonsensical impediments or irritation in the way of treating.   If we do anything
in the meantime, while attempting to treat, I would strengthen
our defensive strength at least, if not offensive.

I am, Sir, respectfully your friend obed servt.

URIAH TRACY.

R. KING TO T. PICKERING.

N. YORK, Feb. 7, 1806.

DEAR SIR :

We are, as we ought to be, inquisitive & anxious concerning
the Plan, or system of measures, that the nation may pursue in

* Genl. Smith of Md., Report of Com. on that part of the Resn. & Message
Jan. 15th relating to Spoliations &c.

† " That it is expedient to prohibit by law, the importation into the United
States of any of the following goods, wares, or merchandize, being the growth,
produce, or manufacture of the United Kingdoms of Great Britain and Ireland,
or their dependencies : . . .   The said prohibition to commence from the
day of   unless previously thereto equitable arrangements shall be made
between the two governments, on the differences subsisting between them ;
and to continue until such arrangements shall be agreed upon and settled."

the present posture of our affairs ; for it is scarcely credible that the public honor and safety, instead of being well guarded by well concerted and prudent arrangements, should be suffered to become the sport of the casual, intemperate and inefficient measures of inexperienced individuals : and yet the several messages of the Pr. look as if every subject were to be submitted to Congress, without the disclosure of the views of the Executive ; which by the letter and spirit of our Govt., is charged with our foreign affairs. Your Bill respecting 100,000 Militia, together with the Bill presented by Mr. Wright, and the Resolution offered by Mr. Gregg, are so far as I am informed justly appreciated in this quarter. Some persons here have supposed that Congress will be able to agree in no precise measures—that the Executive will be undecided and filled with solicitude and that Col. Burr, who is always prompt as well as decisive, will avail himself of this miserable state of things, to decide for the President, as well as to provide for himself.

If the President and his friends are reduced thus low, they are weaker and baser than I could possibly have imagined.

Always faithfully &c

R. K.

P. S.   We are upwards of 70 days without authentic European news.   The posture of affairs at Christmas past will afford Data on which to reason, and we must expect news to that date soon.

COL. PICKERING TO R. KING.

CITY OF WASHINGTON, Feby 8, 1806.

DEAR SIR :

It was natural to suppose that thinking men would feel, not curiosity, but anxiety concerning the measures contemplated by the Government, in the present momentous situation of our affairs ; and before receiving this evening your letter of the 7th, I had determined to communicate to you as full a detail as was practicable of what was going on.

As to a " plan or system of measures," you might as well search for it in chaos itself as at the seat of government. About three or four weeks ago, I dined at the President's. Adverting to subjects before Congress, tho' I believe more especially to our disputes with G. Britain, he said there was such a diversity of opinions among members, and they had so many plans, he doubted whether a majority would agree in any one. I am inclined to think this opinion correct. I feel very confident that neither a general non-intercourse, nor a general or specific non-importation will be agreed to. The Southern planters will not suffer their tobacco, rice & cotton to lie on their hands, when Britain presents the fairest & best market. And they are not so silly as to suppose (as do some of our honourable legislators) that Great Britain will continue to receive into her ports, all the productions of the U. States, while we shut ours against the manufactures & productions of her dominions. This brings into view the resolutions reported to the Senate on the 5th, a copy of which I enclose. (Genl. Smith's Resn.) Mr. Gregg's you will have seen in the newspapers. Those brought into the Senate were laid on our tables on the 6th. . . . but really I have not had time to attend to the subject till this evening; as I meant to accompany the communication with a long letter of information on the subjects which have excited your anxiety.

All America has heard of the closed doors of the House of Representatives ; and the fruit of their discussion being a Bill, it was sent to the Senate, with a confidential message to declare its object—none being expressed in the Bill itself ; except that its title stated it to be, to provide for expenses for foreign intercourse ; and that the body of the bill appropriates two million of dollars to enable the President (at whose disposal the money is placed) to commence with more effect (as the confidential message of the House informed us) a negociation for the purchase of all the Territory belonging to Spain on the Atlantic & the Gulph of Mexico, and eastward of the Mississippi, that is to say the two Floridas. I disclose no secret ; for Saml. Smith told us last Friday (when the bill was passed) that though the doors of Congress had been closed, the subject of their deliberations was well known : and *here*, we all know that the Spanish minister Yrujo is perfectly informed concerning it ; and no doubt his letters are now far on the ocean for the information of his government. It is full two weeks since I was told that he said " We should not get the Floridas for two, nor for five, nor for seven million of dollars " ; and the matter being thus known to Spain, there can be no use in the attempt to keep it a secret at home—unless it be to conceal from the sovereign people the impolitic and unjustifiable projects of their beloved chief Servant.

This bill (or rather the resolution on which it was founded) was the subject of John Randolph's determined opposition—sarcastic reproaches on its advocates, and of strains of eloquence—never before heard from him in that House : such is the report of members. Barna Bidwell was the midwife to deliver the President of this brat & present it to the House. In the course of its nursing, it was said that the President had a desire towards it & wished it might be fostered & grow to maturity. The like intimations were given in the Senate by some of the Ministerial members.

Mr. Tracy, Mr. Hillhouse & Mr. Bayard were the principal opposers of the bill. They dwelt chiefly on the violation of the Constitution by such a pretended appropriation. For, they observed, that nothing in the bill being designated, except the the expenses of foreign intercourse, the President could not apply a dollar of the money to buy land. The words themselves, as well as uniform practice, had given a definite meaning to "foreign intercourse." It was true, they observed, that a similar appropriation had been made three years ago, (act of 26th Feby. 1803) but the President himself had told us, that not a dollar of it had been expended. Tracy & Bayard offered several amendments, in order to express the object explicitly, or by plain construction, and render lawful the application of the money appropriated. But clear statements and cogent reasons availed nothing. For the leaders, met, as it would seem, by an unexpected opposition, held a *caucus* and fixed a majority to vote for the bill, without the alteration of a word ; for they were apprehensive, if it went back to the House, that it would now be wholly rejected. It was carried there by a majority of about 14 ; but many, it was said, had repented. In the Senate 17 voted for it ; 3 fled the final question ; and one, who it was understood would in the end have voted against it, was gone from the city ; eleven gave their nays. So it may be considered as having passed by a majority of only two or three. The opposition in the Senate delayed its passage for about a week ; altho' one member more than once told us that the President wished it to be speedily passed and another added that he wanted it to "send off." One member said he should advise the P. to let the bill be dropped ; for he could *go to market* better without than with it. The President thought otherwise ; he had kept himself out of sight (tho' the suggestions of his friends showed he was behind the curtain), that if the project failed or proved disastrous, he might be screened from responsibility.

Genl. Sumter (whom you will recollect) spoke on Friday (the day it passed) against the bill. He spoke like a sensible, military man, as one well acquainted with the nature of the country proposed to be purchased ; with the difficulty of defending it, and said that at present " we were better without it." I should wrong him, were I not to add, that his sentiments were delivered with perfect propriety & modesty, and with a sincerity that could not fail to have affected every hearer. But the bill had been *decreed*.

Mr. Tracy (I should have mentioned) as well as Mr. Bayard, and especially the former, took a view of the actual State of the Treasury—the measures for defence to be provided for,—the insufficiency of funds, and the probable defalcation of revenue in the current year. But *back-door* influence is generally capable of surmounting all obstacles in the Senate. This body, by its constitution was (I presume) expected to act with superior independence ; but doubtless it is much more obsequious than the House. Its connection with the President is closer, and the paucity of members composing it renders it liable to be assailed with vastly greater ease and effect.

As I have not yet committed my own observations, in opposing the bill, to paper, I will do it now, while they are within my recollection ; and I will thank you to preserve this letter ; as I may possibly have occasion to recur to its details, and I cannot go through the labor of taking a copy.

I should first mention what leaked out from the President's adherents in the Senate, in ordinary conversations. That advice had been received from Paris stating, that if our Government wished to acquire the Floridas, the Government of France would procure the cession to be made. By information from the agents of Nicklin and Griffith at Paris, it appeared that a negotiation was already commenced : with an intimation that in this way only they and others would obtain the arrears due from the

French Government. Saml. Smith, speaking of Armstrong's letter to Marbois, on the claim of N. & G., said, in my hearing, that James Swan had presented a claim for half a million of dollars, and Capt. Barney one for upwards of a hundred thousand dollars : that neither of these two claims were within the provisions of the convention ; and yet were admitted. That it was known that the Livingston family had early purchased a number of good claims and one to a large amount from Barney. Reprobating Armstrong's conduct in the case of Nicklin & Griffith, Smith said, that as soon as it was known to the President, he caused the Secretary of State to write to Armstrong to correct, or pointedly disapproving, the procedure.

Mr. Hillhouse, in the course of his observations on the Secret Bill, mentioned the information that a negociation for the purchase of the Floridas had already been instituted at Paris, and that in this way, merchants hoped to get their arrears ; and said that from the manner in which this business was proceeding, it was evident the two millions proposed to be appropriated, were to be applied in *douceurs.*

Genl. Adair from Kentucky (a new member and apparently thoughtful and stable) objected against the bill on the strong ground of its unconstitutionality ; because from information he had received & relied on, tho' he could not divulge it, he had no doubt that the purchase of Louisiana had cost us five millions extraordinary in consequence of the previous appropriation of two millions, and the like effect would follow that proposed in the bill before us ; because he thought it highly improper to pay any money before the treaty, if one should be formed, was approved of by the Senate. Suppose, said he, that this bill should pass by a small majority, less than two thirds—that the two millions should be expended ; and the treaty be finally rejected by the Senate ; the two millions would be lost.

Mr. Tracy, (taking up the suggestion of Adair) expatiated a little farther. He said the idea of the French Government paying the monies due to American merchants was fallacious ; that we had better have undertaken to pay them ourselves ; that France undertaking to pay them caused the addition of the five millions, and that her stipulating to pay only $3\frac{3}{4}$ millions, occasioned a loss of one and a quarter million to the U. States ; and that the like preposterous course of proceeding, repeated under the present bill, would occasion a similar loss.

I had myself viewed the purchase of the Floridas under the same aspect in which they had been presented by General Sumter and he had anticipated some of my observations.

But I must go back a little, one member asked how the money could be employed in bribery? the President would take care to whom he entrusted it, and he was to account for it! another member asked, where was the room to admit the charge of bribery? The President would take care to preserve it; and as to the purchase, France would acquire a good title and convey the same to us.

I objected on two principal grounds—the *immorality* and the *impolicy* of the measure. It was admitted on all hands that the purchase was to be effected through the French Government. But France was not the proprietor; why then negotiate with Mr. Talleyrand?—perhaps the ablest, certainly the most corrupt minister in Europe; who possess a princely fortune, acquired in a similar way, and by rendering half the princes of Europe his tributaries. Gentlemen asked how there could be any bribery in this case? I desired them to recollect the proceedings under the convention for paying the debts due by France to our merchants. The 10th article was *ostensibly* cautious to prevent the admission of improper claims—claims not within the description of the convention: and yet, at the close, opened a wide door to corruption. That this instrument was doubtless drawn up by Talleyrand himself, or at least, this article; for therein it was provided that if any claim examined by the American board, was not approved by them or by our agent, yet if the *French Bureaux* should think it ought to be liquidated, it was, indeed to undergo the revision of the American board, be by them reported to the American Minister—and by him to the Minister of the *French Treasury, who was finally to decide.* That this particular provision was doubtless inserted by Talleyrand, on purpose to admit unfounded claims *on his own terms.* I reminded them of General Armstrong's extraordinary and disgraceful letter, holding out principles which could not be ascribed to error of understanding. That if a fair bargain was in this case intended, we would go to Madrid to negociate for the purchase—not to

Paris, that hot-bed of corruption. That it was known, however, by the uniform conduct of Spain from the first purchase of Louisiana, that she was extremely averse to let any part of it, or of the Floridas come into the hands of the U. States. That she had protested against the treaty of 1803 ; and in her opposition gave the copy of a note from St. Cyr, the French ambassador at Madrid in 1792, in which he, in the name of the first Consul, solemnly declared that France would never transfer Louisiana to any other power than Spain herself. That altho' she at length ceased her opposition, she had not relinquished her claim. That we knew from the communication before us, that in case of a rupture with Spain, France would take part in the war : and hereafter, whenever a convenient opportunity offered to renew her claim to the Floridas, Spain would do it, and on the ground of *duress,* under the actual state of things ; which a future monarch of France might be well disposed to listen to ; and on our complaint, might justly retort—you knew it was a corrupt and a forced transfer—We knew perfectly well, that if we applied to Spain herself, no consideration which we could offer would induce her to cede to us those provinces ; and therefore it was that recourse was to be had to the authority of France to enforce the sale.

That the value of the Floridas was by no means commensurate with the monies they would cost. The President had informed us (in a pamphlet accompanying the Louisiana treaty in Oct. 1803) that except about thirty miles square in West Florida, next the Mississippi, and wholly or chiefly above the isle of New Orleans, and some narrow strips on the margins of rivers, the residue of both the Floridas was mere sand—with indeed plenty of pine trees and some pasturage for cattle. On this I remarked : That West Florida, if settled and improved at all, would be almost wholly occupied by emigrants from the U. States, and that the products of their lands would go to the market at New Orleans, and consequently be as beneficial to us as if their territory were a part of the U. States. That if at any time the Spanish Government forbade this commerce and sent up vessels to W. Florida, on the Mississippi, we might levy a duty upon them equal to what they should demand of our vessels going up the Mobille : for I had been able to discover nothing in any treaties, which would give Spain a right to navigate the Mississippi from the sea up to West Florida, seeing we were now the proprietors of both banks of the river. In answer to one Gentleman, who had suggested that the Floridas were necessary for our commerce between the Atlantic States & Louisiana, on account of the harbours, I remarked, that the harbours were few, and one only, as far as I had been informed, afforded deep water—that was Pensacola. That as well by the common duties of national hospitality, as our treaty of 1795 with Spain, our vessels, in case of necessity, would always find shelter in those ports both in peace and in war—unless that war should be with Spain herself; in which case we should go and take possession of those harbours and of the Floridas themselves : and that this would cost fewer lives and less treasure than would be necessary to maintain the garrison in time of peace. Besides that, if we owned the Floridas, the forts would only accomodate small garrisons—for we should not incur the expense of large works & numerous garrisons ; and consequently, in the first moments of a rupture with Spain or any other naval power we should easily be dispossessed.

I have more to add but the time fails me, and you will not regret the interruption of a long, & I fear tedious detail, I will renew it without much delay. In the mean time, I hardly need intimate to you that this communication is *confidential*. I have made it as a matter of *public duty* towards one who has sustained so great a share in the Councils and diplomacy of our country, in the present interesting, perhaps I may say perilous, posture of our affairs ; when the men at the helm have neither spirit nor practical talents to form & direct those plans and operations, which the situation of the country demand for securing its just rights and safety. I shall be solicitous to know that this letter gets safely to your hands.

Respectfully yours,

T. P.

T. Pickering to R. King.

Senate Chamber, Feby. 11 1806.

Dear Sir :

In my letter of the 8th I mentioned an inclosure of certain Resolutions reported by Genl. Smith to the Senate, which, in my haste to seal my letter for the mail of the 9th, I omitted. They are now inclosed, together with the motions of Mr. Clay, representative from Philadelphia, of Mr. Nicholson of Maryland and Mr. Crowninshield from Salem. With these Mr. Gregg's should be connected. The whole manifest the confusion of ideas prevalent in the National Councils ; and confirm a sentiment in my last, that you might as well expect to find a system in chaos itself, as in our enlightened Government. If the President had any plan, which he would assume the responsibility to propose, I have no doubt of his securing a majority to adopt it.

I have not yet found time to resume my narrative of Congressional proceedings begun in my last.

With great Respect & Esteem &c

T. PICKERING.

R. KING TO T. PICKERING.

N. YORK, Feby. 14, 1806.

DEAR SIR :

Though I fear I am too late for the mail, I send you a line to say, I have duly recd. and that I am greatly obliged to you for your letters of Feby. 8 & 11. Except one friend Wolcott, I converse freely with no one on these subjects.

Yrs. always

R. KING.

T. PICKERING TO R. KING.

Confidential.

CITY OF WASHINGTON, Feby. 13, 1806.

DEAR SIR :

I have not until this evening, found an opportunity to resume my narrative of occurrences on the passage of the Secret Bill : and so many days have elapsed, I do not precisely recollect at what point I closed my former letter. I must therefore pray you to pardon any repetitions, as well as defects of order in the details of both letters.

General Sumter had anticipated the observations I had intended to offer to show that it was not necessary, nor expedient, at present, that we should become the proprietors of the Floridas by *purchase ;* but I had not extended my views so far as Genl. Sum-

ter, who said "we were better without them than with them."
But it was evident, & so I expressed my opinion, that their poses-
sion was not necessary for the present security of our trade to
New Orleans : that every harbour on the coast of these provinces
was open to our vessels seeking shelter from storms, or from an
enemy ; that in time of peace, we should certainly not incur the
expense of extensive and strong fortifications at the several ports ;
and consequently these would fall instantly before any naval power
with which we should be engaged in war ; that it would cost
fewer lives & less money to attack and take them in a future war,
if necessary for the security of our commerce ; and if worth taking,
we should then make adequate provision for holding them : that
the country in general was nearly a barren sand, excepting the
margins of some rivers, and a tract of about 30 miles square
lying on the Mississippi above the Isle of New Orleans : that the
products of the latter could naturally descend to the town of New
Orleans, and enter into the commerce of our merchants ; that any
restraints on the navigation of the Mobille, which the Spaniards
impose, might be counteracted by equal restraint on their navigation of the Mississippi, seeing we owned both banks of the river ;
that in the hands of the Spaniards, the Floridas served, as Genl.
Sumter had remarked, as a frontier to Georgia and the Mississippi
Territory. It had been also observed by others in the debate
that we were rendered feeble by the dispersion of our population,
and should rather circumscribe than extend our territory.

I noticed the information we derived from the documents received from the President, showing the designs of the French
Ministry, to keep open the means of dissension between the U. S.
and Spain, that their interference might again become necessary.
In consequence of the pressing applications of Monroe and Pinckney at Madrid, the Spanish Minister at Paris had presented a
" querulous " note to Talleyrand, desiring the French Government to declare its interpretation as well of the Treaty of St.
Ildephonso, as of that by which France ceded Louisiana to the
U. S. in respect to boundaries ; but that Genl. A. said no answer
had been given and he believed none would be given : excepting
in regard to West Florida, to which Talleyrand said explicitly we
had no pretence of title : that in fact by the treaty of St. Ildephonso, Spain had only retroceded Louisiana : and France had

in 1762 *ceded* to Spain only the island of New Orleans on the East side of the Mississippi ; that his *silence* in respect to the *western* boundary of Louisiana (whence the *President inferred* that our claim was not denied) was calculated merely for another job. While we claimed to the Rio Bravo, Spain insisted that we had no right westward of a line which beginning in the Gulf of Mexico, between the rivers Carecut or Carcuse and the Armenta or Marmeatoo, ascends towards the north between the Adulo and Nachitoches, until it cuts the Red River ; and thence the boundary remained to be ascertained by commissioners ; leaving us (as Mr. Jefferson expressed it in his message) only " a string of land on the West side of the Mississippi : " altho' the President two years ago informed me that " he had traced the *rightful bounds* of Louisiana, by *authentic documents* so far as Spain was concerned." And we knew that *these* " rightful bounds " extended westward as far as the Rio Bravo ; for our Ministers at Madrid had insisted on that extention and pronounced the counter-claim of Cevallos " absurd " ; while the latter said that he had supported the rights of Spain, as far as the line afore described, " by irrefragable arguments." (By the way tho' the President told us that he had communicated every document necessary to enable us to form a correct judgment on this subject, he had not communicated to us his instructions to Monroe and Pinckney—nor the facts or evidences on which they advanced our claim—nor their arguments in its support—nor the counter facts, evidence & arguments of Cevallos : to obtain them I offered a resolution to request the President to furnish us with them ; but it was negatived).

In the course of my observations, I said that we had been told that the great object in purchasing Louisiana, by extinguishing all causes or occasions of collision, was to ensure to us *perpetual peace ;* and yet two years had not elapsed before this very purchase had brought us, apparently, to the verge of hostilities ; and I was persuaded that the forced Purchase of the Floridas by the authorities of France, which was the object of the Bill, would lay the foundation of a future dispute and war with Spain, unless we would again buy it off. We know from the close alliance of France and Spain, as well as by the explicit declaration of Talleyrand, that in case of a rupture France would take part with Spain ; and when quite at leisure might even stimulate a rupture for the very purpose of aiding Spain in order to resume the possession of Louisiana and the Floridas by conquest. St. Cyr, when, in 1802, at Madrid he assured the Spanish Government in the name of the First Consul, that France would never "alienate Louisiana," gave as a reason—and the sole reason—why France desired the retro-cession of Louisiana, that she respected a possession which had constituted a part of the French Territory."

I have now given you the substance of what occurred in the Senate upon the Secret Appropriation Bill. As I said in my letter of the 8th, I communicate this information to *you*, as *a public duty*, thinking that under such an administration as we now have measures evil and unwarrantable in themselves, and which debase the character of the Country and thereby put even its safety in jeopardy, ought not to be locked up in the President's Cabinet, and in the breasts of a set of men, the greater part of whom have neither discernment to see wherein lie the real interest, the honor and safety of the country, nor independence and spirit to support them. Possessed of the facts I have stated, *you* will be better able to form correct opinions of events. Should these be inauspicious —should they threaten great public mischief it is possible you may suggest some expedient to divert it. Whoever knows Mr. Jefferson, knows that he is utterly incapable of keeping the helm in a storm, or even in a merely clouded horizon. Even democrats in themselves but just above contempt despise him. His weakness, timidity and inordinate desire of preserving his popularity have, as I expected, induced him to avoid responsibility by asking counsel of Congress : or, if dictating any measure, by doing it behind the curtain. "Thus low are reduced the President and his friends ; " " and therefore weaker and baser than you could possibly have imagined."

I think he will not trust Armstrong with the disposition of the two millions. As probably he may place very high confidence in Monroe, the latter may be directed to go from London to Paris ; and thus give a pleasanter opening to an extraordinary mission to negotiate a treaty with the British Government. This hitherto he has avoided, (a treaty) : I have supposed lest he should hazard popular odium—remembering the baleful effects of Mr. Jay's treaty—doubtless excited by him and his partizans to aid in pulling down the federal administration. But I little suspected that this motive would have been avowed by any of his friends. Sam Smith however this day made the precious confession !

The Senate were discussing the second resolution reported to the Senate by Smith, to *"request the President to enter into arrangements with the British Government, for the purpose of adjusting all our differences with that power."* The word *treaty* had been squeamishly avoided by the Comtee. though that was what they meant by arrangements, and Smith repeatedly used *treaty* in the course of his observations in favour of the adoption of the resolution. Among other reasons, he remarked, that calling to mind the dissatisfaction occasioned by a former treaty, the President might feel a reluctance to enter into another with Great Britain ; but that the sense of the Senate, deliberately expressed, by adopting the resolution, might remove the embarrassment. This was the sentiment tho' not given in his words, which I do not recollect : but he was perfectly understood and excited a smile among the few federal members. I had intended to mention the same reason and express my willingness to take that share of responsibility, which would fall on a Senator from a great commercial State ; especially as its chief merchants, in their memorial, had prayed for such a mission to London. I had considered how I should do this in the most delicate manner ; but was very happy to be anticipated by General Smith.

This second Resolution, on different pretences, is much opposed ; and, after being discussed an hour or more, on two different days, still remains undecided ; and yet, I believe that its opposers desire a negotiation with G. Britain for the objects expressed in the resolution.

My Colleague (who with Tracy, Baldwin, Logan, Mitchell, S. Smith and Anderson was the Committee as I believe I mentioned in my former letter) is an advocate for the third resolution—the non-importation of enumerated articles ! But there are so many projects on this subject, I trust none of them will be adopted. That many country members (as is the fact) should be advocates of the measure, and even shortsighted merchants—may elicit no surprise : but really I did not expect that a man of the enlightened mind of Mr. A. would have entertained such an idea. John Randolph, observing my townsmen Crowninshield quite fierce for Gregg's motion, said to one of my friends in the House,

"That he (Crowninshield) was like a hog swimming over a river who would cut his own throat." It seems to be a known fact that a hog, when swimming, strikes his neck with his hoofs ; and, if obliged to swim far, will actually cut through the skin at the throat and eventually kill himself.

Last evening I received, under your cover, an answer to "War in Disguise." I hastily ran through it this morning and shall read it again deliberately. I presume you did not mean that the author should be concealed from me. Some things appeared to be placed in a strong point of view, others to demand further, or a more expanded elucidation to be well understood by the bulk of readers. Authors who have a clear and comprehensive view of their subject are apt to presume too much on the discernment of their readers. This, in a popular work, must always be unfortunate. You will not judge it improper if I venture to make a few observations upon the pamphlet,—if on second perusal any pertinent ones should occur.

Very truly yours

T. PICKERING.

R. KING TO T. PICKERING.

N. YORK, Feby. 17, 1806.

DEAR SIR :

This acknowledges the receipt of your letter of the 13th, those of the 8 and 11 have been acknowledged. I make haste, as the French say, to correct an impression, if it exist, that I am the author of the answer to War in Disguise. I know the author presumed the stile would make him known to you : as I sent a copy of this pamphlet to Mr. Tracy, and another to Mr. Madison, I pray you to take an opportunity of saying, in my behalf to each of these gentlemen what I have just said on the subject to you, lest from the mere transmission, it sh'd be supposed that I am the author, a merit that belongs to another.

Yrs RUFUS KING.

R. TROUP TO R. KING.

ALBANY, Feb. 11, 1806.

DEAR SIR :

. . . We have nothing new here, but a report that the Clintonians and Burrites have formed a coalition : this report is generally believed. De Witt Clinton has undoubtedly broken peace with the Livingstons and he is preparing for a Bonapartean campaign at the next election. The issue of the contest from present appearances will be fatal to the Livingstons, as I fear Bonaparte's late campaign has been to the House of Lorraine. Lewis is as light as the drum in his speech, and he does not appear to possess a single talent for managing the corrupt party he is connected with. This by the by does him no dishonor. It verifies however the remark often made, that no man who aims at independence of conduct will long bask in the sunshine of the people's majesty. Judge Benson will tell you the precious confessions which Lewis is constantly making when alone with the federalists. I have listened to them until my contempt for the government has been lost in pity for the man !

With the most sincere regard

ROBT. TROUP.

CHAPTER XXXI.

T. PICKERING TO R. KING.

CITY OF WASHINGTON, February 20, 1806.

DEAR SIR :

This morning I had folded a letter to you, written for the sole purpose of apologizing for the distant surmise that you wrote the Answer to War in Disguise. Afterwards while at breakfast I received your favour of the 17th, telling me that you were not the author. Mr. Tracy, sitting next to me, I put your letter into his hands.

In fact I had reluctantly yielded to the conjecture that you were the author, in consequence of the confident assertion (as I had heard) of Dr. Mitchell, and the opinions, or, literally, fears of others. The style was so different from yours, I admitted it only as merely possible. Very soon, however, we were generally satisfied that it was the child of G. M. His features are impressed on every sheet. With a brilliant and cultivated mind, he has a coarseness of sentiment which is incompatible with dignity.

The chasteness of your taste and your diplomatic habits were utterly irreconcilable with the production in question.

We have for a month been at work upon the St. Domingo Bill; during which time it has passed the Senate by ayes 21, noes 8. I have heretofore intimated to you the perfect obsequiousness of the Senate. Its advocates affected to be influenced merely by motives of policy, as well with respect to our own black population, as to France—and good faith : while in fact the terrors of Bonaparte's arm, (openly avowed by Wright) undoubtedly influenced the measure. Should he fall, or be *Burgoyned*, the Bill may die in the House of Representatives. . . .

Adieu.

T. PICKERING.

T. PICKERING TO R. KING.

CITY OF WASHINGTON, February 20, 1806. Thursday Evening.
DEAR SIR :

The call for the mail obliged me to close abruptly my letter o. this date.

Of the character of the humour in the answer to War in Disguise, perhaps the following anecdote may furnish a pretty correct idea.

I have the pleasure of lodging under the same roof with all the Senators and Representatives from Connecticut, as well as a part of the Representation from Massachusetts and New Hampshire. We had just read, in Coleman's paper of the 8th, his Literary Notice of the answer to "War in Disguise." "The strain of ridicule (said he) in pages 63.4. is equal to anything we ever met with, and which we defy the greatest of the British advocates to read without downright laughter, at the absurdity of the arguments here exposed."

Just then I opened your packets containing the Answer. Immediately I turned to those pages & read ; expecting a burst of laughter, the pleasure, in such cases, being always the more poignant when numbers participate. I read ; but no one was moved ; each gazed at the other with disappointed expectation. I supposed I had not understood the passage & so failed in the reading. At that moment Tracy came in. I read it again : and

still they remained unmoved. "Why don't you laugh?" said I
to Tracy : "You did not tell me when to laugh," was his answer!

Upon a second reading of the Answer to War in Disguise,
more exceptionable passages appear than on the first perusal.
The words and passages, liable to criticism are numerous ; and
tho' the same expressions might be admitted in conversation, they
are great blemishes in a work of this kind. It was evidently
written in haste ; and with a little pains might have been corrected ; but is not the disposition of the author adverse to a
patient examination? I presume he did not submit the pamphlet
to the correction of any of his friends. And if he did, to point
out errors and faults is an ungracious task, which perhaps not
one in a hundred would venture to perform, unless towards a very
intimate friend ; and a friend, too, sufficiently ingenuous and
modest to receive correction without taking offence.

Does not the author quibble, where he says (p. 12) that the
"*Masterly acquaintance of the Judge* (meaning I presume, Ld.
Mansfield) *with the law of Nations*, was known and revered by
every State in Europe," is one thing ; and "that his *decisions* were
celebrated for their equity and wisdom, is another and a very different thing?" Is it possible to conceive how his masterly
knowledge could be (not *admired* but) *revered*, unless it was displayed in *wise* and *equitable decisions?*

p. 19. "Slily," applied to Sir Wm. Scott. It would be impossible for me, (like the author of the answer) to feel "a high
respect" for any man, however great his talents, if he were *sly* or
meanly artful. If the author meant only that Sir William had
artfully confounded, he is chargeable with a vulgarism in using
the word *slily*.

pages 22. 23. 24. These pages being simply filled with assertions and questions do not carry conviction to the mind—at least
not to mine. I cannot discern any force in the author's reasoning
from the contraband trade of smugglers, and it is not possible that
his own fancy was dazzled with the lively (or to preserve the
metaphor), the sparkling antithesis which, in p. 24, concludes his
questions.

"With every superiority at sea *his heart could wish*." These
last words are too much in the conversation style to be introduced into a disquisition on the law of nations.

p. 27, "Yankees," too, being a nickname should not have found admission into grave discourse.

The ludicrous criticism on "possessing a monopoly which had been destroyed," might have been spared. When an author's meaning cannot be misunderstood, the inaccurate use of a word seems not to be a fit subject of ridicule. The British might correctly *possess* a monopoly of which they had *deprived* their enemy.

These are *specimens* of the faults which have struck me. It is much to be regretted that so fine a composition as "War in Disguise" had not received an answer written with equal elegance, dignity & precision.

Very truly yours
TIMOTHY PICKERING.

URIAH TRACY TO R. KING.

WASHINGTON, March 12, 1806.

SIR :

My health when I passed thro' New York, & ever since, has been so frail that I have written scarcely to any person, but to my family. I have to thank you for the answer to War in Disguise, for which I am indebted to your goodness.

This answer was at first attributed to you, tho' I was not of that opinion. I always supposed that Gov. Morris wrote it. There is merit in it and I regret that more time was not taken to increase its merits. Madison's Book, I suppose you have seen, that was written in a hurry, *this answer* was written in a hurry, and, unfortunately for us everything done among us has been done in a hurry, which respects *Neutral Rights.* I had indulged a hope that you, or some man equally acquainted with the subject, & who was not in a *hurry*, would have favored us, either with an answer to *War in Disguise*, or with a dissertation upon our Neutral Rights ; with a Statemt., such as the subject is capable of, and not composed in a *hurry*, as to *style* or *argument.*

As the subject is now before the public, it is all adapted to a mob ; *Neutral Rights are invaded* is the cry & *you must rally round our rights.*

I most sincerely wish that the time may come, and that I may live to see it, when we shall understand our *rights* of every description, & possess the proper spirit to defend them. Now neither the one, nor the other, has any existence.

Our administration is far behind the people at large, both in understanding & in spirit. I mean that distinct understanding of the subject, which might be expected from men in an elevated station, and that *spirit* which ought to be the portion of all, or our nation is truly in a bad way.

Sneaking behind, to avoid all hazard to darling popularity; shrinking from all official & reasonable responsibility; a language unintelligible, capable of constructions to meet any event, are a few of the leading traits of character of our President, administratn. and also of the majority of both the Legislative branches.

Now, Sir, a Nation, under such circumstances, if the manly, independent spirit of former days was predominant, would extricate itself from such a set of impediments, would indignantly spurn from them such leaders & rally round men who were both able & willing to behave with propriety. But here is the distressing fact : our Country has, by the debauching force of *party*, by the fatal effects of demoralizing Democracy, by the babyish nonsense of *peace, peace*, the watchword of Democrarcy ; by the fatal encouragemt which *vice* has received by the ruling party for five years past, & the discouragement which virtue has, during the same time, recd. from the brow-breatings of vicious scoundrels, thus supported & encouraged, by all these and more, our country is unhinged, is let down to such a degree, that no manly exertion can be expected.

I know that this is croaking ; but when truth will justify in this, & in no other conclusion, ought we to shut our eyes to the truth however humiliating?

I am a sick man, & allowance must be made for the view I take of any subject, as I look thro' a medium, jaundiced not only to my bodily vision, but to my *mind's eye*. If you can set me right, you who are in health & see things without the conflicts, in which I am daily engaged, I shall most cordially thank you.

I am now in the Senate Chamber & the Senate are debating upon the nomination of John Armstrong, as a Commissr., with James Bowdoin, to treat with Spain for territory, boundaries, spoliations, &c. &c., ; whether we shall midwife him or not, is not certain, but as he is proved to be a very great rascal, I think he must be appointed ; from the same principle, which induced the nomination by that immaculate Executive, who has sent us this nomination after knowing every fact, damning fact, which instead of a new nomination, ought to have instantly produced a recall. "*It is a hard winter, my masters, when bear eats bear.*" This moment ½ past 3 P.M., the question of John Armstrong's appointment is postponed until to-morrow.

Yrs. Sincerely
URIAH TRACY.

R. KING TO T. PICKERING.

NEW YORK, March 13, 1806.

DEAR SIR :

Mr. Wolcott some days ago told me that he would write to Mr. Tracy on the subject of the Leander & Miranda's expedition, and as I presume you would see this letter, and preferred for particular reasons, not to write myself, I have said nothing to you of this Project.

The late news from Bordeaux, and which you will have seen in the N. Papers, and according to which Bonaparte remains master of the Continent, has dissipated the Rumours concerning Miranda's views, which have for some weeks engaged the public attention. There are Persons here who hesitated in giving credit to this French news : but the armistice, if not a most gross fabrication, is conclusive ; it cannot be many days before we shall have arrivals from Eng. that will give us intelligence down to February, including the speech and debates at the opening of parliament.

Within a day or two we have heard much of your decisions, and particularly of the denunciation of the Executive by its former friend Mr. Randolph. As to Measures, so far as I can observe the public, none are expected, or at least none that will be either advantageous or honorable to the Country. Every man you meet seems ashamed of the feeble, hypocritcal and mean Proceedings of the Executive. With sentiments of sincere esteem & respect

I remain, dear Sir, your obed. & faithful servant
RUFUS KING.

U. Tracy to R. King.

Sir :

Ecce iterum Crispinus—This day the Senate have expended in a debate upon John Armstrong's Nomination : as I stated to you last week, perhaps no man's character & conduct ever met with a more thorough investigation, & nothing is more clear, than that the Senate, a very considerable majority of them, are sick, quite sick of the man, & really wish the nomination at the devil, and many go further, and send the *nominator* after the nomination ; & these good Democrats too.   The vote now taken 3 o'clock P.M., and stands thus, for Armstrong fifteen votes, against him fifteen votes—so the Vice president had to decide it & he decided it in favor of John Armstrong.   So John Armstrong is appointed.

Yours sincerely,

Uriah Tracy.

Both New York Senators & the Vice Pres. were in favor of Armstrong : so the three votes of New York carried him !

T. Pickering to R. King.

Dear Sir :

Yesterday I sent you, in 5 packets (I think that was the number) a pamphlet the subject of which has probably engaged as great a share of the President's attention, as all the concerns of the " good old States " (as Randolph called them) whether considered in respect to their internal or external relations.   You will see noticed the various Indian languages *radically* different. When I last dined with him (5 or 6 weeks ago) he said he had already ascertained about a hundred.   When some of my fellow lodgers dined with him soon after, that number was materially reduced.   I believe there are 15 or 16 noticed in Capt. Lewis' Narrative.   Mr. Jefferson's object (I should say one of his objects) in his Louisiana inquiries, I take to be, that, if so many *original* languages exist in America, and if we calculate how many ages must elapse before one original language could be radically changed ; it will follow that the Mosaic account of the creation and the chronology founded thereon must be extremely erroneous! . . .

I will inclose you a bill brought into the Senate by Saml. Smith " For the encouragement of the Shipping & Navigation of the U. States." The third reading is to be on the last day of this month ; it being postponed for the purpose of gaining information.   Independently of the general knowledge you possess on this subject, I remember you had occasion officially to turn your attention to our commercial intercourse with England, while you were in London.

I pray you therefore to favour me with your sentiments on the provisions of this bill ; and at as early a day as may be.   At present it can be of little or no consequence, for scarcely a foreign ship enters our ports ; and it seems premature to make regulations now, to operate on commerce after peace shall take place, when in our commercial relations such very material changes may take place.   Have we not as much carrying trade as we can manage ? or if not, would it be expedient to increase it largely (if it were possible for this bill to produce that effect) seeing the event of peace might pretty suddenly deprive us of an essential portion of it.   Besides I take it, what we should most desire of England, France and Spain, would be the permanent admission of the products and manufactures of *our own country in our own vessels*, into the ports, especially the colonial ports, of those nations.

In explaining the grounds of his bill, Mr. Smith said, that all the European nations, excepting England and France, did permit us to carry to them the products and manufactures of other countries, as well as our own.   At the present moment all the products and manufactures of G. Britain & her dominions are prohibited an entrance into France & Spain, & I do not know but some other dependent countries of France.   Have the goodness to communicate to me as early as may be, your views of the subject.   What will be the effects of this measure, if adopted ? what its advantages ? what its disadvantages ?

With sincere respect and esteem &c.

T. PICKERING.

R. King to T. Pickering.

New York, March 20, 1806.

Dear Sir :

In a few lines I wrote yesterday to Mr. Tracy, I communicated the purport of the only important news from England. Yesterday by a short arrival from Bordeaux we have later news both English and French than had been received from England. I inclose to you the morning Paper which announces all I know concerning a state of Europe, that, in my view, is the most extraordinary & menacing to the freedom and Independence of mankind that has existed in modern times.

As no nation is more reasonable more docile, more loyal than England, when wisely governed, so none has greater firmness, longer patience, nor higher courage than our ancestors ; and notwithstanding it has pleased the Almighty to take from them, almost at the same moment, their first Statesman, their most fortunate Admirals, and their ablest General, I feel a strong presentiment and hope that the high spirit and ancient glory of the Nation will enable them to contend against, & finally to triumph over their gigantic adversary.*

* These sentiments repeat the estimate he formed of the English people during his residence in England, as evinced by the following in his handwriting—

It is equally difficult here as in America to form satisfactory opinions respecting the events which are passing in Europe ; and the reason is this, that no exact views, no assured object, no settled system of Politicks, exist in this, or any other of the Great Powers of Europe. The whole is a miserable shifting from expedient to expedient—a course varying with every new incident,—a struggle for an ill understood and inexplicable End. The nearer I see these great nations, the less respectfully do I consider them. At a distance where information was less accurate, and the space for conjectural interpretation much wider, we entertained ourselves in searching for the solution of events which instead of being foreseen or influenced by premeditated causes, have been the mere result of those blind and ill managed efforts which continue to astonish and destroy mankind. I am not deceived in my estimate of England. They are a nation of immense resources, of ancient pride, of powerful habits in favor of their Government, of infinite credulity, of unbounded confidence, and destitute of a single mind capable of making a proper use of these National Faculties at a period more important and interesting to human happiness than has before existed.

It is certain that the objects, for which the war has been prosecuted have varied so often, that those at the helm here can assign no national motive at any one period, that will justify the prosecution of the war at another. I had

The new Ministry unites the Strength and Talents, as it does the Parties and Confidence of the Nation.

With sincere regards, I remain, Dr. Sir Yr. faithful Servant
RUFUS KING.

T. PICKERING TO R. KING.

WASHINGTON, March 21, 1806.
DEAR SIR :

I inclose a Report of the Senate concerning Hamet Caramelli. It is drawn, substantially, by Bradley, and agreed to by all the comtee. (as Tracy tells me) except Baldwin.* A variety of facts and circumstances, but which I cannot attempt to enumerate, induce my belief that Lear's conduct originated in the basest motives. His *reported* treachery to Washington, in communicating (withdrawing from their sacred deposit) papers to Jefferson, has laid the latter under obligations. Mr. J. in his message on Hamet's case, attempted, with much labour, to vindicate Lear ; but in vain : he stands condemned by every man who can think and act independently.

Dr. Thornton (whom Wolcott knows) who is charged with that breach of duty in the department of State, which relates to the issuing of Patents, last December told Genl. Eaton a variety of things relating to Miranda's project, and asked Eaton if he would

believed that England went into the war in order to preserve her own Govt. but if there ever existed the danger that we have imagined on that head, which I am inclined now to doubt, it has ceased to be worthy of attention.

The English people are in no danger of imitating the French from choice—when I speak of the people, I mean to exclude the efficient body of the nation—I equally exclude the philosophers and the indigent. Laying them aside as this nation can do, there remain the vigor, the strength and the great Body of the nation—inclined to preserve order, interested in upholding their Govt. and animated with a generous devotion & courage to defend their country agt. domestic as well as for. Foes. It is true that the suffrage is far from being equal here, and the Election is not in this view an infallible rule to ascertain the public opinion—yet with proper allowances the return of the Members of Parliament gives a pretty sure guide whereby we may infer the national sentiments—making every possible allowance, the late Election, which we are confidently told diminished the opposition, diminutive in members as before it was, the inference is altogether favorable to the attachment of the nation to the existing order of things and demonstrates their disposition amid reverses and misfortunes to uphold the Authorities of the Constitution.

* See Annals of Congress 1805-6 for the history of this claim, pp. 48. 185.

engage with Miranda in an expedition to Spanish America? "Yes (said Eaton) if the Government will give us a commission." Thornton said that several millions of dollars were raised by the Spanish Colonists and that a large sum had been lodged in New York to meet the expenses of the expedition. That the Colonists were prepared and waited only for Miranda to hoist the flag of Independence to rise and throw off the Government of the mother country.

Dr. Thornton is not a little of a visionary—and allowances are to be made ; but I am persuaded that his testimony would throw light on the subject, and be useful to Col. Smith & Ogden on their trials—which we hear are to take place next month.

Respectfully yrs.

T. Pickering.

R. King to T. Pickering.

New York, Mar. 22, 1806.

Dear Sir :

I am particularly obliged to you for the President's Message, communicating the Discoveries in Louisiana. . . .

" The Sty," to use Randolph's phrase, is as I hear very noisy on the subject of Armstrong's appointment, which is regarded as an avowal and justification of his Conduct. There are several subjects on which I should be glad for information. The disclosures that your debate may have made respecting Armstrong is one of them. Was it at all explained how Armstrong was authorized, or what motive induced him, to assume the extraordinary power he has employed in the distribution of the 4 Mil. Dollars ?

We have seen Eaton's letter to the Secy of the Treasy., which states that the Treaty with Tripoli contains an article by which the Bashaw engaged to deliver up the wife and children of his Brother, and that in order to obtain this stipulation, which was to satisfy the ex-Bashaw, Lear gave a Defeasance, by which the article became void.

It is also rumoured that the Treaty was submitted to the Senate for Ratification, without a communication of the Defeasance. On these and other interesting Points concerning our foreign affairs, I should be obliged by exact information, as I have it in contemplation after the close of your Session to make a Review of our foreign Relations.

On examination of the English News, I am not without considerable Hope that the new ministry will inspire new vigour as well as confidence into the Nation. If the ministers can agree in the Cabinet, the administration will be more powerful and more popular than has existed since the Ministry of Lord Chatham : in such event, indeed in any event, the Folly and Rashness of your Resolutions and projects at Washington, will be more fully exposed.

The men who promote these measures are equally ignorant of the character of Englishmen, and the interest of America. Without these miserable provocations Mr. Monroe, if he has abilities, may avail himself of the present juncture ; with them, neither he nor any other person can succeed.

Very faithfully yrs
RUFUS KING.

T. PICKERING TO R. KING.

WASHINGTON, March 24, 1806.

DEAR SIR :

I have been favoured with your letter of the 20th. We had heard of the death of Mr. Pitt. It did not alarm me. For tho' I consider the independence of the U. States as absolutely dependent on the ability of England to maintain *hers,* against all the efforts of Napoleon, yet I have at no time entertained an exalted opinion of Mr. Pitt as a Statesman *to plan and direct great military enterprises ;* and to *select* and *in defiance of all opposition to call forth the requisite talents to execute them.* With an eloquence powerful perhaps as his father's, did he not want much of that *vigour* which enabled the latter successfully to execute the bold project he conceived ? With great talents, I expect more *efficiency* in Lord Grenville. Perfectly relying on your judgment of the preeminent talents, strength and popularity (founded on a personal knowledge of the men) I rejoice that such a ministry has been formed. It furnished just ground for the confident hope you express (in which I cordially join) " that the high Spirit and ancient glory of the Nation will enable them to contend against and finally triumph over their [and the World's] gigantic adversary."

But what will be the effect on our commerce? It is said (by the way of Bordeaux) that the British are releasing all American vessels. Will this relaxation continue? I trust not. It commenced prior to Mr. Pitt's decease : probably influenced by the Catastrophe of the Continental War. The Captures and condemnations may not instantly be renewed. Lord Grenville * and his associates will deeply consider the subject as essentially connected with a continuance of the War. Doubtless their measures may be influenced very much by those of Bonaparte. If the latter commands the Ports of the Continent, from the Baltic to the Adriatic, to be shut against the commerce of Britain (and he has only to command to be obeyed) doubtless the British will interdict the commerce of neutrals, at least with all the belligerent nations. *Necessity* will be declared to be the ground of the interdiction. And will it not be an adequate plea? It will be done openly, frankly, boldly ; and such time being given that neutrals shall not complain of being taken by surprise. In a word the principles of War in Disguise will be adopted : "and if we feel no wish to succour our parent State, when fighting for her liberty and her existence," shall we not "at least desist from wrongs [or measures] which augment her dangers and frustrate her defensive efforts"? I, for one, shall bid her God speed. When she is spending, liberally spending, her blood and treasure, *in fact* for our safety and independence, shall we be restive, because she denies us an *accumulation of profit* beyond that which arises from our regular, permanent course of Trade? If we had an administration that regarded anything in comparison with its' own immediate personal interest and popularity and the indulgence of its hateful passions, satisfactory arrangements, I am fully persuaded, might be made with Great Britain. But I do not believe these will be attempted thro' any other agent than the miserable minister now at that Court. Would you believe it? A very few days only had elapsed, after Mr. Pitt's death, and when the new Ministers had scarcely taken their seats in their offices, before Mr. Monroe applied for his answer to his letter (or remonstrance) to Lord Mulgrave! this is the out-door information.† Yet this is the man who is to be the next President of the

---

* You will recollect his Lordship's decided sentiments on neutral commerce in his celebrated Speech on the Treaty with Russia in 1801.

† P. M. This out-of-door report is incorrect. The President sent Monroe's

U. S. ; the man whom Mr. Nicholson lately pronounced (in the House of R.) second to no one in the United States, and who appears (from all I hear) to be the favourite of Mr. Randolph. Hence the contempt with which you will have observed he has treated Mr. Madison—the competitor of Monroe for the Presidency. This I take to be a great, if not a principal cause of the schism among the democrats. Bidwell, Varnum and the majority of the democrats from the great States of Massachusetts, New York and Pennsylvania are the friends of Madison. Randolph and his special adherents are the friends of Monroe : and while these two divisions of democrats are thus early canvassing for the next President, the actual President is exploring the wilds of Louisiana—its salt plains—its rock or mineral salt—its immense prairies—in which he has discovered the earthly *paradise*—its numerous tribes and remnants of tribes of Indians & how many languages they speak—the hot springs & the warm mud-puddles in their vicinity—and the wonderful phenomena in one of a small or " very minute shell fish " in shape resembling a muscle, but having four legs ; and in another " a vermes about half an inch long, moving with a serpentine or vermicular motion " !

Should Monroe be our next P., Randolph, I presume, must be his prime-minister, and Nicholson Secretary of the Navy. Gallatin (whom R. lately eulogized) must remain Secy of the Treasury ; for they have no Southern man of ability and industry to fill his place. They would not be much embarrassed to find a successor to Mr. Dearborn—*Confidential*—at present. On Saturday while the doors were closed, Mr. Randolph said, that about the middle of December, he called on Mr. Madison, who told him *that the French Government had forbidden our negotiating directly with Spain : that we must negotiate thro' the medium of the French Govt., which wanted money, and that we must give it.* Randolph added " I had not much confidence in him (Madison) before, and from that time I have had none " : at that moment, with an indignant motion, throwing his hat across the hall !

Adieu   T. PICKERING.

You will connect this anecdote with the affair of the secret appropriation of 2 millions.

original letter dated Jany. 28 to the two Houses—in which he mentions that he shall soon apply for an answer. The letter was returned to the President ; the doors were closed ; but nothing important was announced.

R. King To Pickering.

New York, Mar. 25, 1806.

Dear Sir,

I yesterday received Mr. Gallatin's Report and Genl. Smith's proposed navigation Law, which you obligingly sent to me, and today I have recd. the Report of the Commn. concerning the Tripolitan affairs, and the last part of Mr. Randolph's speech.

If I may conjecture the conduct of Congress from what in my own opinion I think it should be at the present moment, they will at once suspend the Resolutions, Bills & Debates, until they receive accounts from England of the Temper and views of the new ministry towards the U. S. I can suppose a system, which, if adopted by the new ministry, would require the best understanding and Harmony with America, and which would therefore offer a most favorable opportunity for the satisfactory adjustment of our intercourse with that country. In this state of things, it would be impolitic and extraordinary, if Congress, instead of giving the Executive an opportunity to effect such arrangement, should adopt any measures that might defeat an advantageous settlement of our concerns.

In respect to the Bill offered by Genl. Smith, were the time a proper one for its discussion, I am by no means satisfied that it would be advantageous. If, as I conjecture to be the fact, England at no time imports into the U. States any Goods not the growth or manufacture of her own Dominions, it would be of no effect as respects her, and in reference to other countries, whose ships sometimes resort to our Ports, if they have no such Regulation, our adoption of it might suggest to them the expediency of their doing it also ; and should this be done, we, being carriers of articles not produced nor manufactured at home in a larger proportion than they are, should be sufferers in a like proportion.

Suppose the law generally adopted, the question between us and England will be immediately settled ; for we shall not be able to import Sugar, Coffee, Teas, India Goods, &c, which now make so considerable a share of our exports. I must close, as I fear I may miss the Post.

Yours &c

Rufus King.

C. Gore To R. King.

Boston, March 26, 1806.

My Dear Friend :

I was really gratified by the Receipt of your last Letter, for although I had no apprehensions that you had acted incautiously, and knew that you had communicated to the Government Intelligence of Miranda's Plan, yet it was unknown to me that you possessed their acknowledgment of having received this information. Their Baseness and meanness seem only to be exceeded by their extreme weakness. That any of our Countrymen can still submit to remain the Dupes of such Imbecillity affords new evidence of the Degradation to which Democracy will sink its adherents. Another Testimony of the Contempt of our Chief for Public Opinion we have in the Appointment of Mr. Armstrong. James Lovel, some time since, wrote Mr. Jefferson a congratulatory Letter on the appointment of Austin to the Loan Office ; saying it was the highest Evidence that could be offered of the Supremacy of the Executive of the U. States ; for a man more universally and more deeply despised than Austin, did not exist in this part of the Country, and that a Government, which could name & keep in Office, a Character, known to be so base, must be stronger than any Despotism within his knowledge.

We are now in the Fever Heat of our annual Election, and such are the Charges against Sullivan, & so well supported, that no man who has the least Regard to Property or Reputation, one would think could vote for him ; and yet he will probably have more than 30,000 Votes.

I shall endeavour to keep out of the Legislature, but I am afraid it will not be in my Power. The last year we obliged many to go into the House of Representatives, and had we not chosen 26, we should have had a Democratic House, of course a Democratic Senate and a Democratic council. I do not know that our chance is better this year, and that any Reason exists why the same means should not be resorted to.

The Supreme Court is now in Session, and Sedgwick, as usual, swearing he will resign : possibly He has declared this so frequently and so publickly that he will be compelled to do it, contrary to his more mature judgment.

The dreadful Fate of the Coalition leaves nothing to be hoped for from the Continent of Europe, against the Despotism of Bonaparte. The Views & Intentions of England, under the new administrations, for any intelligence we obtain, are the mere Subject of Conjecture. Our merchants are afraid of a Peace and well they may be, for notwithstanding many Losses & Embarrassments, their Voyages were generally prosperous. Their Shipments of W. India Produce netted them a profit of a sum from 25 to 50 per cent. . . .

Ever and faithfully yrs.

C. GORE.

C. GORE TO R. KING.

BOSTON, 15 April, 1806.

MY DEAR FRIEND :

. . . While we endeavour to derive Consolation from reflecting on some Errors on the part of the Federalists, and attempt to impute to those the present gloomy Prospect, it is impossible not to perceive, in the existing State of things, under all the circumstances of the Times and the great Difference in the Pretensions of the Candidates to the Confidence of Mankind, the most damning Proofs of the Triumph of Vice over Virtue, and the same Presages of a total Prostration of the Rights of Freedom & of Property to the insatiable Lust of a base & cowardly Despotism, owing its Origin & Support to the meanest and most degraded Passions of the human Heart.

You may wonder that, with a full view of the present & future State of our affairs, I would enter into public Life again. In the first Place, I conceived it would be impossible to avoid a Seat in the House, if I insisted in declining the Duty of a Senator. If it were possible for the Federalists to retain the name and Forces of the Government, in the Crisis which cannot be very distant, it might be of incalculable Benefit to the Cause of Order : and it appeared to me of great importance that Men of Consideration should not resign the Government into the Hands of a different Class, unless they were confident that great Good would result from suffering our Institutions to be destroyed by the Weakness of our Party, or the Violence of the Democrats. In fine, and what was perhaps of more weight in my own mind, it appeared to me that we ought not by deserting our Friends &

our Country in the Hour of peril, to surrender a claim to their confidence when our Advice & Experience may be of use to them & ourselves, and by such Desertion reserve for a future Day the bitter Reflection that had we not shrunk from Exertion, we might have prevented or softened the existing calamities.

We see by the Papers that the Govt. is base & mad enough to persist in persecuting the Persons concerned in Miranda's Enterprise. I cannot but think this is one of the Rocks on which our Chief and his aids are likely to wreck their Pretensions to Confidence, and I look with much Interest to the Denouement of the Business. Congress affords, as the Stories are told to us, a most disgraceful Picture of Imbecillity, Outrage & Meanness ; and what is truly unfortunate to our Reputation at least no man appears to state to the Public, or on the Floor of the House, the Principles on which our Conduct ought to be regulated, and to expose in a just & proper manner the flagitious and degrading Behaviour of our Government.

> Farewell, ever & truly yours
>
> C. GORE.

T. PICKERING TO R. KING.

WASHINGTON, April 19th, 1806.

DEAR SIR :

Some time ago I promised to give the information you requested respecting the application of the Louisiana fund by General Armstrong.

It was stated by Genl. Smith (while Armstrong's nomination was before the Senate), that our Government knowing, or expecting, that the fund would not be equal to all the claims upon it, proposed to the French Government that *all* the claims should be examined, and the sums due ascertained, before any payments were made ; and that if the whole amount surpassed the fund of $3,750,000, the loss should be *averaged*. To this, he said, the French Government would not agree ; insisting that the bills should be drawn as fast as the liquidations were made, conformably to the Convention. This must refer to the 9th Article ; in which you will see the English translation is not of the same import as the French original ; this being "a mesure que," &c.—

which is translated " In proportion." In a variety of places you will observe it to be a very careless and faulty translation. You will also notice the unpardonable negligence of Livingston & Monroe in the *preamble* of this Convention, the object of which is declared to be, to comply with the *second* & fifth articles of the Treaty of Sept. 30, 1800, altho' the *second* was expunged before that Treaty was ratified. By the 4th article of the same Treaty, it was stipulated that " property captured and not yet definitely condemned," should be mutually restored ; but in the fifth article of the Louisiana Convention, this stipulation was either carelessly neglected, or purposely set aside by this clause, " The said 5th Article (of the Treaty of 1800) does not comprehend prizes, whose condemnation has been or *shall be* confirmed."

But notwithstanding the refusal of the French Govt. to admit the deficiency of funds to be averaged upon all the claims, and its determination that the bills should be drawn as fast as the liquidations were made, yet our enquiries produced the information, that Mr. Livingston did not draw a single bill ; and that tho' Mr. Armstrong arrived in Paris in the autumn of 1804, yet he drew no bills until May 1805.

Since Armstrong's nomination to Spain has been approved, we have had laid on our tables a document exhibiting the draughts he has made and the times of drawing. The supplementary documents showing the sums allowed for the embargoed vessels, you will see was occasioned by the disagreement between Marbois and Armstrong as to the persons in whose favour the bills ought to be drawn ; in which matter Armstrong was doubtless in the right ; the original powers being given to Fenwick by the *masters* of the vessels, at the period when the embargoes took place ; and who or whose representations, ought not, at this late day, to receive the property of the *Merchant owners.* An Act has recently been passed to authorize the Sec'y of the Treasury to pay these claims. . . .

It is said Wm. Pinkney (late one of our Commissioners in London) is to be appointed Minister Plenipotentiary to Great Britain—Monroe to return in the Fall.

4 P.M. Mr. Pinkney has been nominated *in conjunction with Monroe* to negotiate on our differences with the British Government. I have just got the message and will give you the words :

Monroe & Pinkney are nominated "to be Commissioners Plenipotentiary & Extraordinary for settling all matters of difference
between the United States and the United Kingdoms of Great
Britain and Ireland, relative to wrongs committed between the
parties on the high seas or other waters, & for establishing the
principles of navigation & commerce between them."

5 P.M. The Senate have struck out (on the second reading)
the two sections of the bill for repealing the duty on salt, and
allowing a bounty to our fisheries and salted provisions. As the
bill passed the House so triumphantly (about 84 to 11) I presumed it would, on the same popular ground, be passed by the
Senate. The votes 16 to 9.

Very truly yours,
T. PICKERING.

NOAH WEBSTER TO R. KING.

NEW HAVEN, May 5th, 1806.

SIR :

The circumstances of the United States are critical and seem
to require some union of sentiment & concert of measures among
the real friends of public safety & National character. I have
seen the spirited & appropriate resolution of the federal gentlemen, on the occasion of the outrage lately committed by the
British ship in N. York Harbor, but have not yet heard of the
issue of the election in the city—an issue which I deem important.

I take the liberty however to request your opinion on the expediency of attempting to procure some expression of the public
sentiments of this State. Our Legislature will meet next Thursday, & there can be no doubt of their readiness to take any
step in the present crisis, which on deliberate consultation shall
be deemed prudent. The federal strength in Massachusetts, if
not totally overwhelmed, is extremely impaired, & Connecticut
alone stands firm with a commanding majority. The great question seems to be whether the time has arrived, when the current
of public opinion in favor of the present administration can be
arrested & turned. Can the folly, the imbecility, & the corruption which have reduced us to a most deplorable condition, be
made to appear with such evidence as to silence and confound
the adherents of the present administration ? Is there any thing

now existing which can change or commence a change of the confidence of that class of people in their leader?

As a general rule it is clear that the Legislatures of the States should not interfere with the measures of the national Government. But are there not emergencies when such interference is not only right but indispensable? And to what point of public danger & national humiliation must we be reduced before an expression of the public will, by the constituent members of the confederation becomes expedient or justifiable?

I have not time to suggest the views I have of the subject. The opinions of gentlemen here are various on this question, & it deserves to be considered in all its aspects before any other step is taken. I have thought it so important as to ask your opinion, &, if you please, the opinions of other influential gentlemen in New York, whether at the approaching session of our Legislature, it is best to express the opinions of that body on the extraordinary measures of the general government, which appear to me to have actually yielded up our Independence—in violation of the highest duty imposed on the administrators of that Govt. by public confidence and the constitution.* Your answer addressed to me at Hartford will oblige

Sir your most obed. Servt.,

NOAH WEBSTER.

* Endorsed by R. K. " Ansd. that nothing should be done without approval by Ellsworth, The Govr., &c."

CHAPTER XXXII.

Miranda wrote to Mr. King, August 23, 1803, from London :

" La conduite ou la bêtise, mon chère ami, va son train ici—de manière que je suis decidé a partir par le premier convoi, avec ou sans secours (for Trinidad). Leur conduite me parait a cette heure suspect, et Dieu sçait si elle n'est pas perfide ! Ainsi je vous conjure au nom de votre patrie et de la mienne de nous faire parvenir des secours au plutôt—Le point ou il faut les diriger est l'isle de Trinidad."

What he asked for were ships loaded with flour and, most urgently, four thousand muskets with bayonets, ammunition for them, priming powder, pikes—and a hundred or two hundred brave Americans. On the same sheet under date of August 30, he says that he has finally made a definite arrangement with the Government to transport him in a frigate to Trinidad, has received from it a small sum of money, and that he has had promised money and men at the Island. He therefore earnestly entreats Mr. King to have forwarded to him "sans faute deux batimens Americains pour le moins, avec quelques armes, et quelques dizaines (sinon des Centaines) de braves enfans de Colombia."

He encloses a statement of the cost of 5000 men with necessary arms &c., for one year, about $4\frac{1}{2}$ millions of dollars, &c.

On the back of this letter, " Rec. Oct. 8th 1803," is endorsed. N. B. The writer has no authority to make to me these propositions ; nor have I inclination to comply with them. Indeed, I could not were I inclined, such supplies being contrary to Law. (Signed)   RUFUS KING Oct. 9, 1803.

Several letters relative to Miranda's affairs both from Mr. King and Mr. Gore will be found on pages 429 to 435 of this volume. But as nothing new occurred to change the relations of Great Britain with Spain, Miranda made no new communications to Mr. King until on July 13, 1805, he writes, that after " inconceivable and unsupportable delays he was about to sail for New York," and asking him to inform those who had promised to assist him " that the time for action had arrived." In a postscript dated August 8th, he says, " the time for our departure is fixed for the 15th of this month."

Mr. King communicated this letter " in secret " to the Secretary of State.

Copy.

R. KING TO J. MADISON, SECY. OF STATE.

Secret.

JAMAICA, L. I., Oct. 15, 1805.

SIR :

You will probably recollect that soon after my return to England, I communicated to you the extract of a letter that I had received and which related to an object respecting which we cannot be indifferent. For some time past I have heard nothing farther on the subject. A few days since, however, I received a letter from the same person dated London August 8, the following extract of which I have thought it expedient confidentially to communicate to you.

" Aprés des inconsequences et des retards inconcevables et insupportables, nous voilà sur le point de partir. . . . Je compte m'embarquer dans le courant de ce mois." " P. S. C'est pour le 15 de ce mois (Aôut) que notre depart est fixé."

Whether any adequate succour has been furnished by England or favorable expectations are derived from a supposed state of things between the U. S. & Spain is what at present I have no satisfactory means of deciding. I may, however, shortly receive more exact information.

With sentiments of Respect & Esteem &c.

RUFUS KING.

Miranda, tired, as has been seen, of waiting for the assistance he had hoped to receive from England, sailed for America, to ascertain there what arrangements he could make to forward his plans. He arrived in New York on Nov. 9, 1805, bringing with him a long letter dated Aug. 14, from Mr. N. Vansittart to Mr. King, giving him a general view of the past relations with Miranda and of the state of ministerial and public opinion in England relative to the liberation of the Spanish Provinces.

N. VANSITTART TO R. KING.

LONDON, Aug. 14, 1805.

MY DEAR SIR :

I have often blamed myself for my long omission in writing to you as well as to some other valuable friends who are abroad, but have found myself embarrassed, not only by the frequent pressure of business and other avocations, but perhaps in a still greater degree by the uncertainty of my own situation. It would have appeared reserved and perhaps unkind to have said nothing of my own position and views, and yet for the last eighteen months I could scarcely have given any account of myself which would not have misled my correspondent at the time the letter could reach him. I should have been happy in writing to a friend whose good opinion I so much value to have entered into such an explanation as to show that this uncertainty has not arisen from any unsteadiness in my principles, or inconsistency in my conduct, but has been the unavoidable result of the circumstances in which I have been placed, had not the occasion of my writing been of a very peculiar kind and connected with circumstances of much greater importance than the fortunes & estimation of any individual.

This will be delivered to you by our common friend, Genl. Miranda, who has at last embarked with scarcely any other means than the resources of his own mind in the execution of the great plan which for so many years he has meditated for the liberation of his country.

You are, I believe, as well acquainted with the prospects of support held out to him long ago in this kingdom as well as on some occasions by certain continental powers, as well as with the preparations made for that purpose by the English Government for a short time preceding the signature of the last peace. But I presume you have not heard that soon after the renewal of the war, I obtained leave to make a private provision of Arms, Clothing & Stores for 5000 men as a preparation in case a rupture with Spain should take place. The Government however entertaining a hope (on grounds which never appeared satisfactory to me and which I shall not now discuss) that the neutrality of Spain might be preserved, directed the articles which had been collected to be applied to other currrent services previous to the change of administration which took place last year. You will learn from Genl. Miranda what has since passed between him and the members of the present ministry. He had for some time after the commencement of hostilities with Spain reason to hope for active & cordial assistance, but the attention of the Government has been so much engaged with different, & I fear, unattainable objects that he has at last determined in utter despair of their taking any decisive steps, to try what can be effected by such resources as America can furnish and may be willing to afford him either as an enterprize sanctioned by public authority or undertaken by individual adventures.

You will be the best judge what support he will be likely to meet with in America, and your influence will be of the utmost importance to him. You are also by your long residence in England, and your intimacy with men of different sentiments and parties, no inadequate judge how far such a plan, supposing the execution of it to be successfully commenced would derive en-

couragement and aid from this country. But on that subject I
will shortly state the best opinion I have been able to form. Our
mercantile body are naturally anxious for an extension of trade
and look with great anxiety to a removal of the restraints which
in a great degree exclude them from the rich market of S. America ; and a great body of our most reasonable and judicious men
consider a well combined system of independence as the best and
only effectual security to preserve those immense territories from
falling, like the mother country, under the dominion of France
and furnishing resources sufficient to enable that ambitious and
domineering power to complete the subjugation of Europe. They
therefore consider this country as bound to support such an
attempt not only as a justifiable measure of hostility but on the
strictest principles of self defence.

On the other hand there are not wanting men of great weight
and authority, who have such a dread and abhorrence of any
thing which bears the name or approaches to the semblance of
revolution that they think all such ideas ought in the most pointed
manner to be *discountenanced*, if not directly *resisted*. It is vain to
argue with them, that the natural and inevitable course of events
leads to separation of populous and rapidly increasing Colonies
from a feeble, decrepit and degraded government ; that we might
as well attempt to stop the tide, as to stop the progress or long
secure the subjection of countries so circumstanced, but that it is
in some degree in our power to select the time and influence the
direction of their great change, and by rendering it more easy and
more beneficial to secure the gratitude and attachment of the new
Power, whose formation we could not prevent, for they will
answer that the effects of the change are so uncertain, and the
evils attending may and probably will be so terrible that we ought
on no account incur the guilt and risque the consequences of co-
operating to produce it.

Of the great parties which divide our State, I have good reason
to believe that the leaders of the present ministry incline to the
first opinion ; as it appears from circumstances within my own
knowledge, that they had not long since a serious intention of furnishing Genl. Miranda with the succours he required, and only
relinquished the plan from an unwillingness to divert the force
which they judged to be necessary from other objects which they

considered more immediately important. The sentiments of the late Administration sufficiently appear from the conduct they pursued at the close of the last war, but I must do them the justice to add that on the conclusion of Peace every idea inconsistent with the strictest discharge of the duties of amity towards Spain was entirely relinquished.

With the sentiments of the opposition parties I am less intimately acquainted ; but I have always understood Mr. Fox and his friends to be favorable to emancipation of S. America, and it seems conformable to the general tenor of their principles that they should be so. Lord Grenville not long since took an opportunity in the House of Lords to declare vehemently against it, to the surprize of many persons who had understood him to express different sentiments in private on former occasions.

But whatever may be the sentiments of particular men previous to the attempt, I have no doubt that obvious views of great national advantage will occasion nearly a general concurrence in its favor in case of a prosperous commencement, and that unless Peace should be concluded and a question of public faith occur, the general disposition of the country will in a manner compel almost any government to give a vigorous support to the enterprize.

In one important respect it will derive unavoidable assistance from our forces, viz. that both our blockading squadrons in Europe and our fleets in the West Indies will be nearly as vigilant and useful in intercepting any succours which the Spaniards or French may attempt to send to the Colonies as if they were stationed for that express purpose.

You will perceive, my dear Sir, that I have addressed you throughout not only with the freedom of a friend, but the sentiments of an Englishman, from a firm conviction, that in this instance (and I believe if rightly understood in every other) the views and interests of this Country and the United States must be indissolubly united. Believe me, my dear Sir,

With great Esteem, very Sincerely yours,

N. VANSITTART.

Mr. King has endorsed on this letter

" Recd. by Miranda Nov. 10th, sent inclosed to Mr. Madison for, the Pres. Perusal Nov. 25, received from Mr. Madison Decr. 5th."

Copy.

R. KING TO J. MADISON, SECRETARY OF STATE.
Private.

NEW YORK, Nov. 25, 1805.

SIR :

I had the honour to write to you on the 15th of last month, since when I have received by General Miranda, who has arrived here, a letter from Mr. N. Vansittart, a member of the British Parliament, and who was likewise a member of the late Administration of Mr. Addington. Mr. Vansittart being a man of distinguished probity and in a situation to understand fully the subject on which he writes, I send you his letter for the President's perusal, requesting that it may afterwards be returned to me.

With great respect, &c.

R. KING.

It will thus be seen that whatever agency Mr. King may have had in assisting Miranda, there is no evidence of his willingness to engage in an enterprize undertaken against a friendly nation without the knowledge of his own government. He was certainly warmly interested in the proposed liberation of the Spanish South American Colonies, and had been for years ; but it does not appear that he contemplated a successful issue without the leadership of Great Britain to cripple the resources of her great enemy and, as Mr. King thought, of his own country, which France would obtain through her power over the Spanish Colonies—Spain being then a mere puppet in the hands of France.

Miranda wrote to Mr. Gore from New York 27 Nov., 1805, the first direct communication after his arrival there.

Vous avez appris sans doute, mon cher ami, que je suis arrivé ici depuis le 9 du courant. Nous avons arrangé deja nos affaires de manière que je puisse partir d'ici vers le fin du mois prochain sans faute. Deux batimens armés et trés bien equipés sont prets pour cet objet ; tout ce qui nous manque (et que j'espére obtenir par vos amis de Boston) est le compliment des armes, et un peu d'argent pour partir sans delai. Ce dernier article ne sera pas

même necessaire si on nous offre le moindre assentiment à Washington ; puisque dans ce cas on nous promet dans cette ville ici
tout les secours pecunières qui sont necessaires.   Enfin pour que
vous soyez parfaitement instruit de ce que nous avons ici, et de
ce qui nous manque pour faire notre *debut* avec succes, nous
sommes convenus (notre ami d'ici et moi) que le Major Armstrong, porteur de celle-ci et un des cooperateurs, personne mûre
et discrète, passe chez vous pour donner toux les renseignmens et
toute l'information necessaire sur cet objet afin que l'ensemble
marche avec un accord parfait.

Comme le risque est plus considérable et le *service* bien plus
important dans cette première occasion que par la suîte, il faut
aussi que les profits soient en proportion—et je croirai qu'un
cent pour cent et même d'advantage, ne serait pas un trop haut
prix.   Vour ferez en tout cas comme vous jugerez ápropos.

Voici une lettre pour mon ami le Genl. Knox, qui pourroit
peut-être seconder nos efforts dans le moment actuel ; mais si
vous croyez cette démarche inutile ou peu necessaire, vous
pourrez la supprimer.   C'est avec l'avis de notre ami commun ici
que je l'ai écrite et que je fais tout, desirant que la chose se fasse
avec sagesse et bonne direction pour que la necessité soit notre
recompense.   Je part demain pour Washington, et vous aurez de
mes nouvelles sans faute.

Agissez en tout cas, je vous prie, avec promptitude et energie
puisque le moment est precieux et les avantages incalculables !

Voici le moyen que notre Commodore propose pour envoyer
les armes de Boston ici *—et pour prevenir l'effet de la loi qui
exige une caution, &c.

Yours most sincerely,

M———A.

---

*A vessel to be cleared out from Boston for N. Orleans ; pass thro' the Sound,
come to anchor in the passage before arriving at Hell Gate ; a person dispatched
from her to N. Y. to inform of her arrival, &c, and then wait further orders.
No difficulty can possibly arise. She will pass through the Sound when the
ship leaves the port of N. Y., and join at the Hook. No law exists to prevent
vessels carrying the articles in question from Boston to N. O. No law exists to
prevent her passing through the Sound for any reason which may be given or
asked.

J. S.

RUFUS KING TO C. GORE.

NEW YORK, Nov. 29, 1805.

DEAR SIR :

Some short time since I recd. a letter from Mr. Vansittart, explaining pretty fully the sentiments of the leading men of different parties in England concerning S. America. Mr. Addington's friends were decided in the event of a Spanish war to afford G. M. succour to attempt the long meditated Revolution. Mr. Pitt also promised that assistance should be given as soon as a war with Spain took place, and the assurances were continued till the new coalition was founded, when G. M. was told that such were the engagements of England that she was not at liberty to divide her attentions or her resources. G. M. immediately determined to embark for the U. S. Mr. Vansittart believes that the Revolution of S. Amer. would be highly popular in England, especially among the manufacturing and commercial part of the nation, and that if a beginning were made, the Government, whatever might be its sentiments, would be obliged to countenance, and even to support the measure. Mr. Vansittart's reasoning which leads to this conclusion appears to me judicious.

In this condition of England G. M. has arrived here, altogether without means, except his personal knowledge and talents, in order to embark in the enterprize he has so long and so maturely considered. There are three courses before him one of which he seems resolved to pursue.

1. To make the attempt with the countenance and support of the U. S.

2. To make it with the cooperation of individuals.

3. To make it without foreign succour wholly depending on the disposition and aid of the inhabitants.

The General left town this morning to sound the administration. I have no means of forming a satisfactory opinion in what temper he will be likely to find our Chiefs. He yesterday showed me the copy of a letter he had written to you, and I have thought it due to the occasion as well as to our friendship to lose no time in sending you this communication.

With unfeigned attachment &c.

RUFUS KING.

J. Madison to R. King.

Private.

WASHINGTON, Decr. 4, 1805.

SIR :

I have received your favor of the 25th ulto. inclosing one to you from Mr. Vansittart, which I now return as you requested, after having submitted it to the perusal of the President. As it is of importance to understand the way of thinking in Great Britain with respect to Spanish America and what the Government there does not at this particular time mean to undertake as well as what under other circumstances it may probably undertake towards the object pursued by Genl. Miranda, the communication of Mr. Vansittart's information relative thereto claims acknowledgments which I pray you to accept with assurances of the high respect with which I have the honor to be

Your most obt. Servt.

JAMES MADISON.

Miranda to R. King.

Private.

NEW YORK, ce 30 Decr., 1805.

I'ai vu mes Cooporateurs hier en vous quittant, et je les ai trouvé tous decidés à suivre sans relache cette patriotique entreprise, avec un zêle vraiment heroique.

Mais comme la promptitude, ainsi que l' *étendue* des apprets, tient en quelque sort dans ce moment aux supports que je puisse leur procurer de mon coté, je vous supplie de ne pas negliger aujourd'hui la démarche dont nous sommes convenus hier au soir, afin qu 'ils puissent definitivement fixer dans la journée le nombre de batimens et la quantité des armes qui doivent être prêtes dans 10 jours.

Je ne vous fais point d'apologie sur mon importunité, puisque vous connoissez l' importance de l' objet et la presse du tems.

A vous invariablement

MIRANDA.

P. S. Ci-joint est le maximum de leur demande.*

Cash 5000, 60 D. 5000., 90 D. 5000, 120 D 5000.

"* I saw my cooperators yesterday after leaving you, and found them all de-cided to carry on without delay this patriotic Enterprize with a zeal truly heroic. But as promptness, as well as the *extent* of the preparations, depends in some

On the back of this letter Mr. King has written

" Miranda 30 December 1805. Respecting succours ; ansd. verbally, that as our Govt. having an opening to do so, had not intimated to any of my friends in confidence even that the supplies might be made in discretion, and privately, there was a difficulty in making the same which would prevent it being done."

The last letter from Miranda relative to his expedition announces his departure.

MIRANDA TO R. KING.

OFF THE HOOK, 2 of Febr., 9 o'clk. A.M.

DEAR SIR :

Nous voilà hors du port et en compagnie de 180 enfans de Colombia—une meilleure suite à tous égards que celle qui accompagnoit le Vainqueur de Pompé quand Ciceron lui donna à diner dans la Ville de Formiæ.   Que la Providence nous seconde et nous ferons mieux peut-être.*

Ever yours
MIRANDA.

In an appendix, will be found a paper written by Mr. King on March 5, 1806, detailing his intercourse with Miranda from the time of his arrival in New York until his departure, and also Mr. King's examination before the Judge of the District Court of New York by the District-Attorney relative to matters connected with sailing of the *Leander* and his connection with General Miranda before the departure of the vessel.

degree at this moment upon the assistance I can provide on my side, I beseech you not to neglect today the steps we agreed upon last evening, in order that they may be able to fix definitively during the day the number of vessels and the quantity of arms that should be ready in 10 days.

I make no apoligies for my importunity, as you know the importance of the object and the pressure of time.

P. S. Annexed is the maximum of their requirement."

* " Here we are outside the harbour, with 180 children of Columbia in company : a better following in all respects than that which accompanied the Conqueror of Pompey when Cicero entertained him at dinner in the City of Formiæ. May Providence help us and we shall do better perhaps."

It may be here stated that relying upon the assertion of Miranda, that though the Government would not assist, they would wink at what was done provided that discretion were used in making preparations for the Expedition, friends in New York advanced him money; two small armed vessels went out to St. Domingo to enlist men there, and were followed by the ship *Leander*, in which Miranda and his men with arms and munitions of war embarked. Messrs. Ogden and Smith, who had been his agents in furnishing the vessel and providing the men and arms, etc., were after the sailing of the vessel subjected to a judicial inquiry on the ground of an infringement of the laws of the United States; but were acquitted by the jury, as it was not proved satisfactorily that the laws of the United States had been broken. While the matter was pending in court, the judge refusing to admit proof of the connivance of, or the tacitly favoring the expedition by the Executive, an attempt was made to obtain the interference of Congress to arrest the proceedings, by the presentation, in the House of Representatives, of a memorial, on the last day of the Session, from Messrs. Ogden and Smith, asking for relief from a prosecution in the Circuit Court of the United States for the district of New York, "for an alleged infraction of the laws of the United States in which, if guilty, they have been led into error by the conduct of officers of the Executive Government," etc., thus distinctly charging certain officers of the Government with a knowledge of the *Leander's* sailing, time enough to have prevented it, meaning more definitely the President. A short but sharp debate ensued, the basis of which was a denial of the charge, unsupported by evidence and calculated not only to incense the country against the administration but against the tribunals of justice in which the case was pending. Let the case be decided there and not be prejudged. If unjustly decided, "then it would be time enough to interfere." The resolutions below were passed by an overwhelming vote.

"Resolved, That the charges contained in the memorials of

Samuel G. Ogden and of William S. Smith are, in the opinion of
this House, unsupported by any evidence, which, in the least degree, criminates the Executive Government of this country."
75 to 8.

" Resolved, that the said memorials appear to have been presented at a time, and under circumstances insidiously calculated
to excite unjust suspicions in the minds of the good people
of this nation, against the existing Administration of the General
Government." 70 to 13.—Annals of Congress, 1st Session, 1805,
1806, p. 1092.

To close this incident in the life of Mr. King, the details
of which will be found in the Appendix, the following letters
are given.

R. KING TO C. GORE.

N. YK., Mar. 9, 1806.

MY DEAR SIR :

Observing the reports contained in the Newspapers respecting
Miranda's Expedition, and that the equipment of the Leander
has become matter of judicial enquiry, you may perhaps think it
irregular that I say nothing to you on the subject, especially as my
own name has been mentioned in relation to the business.

It is not new to you that Miranda left England in utter dispair
of obtaining succor there to enable him to carry into effect his long
meditated views ; his hopes were that adequate assistance might be
had here, either directly from Government, or thro' private individuals. As soon as I understood directly his object, I at once
told him that no prudent individuals would engage with him, at
least that I could not recommend to any of my friends to do so,
without the countenance and protection of Government, and therefore advised him to proceed to Washington, and to lay his whole
views before the Govt. This he concluded to do ; and in order
that the Government might be fully acquainted with the temper of
England and her Government on the subject of Miranda's plan,
as well as with Miranda's views in coming to the Secretary, I transmitted to Mr. Madison a letter that I had received from England
fully disclosing the same, with a request that after being laid before the President, it might be returned to me. This was done

with acknowledgments, &c, before Miranda arrived at Washington.   On his arrival there he took an early opportunity of opening his whole plan to the Government and concluded by asking their assistance, &c.   Time being taken to consider the subject, he was answered that Govt. could or would not grant the succour he demanded, but that private persons might.   What is here stated of what passed between the Govt. and Miranda rests solely upon his report to me, which however I fully credit : my understanding being that Govt. would not act, but that it would wink at the things being done by individuals.   This report being transmitted by Miranda to Ogden, Smith and Lewis, the Leander was equipped and Miranda sailed about the 2nd of February.   While the business was going on, he, M., urged me to engage my friends to assist by a loan of money, which I decidedly declined, because I believed that Govt. would betray those, who should act in the persuasion that they did not disapprove the measure.   He wished me to converse with his associates, which I also refused.   About a week before Miranda sailed, he wrote two letters, one to the Prest. the other to Mr. Madison, which assure them that he had in all things acted according to the intention of Govt. which he hoped he had duly or correctly understood &c.   Of these letters he left copies with me.   Three or four weeks after the date of these letters, and when Miranda was fairly off, an enquiry has been instituted and Smith and Ogden have been arrested, as agents in this transaction.   In the course of the examination, Smith having stated to the Judge that Miranda told him that he had communicated to me his project, as well as what had passed at Washington I was called as a witness.   My examination was short and pointed to Miranda's communication of the expedition.   I with others was recognized to attend the next court as a witness.   The affair has created much attention.   I understand the general impression is unfavourable to the honour of Govt.   I felicitate myself that the sentiments I entertain of our Chief have kept me within the limits of extreme caution.   I cannot with honour be a volunteer on this occasion agt. Govt., but if I am called as a witness on the prosecution they institute, all reserve will be at an end ; the whole must be told, and being told cannot leave any doubt of the unworthy conduct of Govt. in this affair.   This is entirely confidential.

R. King to T. Pickering.

NEW YORK, March 13, 1806.

DEAR SIR :

Mr. Wolcott some days ago told me that he would write to Mr. Tracy on the subject of the Leander & Miranda's expedition, and as I presume you would see this letter, and preferred for particular reasons, not to write myself, I have said nothing to you of this project.   .   .   .

C. Gore to R. King.

BOSTON, March 26, 1806.

DEAR SIR :

I was really gratified by the receipt of your last letter, for although I had no apprehension that you had acted incautiously, and saw that you had communicated to the Government intelligence of Miranda's plan, yet it was unknown to me, that you possessed their acknowledgment of having received this information. Their baseness and meanness seem only to be exceeded by their extreme weakness.   .   .   .

C. Gore to R. King.

BOSTON, April 15, 1806.

.   .   .   We see by the papers that the Government is base and mad enough to persist in persecuting the persons concerned in Miranda's Enterprise. I cannot but think this is one of the rocks on which our chief and his aids are likely to wreck their pretensions to confidence ; and I look with much interest to the denouement of the business.   .   .   .

R. King to N. Vansittart.

Sept. 30., 1806.

DEAR SIR :

It is a long time since I have had the pleasure of hearing from you, tho' I often see your name in the Proceedings of Parliament. I wrote to you after Miranda left this Country, acknowledging the receipt of your Letter by him, and informing you that I had taken the Liberty of communicating it confidentially to the President.

In consequence, it is believed, of complaints to our Govt. respecting Miranda's Expedition, a prosecution was ordered to be instituted against two persons, charged with having assisted him in preparing the same. After a long trial, both were acquitted ; the accused are understood to have justified or excused themselves by offering to prove that Govt. was privy to their conduct. But the Court declared the Statute to be the only Rule for its decision and (without enquiring into the allegation of privity) were the approbation even of Govt. proved, declared it would neither justify nor excuse. Whether the Jury dissented from this interpretation of the law, or were moved by good-will in favour of Miranda's Enterprize, or deemed the proofs insufficient is matter of conjecture. The Business has excited a good deal of attention, and Govt. has not wholly escaped censure.

As to the Expedition, after various disappointments, and several unsuccessful attempts, it still continues to be the fruitful source of contradictory Rumours. After getting possession of Coro, Miranda evacuated it and reimbarked early in August. Yesterday we had a Report that he had relanded and was joined by a large body of the Inhabitants. The inconsiderable force under Miranda's Command, is not sufficient to inspire confidence, and however well disposed toward him, the Inhabitants may be, they seem afraid to risk the consequences of joining him. If your negotiations for Peace fail, I cannot but believe that your administration will turn its attention seriously and efficaciously to this great object. Were I an English Minister I would not rest till the Resources of S. America were wrested from the hands of France, for they can no longer be regarded as those of Spain.

With sincere regard your faithful servt.

RUFUS KING.

CHAPTER XXXIII.

Tudor to King—Carrying Ice to the W. Indies—Dr. Romeyn to King—Election as Manager of the American Bible Society—King to Romeyn—Declines the Office, though approving the Object of the Society—Action of the Episcopal Church to circulate the Bible with the Common Prayer Book—Gore to King—Pinckney to London to assist Monroe—King Receives Degree of LL.D. from Dartmouth, Williams, and Harvard Colleges—Trustee of Columbia College—S. Smith to King—Death of his Son—Tudor to King—Failure of Application relative to Ice Monopoly—Speculations on European Affairs—Williams to King—British and American Commissioners said to have made a Treaty—King on an Outrage against Personal Liberty, in the Case of Alexander, a Lawyer in N. Orleans arrested by Gen'l Wilkinson.

WM. TUDOR, JR., TO R. KING.

BOSTON, June 12, 1806.

DEAR SIR :

Expecting to embark in the course of ten days for England, I am very desirous to obtain some letters from you,* of what kind and for what purpose I cannot better describe than by asking your indulgence while I retail as briefly as possible the motives of my voyage.

About a year since my Brother & myself agreed to attempt to transport Ice to the West Indies. Various circumstances had for some time previous given rise to this scheme, and we gradually convinced ourselves that with proper precautions we might succeed. . . . It will be readily supposed that no small difficulty was encountered in persuading the Governments of the various colonies to listen to a plan considered at first as the wildest extravagance. Indeed I found but three persons in all the Islands I visited, who at the first moment embraced the idea and conceived it practicable. These were Genl. Ennouf, the Gov. of

* Endorsed, " Ans'd, enclosing letter to W. Windham."

Guadaloupe, Lord Lavington at Antigua and a planter, a man of science, at Jamaica.

We have obtained from the Govt. of Martinique, Guadaloupe & St. Domingo the exclusive privilege of importing & selling Ice and fresh provisions packed in the same for the term of ten years. In the English colonies we have made only three applications at Barbadoes, Antigua & Jamaica. At Antigua . . . I had the honor of conversing with Lord Lavington fully on the subject; he gave me & the project a flattering reception & told me did not doubt I should obtain an act in my favour, but as it must be passed with a "suspending clause," coming under the head of a "new and extraordinary nature," he would follow it home, to the Board of Privy Council, with a particular letter in its favour.

At Jamaica I conversed with the most influential members of the Govt. of the Island. My friends had procured for me, a letter from Mr. Merry to Sir Eyrecoote, who received me with much politeness, though he thought it a "strange thing." As I had just received advices, it was in my power to inform him of the safe arrival of a cargo of Ice and provisions at Martinique, and of course that the experiment was decided. He told me it would be a matter of consultation and that he saw no objections. He made many enquiries about America and asked me particularly after you, telling me he had had the pleasure of dining with you frequently in London.

I saw the most influential members of the Jamaica Assembly, and they all thought I might confide in the good will of the Island towards our enterprise. They doubted, at least one of them did, whether I should obtain the act I wanted because it could not be passed without the *suspending clause*, and as the Gov't of the Island deny to the mother country the right of controul, which is given by this clause, they were extremely cautious about passing any act that would agitate the question. They told me I should without doubt obtain a resolution of the Assembly in favour of the enterprise, and a second instructing the agent of the Island to back any application I should make at home. . . . By the *exclusive privilege*, I mean exclusion of all individuals & vessels except those of the nation by whom it is granted ; so that while we open a new branch of commerce to their own subjects, we make no interference with their rights, but only ask exclusive

favour as regards all others.   We undertook this novel enterprise
at the hazard of considerable pecuniary loss, and eternal ridicule
if we did not succeed, and we ask of each Govt. as our reward, a
privilege for a certain term over foreigners alone.   .   .   .

From what has been said (I beg leave to add confidentially),
you know better than myself what would serve me in my application to government.   I know I could carry no letters which would
be of so much service to me.   .   .   .

With great respect, yr. humb. Servt.,

WILLIAM TUDOR, JR.

DR. ROMEYN TO HONBLE. RUFUS KING.

NEW YORK, July 17, 1806.

DR. SIR :

In compliance with the direction of the Board of Managers of
the American Bible Society, I have the honour to inform you
that the Convention which formed that Society elected you one
of the Managers.

The Board fondly cherish the hope that this National Institution meets with your approbatton, & that you will unite with them
in their labour of love and work of faith.   I need not add that
your acceptance of the office will be highly gratifying to the
Board & afford a powerful stimulus to their zeal and activity in
forwarding the great and good cause of furnishing the destitute
with the Word of Life.

I am Dr. Sir your obedt. Servt.,

M. P. ROMEYN, Secy &c.

R. KING TO REV. DOCTR. ROMEYN, SEC.

SIR :

I have received your letter of the 17th instant, which informs
me that I have been elected a manager of the American Bible
Society ; and calls on me to make known whether I accept the
appointment.   The object of the Society's labours well deserves
and receives my approbation ; but as I am connected with the
Body of Episcopalians, and the Bp. to whose opinions in matter
of cyder and discipline I am inclined to defer, has signified to us,
that the object whose attainment is the common desire of all

may be more fitly promoted in the mode he has been pleased to indicate, I think it expedient to observe his counsel and to decline the charge of a manager of the American Bible Society.*

With great respect & Regards I am, Sir, yr. obed. Servt.

RUFUS KING.

DR. ROMEYN TO HON. RUFUS KING.

NEW YORK, July 31, 1806.

SIR :

The Managers of the American Bible Society most sincerely regret that any considerations should have existed to deprive them of the aid of your co-operation, & the honour and influence of your name, as a member of their Board. Their disappointment has its relief, however, in the assurance that "the object of the Society's labours well deserves and receives your entire approbation." I have the honour to be, Sir your obed. Servt.

M. P. ROMEYN, Sec D. C.

* In explanation of the above correspondence and of the position taken by Mr. King, it may be stated that Bishop Moore was then contemplating and urging the establishment of a Society in Connection with the Episcopal Church whose purpose should be to print and circulate the Bible and with it the Prayer Book. This society was actually formed in 1809, and the First Report of its proceedings was made in 1811. In it occurs the following paragraph :

"We would beg leave, however, to express the opinion that Episcopalians, in their charitable efforts to diffuse the blessings of Christianity, should unite the Book of Common Prayer with the Bible. It is certainly the best summary of the doctrines and precepts of the Bible that ever was produced : and in the spirit of true piety, equally untinctured by enthusiasm on the one hand, and lukewarmness on the other, it is superior to all the productions of the human mind." p. 11.

In the list of subscribers to this Society, given in this Report is found the name of Rufus King, as an annual subscriber of $50.

Asst. Bishop Hobart in an address before the Auxiliary New York Bible and Common Prayer Book Society in March 8th, 1816, says.

"We, who unite the distribution of the Book of Common Prayer with the Bible, advance a step further in this work of Christian Benevolence. We desire to make known to all men, not only the Word of God, but the Church of God, which we think the Book of Common Prayer sets forth in evangelical and primitive purity both in respect to doctrines, ministry and worship. In this union of the two objects, so far from being influenced by narrow prejudice and illiberal views, we think we follow the method which the Scriptures point out, and to which common *sense* and the natural course of things lead."

C. GORE TO R. KING.

WALTHAM, August 24, 1806.

MY DEAR FRIEND:

. . . When Pinckney was named for London, I presumed it was merely to assist Mr. Monroe in his Negotiation, but I shortly after was told, that He made an agreement with the President, to be the resident Minister. Knowing the Number of Dependants on him for Subsistence, and having heard, that his Business was extremely profitable (some say to the amount of 15,000 dollars per annum) I concluded that the motives, which could lead him to forego such Claims, in so fair a way of being gratified, for the narrow Support of his present Office, must be very strong : and probably stronger would not be required to induce an Abandonment of those Principles & that Conduct which, He must be convinced, afford the only rational Ground for the Freedom, Honour & Interest of the Country.

I can form no conjecture what the British Ministry will be disposed to do, under the Circumstances that our weak & pitiful Administration have been pleased to place the two Nations. Should Mr. Fox adopt the Course, which would seem most natural, there can be little Doubt, but our government would as meanly retract, as they have unadvisedly hazarded their present system. Our Merchants are now trembling at the Expectation of a general Peace, which would greatly derange their Plans and Enterprizes, as these are founded on the Basis of a continued War in Europe for several years.

The Conduct of the Democrats in the Legislature, on the Governor's Election, was such as to do them some Disservice in the public opinion. Sullivan & Austin are endeavouring to avail themselves of the Death of the Son of the latter to blacken the Federalists and promote their political Views, but I cannot permit myself to doubt that when a public Trial shall disclose every Fact of the Transaction, which led to that event, every man will be satisfied, that it was the individual meanness, and base lying spirit of old Austin, with respect to Selfridge's professional conduct, wherein Politics or Party were no way interested, that produced the Quarrel between these two ; and to the same false & dastardly Temper of old Austin, joined to a malignant Desire of Revenge at any Expence, but his own personal Safety, will be imputed the Destruction of his Son.* . . .

Your faithful Friend
C. GORE.

The Govr. of H. College, on Commencement Day, confer'd the Degree of L.L.D. on Judges Marshall, Patterson, & yourself.

The announcement made by Mr. Gore, that Mr. King had had the Degree of L.L.D. conferred on him by Harvard College, gives an opportunity here to say that a similar honor had been bestowed upon him by the Corporation of Dartmouth College in 1802, and by Williams College in 1803, as the following correspondence shows:

EBEN'R. FITCH TO RUFUS KING, ESQ., L. L. D.

WILLIAMS COLLEGE, WILLIAMSTON, Sept. 28, 1803.

SIR :

I have the pleasure officially to inform you that the Corporation of Williams College, at their late Commencement, conferred on you the Degree of Doctor of Laws. Our regulations require that a Gentleman on whom a Doctorate in any of the learned profes-

---

* C. GORE TO R. KING.

BOSTON, Aug. 5, 1806.

MY DEAR FRIEND :

 . . . Yesterday a Mr. Selfridge, a Lawyer of this Town, having had some Difference with Benjn. Austin, in which He had acted with his Characteristic Baseness and Falsehood, published in the Paper, that this Benj. Austin was a Scoundrel, Liar, &c. Austin's Son, a stout young man, armed Himself with a Club and went to attack Selfridge ; the latter shot the former through the Body, and He died almost instantly. There are various Stories, as you will suppose, relative to the Transaction, and unfortunately those only which made against Selfridge were detailed to the Jury of Inquest, which were that Selfridge fired at Austin before He struck or offered to strike ; while others say that Selfridge received two or three blows, and actually retreated to the wall, warning his Antagonist, that He would shoot Him, if He persisted, before He discharged his Pistol. Endeavour will not be wanting to make this a Party Affair, but I think after the first Passions have subsided, it will not be attended with the effect expected ; for Ben. Austin's Conduct was base and mean in the extreme, and the Son was undoubtedly set on by the Father to beat this man, who was feeble and in no degree a Match for the Son at cudgelling.

Yours truly
C. GORE.

sions is conferred, should have been nominated at a previous meeting of the Board.   You were duly nominated at our Commencement in Sept. 1802.   Soon after it came to our knowledge that the Corporation of Dartmouth College had anticipated us in our intentions.   But the Corporation of this College, duly appreciating the eminent services rendered to your Country in your late important Embassy to the Court of London, and your acquired reputation for general jural and political science, were unwilling not to give you this small, but unequivocal testimony of their high esteem, repect and friendship.

With great respect and consideration, I am, Sir, your most obedient & very humble servt.,

EBEN'R FITCH.

To this Mr. King responded :

R. KING TO EBEN'R. FITCH.

WILLIAMS COLLEGE, NEW YORK, Oct. 12, 1803.

SIR :

I have had the honour to receive your letter of the 28th, of Sept., and I entreat the favour of you to present to the Corporation of Williams College my most respectful acknowledgment and thanks for the honour it has been pleased to confer upon me : an honour which I must altogether ascribe to the indulgent partiality of the Corporation, rather than to any acquirements that give to me a title to this distinction.

Be pleased, Sir, to accept my thanks for the polite and friendly terms in which you have communicated this act of the Corporation, and to be assured of the respect and esteem with which I have the honour to be

Sir, your obedt. & faithful Servt.,

RUFUS KING.

The Rev. Dr. Beach wrote to Mr. King, that on August 4, 1806, he was elected a Trustee of Columbia College.   He continued to act as such until the year 1824, when he resigned.

S. SMITH TO R. KING.

BALTIMORE, 24 Nov., 1806.

DEAR SIR :

The shock arising from the loss of my beloved son has been severely felt ; indeed, my Dr. friend, I find it difficult to find com-

fort in my own mind. Your letter has been a balm to my affliction. It has afforded that consolation which cannot fail to gratify.
It gives to my son that character, from a stranger, which his Parents,
had too fondly cherished as their consolation in their advanced
age and as the protection to six daughters. They have now only
one brother, young, lively, amiable, but as all youths of twenty
are, less steady than when more advanced ; so is he less than his
brother.

By the advice of those who have suffered similar losses (for this
is my first) I am endeavoring to chase away Grief by an attention
to Business—the mind whenever unoccupied reverts to its loss.
But I will be comforted, I will find it in the friendship of men
such as you are, my friend, and in the good qualities of my remaining family. I pray you to present me respectfully to your
amiable Lady and to believe me

your friend,

S. SMITH.

W. TUDOR, JR., TO HON. R. KING.

LONDON, December 3, 1806.

DEAR SIR :

The letter of introduction you did me the honour to give me
to Mr. Windham, I left with a card soon after my arrival. The
apprehension you mentioned in the letter to me, that I should
find some difficulty in engaging their attention to my application,
occupied as they were by the events of the war, I have realized
in some degree. I had one interview with Ld. H. Petty, which
was attended with a great deal of politeness on his part, but terminated with the interview. Mr. Windham, I have never heard
from. I found it necessary to make my application to the Board
of Trade, and had two or three conversations with Lord Auckland
and Sir Joseph Banks on the subject and obtained my wish from
that Board to carry on the enterprise in the form of an order of
Council. In addition to the events of the war, they have had strong
contested elections to carry on, so that it would have been unreasonable indeed to have expected their attention to a subject
of a private nature.

W. Tudor to R. King.

London, December 5, 1806.

Dear Sir :

. . . I could not find a person who believed at the beginning of the war that Prussia would be successful, but that she should be overthrown in one battle, that her whole army should be captured, her towns taken, her kingdom ravaged and her power annihilated in the space of one month, is a calamity that no one contemplated. Indeed even for the account of these disasters, they are indebted to the enemy. Lord Morpeth whom they sent to the Prussian headquarters found the army retreating after the first battle and he never stopped running not even to look behind him, till he got fairly onto the Island. In consequence they have only had the French Bulletins for information, and they have never certainly known to this day, where the King of Prussia is, or what are his intentions. As to the King personally, perhaps no man in Europe pities him, and he furnishes a useful lesson of what is the result of such conduct as he has pursued and such counsels as those of Count Haugwitz and Mr. Lombard. The total want of information from the Continent leaves the public nothing but conjecture about the future movements of the King of Prussia, of Austria and Russia. In the meantime the " Gingerbread Baker," as the caricaturists have called him, is preparing a new batch of Kings & Knights.

The dissolution of Parliament has produced a larger majority for the Ministry. Mr. Percival and Lord Castlereagh are the leaders of the opposition. It is not generally believed that the present " *broad-bottomed* " administration can hold together very long. Since the death of Mr. Fox the Grenvilles have had the decided superiority. Fortunately this nation are at present warlike in their humour. The capture of Buenos Ayres elated them excessively. The recent seizure of property at Hamburg has made them shrink a little. So long as they continue to keep Napoleon at bay, there are hopes for the future. But in a free nation, the materials of faction always exist, and a free and rich nation have an unequal contest with the power, the ambition, the talents and the despotism of their enemy. They are too easily depressed, tho' they are unwilling to allow it themselves, and it makes one fearful of the event when so great an effect was produced by the late business at Hamburg. If B. *dictates* a peace to them, we must take our turn, and there must be different characters at the helm, from what now hold it, to save us from destruction. . . .

With the greatest respect yr. mt. hble. Servt.,

W. TUDOR, JR.

S. WILLIAMS TO R. KING.

LONDON, 10 Dec., 1806.

DEAR SIR :

I have your letters of 26 & 30 Sep. The Exportation of Grain is prohibited, and it is with difficulty that leave is obtained to ship seed oats to Ireland ; but I shall endeavour to ship yours in 2 or 3 of the New York Ships, as Ship's stores or as Clover Seed. The Hives &c are not to go at present. I sent Mr. Lyman similar Hives a few years ago, which I bought of Wildman in Holborn. Mr. L. had them in his Garden at Waltham, one or two years, but he found that the Bees ate or stung his fruit so much that he was induced to give away the Hives.

The Newspapers will shew you the rapid Flight of Bonaparte to Universal Empire. He may march to China, if he desires it and would soon visit you, if John's Ships were not on the route or if John would lend him a few, as he intimated to Ld. Lauderdale. Ld. L. was told at Paris that Bonae. wd. furnish soldiers if England wd. Ships to conquer the U. S.

I send you a Pamphlet "The State of the Negotiation," which at first was supposed to have been published under the Sanction of the Ministers. They say it was not.

It was reported yesterday that the B. and A. Commissioners had agreed upon the terms of a Treaty. They had not on Sunday when I saw Mr. Monroe. The B., as you may suppose, do not readily consent to a relaxation of the rule of 1756. It is said they may relax so far that the landing of colonial produce, securing the Duty, & re-shipping it in other bottoms, shall be considered as a termination of the voyage, and allow the Importer, or any other, to export it to Europe. They may insist upon a Duty being laid on the Exports. Entre nous, Mr. M. & Mr. P. asked me last week whether the Amern. Merchants would be willing to pay 2 or 2½ pr. cent. on the Export of Colonial Produce in case they could not otherwise agree with the B. Commrs.

Understanding from them that the Deduction of the Draw-back, which amounts to about 1 pr. cent. would not be made if Congress chose to discontinue it, I told them that I thought it would not be a material objection, as it would be a charge of only 1 or 1½ pr. ct. more than the produce now pays on Exportation.

Should they agree to the Duty, Congress will I suspect continue the Deduction in order to get as much as they can from the Merchants.

The India Trade may remain as fixed by Mr. Jay.

The impressment of Seamen & compensation (costs and Damages) for the detention of our Ships may rest in statu quo, or be reserved for future discussion—a dutch ad referendum.

The Blockade of the British Isles by Nap's Decrees will have no other effect than giving 4 or 5 pr. ct. to the British Under-writers.

If the British can venture to spare so many Troops, they will endeavour to take Spanish So. America. You may have to settle the Bound. of Louisiana with them. . . .

I am, Dr. Sir. your faithful Servt.,
S. WILLIAMS.

Aaron Burr's plot to establish an independent government west of the Alleghanies, to include a part or all of Mexico, was brought to a close by the action of General Wilkinson in New Orleans. He had been looked upon as one of the leaders and was cognizant of all the plans, but at the last moment, whether through fear or loyalty, he caused the arrest of Bollman and other agents of Burr. A writ of habeas corpus was sued out in the Superior Court, but General Wilkinson stated that he "had arrested them as a step towards the defense of the city, on a charge of misprision of treason," refused to give them up and sent them as prisoners to Washington. One of the lawyers, James Alexander, who had been instrumental in obtaining a writ of habeas corpus, by which one of the accused had been liberated, was arrested for the act and held as a prisoner.* Under what circum. stances, Mr. King was led to express an opinion on these high-handed measures, other than as a general disclaimer against them, does not appear. But among his papers, is found the article which follows, and which clearly shows his view of the outrages against personal liberty.

The baneful effects of Faction are in few cases more manifest than in the ease and safety with which the most important principles of a free government may be violated by the Idols of popular worship. That unprincipled and ambitious Demagogues should endeavour to stir up and alarm the prejudices of the People, for the purpose of destroying the reputation of their political competitors and advancing themselves to Stations of trust and honor, is what no man acquainted with the history of past times will be surprized at. But that these same men, after attaining the object of their immoral ambition, should openly dare to commit the very offences, which they had falsely imputed to their opponents, would seem to be incredible, did we not from day to day behold the proofs of the profligate inconsistency.

All may not, but many will, remember the criticisms and objections, the doubts, the anxiety and the fears expressed by the Antifederalists, *who now call themselves Republicans,* on the publication of the Constitution of the U. S. In this State, especially, the deepest solicitude was manifested lest by the creation of a federal city, a federal judiciary, a federal army and other federal powers, the civil Rights of the Citizens should be abridged. Great and unwearied exertions were made by the Federalists to answer these objections and remove these impediments to the adoption of the federal constitution, and as the spirit of Faction had not at that period acquired the ascendency over men's minds, which it now unhappily possesses, these exertions of the Federalists prevailed and the sober understanding of the American People approved and adopted the Constitution, which went into immediate operation under the auspices of its Framers and Friends. To soothe the mortified pride of the Antifederal Lead-

* Hildreth's *Hist. of U. S.* 2d Series, vol. ii., p. 612–13. Genl. Wilkinson's Affidavits *Annals of Congress,* 1806–7, p. 1013.

ers, to promote harmony amongst the States, sundry amendments of the Constitution in the nature of a Bill of Rights were proposed and afterwards adopted.

The 5th Article of these amendments declares " that no person shall be deprived of his liberty, without due process of Law."

The 4th Article declares that the persons of the Citizens shall be secure from unreasonable seizure ; and that a warrant of arrest shall not issue, but on probable cause and supported by an oath."

The 6th Article declares that in all criminal prosecutions, the accused shall enjoy the right of a speedy and public trial by an impartial jury of the State and district in which the crime shall have been committed, and shall have the assistance of counsel for his defence."

These provisions which were already established and recognized as law throughout the U. S., if not expressed in the new Constitution, were in no respect impaired by it ; and so long as the Government continued in the hands of the Federalists, these were like every other provision of the Constitution preserved inviolate.

The present chiefs and favorites of the People, by the aid of foreigners, imputed many errors to the federal administration, and amongst other false charges, ascribed to them a deliberate purpose to abridge, by the sedition Laws, the personal liberty of the Citizen. These charges united with others equally unjust excited jealousies and fears among the People, who in the end transferred the administration from the real friends of Liberty and their Country to the men who now so unworthily possess the Government.

It is earnestly desired that the eyes of the motley and stupid worshippers of Mr. Jefferson, if for a moment they can be turned from the Idol of their false adoration, may be fixed upon the late *Executive Proceedings*, in the arrest, imprisonment, transportation and severe secret military confinement of Alexander, Swarthout and Bolman ; proceedings of the Executive, unprecedented in the annals of a free country, that breaks down the tallest and strongest barriers of our Liberties, at the same time that it shews an ineffable contempt for the Constitution, the rights and the understanding of the Citizen, inasmuch as the same has passed at the very seat of Government and under the noses of the Representatives, and Judges of the nation.

Of right and according to the provisions of the Constitution, Alexander, Swarthout and Bolman, admitting even that they had committed Treason, could be arrested, tried and punished only in the district where the treason was committed. The Federal Town is a territory over which Congress have exclusive Jurisdiction ; its inhabitants are without political rights, being governed by laws, in the making of which they have no representation or influence. Alexander, Swarthout & Bolman committed no treason at Washington and are not liable to be carried from New Orleans to Washington for trial, for a crime committed at N. O. As well might the inhabitants of New York be taken up by the federal officer at Ft. Jay, put on board a Gun Boat and sent by sea to Baltimore and from thence to Washington, and be there tried for a breach of the Revenue Law, or any other offence against the U. S. The one is not a greater nor grosser violation of the personal Rights and Liberty of the Citizen than the other ; and any argument that would justify the one will justify the other ; none however can be offered to excuse, much less justify, either.

Instead of the persons (charged with treason in a vain, ridiculous nugatory military declaration) being arrested and proceeded against at N. Orleans, where the judiciary is completely competent and free from all suspicion of disloyalty, and where alone they can be lawfully tried, what has been the course, and what have been the sentiments and language of the Centinels of freedom on this occasion ? As nearly the same proceedings were adopted in all three cases, a statement of the case of Mr. Alexander, which is the last of the three, will be sufficient to furnish an adequate knowledge of them all. It is possible that in some immaterial circumstance there may be some inaccuracy, the business having been transacted with much secrecy and great pains taken to hide it from the public eye.

Mr. Alexander is a young man of very considerable talents, who, if not born, received his education in this City, and is known to many of its respectable inhabitants. Being here admitted to the Bar, he commenced his practice with reputation and would without doubt have arrived at eminence in his profession, had he continued to reside in this City ; from which he removed to N. O. soon after its cession to the U. S. There his talents and learning gave him distinction and he is ranked among the first lawyers who practice in the Courts of that District.

Genl. Wilkinson, without the slightest evidence of guilt, but with the view, as it would seem of removing this gentleman, who was known to be an able lawyer and whose principles would oblige him to offer his assistance to protect the civil rights of his fellow Citizens against the tyranny and oppression of the military, caused Mr. Alexander to be arrested, not by civil process, but by the military force acting under a vain, ridiculous, unprecedented and illegal military order, and thus having him in his custody transported him by sea, and in a course that carried him out of the limits of the country, to Baltimore, where by a military force, he was precluded from vindicating his rights by an appeal to the Laws, and from Baltimore secretly sent in military custody thro' the State of Maryland to Washington, and there, by authority derived from the President, confined in the Marine Barracks, guarded by a military force, and denied all intercourse and communication with the faithful friends of Liberty and law. While this outrageous scene was passing, an effort was made, and it is religiously believed at the instigation of the President, to pass an act to suspend the Habeas Corpus, not within the District of Orleans, not in the Western Country alone, but throughout the U. S.—a measure, had it passed, that would have put every man in the U. S., who is not ready to fall down and worship the Idol of Democracy, in the power of the Executive, which might by an order from the Secretary of War, or other automaton Minister, have seized any Citizen in any of the States, however virtuous, however innocent, transport him to Washington and there confine him in Barracks or Bastiles, without bail or mainprize—without communication with his friends, without any other of the supports of life, than those which were scantily afforded to the persecuted   or to the Mysterious Man in the Iron Mask.

How the Senate of the U. S. could have passed an Act which would have permitted such deeds of tyranny, is strange and incomprehensible. That body with all its weakness, meanness, and subserviency, contains men devoted to the freedom of their country and worthy of its highest confidence. The Bill failed in the H. of Reps., who in checking this act of tyranny, have atoned for much imbecility and folly that had before been exhibited.

By some means Mr. Chas. Lee, the late Attorney General had become acquainted with Mr. Alexander's situation, and went to confer with him in his dungeon ; but the myrmidons charged with his custody refused to admit the Minister of the Law to visit or speak with the prisoner, and insolently supported the denial at the point of the bayonet.   These facts were reported to the Supreme Court, and being about to become matter of investigation, a letter was despatched from the Sec'y of War, by whose direction may be guessed, directed to the Officer charged with the military custody of Mr. Alexander, and instructing him to carry Mr. Alexander before Mr. Justice Ducket, one of the Judges of the local court of the federal City.   This mandate was obeyed, and as the letter contained no charge against Mr. Alexander, instead of discharging Mr. Alexander, as it was his duty to have done, the complaisant Judge endorsed upon the letter that the officer had obeyed his orders ; whereupon the officer, well understanding his part, informed Mr. Alexander that since the Judge declined renewing or giving any orders concerning him, he would no longer be troubled with his custody at the Marine Barracks, and accordingly left Mr. Alexander once more a freeman.

The confinement of a citizen without due process of Law is false imprisonment.   Due process of Law in cases of imprisonment is a warrant in writing, under the hand and seal of a competent civil magistrate, expressing the cause of commitment, in order that the same may be examined into, if required, by a writ of Habeas Corpus.   In England by the 31 Chap. 2, C. 2, to send a prisoner to Scotland, Ireland, or beyond the Sea, is illegal ; and whosoever commits a person contrary to that Statute, is disabled from bearing any office, incurs the penalties of a premunire, and is incapable of receiving the King's pardon : and the person injured has his suit agt. the offender and all his aiders and abettors ; and shall recover treble costs, besides damages, which no jury shall assess at less than £500. sterling.

If Mr. Alexander does not pursue his gaolers and all their aiders, advisers, and abettors, he merits the scorn of his country in addition to all he has suffered.   He owes it to himself as a freeman, and what is more, he owes to liberty and his country the vindictive pursuit of his detested oppressors.   For, says the learned Blackstone, if once it were left in the power of any, the highest magistrate, to imprison arbitrarily whomever he or his officers thought proper, there would soon be an end of all other rights and immunities. Some have thought that unjust attacks even upon life, or property, at the arbitrary will of the magistrate, are less dangerous to the Commonwealth, than such as are made upon the personal liberty of the subject. To bereave a man of life, or by violence to confiscate his estate, without accusation or trial, would be so gross and notorious an act of despotism, as at once to convey the alarm of tyranny throughout the whole kingdom ; but confinement of the person, by secretly hurrying him to gaol, when his sufferings are unknown, or forgotten, is a less public, or a less striking and, therefore, a more dangerous engine of Arbitrary Movement.

It is evident that this paper must have been written during the discussion in the Senate and House of Representatives of an act to suspend the writ of habeas corpus for three months, probably to meet these cases, an act passed by the Senate in secret session, but rejected almost unanimously by the House. Messrs. Bollman and Swarthout were discharged by the Supreme Court on a writ of habeas corpus, and Mr. Alexander " without any opposition on the part of the government,"

This paper, therefore, properly belongs to the history of 1807—as these discussions arose during the early months of that year.[*]

* Hildreth Hist. of U. S., vol. ii., 2d Series, pp. 625–6.

APPENDIX I.

Although there are no records in. the way of letters or
diary of the time passed by Mr. King in Paris, there are
some notes which have been preserved and may be found
interesting. They are taken from Mr. King's Memorandum
Book, and are headed " BRIBERY IN POLITICS." He says:

Sir Jno. Dalrymple asserts that Louis 14, by Barillon, his
Ambassador in England, bribed Sidney, Russell, Hampden and
other illustrious Patriots of the Reign of Charles II. Mr. Fox
went from London to Paris in 1802, for the purpose as he avowed
of examining the Documents in the Scotch College (Barillon's
Correspondence) to wh. Sir John Dalrymple refers and on wh. he
grounds his assertions.

While at Paris he told me that he had examined the correspondence and was convinced that the Patriots did receive Barillon's money, and added that he thought them justifiable in doing
so. Charles II. wished war with France in hopes that this state
of the nation wd. better assist him in recovering the Prerogatives
lost in the civil war. The Patriots seeing his views opposed the
war and the King of Fr. did not wish it. In this state of things,
it was fair for Barillon to offer & them to take French money to
be used not for their private purposes, but applied in acquiring
an influence agt. a war with France. Mr. Fox declared that he
did not believe that a penny was applied to the private use of
the Patriots, but that the whole was employed in opposing the
views of the Crown, and the opposition, being patriotic, he
thought the receiving French money justifiable.   R. K.

In connection with this, and in corroboration of the received opinion that there was truth in the statements of

Dalrymple, there is an entry in Mr. King's Memorandum Book under date of Dec. 28, 1801, which relates to this, and also contains a statement of a somewhat similar circumstance in the War of the Revolution of the United States. It is headed:

CORRUPTION—SYDNEY AND BARILLON—Dec. 28, 1801.

Dined with Wilberforce—Mr. Otto, myself, with Mr. Wilberforce the whole party—Conversation Miscellaneous—Among topics, the Papers respecting the time of Charles I. & II. which are in the Scottish College Paris were mentioned. Dalrymple has given an account of some of these and particularly of Barillon's letters and of the money he paid to the great patriots of England. Mr. Wilberforce said Mr. Fox was employed in composing the history of that period and purposed going soon after the Definitive Treaty to Paris to examine these papers. I suggested some doubt of the truth of Dalrymple's account. Mr. Wilberforce said no doubt was entertained in Eng., that his report was a faithful one, but some persons doubted whether Barillon, the Fr. Ambassador, really paid the money to the persons to whom he charged it, thinking it more likely that he put it in his own pocket ; that for his own part he was disposed to believe that Sydney and the others did receive money from France, not for their private purposes, but to support their opposition to the Court, as the King certainly did procure money from abroad to enable himself to oppose them. Otto said he could entertain no doubt that such was the fact ; (addressing himself to me in a low voice as Mr. W. slipped into an adjoining room) even some of your patriots did the same thing. They applied to us (the Fr. Embassy in America) in this way—we can go on no farther without succour—our party will fail or lose ground unless supported, &c., and what, continued Otto, can a minister do in such circumstances ? he has but one course, he must give money, &c. I did not push the conversation any farther, intending to take a more convenient opportunity to renew it with Otto.

It does not appear that this conversation was renewed. But it was apparently deemed of credibility—for Mr. King, as he has several times said, had a high regard for the integrity and trustworthiness of Mr. Otto.

APPENDIX II.

INTERVIEW BETWEEN GALLATIN AND KING—1803.

Mr. Jefferson, writing on Aug. 1803, from Monticello to Mr Gallatin* says among other things:

I hope you will make every possible occasion of getting information from Mr. King as to the views and dispositions of England, and of satisfying him of the perfect friendship of this administration to that country. The impressment of our seamen, and the using our harbors as stations to sally out of and cruise on our own commerce, as well as on that of our friends, are points on which he can perhaps give useful advice.

Mr. Gallatin on Aug. 18, 1803, the same day, not in answer to the above,† writes to Mr. Jefferson, giving an account of an interview with Mr. King which shows that he was seeking such information as was asked for.

. . . Mr. King seems to think that he might have renewed the commercial treaty on conditions satisfactory to America. Great Britain has not made any approach of late on that subject ; he thinks the Government has not even thought on the limitation by which it will expire, and that Mr. Merry will have no instructions on the subject. He is of opinion that in the East Indies the want of a treaty will not place us on a worse footing ; that there is no danger to be apprehended on the subject of provisions being considered as contraband ; and that the improvement in the West India courts of admiralty will relieve us from many of the embarrassments experienced by our trade during the last war. The only ground on which he feels any apprehension is that of impressments ; and had he not been on the eve of his departure, he might, he thinks, have succeeded in making some arrangement ; the greatest obstacle to this resulted from the prejudices of Earl St. Vincent. Mr. King considers the present administration in England as the most favorable that has existed or can exist for the interests of the United States, but he does not rely much on their permanence ; the members who compose it are respected men of integrity, but have not the perfect confidence of the

* *Writings of Albert Gallatin*, by Henry Adams, vol. i., p. 139.
† *Ibid*, vol. i., 140–143.

people, nor particularly of London ; their abilities being considered as unequal to the crisis. Mr. King himself, speaking of them, whilst conversing of the British manifesto, called them "little men." He asked me who was to be his successor ; I answered I presumed either Mr. Livingston or Mr. Monroe. He said that Mr. L. would do very well, his deafness excepted, which was a strong objection. His British Majesty asked him twice who would be sent, and expressed satisfaction in case Mr. L. were the man ; but when he saw Mr. Monroe's name announced in the newspapers for the mission, he inquired particularly of his character and asked Mr. King whether he had not been opposed to him in politics. Upon being answered that those differences of politics had only been shades of opinion and that Mr. Monroe was a man of great probity and integrity, "Well, well, if he is an honest man he will do very well," was the reply ; and Mr. Hammond assured afterwards Mr. K. that Mr. M., if appointed, would be perfectly received. Yet Mr. K. seems to apprehend that there is still some *prevention* which may render his situation less comfortable and his services less useful than those of another person.

I repeated to him verbatim the commercial article of the treaty, expressed my wish that it had been communicated to him when he made his communication to the British government, and asked whether he thought that the article could possibly create any difficulty. He answered, without the least hesitation, that it could not, that it was perfectly defensible, must be considered as part of the purchase money, and expressed his full conviction that the British government would not cavil at it. He observed that Messrs. Livingston & Monroe had in their letter to him used the word "claim" to which, in his letters to Lord Hawksbury, he had substituted the word "right." I was almost tempted to believe from his conversation that Mr. L. had communicated the treaty to him. . . .

On the subject of Louisiana generally, Mr. King's opinions both as relating to New Orleans and the upper Country west of the Mississippi, seem to coincide with yours. He hinted, however, that more advantageous terms might have been obtained,* and

---

* Mr. Cutter in a letter to Dr. Torrey, Washington, Oct. 31, 1803, says " The purchase of Louisiana may prove a good thing, and it may be attended

openly said that if our ministers did not think it safe to note the object by insisting on a reduction of the price, they had it at least in their power to present the mode of payment ; that money might have been raised in England on much more advantageous terms if the mode had been left open to us ; that Cazenove who was Talleyrand's privy counsel and financier must have suggested the species of stock which was adopted, &c. He then asked me what could have been the reason which induced our ministers to agree to make an immediate cash payment for the American debts, instead of paying them in stock or more convenient instalments, as the creditors would have been perfectly satisfied to be paid that way, and *that* object at least did not seem to be one on which the French government would insist. I told him that I really could not tell, for I knew that mode or some similar one had been contemplated by the administration, and I had not understood that any explanation on that subject had been received from our ministers. On my mentioning that the French Cabinet seemed to have believed that the question of peace or war was in their power, and that our ministers being naturally under a similar impression, might have been induced to yield to more unfavorable terms than if they had contemplated war as certain, he observed that on the arrival of every messenger from France the correspondence of Lord Whitworth and Mr. Talleyrand had been communicated to him by the British Ministry, and that by the return of every messenger he had communicated its substance to Mr. Livingston, as well as his opinion of the certainty of war. We both concluded our conversation on that subject, by agreeing that Mr. Livingston's precipitancy had been prejudicial to the United States. And he observed that Florida must necessarily fall into our hands, and that he hoped too much impatience would not be evinced on that subject.

Mr. King lent me the rescript of the Emperor of Russia offering his mediation. It is too long to be transcribed. Although he says in one place, " qu'il avait déjà chargé une fois son ministre de communiquer ses sentiments au Gouvernement Fran-

with very serious evils. I consider the price much too high, and find that it is Mr. King's opinion (our late minister at London) that it might have been obtained for a much less price."—ED.

çais sur la nécessité qu'il y aurait de faire diverses causes d' inquiétude, qui agitaint les Cabinets de l' Europe," I should think from the whole tone of that document, that he will not approve the grounds on which England has placed the renewal of the war.

APPENDIX III.

This letter would have had a better place among those of its date, but it contains a number of interesting details, given by Mrs. King, which to her family, at least, will be a valuable contribution showing the happy relations of the home life.

MARY KING TO CHARLES KING, HARROW, ENGLAND.

BROADWAY, NEW YORK, December 6, 1803.

MY DEAR CHARLES :

We yesterday had the pleasure of receiving John's letter of 17th Sept. written, as I suppose, to come by Mr. Merry, but which was probably too late for him and was forwarded by the October Packet. I observe that you are again at Harrow and continue as well pleased as ever with Dr. & Mr. H. Drury's treatment. I hope nothing will occur to interrupt this harmony. Pray tell me candidly how you were pleased with the Abbé, and whether you think you gained anything while there ; by the conclusion of the approaching holidays, I expect you will be able to speak, if not write, French. We often wish that it was among the list of possibilities for you to pass the Christmas holidays with us, and return again to Harrow. We shall feel your absence on this occasion very sensibly, as I may add we do on every other. Often indeed in my rambles do I miss the beau, who used so patiently and willingly accompany me in my long walks to Kensington Garden &c. It is not much the fashion for ladies to walk here, and I cause great astonishment in walking so much and alone. Pug sometimes goes with me, but thro' the summer, it interfered so much with his school hours, and I was compelled to walk alone or stay at home. I don't find that your Papa's desire of moving has increased much. On an average twelve out of the sixteen hours he is up, are generally passed upon his chair ; as his knee has given him no trouble, I have advised his using it a little more, and occasionally he has walked for an hour or two, but not often. He has try'd it more while we were moving than for a long time before. I believe I mentioned to you that we had taken Mr. Livingston's house in Broadway, where we removed last Monday week, and are just beginning to feel ourselves a little at home.

Our City again enjoys good health ; the frost, as usual, put an end to yellow fever ; and I wish we could flatter ourselves with the hope that it would never return. The weather for the last two months has been uncommonly fine, and the sun and un-clouded sky in the month of November, were rather a novelty to me, who from so long an absence had almost forgotten its appearance : the Fall in our country is undoubtedly the finest season, and more delightful weather could not be experienced in any climate than we have enjoyed and are still enjoying at this moment ; it is more like May than December ; very little frost and not a flake of snow has yet fallen. Edward has been long anticipating the pleasure of a ride in a Sleigh ; for as yet he has no idea of what it is. We have had the supreme felicity of a visit from Jerome Bonaparte—that is our City—for myself I have not had the satisfaction of a single peep at him ; and he was pleased to express great delight at the attention he received here ; so much so that he intended to make it his residence for the winter ; but yesterday I understood he had embarked in one of our Merchantmen bound to France.

Whenever you hear from James pray communicate it to us, for I see no other chance of ever receiving any intelligence from him ; what the cause is I cannot imagine. Mr. & Mrs. Payne are gone to pass the winter at Washington, they did us the favor of staying two nights with us in the country on their way thither. She is well looking and agreeable and he seems perfectly happy. The lady was a widow & had a daughter by her first marriage ; she is about five or six years old and a more interesting child I never met with. Mrs. Gore's natural fondness is such for chil-dren, that I am sure she will attach herself strongly to this little girl.

I have written to Mrs. Gore repeatedly but have not received one line from her since July. I intended writing again by this

Packet, but I find I shall not have time ; you must therefore offer her our most sincere remembrances and best wishes for the re-establishment of her health, which with some concern we learned had been interrupted by a violent attack of Influenza. You cannot confer a greater obligation on me than to evince by a scrupulous attention to all Mrs. Gore's requests, a strong sense of her maternal kindness ; for in my absence it must be considered as such.

We had thoughts of sending you some apples and cranberries ; but on reflection your Papa thinks the latter may be bought in Oxford Street for less money than the duty and Custom House fees would amount to ; and the great uncertainty of the former reaching you good for anything, in addition to the expense alluded to above, has prevented our fulfilling that intention. You must therefore endeavor to console yourselves with the golden pippin instead of those from Newtown.

Frederick, or little Fitty as he calls himself, has become a great chatterbox ; every word he hears, he repeats and he really speaks much plainer now than Edward did at three years old. I am sure you would give one week's allowance to have a kiss of the blessed one ; regularly night and morning he blesses his Uncle and Aunt Gore with his dear brothers. Edward talks of finishing this letter ; but least he should not, begs to join us in the most affectionate remembrances to you & John.

Always unfeignedly your M. K.

APPENDIX IV.

By an oversight the following letter has been left out of its proper position on page 352. It is important as showing that Mr. King positively declined to be a candidate for the office of Governor of New York.

R. KING TO A. HAMILTON.

NEW YORK, March 1, 1804.

DEAR SIR :

Since my letter of the 24th (February) I have received yours of the same date ; and after maturely reflecting upon the subject, and consulting one or two of our friends here, I am confirmed in the sentiment that I ought not to consent to be a candidate for the Governorship, should the federalists think of offering me.

This being my determination, it is right that I should apprize you of it, in order that our friends may not make an offer which I should be obliged to decline.

If you consider to what the office of Governor has been curtailed, and what in the actual state of parties must be his condition, if a man of virtue and independence, I cannot but persuade myself that you will see insuperable objections to my consenting to be thus disposed of.

With sentiments of Regard, &c.,

RUFUS KING.

APPENDIX V.

LOUISIANA.

RIGHTS UNDER THE CONVENTION OF PURCHASE.

In the year 168– Monsr. La Salle coming from Canada embarked at the confluence of the Illinois & the Mississippi, and descended the latter River to its mouth. In virtue of this voyage a large tract of Country on each side of the Mississippi was claimed and afterwards possessed by France under the name of Louisiana. The villages of St. Louis & St. Genevieve on the west bank, and Kaskaskia & Kahoka on the east bank of the Mississippi were planted in the close of the 17th Century. In lower Louisiana, upon the sea coast & its vicinity, French posts & settlements were early established as far east as the Apalachicola, and as far west as Natchitoches. The boundary between Florida & Louisiana was for a series of years matter of controversy between France & Spain, but is understood to have been settled between them about the year 1748, by agreeing upon the River Perdido & a line from its source to the Alleghany Mountains.

Such was the State of Possessions & claims respecting Louisiana at the commencement of the 7 years war ; In the preliminaries at the conclusion of which, by the Treaty of 1763, France &

Spain ceded & guaranteed to England all the Territories belonging and claimed by them respectively upon the continent of
Amer. & East of the Mississippi ; so that in addition to Canada
& its Dependencies—a subject distinct from that of the present
investigation—France ceded to Eng. all that part of Louisiana
wh. was on the East side of the Mississippi (the City and Island
of New Orleans excepted) and Spain in like manner ceded to
Eng. Florida.   Whatever therefore were the Rights of France
and Spain in relation to these Territories, and whatever may
have been their boundaries, England thenceforth became the
owner & possessor of the whole country (the City and Island
of N. O., East of the Mississippi excepted).   But on the day of
the date of the Preliminaries, Nov. 3, 1762, by which France
ceded East Louisiana to Eng., she also by another Act ceded the
whole country of Louisiana, together with N. O. & the Island in
wh. the City is placed to Spain.   By turning to the Preliminary
Treaty of 1762 between F., S., & G., it will be seen that these
cessions to England are correctly stated, and by reading the
King of Fr.'s, letter dated April 21, 1764, to Mr. D'Abadie, his
Director Genl. & Commandant in Louisiana, it will also be found
that the cession to Spain is also correctly stated.   This letter will
be found in the Annual Register Vol. 8., p. 271.

  Suffice it to observe in this place, that the Territories ceded to
England and to Spain belonged to France on the 3 of Nov. 1762,
the day of both cessions.   All Louisiana was owned & possessed
by France ; by two acts of the same date, and to each of which
Spain was a party, France divided Louisiana, ceding and guarantying the Eastern Part thereof clearly & distinctly to England,
and the Western Part thereof, including the city & Isl. of N. O.
to Spain.   As Fr. owned the whole of Louisiana, if she conveyed
& with the privity of Spain too, a part thereof by metes and
bounds to Engd., however vague and comprehensive the Terms
may have been by which she at the same time conveyed
Louisiana to Spain, France could not convey nor could Spain
acquire more than the Residue of Louisiana, after deducting
what was contemporaneously conveyed to England.   As this conclusion seems too plain to require the production of authorities
or further illustration, I pass on.   The ceded Territories upon
the East side of the Miss. were afterwards taken possession of by

England. The " Special Act " by wh. West Louisiana was ceded to France has never been published. According to the letter from the K. of Fr. to Mr. D'Abadie, a copy of this Instrument was sent to N. O. with orders that it sho. be there enregistered. Whether this was done, and whether the Record still remains, are matters concerning wh. we have no information ; tho' doubtless our Govt. must have ascertained these facts.

By referring to Hutchins' Historical Narrative and topographical Description of Louisiana & West Florida, pub. at Phila. in 1783, as well as to an extraordinary Publication, entitled Memoire Historique & politique sur La Louisiane, (printed at Paris in the year 1802, when France had prepared an Expedn. to take Possession of Louisiana) it will appear that there was something unusual, not to say mysterious, in the delays as well as in the manner in which Spain took possession of Louisiana, and one might from these circumstances, as well as from the want of publicity of the Act of Cession, be lead to entertain Doubts, as it appears from Mr. H's. Memoire, that the Inhabitants of Louisiana did, concerning the Date as well as the authenticity of this Act of Cession.

Soon after the Treaty of Peace in 1763, and while France still remained in possession of New Orleans, and West Louisiana, England took possession of all the French Posts upon the East side of the Mississippi, as also of the Span. Posts in Florida. It was in the Summer of 1763, that East Louisiana & Florida were delivered up by France and Spain to England, but it was not until Genl. O'Reilley's arrival with 4m. Spanish Troops at N. O. July 23 1769, that N. O. and Louisiana were taken possession of by Spain ; so that N. O. and W. Louisiana remained 6 years in the possession of France after East Louisiana & Florida had been delivered up to & possessed by England. These facts are established by Hutchins' Narrative, as well as by other authentic publications.

By the Proc. of Oct. 7, 1762, England established two Provinces by the name of E. & W. Florida, Georgia being the northern Limits of E. Florida & the 31st degree of lat. the Northern Limits of W. Florida, and the Apalachicola River the division line between them. It may aid the purpose of this Disquisition to observe that the Territory of West Florida consisted of that part of Louisiana, lying south of the 32° of Lat. and between the Mississippi and the waters east of the Island of N. Orleans the West, and the River Perdido and a line from its head to the Allegany on the east, together with that part of Spanish Florida lying between the last mentioned line and the River Apalachicola. It may further assist in this Elucidation to remark that the Proc. of Oct. 7, 1763, above referred to, restrained the Colonies from granting any part of the lands lying upon the East bank of the Mississippi and to the North of W. Florida—the same being reserved with other lands for the future disposition *of the Crown.*

During the American War, Eng. being in possession of the Floridas, Gen. Guloeg the Span. Govr. of Louisiana conquered the Province of W. Florida, and at the conclusion of that War, the Floridas were ceded by Engl. to Spain, & the Mississippi on the West & the Floridas on the S. were made the boundaries of the U. S.

It should be here remarked that the Territory on the East bank of the Mississippi, once included in Louisiana, ceased, after its cession to Eng., to be known or described by that name. From that Period New Orleans & the Territory west of the Mississippi have been called and known as Louisiana; and no Diplomatic or other public act has from that date given the name of Louisiana to any portion of the Territory ceded by Fr. & Sp. to Eng. by the Treaty of 1763; but on the contrary that since the year 1763, an unbroken series of diplomatic and other public Acts, comprehending every public Act of the U. S., which has had relation to the subject, have uniformly ascribed to Louisiana the eastern Boundary assigned to it by the Treaty of 1763, and with equal uniformity have recognized & described the adjacent Territory eàst of that Boundary by other names. By the 2nd Article of the Treaty between Sp. & the U. S. it is provided "that the Southern Boundy. of the U. S., which divides yr. Territory from *the Span. Colonies of E. & W. Florida* shall be a line beginning at the River Mississippi at the 31st degree of No. Lat. &c. The 5th Art. again speaks of the boundaries of *the two Floridas.* Furthermore, It is understood (tho' we cannot state our information as completely authentic) that the Govt. of the Floridas has been confided to the Govr. of Cuba and not to the Gov. of Louisiana; so that not only in name but local Govt., the Floridas have been maintained as a Territory distinct from that of Louisiana.

How far the Laws of the U. S. may have at any time taken notice of or mentioned the Floridas, we have not examined; but there is reason to believe that the Instructions & Acts of the Old Congress, as well as the Instructions and other Acts of the President of the U. S., for a series of years past, have described the Territory south of the southern Boundary of the U. S. as E. & W. Florida. In a Memoir respecting Louisiana drawn up by Chañ Livingston, printed in the French language, and presented to the French Govt., while he was our Minister at Paris, he observes p. 16, " la possession de la Louisiane est néanmoins tres-importante pour la France, si elle en tire le seul parti que la saine politique semble lui dicter. Je parle de la Louisiane propre, dans laquelle jè ne comprends point les Florides, parceque je pense qu' elles ne font pas partie de la Cession." *

By the Treaty of 1763 between E. F. & Sp., the navigation of the River Mississippi from its source to the ocean was declared common to England and France—by the Treaty of Peace between England & the U. S. the navigation of the River Miss. was also declared common to Eng. & the U. S.; but as by the Treaty of 1783, between England & Spain, the former ceded to the latter East & West Florida, France having before ceded Louisiana to Spain, She became mistress of both banks of the Mississippi, and asserted a Right of closing its mouth against the American navigation. It is needless to do more than merely to recall this subject, to the public Recollections, and to add that the Treaty of 1783 between the U. S. and Spain removed this obstruction & secured to the U. S. the free navigation of the Mississippi, together with a Right of Deposit at New Orleans for 3 years, and afterwards either there or elsewhere on the Banks of the Mississippi.

At the Expiration of the Term of Deposit at N. O., new difficulties arose on that subject & negotiations respecting it were confided to Mr. C. P., the Amer. Minister at Madrid. While the

---

* " The possession of Louisiana is nevertheless very important to France, if she pursues respecting it the only course which a wise policy appears to suggest to her. I speak of Louisiana proper, in which I do not comprehend the Floridas, because I think they make no part of the Cession."

Point remained undetermined, Sp. ceded back to Fr. Louisiana, including the City & Island of N. O ; and Fr. in the beginning of 1802 prepared an Expedition to take possession of the Country. Negotiations were now transferred from Madrid to Paris, and Mr. Monroe was joined to Chancellor Livingston for the purpose of purchasing the City & Island of N. O. This venture was terminated by the cession of Louisiana to the U. S. ; and the decision of the question whether any part of the Territory ceded by France & Spain to Eng. by the Treaty of 1763, was ceded by Fr. to the U. S. by the Convention of 1802, must determine the validity of our claim to West Florida, and the justice of the present proceedings to occupy that Country as the Property of the U. S.

To determine this Question, we must refer to the Act of cession from Fr. to the U. S. ; which again refers us, not to the Act of Cession of Spain to France, which is not communicated to us, but to a paragraph of that Act stated to be dated Oct. 1, 1800, by which Spain retrocedes, or cedes back again to Fr. Louisiana " with the same extent that it then had in the hands of Spain, and that it had when France possessed it, and such as it should be after (pursuant) the Treaties subsequently entered into between Spain and other States."

The description of Limits is a triple one, and in order to give to it a just and definite interpretation, the several parts must be reconciled ; for it is wholly *inadmissible* that the members of the Description of Limits are irreconcilable, or in other words, that the extent of one is greater than that of another. This would be to assert that Louisiana had two limits, the one greater than the other, which would be absurd ; as it would be to assert that a Territory may be greater or less than it actually is. Three points are then to be ascertained and reconciled.

1. What were the Limits of Louisiana in the hands of Spain in Oct. 1800 ?

2. What were its Limits when in the hands of France ?

3. What ought to be its limits pursuant to Treaties between Spain and other States after it became her Property ?

It has been already stated that before the year 1763 Louisiana comprehended a large Territory on the east Bank of the Mississippi, extending from its mouth to the Illinois Country inclusive & belonged to Fr—by that Treaty, this part of Louisiana, including the Territory of W. Florida, was separated from it & ceded by Fr. to Eng. ; contemporaneously with this Cession, Fr. ceded Louisiana including the City & Island of N. O. to Spain : taking these two Acts of Cession together—wh. we are bound by the maxims of Construction to do, both having relation to one subject, being of like date and the same parties—it is manifest that the Eastern Boundary of Louisiana is established to be the River of the Mississippi from its source to the Ocean. Louisiana thus defined upon its Eastern Boundary, altho' the Act of its Cession to Spain bears the date of Nov. 3, 1762, remained in the possession and under the Govr. of France almost 7 years afterwards, Count O'Reilley not having arrived until July 1769. At this epoch Louisiana thus bounded upon the Mississippi was taken possession of and passed under the Govt. of Spain—the adjacent Territory to the East thereof being at that time in the possession & under the Govt. of Eng., and the southern part thereof having been included within the British province of W. Fl. This State of possession & of Names continued until the American War, in the course whereof Spain conquered W. Florida, and by the Treaty of Peace in 1783, England ceded East & W. Florida to Spain, the Territory to the Northward thereof and adjacent to the Mississippi, having been ceded by Eng. to the U. S.

Spain took possession of East & W. Florida in the year   , and instead of incorporating them or any part of either of them with Louisiana, placed them both under the Havannah. For this Fact we refer to a Document in the possn. of our Govt.—a letter from the Spanish Minr. Cevallos to Messrs. Monroe & Pinckney. This Fact is moreover acquired from other sources of information, as well as from the general Notoriety of the Measure. If W. Florida has at no time since its cession by England to Spain been reunited to Louisiana—as must be the fact, inasmuch as it has been placed under a difft. Govt. and preserved its new name —it follows that at the date of its retrocession to Fr. Spain possessed it with the same Limits which it had when she first acquired it—that is to say, with the Limits assigned to it by the Treaty of 1763—and consequently with the exclusion of W. Florida.

The second clause furthermore provides that the Limits of Louisiana shall also be the same as it had when possessed by France. Now it has been shown that Louisiana while in the possession of France had different Limits before the Treaty of 1763 —Louisiana covered both Banks of the Mississippi, after that Treaty it contained nothing except the City Island of N. O. upon its eastern Bank. France, as has also been shown, possessed & governed Louisiana after as well as before the cession of the East Bank to England.

As no particular period in the possession of France is named, according to the Rules of Interpretation in such cases, that time of possession must be adopted, by which the two clauses may be reconciled. Now as we have shown that the Mississippi formed the Eastern Limits of Louisiana at the time of its retrocession by France after the Treaty of 1763, it accords with the Rules of sound Construction to take this period of the French Possession as that referred to in the Act of Cession. By doing so we reconcile the two clauses ; whereas by adopting a Period antecedent to the Treaty of 1763, when both Banks of the Mississippi were included in Louisiana, we not only render the two clauses inconsistent, but moreover establish a construction by wh. Spain cedes to Fr. what does not belong to her, but to the U. S. ; for the Kaskaskias & Kahokia, with the Eastern Bank of the Miss. from the highest of these Villages to the southern Boundary of the U. S. were indisputably within the Limits of Louisiana before the Treaty of 1763—and as indisputably ceded by Fr. to England & by England to the U. S. Such a construction would be odious ; since we are not at liberty to suppose that one Nation can grant what belongs to another. Furthermore the Treaty cedes with the same Limits as Louisiana actually had in the hands of Spain, and also with the same Limits it had when possessed by France ; now, if the Limits are to be in both cases the same, one cannot be greater than the other ; this would be to contend that equal quantities could be unequal, which is absurd.

Having given what we have seen to be the just Construction of the 1 & 2 clauses of this article, we proceed to examine the Import of the 3d clause. The Limits are to be as they ought to be according to the subseqt. Treaties between Spain & other Powers, France possessed Louisiana till 1769—the subsequent Treaties are the Treaties of 1783 between Sp. and England and of 1795 between Spain & the U. S. By the Treaty of 1785 Spain acquired W F. : to be as they ought to be according to that

Treaty W F. cannot be included. By the Treaty of 1795 the
W. Limits of the U S. are fixed, and the Northern Boundary of
W. Florida : to be as they ought to be according to this Treaty
W. Florida is in like manner excluded, both Treaties naming and
deciding upon W. Florida as a Territory distinct from Louisiana.
Then as the Treaty of 1801 did not affect the Rights of the U. S.
acquired under the Treaty of 1795, in like manner it would not
affect the Rights of Spain acquired under the Treaty of 1803.

APPENDIX VI.

LOUISIANA.

VALUE OF THE ACQUISITION & EFFECT ON THE
POLITICAL UNION.

Nations are not always sensible of those changes which in some
sort control and fix their destiny : indeed these consequences are
rarely foreseen or understood, for so limited and imperfect is the
understanding of even the most enlightened men that it is not
always easy for them to distinguish events of ordinary import
from those which overrule and decide the character and fortunes
of States. Notwithstanding we live in perilous times, and are
almost indifft. witnesses of the most extraordinary & important
changes in human affairs, we cannot be wholly inattentive to
what immediately regards our own immediate interest. Situation
as well as the Policy adopted by our Govt. clothe with indifference the Politics of Europe, but we all possess a lively regard and
vigilant attention to what concerns our own country.

We have recently been informed from the seat of Govt. that a
Treaty has been concluded with France, by which not only New-
Orleans but all Louisiana, as ceded by Spain to France, has been
ceded to us. This information is. of greater significance than
seems to be commonly imagined. The entire and exclusive
control over the navigation of the Missi. is indispensable to our
political union ; a treaty which secures this great object is therefore justly regarded with favour. It is proposed to examine the
merits of the opposite opinions, which have been entertained

concerning the best mode of attaining this End.   Neither is it of importance, in respect to the object of this paper, to inquire whether the treaty wh. has been concluded, has been brought about pursuant to the preconceived views and instruction given to the negotiators, nor whether it may not have been owing almost exclusively to a state of things which could not have been foreseen, and which is altogether foreign and independent of the views of our own Cabinet.

Laying these inquiries wholly aside, it is of importance to look at the acquisition we have made and to consider at the outset its extent, its use, and its probable effect upon our politi. union.

1st. The newly acquired Territory, with the exception of the Island of N. O., is wholly on the west side of the Miss. & is bounded southerly by the Gulph of Mexico, easterly by the Miss. in its whole length, and northerly and westwardly by unascertained lines, separating Louisiana from Canada in the north and the Spanish Territories to the west.

The two Floridas bounded northwardly by the southern line of the U. S. and eastwardly and southwardly by the Ocean, and westwardly by the Miss. & the Lakes Maurepas & Ponchartrain, were never included in Louisiana, were not ceded with it to France and still remain Provinces of Spain.   As we have now added Louisiana to our Territories, the Floridas are now surrounded by us & the ocean on every side.   The Region west of the Miss., which has been claimed as within Louisiana is probably as considerable as the whole of the U. S. and is reported to be superior in soil & climate to the country East of the Miss.

2nd. The object we desired and were bound to acquire in order to maintain the Union of our Country, was the control over the mouth of the Miss. ; in other words, we wanted the Dominion of N. Orleans.   Without this the people living on our Western waters must have been under the control of the Masters of New Orleans, and to avoid greater difficulties might have been obliged to withdraw from our Union & become subjects to another Power.   If New Orleans and the Floridas had been acquired and nothing more, this object would have been attained : indeed the acquisition of N. Orleans wd. have been sufficient, for the Floridas would have soon followed, and, without trouble or expense, fallen into our hands.   It was· not Territory for the

sake of Territory, wh. we wanted ; New Orleans in this respect
is of small consequence, but as the Nation, wh. must possess the
Domin. over the trade and Navigation of the Miss., its acquisition by us was indispensable. At a future day the Floridas,
and especially W. Florida which commands the mouths of several Rivers ascending far within the limits of the U. S., wd. have
become necessary additions to our Territory. At present the
acquisition was not wanted, and before it wd. be, Events will
inevitably occur wh. must change entirely the state of the American Continental Colonies, and wh. would naturally unite the
Floridas to our Territories. The inference from this remark is
that New Orleans alone, or at the most New Orleans and the
Floridas were all we required to give us the control over the
Trade and Navign. of the Miss. But we have all Louisiana in
addn. What is the value or advantage of this acquisition, to
what use shall we apply it, may it not prove pernicious instead of
beneficial?

The Region is extensive and possesses properties wh. may render it more inviting to settlers than the country within our former
limits. Will you open land offices & sell it or any part of it, will
you lay it out in new States, will you sell only to yr. own Citizens, or only to Foreigners, or indifferently to both, will you
divide the Country into Departments, and appt. indt. Superin-
tendents and trading houses, will you place Garrisons there to
protect the settlements wh. have been made since the time of
Louis, the XIV, will you carry on indian wars with tribes whose
names and numbers you are yet unacquainted, will you in this
respect do what neither the Conquerors of Mexico, nor their Posterity have yet been able to do, reduce to submission the Sav-
ages within Louisiana, who for more than two Centuries have
maintained a war with the Spaniards? Or will you by law prohibit the migration to and settlement of the People beyond the
Miss. : are you willing to do so, and if so, will you (be) able to
adhere to this System? Will you post a cordon of Troops upon
the Bks. of the River with orders to stop emigration and to
remove the settlers who shall pass?

It is true that the Proprietors of new Lands in every part of
the Union may be in favour of this Prohibition, as the opening
of new and better Lands West of the Miss., and in the vicinity

of the Spanish mines, may depreciate the Lands which wd. otherwise be sold and settled within the U. S.

But you encourage emigration, and invite the unhappy of other countries to fly hither for repose. Will they be content with these prohibitory laws, operating in favor of the few ; will not these be joined by others whose voices may be as loud as those of the landholders, & will not the spirit of speculation, to which neither lands nor seas afford limits, be awakened to fix itself upon this Western region ? In short so long as this Region belongs to us, shall we not be engaged in a perpetual conflict concerning its defense or its settlement ?

The Territory is of value for settlement or solitude, or we ought not to possess it. Of what value can it be as a solitude ? As long as it is our Territory we can prevent its settlement, if deemed advisable : if it be of no worth to settle, it is an affair of importance that we can prevent its settlement by others. If the country be such as it is represented, either France or England might plant colonies there deriving the greater part of the settlers out of the U. S. Our population would not only be drawn away but it wd. contribute to raise up a dangerous Rival on our Borders. Two remarks may be made by way of reply : first no European Nation will long maintain a Colony on the Continent of America ; were it necessary to adduce the grounds of this assertion, they could be readily exhibited.

2nd. Were it otherwise, no colony can be planted upon the Waters of the Miss. wh. wd. not be controlled by the Power commanding the mouth of the River. The same embarrassment wh. we lately experienced wd. be felt by any such colony wh. would bear the same relation to the Power, which should be Master of N. Orleans, that our Western states wd. have borne towards France had she prosecuted her Louisiana colony.

The result is that little or no danger could have been apprehended from the colonization of Louisiana by any for. Power, the U. S. being Masters of New Orleans, and consequently that the Dominion of the Country, for the purpose of preventing its settlement, is of no value.

But why should we not settle the country ? A single or simple Govn. can exist only over a confined Territory ; but our federal system may suit extensive and remote Regions. The experiment has already combined distant Territories and may unite regions still more distant ; who can mark the limits of the federal system ? Or say it may not be carried far beyond any notions that we have entertained in reference to political associations of a character materially different ?

This Enquiry opens too wide a range for present discussion. Suffice it to remark that Experience alone is the safe guide in human affairs and wanting that, if want we do, prudence should restrain us from rash experiments. A little common sense and common experience will be our best monitors. These admonish us that we have already a sufficiently extensive Empire ; our new settlements have been created out of the Resources of the old, as well as protected and defended by their power. Perhaps we have seen the worst of Indian wars and those Burthens unavoidably incident to these remote and detached settlements— nurtured by the old States, the new ones begin to taste the blessings of order and Govt., and are growing willing, as well as able, to contribute to their support : property is acquiring a fixed and reasonable value, founded upon the neutrality of supply and demand. But if in this promising state of things you throw open the acquired Territory of Louisiana, and thereby invite to its settlement, the scene is changed ; new lands throughout the U. S. will become of little value ; those which have been sold to settlers will be given up & never paid for, and the Purchasers will, from a spirit that has shewn itself from the earliest settlement of the Country, march westward in pursuit of Regions better than those they leave behind or pass over. Is this no injury to the present landholders, will this work no change in our social condition ?

APPENDIX VII.

CESSION OF LOUISIANA.

THE PRICE, MERITS OF NEGOTIATING MINISTERS, AND POLICY OF PURCHASE.

Certain reflexions are suggested by the temper with wh. the Country has received the information of the Cession of Louisiana to the U. S., a measure that in no point of view in which it may be considered, can be regarded as indifferent. The Public seems to have stopped short of the most import. considn. in relation to the cession and to have employed itself with inquiries respecting the Price of the Cession, the respective merits of the Ministers employed to effect it and the Policy of the Govt. in resorting to negotiation in preference to another course that was recommended. These points tho' of secondary consequence deserve examination, each of them with a reference to the avowed Principles of our Executive. Beginning with the last,

It is the natural result of a plan, having regard to the existing state and probable course of affairs, which ought to decide its merits. The interposition of a cause, wholly unforseen, which operates favorably, adds no merit to the plan, any more than the like cause operating unfavorably wd. detract from it. The Peace of Europe had been recently concluded when Mr. Monroe's mission was projected, and it may with confidence be asserted that no expectation was entertained either here or abroad, that it wd. be so soon interrupted. On the contrary it is known that the whole scope of the Instructions was founded upon the presumed continuance of Peace in Europe and the opinion that France thus at peace, our Envoys wd. be able to affect the Relinquishment of the Project of colonizing Louisiana, and the cession of New Orleans and the Floridas to us.

The question of the merits of the Project being therefore on this point, wd. or wd. not the Envoys have obtained the Relinquishment of the Expedition and the cession of New Orleans & the Floridas, had the peace between Fr. & Eng. continued ; in other words, would the Expedition which was about sailing from Holland to Louisiana have remained in Port, had not the fear of the Eng. fleet kept it there.

As some criterion to form a right Judgment on this point we may be assured that the mission of Mr. Monroe was known in France several months before his arrival there ; the Despatches of Mr. Pynchon have seasonably and fully apprised his Govt. of its object as well as of the means by which it was expected to be attained ; that reiterated and vigourous remonstrances agt. the Expedition were made by our Ambassador, Mr. Livingston, before Mr. M.'s arrival ; that the memorials and memorialists were alike disregarded, and equally so in any former missions to France, that the idea of selling Louisiana to the U. S. was treated with ridicule and contempt and likened to what was termed the base conduct of Charles the 2nd who sold Dunkirk to France ; that the Expedition was hurried on, Mr. Livingston was plainly told that it wd. proceed and that in regard to our claims of a Deposit at N. O., Bernadotte wd. be immediately despatched as Envoy to Washington ; and that, as soon as the Prefect of Louisiana and the Envoy had reached their posts, made the requisite Enquiries on the spot respecting our claims, and sent their Report to Paris, an answer would be given to us ; and until the war with Engd. became inevitable no single circumstance occurred to afford the slightest ground of hope that France would listen for a moment to the Proposal of our Envoy.

Upon these facts all impartial men must perceive that had peace continued, the mission would have totally failed, and that the relinquishment of the French Expedition to Louisiana and its cession to us, is solely to be ascribed to the war with England.

In regard to the respective merits of the Envoys, in negotiating and signing the Treaty, the statement already made seems sufficiently to point out the influence that prevailed with France to give her Consent ; and when it is added that the overture to cede Louisiana came from France and not from our Envoys, it cannot be difficult to settle the partition of Praise between them. Yet it is due to the character of Mr. L., whose zeal upon this subject had prompted him to use unwearied and various exertions to convince France of the impolicy of the Expedition to Louisiana, to declare that their business was so far settled before Mr. M.'s arrival at Paris, that nothing remained for him to do when he appeared there, but to give his consent and signature to the contract.

As to the price, tho' perhaps this also is open to fair objections —and to very strong ones on the avowed principles of the Executive respecting the increase of the public Debt—it must be admitted in regard to the Public welfare that these objections are inferior to all others that arise in the examination of this important transaction.

If France was compelled by the war with Eng. to suspend or relinquish the projected Expedition, this circumstance secured to us almost every advantage we could desire in pressing France and Spain to consent to such an arrangement respecting New

Orleans and the free navigation of the Miss., as we had a right to demand.

The Debates of the Br. Parliament upon the Treaty of Amiens had shown the strong aversion of Eng. to the occupation of Louisiana by France, and must have satisfied both France and America that, unless vanquished, Eng. wd. not consent to Louisiana being colonized by her Rival.

So far as Title was the object, we already had it by the Treaties with G. B. & Spain ; for the Right of Deposit at N. O., obtained by the Span. Treaty, reserved a power to Spain within a limited time to discontinue this Right at N. O., assigning an equivalent Deposit at another place, yet the time, within which this change might have been made, elapsed without its being done, and in consequence thereof the Right of Deposit became absolute and unchangeable ; so that France who recd. the cession from Spain posterior to the Treaty with us, took it subject to our Rights under an elder treaty.

So far then as respects the Right of Deposit at New Orleans, and the navigation of the Miss., the case stood thus : we had as complete a title to the enjoyment of these Rights, as to the Deposit at New York and to the Navigation of the Hudson ; but being menaced with an interruption of the Right of Deposit, we sent a mission to effect a removal of unjust Impediments, and the question of how much or how little money ought to be given upon a mere mercenary calculation—(laying aside wholly the principle of honour, the only one worthy of being consulted in regard to the invasion of an important natural Right) is perhaps on the view of the subject we have taken not very difficult to be determined, as it is believed that very few wd. be found who under the known & favourable circumstances of the negotiation wd. have consented to a larger sum than Congress deemed sufficient when those Circumstances were unforseen.

Whether it wd. not have been more natural as well as economical to have given money to France and six per cent. to our own citizens whom we are to pay what France owed them instead of the inversion of this course, can admit of no sort of doubt : that the mode which has been preferred is both bad economy and in other respects injudicious might be easily demonstrated.

The observations made in a former Paper were calculated to

shew that the Cession of Louisiana (regarded as a confirmation of our Right to navigate the Mississippi, and as a conveyance of New Orleans in Sovereignty instead, as a confirmation of our Right to use it as a free Port) ought not to be considered as what men of Business call a good Bargain on our side ; that the overture to sell came from France, when by reason of the war which had become inevitable, she was obliged to relinquish her plan of colonization, and consequently that the respective friends of the Envoys have no room to contend for an unequal division of credit between them ; and that the cession which has been made so far from conforming the Policy of the Mission to France, may, if considered in reference to the condn. of France at the date of the Negotiation, be regarded as proof of the Superior wisdom of those who recommended a different course.

Before we proceed in the examination of the Policy of our accepting the Cession of Louisiana it may be proper to enquire whether the President's views and Ins. to the Envoys were directed to the acquisition of the country beyond the Miss., or whether the proposal to annex this immense Region to the U. S. did not for obvious or concealed reasons originate with France. Altho' we have not seen the Instructions to the Envoys, nevertheless sufficient has elapsed to disclose in various ways whatever may have been the President's private sentiments (of which we profess to be ignorant) that the Envoys had neither Instructions nor Power to ask for or receive an acre of Land.*

APPENDIX VIII. (*to Page 407.*)

HAMILTON'S ESTATE.

O. WOLCOTT TO R. KING, HARTFORD.

NEW YORK, July 12, 1804.
MY DEAR SIR :

I addressed a line to you yesterday, but I suppose it to be my duty to inform you that our friend Hamilton expired to-day about 2 o'clock. The feelings of the whole community are agonized beyond description ; for the first time Envy is silent ; all remember with gratitude the talents and services of the deceased Hero,

* This ends abruptly—The Sequel is not among the papers.—Ed.

and mourn the untimely end of the pride and ornament of our Country.

Our friend fell by the first fire. The ball passed through one side and lodged in or near the spine. He was brought to his friend Mr. Wm. Bayard's house and the few hours of life and reason which remained were chiefly spent in religious Exercises.

Present my condolence to Judge Benson and rest assured of the high esteem and attachment of Dr. Sir

Your faithful

O. W. Wolcott.

O. Wolcott to R. King, Boston.

New York, Aug. 14, 1804.

Dear Sir :

I inclose a memorandum of the subscription here : no person has been solicited and many persons who will doubtless subscribe are out of town. I have heard it said by those who know the opinion of the city that about $30,000 may be expected.

A diversity of opinion exists in Phila. respecting the course proper to be pursued. Mr. Lewis, Mr. Rawle, Mr. Tilghman, Mr. Waln, and Mr. Girard are a committee of a select number of gentlemen to consider and recommend what they ought to do. I know nothing of the nature of their difficulties. From Baltimore nothing of consequence is to be expected.

This is certain that it will require considerable management to render Genl. Hamilton's Estate Solvent. Genl. Schuyler can doubtless borrow money, but of what advantage would it be to increase a mass of unproductive property and diminish the sources of immediate income ? But it is unnecessary to reason on a question of this nature. Those who are to consider it are good judges of what is proper.

I shall leave this place in a few days for Connecticut to attend upon Mrs. W. whose health is feeble. If you have occasion to write on this subject, a letter to Mr. Gracie or Genl. Clarkson will be immediately attended to.

With high esteem &c.,

O. W. Wolcott.

In a postscript, Mr. Wolcott sends a list of the subscribers all well known New Yorkers, with the amount each contributed—

There are eight for $1000, each, among whom is Mr. King, one for $750, eleven for $500 each, a number for smaller sums, amounting in all to $16,100.—These names are all of leading citizens and friends of Genl. Hamilton.

O. WOLCOTT TO R. KING.

NEW YORK, Aug. 14, 1804.

DEAR SIR :

I wrote you yesterday, but having since had an interview with Genl. Clarkson and Mr. Gracie, I am able to state further particulars. Genl. Schuyler's property has probably been overrated. It is certain he owes money and has no funds at command. Every vestige of our friend's earnings will vanish unless the proposed contribution is successful. The country seat is secured for the indemnity of the endorsers of discounted paper, which amounts to $20,000. Mrs. Hamilton's attachment to this country seat you well know. The necessity of selling it would excessively distress her. I am now assured that the suggestions which some persons have made that the family would be offended are utterly without foundation : that on the contrary they will consider pecuniary assistance under their present circumstances as in justice they ought, merely as a manifestation of the gratitude and respect of the contributors to the character of the Decd.

Alexander, son of the \Genl. was graduated the first of this month. He was destined by his father for a merchant. On many accounts it will be best that he receive his education for this profession out of the city. I pray you to inquire whether a respectable place can be obtained for him in Boston. He is now about 18 years of age. I make this request on the suggestion of the family.

With highest esteem &c.,

O. W. WOLCOTT.

APPENDIX IX. TO P. 485.

MIRANDA AND THE SAILING OF THE LEANDER.

There is among Mr. King's papers an account of his relations with Miranda, in reference to his plans and conduct in arranging for and carrying out his Expedition, which as is well known sailed from New York, and for many reasons, (one of the chief of which was Miranda's unfitness to command such a venture) failed and was disastrously broken up. There was published in Boston, (a second edition in 1810), an account of the Expedition in a series of letters, written by a member of the expedition, detailing the daily events, the causes of failure and the capture of most of those engaged in it. Mr. King's account is as follows :

General Miranda arrived at New York from England Nov. 9th 1805, and the next day called on Mr. King, whom he had known in London, and delivered to him a letter from a respectable English gentleman dated Aug. 14, 1805, of which the following are extracts.*

The General's communications to Mr. King corresponded with the tenour of the foregoing extracts ; and he further stated that the Province of *Caraccas*, his native country, was suffering beneath the most oppressive tyranny, that the Inhabitants, were generally disaffected, that they were ready to throw off the Spanish Government and invited him to return and co-operate with them in asserting their liberty and independence, and that he had come to the U. S. to obtain the requisite succours to enable him to effect the Revolution.

Mr. King told Gen. Miranda that private persons, whatever might be their sentiments concerning the enterprize in which he was engaged, could not with safety afford him the assistance he wanted, as the U. S. was at peace with Spain, and the laws prohibited the setting on foot of an Expedition of this nature, and recommended to him without delay to proceed to Washington and lay open his views to the Government.

At a future interview General Miranda informed Mr. King that he had disclosed his object to Commodore Lewis and Col. Smith who had made him acquainted with Mr. S. G. Ogden ; that Ogden and Lewis owned two or three stout armed ships, that they entertained sentiments favourable to his purpose, that if he had friends he could soon procure the men and arms he wanted, and with this succour that he should command a force superior to that which Dion possessed when with Plato's approbation he returned to Syracuse, his native City, and overthrew the Tyrants. Mr. King repeated to Gen. Miranda that he ought to consult the

---

* These are omitted as they are from Mr. Vansittart's letter.

Government before he attempted anything ; that however true it was, that all Greece applauded the enterprize of Dion, and its wisest citizens assisted or accompanied him, neither men, nor States, nor the discipline and devotedness of Freedom were the same now as then ; that we possessed as little of the purity of ancient Patriotism as of its invincible courage aud tho' there was a time when it might have been both safe and honourable to have erred with Plato, those days were gone, and a mere regard to personal safety with the coldest and lowest calculations of prudence had become virtues of higher rank than those which once animated the Sages of antiquity.

General Miranda afterwards informed Mr. King that he had concluded to go to Washington and to lay open his intentions to Government, and asked Mr. King to give him a letter of introduction to the Secretary of State, which was declined.

General Miranda having determined to ask the countenance and succour of Government, with the view of apprizing the President of the General's actual situation, as well as of the purpose for which he came to the U. S., Mr. King transmitted to the Secretary of State for the President's perusal, the original letter that he had from England disclosing Miranda's views. Mr. King's letter was dated Nov. 26, 1805, the Secretary of State's letter returning the enclosure after the same had been perused by the President was dated Dec. 4, 1805.

General Miranda left N. Y. for Washington Nov. 28, arrived there Dec. 6, left it Dec. 20, and returned to N. Y. Dec. 23, 1805. He informed Mr. King that, immediately after his arrival at Washington, he visited the President ; after which he visited the Secy. of State, and left his address with a letter of introduction from Dr. Rush of Philadelphia ; that at the interview which followed he informed the Secy. of State that he had desired to make an important and confidential communication to the Government as soon as the President should permit it to be received ; that at a future interview the Secy. of State informed him that having consulted the President he had been authorized to receive his communications ; that General Miranda then opened to the Secretary of State his object in coming to the U. S., exposed the condition of the Province of *Caraccas*, the general discontent of its Inhabitants and the ease with which it might become independent, and concluded by asking the countenance and succour of the Government. The manner and tenour of the observations made by the Secretary of State on this occasion were considered by M. as encouraging and satisfactory.

That at a subsequent interview the Secretary of State, who seemed more reserved than before, informed Gen. Miranda that he had communicated to the President what had passed in their preceding conference, that the President's sentiments could not be doubted, but that Government could afford neither sanction nor succour to the enterprize in which he was engaged.

General Miranda remarked that without the countenance of Government individuals might be unwilling to assist him ; the Secretary replied that the U. S. was a free country, where every one may do what the laws do not forbid. Genl. Miranda observed that the Bill then depending, prohibiting the exportation of arms and ammunition, might impede his measures. The Secretary answered that the Bill might not become a Law.

General Miranda said he had conferred with certain persons in New York respecting his views and if Government would privately make him a small advance, he might with their assistance find the supplies he wanted. The Secretary replied that the merchants would advance money whenever they became satisfied that they had an interest in doing so, and enquired what supplies he might want, and who were the Persons with whom he had conferred. General Miranda answered that he wanted a few officers, a small number of privates, together with a quantity of arms and ammunition, and that he had conferred with Commodore Lewis, Col. Smith and Mr. S. G. Ogden. The Secretary expressed himself favourably concerning the fitness of these persons for the Expedition, adding in reference to Lewis and Ogden, that it would be better than the St. Domingo trade, and that Col. Smith was more qualified for military service than for the Custom House.† General Miranda said that Col. Smith would go with him, if he could have leave of absence, which he regarded should be granted under the pretext of having business at New Orleans. The Secretary replied that such permissions were unusual—and the conference ended with an intimation on the part of the Secretary of State that whatever might be done should be.

† He was an officer in that at New York.

discreetly done and with the understanding on the part of Miranda, that altho' the Government would not sanction, it would wink at the Expedition.

Miranda remained at Washington 14 days, dined twice with the President ; the second time being after the Secretary of State had laid before the President the communication received from Gen. Miranda. He also dined with the Secretary of State the day before he left Washington—having waited there two days to attend the dinner.

As soon as General Miranda returned to N. York, he settled his plan with Commodore Lewis, Mr. Ogden and Col. Smith. Commodore Lewis sailed soon after for St. Domingo, with two armed ships, the Emperor and the Indostan, with instructions from Miranda to engage the mulatto Chief Petion together with a corps of persons of colour to co-operate in effecting the Revolution of the Province of Caraccas. General Miranda, his associates American Officers and Privates, together with a supply of arms and ammunition followed in the ship Leander commanded by Captain Lewis, brother of the Commodore.

After Miranda's return from Washington, he stated to Mr. King his apprehensions that he should be embarrassed from the want of funds, and requested that Mr. King, thro' his friends, would endeavour to effect a loan for him, which in addition to other means might be sufficient to carry his preparations to a pitch that would render his success infallible.

Mr. King explained to Miranda, in declining his request, the reasons why it would be unfit and inexpedient in him to take any part in, or in any way promote the enterprize in which he was engaged. Mr. King did not however hide from General Miranda the cordial interest that he had long cherished in favour of the Emancipation of South America, nor did he conceal the hope he entertained and which arose out of the posture of public affairs, and his opinion respecting the true political and commercial system of this Country, as Spain had given to the U. S. just. cause of war, that the power and resources of the nation would be employed in breaking asunder the weak and degrading chains which for more than three centuries had bound the new world to the old.

Of funds without which he could not proceed, Miranda remarked, that his chief and best property consisted of the extensive and valuable Library with which Mr. King was acquainted, and that he would try to raise money upon it.   If he succeeded in the Enterprize to which he had devoted himself, he should be able to redeem this Library ; if he failed he should not want it ; he added that on this principle, he would draw Bills for £.2000. Sterg. on persons in London, whom he named, and in whose care he left his Library and other effects, and requested Mr. King to express his opinion of the value of the Library to any person who might call upon him to ask it.   Soon after Mr. Daniel Ludlow called on Mr. King and enquired of him respecting Miranda's property in England, Mr. King answered that he knew of no property belonging to him, except a valuable Library that he possessed when Mr. King left England.   Mr. Ludlow asked Mr. King if this Library was worth £2000. Sterling ; Mr. King answered that in his opinion it was worth that sum and more. Mr Ludlow asked Mr. King if he knew the persons whose names he mentioned on whom Miranda had drawn for £2000. Ster. Mr. King answered in the affirmative, and that they were friends of Miranda.   Mr. Ludlow then asked Mr. King if he would purchase Miranda's Bills were he in want of Bills on London ? Mr. King replied that were he in want of Bills he should not trust his own judgment but consult with Mr. Ludlow or some other merchant respecting such as might be offered to him.

Mr. King afterwards understood from General Miranda that Mr. Ludlow had purchased the Bills, and that the General had pledged the Library to the Drawers as a security for the repayment of the money.

About this time, or earlier, Miranda told Mr. King that he was sending an agent to Boston for the purpose of raising money and asked him to furnish the agent with a letter of introduction to one of his friends in Boston ; this was declined, and Mr. King afterwards understood from Miranda that the mission proved ineffectual.

General Miranda informed Mr. King that in addition to the £2000. drawn on the security of his Library, he had drawn on a Banker in London for what he had not expended of a letter of credit for £800. Sterling which he brought from England, and also for two or three thousand pounds sterling upon a person in Trinidad, whose name was mentioned but not recollected.

On the 23d of January General Miranda called on Mr. King and showed him two letters which he had written and which he said he should send by the mail to the President and Secretary of State, both dated January 22, 1806, and added that he would as he afterwards did give to Mr. King copies of these letters. The Leander left the Hook Feb. 2, 1806.

The following are copies of the letters from General Miranda to the President and Secretary of State.*

Translation—Copy—Private—

FRAN. DE MIRANDA TO THE HON. JAMES MADISON, ESQ. &C. &C.

NEW YORK, January 22, 1806.

SIR :

On the point of leaving the U. S., allow me to address a few words to you, to thank you for the attentions that you were pleased to show me during my stay at Washington.

The important concerns, which I then had the honour to communicate to you, I doubt not will remain a profound secret until the final result of that delicate affair.

I have acted upon this supposition here, by conforming in everything to the intentions of the Government, which I hope to have apprehended and observed with exactness and discretion. The enclosed letter contains a book which I have promised to the President of the U. S., and which I pray you to transmit to him.

Have the goodness to present my respectful compliments to Mrs. Madison and to believe me with high consideration and esteem, Sir,　　　　　Yr. very humb. & ob. Servt.

FRAN. DE. MIRANDA.

Translation—Copy.

MIRANDA TO T. JEFFERSON ESQ., PRESIDENT OF THE U. S.

NEW YORK, January 22, 1806.

MR. PRESIDENT :

I have the honour to send you with this " La Storia naturale e civile del Chilé," of which we conversed at Washington. You

---

* These letters are in French, which with the translations into English, are in this manuscript.　But as the translations express faithfully the originals, they only are here given, for want of space—Ed.

will perhaps find more interesting facts and greater knowledge in this little volume than in those which have been before published on the same subject concerning this beautiful Country.

If the happy prediction which you pronounced on the future destiny of our dear Colombia is to be accomplished in our day, may Providence grant that it may be under your auspices and by the generous efforts of her own children. We shall then, in some sort behold the revival of that age, the return of which the Roman Bard invoked in favour of the Human Race :

> " The last great age foretold by sacred rhymes
> Renews its finished course ; Saturnian times
> Roll round again, and mighty years, begun
> From this first orb, in radiant circles run."
>
> Dryden.*

With the highest consideration and profound respect,
I am, Mr. President, yr. very humb. & very ob. servt.,
(signed) Fran. de. Miranda.

On the 3rd of March, 1806, Mr. King received the following note from the District Judge—viz. : The District Court, which is at present sitting at No. 14 Dey Street would wish to see Mr. King as a Witness in some important business as soon as possible—Monday 3rd March.

Mr. King immediately attended, and being informed by the District Attorney that the enquiry related to the Destination of the Ship Leander and the views of General Miranda, was asked if he knew the General ? Mr. King asked if any prosecution existed against General Miranda ; the Judge replied none at present, but that facts might be disclosed that would originate one. Mr. King observed that he should think himself bound to answer such questions as the Court might think proper to propound, but that he knew nothing concerning the Leander, or General Miranda's views, except what the General had confidentially communicated to him, and which he could not therefore disclose, unless in obedience to the injunction of the Court. The Judge replied that the Court would expect answers to the questions it might ask.

* Quoted in Latin from Virg. Eclog. 11.

The Attorney General then repeated the question, whether Mr. King knew General Miranda? Mr. King, being first sworn, answered that he had known the General many years, and for several during his residence in England. Is Miranda a native of Caraccas? Mr. King answered that he had understood so from him. When did Miranda arrive at New York? In November last. Did he disclose to Mr. King the object of his coming to the U. S.? He did. What was his object? He represented to Mr. King, that his native Country was oppressed by the Spanish Government and was in a condition and ready to throw off the yoke; that he had been invited by his countrymen to return and join them in effecting the Revolution; and, to comply with the invitation, he wanted a few Officers, a small number of privates and a quantity of arms and ammunition. Mr. King told General Miranda that individuals could not with safety furnish these supplies, and recommended him to go to Washington and make a full disclosure of his business to the Government.

Did Miranda go to Washington? He informed Mr. King that he did. When did he leave New York for Washington? Towards the end of November. Did he disclose his business to Government? He told Mr. King he had. What answer did he receive from Government? That Government did not sanction the Enterprize, but that it would assist at Miranda's procuring the supplies from individuals, provided the same was done discreetly. Did Miranda declare who were his associates? He did. Who were they? Commodore Lewis and his brother, Mr. L. G. Ogden and Col. Smith; he added that he had mentioned those names to Government, which thought them suitable persons for the business. What quantity of arms and how many men are on board the Leander? Mr. King answered that he did not know. Did Miranda mention the destination of the Leander? He did. What was her destination? A port in St. Domingo and from thence to the Coast of Caraccas. Did he mention the purpose of his going to Caraccas? He did. What was it? To co-operate with his countrymen in accomplishing a Revolution. Did you understand that force would be used against the existing Government? Most certainly, if necessary to overturn it.

The interrogatories being finished, Mr. King requested that they might be read over together with his answers that the latter might be corrected if misconceived or erroneously expressed. This being done, instead of the answer given by Mr. King to the Question, "What answer did he receive from the Government?" the judge omitted the latter clause and varied the form so as to read "the Government repelled the overture." Mr. King pointed out the variance and desired the answer might be set down as he delivered it. The Attorney General observed that as Mr. King's testimony was material only in respect to the destination of the Leander, he doubted whether it would be necessary to take his deposition, as he would be recognized to give his testimony in Court. The Judge assenting, Mr. King was recognized and the paper containing his examination was thrown into the fire.

MARCH 5, 1806.

APPENDIX X.

REVIEW OF THE FOREIGN RELATIONS OF THE UNITED STATES.

Among the papers of Mr. King, the following interesting review of the foreign relations of the United States will give his opinions on many of the questions which were engaging the attention of the Government, and in the proper solution of which he differed from the Administration. Though the paper begins abruptly with a discussion of certain articles of a proposed treaty, it gives a well-considered view of their effect upon maritime law, and consequently upon our commercial relations, and therefore it is here published as evincing the interest he took in public affairs, although he was not in public life. When it was written, and probably published by him is uncertain, but it may have been subsequent to the date of his letter to Mr. Pickering on p. 506 of this volume, in which he says: "I have it in contemplation, after the close of your Session to make a review of our foreign relations."

The 14th article provides that free bottoms make free goods. Every man who remembers the humiliated situation of our Country in the years 1794 and 1795, will recollect the fervour with which that regulation was asserted and contended for, as one of the most important provisions of what was called the Modern Law of Nations. England was decried because she would not admit, France applauded for supporting, it. But how far she has conformed her conduct to this Rule, appears in the long list of captures before us. We omit the Catalogue and cite only the case of the Ship Two Friends, McNiel, Master : a regular trader between London and South Carolina, taken with a most valuable cargo, by the French Privateers, which blockade the harbour of Charleston. The assertion that she had not a certificate from the American Consul in London to prove the cargo neutral property is a frivolous pretext, circulated by the corrupt instruments of our Administration, and from the same motives, which led to the base but unsuccessful attempt in the to persuade the public that the Two Friends is a British and not an American ship. No such certificate was necessary : the ship was provided with a passport in due form proving her to be American property; wherefore according to the Convention with France, the bottom being free the cargo was free also. It might have been enemy's property or even contraband of war, still as the Ship was American and bound to an American, not an enemy's port, the capture was repugnant to the Article before us.

The members of our present Administration constantly manifested the desire to establish a new maritime code. They have in this respect shown as much fondness for French fashions as their Wives, and snapped at every hook baited with the phrase, free ships, free goods. But it is prudent even for Powers of the first order (much more for others) to avoid innovating on the established Law of Nations. Public opinion is of such importance that Sovereigns frequently endeavour to conciliate it by labored manifestoes. Few are so hardy as to bid it defiance, and fewer still can do so with impunity. When a treaty between two nations is founded on and conformable to the acknowledged public Law (which like our common Law has been matured by the wisdom and experience of ages), the violation of it is generally acknowledged, and other nations are interested in punishing the perfidy. But when new fangled notions are foisted into national compacts by the art of a duping Power operating upon the folly of its dupe, no sooner is the bargain broken than surrounding nations applaud the breach, because it restores old principles. They justly deride the awkward lamentations of those who had set themselves up for teachers and models to their superiors. We shall not examine the solidity of the favorite position, that a free ship makes free goods, because some of our friends have wished to establish it, without reflecting that if ever we should be at war, it would destroy our best means of aggression. But we must notice a difficulty which cursory observers may not perceive, tho' it ought to be weighed by those who assume the character of Statesmen. It is evident that a new principle of maritime Law cannot be established against the will of the first maritime Powers. It is equally evident that they will not assent to a principle which takes from them the advantage of their naval superiority : and it is not less evident that such superiority can be of little use if an enemy's commerce can be carried on in perfect safety under cover of a neutral flag. It is, moreover, a wilful blindness not to see that the attempt to make goods of an enemy free from capture when on board of a neutral ship, were levelled at the naval power of Great Britain, and by necessary consequence at her existence. Whether it be our interest that she should perish, is a question which shall not at this time be considered. But will any man of sound mind pretend that if the naval empire of France were established on the ruin of Britain, this new principle would be respected by France ? Are we not on the contrary warranted by experience to say that she would break the cobweb ties of a treaty as freely as any one of her admirers can break the Lilliputian ties of an oath.

We are neither the advocates nor accusers, much less the panegyrists or calumniators of any Prince, Power or Potentate. Born and educated in America we are bound to this our native Country by interest, duty and affection. Our partialities, our predilections, our attachments are to her. If we could pretend equal love to another, we should hold ourselves as unworthy of confidence as any of those who born abroad come canting to our shores their dear, dear love for America, and who better to gull and dupe this credulous people have the infamy to pretend a hatred for the land which gave them birth. But that strict impartiality, which we feel and avow, will not permit us to shut our eyes against the light of truth.

We will not indeed look at these reproaches which the nations of Europe cast on each other, but we must look at the facts which regard ourselves ; and if we respect their evidence, we must acknowledge that England has been more faithful to her Treaties with us than some other Powers. She has indeed been less profuse of promise, but she has been more fruitful in performance. Treaties made with her do not hold out such prolific hopes as those which delight our visionary Rulers but they give security. England, who is unquestionably the dominant Power at sea, does not restrict us in the exercise of our right as neutrals to navigate as freely, as in time of peace, from the ports of one enemy to those of another. She will not hold to the novel doctrine that a neutral flag shall protect the property of an enemy, and which, adopted as a principle, would in practice be exclusively advantageous to the inhabitants of the North of Europe ; because from the low price of labor and materials, they can carry merchandize cheaper than we can, and because (their navigation laws differing widely from ours) they naturalize a foreign Ship with as much facility as we do a foreign vagabond. But tho' England makes Prize of her enemies' goods, she does not condemn the neutral ship, which has taken them on board, nor even withhold the stipulated freight. With other Powers we have made Treaties according to which not only our neutral ship is sacred, but even a portion of her sanctitude is extended to the iniquitous cargo sufficient for its salvation, and what is the consequence? These darling Treaties of high promise are violated with as little remorse as that of a schoolboy in drowning a blind puppy ; and with as much contempt for our representations as his for the howling of its dam, because like the miserable bitch we bark, but dare not bite.

After all, if certain Powers would stop at the mere breach of Treaty, those who to get money, or to save it, will submit to disgrace might patiently bear the loss of our national honor. But alas the arrogance of one party is generally proportioned to the meanness of the other. We have seen decrees to confiscate American Ships should a single rope yarn of British Manufacture be found on board ; and although the violations are not quite so outrageous, they deprive us of advantages to which we are entitled by the Law of Nations, as well as those conceded to us by

Treaty, and being submitted to invite, and will excuse if not justify such further violations as interest or caprice may dictate. And here let it be asked, of what use to make Treaties with Powers void of faith? Is it not better to adhere to the established Law, and exert our force against those by whom it shall be violated? Is it not—but we forbear; since to mention what ought to be done, and what our honorable Nation would do, might look like a libel on our *wise* and *virtuous* and above all our *magnanimous* administration.

The 18th Article regulates the manner of visit and search. This important stipulation is also shamefully disregarded. Not only the masters of American ships are forced to leave their vessels and go on board French cruizers with their papers, but armed detachments are sent on board of American vessels to plunder their cargoes and insult and maltreat their crews. When Capt. Pigott of the English Frigate Hermione offered personal violence to Jessup, the democratic papers resounded with clamorous outcry. The federal Administration made a strong remonstrance to the British Govt.; enquiry was ordered; redress was promised and would probably have been given, had not the murder of Capt. Pigott by his own crew placed him beyond the power of human tribunals. But now that we are constantly exposed to, and daily experience French and Spanish atrocities, what have these Gentlemen done with their sympathy in the sufferings of their countrymen? Is it asleep, or peradventure gone on a journey, to wait a nod of favour from the imperial Court? Their newspapers, once so loud in complaint, are silent : we hear of no appeals to the national sentiment, no remonstrance by our Government to those of France and Spain. Are stripes then less degrading from the hands of a Frenchman or Spaniard than from those of a Briton?

By the 19th Article, every American vessel under convoy of a national ship is exempt from visit and search by French cruizers, why then is our commerce unprotected? Why have we no Frigates cruizing along our own coasts? Why is the property of our merchants exposed to plunder and our national character to disgrace? Is there a nation, was there ever a nation with such ample means of self defence reduced to a state of such utter contempt?

It would seem as if a plan had been laid to expose us to every possible insult, and to torture every nerve and fibre of national sensibility. When a Frigate and store ship were destined to the Picaroon war of Tripoli they were sent separate, and as if fearful that the plunder of merchants might wound only that description of citizens, the national property is exposed, so that the whole nation might suffer, and every citizen drink of the cup of shame. If such was the plan, it has succeeded beyond all reasonable expectation. The store ship was taken, and has been retaken ; we are to receive her back therefore as a boon of British bounty, on paying the price of salvage acknowledging the efficacy of that force which we dare not employ.

We proceed to the Louisiana Treaty, by which *French debts* due to American citizens to the amount of nearly twenty millions of Livres are assumed by the United States. It will be remembered that the federal Administration with a view to establish public credit, and to adjust the State accounts, assumed the debts of the several States. This measure was nevertheless loudly censured by the exclusive patriots, who are now silent, or ready to approve the assumption of French debts. It is true that American citizens were expected to be benefited by both assumptions. It seems, however, a little difficult to explain upon any honourable principle the approbation of a measure when it assists the credit and finances of a foreign nation, and the condemnation of it when beneficial to our own. It will not be alleged that the U. S. received an equivalent in one case, and not in the other ; in the instance of the State debts, the amount assumed was charged to the several States, and liquidated in settling their accounts ; so in the other example the sum assumed is discounted in the purchase of Louisiana. There are indeed some men so malicious as to say, that the assumption of French debts gave no relief to France, because regardless of her engagements she did not conceal the determination to delay payment so long as might suit her convenience ; and the system of delay once adopted might easily have been easily extended so as to be in effect a denial. They say too that the real relief was felt by our Administration, who were thereby liberated from the irksome task of presenting fruitless claims to citizen Talleyrand, who received and put them in his pocket with every circumstance of neglect and indifference.

Nay these malicious men go further and pretend that the 20 millions of Livres were superadded to the price, in the lumping bargain for Louisiana, so that in fact we received no consideration for paying French debts to our citizens.

We are, however, far from believing the insinuations of such men ; still less will we listen to certain ugly criminating allegations, which would resolve the public conduct of great officers into a mean pursuit of private interest. By the Louisiana Treaties two things are incumbent on France. 1st, to assist us in settling the boundaries, so that we may possess Louisiana as France would have done ; 2nd, to facilitate the liquidation of debts she owes to our citizens, so that they may obtain payment from their own Treasury.

Mr. Livingston, who (as we have already observed) had settled the terms of the Louisiana Treaty before the arrival of his colleague, Mr. Monroe, took care to insert a clause, which if duly observed at Washington, would have rendered all negotiation about the limits unnecessary. This clause wisely required that France should give us actual possession of all Louisiana before she could call for payment ; according to the terms of the Treaty, and in consistence with its true spirit and intent, we justly claimed the country between the Mississippi and the Perdido as part of Louisiana (a country of greater value to the U. S. than the whole territory lying west of the Mississippi). This as well as New Orleans and the western bank of the Mississippi was in possession of Spain and occupied by Spanish troops. New Orleans and the western bank of the River were, in conformity with the Treaty of St. Ildefonso, surrendered to France by the Spanish Commissary and then delivered over to us by the French Commissary. But our troops were not even permitted to set their feet upon, or pass through any part of the country between the Mississippi and the Perdido on their way to take possession of Louisiana. The Spanish garrison continued to possess it, displaying their flag within view of our troops as they passed them. By thus leaving this part of Louisiana in the hands of Spain, when we took possession of New Orleans and the western bank of the Mississippi, our Administration indirectly acknowledged the right of Spain to the country, and thereby cast such fresh doubt upon our own title as could not but operate to our disadvantage. Still, however, the staff was in our own hands as the money was in our treasury. The possession of New Orleans and of the western bank of the River being delivered to us, our Adminstration should have demanded the surrender of the country between the Mississippi and the Perdido, as a preliminary condition to the payment of the purchase money, according to the terms of the Treaty, which expressly declared that Possession of Louisiana should be delivered before the money was paid. This was the plain, simple course and had it been pursued we should now have been in full & quiet possession of all Louisiana. Why this course was not adopted, we are at a loss to conceive. But in fact it was not adopted. We obtained possession of only a part of the Territory we had purchased and though we were not obliged to pay a dollar before the delivery of the whole, our administration paid every cent, and thereby put it in the power of both France and Spain to say, what they do say, that we have received possession of all that was intended to be ceded ; nay that our payment of the purchase money, which was not demandable till the ceded country had been delivered, was a full acknowledgment that we had already got all that we considered ourselves entitled to claim. Our economical Administration having thus precipitately poured out our treasure and abdicated our rights, dispatched in their profound wisdom their fac-totum Monroe to correct the procedure. This facetious, polite and sagacious personage was it seems to persuade some of the ablest Ministers in Europe to forego the advantages which we had so weakly given them and obtain the surrender of a valuable Territory, which our Government had left in their possession by a neglect which, if they were federalists, we should call criminal.

Proceeding from London to Madrid Mr. Monroe took Paris in his route, and though it was notorious that his character and connexions in that metropolis rendered his presence disagreeable to the Government, an article found its way into one of the French papers, stating that he had been most graciously received by the Emperor.* Unexperienced men formed expectations from this

* In the *Moniteur*, the official paper of France, after mentioning sundry presentations by the foreign Ministers and Ambassadors at the Emperor's Levee, it is said, "Mr. Armstrong the American Minister was permitted to present Mr. Monroe," etc. A phraseology so extraordinary seems to have been

article (which every American in Paris knew to be false) favourable to the object of Mr. Monroe's mission ; reflecting ones however looked a little further, and seeking for Bonaparte's views in the calculation of his interest, endeavored to discover how this would be affected by the good will of Spain, or that of America— if the latter were too profitably employed, too prudent, or too remote to be drawn within his vortex, this was not the case with the former. The favour of Spain therefore became an object of his careful attention, and would of course be more assiduously cultivated than that of America.

Mr. Monroe, however, presented through the American Minister at Paris a memorandum to the French Government, setting forth the limits of Louisiana and claiming the good offices and interference of the Emperor Napoleon with the Spanish Court in fixing the same. But the memorial was treated with contemptuous silence, so that after patiently waiting for and humbly soliciting an answer, the Knight of the Sorrowful Countenance was obliged to jog on to Madrid without one. There the claim was renewed and answered by a flat denial ; in which, as was stated, France fully concurred. We presume that this will be decisive and that our magnanimous Administration will in all humbleness submit. At a convenient season France and Spain may send half a dozen French regiments to Mobile, and our wise statesmen, who already have paved the way for it by removing their custom house from Mobile to Fort Stoddard, be at once convinced and easily convince their followers that their Title is defective, and that prudence, republicanism, the principles of humanity and true economy require that we should advance as many additional millions as may be demanded for a second sale ! Thus one of the most antient and important parts of Louisiana, for which we have paid 15 millions of dollars, is lost, or rather has been most weakly and negligently thrown away. But the loss of the country and loss of money tho' great, are of little consequence compared with the loss of reputation ; for when before has it happened that a nation has gratuitously given a certainty for an uncertainty, accepted the imperfect in lieu of the perfect

inserted with the double view of counteracting the above publication and of apologizing to the courts of Europe for suffering such a man to appear at the Tuilleries.

performance of a condition ; or referred to negotiation and the consent of those, whose interest was opposed to its own, a point, the decision of which was completely within its own power.

In respect to the assumed debt, notwithstanding the diligence of the Board of Commissioners and the appointment of successive Ambassadors, the business is still embarrassed by a series of frivolous pretexts, and tho' some partial payments have been made, the far greater part remains in suspense.

The creditors become daily more impatient, one day hoping, the next in despair, and will probably be kept in that condition, till they shall consent to sell their claims for a fourth of their amount. Then, and not before, the American Minister will be permitted to draw the bills. It is true that in this way our merchants will be robbed without shame or remorse, but the sooner they submit the better, for they may easily convince themselves by the neglect they experience on other occasions, that nothing effectual will be done for their relief.

We come now to our political relations with Spain, and if the importance of discussions with a foreign Power are to be inferred from the number and dignity of the Envoys employed, those with Spain must be of no ordinary magnitude ; our Administration estimating more the pride than the ability of Spain have sent her the Titles if not the Talents of our Country. At first, the chaste and generous Charles Pinckney, cidevant Governor of South Carolina, who soon brought the business, as he supposed, to a most satisfactory conclusion. His Spanish convention has been published, and reflects equal credit on the negotiator, on those who approve and on him who ratified it. This notable Convention excluding many of our claims from redress, refers the greater part to future negotiations ; an expedient for giving them up forever, which to every man of common information the refinement of Courts makes use of in such cases.

The remonstrance of our merchants against this Convention was of no avail ; but our wise Administration having ratified it, and thereby sanctioned the surrenders it makes, thought proper, as in the case of Louisiana, to negotiate anew for what they had so improvidently abandoned : for this purpose another Ex-Governor of no little State, but of great dominion, and who had already given an earnest of his diplomatic skill was dispatched ; and scarcely had this pair of Excellencies commenced the business of their mission, when a third Envoy, not himself indeed a Governor, but the son of a Governor, was appointed, whether to unite with, or to succeed the other two, or as an umpire, we have not been able to learn. Mr. Monroe having passed thro' Paris, as we have mentioned, opened in concert with Mr. Pinckney his negotiation at Madrid for the purpose of revising the Convention, and enlarging its provisions, as well as for settling the limits of Louisiana.

It is stated that 240 American vessels, amounting now to upwards of seven millions of dollars, have either been seized under Spanish authority, or sent by French Cruizers into Spanish ports and then condemned by French Consuls. About one third of their plunder was made by Spain, the other two thirds by France. Mr. Monroe has negotiated with his usual success. Spain, it is said, refuses now even to adhere to the Convention made with Mr. Pinckney ; but at any rate, as to the enlargement of it, so as to include the vessels captured by the French and condemned and sold in her ports, she denies that she is at all responsible and fortifies her refusal by the extract of a dispatch from Talleyrand to Cevallos, which declares that France would see with displeasure any interference on the part of Spain, affecting the validities of the capture or condemnation of prizes, made under authority of France, and that she would not fail to signify to the American Government her dissatisfaction at any claim it may set up against Spain for matters which had already been adjusted between France and the United States. It is presumed that the Imperial reprimand has been, or soon will be, signified at Washington, and if so, we shall probably hear no more of this negotiation ; unless indeed they can fall on some contrivance to throw the blame of their miserable blunders upon the Federalists.

As to Louisiana, we claim an indefinite western and northern extension, and comprise within its eastern limits a great part of west Florida. Spain, as we have already observed, denies our claim ; and assigns the River that falls into St. Barnard's Bay, about 80 leagues west of the marshes at the mouth of the Mississippi, as the boundary in that quarter, and runs the line up northwardly along the western limits of the old French Settlements : she also assigns the Mississippi, and eastern shore of the Island of New Orleans as the eastern boundary of Louisiana, insinuating at the same time that for a suitable compensation Spain might be prevailed on to cede the whole of W. Florida to the U. States. This decision of Spain, as seen by every man of common sense in the country, appears to have surprized and confounded our Envoys, who in May last were preparing to leave Madrid, and according to the latest account Mr. Monroe has actually left on his return to England.

The boundaries of Louisiana remain undecided ; and Spain, it may be presumed, will continue to seize our ships, and to permit the French to condemn and sell them, in her European and West India Ports. Nay should Spain stop here, our magnanimous Rulers may applaud her moderation.* But whenever one of the officers, a Governor, an Intendant, or anything else, may think proper to interrupt the navigation of the Mississippi, he will do so ; for his right and his means are as good as before. Thus while Capt. Lewis and Company are so profitably employed in catching Magpies, and picking up rams' horns on the banks of the Mississippi, our illustrious President finds all his hopes & projects blasted by the single stroke of a Spanish pen. Farewell lead mines, farewell prairies, and you too, ye mountains of salt, a long farewell !

* " We have already said that we do not pretend to penetrate the arcana of State secrets, and therefore we shall not take upon us to assign the reason why the Spanish negotiations have failed. It seems indeed unnecessary, for since no man of common sense and information had any hope of success ; none such can be surprized at the failure. We however deem it an act of justice to communicate the reason which has been assigned by the confidential friend of our Administration in this City. He, it seems, lays all the blame on the Marquis Yrujo, Minr. of his Cathc. Maj. to the U. S., and is very wroth at the aforesaid Marquis who it appears has given to his Court a circumstantial detail of the men and things that govern America. It has been insinuated that he presumed to qualify our wise and magnanimous President as a whimsical coxcomb, and miserable coward without sense to understand, or spirit to defend the interests entrusted to his care ; as one who in the vain pursuit of a little pleasing popularity, sacrifices the honour of the nation, to a six penny economy. It has also been insinuated that the said Marquis has audaciously declared that the ruling Faction, conscious of not having the talents or enough of the confidence even of their own supporters to manage a war, will give up anything to avoid it ; that our nation generally is so immersed in the pursuit of money, and so devoid of public spirit, that a Senator of one of the most powerful States de-

The next of our foreign relations that present themselves, are with Holland, our commerce with which country is subjected to unequal and peculiar burthens. By our Treaty no other or higher duties are payable upon articles imported into Holland from the U. States, than upon like articles imported from all other countries. Instead of observing this just and equal stipulation, Coffee, Sugar and Cotton, carried from the U. States to any of the Dutch European ports, pay between two and three per cent higher duties than the same articles imported from any other nation ! ! This discrimination is attempted to be vindicated by an ancient law that gave to the Dutch West India Company a duty of between two and three per cent on certain goods imported from any country lying west of a meridian passing thro' one of the Western Islands. This law was unquestionably annulled so far as regards the U. S. by the subsequent stipulation of our Treaty just cited, and which stands in contradiction to it ; and there is reason to believe that the discrimination would long since have been abolished on a proper representation to the Dutch Government. Our Administration is informed of this abuse ; but we hear of no remonstrance against it, and the injury is permitted to subsist. Let any man acquainted with the immense quantities of Coffee, Sugar and Cotton, annually imported from the U. S. to Holland

---

clared, in a public debate, that the American people will not submit to the payment of taxes for carrying on a war. Nay it has been insinuated that this same Marquis attributes the power and influence of the ruling faction in America, to a compliance with this base disposition, and to the continued sacrifice of honourable principles, to the love of ease and love of money, which are said to form prominent features of American character. In short, the Marquis is reported to have told his Court, that whatever sounding language the Triad of American missionaries might use, if Spain remain firm to her purpose, she might rely on it, the American Administration would recede.

"Spain it appears has followed his advice, and continued firm. The democratic Gentleman, above alluded to, thinks this conduct of the Spanish Minister abominable ; and indeed, if he has been guilty of falsehood, we think so too. But, if he has told the truth, he has done what every able Minister and every honest man, in his place would have done. We think therefore the Administration, before they censure the Marquis, should first ascertain what he really has written, and if it be what has been suggested, prove by a wise and manly conduct that he has told scandalous and malicious Lies ; for they cannot in this case, as in that of poor Croswell, take advantage of the maxim that a libel is the more a libel in being true."

take the trouble to compute the amount of an ad valorem duty of two and a half per cent on the same, which we have paid and still pay to the Dutch Govt., which we are not, and never were liable to pay, and the aggregate amount of which is therefore a total loss to the American Merchants, the sum will astonish the public, tho' it may have no influence on our wise and economical Administration.

But it is needless to dwell on this, which has become a trifle, now that in imitation, or rather in obedience to France, our Treaty with Holland has been wholly set aside, or at least violated in so barefaced a manner, as to justify, and perhaps to require the rejection of it on our part. On the whole we believe it will be impossible to find in diplomatic history, during a similar period, such a series of blunders, with a complication of folly and meanness, as America has presented within the last four years. We are already far advanced towards a state in which it may be difficult with the best talents of our country to extricate the nation from surrounding dangers. Should we point them out, we might be treated as alarmists, visionaries and false prophets ; we forbear therefore to attempt it but desire when evil betides America, it may be remembered that we have shown some of the steps, which have led to her ruin.